09

Challenges and Policy Programmes
of China's New Lead

Challenges and Policy Programmes of China's New Leadership

Edited by

Joseph Y. S. Cheng

City University of Hong Kong Press

First published 2007
Printed in Hong Kong

ISBN: 978-962-937-136-4
1005476390

Published by
City University of Hong Kong Press
Tat Chee Avenue, Kowloon, Hong Kong

Website: www.cityu.edu.hk/upress
E-mail: upress@cityu.edu.hk

Table of Contents

Preface

The new leadership team under Hu Jintao and Wen Jiabao began to consolidate power and make its mark on China's policy programmes since the autumn of 2002. This has become more prominent after the retirement of Jiang Zemin from the chairmanship of the Party Central Military Commission in 2004. The Chen Liangyu case in late 2006 seems to have confirmed that Hu and Wen will have the decisive say in shaping the leadership lineup to be announced in the Seventeenth Party Congress in the autumn of 2007. While there is a well-established consensus on the challenges and problems facing China, the priorities and the policy solutions defined by the new leadership nonetheless have their distinct features. This volume tries to analyze the new leadership's perceptions of the challenges facing it, how it defines its priorities, builds up political support for its policy programmes and overcomes the resistance of vested interests. Attempts have also been made to evaluate its achievements so far.

China's economic development has certainly been impressive in recent years. But the leadership is aware of the challenges and sharpening contradictions involved. At this stage, the emphases are on sustainable development and improvement in efficiency. It understands that the gaps among regions, between the coastal and interior provinces, between the urban and rural sectors, and between the rich and poor have been widening, hence its appeal for the establishment of a harmonious society. The state is ready to allocate more resources to help the under-privileged; and given its much increased revenues and foreign exchange reserves, it can afford to improve the quality and coverage of the social security system. But the leadership has no plan for democratic reforms, and will not accept any erosion of the Party's monopoly of political power. In fact, it has stepped up pressure on the mass media, the non-governmental organizations, and the dissidents.

This edited volume involves a team of China experts contributing chapters on their respective areas of expertise. It is hoped that it will serve as a good starting-point for informed discussions, and therefore will be an attractive reference book for China courses at the undergraduate level in local and Western universities. It also aims to serve as a useful and convenient reference for the general public such as bankers, business executives and journalists interested in China.

Finally, I would like to take this opportunity to thank the staff of the City University of Hong Kong Press for their hard work and dedication throughout the publication process, especially Mr. Patrick Kwong, the director, who has offered much valuable advice and assistance. Thanks are also due to all the authors for their support and co-operation, especially in meeting the numerous deadlines set within a tight editorial schedule. Last but not least, this book would have been impossible without the valuable contributions from my colleagues at the Contemporary China Research Project, City University of Hong Kong.

Joseph Y.S. Cheng
January 2007

Challenges and Policy Programmes
of China's New Leadership

1

Introduction: Economic Growth and New Challenges

Joseph Y. S. CHENG

The assumption of power by the fourth-generation leaders in 2002 coincided with the broad recognition of China's impressive economic growth. The Chinese economy, fuelled by record exports and strong investment, grew 9.9% in 2005, overtaking that of Britain as the fourth largest in the world. The National Development and Reform Commission forecast a slightly slower growth rate of 8.5%–9% in 2006. Many experts in fact believe that a slowing of China's growth rate to 8% would be healthy, while they also expect China to be able to maintain an average growth rate of above 7% in the coming decade.[1]

In recent years, the academic community in China is concerned with the country entering into a complicated and challenging stage of development. In 2003, per capita gross domestic product (GDP) in China amounted to US$1,090. Chinese academics are aware of the historical experiences of many countries in the world that after reaching the level of US$1,000 per capita GDP, a number of phenomena had emerged including the deepening of social stratification, expansion of the middle-class and its influence, the rise and development of various lines of cultural thought, exacerbation of the widening gap between the rich and poor, etc. These phenomena in turn had led to political turmoil, sharpening of social contradictions, rising tension among ethnic groups, and so on. The lessons drawn are that in this stage of development, the risks of high disharmony in society would be considerable. Chinese academics are eager to learn from the experiences of various countries in dealing with such risks.[2]

They observe that since the 1970s, economic growth in a number of countries and regions including the "four little dragons of Asia", Malaysia and Thailand further accelerated after their per capita GDP had surpassed the US$1,000 level. But in other countries such as Brazil, Argentina, Mexico, Indonesia and the Philippines, economic development stagnated after their per capita GDP had reached the US$1,000 mark. Argentina, for example, reached the significant mark in 1961, but its per capita GDP growth rate was only around 1.9% in the following four decades and more. The situations in Brazil and Mexico were similar. They too reached the significant level in the 1970s; but subsequent economic growth has remained low, with average annual rates of about 3%. Chinese scholars are especially concerned with the expanding gap between the rich and poor. They note that after reaching the per capita GDP level of US$1,000, the respective Gini coefficients were between 0.35 and 0.45 in Brazil, Mexico and Argentina. Then the situation further worsened, and their Gini coefficients rose to the range of 0.45 to 0.6. Today, the Gini coefficient in China is approaching 0.47,[3] which obviously is a very dangerous level especially in view of its claim as a socialist country. Moreover, corruption is rampant in China. Chinese scholars are therefore concerned that China should not repeat the mistakes of Latin America.

Despite spectacular economic growth, signs of sharpening social contradictions are obvious. Public Security Minister Zhou Yongkang admitted at the end of 2005 that mass incidents, including protests, riots and mass petitioning, had risen 28% in 2004 to 74,000, while only 10,000 had been recorded a decade ago. Participants in these mass incidents amounted to 3.76 million. Disgruntled villagers deprived of land with meagre compensation, migrant workers petitioning for back pay, laid-off workers at state-owned enterprises (SOEs), and well-organised demobilised soldiers demanding welfare payments were believed to be the main groups behind these mass incidents.[4]

The explanation given by a spokesman of the Ministry of Public Security, Wu Heping, on 7 February 2006 was interesting. Wu recognised that rural riot was "a concept that does not exist", and his analysis was as follows: "In the phase (of fast economic development), the interests, relations and positions of different parts (of society) are undergoing adjustment. In the process of adjusting, there will accordingly be an increase in (the number of) common people who, in order to defend their own interests, express their pleas to government and relevant departments through various channels." Wu believed that "all these problems can be solved gradually in the framework of a 'harmonious society'".[5]

While presenting the Proposal on the Eleventh Five-Year Programme at the Fifth Session of the Sixteenth National Congress of the Communist Party of China (CPC) Central Committee in October 2005, Premier Wen Jiabao called for the stepping up of national efforts to build a harmonious society, indicating that employment, social security, poverty reduction, education, medical care, environmental protection and safety would be given priority. On social security, Premier Wen emphasised the improvement of the insurance system of pension, basic medical care, unemployment, industrial injuries and birth, the tackling of the social security issue for migrant farmer-workers in cities, as well as the setting up of a social security system supporting minimum living standards in rural areas.[6]

These measures were aimed at reducing the polarisation of society. According to the National Development and Reform Commission, the income of the richest 20% of the urban population accounted for 59.7% of the overall income of urban residents, while that of the poorest fifth accounted for only 2.7%.[7] Further, less than 0.5% of the families owned over 60% of the nation's wealth in private hands, and 70% of this private wealth was in the hands of those families with financial assets exceeding US$0.5 million. This concentration was 10 times as much as that in the United States.[8]

While there is an acute awareness of the challenges brought about by rapid economic development and the widening gap between the rich and poor, the Chinese leadership has no intention of introducing political reforms. Apparently it has been suffering from an exacerbating sense of insecurity while the CPC continues maintaining a monopoly of political power. In view of the crackdown on the mass media, political discussions on the Internet and dissidents in 2004 and 2005, expectations of the new leadership among the liberal intelligentsia in China and in overseas Chinese communities have been in sharp decline. The handling of Zhao Ziyang's funeral in early 2005 and the subsequent toned-down commemoration of the ninetieth birthday of Hu Yaobang demonstrated that the new leadership was still worried about potential political protests and the demand for the reversal of the verdict on the Tiananmen Square Incident.

The combat of corruption remains a significant issue in the new leadership's policy agenda. A system of accountability supported by the rule of law is essential to achieving the objective, and this unavoidably involves progress in democratisation. Even if the leaders are reluctant to accept the democratisation process, at least the mass media and the local people's congress system should be exploited to serve as monitoring and checks and balances mechanisms. Apparently the new leadership is too eager to preserve the Party's monopoly of power or reluctant to challenge the vested interests to allow severe reports and criticisms of corruption cases by the mass media and local people's congresses. As the media are afraid to challenge the local authorities to which they are accountable, they were tempted in recent years to expose cases of corruption and abuses of power in other provinces. In 2005, this practice was terminated by the Party's Central Propaganda Department. Given such restrictions, corruption obviously has been worsening and the vested interests have been strengthening.

Challenges in the Political Scene

There is a common view in China that given the formative years and educational background of Hu Jintao and Wen Jiabao, they will likely retain their orthodox Marxist-Leninist mindset. It is impossible to expect them to engage in Mikhail Gorbachev-type political reforms; even significant though moderate steps of democratisation such as nationwide direct elections of town and township heads will be difficult. According to this view, Hu and Wen's ideal is to return to the good old days of the 1950s when the Party was in full control, and the vast majority of Party cadres were uncorrupt, dedicated and selfless.

Two major political projects initiated by Hu Jintao apparently are in line with achieving this ideal scenario. On December 26, 2005 (the 112th birthday anniversary of Mao Zedong), the Institute of Marxism-Leninism-Mao Zedong Thought of the Chinese Academy of Social Sciences was raised in status to a Marxism academy; its establishment was expanded from 75 professorial-rank researchers to 200. The Party Central Committee actually launched a ten-year project in early 2004 for Marxist theoretical research. The project has five major tasks, including revised translation and re-interpretation of Marx's classic works, preparation of basic theoretical teaching materials for tertiary institutions on philosophy, political economy and scientific socialism as well as a whole series of teaching materials for tertiary institutions on sociology, law, history, contemporary Chinese history, journalism, etc. [9] The Chinese leadership still believes in the strengthening of ideological work to consolidate the legitimacy of the CPC regime; it also seeks to find theoretical justifications for their policy programmes today.

Meanwhile, a mild rectification campaign in the form of a self-improvement education drive has been going on to improve the vanguard character of the Party members. In January 2005, the 69.6 million Party members were asked to study the Deng Xiaoping theory, the "three represents" thesis of Jiang Zemin, and the scientific development perspective of Hu Jintao. An important objective of the campaign was to tackle the problems of the weakening Party organisations at the grassroots level and the wavering ideological conviction of the Party members. By the end of 2005, the second stage of education activities had been completed, in which more than 30 million Party members from urban grassroots Party organs and those at the town/township level participated. The third stage started in November 2005 and would finish in June 2006. More than 26 million Party members from the rural grassroots Party organs were involved; and the campaign has been aligned with the construction of "socialist new villages".[10]

It is not expected that these efforts will yield many results. The local governments and university students are not interested in Marxist education, and many universities have already abandoned courses on Marxism.[11] Most cadres are not serious with the self-improvement education drive too. Their attention tends to concentrate on career opportunities associated with the personnel changes in the coming Seventeenth Party Congress in 2007. Since Jiang Zemin's retirement from the chairmanship of the Party Central Military Commission in the autumn of 2004, Hu Jintao has been able to make his own appointments to consolidate his power base; he has not been bold enough to remove Jiang's corrupt protégés though. In these promotions, the new leadership apparently wants to institutionalise the practice of frequent transfers between central positions and local assignments; the reshuffles are also designed to strengthen the implementation of central policies at the local level. It has been observed that those who had served in the Communist Youth League, with respectable qualifications in economics and law, were favoured in the recent promotion exercises; and there may well be a trend that there will be fewer engineers and more social scientists/management experts in the leadership. These newly-promoted cadres are expected to facilitate further economic reforms, especially in trade, finance, foreign exchange, banking, rural economy, etc.

At the Seventeenth Party Congress, Hu Jintao, Wen Jiabao and Li Changchun will be the only members of the Standing Committee of the Political Bureau below 65 years of age. The age gap between them and Political Bureau members such as Chen Liangyu, Liu Yunshan, Zhang Dejiang, etc. is substantial, hence there will be a good chance that Hu Jintao will not retire even in the Eighteenth Party Congress. The fifth-generation leaders will likely be selected from the present central ministers and provincial heads who are at the age of 55 years or so. The best arrangement will be for them to join the Political Bureau in 2007, and have a period of ten years to prove their credentials. The political gossips at this stage are that Hu Jintao, Wen Jiabao, Zeng Qinghong and Wu Bangguo will stay, while Jia Qinglin, Wu Guanzheng, Luo Gan, Huang Ju and Li Changchun will retire from the Standing Committee of the Political Bureau. The probable replacements will be Zhang Dejiang, Zhou Yongkang and He Yong. In the State Council, Wen Jiabao will remain as Premier, while Yu Zhengsheng and Bo Xilai will be promoted deputy premiers.[12] There may well be further changes before the Party Congress.

In the absence of major political reforms, some administrative innovations have been introduced in recent years. In the Sixteenth Party Congress in 2002, the Chinese leadership proposed systems of fixed terms, resignation and responsibility for leading cadres in the Party and government. In 2004, the "Temporary Regulations on the Resignation of Leading Cadres in the Party and Government" were promulgated, stipulating that the principal responsible officials have to resign to assume responsibility for serious neglect and mistakes in the management and supervision work in market regulation, environmental protection and social management leading to major damages. In April 2005, the "Civil Service Law" was adopted (to be implemented in the beginning of 2006), and resignation assuming responsibility becomes a part of the civil service management system in legal form. In the following December, Xie Zhenhua, director of the State Environmental Protection Administration, became the first ministerial-rank official to resign under such provision, assuming responsibility for the Songhua River pollution incident in the Northeast.[13] At the end of 2005, the Party Central Committee was drafting the methods of implementation concerning the "CPC Intra-Party Supervision Regulations (on trial)". In this exercise, the Party would adopt provisions to allow Party members, Party representatives or Party committee members to initiate demands for the recall or dismissal of cadres to be presented to the relevant Party organs.[14]

To improve the quality of cadres, there has been a general

emphasis on academic qualifications and overseas experiences. The younger generation of cadres who are eager to seek promotions have certainly been responding. Many of them have postgraduate degrees and considerable exposure to the international scene. This not only applies to central government officials, but also to provincial and city officials. The coastal provinces and cities took the lead about a decade ago; now even the interior provinces and cities follow suit. This development has been facilitated by the growing revenues of the local governments. At the same time, many training programmes are organised for all levels of cadres. It was reported that in 2003–2005, 176 new full and alternate members of the Sixteenth Central Committee had participated in seminars on various ideological topics; similarly more than 2,000 new deputies of the National People's Congress and delegates to the National Committee of the Chinese People's Political Consultative Conference, almost 600 provincial- and ministerial-level cadres, and over 540,000 cadres at the county/section (*chu*) head level had taken part in various seminars and training programmes. [15] These programmes served the purposes of high-lighting the importance of life-long education for cadres as well as ensuring that the thinking of the cadre corps would be in line with the Party leadership.

The latter has become increasingly difficult as the phenomenon of "there are policies from above, but there are all kinds of counter-measures from below" has been worsening. In view of the expanding economic autonomy of local governments in the context of market reforms, they have been emboldened in resisting unfavourable policy initiatives from the government. In education, for example, six years after the announcement of a tertiary students' loan scheme, eight provincial units still had not implemented the policy by the end of 2005. It is an open secret that Shanghai has been refusing to co-operate with the central government's macro-economic adjustment policies; Shanghai wants to continue its ambitious economic development plans and is reluctant to reduce investment in infrastructural projects.[16] In mid-2005, a Guangdong provincial government official told the author it was fortunate that the provincial government had not fully followed the instructions from the central government and had continued to build a number of electricity-generation plants; as a result, the province's electricity shortage was less severe.

This problem was so serious that the official media in China openly discussed it. A commentary in *Zhongguo Qingnian Bao* on 17 November 2005 acknowledged that, in recent years, central government policies had been encountering problems in implementation at the local level. This might be related to inadequate understanding of the policies on the part of local governments, the existence of too many layers of governments, and the incongruence in interests between the central and local governments. But the root cause was the under-development of the rule of law, so that some local governments considered themselves above the law. The commentary suggested that it would be a top priority to establish the authority of the central government in the promotion of the rule of law. Less than a month later, *Liaowang Weekly* also published a commentary severely criticizing the protection of local interests at the expense of the central authorities. On one hand, in the cases of land appropriation and urban renewal, there was insufficient concern for the interests of the people, thus damaging the image of the central government. On the other hand, in the case of macro-economic adjustment, some local governments considered that they could only seize the initiative by not strictly following the central government's directives.[17] Thus there is a danger that the central authorities may be gradually marginalised by local interests, especially when the central leadership is perceived to be weak.

Economic Challenges

In October 2005, the Sixteenth Central Committee of the CPC adopted the "Proposal on the Eleventh Five-Year Programme on National Economy and Social Development" (henceforward referred to as "the Programme"). The Programme is candid in admitting serious economic problems in the state while it enjoys high economic growth (9.1% in 2003, 9.5% in 2004 and 9.9% in 2005). Domestic problems include the unbalanced development of urban and rural areas, extensive mode of economic growth, irrational economic structure, weak creativity, great difficulties in agriculture and the rural areas and among the peasants, and significant employment pressure. In terms of the global environment, the Chinese leadership anticipates that the global economy will develop in a more uneven manner, and competition for natural resources, markets, technologies and human resources will be stiffer. Trade protectionism is expected to take new forms.[18]

Under the banners of implementing the scientific concept of development and building a harmonious society (slogans representing the new economic development strategy), the Chinese leadership hopes to correct the imbalances generated by the twenty-seven years of rapid growth (1979–2005). To narrow the gap between the coastal and interior provinces, the Programme pledges to boost the development of the western region, revitalise the traditional industrial base in the northeastern provinces, and promote the rise of the central region. The central government will continue to support the central and western provinces in economic policies, capital investment and industrial growth. Premier Wen Jiabao indicated that the interactive mechanism of regional co-ordination would be improved.[19]

Many western provinces in recent years have been able to achieve economic growth rates higher than the national rates largely because of the inflow of investment funds for major infrastructural projects and the rise of raw material prices in international markets. Some central provinces like Jiangxi have also been able to benefit from the re-location of labour-intensive industries from the prosperous coastal provinces, achieving a "flying geese" pattern of development. But the interior provinces have been handicapped by an eastward outflow of talents. In a way, they have been subsidizing the eastern region through educating their well-qualified labour force. Further, the development of small and medium-sized private enterprises is still backward. Meanwhile, environmental degradation remains a problem in the western region.

A survey conducted by the Ministry of Science and Technology on the eleven provincial units in western China between June 2004 and February 2005 offers an interesting picture of the difficulties in the under-developed interior, the issue of regional differences, and the problems facing China's development strategy in the next stage. Take the most basic issue of drinking water as an example, 37.4% of the households in the western provincial units had hidden safety concerns, and 48.4% of the rural households had such problems. 28.7% of the households in the western provincial units did not consistently drink boiled water, and 35.5% of the rural households shared this practice.

The overall unemployment rate in these eleven provincial units was 2% (5.9% in the urban areas, and 0.8% in the rural areas), not taking into consideration seasonal unemployment and under-employment. The overall Gini coefficient was 0.435–0.396 in the urban areas and 0.419 in the rural areas. Although 62.9% of the households believed that their economic conditions had improved in the past five years, the average urban household annual income was 17,964 yuan, and the average rural household annual income was 9,525 yuan. 42% of the households were in debt. Urban residents borrowed money mainly for building/buying houses, medical treatment, children's education and business purposes. Their rural counterparts were in debt because of purchases of agricultural production materials, expenses on medical treatment and children's education, etc.

Illiteracy remained a serious problem. For those over 15 years of age in western China, 15.9% had difficulties reading a letter, and 25.9% could not read a letter. Difficulties in access to education and medical services are reflected by the following statistics. The education expenditure of a primary school student per annum cost 4% of the average annual household income; that of a junior high school student 11%, a senior high school student 24%, and a university student 74%. For those who were injured or sick affecting work and daily life in the past thirty days, 23% had not gone to see a doctor, among whom 43.1% indicated that economic considerations were the cause.[20]

While China has been very successful in attracting foreign investment in support of its development through imported expertise and technology, there is an increasing concern at this stage that China will remain the low-technology, labour-intensive workshop to the world. In January 2006, speaking at a national conference on innovation, Premier Wen Jiabao indicated that "independent innovation (*zizhu chuangxin*)" would be core to China's development strategy in the next fifteen years.[21] In the following month, a document entitled "Outline of National Medium and Long-term Science and Technology Development Plan" was released, revealing an ambitious plan to close the gap with developed countries and transform China into a leading technological power. China would gradually increase its investment in research and development from just 1.23% of its GDP in 2004 to 2.5% (900 billion yuan) in 2020, and limit its dependence on foreign technology at the 30% level by then.[22]

The Outline identifies many focus areas of research, including space projects, information technology, genetic engineering, nuclear technology, national defence and energy conservation. It is significant that between 60% and 70% of the research and development funding would come from enterprises, while the increase in central government's fiscal input would mainly serve as a policy guide. In sum, the Outline offers a plan to lay the foundation for China to emerge as a major power in science and technology in the middle of the twenty-first century.

Weaknesses in innovation as well as in science and technology are not the only handicap for sustainable economic growth. The lack of efficiency in investment has been an increasing concern. During their economic take-off stages, Japan and Korea achieved even faster growth than China today, but with a lower level of investment. China has been very successful in attracting foreign direct investment, which amounted to about US$60 billion in 2005. However, with a savings rate of over 40% of GDP, there is no shortage of investment funds. The problem is the inefficiency of the domestic financial institutions in allocating capital. China's incremental capital-output ratio is high and rising. According to the

World Bank, the ratio rose steadily to 5.4 in 2002 from 3.96 in the first half of the 1980s. SOEs account for about 25% of output, but they receive 65% of the lending from the banking sector. Meanwhile, the banking system's non-performing loans are officially estimated at about 25% of total loans, but many foreign experts put the figure at about 40%. At this level, the banks in China are already considered bankrupt.[23]

The investment-driven high growth tends to generate over-capacity problems, which in turn force Chinese enterprises to export more. In view of the trade conflicts with the United States and the European Union, Chinese leaders appreciate that future economic growth should depend less on investment and exports, and more on domestic consumption. GDP's dependence on foreign trade has exceeded 70%; and the population's consumption as a proportion of GDP has been falling. In 1979–2004, the population's consumption increased at an average annual rate of 7% (calculated on the basis of comparable prices), while GDP grew at an average annual rate of 9.4%. Consumption as a proportion of GDP was 50.8% on average in the 1978–1990 period; and it fell to an average of 46.2% in 1991–2004. The lowest rate of 43.1% was recorded in 2004.

The decline in consumption is partly related to the widening gap between the rich and poor, especially the expanding divide between the urban and rural sectors. According to the researchers of the Institute of Economic and Social Development, National Development and Reform Commission, the income ratio between urban and rural residents continued to expand from 3.2 times in 2004 to 3.3 times in 2005. In 2005, within the urban sector, the average per capita income of the top 20% of the urban households was about six times that of the lowest 20% of the urban households; while in the rural sector, the average per capita net income of the top 20% of the rural households was about seven times that of the lowest 20% of the rural households.[24] Raising the incomes of the rural sector and the urban poor will certainly help to stimulate domestic consumption and reduce the dependence on investment and exports for sustainable growth, which is in accord with both the above economic objective and the political objective of reducing contradictions and building a harmonious society.

The new leadership has clearly indicated its intention to reverse the previous trends by demanding industry to support agriculture, and the urban sector to support the rural sector. A larger proportion of the state's investment fund will go to the rural sector to strengthen its infrastructure. At the same time, through the reform of the taxation system, the peasants' financial burden arising from taxes and levies will be considerably reduced. More important still, the rural labour force will be allowed to move into towns and small cities in search of employment. Urbanisation is now perceived to be a positive development. More resources too will go to the support of social services in the rural sector, especially education and medical services.

Migrant labourers have been a conspicuous phenomenon reflecting the poverty and under-employment in the rural sector. A rough estimate was that there were 120 million migrant labourers in 2005, with half of them moving beyond the provincial boundaries.[25] In recent years, the central government accepts that the movement of the surplus labour from the rural to the urban sector is an important way to promote urbanisation and economic development. Hence, it has been adopting active measures to improve the employment environment for this labour movement and to protect the rights of migrant labourers. These measures aim to:

a) settle the wage arrears owed to migrant labourers;
b) get rid of the illegal intermediaries and offer free employment services for migrant labourers;
c) remove the irrational restrictions and charges which discourage the migrant labour flow;
d) strengthen job training for potential migrant labourers;
e) provide free education for the children of migrant labourers;
f) study ways to include migrant labourers into the urban social security system;
g) continue to reform the household registration system so as to enable migrant labourers to enjoy equal rights and responsibilities as local residents; and

h) promulgate and implement labour legislation such as the Regulations on Labour Security Supervision (*Laodong Baozhang Jiancha Tiaoli*) released by the State Council on 1 November 2004.

Despite the above measures, migrant labourers today still encounter considerable discrimination, and there is a long way to go before they can enjoy equal treatment as local residents. Though their wages have been rising in recent years, the urban cost of living has been increasing rapidly too. Since 2004, there has emerged a shortage of migrant labour in some areas in the Pearl River Delta and Yangtze River Delta mainly because wages have become less attractive due to rising urban cost of living and improving employment conditions and remuneration in the rural sector. At the same time, violations of migrant labourers' rights remain rampant, including refusal of and delays in payment of wages, unreasonable overtime work, poor working conditions, absence of proper labour contracts, etc. Migrant labourers must better equip themselves too to meet the demand of the restructuring of manufacturing industries. A survey in 2004 revealed that 2% of the migrant labourers were illiterate or semi-literate, 16% had a primary education, and 65% of them had a junior high school education. Only 28% of them had received training in technical skills.[26] The provision of technical training will be increasingly important. China's demographical structure reveals trends both for optimism and serious caution. In the first place, while China's population reached the 1.3 billion mark on 6 January 2005, the peak might come earlier and at a lower level than anticipated earlier. The more optimistic forecast predicts that the peak would arrive in 2025 at the level of 1.387 billion. The middle-of-the-road forecast estimates that the peak would arrive in 2030 at the level of 1.447 billion; while the more pessimistic estimate places the peak in 2045 at the level of 1.575 billion. Most experts hold the view that the situation should be slightly better than the middle-of-the-road forecast; and this represents a much improved situation than the earlier forecast of the peak in 2050 at the level of 1.6 billion based on the fourth census in 1990.[27]

On the other hand, the population is ageing rapidly. The population of people aged 65 years and above reached 7.69% in 2005, and it is expected to rise steadily to 10.42% in 2017, 20.13% in 2035 and 24.28% in 2050. This ageing process takes place at a speed that approximates the world record. The proportion of people aged 65 years and above in China will take 27 years to rise from 7% to 14% (2001–2028); the corresponding length of time in Japan was 24 years (1970–1994); in the United Kingdom 45 years (1930–1975); in France 115 years (1865–1980); and in the United States about 65 years (1945–2010). The size of this aged population in China will certainly be large; it grows from 35 million in 2000 to 100.94 million in 2005 and 335.78 million in 2050.[28]

The situation in China is all the more worrying because the ageing process takes place before it has become a prosperous and developed country. When the proportion of those aged 65 years and above reached 7% in Japan in 1970, its per capita GDP was US$1,900; and when the proportion reached 14% in 1994, its per capita GDP was well above US$35,000 (US$38,000 in 1995). However, when China was on the threshold of an ageing society, its per capita GDP was only at the US$1,000 level; and when the proportion of the Chinese people aged 65 years and above reaches 14% in 2028, its per capita GDP would probably just exceed US$3,500.[29]

The quality of the population is obviously another important consideration. Chinese leadership advocates a policy of "strengthening China through science and education (*kejiao xingguo*)". Before the recent plan to raise investment in research and development in 1999, it started to increase the number of tertiary students in a very aggressive manner. From 1999 to 2004, undergraduate students in tertiary institutions in China increased by 220%, and graduate students by 310%. In the previous six years (1993–1998), the growth was only 34.4% and 86% respectively.[30] The development of tertiary education is essential to China's economic development, especially in upgrading its industries and developing its business services. However, this rapid expansion of tertiary students' intake has adversely affected the quality of university education, and generated mismatches in manpower demand and supply and substantial unemployment among fresh graduates. This is a common problem in Third World countries, but the Chinese authorities have not been able to learn the lesson from their experiences.

In 2005, university graduates in China amounted to 3.38 million, 20.7% more than in 2004; and the anticipated number in 2006 is 4.13 million. In the Eleventh Five-Year Programme period (2006–2010), China will produce more than 25 million university graduates. Yet, at the same time, the number of unemployed graduates has been rising rapidly, from 0.3 million in 2000 to over 0.52 million in 2003 and 0.69 million in 2004. In the first place, the expanding supply of graduates begins to generate an oversupply in some cities and sectors. In recent years, Party and state organs, as well as SOEs, have been under pressure to reduce their establishments to cut expenditure, and they used to be the major employers of fresh graduates. Meanwhile, the employment situation remains very tight because of the large number of people entering the labour market, surplus labour from the rural sector and the substantial pool of the unemployed. Tertiary institutions have been criticised for their inflexibility, concentrating on the expansion of similar programmes while neglecting practical work skills and the cultivation of an innovative spirit among their students. Employers are increasingly reluctant to spend on the training of new recruits too.[31]

The central government attempts to offer certain favourable conditions to direct fresh graduates to seek employment in the western provinces and the rural sector, but these conditions do not seem to have much appeal. In contrast to the employment difficulties among university graduates, there is a shortage of technicians in the coastal municipalities. There was, for example, a shortage of up to 100,000 technicians in Beijing in the summer of 2005. This shortage had been related to the decline in funding support for vocational training. In 1997, vocational education was given 11.17% of the national educational budget; this proportion dropped to 6.35% in 2002. Experts believe that vocational education needs more money than ordinary education, up to the ratio of three to one at the senior high school level. In China, the opposite was the case. In 2003, each ordinary senior high school student was allocated 265 yuan from the national educational budget, but a vocational senior high school student only received 239 yuan.[32] Further, while the Ministry of Education and the Ministry of Labour and Social Security have their respective vocational school systems, technical skills certification and accreditation are in the hands of a number of ministries too.

Finally, China's economic development strategy at this stage begins to place much more emphasis on being resource efficient and environmentally friendly. As the Chinese people's living standards improve, the demand for environmental protection has been growing, and this demand has been gradually transformed into group action. The pollution of Sunghua River in the Northeast by poisonous chemicals by a subsidiary of the China National Petroleum Corporation in Jilin in November 2005 attracted both domestic and international attention.[33] China has to import more than 40% of its oil, but its energy consumption per unit of GDP is 2.4 times higher than the world average. Yet there is no planning and research on the development of energy-saving standards, the system in place is far from satisfactory, and most energy-consuming industrial equipment does not have energy-efficiency standards. The State Council has just started to formulate various policies on the saving of resources to regulate market and consumer behaviour. Similarly, the National Development and Reform Commission, together with other ministries, recently released a "Guideline Regarding China's Policy on Water-efficient Technology", which aims to achieve a "small increase" in industrial use of water, "zero growth" in agricultural use of water, and a gradual decline in urban residents' use of water within the 2005–2010 period.[34]

The Chinese authorities hope to adjust the prices of resources and introduce tax reforms in support of the resource-efficient and environmentally-friendly development strategy. There is an increasing awareness that the prices of resources in China cannot accurately reflect the market demand and supply conditions as well as the scarcity of the resources. Chinese leaders now accept that the ultimate solution is the marketisation of the prices of resources, allowing prices to be determined in market competition, with the foci on the prices of water, electricity, oil and natural gas, coal, and land. Tax measures will soon be introduced to promote the conservation of resources through improving the efficiency in their utilisation.

In sum, Chinese leaders are acutely aware of the problems and imbalances generated by almost three decades of rapid economic growth, as well as the challenges of the next stage of economic development. They seem to have the answer too, and the crucial issue is to overcome the vested interests and continue to push for reforms.

Social Challenges

The new leadership's advocacy of the building of a harmonious society reveals the danger of sharpening contradictions in Chinese society today. According to a study group of the Institute of Sociology at the Chinese Academy of Social Sciences, China's social structure at present consists of ten social strata:

a) state and social administrators (2.1%);
b) managers (1.6%);
c) private-sector entrepreneurs (1%);
d) professionals and technicians (4.6%);
e) office personnel and general white-collar groups (7.2%);
f) individual/household entrepreneurs (7.1%);
g) commercial/service sector workers (11.2%);
h) industrial workers (17.5%);
i) agricultural labourers (42.9%); and
j) the underemployed/unemployed in the urban sector (4.8%).[35]

Ideally, the social structure should be olive-shaped, with the vast majority in the middle, and small minorities at the top and bottom.

The social structure in China today is far from ideal; there are still far too many people in the lower and lower-middle social strata, while the upper-middle strata are too small. In this context, there is a common consensus in China that the four principal social contradictions are: a) imbalances in income distribution and the widening gap between the rich and poor; b) the heavy financial burden of education, and the uneven opportunities available; c) difficult access to medical services and their high cost; d) excess of labour supply over demand, and the serious gaps in social security.

Regarding the imbalances in income distribution, Chinese people in the same occupations receive vastly different remunerations because of their respective social status, locations and involvements in different sectors. In 1985, the ratio of average per capita rural net income to average per capita urban income was 1:2.57; it gradually expanded to 1:3.23 in 2004. If one takes into consideration various types of transfer of payments and subsidies to the urban sector, the ratio may well become 1:5. These imbalances are generally regarded as the most important factors of social instability. In the event of an economic slowdown, they may easily lead to riots and protests.

In the education sector, surveys show that the respective chances of receiving tertiary education in the urban and rural sectors are in the ratio of 5.8:1, and it deteriorates to 8.8:1 regarding entry to the best universities. A study in Anhui province reveals that a university student had to spend 48,000 yuan to complete his four years of education. In the same province, the average per capita rural net income per annum in 2004 was only 2,668 yuan, so it cost a peasant his income for 18 years to support his child to complete university education.

While the population in China amounts to 22% of the world total, medical resources only make up 2% of the world total. Further, 80% of the country's medical resources are concentrated in cities, and 80% of such urban resources are concentrated in major hospitals. Medical care, or the lack of it, is an important issue causing much dissatisfaction among Chinese people.

2006 is the year when the number of new entrants to the labour market reaches its peak. In the near future, China expects an increase of 10 million new workers per annum, while another 14 million will be made redundant. Despite the impressive economic growth rates, the economy can only generate 10 million more jobs every year, resulting in an excess supply of 14 million workers. These statistics and observations[36] help to illustrate the seriousness of the social problems, and it is worthwhile to examine their causes and the Chinese authorities' responses.

Social Inequalities

In 2004, contributions from the primary, secondary and tertiary sectors to China's GDP were 15.1%, 52.9% and 32% respectively. In the same year, the three sectors provided employment for 46.9%, 22.5% and 30.6% of the total labour force respectively,[37] meaning that 46.9% of the labour force was producing only 15.1% of the GDP, which is the structural cause for the poverty among peasants. This structural factor has been exacerbated by the gap in development between the coastal and interior provinces discussed earlier.

The obvious solutions are to facilitate labour movement from the rural to the urban sector and to accelerate the development of the interior provinces with more resources from the central government. The Chinese leadership has been actively pursuing policies to realise these objectives (as discussed in the previous section), but they will take time to achieve results. According to the National Bureau of Statistics, urban employment in 2004 reached 264.76 million, with rural migrant workers numbering 120 million. In the manufacturing, construction and service industrial sectors, 63.6% of the labourers were rural migrant workers.[38] In view of the discriminations against the latter, it has been said that the urban-rural divide has re-emerged between local residents and outsiders in the cities.

The Chinese leadership now accepts an accelerated rate of urbanisation (41.8% in 2004). It endorses the experts' views that urbanisation in China seriously lags behind industrialisation, and adversely affects the modernisation process. The low rate of urbanisation slows down the expansion of the tertiary sector based on modern service industries, reduces new employment opportunities, and lowers people's consumption which goes against the objective of stimulating domestic demand.

In 2005, eleven provinces including Guangdong, Jiangsu, Zhejiang and Hunan had already introduced policies to reform the local household registration system. Apparently, there were no serious problems arising from the increase in demand for urban social services. There is thus perhaps a better foundation to ask for a complete overhaul of the system and to formally abolish the urban-rural divide through legislation by the central government. Interim measures would probably concentrate on removing the discriminations against the rural migrant workers.

Socio-economic inequalities have a significant psychological dimension too. Various opinion surveys in China reflect strong dissatisfaction with the widening gap between the rich and poor. In spring 2005, for example, *Zhongguo Jingji Shibao* (China Economic Times) and Sohu.com Inc. jointly conducted a Web-based questionnaire survey on the most concerned topic regarding the establishment of a harmonious society. The 3,700 respondents identified the following five topics: the gap between the rich and poor (identified by 23.73% of the respondents); social security and re-employment (14.59%); environmental protection (14.19%); rural sector and agricultural/peasant issues (11.73%); and adjustment and control of the real estate market (8.84%). Slightly later, China Society Research Institute conducted a questionnaire survey in ten major cities on the focal points of attention of the current annual sessions of the National People's Congress and the Chinese People's Political Consultative Conference. The 1,500 completed questionnaires indicated that the vast majority of the respondents were most concerned with the following issues: the expanding income gap between the rich and poor and injustice in social distribution (identified by 91% of the respondents); real estate and property issues (89%); employment and re-emplyment (83%); price fluctuations (81%); etc.[39]

The significant concern over of this widening gap between the rich and poor is related to the common perception that the gap has been widening rapidly, and that this widening gap is mainly the result of corruption and the use of other illegal means to get rich. Opinion surveys also demonstrate that few people consider that differences in abilities and performances are the major reasons for the socio-economic disparities. In a society which claims to be building socialism, with an emphasis on egalitarianism up to 1978, Deng Xiaoping's advocacy of "letting a segment of the population get rich first" is no longer perceived as providing the momentum for reforms and the incentive for hard work, but more as a problem of the market economy where corruption is rampant.

Education and the Middle Class

Education is considered the most important channel of upward social mobility in China today, very similar to the situation in the "four little dragons of Asia" since the late 1960s. During the Tiananmen Square Incident in 1989, the salaries of China's urban educated were low; and it was said that street hawkers selling cooked eggs earned more than the top scientists engaged in the nuclear-weapon programmes. Since then, there has been a deliberate government policy to favour the urban educated through handsome salary increases and lucrative perks including housing. As Jonathan Unger observes, China's educated middle class is elitist, and many of its members do not want democracy. If unrest like the 1989 incident occurs again, much of the middle class would be on the government's side.[40] This is reassuring to the Chinese leadership, which fears most that Chinese intellectuals and university students would stand at the forefront of organised unrest generated by the grievances of poor peasants and unemployed workers.

The material rewards for education, the restored traditional respect for intellectuals, and the prevalence of one-child families all contribute to the significance of education opportunities. The high cost of education is not only a heavy burden for the poor families, it has also reduced their chances of upward social mobility. A market economy calls for "small government, big society"; and as state inputs into education fail to grow, the increasing cost of education has to be borne by individual families, thus exacerbating the socio-economic inequalities.

The state authorities for two decades have been trying to raise budgetary expenditure on education to 4% of GDP. In 2003, the proportion stood at 3.28%, 0.04% below that in 2002; in 2004, the proportion further declined a little.[41] Funding for free education in the rural sector has been an old problem. Today over two thirds of the financial burden falls on the rural county governments which are usually poor. A survey of the rural areas conducted by the Legal System Office (*Fazhiban*) of the State Council reveals the following consequences of inadequate funding: many rural schools suffered from serious inadequacies of public funding, while some had no public funding at all (this meant that they had to transfer the burden to students' parents); some schools had dangerous buildings and were in debt; pay for teachers were delayed and could not be released in full; and parents' heavy burden led to student dropouts. A task force on case studies of the state's important education policies surveyed 17 junior high schools in the rural areas in six provinces which showed a student dropout rate of 43%, with the highest being 74.37%, vastly exceeding the 3% policy goal of providing nine years of universal free education. At the same time, because of the loss of teachers in rural areas, there has emerged a group of unqualified replacement teachers amounting to 550,000 to 600,000. They normally work in the distant, backward mountainous areas, mostly in one-teacher schools, with a monthly salary of one to two hundred yuan or less.[42]

In the National People's Congress annual session in March 2005, 740 deputies participated in amendments to the Free Education Bill. One of the deputies, Zhu Yongxin, estimated that on the basis of 500 yuan per primary school student per annum, tuition fees covering nine years of universal free education would cost 67.5 billion yuan, and they would cost only 20 billion yuan if limited only to the state-designated poor counties. This cost should be borne completely by the state budget.[43]

At the other end of the spectrum, there are senior high schools which cost a few hundred million yuan to build one, and even kindergartens which cost about one hundred million yuan each. There are also parents who pay hefty sums of money (*zexiaofei*) to enroll their children in prestigious schools. These phenomena have become talking points in big cities as they reveal a grossly unfair distribution of education resources, reflecting the widening gap between the rich and poor. In this connection, the education experiments in Tongling City in Anhui are interesting. Tongling is possibly the only city in China where students cannot choose schools. The education authorities in Tongling attempt to distribute education resources in a balanced manner, according priority to the assistance of weak schools. Teachers and principals are rotated, and the best of them go to help the schools falling behind. Finally, a high proportion of student quotas in prestigious senior high schools are equally distributed among all junior high schools (60% in 2005 and the ratio would continue to rise), so that a certain ratio of graduates in every junior high can get into the prestigious senior high schools, thus removing the incentive for parents to choose schools for their children.[44]

The declining quality of education, caused by the heavy emphasis on university entrance examinations results, is another controversial issue. The work burden of primary and high school students has been rising. They have to attend extra lessons often involving substantial costs to parents. Schools are keen to do well in all kinds of competitions, and university entrance rates have often become the most important criterion in assessing the performance of schools and local education authorities. In some cases, senior high school principals and teachers are sanctioned for the fall in university entrance rates of their students. As a result, the comprehensive development of students has been neglected, and teachers often focus on heavy assignments and public examinations drills. Education is certainly not enjoyable from students' point of view.

Medical Services

The marketisation of medical services is probably the worst aspect of market reforms in China, generating a lot of complaints and grievances. The fundamental problem is: in both urban and rural areas, the new medical insurance systems have yet to be developed satisfactorily, hence their coverage has been limited. A majority of Chinese citizens today do not have coverage of any kind, and they have to bear all medical costs when they fall ill. At the same time, medical service providers, now especially hospitals, have been fully marketised; funding from the government now constitutes an insignificant part of their revenues. Their incomes are mainly derived from their services and sales of pharmaceutical products.

Under such circumstances, there is a natural tendency for medical service providers to maximise their incomes, including asking patients to do repeated and unnecessary check-ups and prescribing expensive drugs. Access to medical services has become increasingly difficult and expensive, and this is a major complaint in the Chinese society today. In this unregulated market of medical services, resource allocation has been distorted. Most resources have gone to hospitals in the cities, especially to the most prestigious, best-equipped hospitals in the coastal metropolises, leading to declining resources for medical services at the grassroots level and in the rural areas.[45]

A survey in early 2005 demonstrated that 65.7% of the Chinese population did not have any kind of medial insurance; about one quarter of the respondents abandoned medical treatment because they could not afford it.[46] The Chinese leadership is aware of the significance of the issue, and it has begun to actively help to provide co-operative medical insurance in both the urban and rural sectors.

In the former, reforms in the health insurance system began in the early 1990s; the basic orientation was to develop a society-wide system to replace the practice of insurance being provided by employment units. Hence these reforms were largely measures introduced in support of the reform of SOEs. At the end of 1998, the central government decided to establish a basic medical insurance system for urban employees aiming at wide coverage, i.e., covering all employees including those of Party/state organs and public-sector institutions. Whether individual entrepreneurs, the self-employed and employees of township/town enterprises should be included or not would be decided by local governments. Urban employees involved have been expanding gradually; and at the end of September 2005, the system had 133.41 million participants, 9.37 million more than at the end of 2004.[47] This coverage (slightly more than 40%) is still quite far from the policy objective of "wide coverage".

As is usually the case in China, progress has been slow as apparently high priority had not been accorded by the leadership. In the private sector, especially among foreign-invested enterprises, there is a tendency to turn to commercial insurers. As their employees are young, their payments to insurance companies are less. For the same reason, they may even choose to absorb the cost and the risk themselves without securing any insurance at all. In the state sector, progress has been slow because of the incumbent employees who represent the vested interests benefiting from the old system and are naturally resistant to reforms. For enterprises in financial difficulties in the state and collective sectors, they may not even be able to pay the pages and are therefore reluctant to join any medical insurance scheme for their employees.

Experts have criticised the serious omissions in the initial policy design too. The policy promulgated in 1998 attempted to cover urban employees (*zhigong*) only, and therefore neglected the self-employed, the migrant workers, etc. In recent years, some relatively prosperous local governments have been trying to involve these neglected categories as well. More important still, the initial policy had no consideration for the families of the urban employees and the old people who had no employment units to support them. These blind spots have yet to be tackled.

Before the economic reforms in the late 1970s, it was claimed that the rural co-operative medical insurance system covered 90% of the rural population. With the dissolution of the people's communes, the system obviously could not be maintained. In 1993, the coverage of this rural co-operative medical insurance system fell to 9.8% of the rural population. It further declined to 6.6% in 1998; and in response to the central government's strong promotion, it rose back to 9.5% in 2003.

In January 2003, the central government declared its policy of establishing a new rural co-operative medical insurance system, and gradually expanding its coverage through the spread of experimental sites. The ambitious objective is to cover the entire rural population by 2010. The most important innovations include shifting the organisation and administrative work from the township/town level to the county level, and providing state support through subsidies. At the end of June 2005, 163 million people in the rural sector had participated in the system, supported by 5.038 billion yuan of state funding.[48]

At this stage, resources on a per capita basis are limited to 30 yuan per annum (20 from the central government, and 10 from each individual peasant). According to national statistics in 2004, the rural population in China spent on average 130.6 yuan per capita on medical services. The present level of resources is certainly far from adequate in offering satisfactory medical services. There are other serious problems too. Since this is a voluntary system, there are many types of reasons for peasants to refuse participation. The present level of participation has been exaggerated because there are many cases of local governments forcing the rural residents to take part in order to secure the central government subsidy and to claim good performance in meeting policy demands from the above. As the present system largely serves as a safety net and only covers major illnesses, those who are relatively healthy feel that they have not been well served. Regarding the poor peasants, they still cannot afford their required shares of the costs involved in major illnesses and operations and have to choose to give up seeking medical treatment, so the system cannot help them either. In the case of poor local governments, they too have difficulty absorbing the additional financial burden.

The current medical services provided in China are a very significant example of failure in the marketisation of essential social services. They also reveal the limitations of "small government, big society". Economic development and the building of a "harmonious society" as claimed by the new leadership cannot be perceived to have benefited two thirds of the population who find access to medical services difficult and often beyond their means. Worse still, improvements can only come slowly.

Conclusion

At the end of the Cold War, Francis Fukuyama concluded that the evolution of human societies through different forms of government had culminated in modern liberal democracy.[49] China seems to have convinced the world that it will be an exception, at least in the foreseeable future. While the Chinese leadership refuses to allow any erosion of the CPC's monopoly of political power, it has been very skilful in meeting the emerging challenges in the era of economic reforms and opening to the outside world.

In the beginning of this era, Deng Xiaoping and his supporters realised that the legitimacy of the Communist regime had to depend on its ability to deliver the goods. The CPC attempted to secure its legitimacy by improving the people's living standards through economic development. Up till today, Chinese leaders continue to try to achieve an economic growth rate of 8% per annum. In the final years of Jiang Zemin as the top leader, he attempted to introduce the "three represents" theory and to recruit entrepreneurs into the Party so as to broaden its base of support.[50] Obviously, entrepreneurs, managers, professionals, Party cadres, state administrators, etc. have now constituted the backbone of China's expanding middle class, and they have much benefited from the country's impressive economic development. Hence they are in support of the *status quo* and do not want to see radical reforms.

Hu Jintao and the other Chinese leaders today are well aware of the sharpening social contradictions, that is why they are now trying to build a "harmonious society" with more assistance to the under-privileged groups mainly through the establishment of a social security net. Efforts are made to maintain a better balance while avoiding undue emphasis on economic growth rates alone, including higher priority accorded to environmental protection, higher efficiency achieved in the utilisation of natural resources, more encouragement of internal consumption, greater dependence placed on the domestic market, etc. The Chinese leadership also attempts to continue to maintain a friendly international environment in the future by establishing various kinds of strategic partnerships and partnerships with the major powers of the world and offering re-assurances to downplay the "China threat" perception among its Asian neighbours.[51] It is commonly recognised that these policy orientations are in the right direction. The question is how successful they will be in maintaining political stability in the absence of genuine political reforms.

The rapid increase in protests, riots and mass petitioning not only reflects exacerbating social contradictions in the context of the widening gap between the rich and poor, it also demonstrates the empowerment of the under-privileged groups with rising anger against corruption and abuse of power.[52] The Tiananmen Square incident in June 1989 was triggered off by the outrage against corruption and the demand for democracy. Today the Chinese leadership still refuses to respond to the request for a reversal of the official verdict on the incident. Similarly, it suppressed discussion on the Cultural Revolution during the fortieth anniversary of its launch and imposed many restrictions on the funeral of Zhao Ziyang. This pattern of behaviour reveals its strong sense of insecurity. It is generally believed that Beijing has been very concerned with the recent "coloured revolutions" in the post-Soviet states.

There are significant paradoxes regarding corruption in China. In the first place, the spread of corruption does not seem to have hampered China's economic development. Further, more economic liberalisation apparently has led to more corruption in China. Regarding the causes of corruption, the so-called new left or social democrats in China blame the authorities' blind faith in the market, especially after 1992, pointing to the decline in resources at the disposal of the central government to offer more social services to promote a more equitable re-distribution of income, as well as the loss of control over local cadres. The new right or neoliberals, on the other hand, criticise the over-extended role of the government and advocate a reduction of state power. These intellectuals emphasise property rights and push for privatisation.[53]

The leadership, however, follows Deng Xiaoping's advice and continues to avoid open ideological debates. It tries to generate resources to implement policies bringing relief to the poor. This task has been made easier by the rapid economic growth. The real pressure will come when the economy slows down. As observed by Samuel P. Huntington, revolutions often occur when a period of sustained economic growth is followed by a sharp economic downturn.[54]

Notes and References

1. *South China Morning Post* (an English newspaper in Hong Kong), 26 January 2006.

2. Xiao Guoliang and Sui Fumin, "Chuyu shizilukou de Zhongguo jingji – 2005 nian hongguan tiaokong zhengce fenxi (Chinese economy at the crossroads – policy analysis of macro-economic adjustments and control in 2005)", in Governance in Asia Research Centre, City University of Hong Kong and Centre for Public Policy Study, Chinese Academy of Social Sciences (eds.), *Zhongguo Gonggong Zhengce Fenxi 2005 (Analysis of Public Policies of China 2005)* (Hong Kong: City University of Hong Kong Press, 2005), pp. 35–39.

3. Gu Yan and Yang Yiyong, "Shouru fenpei lingyu de xin qingkuang, xin tedian jiqi duice" ("New trends in income distribution and related policy recommendations"), in Ru Xin, Lu Xueyi, Li Peilin, et al. (eds.), *Shehui Lanpishu – 2005 Nian: Zhongguo Shehui Xingshi Fenxi yu Yuce (Bluebook of China's Society – Year 2005: Analysis and Forecast on China's Social Development)* (Beijing: Social Sciences Academic Press, 2004), p. 222.

4. *Central Daily News* (a Chinese newspaper in Taipei), 16 December 2005; and *South China Morning Post*, 8 February 2006.

5. *Ibid.*

6. "Wen explains proposal on 11th 5-year plan", see http://www.gov.cn/english/2005-10/20/content_80097.htm.

7. *South China Morning Post*, 8 February 2006.

8. *Dalu Qingshi* (*Mainland China Situation*), published by the Mainland Affairs Council, Government of Taiwan, January 2006 issue, p. 2.

9. *Oriental Daily News* and *Wen Wei Po* (Chinese newspapers in Hong Kong), 5 November 2005; *Ta Kung Pao* (a Chinese newspaper in Hong Kong), 25 November 2005; and *New China News Agency* dispatch, 16 November 2005.

10. *Ibid.*, 28, 29, 30 November and 20 December 2005.

11. *The Sun* (a Chinese newspaper in Hong Kong), 5 November 2005.

12. *China Times* (a Chinese newspaper in Taipei), 5 January 2006.

13. *New China News Agency* dispatch, 2 December 2005.

14. *Oriental Daily News*, 7 December 2005.

15. *New China News Agency* dispatch, 5 December 2005; and *China News Agency* dispatch, 21 December 2005.

16. *Hong Kong Economic Times* (a Chinese newspaper in Hong Kong), 18 November 2005.

17. *The Sun*, 11 December 2005; and *Hong Kong Economic Journal* (a Chinese newspaper in Hong Kong), 13 December 2005, quoting *Liaowang Weekly* (Beijing), 5 December 2005.

18. "Guiding proposal issued for next 5 years", http://www.gov.cn/english/2005-10/19/content_79375.htm.

19. "Wen explains proposal on 11th 5-year plan".

20. Wang Fenyun and Zhao Yandong, "Xibu 11 sheng (shi, qu) chengxiang jumin shenghuo zhuangkuang diaocha (Living conditions in rural and urban China – survey from 11 provinces)", in Ru Xin, Lu Xueyi, Li Peilin, et al. (eds.), *op. cit.*, pp. 17–29.

21. David Kang and Adam Segal, "The Siren Song of Technonationalism", *Far Eastern Economic Review*, Vol. 169, No. 2, (March 2006), p. 6.

22. *South China Morning Post*, 10 February 2006; and *Ming Pao* (a Chinese newspaper in Hong Kong), 10 February 2006.

23. Hugo Restall, "India's coming eclipse of China", *Far Eastern Economic Review*, Vol. 169, No. 2 (March 2006), pp. 12–15.

24. See Li Peilin, "Zhongguo zhanzai xin de lishi qidian shang – 2005–2006 nian Zhongguo shehui xingshi fenxi yu yuce zongbaogao" ("China at the Historical Turning-point – Analysis of Social Situation in China, 2005–2006"), in Ru Xin, Lu Xueyi, Li Peilin, et al. (eds.), *Shehui Lanpishu –*

2006 Nian: Zhongguo Shehui Xingshi Fenxi yu Yuce (*Bluebook of China's Society – Year 2006: Analysis and Forecast on China's Social Development*) (Beijing: Social Sciences Academic Press, 2005), p. 9.

25. Gu Yan and Yang Yiyong, "2005–2006 nian: Zhongguo shouru fenpei wenti yu zhanwang" ("Income distribution in 2005–2006"), in *ibid.*, pp. 277–278.

26. Mo Rong, Liu Jun and Chen Lan, "Jiuye xingshi: guanzhu nongmingong de jiuye wenti" ("Employment: more attention to rural migrants"), in *ibid.*, p. 113.

27. *Ibid.*, pp. 113 and 117–120.

28. Zhang Yi, "13 Yi zhihou Zhongguo renkou de xin tezheng" ("New characteristics of demographical structure"), in *ibid.*, p. 99–100.

29. *Ibid.*, pp. 102–105; and Zhang Weimin, Xu Gang, Yu Hongwen and Cui Hongyan, "Renkou biandong yuce" ("Forecasts on population changes"), in Tian Xueyuan and Wang Guoqiang (eds.), *Quanmian Jianshe Xiaokang Shehui Zhong de Renkou yu Fazhan* (*Population and Development in the Comprehensive Construction of a Relatively Prosperous Society*) (Beijing: *Zhongguo Renkou Chubanshe*, 2004, pp. 121–122).

30. Huang Yanfen and Li Hongmei, "Jinrong fengxian xin biaoxian: guore de gaoxiao quandi daikuan (New problems in finance and banking: loans to universities)", in Ru Xin, Lu Xueyi, Li Peilin, et al. (eds.), *op. cit.*, (2005), p. 301.

31. *Dalu Qingshi* (*Mainland China Situation*), op. cit., pp. 46–48.

32. Ji Kesian, "Jiye jiaoyu qidai xin tupo (Vocational education expects new breakthrough)", *Xiandai Jiaoyu Bao* (a Chinese newspaper in Beijing), 31 August 2005.

33. *China Times*, 24 November 2005.

34. Yan Shihui, "Jianshe ziyuan jieyue he huanjing youhao xing shehui" ("Establishing an Energy saving and environmentally friendly society"), in Ru Xin, Lu Xueyi, Li Peilin, et al. (eds.), *op. cit.*, (2005), pp. 178–179.

35. Lu Xueyi, "Tiaozheng shehui jiegou, goujian shehuizhuyi hexie shehui" ("Adjusting social structure for the construction of a harmonious society"), in *ibid.*, p. 203.

36. *Ibid.*, pp. 193–208; Li Peilin, *op. cit.*, pp. 1–14; and *New China News Agency* dispatch, 30 October 2005.

37. Lu Xueyi, *op. cit.*, p. 196.

38. *Ibid.*, p. 200.

39. For details of the two surveys, see Wang Junxiu, "Dangqian Zhongguo

shehui xintai fenxi baogao" ("Current socio-psychological analysis"), in Ru Xin, Lu Xueyi, Li Peilin, et al. (eds.), *op. cit.*, (2005), pp. 68–69.

40. See Jonathan Unger, "China's Conservation Middle Class", *Far Eastern Economic Review*, Vol. 169, No. 3, (April 2006), pp. 27–31.

41. Yang Dongping, "Zouxiang gongping: 2005 nian Zhongguo jiaoyu fazhan baogao (Towards social justice: education in 2005)", in Ru Xin, Lu Xueyi, Li Peilin, et al. (eds.), *op. cit.*, (2005), p. 236.

42. *Ibid.*, pp. 239–240.

43. *Ibid.*, p. 240.

44. *Ibid.*, p. 239.

45. Gu Xin, "Zhongguo yiliao tezhi gaige: xianzhuang yu tiaozhan (China's public health reform: current situation and challenges)", in *ibid.*, pp. 209–210.

46. The survey was conducted by Horizon Social Survey Co. in February 2005 in seven cities and townships/towns in seven provinces. The survey data was released in a Central Television programme *Dongfang Shikong (Eastern Universe)* on 30 September 2005; see http://www.lm.gov.cn/gb/insurance/2005-09/30/content_87469.htm.

47. Gu Xin, *op. cit.*, p. 212.

48. *Ibid.*, pp. 214–215.

49. Francis Fukuyama, *The End of History and the Last Man* (New York: Free Press, 1992).

50. See Jiang Zemin's speech on the eightieth anniversary of the establishment of the CPC in *Remin Ribao* (Beijing, 2 July 2001).

51. See the author and Zhang Wankun, "Patterns and dynamics of China's international strategic behaviour", *Journal of Contemporary China*, Vol. 11, No. 31 (May 2002), pp. 235–260.

52. Gordon G. Chang, "Halfway to China's Collapse", *Far Eastern Economic Review*, Vol. 169, No. 5 (June 2006), pp. 26–27.

53. Yan Sun, "Corruption, Growth, and Reform: The Chinese Enigma", Current History, Vol. 104, No. 683 (September 2005), pp. 257, 262.

54. Samuel P. Huntington, *Political Order in Changing Societies* (New Haven: Yale University Press, 1968); and Samuel P. Huntington, *The Third Wave: Democratization in the Late Twentieth Century* (Norman: University of Oklahoma Press, 1991).

2

The Traits and Political Orientation of China's Fifth-generation Leadership

Willy Wo-Lap LAM

Introduction

At the time of the 18th National Congress of the Communist Party of China (CPC) slated for 2012, both President Hu Jintao and Premier Wen Jiabao will be 69, meaning they will be stepping down from the Politburo if existing criteria on rejuvenation are followed. For convenience of classification, top cadres who have run China after the longish "Jiang Zemin era" (1989–2003) are identified as the *disidai* or fourth-generation leadership – and that coming after the Hu-Wen team, the *diwudi* or the Fifth-generation corps. This paper will look at the background, traits as well as political orientation and agenda of fifth-generation leaders, particularly those with good ties with supremo Hu. More significantly, the question of whether the successors of Hu and Wen will be able to accomplish the unfinished goals of the Fourth Generation will be examined. Equally important will be the issue of how different the young turks will be from their forebears – and whether their enhanced policy input in the 2010s will spell a difference in areas including economic and political reform.

Since it has been a long-standing Chinese tradition for up-and-coming politicians to lie low, to remain humble – and not to be seen as upstaging their seniors – few among the potential leaders for the 2010s have impressed domestic or foreign observers with a distinctive personality or clear-cut policy orientation. However, it is possible from a careful examination of current Chinese politics as well as the factions and groupings from which future leaders will likely emerge to make fair and balanced projections of how Fifth-generation cadres will behave. Particularly given the growing importance of China on the world stage, as well as the popularity of the "China threat" theory, it is imperative that more light be shed on the men and women who will succeed the Hu-Wen team.

Challenges Facing
the Next Generation of Leaders

By late 2006, the Fourth-Generation leadership – often referred to as the "Hu-Wen team" – had already been in power for four years. Given the likelihood that both Hu and Wen will serve until the 18th National Congress of the Communist Party of China (CPC) in 2012, it is perhaps injudicious to pass too early a judgment on their accomplishments. However, it is also true that much of the essence of the so-called *huwen xinzheng* ("Hu-Wen New Deal") has become apparent – to the extent that it has become meaningful to analyze both the good points and demerits of the Fourth-Generation leadership. For example, the Hu-led Politburo has won plaudits for their *yiren wenben* ("putting-people-first") credo as well as their "scientific view of development," which means that the party and government are paying a lot more attention than previous administrations to boosting the living standards of the disadvantaged sectors and to promote social justice.[1] The Hu-Wen team has by and large acquitted itself well in maintaining a high growth rate and in generating new jobs. This is despite the fact that the State Council has at least in the views of Western economists and government officials, been too cautious in economic reform, particularly in allowing market forces to play a bigger role in the capital, stock and currency markets. Moreover, Hu, as Head of the CPC Leading Group on Foreign Affairs, has in particular achieved notable results in the foreign policy sector.

At the same time, it is true that the shortcomings of the Hu-Wen regime have also become obvious. And the evolution of Chinese politics since the 16th CPC Congress has cast doubt on whether this leadership could by 2012 change its ways or otherwise make amends for their shortfalls. Just take the example of political reform, on which the world's attention is focused as a bellwether of which way China is going. When Hu first took over from the conservative ex-president Jiang Zemin, there were great expectations that this "China's Gorbachev" might move faster in areas ranging from ideological liberalisation to fostering a pluralistic society. However, particularly since mid-2004, Hu – and such of his Politburo colleagues in charge of propaganda and security as Luo Gan, Li Changchun, Liu Yunshan and Zhou Yongkang – has turned back the clock on liberalisation by arresting and harassing a large number of liberal academics, intellectuals, as well as members of activist NGOs and professional organisations. A number of initiatives begun in the Jiang years, for example, expanding village elections to the level of *xiang* (townships) and *zhen* (towns), have been shelved.[2]

The one question that most haunts members of the Fourth-Generation leadership may be: will theirs be merely a transitional epoch? In other words, because of ideological straitjackets as well as force of circumstances, the likes of Hu and Wen might not have the opportunity to demonstrate their worth and come up with thorough-going reformist agendas during the time allotted them from 2002 to 2012. Constraining factors include not only socio-economic instability but the unwillingness of the ruling elite – what some political scientists have called a "collusive bloc" of CPC cadres and business leaders – to introduce changes that may detract from their monopoly on power.[3]

The argument can be made that because of their background and training – as well as shifting international realities – *diwudai* or Fifth-Generation cadres might be better placed – and timed – to finish the new long march of reform. While no definition of the *diwudai* has been given by the official media, the Fifth Generation can generally be characterized as cadres now in their late-30s to the early 50s. Most *diwudai* cadres attended college in the mid-1970s and 1980s – and joined the CPC from the late 1970s onwards. In terms of education and professional experience, members of the *diwudai* are better qualified than their forebears. Many have master's or doctorates in the social sciences – as distinguished from the fact that practically all Third- and Fourth-generation titans were engineering graduates. While most *diwudai* cadres were trained in Chinese universities, a good proportion have attended at least short-term courses – or worked – in Western or Asian countries. Many of them have had ample experience in interacting with Western businessmen or academics – and quite a few can speak English with ease. The single most important influence in their life and career is Deng Xiaoping's reform policies rather than earlier events such as the Cultural Revolution of 1966 to 1976. Moreover, relatively few of them share President Hu's apparent attachment to many aspects of Maoism, including Mao's teachings such as "democratic centralism."[4]

Compared with their predecessors, Fifth-generation cadres have had substantially more exposure particularly to the U.S. and Europe. Among the estimated 400,000-odd Chinese who have gone abroad for education since the early 1980s, about 180,000 have returned to work in China. And a considerable number of these so-called "returnees," or holders of American and other foreign degrees, might be inducted to leadership circles toward the end of the present decade.[5] It is possible that given their knowledge of the Western economy and society, reform on a wide variety of areas might be speeded up. Moreover, it is likely that owing to factors including the spread of the Internet and enhanced contact with foreign culture post-WTO, Chinese as a whole may be more attuned to the requirements of globalisation. Compared with their *disidai* predecessors, *diwudai* stalwarts might have a better understanding of the fact that it would be quite impossible – if not self-destructive – for the CPC to maintain the kind of monopoly on power, resources and information that was still possible in the early 2000s.

How far the *diwudai* could go in the 2010s depends, of course, on how well the masters of Zhongnanhai are handling social unrest particularly in the countryside. It will take at least until around 2010 before the fruits of the Hu-Wen team's *yiren weiben* ("putting people first") and "scientific" development theories could start reversing the trend of worsening social polarisation – if not class warfare – that is the unfortunate side-effect of what some commentators have called the primitive stage of Chinese-style capitalism. Given that the knee-jerk reaction of the average CPC cadre – including one who has attended college in the West – is to beef up control and suppression mechanisms, whether Fifth-generation leaders are in a position to introduce genuine political reforms remains a big uncertainty.

The younger generation of leadership also has to deal with the responsibilities that come with China's emergent "regional superpower" status in the Asia-Pacific region. Competition between China on the one hand, and the U.S. and Japan on the other, will heat up further by the early 2010s. For reasons including securing the requisite *Lebensraum* for economic development such as energy supplies –plus the imperative of reining in Taiwan independence – Beijing is expected to adopt more aggressive defense and foreign policies.[6] A big test of the *diwudai's* ability to advance the course of reform will be whether they would fall for the growing demands of nationalism – seen as the only cohesive force in this far-flung country in this post-socialist era. Should Fifth-generation cadres succumb to the nationalistic temptation, their achievements in both economic and political reform may be adversely affected.

Traits of the Fifth-generation Leadership

The Fifth-Generation leadership is tipped to begin running China from the early 2010s. In the wake of China's WTO accession in late 2001 – and the need for the party, government and enterprises to recruit thousand upon thousand of English-speaking, globally-minded professionals – the proportion of senior posts being given to officials in their early 40s or even late 30s is expected to increase dramatically. Indeed, by the end of 2006, there were several cadres around 45 years of age who had already been appointed to vice ministerial-level posts or above. Among those born in 1960 were Acting Governor of Hunan Zhou Qiang, Vice-Minister at the State Environmental Protection Agency (SEPA) Pan Yue, Vice-Minister at the State Council Office for Taiwan Affairs Ye Kedong, Vice-Party Secretary of Tibet Hao Peng, and Vice-Minister at the Ministry of Justice Zhao Dacheng. Other rising stars include Minister of Agriculture Sun Zhengcai (born 1963), Party Secretary of the Communist Youth League Hu Chunhua (1963), Vice-mayor of Beijing Lu Hao (1967), and Vice-Governor of Tibet Deng Xiaogang (1967).[7]

Given that most *diwudai* cadres have developed their careers in the epoch of market reforms, it seems reasonable to assume that it is in their vested interests to continue with economic liberalisation. This is particularly true for those with experience in departments such as foreign trade or financial regulatory agencies, which either did not exist or were not considered important in the pre-reform era. However, it is a testimony to the time-tested bureaucratic philosophy of "never taking the lead" that by 2006, few among the bright young men and women tipped for the big times had yet displayed a knack for bold thinking or novel problem-solving.

A key factor behind the traits and outlook of Fifth Generation cadres is their background and political affiliations. Given the predominance of President Hu in Chinese politics after the retirement of ex-president Jiang in September 2002, it is not surprising that the majority of the fast-rising officials come from the so-called Hu Jintao or Communist Youth League (CYL) Faction (see following section). In order to fully appreciate the peculiar nature of the Hu or CYL Faction, it is perhaps instructive to first look at other cliques. By 2006, it was obvious that quite a few traditional nurturing grounds for leaders might be losing their effectiveness. Take, for example, the talent pool known usually as the "gang of princelings," or the sons and daughters of senior cadres. By the early 2000s, quite a large number of these "high-born" cadres had gone into business rather than the much more risky world of politics and government. Examples included the offspring of former premier Li Peng, whose reputation as "Tiananmen Square butcher" has stuck with Chinese and foreigners alike. Daughter Li Xiaolin, for example, has emerged as a successful businesswoman in the electricity sector.[8]

Prominent princelings in their late 40s and early 50s who have already occupied vice-ministerial positions or above include Zhejiang Party Secretary Xi Jinping (born 1953), Chinese Academy of Science Vice-President Jiang Mianheng (1957), SEPA Vice-Minister Pan Yue (1960), Vice-Political Commissar of the PLA's General Logistics Department, Major-General Liu Yuan (1951), and Political Commissar of the PLA Air Force Liu Yazhou (1952). They are respectively the son of party elder Xi Zhongxun; son of Jiang Zemin; son-in-law of General Liu Huaqing; son of the late president Liu Shaoqi; and son-in-law of late president Li Xiannian. However, as Chinese society becomes more pluralistic, the general public's antipathy toward "dynastic politics" has increased. And it is little wonder that most sons and daughters of the current Politburo – who might have developed into *diwudi* stalwarts – have kept a low profile at least in the political field.[9]

Another erstwhile hotbed of talent, the *Shanghaibang*, "Shanghai Faction," is tipped to decline in significance following the full retirement of ex-president Jiang – and the expected retirement from the Politburo Standing Committee and Politburo of a number of Shanghai Faction stalwarts at the 17th CPC Congress in 2007. For example, Vice-President Zeng Qinghong, Executive Vice-Premier Huang Ju, and the Chairman of the Chinese People's Political Consultative Conference Jia Qinglin are tipped to call it quits on that occasion. For obvious reasons, unpopular Fifth-generation Shanghai Faction affiliates with excessively close ties to ex-president Jiang are expected to fade away. Foremost among them is Jiang's eldest son Jiang Mianheng, who is widely thought to have leapfrogged up the business – and later political – ladder owing to his father's special position.[10]

Indeed, the Shanghai Faction's relative eclipse seems probable despite the fact that *Shanghaibang* stalwarts such as Zeng Qinghong and National People's Congress Chairman Wu Bangguo have been grooming potential *diwudai* cadres from the early 2000s. As of 2006, younger-generation Shanghai Faction affiliates with potentials for promotion include Shanghai Mayor Han Zheng (who, however, is also close to the Hu Faction); Party Secretary of Jiangxi Meng Jianzhu; Director of the CPC General Office Policy Research Unit Wang Huning; and Vice-Mayor of Chongqing Huang Qifan. Most members of this group, such as Meng (born 1947), are already in their mid-50s; and only Mayor Han (1954) and Wang (1955) enjoy the age advantage.[11]

Given the fact that Shanghai-related politicians and intellectuals have played such a big role in Chinese politics since the 1960s, it would be a pity if the Hu-Wen leadership were to sideline the clique simply for factionalist considerations. After all, quite a few former underlings of ex-president Jiang have displayed reformist tendencies. Wang, a former professor at Fudan University, for example, fed ex-president Jiang a number of forward-looking proposals for political reform. These have ranged from expanding village-level elections to modernizing the structure of the PLA.[12]

Faring better than the Shanghai Faction is a solid body of financially-oriented technocrats who first gained national prominence as the bright young men and women working under former premier Zhu Rongji and former vice-premier Wen Jiabao. Most of them have had long experience in departments such as the Ministry of Finance, the banks, foreign trade units, as well as regulatory bodies such as the China Securities Regulatory Commission (CSRC). A number of Zhu – and Wen – affiliates who straddle the Fourth and Fifth generations have already risen to senior slots in the State Council. Prominent among them are Head of the National Development and Reform Commission Ma Kai (born 1946), Executive Vice Minister of Finance Lou Jiwei (1950), Chairman of the China Construction Bank Guo Shuqing (1956), and the Vice-Chairman of the National Council for the Social Security Fund Gao Xiqing (1953). Up-and-coming Fifth-generation affiliates of what can be loosely called the "Zhu-Wen Faction" also include People's Bank of China Vice-Governor Wu Xiaoling and the Assistant Minister of Commerce, Yi Xiaozhun. However, these technocrats will probably function more as executors of policy rather than originators of new ideas on reform, particularly socio-political reform.[13]

Last but not least, the *haigui pai* or "returnees from abroad" is set to pack a punch in the 2010s. By the mid-2000s, a few dozen returnees had advanced to vice ministerial-level posts or above. Well-known Fourth-Generation *haigui pai* ministers have included the Governor of the People's Bank of China, Zhou Xiaochuan, Minister of Education Zhou Ji, Minister of Science and Technology Xu Guanhua, and the Ambassador to the U.S. and former Vice Foreign Minister Zhou Wenzhong. Fast-rising Fifth-Generation returnees who have made good include Vice-Mayor of Shanghai Yan Junqi, who studied in Sweden; Hunan Vice-Governor Gan Lin, a graduate of Nottingham University in England; and Jiangsu Vice-Governor Zhang Taolin, who has a German doctorate.[14] Given the overall pliability of Chinese cadres, *haigui pai* affiliates do not seem to have suffered discrimination because of possible suspicion by some of their more conservative superiors that the neophytes might have been exposed to heavy dosages of "bourgeois liberalisation" while studying in such hotbeds of capitalistic decadence as New York, London or Paris.

The Predominance of the Communist Youth League (CYL) Clique

It is not surprising that among various CPC factions, the CYL Clique has been most successful in propagating *diwudai* successors. After all, the very function of the league is to identify potential leaders from the younger generation. The political fortune of the entire faction has gone up tremendously following the rise of President Hu. A number of Beijing-based officials who are in their late 30s to early 50s are CYL alumnae and considered Hu protégés.

Foremost among them are the Vice-Director of the CPC General Office, Ling Jihua (born 1956), Party Secretary of Chongqing Wang Yang (1955), Vice-Head at the CPC Organisation Department Shen Yueyue (1957), and the President of the Chinese State General Administration of Sport Liu Peng (1951).[15]

Having himself served for long years in the provinces, Hu has been particularly conscientious in grooming CYL alumnae for important regional slots. By 2005, there were more than 20 league affiliates holding positions such as party secretary, governor, or mayors – or the relevant deputy positions. The regional strength of the CYL Faction was augmented following a spate of reshuffle after Hu became CMC chief in September 2004. Young turks with potential included Party Secretary of Liaoning Province Li Kejiang (born 1955), Party Secretary of Jiangsu Li Yuanchao (1951), Party Secretary of Tibet Zhang Qingli (1955), Governor of Qinghai Song Xiuyan (1955), Governor of Fujian Huang Xiaojing (1946), Party Secretary of Guangxi Liu Qibao (1953), Party Secretary of Shaanxi Yuan Chunqing (1952), Vice-Party Secretary of Beijing Qiang Wei (1955), Vice-Party Secretary of Shandong Jiang Daming (1953), and Mayor of Lhasa Luosang Jiangcun (1957).[16]

The profusion of CYL members on the rise has given rise to this question: are they any good? What some critics call the intrinsic deficiencies of the leaguers still obtain. This is a reference to the fact that owing to their background and experience, most league alumnae are career party functionaries and party affairs specialists well-versed in areas including ideology, propaganda and organisation.[17] Quite a few of them followed the career trajectories of famous CYL politicians including Hu himself and former PSC member Hu Qili: they started their political careers as student leaders at famous universities such as Tsinghua or Peking universities. Such is the case, for example, of prominent Hu protégés Li Keqiang and Ling Jihua. And quite a number of league stalwarts, for example, Li Yuanchao, Liu Qibao and Liu Peng, have had experience working in the culture, media and propaganda fields. By contrast, relatively few CYL affiliates have had exposure to economic, finance or foreign trade departments. While most of them may be familiar with how market forces work – and are supporters of economic liberalisation – league affiliates almost invariably take as an article of faith not only the imperative of the survival of the CPC as the ruling party but also the fact that party organs should play dominant roles in almost all aspects of the polity.[18]

Moreover, there is evidence that after cataclysmic events including the 1989 pro-democracy movement and the fall of the Soviet bloc in the early 1990s, a wave of conservatism has swept the CYL and its affiliates. Bona fide liberals such as Hu Yaobang and former head of propaganda Zhu Houze – who was also put under surveillance on orders from President Hu – seem to have become very much a rarity. As of early 2005, there is little to support the optimistic projection that younger-generation CYL stalwarts such as the two Li's of Liaoning and Jiangsu possess the breadth of vision and willingness to embrace the new-fangled that characterized Hu Yaobang and Zhu Houze.

Apart from Youth League associates, Hu has also promoted former associates and underlings who had worked with him in western provinces. After all, the president spent more than a dozen years in the provinces of Gansu, Guizhou, and Tibet. Members of this so-called Northwestern Faction included the just retired Party Secretary of Sichuan, Zhang Xuezhong, Director of the New China News Agency, Tian Congming, Governor of Gansu Lu Hao, and the First Vice-Chairman of the State Banking Regulatory Commission, Yan Hanwang. Particularly among young turks below 50 years of age, however, the Northwest Faction pales in importance alongside Hu's CLY protégés.[19]

Moreover, the CLY faction may have the same problem of legitimacy that haunted the Shanghai Faction under ex-president Jiang. Jiang – and subsequently Hu – seemed to have violated the principle laid down by Deng concerning "geographic distribution" in the selection of cadres. Immediately after the June 4, 1989 crisis, Deng noted that leading officials should come "from the five lakes and four seas," a reference to the fact that factionalism would only vitiate the strength of the party. One of the reasons behind the unpopularity of Jiang – and his close associates such as Vice-

President Zeng – is that he has promoted an excessively large number of his cronies from the Greater Shanghai Region.[20]

The same seems to be happening with Hu. Questions have been asked about the competence of the scores of CYL-related officials he has elevated in the run-up to and after the 16th CPC Congress (also see following section). This was particularly the case for Hu cronies installed to slots that required special expertise. Take for example, Yan Haiwang, a former party secretary of Gansu who became vice-governor of the People's Bank of China in 1998 and CBRC vice-chairman five years later. Yan's relationship with Hu goes back to their days together in Gansu. However, partly because Yan had had no expertise in banking, his appointment to top positions in the banking sector was almost entirely due to Hu's recommendation.[21]

Hu's mid-2005 appointment of another CYL protégé, Wu Aiying to the important post of Justice Minister has also raised eyebrows. Wu is yet another of the career party apparatchiks who rose through the ranks of a provincial youth league. Born in 1951 in Shandong, Wu spent almost her entire career in her native province, where she held mostly party-related political jobs. Apart from being a leader of the Shandong CYL from 1982 to 1989, she has looked after the All China Women's Federation and was Chairman of the provincial Chinese People's Political Consultative Conference. Most significantly, the Hu associate has had no formal training in the law whatsoever.[22]

Major Candidates for Leadership Posts

Leading Candidates to Succeed Hu Jintao

The two Lis – Li Keqiang and Li Yuanchao – are the unquestioned frontrunners to be "the next Hu Jintao." Sources close to the Hu-Wen team think it is possible that one of the two Lis may be appointed to the Politburo, even the Politburo Standing Committee (PSC), at the 17th CPC Congress. A close examination of the career and policy orientation of the two Lis will shed further light on what *diwudai* leaders are like – and what kind of changes they may introduce in the 2010s.

Sometimes known as "Hu's clone" and alter ego, Li Keqiang (born 1955) has had a similar background to his mentor. Like Hu, Li remained in college as a political instructor and CYL cadre after graduating with distinction from the Law Faculty at Peking University in 1982. He rose through the ranks of the league to become its chief in 1993. That Li became a ministerial cadre at the tender age of 38 was an unmistakable sign that he was being groomed by Hu for bigger things. Moreover, the Anhui native was made a full Central Committee member at the 15th Congress in 1997 – while it was not until 2002 that his closest competitor for Hu's mantle, Li Yuanchao, became an alternate Central Committee member.[23]

In 1998, Li Keqiang was transferred to populous Henan Province as vice-governor; and he became governor one year later. In the Chinese hierarchy, a young turk with big promise has to spend at least several years in the localities before further promotions in the *zhongyang* ("centre" or central party and government organs) are possible. Li became party secretary, the No. 1 position of Henan, in 2002. And in a sign that Hu was preparing to soon elevate Li to the Politburo, the president's protégé was transferred to Liaoning in late 2004. This move could be critical to Li's political fortune because having worked for six years in a predominantly agricultural province, he now had to prove his mettle in an industrial setting. The Liaoning slot is also important because developing the *dongbei* or northeast is one of the key initiatives of the post-16 Congress leadership. And Liaoning being the most important of the three northeastern provinces, the bulk of state investments in the *dongbei* would be channelled to Liaoning.

Li has many advantages. With a bachelor's degree in law – and a doctorate in economics which he completed while working in the CYL – Li fits the profile of the new generation of cadres well-versed in the social sciences. Having worked in the league for 16 years, he has inherited a vast national network of Fifth- and Sixth-Generation cadres. Moreover, he is the youngest among the dozen-odd cadres that the Hu-Wen leadership is poised to induct into the Politburo in 2007. However, Li lacks solid experience in a economics-related department in the central Government. Perhaps most importantly, his track-record in Henan left a lot to be desired.

For most analysts, the one major event they remember during the six years that Li was in Henan was the Christmas Fire in a downtown karaoke in Zhengzhou in 2000, in which more than 300 mostly young men and women perished. Of more significance is the fact that Li apparently failed to turn around the backwardness of the landlocked province. A key reason behind Henan's lack of progress on the economic and open-door front is, of course, the fact that the central provinces – including Hunan, Hubei, Jiangxi, and Anhui – have been neglected by Beijing authorities. In the Deng and Jiang eras, attention and resources were focused on Guangdong and Shanghai. The Hu-Wen team has been paying more attention to the western as well as the northeastern provinces. Li was thus unable to parlay his special relationship with Hu into getting more favourable policies for Henan. This is despite the fact that shortly before he left for Liaoning, the official media did come out with the new slogan of "enabling the rise of central China."[24]

A more damaging critique is Henan officials' shameful treatment of AIDS victims, mostly impoverished villagers who got hit with HIV viruses while selling blood to make ends meet through the 1990s and early 2000s. It was not until top leaders, notably Premier Wen, began to take a more pro-active stance toward AIDS and other epidemics in the second half of 2003 that Li began to do something about the situation in his province. The short biography of Li that the official NCNA issued upon his transfer to Liaoning noted the many trips he had paid to "AIDS villages" in Henan. Yet most if not all of these journeys took place after late 2003 – and were probably motivated by the need to gain media exposure.[25]

Li Yuanchao (born 1950), is another former CYL luminary who worked under Hu from 1983 to 1986. The unassuming son of former Shanghai vice-mayor Li Gancheng cut his political teeth while serving as head of the league organisation within Shanghai's Fudan University – where he graduated with a mathematics degree in 1982 – and later at the Shanghai CYL committee. At CYL headquarters in Beijing, Li was in charge of propaganda and youth work – and reported directly to Hu. His first break came in 1996, when he was made vice-minister of culture. Li was promoted vice-party secretary of Jiangsu in 2000. And two years later, the man of the future became the Party Secretary and honcho of this rich and well-endowed coastal province.[26]

Li's more assertive personality has meant that his elevation up the hierarchy has been less smooth than that of Li Keqiang. While in Jiangsu, he made a name for himself for aggressive administrative reform, if not political liberalisation as such. For example, he was severe with corrupt officials – and generally effective in fighting graft by going after well-connected cadres who were suspected of leading decadent lifestyles. Li's anti-corruption crusade was so thorough that senior cadres including the province's organisation chief, head of the transport department, the top manager of state assets, and even the director of the provincial anti-corruption bureau were nabbed and given hefty sentences. Li was also instrumental in popularizing public civil-service exams to recruit mid-echelon party and government officials.[27]

That the Hu confidante has yet to master the skills of an able administrator, however, was evidenced by the fact that Jiangsu Province did not acquit itself that well in the well-published campaign to cool down the economy which started early 2004. The crusade was launched by the State Council in view of the fact that a bubble had developed in sectors such as real estate – and that the price of raw materials such as steel, aluminium, cement were getting sky-high. One notorious private-held steel mill, Tieben Iron and Steel Works, ran afoul of the authorities because the 10.6 billion yuan project was sitting on 450 hectares of illegally occupied land in Changzhou, Jiangsu. In mid-2004, the State Council closed the plant – after issuing stiff orders to find out whether Tieben had grown so big because responsible cadres in Jiangsu had violated laws or even taken bribes. There was speculation that Li did not suffer political damage from this incident only because of Hu's backing.[28]

Ten Stars for the 17th CPC Congress

The following Fourth- and in most cases Fifth-generation cadres are tipped for promotion – perhaps even induction into the Politburo – at the 17th CPC Congress. Their background and political orientation will yield an interesting picture of how Fifth-Generation leadership will run the country. [29]

Liu Yandong (f) (born 1945). Director of the CPC United Front Department and a Vice-Chairman of the advisory Chinese People's Political Consultative Conference, Liu served together with Hu on the CYL Central Committee Secretariat in the mid-1980s. In terms of age, Liu belongs to the Fourth Generation. However, because of her late-blooming political career, she is expected to serve beyond the 18th CPC Congress in 2012. While there is speculation that she may become party secretary of Shanghai, it is likely that mentor Hu will want Liu to remain in a key party position after the 17th Congress. Liu is in line to become China's most senior female cadre after the expected retirement of Vice-Premier Wu Yi in 2007.

Wu Aiying (f) (1951). Wu is one of the few female CYL affiliates that Hu has successfully promoted to a senior State Council post. Wu demonstrated her administrative and organisation ability through a series of Youth League and Women's Federation posts in Shandong Province, rising to become deputy secretary-general of the provincial party committee in 1998. She was made a Minister of Justice in 2005. Given the importance that the Hu-Wen team has put on rule by law, Wu is almost sure to get a promotion at the 17th Party Congress.

Ling Jihua (1957). Ling, a long-term Head of Hu's personal office, is tipped to be made Director of the CPC General Office at the 17th Congress. Former directors of the General Office have included luminaries such as Wen Jiabao and Zeng Qinghong. So far, Ling has kept a low profile. While his ostensible main job is preparing documents and speeches for Hu, Ling is also an important political strategist for his boss.[30]

Shen Yueyue (1958). While little known even within China, Shen, the Executive Vice-Chief of the CPC Organisation

Department handles the crucial task of ensuring that Hu's protégés will be installed in key party and government slots. There is a possibility that Shen will get into the Politburo in 2007 if she replaces her current boss, He Guoqiang, whose links with Hu are tenuous. Shen first came to Hu's attention as Head of the Zhejiang Provincial CYL Committee.

Yuan Chunqing (1952). Party Secretary of Shaanxi Province, Yuan could become a prominent representative of the fast-developing western region. The Hunan native worked under Hu in the CYL from 1983 to 1986. He is one of the few members of Hu's inner circle who have experience in the judicial and disciplinary field. Yuan, who has a doctorate in economics from Peking University, was a senior member of China's highest anti-graft unit, the Central Commission for Disciplinary Commission (CCDI) from 1997 to 2001. Seen from this perspective, there is also a possibility that Yuan might become the No. 2 at the CCDI at the 17th Party Congress.

Han Zheng (1954). This young and capable mayor of Shanghai has enjoyed a high profile with foreign businessmen and leaders. Han has links to the Hu Faction through having spent several years in the municipal branch of the CYL. His other big advantage is that the Shanghai native is also acceptable to the Jiang Zemin or Shanghai Faction. Han became Acting Secretary of Shanghai in September 2006 upon the detention of Party Secretary Chen Liangyu on charges of corruption and giving shelter to underlings guilty of economic crimes. There is a good chance he will be cofirmed party boss of the metropolis at the 17th CPC Congress held in late 2007.[31]

Zhang Qingli (1951). Zhang, who was appointed Party Secretary of Tibet in 2006, has ample experience in the northwest. Before this promotion, the Shangdong native worked for many years in the paramilitary Xinjiang Production and Construction Corps (XPCC) in the Xinjiang Autonomous Region, rising to XPCC Commander just a few years ago. The fast-rising star first met Hu in the early 1980s, when they both worked in the headquarters of the CYL.

Zhang Baoshun (1950). Zhang, yet another CYL alumna, was promoted Governor of Shanxi in 2004 and then Party Secretary of the same province just one year later. This former dock worker is one of only a handful of Fifth-Generation CYL affiliates who worked directly under Hu when the latter headed the league in the mid-1980s. Zhao's proletariat root and down-to-earth working style could make him a "latter-day Li Ruihuan," a reference to the legendary carpenter and builder of the Great Hall of the People who made it to the PSC in the 1990s.

Liu Qibao (1953). The Party Secretary of Guangxi Province was the veteran head of the Anhui provincial CYL committee. He is one of only several CYL rising stars who have had substantial experience in central-government departments. From 1994 to 2000, he was a vice-secretary general of the State Council. Liu also had a brief stint as mayor of the famous boom town of Suzhou, many of whose former mayors and party secretaries have been promoted to senior regional posts.

Zhao Leji (1957). At the time of the 16th CPC Congress, Zhao, then governor of Qinghai, was the youngest head of any provincial administration in the country. The Qinghai native was promoted party secretary of the same province in 2003. While the Peking University graduate enjoys a good reputation in the western province, his career trajectory may be affected by his lack of strong connections with major Beijing cliques or power-brokers.[32]

Cadres with Business Backgrounds

The elevation of the following entrepreneurs or former businessmen – most of whom having no close affiliation with existing factions – shows the ability of the Hu-Wen leadership to look beyond traditional party and government cadres for recruitment as top-level officials. This new trend in personnel management began in earnest with the appointment in late 2003 of a successful petroleum executive, Wei Liucheng, as Governor of Hainan. Given the lack of economic and business expertise of the predominant CYL Faction, it is imperative that President Hu give more authority to officials who are former entrepreneurs.[33] Some of the businessmen who may morph into senior cadres are listed below:

Zhang Qingwei. This Fifth-generation specialist in aerospace is tipped for a senior State Council position in the cabinet to be formed in early 2008. Zhang (born 1961) is General Manager of the China Aerospace Science and Technology Corp. He was inducted into the Central Committee in 2002 for his contribution to this sensitive and cutting-edge technology which has immense implications for defense. Zhang also enjoys a special link with the CYL by virtue of his membership in the Standing Committee of the All-China Youth Federation, a sister unit of the league.

Li Yizhong. Head of the National Work Safety Administration, Li is formerly Chairman of Sinopec Corp and Deputy Director of the State-owned Assets Supervision and Administration Commission. The 60-year-old Li's solid industrial and government experience should stand him in good stead if the Hu-Wen team wants more cadres with business experience in the Politburo.

Miao Yu. One of the few Fifth-generation cadres to have both business and government experience, Miao began his career in the automobile trade, rising to become general manager of the Dongfeng Automobile Co. Dongfeng had made headlines the past few years with a series of joint ventures with major Western and Japanese motor works, including Nissan. In early 2005, Miao (born 1955), was appointed Party Secretary of Wuhan, a major hub in central and western China.

Jiang Jianqing. Jiang (born 1953) is President of the Industrial and Commercial Bank of China (ICBC). A locally trained technocrat, Jiang is billed as an exemplar of the first generation of computer-literate banker who is knowledgeable about Western-style financial practices. The career of Jiang, who authored a book on technological changes in U.S. banking, was greatly boosted by the success of the ICBC's listing on the Hong Kong Stock Exchange in 2006.

Zhu Yanfeng. President of China's First Auto Works, Zhu (born 1961) is one of China's most successful entrepreneurs. He has been instrumental in modernizing FAW through attracting foreign capital and technology. Zhu has a bright future particularly if he is later tapped for an administrative job in the central or local governments.

Conclusion:
China under the Fifth-generation Leadership

President Hu, and to a certain extent other top leaders such as Premier Wen, has invested a lot of responsibility – and hopes for the country's future – on a group of untested Fifth-generation cadres. That the bulk of these officials seem to have a CYL link, however, has raised concern in more ways than one. Apart from the "innate deficiencies" of CYL alumnae discussed above, analysts have called attention to the lack of experience of a number of relatively young men and women suddenly put in control of major portfolios.

Take for example, the case of Shen Yueyue, Hu's point woman on personnel matters. Before her "helicopter-style" elevation to the post of Executive Vice-Head of Organisation in early 2003, Shen had been vice-party secretary of Zhejiang and Anhui Provinces. Given her fairly limited if not provincial background, there are doubts as to whether she possesses the knowledge and worldview necessary to push the country forward in the ever-more competitive 2010s. The same goes for another female rising star, China's only woman governor Song Xiuyan (born 1955). The Qinghai Governor does not have a formal college education. And she was spotted by Beijing's talent scouts through her diligent work in the Qinghai CYL as well as in the Organisation Department of the Qinghai provincial party committee. Yet the popular, high-profile Song does not seem to have expertise beyond those traditionally associated with party functionaries.[34]

It is also problematic that so many fast-rising cadres seem to owe their political fortunes in large part to Hu's patronage. Firstly, these Hu protégés will be too beholden to their mentor to develop their own leadership styles – or a distinctive set of ideas and policies on how the country should best be run in the 21st century. These Hu associates and underlings have moved up the ladder owing to obedience and loyalty, not their ability to hack out new paths. A corollary of this conundrum is that having grown up in a greenhouse atmosphere, these cadres may not be able to handle crises well. The likes of Li Keqiang or Li Yuanchao lack the experience of, say, Hu when he was party boss of Tibet, or Wen, when he was handling multitudinous floods and natural disasters while being a junior vice-premier in Zhu's cabinet.

As discussed above, potential *diwudi* leaders of tomorrow suffer from a lack of substantial exposure in areas including finance, foreign trade, energy as well as security and diplomatic affairs. Thus in the near to mid-term – for example in the five years to be covered by the 17th CPC Congress – it will still be Fourth-Generation officials first groomed by former premier Zhou Rongji who will be calling the shots in economic and financial portfolios. Thus a raft of cadres born in the mid-1940s to early 1950s will likely dominate major State Council ministries at the new cabinet to be formed in early 2008. They may include Liu Mingkang (born 1946), Zhou Xiaochuan (1948), Ma Kai (1946), and Lou Jiwei (1950), respectively Chairman of the State Banking Regulatory Commission, Governor of People's Bank of China, Minister at the National Development and Reform Commission, and First Vice-Minister of Finance. Most of these technocrats were trained either by Zhu or Wen when the latter was vice-premier from 1998 to 2003.[35] As of late 2005, however, the CYL Clique – and other factions for that matter – had yet to groom Fifth-generation cadres of the caliber of the above-mentioned technocrats. And the future leaders have to persuade the first generation of successful Chinese entrepreneurs such as the above-mentioned Jiang Jianqing, Zhu Yanfeng or Miao Yu to join the government at high levels.

The rather limited range of expertise – and worldview – regarding most of Hu's protégés perhaps reflects the relative paucity of experience of Hu himself. Although he was picked by Deng in 1992 as a PSC member in preparation for taking power some day, Hu the apparatchik par excellence has had a hard time learning the ropes of running a country after he became party chief in November 2002 and state president shortly afterwards.

The relative dearth of strongmen or strongwomen among Fifth-generation cadres already on the political stage might also mean that they could succumb to the lobbying – or even intimidation – of hard-line elements in the polity. Two groups – PLA generals and nationalists – are expected to make waves in the 2010s. Owing to the Hu-Wen group's relative insubstantial power base in the PLA – and the civilian leadership's need to get the backing of the generals particularly in times of both domestic and foreign crises – military officers are expected to continue enjoying their lopsidedly big share of political resources. Apart from surging military budgets, these special privileges include strong political representation in top organs: for example, two Politburo seats and about 20% of the membership of the CPC Central Committee.[36]

With perhaps a couple or so of exceptions during the Cultural Revolution, there has been no precedent in Chinese politics of a coup or its equivalent, in the sense of military officers dictating what the civilian administration should do. However, Hu himself probably set a bad example by preaching a high degree of symbiotic linkage between the military and civilian sectors, including reviving the Maoist ideal of the "interchangeability" of civilian and military personnel, equipment, as well goals and pursuits.

Given that the social fabric will continue to remain tenuous, Fifth-generation cadres will likely have to follow in Hu's footsteps by relying on the armed forces – including the People's Armed Police – to maintain socio-political stability. And in return, *diwudai* leaders will likely continue the practice of allowing the forces to have a big chunk of the national pie if not also a big say in policymaking. It is not a secret that a sizeable proportion of generals and senior colonels in their 40s and early 50s want to project China's global power a more aggressive fashion; they also advocate hard-ball tactics vis-a-vis the U.S. and Japan. For example, General Liu Yazhou, a noted military theorist, caused a stir in the early 2000s by posting several articles on the Internet that called for more assertive diplomatic and military actions to counter perceived threats coming from the U.S. and Japan. Noting that China must have strong offensive capabilities, General Liu noted that "the sole purpose of power is to pursue even greater power." In April 2004, Liu and several PLA colleagues openly called for an abrogation of earlier China-Japan agreements that relieved Tokyo of the responsibility for compensating China over WWII atrocities.[37]

However, it can be said in favour of Fifth-Generation stalwarts – including Hu's protégés – that they will likely continue with the more positive aspects of the Hu-Wen administration. These include a fairer distribution of resources across the vast nation – and not just putting all the eggs in the basket called the east-China gold coast. Moreover, more attention will be paid to values neglected by earlier leaders from Mao to Jiang, which include social justice, respect for rule by law, and more care for the disadvantaged sectors of society. Compared with previous administrations, there is a larger contingent of cadres among the *diwudai* who have first-hand experience of poor provinces such as Gansu, Qinghai or Tibet. While this reflects the fact that both Hu and Wen worked for substantial years in western China, this change will nonetheless ensure that national resources will be more equitably parcelled out among different regions.[38]

Notes and References

1. For a discussion of the new ethos of a caring, harmonious society, see "Party Chief Hu: Building a democratic, law-based and harmonious society," China News Service, 19 February 2005; "A road map for building a harmonious society," *21st Century Economic Herald* (a liberal Guangzhou paper), 4 March 2005.

2. For a discussion of the evolution of grassroots elections, see, for example, Tony Saich & Xuedong Yang, "Selecting within the rules: Institutional innovations in China's governance," Paper presented at Conference on Local Government Comparisons in India and China, Beijing, January 2003; Yang Fan, "The level of direct elections may be elevated," *Wen Wei Po* (a China-run Hong Kong daily), 20 May 2003.

3. For a discussion about the "collusion" of cadres and business interests in China, see, for example, George J. Gilboy & Eric Heginbotham, "The Latin Americanization of China?" *Current History* (U.S. journal), (September 2004).

4. President Hu's high regard for Mao Zedong was evident in the hagiographic speech that he delivered on the occasion of Mao's 110th day in 2003. See "Hu calls for carrying on Chairman Mao's great cause," *China Daily* (an official Chinese paper), 30 December 2003.

5. For a study of the contributions of the "returnees," see, for example, David Zweig, Wilfried Vanhonacker & Chung Siu Fung, "Reverse migration and technology: the case of China," Center on China's Transnational Relations Working Paper No. 11, University of Science and Technology, Hong Kong, October 2005; Staff reporter, "The road home," *Shanghai Star* (a Shanghai English-language paper), 23 January 2003.

6. For a discussion of the link between economic development and a strong defence, see, for example, Zhang Jian, "The economy and defence should develop in a coordinated manner," *Wen Wei Po*, 11 November 2004; Nan Li, "From revolutionary internationalism to conservative nationalism," Occasional Paper No. 39 (U.S. Institute of Peace, Washington, May 2001).

7. For a discussion of young cadres being tapped by the Hu-Wen leadership for promotion, see, for example, Qiu Ping, *The Fifth Generation of the Chinese Communist Party Leadership*, Xia Fei Er Press, Hong Kong, 2005, pp. 412-428; "Cadres born in the 1960s have entered the decision-making echelon," *Wen Wei Po* (a Chinese-run Hong Kong paper), 25 January 2007.

8. For a portrait of Li Xiaolin, Chief of China Power International, see, for example, Nellie Huang, "Li Xiaolin, Star Power," *Time* Asia Edition, 13 December 2004; Li's brother, Li Xiaopeng, is also making waves as head of the mammoth Huaneng energy company.

9. For a discussion of the princelings, see, for example, Joseph Fewsmith, "Generational transition in China," *The Washington Quarterly* (a U.S. journal) (Autumn, 2002).

10. For a discussion of the political careers of the two Jiang Zemin sons, see, for example, Willy Lam, "Chinese corruption crusade causes new factional infighting," *China Brief* (Washington D.C.: Jamestown Foundation, 20 January 2004).

11. For a discussion of the Shanghai Faction princelings, see Willy Lam, "Factional politics in the CCP," *China Brief* (Washington D.C.: Jamestown Foundation, 8 March 2004).

12. For a discussion of the career and contribution of Wang Huning, see, for example, Cheng Li, "The 'Shanghai Gang': force for stability or cause for Conflict?" *China Leadership Monitor* (Stanford: Hoover Institution, Stanford University, Winter 2001).

13. For a discussion of the potentials of technocrats trained or promoted by

Zhu Rongji and Wen Jiabao, see, for example, Willy Wo-Lap Lam, *The Era of Jiang Zemin, op. cit.*, pp. 366–368.

14. For a discussion of the influence of the *haigui pai* cadres, see, for example, Li Liang & Dong Shuhua, "Eye-catching cadres among ten generations of returnees from abroad," *Southern Weekend*, cited in *Frontline* magazine (a Hong Kong China-watching monthly), August 2005.

15. For a discussion of Beijing-based CYL elite, see, for example, Ting Wang, *Hu Jintao and the Successors of Communist Youth League in China* (Hong Kong: Celebrities Press, 2005), pp. 303–334.

16. For a discussion of the careers and traits of provincial-based CYL affiliates, see Cheng Li, "Hu's followers: provincial leaders with background in the Communist Youth League," *China Leadership Monitor* (Stanford: Hoover Institution, Stanford University, Autumn 2003).

17. For a discussion of the traits and characteristics of CYL-affiliated officials, see, Willy Wo-Lap Lam, "Enter the fifth generation," www.cnn.com, 3 December 2001.

18. For example, various Hu lieutenant and CYL stalwarts are at the forefront of pushing the president's pet program to boost the "advanced nature" of Marxist rectitude among CPC members.

19. Hu Jintao has also promoted large numbers of his associates when he was working in Gansu, Guizhou and Tibet provinces. The highest-ranked of these followers of Hu is the party secretary of Xinjiang, Wang Lequn. For a run-down of his career, see "Wang Lequan: Politburo member of the CPC Central Committee," NCNA, 15 November 2002.

20. Resentment against the excessive fast promotion of CYL Clique members is said to have blocked the promotion of Liaoning party boss Li Keqiang at the 5th Plenary Session of the CPC Central Committee in November 2005; see, for example, Yu Wenxue, "Hu speeds up pace of centralization of power," *Open* magazine (a Hong Kong China-watching journal), November 2005.

21. Yan Haiwang was favoured by Hu partly because both of them had worked together in Gansu Province; for a run-down of Yan's career, see, "Yan Haiwang," Chinavitae.com website 2003 edition, http://chinavitae.com/printer_friendly.php?id=1149.

22. For a discussion of the significance of the rise of Wu Aiying, see, for example, Cheng Li, "Hu's policy shift and the Tuanpai's coming of age," *China Leadership Monitor* (Stanford: Hoover Institution, Autumn 2005), http://www.chinaleadershipmonitor.org/20053/lc.pdf.

23. For a discussion of the early career of Li Keqiang, see, for example, Zong Hairen, *China's New Leaders: The Fourth Generation* (New York: Mirror Books, 2002), pp. 421-465.

24. See "Henan Party Secretary Li Keqiang on the three markers for the rise of central China," China News Service, 11 October 2004.

25. For a discussion of the impact of AIDS on Henan Province – and Li's self defence, see, "Li Keqiang: the most important thing is to let the masses know the facts," China News Service, 12 September 2004.

26. For a discussion of the career and prospects of Li Yuanchan, see, for example, Li Cheng, "Hu's new deal and the new provincial chiefs," *China Leadership Monitor* (Stanford: Hoover Institution, Summer 2004), http://www.chinaleadershipmonitor.org/20042/lc.pdf.

27. Li is one of the several provincial party secretaries keen to introduce more competition for the appointment of cadres. For a discussion see, Dan Qu, "Open nomination and public election of officials in Jiangsu Province," www.chinaelections.org website, 20 November 2004, http://www.chinaelections.org/en/readnews.asp?newsid=%7B052CA905-4FAD-4C4C-A47C-0431D4EA0383%7D.

28. For Li Yuanchao's own views on the "Tieben incident," see Zhao Ran, Zheng Chunping & Guo Bensheng, "Jiangsu will build a harmonious society in 2005," *Xiandai Kuaibao* [*Modern Daily*], Nanjing, 2 January 2005.

29. For a discussion of senior CYL affiliates who are tipped for promotion at the 17th CPC Congress, see, for example, Ting Wang, *op. cit.*, pp. 261–301; Willy Lam, "Hu boosts power as he scrambles to maintain social stability," *China Brief*, (Washington D.C.: Jamestown Foundation, 13 September 2005).

30. For a discussion of the career and prospects of Ling Zhihua, see Ting Wang, *Hu Jintao and his Successors in the Communist Youth League* (Hong Kong: Celebrities Press, 2005), pp 319–324.

31. For a discussion of the career prospects of Han Zheng and other Shanghai-related officials, see for example, Qiu Ping, *op. cit.*, pp. 132–138; 175–184.

32. Some analysts, however, believe Zhao Leji has close ties with President Hu, see, for example, "China politics: Hu builds his power base," *Economist Intelligence Unit Viewswire*, 18 February 2005, http://66.102.7.104/search?q=cache:zcHWsceee24J:www.viewswire.com/index.asp%3Flayout%3Ddisplay_article%26doc_id%3D1988052998+China +%26 +Zhao+Leji&hl=ja.

33. The Hu-Wen team started appointing businessmen to senior government posts in late 2003, when former CEO of oil giant, CNOOC, Wei Liucheng, was made Governor of Hainan Province. For a discussion of Wei's views on economic development, see, for example, "Hainan ready for large-scale development and construction," *China Daily*, 15 November 2004.

34. For a discussion of the career of Song Xiuyan, see, for example, "Hu Jintao's three dark horses," *Frontline* magazine, August 2005.

35. For a discussion of technocrats close to Zhu and Wen, see, for example, Tim Healy and David Hsieh, "Zhu's technocrats," *Asiaweek* (a Hong Kong-based newsweekly) 13 March 1998.; Long Hua, *The Inside Story of the Wen Jiabao Administration* (Hong Kong: Xinhua Colour Press, 2004), pp. 277–323.

36. For a discussion of the high importance that the Hu leadership is attaching to the PLA, see, for example, "Hu Jintao: We should seek the coordinated development of national defence and the economy," New China News Agency, 24 July 2004; Zheng Ying, "The Politburo seeks strategy on making the country prosperous and attaining strong defence capabilities," *Orient Outlook Weekly*, 9 August 2004.

37. For a discussion of Liu Yazhou's military theories, see for example, Alfred Chan, "A young turk in China's establishment: the military writings of Liu Yazhou," *China Brief*, Jamestown Foundation, 13 September 2005.

38. For a discussion of Hu protégés who have substantial experience in the northwestern provinces see, for example, Willy Lam, "Hu Jintao gambles on the West," in www.Asiasentinel.com, 16 January 2007; http://www.asiasentinel.com/index.php?option=com_content&task=view&id=341&Itemid=31.

3

Plus Ça Change, Plus C'est la Même Chose: Political Reform in Rural China

Sylvia CHAN

The transfer of power from the third generation of Communist Party of China (CPC) leaders to the fourth generation at the 16th Party Congress was carefully planned and managed by the Party apparatus. This being the case, one can expect few abrupt changes in policy directions. Emphasis on economic reform and economic growth and de-emphasis on political reform has characterised the entire post-Mao period, and there is no reason to think that the new leadership will embark on a different course. In the list of tasks set for Wen Jiabao's new government in 2003, many pertained to improving the rural economy and increasing farmers' income, while strengthening democracy received only a brief mention.[1] In the new year of 2004, the new leadership announced a series of policies aimed at promoting agriculture, rural industry and rural private enterprises in a document known as the Central Committee Document No. 1.[2] There is, however, not a word in it about improving democratic governance in villages. A year later, another Central Committee Document No. 1 reiterated much of the content of the 2004 Document No. 1, but a paragraph was added to call for expanding democracy in the countryside, while stressing that villagers' self-governance should be firmly placed under the leadership of the CPC.[3]

Villagers' Self-governance or
Village Party Committee Governance?

As a matter of fact, Party leadership of villagers' self-governance is written into Article 3 of the 1998 Organic Law of Villagers' Committees (Organic Law). Soon after its promulgation, the Party circulated a document entitled "Work Regulations for Basic-level CPC Organisations in Rural Areas", which explains what Party leadership means in practical terms. Article 9b of that document says that the village Party branch is to discuss and *make decisions* (my emphasis) on important matters concerning economic construction and social development in the village, [4] thereby annulling the Organic Law's stipulation that the villagers' assembly alone has such power. This Party document has in essence changed the nature of villagers' self-governance into governance by the Party through its village Party branches.

Villagers are of course angry that they are cheated of their democratic rights. They ask why they should bother to elect people who have no power at all to run village affairs, while unelected Party cadres enjoy unchecked power. Elected villagers' committee (VC) members, especially VC directors, are even more resentful. Emboldened by the popular mandate they have received, many VC directors have refused to play second fiddle to village Party secretaries. [5] The rivalry between these two has not only hindered development of democracy, but has often made villages ungovernable. A case in point was the widely-publicised incident of fifty-seven VC heads in Shandong Province collectively tendering their resignation in protest against harassment by rural Party authorities. [6] How to reconcile the irreconcilable demand of the Party for continued dominance in rural politics and the demand of villagers to run their villages democratically and independently has become the most serious challenge village political reform has to face.

Various ways of resolving this dilemma have been proposed and tried out. Basically, there have been three models. The first is to try to legitimise the power of village Party secretaries through quasi general elections. Under this model, voters cast a primary ballot to recommend a candidate for their village Party secretary. The township Party committee then selects a candidate from among those recommended by over 50% of voters. The ticket is then voted on by all Party members. This is known as the "two-ballot" system.[7] In itself, this model in no way resolves the conflict between the two leaders, and in fact may even intensify tension between them, if both believe that they have won an equally strong popular mandate. Related to this model is the so-called "one shoulder" (*yi jian tiao*) model, which requires one and the same Party member to hold both the position of village Party branch secretary and that of VC director concurrently. This is achieved by either making the Party secretary (ideally one who has won the position through the two-ballot system) run for VC directorship in an election, or appointing the elected VC director to be Party branch secretary. Either method is bound to violate norms of democracy. In the former, an election is held to return a pre-determined candidate; in the latter, a candidate is foisted on Party members to be their leader. A third way is to hold a free and fair VC election. If the elected VC director is a non-Party person, she/he will be recruited into the Party and promoted to the secretary position immediately.[8] This method, apart from violating Party members' democratic rights, may also involve forcing the elected VC to join the Party against her/his will.

The least publicised of these three models is the Wu'an model, the brainchild of the municipal Party committee of Wu'an City in Hebei Province. This model acknowledges the co-existence of both the Party branch committee and the VC, and tries to work out institutional arrangements for fair power-sharing between them. It affirms the supreme position – the *diyi bashou* – of the Party secretary in the village power structure, but stipulates that all important decisions are to be made by a joint meeting of the village Party committee and the VC. The meeting is to be chaired by the Party secretary but the agenda are to be set jointly by the secretary and the VC director. All important decisions should be made by a formal vote at the joint meeting following the principle of majority rule. The model also contains specifications of how some of the most hotly contested powers – such as the power to control village finance and the VC official seal – are to be shared. These arrangements usually involve participation of ordinary villagers. For example, power to authorise small amounts of expenditure is delegated to the Party secretary and the VC director jointly, and power to authorise larger amounts is given to the joint meeting of both committees, while expenditures above a certain level have to be approved by the villagers' representative assembly. Before invoices and receipts can be accepted for book keeping, they are to be checked and signed by a legally constituted Finance Management Small Group whose members are, in principle, ordinary villagers.[9]

The Wu'an model is thus an attempt to salvage some democratic elements and autonomy in villagers' self-governance within the strait jacket of Party leadership. It tries to achieve this by depersonalising Party leadership, so that it will become essentially an abstract principle with few practical implications. In practice, the Party secretary will be checked and balanced not only by the VC, but also by institutions involving democratic participation. Similar checks and balances will also be applied to the VC, particularly the VC director.

This model, however, has died a premature death. Zhan Chengfu, a high-ranking official in the Ministry of Civil Affairs (MoCA), has revealed how this has come about.[10] According to him, when the Wu'an model was reported to Hu Jingtao in January 2001, Hu instructed his subordinates to further investigate into the "operating mechanisms of villagers' self-governance under the leadership of the Party". At about the same time, Wen Jiabao referred to leaders of several Party departments and government ministries the incident of collective resignation of fifty-seven VC directors in Shandong Province. Then three departments of the CPC Central Committee joined the MoCA to send a team to investigate the tensions between the Party branch committees and the VCs and to come up with recommendations. From April to August 2001, the team visited more than fifty villages in over twenty cities and counties in four provinces, and submitted their findings and recommendations in a document. In September, Wen Jiabao instructed that "at an appropriate time" after the convention of the 16th Party Congress, this document be circulated first to the four departments/ministry that sent the team, and then to local governments, to canvass opinions. This document, however, never saw the light of day, but Zhan thought that its recommendations were so important that they deserved a place in his report on the development of villagers' self-governance. It appears that the document recommended, among other things, that villagers' assemblies (VAs) and villagers' representative assemblies (VRAs) should be the decision-making bodies. It also recommended that the principle of majority rule should be adopted by village Party committees, VCs and the joint meeting of these two committees, and that no individual should have the final say on any matter. The document further laid down procedural details for the convention of VAs, VRAs, and the two committees, and defined the powers and responsibilities of the two committees. Its recommendations are thus very similar to the Wu'an model and were apparently approved by Wen Jiabao. This is to say that more than a year before Wen was promoted to state premier, he had already formed an opinion as to how villagers' self-governance should develop. Unfortunately, his opinion has not prevailed.

In August 2002, the CPC Central Committee and the State Council instructed those responsible for organising the 2002 VC elections to encourage village Party branch leaders to run for positions in VCs and to support ordinary Party members to stand as candidates of villagers' representatives and villager small group leaders.[11] This document can thus be construed as an endorsement of the "one-shoulder" model and rejection of the Wu'an model. As it was circulated only three months before the 16th Party congress, one can assume that it had the approval of the new supreme leader Hu Jingtao, who was then in charge of Party affairs. This should caution us against talking about "the Hu-Wen leadership" as if there were no difference between them on policy issues.

Villagers' Representative Assembly: Representing Whom?

The 1998 Organic Law authorises the establishment of VRAs to exercise such powers as delegate to them from time to time by VAs (Article 21). The law, however, still upholds the VA as the supreme decision-making body and invests it with certain powers which cannot be delegated to anybody. These non-transferable powers include that of adopting and revising charters of villagers' self-governance (*cunmin zizhi zhangcheng*) and villagers' codes of conduct (*cun gui min yue*); powers to organise VC elections and by-elections, and to recall VC members; and powers to amend or repeal decisions made by VCs and VRAs. The Organic Law also allows only populous and spread-out villages to establish VRAs.

In fact, Article 21 is but a posterior legitimisation of a *fait accompli*. Even though the 1987 experiment Organic Law made no mention of the VRA, in the first few years of its implementation, some local governments had already taken it upon themselves to create such an institution. The justification was that it was too difficult to call a general meeting of the VA with the required quorum to make decisions. Their initiative received the backing of MoCA.[12] By 1998, many villages had instituted VRAs, ignoring the law's restriction of VRAs to populous and spread-out villages. Since 1998, VRAs have been playing an increasingly important role in villagers' self-governance. Many villages have not convened a VA general meeting for years and have allowed VRAs to exercise even some of the non-transferable powers of VAs.[13]

A crucial area where VRAs enjoy great power is in the electoral procedure of VCs. In some villages, VCs were even elected by VRAs rather than in a general election.[14] While this is clearly a flagrant transgression of the Organic Law, other dubious practices violating the democratic rights of villagers may even be legal. The problem is that to date there is no national electoral law governing VC elections, and VC elections are governed by provincial electoral regulations drawn up by provincial authorities. A number of provincial regulations invest VRAs with powers to elect electoral commissions and draw up lists of finalists in VC elections, thus enabling VRAs to influence the outcome of VC elections.[15]

The establishment of VRAs has been touted by the Chinese authorities as a monumental event opening up a greater and brighter future for villagers' self-governance.[16] It is probably true that in villages where voters number over a thousand and even several thousands, it is unrealistic to expect such a large crowd to meet frequently to deliberate and make important decisions. It may also be true that the quality of governance could improve if such decision-making power is delegated to a small number of better-informed and politically more experienced representatives of villagers.[17] VRAs may also be an appropriate institutional channel for day-to-day participation by villagers in the political process through their trusted representatives.[18] The problem is that the current Organic Law contains few provisions to make the VRA a truly representative body. It simply says that populous and spread-out villages may *tuixuan* villagers' representatives (VRs) (Article 21, my italics). It chooses to use the multiple-meaning word "*tuixuan*", which can mean "elect", "select" or "recommend", instead of the unambiguous "elect" (*xuanju*). Neither does it make clear who is to do the *tuixuan*. Most provincial regulations simply adopt the ambiguous wording of the Organic Law. In practice, more often than not, it is township Party officials and village Party secretaries who handpick VRs. Sometimes, sham "elections" may be held to legalise the VR status of their henchmen/women, but often even such formality is dispensed with.[19] As a result, most VRAs today are at best toothless tigers and at worst subservient agencies to carry out the Party's dictates in the name of the voters.

If villagers' self-governance has stagnated and even gone backward, as many of its supporters have now come to realised,[20] can the inchoate township political reform keep the momentum of reform going and be the real catalyst for China's democratisation? This is the question many are now asking.

Problems in Township Governance –
Call for Reform [21]

Townships had been abolished after 1958 and were reinstated as the lowest administration level of government in December 1982. It was then envisaged that the newly-restored township government would be responsible for administration and services, while the people's commune would become an economic entity in rural areas.[22] By then, however, the people's commune had become but a shadow of its former self and soon disappeared without a trace. Responsibilities of economic management were eagerly taken over by township governments. Since then, the size of township bureaucracy has kept growing at an unprecedented speed.

Expansion of township governments has been made possible by fiscal and tax reforms in the post-Mao era.[23] Under new fiscal arrangements between the national and sub-national governments, townships are allowed to have their own relatively independent finance made up of budgetary revenue, extra-budgetary funds and "self-raised" funds (*zichou zijin*), the latter two categories being largely controlled by township governments. But financial autonomy comes with a price: sub-national governments have to take on more expenditure responsibilities. Central government's share of expenditure started to decline rather sharply in the mid-1980s, from 52.5% in 1984 to 39.7% in 1985, and has continued to decline steadily ever since.[24] Such expenditures as public health and education in rural areas have been borne mainly by sub-national governments. For example, in 2002, 78% of townships' incomes, 9% of counties' budgets and 11% of provincial budgets went to education, while the national government's contribution was a mere 2%.[25] As to public health, the percentage of rural population covered by government-subsidised health insurance schemes dropped from 69% in 1980 to 10% in 2000. The annual contribution of the central government to the schemes from 1991 to 2000 averaged a measly five million *yuan* a year, or less than one *fen* per head.[26] Provincial governments were either unable or unwilling to be more generous. One provincial government, for example, required townships to bear three quarters of the costs of building hospitals and clinics.[27] For most townships, however, budgetary revenue alone can barely pay their salary bills, let alone meeting other expenditure responsibilities.[28] Township officials thus have no choice but to find additional sources of income. Hence, the ever-rising illegal fees and charges and all kinds of "self-raised" funds apportioned to rural households.

Nor is the township government the only predator in rural areas. A number of ministries in Beijing have established a network of branch offices at each sub-national level. These offices are nominally under the dual leadership of the local authorities and their respective superordinates in the ministry's administration. This is a Maoist legacy of the so-called dual rule of "vertical" and "horizontal" lines of command. When it was introduced, the intention was for the Party to maintain political control over specialist ministries, through the Party's own network of committees at all levels of administration.[29] These Party committees were and still are responsible to no one but their respective superordinate committees and thus ultimately to the Party centre in Beijing. It is clearly an ideology-driven policy. The everyday governance of townships, however, relies heavily on the work of functional agencies and not on vacuous "political leadership" township Party committees are supposed to provide. In the post-Mao era, as Party authority has weakened considerably, these agencies can afford to ignore township Party committees and answer only to their respective superordinates. Many ministries have authorised their local agencies to collect illegal fees and charges, so as to be self-sufficient and hopefully to remit some of their gains back to their superordinates.[30] In fact, since the tax-for-fee reform (see below), it is mainly these agencies that have kept on collecting fees and charges.[31]

The problem of excessive exaction on villagers has become the major cause of rural discontent since the mid-1980s. Angry villagers would often try to take their grievances to upper-level governments, but they are seen by authorities at all levels as subversive elements and are often suppressed by force. Those who have managed, at great risks, to make their way to upper-level governments have seldom succeeded to have their complaints satisfactorily dealt with, and have often suffered retribution.[32] Driven to desperation, villagers have time and again taken the law into their own hands. Incidents of beating up tax/fee collectors have occurred frequently, and anti-exaction riots involving many hundreds and even thousands have broken out in several provinces.[33]

The extent of rural unrest has shocked the top leaders. From 1985 to 2000, they issued more than twenty notices exhorting sub-national governments to reduce villagers' financial burden, all to little avail[34] Starting from 1995, a tax-for-fee reform has been tried out by various county governments, whereby an increased amount of agricultural tax is levied to replace fees and charges. After many twists and turns, the reform finally became state policy in 2000. But the reform has strained county and township finances even further, for transfers from their superordinate governments have not adequately compensated for revenue losses in fees and charges.[35] Another policy aimed at reducing farmers' financial burden announced in the 2004 Document No. 1 was reduction of agricultural tax by 10% in 2004, with a promise to abolish the tax altogether in five years. In March 2005, Wen Jiabao announced that the promise would be made good in 2006, two years earlier than planned.[36]

Much of the extortion from farmers has gone to support the over-bloated township bureaucracy, the product of a cumbersome and rigid administrative structure. It is estimated that in 2004, there were 13.162 million people on township governments' payrolls, and that 40% of farmers' taxes and charges went to support them.[37] At the pinnacle of this structure is the township Party committee, which has its own organisational, propaganda, disciplinary and even a united front department. The Party committee also controls the militia and armed security guards. The township government has even more agencies under it. The number varies from township to township, but is seldom fewer than twenty and in extreme cases more than fifty. They include various economic management committees, department of finance, offices for public security, family planning, health and education, transportation, etc. etc. Many townships have their own TV and radio stations, and even film-projection teams. The township people's congress, which has no real power and functions, has a staff on state payroll. So have the so-called mass organisations such as the Youth League and the Women's Federation.[38] In addition, there are agencies of various ministries. Such a structure is a recipe for duplication of agencies, functions and staff, conflict of interests and confusion of command. For example, taxes are collected by the township's finance department and various economic management committees, as well as the vertically-controlled taxation office. Several campaigns of simplification have been conducted since the 1980s, but it is only the latest starting in 2000 that has seriously targeted county and township bureaucracies. The goal is to trim county and township state employees by 20%.[39] But a survey conducted in twenty townships of ten provinces between December 2002 and May 2004 shows that the campaign has so far been a dismal failure.[40] In most these townships, there has been no real reduction of personnel. When departments are merged, former staff of abolished departments are retained, for there is nowhere to relocate them. The few old and sick who have been retrenched are still on government payroll, and the vacancies have been quickly filled up by people with good connections. In fact, one reason why township and county bureaucracies have not been trimmed as much as higher levels is that they are intended to serve as dumping grounds for large numbers of redundant cadres from higher levels. As the township *bianzhi*, i.e., approved positions in a state institution, can only accommodate a limited number of cadres,[41] many township institutions, including those under vertical control, have been weaned from state support and subsisting solely on fees and charges, legal and illegal.[42]

As can be seen from above, exactions on villagers are due to shortfalls in township revenues. The shortfalls, in turn, are primarily due to inadequate budgetary allocations from superordinate governments and to the latter shifting their spending responsibilities to township governments. Being at the lowest rung of the administrative structure, township governments have very little bargaining power vis-à-vis their superordinates and have been reduced, in essence, to agents of provincial and county governments to carry out their orders. Policies are designed to protect such a power hierarchy. One such policy is that of cadre management, whereby appointment, reward and punishment of office-holders are the discretion of leaders one level above. Criteria for reward and punishment are set by them. These criteria usually consist of quantified targets for various tasks that subordinates are to fulfil. Some of these, such as birth control targets and control of incidents of social unrest, are "hard" targets, and non-fulfilment of even one such target will cancel out all other achievements.[43] Moreover, targets are inflated at each sub-national level before they are assigned to the next subordinate level, because officials have to vie with their compeers for recognition by their superiors. When targets reach townships, they often become so unrealistically high that they make an impossible demand on townships' meagre resources. Worse still, some targets are set with no regard to local conditions. For example, in the heydays of village and township enterprises in the 1980s, poor agricultural provinces in China's hinterland were under enormous pressure from the central government to emulate their coastal counterparts to expand this sector at all costs. Many village and township enterprises were hastily started by orders from above. Predictably, most of them were plagued by mismanagement, corruption, and lack of technical know-how and adequate capital. Many went bankrupt in a short time. Not only did farmers lose all their forcibly apportioned capital but township governments also incurred heavy debts as a result. The large numbers of failed command investments is partly responsible for the debt crisis township governments have now found themselves in. According to the Ministry of Agriculture, in 1998 township government debts averaged 2.98 million *yuan*,[44] It grew to 4 million in 2001,[45] and 4.5 million in 2002.[46] Moreover, these figures do not include debts incurred by bankrupt and unprofitable village and township enterprises and unpaid salary and utilities bills, and hidden debts usually far exceed reported debts.[47]

Reform of Methods of Selection of
Township Government Leaders

I have argued that Beijing has been responsible for most townships' problems, but the perception of villagers may be somewhat different. Since it is township cadres and their lackeys who come to demand payments, and who seize their personal possessions and sometimes beat them up if they do not pay up, villagers see township cadres and complicit VC members as their enemies No. 1. Most mass demonstrations and riots in the countryside have so far been directed against township officials and occasionally their county superiors, but have seldom targeted provincial and central governments.[48] Township and county governments are thus more keenly aware of the rural crisis and the need to do whatever is necessary to avert it. This explains why almost all township reforms have been initiated by local authorities.

As a matter of fact, there have only been a small number of such reform throughout China and most had taken place before the transfer of power to the current leadership. Of these few experiments, some were more cosmetic than real. Take as an example the reform of the 1998-1999 election of township government leaders and president of the people's congress at Jiepai Township of Sichuan Province.[49] The only reform consisted in disallowing nomination of candidates by the presidium of the township people's congress. Instead, nominations had to come from groups of people's congress delegates. Because previously it was the Party that had dictated to the presidium whom to nominate, the change should have helped to make the elections more democratic. As it turned out, all four groups of delegates nominated the same person for the post of president, who was of course elected unopposed subsequently. In the election of the government head, only two of the four groups nominated one candidate each. When the poll was taken, one candidate was elected unanimously. Not only did no one in the group nominating the loser vote for him, but the nominee – a delegate himself – did not vote for himself either.

The whole exercise was thus a farce. A similar "reform" in which elections were blatantly manipulated by the township leadership to return all candidates of their choice occurred in Xiao Township in Hubei in 2002. But these and other sham reforms have all been reported in the Chinese media and sometimes accepted by scholars as positive experiments.[50] In the following, I shall briefly discuss three reforms that in my opinion were genuine and more significant.

"Open Selection": Baoshi Township and Others[51]

The reform at Baoshi was initiated by leaders of Shizhong district in the city of Suining in Sichuan Province, and approved by the municipal authorities. In early 1998, the head of Baoshi township government was charged with corruption and sacked. The district leadership decided to make the process of selecting his successor more transparent. Party and government cadres and VC leaders within the district were invited to apply for the position, if they were under thirty-eight years old, had the required education qualifications and met certain broadly-defined political criteria. Sixty-seven qualified applicants then sat a written examination to test their knowledge on a variety of topics. The top six candidates in the examination were given two to three days to familiarise themselves with conditions in Baozhi before they faced a selection panel, one by one, to answer questions put to them. The panel was made up of Party and government leaders of Suining and Shizhong, leaders of the city and district people's congresses and political consultative conferences, township Party cadres and delegates to the township people's congress, as well as village Party branch and VC leaders and villagers' representatives. A vote was taken at the end of these interviews. The two candidates receiving the most votes became the final candidates for the position, after they had been approved by the district Party committee. The ticket was then voted on by the township people's congress. In the end, a twenty-nine-year-old district cadre emerged as winner. A few months later, the Shizhong leadership applied the same method to the selection of two township Party committees secretaries and one township government head.

"Direct Election": The Buyun Experiment[52]

At the end of 1998, the Shizhong leaders decided to try out direct election of township government heads. They were, however, not the first to hit upon this idea. In 1997, leaders of Shenzhen City in Guangdong Province had applied to do the same, but their application had been rejected by the National People's Congress. Why the Shizhong leaders should have put their careers on the line to embark on this project is not entirely clear.[53] The national acclaim and local popularity the previous reforms had won them might have motivated them to take this bolder step. We also know that rural discontent in the province had been widespread and had erupted into several large-scale mass protests and riots, the most notorious and violent of which broke out in 1993 in Renshou, a county not far from Suining.[54] Since popular resentment against township officials was behind most these incidents, it was politically expedient to try to placate villagers by giving them some say in choosing these officials. This would on the one hand make officials more responsive to voters' demands and, on the other, when things do go wrong again, villagers would feel partially responsible for having picked the wrong people, and not sheet all blames to township leaders and their superordinates.

Fully aware of the risks involved, the Shizhong leadership had been very cautious from the start. They picked a small township in a far-flung rural area to conduct the experiment, so that any possible political fallout could be easily contained. This township was Buyun. In 1998, it had no telephone lines and was connected to the outside world only by dirt roads. It had ten villages with a total voting population of just under 12,000, of which 4,000 had immigrated.

The decision and regulations for the direct election were announced on the first day of December 1998. All eligible voters of 25 years of age and older who had the minimum education qualifications of senior high school or equivalent were encouraged to nominate for the position, but their nomination would have to be endorsed by either an organisation or thirty eligible voters. A panel of one hundred and sixty-three people pre-selected two finalists from the qualified candidates. This selectorate included leading members of the township Party and government and members of the presidium of the township people's congress. It also included three leaders of each VC, all village Party branch secretaries and villager small group leaders, as well as three villagers' representatives from each village.

In the end, fifteen people nominated. Each of them made a twenty-minute speech outlining their policies before the selectorate and answered questions put to them. The meeting was held in a school playground and was watched by a crowd of several thousand. Two candidates obtained the required majority vote in the primary ballot and became the finalists.

The Shizhong district Party committee, however, had the right to nominate one candidate, who would automatically be a finalist without the scrutiny of either the voters or the selectorate. Though there had been talks about making the selection procedure of this candidate more transparent and competitive, it has not been revealed how the candidate Tan Xiaoqiu was selected. Tan had been transferred to Buyun to be the deputy Party committee secretary not long before, and was to be appointed township government head before the decision for direct election was made.

A ten-day campaigning by the three candidates followed immediately. It mainly consisted of two public debates held on market days at the township seat and one in each village. Rules for the debates were drawn up by the township electoral commission in consultation with the candidates, and costs for these prescribed debates were covered by the district government. Candidates could also mobilise friends and relatives to campaign for them outside these debates. By all accounts, candidates' campaigns were intense and by and large orderly. The voting procedure in the final election, too, appears to have conformed largely to international standards: use of polling booths was compulsory; vote by proxy and "roving" ballot boxes were banned, and officers filling ballots for illiterate voters were closely supervised. In the end, Tan Xiaoqiu won 50.19% of votes and became the first directly elected township government head in China.

But there was a hitch. According to the Chinese constitution, a township government head is to be elected by the township people's congress. To circumvent this obstacle, Tan appeared before the congress four days later, and obtained a unanimous "confirmation" of his position. The elected head was thus still responsible to the congress, and could be impeached and recalled by it.

In 2001, when election of heads of township governments was again due, the Party's Organisational Department and the National People's Congress jointly sent an investigation team to Buyun, apparently to try to prevent a repeat of the "unconstitutional" 1998 election. The team found overwhelming support by the people for direct election, and reached a compromise solution with the Shizhong leaders. As in the 1998 election, qualified people could freely apply for the position in 2001. A selectorate of one hundred and sixty-five chose two from the twelve applicants. The Party committee nominated no candidate, probably because there was no need to, as the incumbent head Tan was among the applicants, and was set to be chosen by the selectorate consisting of a large number of Party leaders and members. The two candidates then held seven debates before voters cast their votes to pre-elect one candidate. Tan won the pre-election, was recommended by the district Party committee to the township people's congress as the sole candidate for the position, and was elected by the congress.[55]

The "Three-ballot" System: Dapeng Township[56]

The Dapeng model is also known officially as the "two-ballot" system. But it is a misnomer, as it really involved three ballots.

Dapeng Township is located in Longgang district in the city of · Shenzhen in Guangdong Province. As mentioned above, Shenzhen leaders' proposal to hold direct elections of township government heads was vetoed by the National People's Congress. Thereupon, they decided to try out in early 1999 this three-ballot model.

First, the Longgang district leadership lay down qualifications for that position, saying that preference would be given to Party members. Eligible voters were encouraged to nominate candidates by anonymous votes. Participation rate in the nomination was an amazingly high 95.8%, and seventy-six people were nominated. The incumbent township government head Li Weiwen received over three thousand and three hundred votes out of a total of over five thousand, leading by nearly three thousand votes over the next most popular nominee. The district leadership short-listed five nominees receiving over one hundred votes. (Only six people received over one hundred nominations, but one was disqualified because of age.) These five people each delivered a campaign speech before one-fifth of the electorate, consisting of township Party members, township cadres, VC leaders, villager small group leaders, and one voter from every household. This group then pre-elected by secret ballot one candidate out of the five. The winner Li Weiwen was recommended to the township people's congress by the township Party committee as the sole candidate for the position, and was duly elected by the congress.

Township Political Reform Since 2003

The Aborted Reform in Pingba

The most daring reform that has been attempted so far took place in Pingba Township in Sichuan Province. The township is in Chengkou County under the jurisdiction of Chongqing, one of the four cities directly administered by the national government. The reform was initiated by the Party secretary Wei Shengduo. He wanted it to be a comprehensive reform of the township political system. He proposed to reform the electoral procedures not only of township government heads but also of other township political leaders, including the Party secretary. He also intended to reform the entire township power structure and its operating mechanisms. The reform programme allowed all Party members to apply for the position of township Party secretary, authorised the township Party congress to pre-select one or more candidates, and provided for pre-election of the finalist by all voters. The final ticket was to be voted on by all Party members. The programme also introduced measures to ensure collective leadership and accountability of the Party committee. It proposed to establish a standing committee of the Party congress consisting of members of the Party committee and one representative from each Party branch. This standing committee was to meet every three months to discuss issues and make decisions. It was to be invested with the power to interpellate, impeach and dismiss Party committee members, and power to initiate a vote of confidence in the Party committee. The programme's proposals to reform the government and the people's congress included direct election of the township government head by all voters, the procedure of which was to be similar to that adopted in Buyun in 1998 but without the ritualistic confirmation of the elected candidate by the township people's congress. This elected township government head was to nominate his cabinet and his nominations were to be approved by the township people's congress. The programme invited all eligible voters to nominate for people's congress delegate positions and allowed aspiring delegates to freely conduct their own campaigns. It provided for self-nomination or joint nomination by congress delegates for the position of president of the congress presidium, and direct election of this office-holder by congress delegates. It proposed to create a standing committee of the congress consisting of one delegate from each electoral district, which was to meet bi-monthly to discuss issues and make decisions. Discussion sessions were to be open to the public. The congress and its standing committee were to be empowered to impeach and recall government leaders, and to initiate votes of confidence in the government. There were provisions for dissolution of government and appointment of a care-taking government in case of a vote of no confidence. Significantly, the programme recommended separating the functions of the Party committee from those of the government and the people's congress. The Party committee, it said, was to make and submit proposals to the people's congress, and the latter was to discuss and vote on the proposals. The government was to carry out the resolutions adopted by the people's congress without interference from any quarters. The Party's duty was to watch over the government to make sure that it executes the decisions of the people's congress diligently and properly, and supervise township cadres and Party members so that they do not engage in corrupt and unlawful practices.[57]

It can be seen that the proposed Pingba reform goes farther than the ones carried out in Buyun and Dapeng. In the latter two cases, the only democratically elected office-holder is at best second in command in the township power structure. What would happen if s/he should disagree with the Party secretary's inappropriate decisions? Even if s/he had the courage to defy them, would s/he get the support of her/his colleagues, who are beholden to the Party secretary for their positions? S/he is supposed to be responsible to the township people's congress, but can an undemocratically-constituted congress truly represent the will of the people? Clearly, whatever personal qualities the elected township government head may have, and however much popular support s/he may enjoy, s/he can only work under the severe constraints of an undemocratic system and is powerless to rectify the ills stemming from that system. On the other hand, in the Pingba reform, voters would have some control over all their leaders, including the most powerful Party secretary. Their input in the political process would be guaranteed not only at elections but also on a daily basis through such institutions as the reformed people's congress and its standing committee and the reformed Party congress and its standing committee. More important still, the Pingba reform programme is the only one to date that has tried to introduce institutional mechanisms to restrict the Party's power and supervise the Party's exercise of power. This is not to say that the Pingba model is perfect. One obvious flaw is that it contains no provision for rejection by the people's congress of proposals submitted to it by the Party. But Wei

Shengduo later explained that if a proposal should be rejected, the Party would make changes and resubmit it.[58]

On 18 August 2003, the reform programme was unanimously endorsed by the Party congress and the township people's congress. Two days later, election of the Party secretary and the government head began in earnest, without prior approval from county leaders. This election was about fourteen months ahead of the scheduled election to be held at the end of 2004. Wei reportedly said that he merely intended it to be a drill in preparation for the 2004 election. This could be the reason why not many people were interested enough to enter the race. Wei was the only candidate for the position of Party secretary, and the incumbent township government head had to compete with another person for the government head position. The poll was to be taken on 29 August. In the afternoon of 28 August, five or six county leaders came to Pingba and ordered the cancellation of the election. Wei was detained at the county seat for investigation, and a new township Party secretary was appointed by the county Party committee. Although Wei was eventually released, he lost his job.[59]

The Xian'an Reform[60]

A very different reform took place in the townships under the Xian'an district of Xianning city in Hubei Province in 2003. Xian'an is one of the poorest districts in Hubei, and the tax-for-fee reform has worsened its financial situation. At the time of the reform, its annual budget shortfall had been some thirty million *yuan*, and its township debts totalled one hundred and fifty million *yuan*. It was this financial crisis that drove the Xian'an leaders to launch the reform. The chief architect of the reform was the district Party secretary Song Yaping. His short-term objective was to cut spending by trimming township bureaucracy. His long-term vision was to abolish township government altogether and replace it with something like a county government agency.[61] Whether his vision is good or bad is beyond the scope of this paper. We shall only look at the political implications of the Xian'an reform programme in 2003. The reform is dubbed the "four-in-one" model. In plain language, it means subsuming under the township Party committee the township government and even the people's congress and the political consultative conference that are supposed to facilitate participatory democracy. This is to be achieved by making the Party secretary serve concurrently as township government head, and the two deputy secretaries serve concurrently as president of the township people's congress and head of the township political consultative conference respectively. Other members of the Party committee will also become concurrent deputy heads of the township government, and leaders of various "mass organisations". All Party committee members are to be elected through the two-ballot system, and those holding government positions to face all voters in a general election in addition. At the same time, the large number of departments formerly under these four institutions are to be merged into four only, and all positions in them are to be competed for by former employees through the open selection system. The many functional agencies, too, are to be gradually separated from the township administrative system and run as self-supporting services or economic units. It is said that the reform has successfully retrenched 44% leaders and 49.39% ordinary township employees, reducing the annual salary bill by nearly three million *yuan*. Economically, it can be said to be a resounding success.

From the Party's point of view, the reform may be an even greater success politically. According to a report, township leaders are happy that they are more united and work more efficiently after the reform, because "there is only one voice. What the Party committee wants is also what the government wants".[62] They must have forgotten Mao Zedong's teaching that the Party would do well to listen to more voices.[63] To be sure, the Xian'an model probably does no more than acknowledging the reality of the Party's monopoly of power. But even the Party's supreme leader Deng Xiaoping regarded over-concentration of power in the Party as a bad thing.[64] The Xian'an model, however, moves in the opposite direction to institutionalise such monopoly of power. Even though the reform programme provides for two ballots to choose Party committee members, these provisions would at best protect the democratic rights of Party members, who make up but a fraction of the population. The only role non-Party voters have in choosing these leaders is that their representatives may join Party members to recommend candidates, but it is up to the township and district Party committees to pick the finalists. True, the reform programme also requires Party committee members who are to hold concurrent positions in the other three institutions to be elected to those positions by all voters. But when the whole reform hinges on the arrangement for Party leaders to become concurrent leaders of the other three institutions, these elections can never be genuinely free and fair.

It appears that the Xian'an model has been endorsed by the Hubai provincial authorities. At the end of 2003, a notice was issued by them to instruct townships in Hubei to carry out reform along the line of Xian'an, and to complete it by the end of 2005.[65]

Conclusion

At the heart of the call for township reform on the part of China's political and intellectual elites is the problem of rural poverty threatening social stability, referred to in Chinese literature as the problem of three *nong*'s – *ngmin* (farmers), *nongcun* (villages) and *nongye* (agriculture). The primary objective of their envisaged reform is to alleviate farmers' financial burden. Unquestionably, Chinese farmers have been overtaxed, but high taxes are not the only, nor the most important, cause of rural poverty. To a certain extent it is a problem common to all populous, resource-poor and land-poor developing countries. In the case of China, however, the problem is partly policy-induced. On this score, the overall urban-orientated developmental strategy adopted by the post-Mao regime has to bear major responsibility. This strategy is inherited from the Mao era, but in its selective de-Mao-isation, the post-Mao leadership has not only not jettisoned it but has in some respects strengthened it.[66] In all fairness, since 2003, the Hu-Wen leadership has taken some measures to correct this bias. It has increased investments in agriculture.[67] It has relaxed restrictions for villagers to migrate to cities, and introduced measures to protect rural migrant workers.[68] Funding for education and medical care in rural areas has also increased somewhat.[69] But what they have done is too little; one can only hope that it is not too late.

The current leadership has been trying to avoid, or at least to postpone, genuine political reform for as long as possible. Meanwhile, their attempts to fix what are fundamentally political problems through economic, administrative and organisational adjustments have not been very successful. The policy to streamline township bureaucracy is a case in point. As this chapter has argued, behind the intractable problem of an over-sized township bureaucracy is the fundamental political question of how power should be shared between the ruling elites and the people, between the Party and government and between various levels of government, and how abuse of power can be prevented. Similarly, the problem of farmers' financial burden is mainly a function of state-instituted distributive injustices. The injustices arise because the state prioritises pursuit of national wealth and power over the wellbeing of individual citizens.

But more and more Chinese citizens, including those in the countryside, are demanding political reform. The Chinese leaders cannot completely ignore their wishes, nor can they ignore pressure from the international community to liberalise the system. They therefore want to be seen to be on the side of political reform while at the same time make sure that any reform will not jeopardise the Party's hold on absolute power. When they perceive that villagers self-governance may weaken the Party's dominance in rural politics, they move to introduce the so-called "one-shoulder" model and transform the villagers' representative assembly into an assembly of the Party's obsequious servants, so that villagers' self-governance may still retain some trappings of democracy but with little democratic substance.

It appears that in township reform in the last few years, some Party leaders have adopted the same tactics. For instance, in the case of the Buyun and Dapeng reforms, one may wonder why the Party, which has never been famous for its fastidious adherence to law, should have insisted on township government heads being elected by the township people's congress, even though in both cases it was merely a formality. A possible answer is that these proposed reforms would give voters decisive influence over the choice of the final candidate. Township people's congresses, on the other hand, are still under the firm grip of the Party. A Party-dictated vote in the congress could thus be used as the last resort to block the passage of people disapproved by the Party to leadership positions in township governments. This is why the Pingba reform had to be nipped in the bud when it threatened to curb the Party's power and give the people a great deal of control over both the government and the people's congress. This is also why the Xian'an model, which consolidates Party control over both the government and the people's congress, has been welcomed by some provincial leaders. Significantly, as provincial people's congresses have become more assertive of their rights to participate in the political process,[70] there are signs that Beijing is now moving to strengthen Party control over them. Under Hu Jintao, the number of provincial Party secretaries who are also presidents of the provincial people's congresses has increased from nine to twenty-four.[71]

Reportedly, in his meeting with Tony Blair in Beijing in early September 2005, Premier Wen Jiabao told his guest that direct elections would be held at the township level.[72] It is not clear what office-holders are to be directly elected in his envisaged direct elections, and it is questionable if Wen Jiabao's pronouncements on political reform count. But it is conceivable that the Party will gradually allow more and more townships to hold direct elections of one kind or another. The question is what kind. The kind of direct elections that we have seen in Xian'an is, in my view, one that China can do without.

Acknowledgments

The author wishes to thank Bick-har Yeung, the East Asian Librarian of Melbourne University, and Shirley Lee of the City University of Hong Kong for their kind assistance in locating a number of Chinese references.

Notes and References

1. The full text of Zhu Rongji's report is printed in *Renmin ribao* (*People's Daily*), 20 March 2003, pp.1–3.

2. *Zhonggong zhongyang guowuyuan guanyu cujin nongmin zengjia shouru ruogan zhengze de yijian (Opinions of the CPC Central Committee and the State Council on Some Policies Concerning Accelerating the Rise of Farmers' Income)* (2004 Document No. 1) (Beijing: Renmin chubanshe, 2004).

3. *Zhonggong zhongyang guowuyuan guanyu jinyibu jiaqiang nongcun gongzuo tigao nongye zonghe shengchan nengli ruogan zhengze de yijian (Opinions of the CPC Central Committee and the State Council on Some Policies Concerning Further Strengthening Rural Work and Raising the All-round Productive Capacity of Agriculture)* (2005 Document No.1) (Beijing: Renmin chubanshe, 2005).

4. "Zhongguo gongchandang nongcun jiceng zuzhi gongzuo tiaoli" , *Xinhua News Agency*, Beijing, 29 March 2001, http://www.chinarural.org/fgzz.htm.

5. A recent in-depth study of conflicts between village Party committees and VCs is Jing Yaojin, *Dangdai Zhongguo nongcun "liang wei guanxi" de weiguan jiexi yu hongguan toushi (A Micro Analysis and Macro Perspective of the Current Relationship between the Party Committee and the VC in Rural China)* (Beijing: Zhongyang wenxian chubanshe, 2004). Studies in English on this topic include Guo Zhenlin with Thomas P. Bernstein, "The impact of elections on the village structure of power: the relations between the village committees and the Party branches", *Journal of Contemporary China*, Vol. 13 No. 39 (2004), pp.257–275; Björn Alpermann, "The post-election administration of Chinese villages", *The China Journal*, No. 46 (2001), pp.45–67; and Jean C Oi and Scott Rozelle, "Elections and power: the locus of decision-making in Chinese villages", *The China Quarterly*, No. 162 (2000), pp. 513–539.

6. "'Cun guan' weihe yao cizhi" ("Why 'village officials' wanted to resign"), *Renmin ribao*, 21 March 2001, p.9.

7. Jing Yaojin, *Dandai Zhongguo nongcun* . . . , pp.81–112; Li Lianjiang, "The two-ballot system in Shanxi Province: subjecting village party secretaries to a popular vote", *The China Journal*, No. 42 (1999), pp.103–117.

8. Jing Yaojin, *Dandai Zhongguo nongcun* . . . , pp. 113–136.

9. For details of the Wu'an model, see *ibid.*, pp. 137–158.

10. Zhan Chengfu, "2001 nian Zhongguo nongcun cunmin zizhi fazhan baogao" ("Report on the development of villagers' self-governance in 2001"), *Cunmin zizhi yanjiu*, No. 34 (2003), http://www.chinarural.org/readnews.asp?newsid={3FC3C535-A122-45FA-8C6D-F03A4D2366EE}.

11. "Zhonggong zhongyang bangongting guowuyuan bangongting fachu tongzhi jinyibu zuohao cunmin weiyuanhui huanjie xuanju gongzuo, zhongbanfa (2002) 14 hao" ("Circular issued by the offices of the CPC Central Committee and the State Council concerning further improving work for the coming VC elections, No. 14 (2002)") (Circular No. 14, 2002), *Xiangzhen luntan*, No. 8 (2002), pp. 4–6.

12. In as early as 1994, a powerful think tank within the MoCA wrote a lengthy report suggesting how VRAs should be constituted and how they should operate. It cited many examples of existing VRAs. Zhongguo jiceng zhengquan yanjiuhui Zhongguo nongcun cunmin zizhi zhidu yanjiu ketizu (ed.), (The research group on villagers' self-governance in rural China under the Research Institute of China's Basic-level Governance), *Zhongguo nongcun cunmin daibiao huiyi zhidu* (*Report on the Villagers' Representative Assemblies in China*) (*Report on VRAs*) (Beijing: Zhongguo shehui chubanshe, 1995).

13. I have discussed these and other irregularities in Sylvia Chan, "Villagers' Representative Assemblies: towards democracy or centralism?", *China an International Journal*, Vol. 1, No. 2 (2003), pp. 179–199.

14. For example, Zheng Mengxiong, "Laobaixing de shiqing rang laobaixing ziji dangjia zuozhu – guanyu Tiaodaizhen jianli cunmin daibiao huiyi de diaocha yu sikao" ("Let the common people manage their own affairs -- investigating into and reflecting on the establishment of VRAs in Tiaodai Township") *Cunmin zizhi yanjiu*. No. 1, (n.p.d.) http://www.chinarural.org/readnews.asp?newsid={75BC460A-5042-11D6-A7E7-009027DDFA1E}.

15. The following provinces give at least one of these two responsibilities to VRAs: Fujian, Hainan, Jilin, Liaoning, Shandong, Shaanxi, Shanghai, Sichuan, Tianjin, Xinjiang, Xizang, and Zhejiang. Provincial regulations governing villagers' self-governance can be obtained from the website of MoCA www.chinarural.org. In this article, the four directly administered cities are treated as provinces.

16. *Report on VRAs*, p. 1.

17. These are pro-VRA arguments put forward by, among others, He

Baogang & Lang Youxing, "Cunmin huiyi he cunmin daibiao huiyi" ("Villagers' assembly and villagers' representative assembly), *Zhengzhixue yanjiu*, No. 3 (2000), pp. 55, 58; Xu Yong, *Zhongguo nongcun cunmin zizhi* (*Villagers' Self-governance in China*) (Wuhan: Huazhong shifan daxue chubanshe, 1997), pp. 83–84.

18. See Tong Zhihui's study on the origin of VRAs in Xuchang County of Henan Province in Tong Zhihui, "Cunji minzhu yanjin zhong de cunmin daibiao huiyi zhidu" ("The VRA system in the evolution of democracy at the village level"), *Cunmin zizhi yanjiu*, No. 27 (2003), http://www.chinarural.org/readnews.asp?newsid={53BC9FEC-C1DD-4218-A845-98B111AB367F}.

19. Sylvia Chan, "Villagers' Representative Assemblies . . . ".

20. Xu Yong, "Cunmin zizhi de chengzhang: xingzheng fangquan yu shehui fayu" ("The growth of villagers' self-governance: decentralisation of administration and maturation of society"), *Huazhong shifan daxue xuebao*, 2 (2005), pp. 2-8; Li Fan (ed.), *Zhongguo jiceng minzhu fazhan baogao 2003* (*Grassroot Democracy in China* – 2003), (2003 Baogao) (Beijing: Dongfang chubanshe, 2004), pp. 21, 29.

21. I use the term "township" here to refer to both *xiang* and *zhen* in China, for they have the same status in the government administrative structure. The difference between them is that a *zhen* usually has a larger population and is more urbanised and industrialised than a *xiang*.

22. "Zhonggong zhongyang guowuyuan guanyu shixing zheng she fenkai jianli xiang zhengfu de tongzhi" ("Notice from the CPC Central Committee and the State Council concerning separating government from the commune and establishing township government", *Xiangzhen caizheng shouce* (*Handbook of Township Finance*) (Chengdu: Sichuan kexue jishu chubanshe, 1987), pp. 1–3.

23. It is beyond the scope of this chapter to go into the many reforms in fiscal arrangements and taxation structures since the early 1980s. For reform in the 1980s & 1990s, see Susan H. Whiting, *Power and Wealth in Rural China, the Political Economy of Institutional Change* (Cambridge: Cambridge University Press, 2001), pp. 75–93, 267–286; Le-yin Zhang, "Chinese central-provincial fiscal relationships, budgetary decline and the impact of the 1994 reform: an evaluation", *The China Quarterly*, No. 157 (1999), pp. 115–141. For tax reform since 2000, see Ray Yep, "Can 'tax-for-fee' reform reduce rural tension in China? the process, progress and limitations", *The China Quarterly*, No. 177 (2004), pp. 42–70.

24. Le-yin Zhang, "Chinese central-provincial fiscal relationships . . .", pp. 120–121. In this article, Zhang argues convincingly that the central government is the winner vis-à-vis sub-national governments in a seemingly decentralised fiscal regime in the post-Mao period.

25. "Yiwu jiaoyu jiujing shi shenmo?" ("What exactly is compulsory education?"), *Nanfang zhoumo*, 14 March 2002.

26. Song Binwen, Xiong Yuhong, Zhang Qiang, "Dangqian nongmin yiliao baozhang de xianzhuang fenxi" ("Analysis of the current situation of medical insurance for farmers"), *Shiji Zhongguo*, http://www.cc.org.cn/newcc/browwenzhang. php?articleid=3096.

27. Cao Jinqing, *Huanghe bian de Zhongguo, yige xuezhe dui xiangcun shehui de guancha yu sikao (China along the Yellow River – Observations and Reflections on Rural Society by a Scholar)* (Shanghai: Shanghai wenyi chubanshe, 2003), p. 680. An abridged version has been translated into English: Nicky Harman & Huang Ruhua, *China Along the Yellow River, Reflections on Rural Society* (London: RoutledgeCurzon, 2005).

28. According to a study by a research group of the Ministry of Finance, most townships in Yunnan, Qinghai and Jilin Provinces owe their employees salaries. In the city of Harbin alone, salaries owed by 70% of its townships total a staggering 147.24 million *yuan*. "Xiangcun zhengfu zhaiwu huajie duice yanjiu" ("Ways to resolve township and village government debts"), *Caijing luncong*, No. 4 (2004), pp. 3–4.

29. See Franz Schurmann, *Ideology and Organization in Communist China*, Berkeley: University of California Press, 1970, pp. 85–90, 188–194.

30. Andrew Wedeman, "Budgets, extra-budgets, and small treasuries: illegal monies and local autonomy in China", *Journal of Contemporary China*, Vol. 9, No. 25 (2000), p. 492.

31. Xiang Jiquan, "Gai 'qi zhan ba suo' wei 'tiao kuai fenli'" ("Reform the numerous agencies and separate horizontal and vertical commands"), *Juece zixun*, No. 5 (2003), p.45.

32. Christopher Buckley, "China's powerless look to legislature", *The New York Times*, March 12, 2002. Gruesome examples of the plight of villagers seeking justice are reported in Chen Guidi & Chun Tao, *Zhongguo nongmin diaocha (An Investigative Report on Chinese Farmers)* (Beijing: Renmin wenxue chubanshe, 2004), pp. 7–30, 57–81, passim.

33. There is a substantial literature on post-Mao rural unrest both in English and Chinese. For a review of English literature on this topic, see Kevin O'Brien, "Collective action in the Chinese countryside", *The China Journal*, No. 48 (2002), pp. 139–154. Other studies include Thomas P. Bernstein & Xiaobo Lü, "Taxation without representation: peasants, the central and the local states in reform China", *The China Quarterly*, No. 163 (2000), pp. 752–760; Yu Jianrong, "Liyi, quanwei he zhixu" ("Interest, authority, and social order"), *Zhongguo nongcun guancha*, No. 4 (2000), pp. 70–76; Sung Kuo-Cheng, "Peasant unrest in Szechuwan and Mainland China's Rural Problems", *Issues and Studies*, Vol. 29, No. 7 (1993), pp. 129–132.

34. Yu Depeng, "Nongmin fudan wenti de shehui he falü fenxi" ("A sociological and legal analysis of peasants' financial burden"), *Ershiyi shiji*, No. 2 (2001), pp. 127–137.

35. Ray Yep, "Can 'tax-for-fee' reform . . . ".

36. Wen Jiabao's report to the National People's Congress, *Renmin ribao*, 15 March 2005, pp. 1–2.

37. "Zhongguo chebing xiangzhen 7400 ge, jingjian jigou jianqing nongmin fudan"("China alleviates farmers' burden by abolishing and merging 7400 townships and downsizing township bureaucracy"), http://www. chinarural.org/readnews.asp?newsid={5EA6EE5A-DF90-4477-907A-924CA9 FDE7B7}.

38. For the township political system and power structure, see, among others, Wang Yalin, "Nongcun jiceng de quanli jiegou ji qi yunxing jizhi" ("The basic-level power structure in rural China and its operating mechanisms"), *Zhongguo shehui kexue*, No. 5 (1998), pp.. 37–51; Wu Licai, "Zhongguo xiangzhen zhengquan de xianzhuang" ("The state of the current township political system"), in Huang Weiping & Zou Shubin (eds.), *Xiangzhen zhang xuanju fangshi gaige: anli yanjiu* (*Case Studies: Reforming Methods of Electing Heads of Township Governments*) (Beijing: Shehui kexue wenxian chubanshe, 2003), pp. 37–75; Li Xueju, Wang Zhenyao & Tang Jinsu, *Xiangzhen zhengquan de xianzhuang yu gaige* (*The Current State of the Township Political System and its Reform*) (Beijing: Zhongguo shehui chubanshe, 1994).

39. *Xinhua Yuebao*, No. 3 (2001), p. 11.

40. Zhao Shukai, "Xiangzhen gaige: jiantao yu zhanwang" ("Township reform: a review and a forward outlook"), www.usc.cuhk.edu.hk/ wk_wzdetails.asp?id=3786.

41. For a discussion of the *bianzhi* system, see Kjeld Erik Brødsgaard, "Institutional reform and the *bianzhi* system in China", *The China Quarterly*, No. 170 (2002), pp. 361–386. Brødsgaard's study focuses on the central and provincial levels but can throw some light on the local levels.

42. For an illuminating micro analysis of the structure of township institutions and their operations, see Cao Jinqing, *Huanghe bian* . . ., pp. 508–525; also pp.91–95, 464–469; *China along the Yellow River*, pp. 94–112.

43. Susan H. Whiting, *Power and Wealth* . . . pp. 100–118; Rong Jingben, Cui Zhiyuan et al., *Transformation from the Pressurised System to the Democratic System of Cooperation*, Beijing: Zhongyang bianyi chubanshe, 1998, pp. 269–283.

44. "Xiangcun zhengfu zhaiwu . . . ", p. 1.

45. Ray Yep, " Can 'tax-for-fee' . . . ", p. 56.

46. Deng Dacai, "Xiangzhen zhaiwu weihe lü jian lü zeng?" ("Why have township debts kept growing despite repeated attempts at reduction?"), *Nanfengchuang*, 28 January 2003.

47. "Xiangcun zhengfu zhaiwu...", pp. 2–4.

48. Fn. 33. Also, Liangjiang Li, "Political trust in rural China", *Modern China*, Vol. 30, No. 2 (2004), pp. 228–258.

49. For details, see Shi Weimin, *Gongxuan* . . . , pp. 336–349.

50. The scholar Tong Zhihui is an exception. He exposed the sham Xiao Township reform in "Zhengzhi tizhi 'xingshihua gaige' de shengcheng luoji—Hubei Xiaozhen 'hai tui zhi xuan' ge'an yanjiu" ("The generative logic of a 'formalistic reform' of the political system—a case study of the 'sea recommendation and direct election' in Xiao Township", *Zhanlüe yu guanli*, No. 6 (2003), pp. 78–86.

51. For details, see Li Fan et al, *Chuangxin...*, pp. 79–91 and Shi Weimin, *Gongxuan...*, pp. 384–410.

52. Li Fan et al., *Chuangxin* . . . , pp. 115–152; Shi Weimin, *Gongxuan* . . . , pp. 428–435; Baogang He & Youxing Lang, "China's first direct election of the township head: a case study of Buyun", *Japanese Journal of Political Science*, Vol. 2, No. 1 (2001), pp. 1–22.

53. Insider information on some behind-the-scene manoeuvres by the major players in this episode is provided by Lianjiang Li, "The politics of introducing direct township elections in China", *The China Quarterly*, 171 (2002), pp. 710–716.

54. Sung Kuo-Cheng, "Peasant unrest . . . ".

55. For procedure of the 2001 election, see " Buyun xiang liangci xuanju de gaikuang, bijiao ji sikao" ("A brief description of the two elections in Buyun: comparson and reflections"), http://www.chinaelections.org/readnews.asp?newsid={B7B7CF4A-01FB-4DBA-82EE-F7070AD88519}.

56. Huang Weiping (ed.), *Zhongguo jiceng minzhu fazhan de zuixin tupo—Shenzhen shi Dapeng zhen zhenzhang xuanju zhidu gaige de zhengzhi jiedu, (The Latest Breakthrough in the Development of China's Basic-level Democracy – a Political Reading of the Reform of the Electoral System of Government Leaders of Dapeng Township in Shenzhen)* (Beijing: Shehui kexue wenxian chubanshe, 2000); Shi Weimin, *Gongxuan* . . . , pp. 411–427; Li Fan et al., *Chuangxin* . . . , pp. 91–96.

57. The Pingba reform programme is printed in Li Fan (ed.), *2003 Baogao*, pp. 196–205.

58. *Ibid.*, p. 217.

59. For details of this episode, see *ibid.,* pp. 227–234; Charles Hutzler, "China frees small-town Party official who tried to hold democratic elections", *Wall Street Journal,* 16 September 2003.

60. Sun Donghai, "Xian'an zhenggai xuanfeng" ("The whirlwind of political reform in Xian'an"), *Juece zixun,* No. 4 (2003), pp. 10–17; Guo Zhenglin, "Xiangzhen zhengzhi gaige de 'si he yi' moshi: Xian'an zhenggai diaoyan baogao" ("The 'four-in-one' model of reform of the township political system: an investigative report on the Xian'an political reform"), *Gonggong guanli yanjiu,* No. 2 (2004), http://www.usc.cuhk.edu.hk/ wk_wzdetails.asp?id=4082; Wu Licai, "Xiangzhen gaige de zongtixing silu" ("A holistic approach to township reform") in Li Fan (ed.), *2003 Baogao,* pp. 235–236.

61. Song Yaping, "Yige quwei shuji de shi'er tiao" ("Twelve proposals by a district Party secretary"), *Juece zixun,* 5 (2003), pp. 38–39; Sun Donghai, "Xian'an zhenggai . . . ".

62. Guo Zhenglin, "Xiangzhen zhengzhi gaige de 'si he yi'...".

63. *Selected Works of Mao Tsetung Volume V,* Peking: Foreign Languages Press, 1977, p. 414.

64. *Selected Works of Deng Xiaoping (1975–1982),* Beijing: Foreign Languages Press, 1984, pp. 152–158.

65. He Hongwei, "Hubei dui xiangzhen shixing zhongda gaige" ("Hubei Province is undertaking a major township reform"), *Nongmin ribao,* 2 December 2003.

66. Notably, in the provision of health care in rural areas.

67. As announced in the 2004 and 2005 Documents No. 1.

68. *2004 Document No. 1,* pp. 7–8. A significant step towards protecting migrant workers was the repeal of regulations that allowed police to detain and repatriate vagrants and beggars in cities, after a migrant worker was beaten to death in a detention repatriation station. *Xinhua yuebao,* 2 (2004), p.168. For reform of the household registration system in the post-Mao period to allow greater mobility of the rural population, see Fei-ling Wang, "Reformed migration control and new-targeted people: China's *hukou* system in the 2000s," *The China Quarterly,* No. 177 (2004), pp. 118–121.

69. For education, see "Guowuyuan guanyu jinyibu jiaqiang nongcun jiaoyu gongzuo de jueding" ("The State Council's decision on further improving education in rural areas"), *Xinhua yuebao,* No. 10 (2003), pp.171–175. For health care, see "Zhonggong zhongyang guowuyuan yuanyu jinyibu jiaqiang nongcun weisheng gongzuo de jueding" (" Decision by the CPC Central Committee and the State Council on further strengthening health care in rural areas", *Renmin ribao,* 30 October, 2002, p. 1.

70. Ming Xia, "Political contestation and the emergence of the Provincial People's Congresses as power players in Chinese politics", *Journal of Contemporary China*, Vol. 9, No. 24 (2000), pp. 190–192.

71. Matthew Forney & Susan Jakes, "Requiem for Reform?", *Time*, No. 4 (31 January 2005), p. 44.

72. Nan Chengliu, "Xiangzhen zhixuan de shitou" ("The momentum of township direct elections is gathering"), http://www.chinarural.org/readnews.asp?newsid={8A165F14-D0BF-47FF-8EA9-5D54CC730F46}.

4

Managing Rights Talk in the "Harmonious Society"

Graham YOUNG
Yingjie GUO

In 2004 the Hu Jintao-Wen Jiabao regime introduced the objective of establishing a "harmonious society" (*hexie shehui*) as the overall guidance for Communist Party rule. As suggested by Hu Jintao:

> A harmonious society will feature democracy, the rule of law, equity, justice, sincerity, amity and vitality. Such a society will give full scope to people's talent and creativity, enable all the people to share the social wealth brought by reform and development, and forge an ever closer relationship between the people and government. These things will result in lasting stability and unity[1].

While there are ample grounds for cynicism about such CCP slogans, "harmonious society" can be taken as an effort to signal at least some sense of the regime's programmatic priorities. It suggests a difference of emphasis from the preceding Jiang regime, with its "Three Represents" slogan, according to which "the Party must always represent the requirements of the development of China's advanced productive forces, the orientation of the development of China's advanced culture, and the fundamental interests of the overwhelming majority of the people in China".[2] The two are not strictly comparable, as "three represents" refers to the nature of the

97

Party while "harmonious society" refers to the Party's social objectives. And the Hu-Wen regime continues to endorse Jiang's formulation. Nevertheless, the rhetoric of "harmonious society" has tended to move away from comfortable confidence in the progress of the "advanced", especially as manifested in economic development, directed by the Party as a collection of economic, social and cultural elites. In particular, the Hu-Wen regime has begun to suggest qualification of the pursuit of economic growth by taking more account of difficulties. A major element of the "harmonious society" is "harmony between man and nature", as the regime appears to give greater priority to overcoming environmental devastation and trying to ensure sustainability of Chinese society, let alone economic growth. The regime has also begun to change the emphasis in "fundamental interests" of the Chinese people by more explicit recognition of consequences and problems of economic development. This has included expressed commitment to ameliorate gross inequalities, regional and social, which have come to characterise Chinese society.

The appeal to "harmonious society" is clearly a response to evident disharmony. The last several years have seen increasing and increasingly strident expressions of grievance by a range of groups in Chinese society. The most overt signs are "mass incidents" of which, according to the Minister of Public Security, there were 74,000 in 2004, involving 3.67 million people.[3] This was an increase from 58,000 such incidents in 2003. They included everything from protest marches to riots to violent attacks on property. The Chinese leadership appears to be increasingly worried by threats to their prime political value, stability – which, in turn, is equated to survival of the regime itself. The "ever closer relationship between the people and government" must be seen as objective rather than description.

There is a wide range of social cleavages encouraging disharmony. These include identity issues, as Colin Mackerras demonstrates with respect to ethnicity. For several years the Chinese regime has been concerned with the perceived disruptive influence of religious groups or spiritual sects, most notably Falungong.

Disturbances in the countryside can have various causes, such as resurgent clan disputes and feuds. But the overwhelming source of expressions of grievance and "mass incidents" has been what Western sources refer to euphemistically as "externalities of development" – that is, protests by the victims of economic growth processes. As discussed in other chapters, there has been at least some movement from rhetoric to policy action to deal with gross inequalities and deprivations, qualifying the growth-at-all-costs approach which has prevailed during the reform era.

In this chapter we focus on the regime's treatment of "rights and interests" (*quanyi*) which has been fitted into the advocacy of a "harmonious society". We suggest that the Hu-Wen regime is taking greater account of the increasing prevalence of "rights talk" in China over the last decade or so. But we are not following a tendency by external (mainly "Western") observers to celebrate increasing references to "rights" as showing greater "rights consciousness" among the Chinese population in the sense of acceptance of international standards of "human rights", then perhaps taking that further to claim pressures for a particular form of "democratisation". While there is no doubt something of that, "rights talk" is much broader and, by the same token, does not necessarily conform to the expectations or wishes of "human rights" proponents. We focus on the regime's efforts to channel and shape rights talk. While "rights" are recognised as things which are important to the Chinese people, the Hu-Wen regime is intent on controlling how "rights" are understood, as demonstrated especially by official preference for the term *hefa quanyi* – "legal/lawful/ legitimate rights and interests".

We first consider the range of rights talk as it has proliferated especially over the last decade. While noting the diversity in conceptions of rights, we concentrate on two prominent themes, the instrumentalism of rights talk and the tendency to regard rights as grants of the state. Rights talk may in some ways threaten the Hu-Wen regime, or at least may have potential for doing so. But the regime also has considerable opportunities not only to acknowledge but also to make use of rights talk for its policy objectives. Its challenge is to control rights talk so that it maintains established instrumental and statist channels.

Rights Talk

There has been a remarkable spread of rights talk in China during the reform era. Among intellectuals, liberals, for instance, demand individual rights, particularly the right to property. Nationalists can openly talk about "national rights" (*zuquan*) as differentiated from "state rights" (*guoquan*). The New Left promotes collective social and economic rights. Party conservatives lament the erosion of the rights of the working people. Going beyond intellectual circles, to take a couple of examples of how far such talk can be applied: a woman in Beijing successfully sued a public house which "violated her right to human dignity" by denying her entry on the grounds that she was too ugly.[4] A Ms Tao claimed compensation after a car accident caused injury to her mouth and teeth, impinging upon her "right to kiss".[5] In his regular column in *People's Daily*, sociologist and self-made sex educator Pan Suiming argues that women have the "right to sex" and the "right to sexual pleasure".[6] A partial list of claimed rights includes human rights, right to development, right to life, citizenship rights, democratic rights, minority rights, peasants' rights, women's rights, children's rights, rights of the disabled, patients' rights, rights of the underprivileged, right to due legal process, ownership rights, consumer rights, right to inheritance, guardianship rights, right to privacy, right to work, right to education, and so on and on.

Such variety indicates not an homogeneous discourse with a singular objective but mixtures of creative, competing or even conflicting discourses, even though these are sometimes mutually compatible or overlap. Thus we should avoid the common mistake of using any one of these as a metonym for Chinese rights thinking, let alone taking for granted that people in China use "rights" according to purported international standards of "human rights".

At the same time, diversity indicates the extent to which rights talk is not merely a creature of the Chinese regime.

Chinese rights talk is novel in the sense that it is a language which the Communist Party had suppressed for more than three decades. Novelty may encourage diversity, because of a lack of inhibitions from accumulated assumptions and understandings concerning the scope and relevance of "rights". Nevertheless, a notion of "rights" necessarily draws upon broader social and political conceptions. And this encourages study of political-cultural influences on rights talk. One suggestive way of approaching this is to look at Chinese discussions of "rights" in the era before the establishment of the PRC.

Analyses of Chinese discussions of "rights" through the first half the 20th century typically identify several main themes. These include, *inter alia*:[7]

- the lack of a deontological view of rights – rather, rights were typically understood in utilitarian and/or consequentialist terms
- an understanding of rights in terms of interests
- conviction that interests understood as rights could and should be harmonised
- recognition of collective as well as individual rights
- rights as grants of the state rather than as protection of the individual from the state
- rights allowing contribution of the individual to the nation
- close linkage of rights and duties
- substantial rather than procedural conception of rights
- attention to both economic and political rights.

None of this is to suggest a "Chinese" view of rights; there are tensions among the items on this list, and there is much scope for inconsistencies of interpretation revolving around all of these themes. Nor are we advocating a culturalist, or more specifically etymological, determinism. With respect to the latter, the discussions of "rights" from the second half of the 19th century was such a departure from Chinese political thought that a neologism was required for "rights" (*quanli*), and it did not have the attendant baggage of implicit understanding of the term in some European languages[8]. Randall Peerenboom suggests:

> . . . the rendering of the concept of "right" as *quanli* prejudices the debate in favour of rights as interests. This is not to say that Chinese speakers are incapable of understanding *quanli* as something other than interests or that the concept of rights as trumps or limits on interests cannot be expressed in Chinese. But the etymological connotation is obviously apt to shape the ideas conceived and expressed in such terms. One can well imagine that if the English word for rights was "weighing-interests," it would be difficult to persuade someone that rights were an anti-majoritarian device that differs in kind from and cannot be weighed against interests.[9]

This point would be reinforced when the favoured term is "rights and interests". But Marina Svensson is highly critical of what she regards as "etymological fallacy"[10], which presents the derivation of the term as a limit on Chinese conceptions of "rights". And it should be noted that Peerenboom does not deny the ability of Chinese speakers to adopt diverse understandings of rights. Still, even if determinism is unwarranted, it is worth bearing in mind the point that there are at least potential implications of the term "rights" which differ from its use in other contexts. The same applies to the broader political-cultural framework. Cultural determinism is clearly untenable, given the plurality of views of rights mentioned above, let alone the development of rights conceptions in several Chinese cultural contexts, such as Hong Kong. Nevertheless, it is possible to see continued reference to themes detected in earlier discussions in current Chinese discussions, as reflection of political-cultural predispositions which may retain some influence in China. That influence may be transcended and countered or negated by other influences. But political-cultural predispositions can also be a resource to be used by the Hu-Wen regime for shaping and limiting rights talk.

In particular, several of the themes listed above are complementary and can be presented in two main overarching approaches, instrumentalism and statism, which are both prominent in Chinese rights talk and most useful to the regime. The emphasis on instrumentalism is, of course, embedded in our title. The term "rights talk" itself indicates the effort to use rights claims as instruments to advance an objective. Often "rights talk" is a pejorative term because it tends to suggest a facile recourse to "rights" in order to satisfy desires or even whims. Thus it tends to imply individual selfishness, as opposed to an implicit deontological notion of rights as general claims with a more clearly articulated moral foundation. In this chapter we do not intend "rights talk" as a pejorative term. It is important to recognise the significance of many of the issues raised in Chinese rights talk – often life-and-death matters. To take the rights most favoured by many external observers, civil and political liberties are obviously of major import to those subject to torture, imprisonment or execution. Rights to adequate health care are important to those who are denied access to medical facilities and those who suffer from resurgence of endemic diseases and growth of new ones. Those who demonstrate or riot in advancing a right to a clean environment are often directly motivated by deaths and disabilities in their families. Workers' rights are important to those who are dying in huge numbers in mines and factory fires. There may sometimes be whims and insatiable, selfish desires, but much of Chinese rights talk is far from trivial.

The conception of rights as interests is obviously consistent with instrumentalism. But, rather less obviously, it also reinforces statism. This can be illustrated with the now stock phrase noted above, *quanyi*, "rights and interests".[11] While conceiving of interests as the basis of rights has been a long-standing theme in Chinese discussions of rights, as Ronald Keith shows it has received new prominence in the regime's formulations since the early 1990s.[12] He describes this as an "incipient challenge to the conventional 'unity of

rights and obligations'"[13]. The linking of rights with duties or
obligations (the closeness of which is demonstrated in the
Constitution, where rights provisions are included in the chapter
"Fundamental Rights and Duties of Citizens") has not been
repudiated; nor has the Constitutional insistence that "The exercise
by citizens of the People's Republic of China of their freedoms and
rights may not infringe upon the interests of the state, of society and
of the collective" (Article 51). Nevertheless, a greater emphasis on
recognition of diverse interests as rights, stimulated by processes of
economic change, might imply corresponding reduction of emphasis
on duties and obligations of subordination of individual to state
interests.

Emphasis on *quanyi*, however, does not lessen the statist
approach to rights but rather changes the framework in which
statism is presented. It could be imagined that the two parts of
quanyi are not necessarily combined – that is, "protecting rights and
interests" could be interpreted as protecting both rights and interests,
although the two are separable. But the constant official iteration of
quanyi appears to suggest the reverse, that rights and interests are
inherently conjoined. This is consistent with the notion that rights
are understood as, or even reduced to, interests. By the same token,
of course, interests are recognised as rights. And this is how the state
retains its role in the determination of "rights".

It would be absurd to give status of rights to *all* interests – such
as subjective interests which can expand to all sorts of material
wants, or interests which include harm to others. Even an
understanding of society which emphasises "harmony", as against
the "Western" tendency to focus on conflict, could not simply elide
all differences and competition among interests. In that case the
interests given the status of rights must be restricted. A standard
liberal response is to restrict according to a criterion of harm to
others; but this is, in fact, not a liberal problem, because rights are
not understood (solely) as interests. Without any deontological
conception of rights, there has to be some sort of criterion for
distinguishing which interests are to be given the status of rights.
The proposition that the state determines rights follows easily and

directly. This can be according to the state's judgment on the relative worth of interests (for example, distinguishing between my interest in adequate nutrition and your interest in accumulating luxury consumer goods), the priorities of competing worthy interests (facilitating trade-off arguments) or according to distinctions between "real" and misguided interests and/or general as opposed to particular selfish interests. Such decisions can be made only by the state, thus confirming the notion that rights are grants of the state. Further, rights as interests can also be weighed against other types of interests (such as economic development or political stability) which the state might promote.

The restriction of which interests are recognised as rights, and the state's responsibility in doing so, is included in the common phrase, mentioned above, in which rights and interests (*quanyi*) are qualified by reference to *hefa*. The adjective *hefa* can mean legal, lawful, legitimate. These terms have different connotations. "Legal" suggests that rights are defined by what is formally prescribed by law. "Lawful" suggests obligation to act according to those prescriptions and also not to make rights assertions beyond what is legally provided. Both of these connotations directly confirm the notion of rights as grants of the state. "Legitimate" might be more ambiguous. There could be a standard of legitimacy apart from legal provision, or independent of state decision. But that would not be consistent with the way in which Party-state sources use *hefa*. In official use the word's connotation of "legitimacy" cannot readily mobilise resistance to a state-sanctioned understanding of rights; it encourages the interpretation of "legitimate" *because* "legal" and "lawful" rather than recognising a competing basis for legitimacy.

Thus, the emphasis on "rights and interests" does not nullify a statist approach to rights. The underlying notion that rights are not inherent in human personhood but are grants of the state is also consistent with other themes in Chinese rights thinking listed above, such as recognition of collective as well as individual rights, conviction that interests understood as rights can and should be harmonised, that rights allow contribution of the individual to the nation. The state can be presented as the bearer of collective interests (and, beyond that, identified with the nation). As the Hu-Wen regime has begun to emphasise, it is also the state's role to foster social harmony. Thus, although the "interests as rights" formulation could have a potential to encourage rights inflation, through pressure to have self-defined individual or group interests acknowledged as rights, the Chinese regime strongly resists any such tendency. Understanding rights as interests allows the regime a continual resource to repudiate particular rights claims. The Party-state arrogates to itself determination of which interests are to be designated as rights. In doing so it must take account of other competing interests, giving priority to collective interests, and asserting real or objective interests as opposed to subjective and possibly misguided desires. The Party-state claims the role of repository of collective and objective interests.

Regime International Rights Talk

Many external criticisms of rights abuses in China give the impression that conceptions of and popular enthusiasm for rights are rigorously repressed by a ruthless and fearful regime. And the task of "international society" is to drag that regime into accepting its obligations in recognising and protecting rights. In fact, contrary to such stereotypes, rights have come to play an increasingly prominent role in Chinese politics. That role is not primarily in terms of rights-conscious Chinese citizens challenging the regime. And notions of rights have become prominent mainly through the actions of the regime itself, rather than through external influence.

This is not to suggest that there have not been significant external influences, which we deal with only briefly here. The Chinese Government's involvement in the "international human rights regime" served to license the early resurgence of rights talk in China. Other international arrangements, especially the WTO, continue to foster legal changes relating to rights. Nevertheless, this is still a long way from the Chinese regime being "socialised" into acceptance of "international human rights standards". The regime has certainly been sensitive to embarrassment in international circles, on the grounds of threats to prestige and influence. It has also presented itself as active in the international human rights regime, including the use of "dialogue" and cooperative arrangements with other countries, and some limited acceptance of external scrutiny of Chinese practices. At the same time, it has proved capable of evasion and avoidance in dealing with foreign critics – through lies, diplomatic manoeuvres, formalism, token gestures to deal with particular prominent issues. It has fostered good relations with regimes condemned by "international society". Against the supposed conformist pull of "international standards", the regime has also been ready to resist and reject foreign influences directly and vigorously, repudiating critics' motives and the sincerity of their accusations.

The regime's approach to the international regime has been statist in a way which fits with statism described above, rights as the grants of states. The usual way of expressing this aspect of statism is to assert the principle of state sovereignty. And this is usually criticised as a means of evading international human rights norms. From the perspective of the Chinese regime, however, rights as grants of the state is a form of political-legal construction of rights which is not different in kind from the political-legal construction of international human rights. In that case, the Chinese official view is that an assertion of sovereignty is not so much a deviation from an accepted international approach to rights, but more a jurisdictional dispute. And a crucial point is to consider the character of the international norms – from the Chinese regime's perspective, what are the main influences in the establishment of the supposed norms, and how they are differentially used by powerful states.

The Chinese regime has been consistently sceptical of normative claims of international human rights, pointing to the inconsistency, hypocrisy and manipulation of the international human rights regime. That has been helped by the critics' selectivity – focusing mainly on civil and political rights with far less concern for social, economic and cultural rights, except when linked to issues such as health and environment which reach beyond China's borders, fashionable issues such as Tibet, or maybe labour rights which are seen as relevant to the jobs of workers in rich countries. The regime's claim that human rights critics are cynical, having the ulterior motive of trying to undermine China's economic growth and world stature, is widely supported among the Chinese people and constantly reinforced by foreign governments' clumsiness, especially as demonstrated by the US Administration.

Many international non-governmental organisations have also been active in China, or have monitored Chinese events from abroad, and have been concerned with rights issues beyond the areas of civil and political rights favoured by foreign governments. In some ways such bodies are more difficult for the Chinese regime to deal with. Many of them are less easily dismissed with accusations of cynicism and hypocrisy. The regime has attempted to counter their influence, especially by censoring communications, with the aim of preventing the spread of critical comments, including those which provide a perspective on rights different from that which the regime promotes. The regime has also been concerned with possible more direct political effects of organisations which are active in China. Thus, the Hu-Wen regime has recently been alarmed by the possibility that issues such as environmental rights can generate demands for broad political changes. The level of concern has been raised by fears of possible emulation of the so-called "colour revolutions" in former state-socialist regimes – Rose in Georgia 2003, Orange in Ukraine 2004, and Lemon in Kyrgyzstan 2005.[14]

Regime Domestic Rights Talk

It is inaccurate, however, to depict the Chinese regime as wholly reactive or defensive with respect to rights. Since the late 1980s, the regime has developed a new stance towards rights in accordance with re-fashioning the relationship between Party-state and society.

Much of this process has been a function of reducing direct Party-state controls and interference. At the same time, and partly based on this reduction, the regime has sought to portray itself as the promoter and protector of Chinese people's rights.

The overarching political fact of the reform era, as is evident in contributions throughout this volume, is the reduction of direct Party-state controls over Chinese society – through the demise of the state-socialist economy and the corresponding erosion of the all-encompassing embrace of *danwei* (work units) and rural *shengchandui* (production teams and brigades) as the orbit and limit of social life, as well as other mechanisms by which the Party-state formerly monitored and controlled almost all aspects of an individual's life. Long ago this massive transformation, in its early stages, was analysed according to the distinction between a "zone of indifference" and a "zone of immunity". The former was "defined by policy decisions, which determine that it is not in the state's interest to interfere in certain spheres of activity", the latter "legitimated and protected by a doctrine of individual rights"[15]. This distinction can still be used in showing some, but not all, of the principal dimensions of rights trends over the last couple of decades.

First, there are certainly areas of social life to which the Party-state is now quite indifferent. To refer to a case cited above, no part of the Party-state is likely to be interested in Ms Tao's kissing capabilities (although raising this issue would surely have been treated as a manifestation of "class struggle" in 1967 or 1975). In January 2005, there was a debate in Beijing's mass media on guardians' rights versus children's right to privacy. It started after Beijing Mobile introduced a new SMS service, "parents-children connect", which enabled parents to find out about their children's whereabouts at any time. Expectedly, the service proved very popular with parents who were typically of the view that it enabled them to exercise their guardianship rights (*jianhuquan*). Also expectedly, most children hated the service and demanded their right to privacy be respected. Neither the Central nor the Beijing Municipal Government intervened in the debate.[16]

During the reform era the zone of indifference has expanded

beyond such personal matters to include most areas of relations between Party-state and society. One pertinent example is rights talk itself – that is, there has been considerable leeway in the expression of views on rights, which is reflected in the diversity described above, including liberal views which are directly inconsistent with the regime's own approach. Indeed, the extent of such expansion of the "zone" raises the question of whether "indifference" remains the proper term, as it suggests that the Party-state chooses whether or not to interfere. The Party-state now has less discretion in the types of choices it might make, because of the extent of economic and social transformation, the huge costs of reversal, and the inability to exercise the sorts of controls it once used. Nevertheless, while regime choices are restricted and there has been an expansion of personal and group autonomy, it is another matter to describe this process as the enlargement of (*de facto*) rights. There remain areas where the Party-state is far from indifferent; and in those areas from which the Party-state has retreated, it is not difficult to imagine circumstances in which it would be willing to pay the costs of greater interference.

Increased indifference does not equal immunity. Chinese people have various types of immunities in formal legal terms, in areas such as freedom of speech, association, religion and so on, but there is ample evidence that the Party-state does not actually respect those immunities. Whatever the legal provisions the Party-state restricts freedoms of speech and organisation which it regards as politically threatening. Vigilant external critics still point to numberless cases of Party-state coercion and suppression, in egregious abuse of international "human rights" standards to which the Chinese Government has formally assented. A stock official responses is that these cases are handled "according to law", which is supposed to make their disposition consistent with the formal-legal provisions for rights protection. But there is no doubt that the "law" here is manipulable according to official policy and preferences.

Thus, violations of claimed rights are routine and common enough to invalidate their status as genuine rights. At the beginning of the Hu-Wen regime many observers perceived the opportunity for a more "liberal" approach to such issues as freedom of speech and association. But, as Jean-Philppe Béja shows, since 2004 the regime has disappointed those hopes, such as by resorting to tightened restrictions on the press and continuing the search for more effective censorship of electronic communications, criticism of the role of "public intellectuals", and maintaining or increasing its regulation of social organisations.

The notion of "indifference" can be adapted to another use different from that suggested above. During the reform era the Party-state has shown considerable indifference to many areas of claimed social and economic rights. In its pronouncements on human rights since the early 1990s, the regime has emphasised the priority of "right to subsistence". Although that can have variable interpretations, at the most elementary level it concerns access to bare living necessities. And the regime can claim some success in reducing the numbers in the direst poverty. But for most of the population the regime has abandoned much of the responsibility for provision of social goods which had formerly been based upon the state and collective economy. As discussed in other chapters of this volume, there have been some measures to establish new mechanisms of social security, although these have a long way to go before becoming widespread and effective. And while there has been a decline of state welfare provisions in urban areas[17], the bulk of the population in rural areas has been even more disadvantaged. In education the move towards market mechanisms has imposed burdens of extra fees and charges, with the result that large numbers of children (especially girls and in rural areas) do not receive even elementary education, regardless of the legal provisions[18]. Similarly, the poor are denied health care because of prohibitive charges, especially in diagnostic tests and medicines, as well as suffering from a declining public health system less able to deal with endemic and epidemic diseases. The Hu-Wen regime has referred to these matters in the context of social inequalities and has begun to make budgetary provisions for some of the most severe problems, but much more will be needed to confront the erosion of social and economic rights, especially in rural areas.

Apart from greater indifference, the Chinese Party-state claims a more positive role as promoter and protector of various forms of rights. The lessening of interference in all social activities has facilitated those claims. The Party-state, having detached itself from many economic (and, to a lesser extent, cultural and social) activities, can no longer be regarded automatically as the target of rights claims or held directly responsible for rights abuses in areas over which it does not exercise direct controls. It is thus able to present itself not as a self-interested party but as promoter of collective or general interests, expressed as rights. Such rights protection applies in areas which are not focused on questions of relations between the Party-state and society; that is, it does not apply in areas understood as directly political in that sense. But it does have a political framework in terms of the regime's emphasis on citizens' rights – defined within the framework of the Party-state and its processes and institutions, primarily through legal provisions.

A good example of the regime's stance as rights protector is that of consumer rights. The much higher level and variety of consumption in China encourages greater awareness of individual entitlement and expectation, phrased in terms of consumers' rights. Such rights are not necessarily directed against nor unwelcome to the Party-state. On the contrary, as Beverley Hooper demonstrates[19], the regime has fostered articulation and organisation of consumers' rights, because this is consistent with its own interests. That includes legal protection, which fits in with the regime's emphasis on citizens' rights. As another example, in the new Trade Union Law the Party-state as law-maker repositions itself as third-party mediator between workers and employers and a protector of the rights of both, instead of a law-maker plus employer (as in the old law) with an interest in preventing workers from exercising their rights (while telling them that they are the masters of the country). The regime has little to lose from tougher laws and actions aimed to force employers to pay wages or pensions and to improve working conditions (although lower levels of the Party-state may have incentive to tolerate such abuses of legal rights). Similarly, the regime has nothing to gain and much to fear from massive, volatile, discontent amongst the country's (estimated) 94–104 million migrant workers whose employers refuse to pay them, or often put their lives at risk.

The regime has generalised its claimed role as rights protector through a wide range of legislation. This has been going on since the early 1990s and has been extended by the Hu-Wen regime. Of most general symbolic significance is inclusion of a new Article 32 in the Constitution of the People's Republic of China, providing that "the state respects and safeguards human rights", at the Second Session of the Tenth National People's Congress, March 2004[20]. At the same Session the NPC revised articles of the Constitution concerning property rights, including greater protection for compensation with the requisition of property and, consistent with the dominance of capitalism in the Chinese economy, extending the protection of private property from the means of living (*shenghuo ziliao*) to the means of production (*shengchan ziliao*). In 2004–5 there have been revisions of legislation and regulations on protecting "rights and interests" of labour, women[21], the disabled, usually making the existing provisions more explicit and detailed. In January 2005 the *People's Daily* began a column on human rights education. And several bodies have established telephone hotlines concerning human rights issues – including the Supreme People's Procuratorate, concerning issues of abuse of power[22].

As this last shows, the Chinese regime has tentatively extended its claims to protect rights to deal with citizen rights against the Party-state itself. Since the 1990s new laws and regulations allow citizens to object to administrative actions and officials who abuse their power, by seeking reconsideration of administrative decisions or taking legal action for redress. The first law was the Administrative Litigation Law, promulgated in 1989 and effective from October 1990. Others include the State Compensation Law, Law on Administrative Penalties, Law on Administrative Supervision and Law on Administrative Reconsideration.

While these laws do allow individuals (and legal persons) to challenge officials and state actions, according to infringement of "lawful rights and interests", the grounds for rights-based challenges are strictly confined. They must be grounded in specific legal provisions – "rights and interests" are not to be considered in any wider context. And any litigation is in terms of "concrete administrative action" (*juti xingzheng xingwei*)[23]. Thus, there is protection of specific legal rights as applying to specific persons.[24] The claims in the 1995 White Paper that the Administrative Litigation Law "is an important law ensuring people's civil rights" and that "People consider (it) . . . as a 'law for people to lodge a complaint against officials'" are, at the least, over-stated.[25]

One of the most significant aspects of such laws is that they effectively confront only part of the Party-state. They do not challenge the regime itself; the restriction to concrete administrative actions means that the Laws are overwhelmingly concerned with the lower levels of the state. The need to distinguish among different parts and levels of the Party-state, a theme which recurs in many chapters of this volume, is especially pertinent to discussions of rights.[26] Indeed, from the perspective of the regime, one of the main purposes of administrative law is to check and discipline lower-level officials and organs in an effort to ensure adherence to Central policy as expressed through laws[27] – as well as shifting blame and ensuring that the target of popular discontent in not the regime itself but those lower levels.

Popular Take-Up of Rights Talk

Many opinion surveys suggest increasing rights awareness among Chinese people.[28] The results indicate majority support for protection of legal rights and for various civil liberties. At the same time, some data suggest greater concern with economic than with political rights. And more significantly, in assessing expressions of opinion in favour of rights, the strength of such opinions must be set against other political values. The data suggest that rights as values are often subordinated to other values, especially economic betterment and social order. Most survey respondents also express reluctance to challenge Party-state authorities. And there is some survey evidence to confirm the prevalence of the perception that rights are grants of the state.[29] Further, while survey data might tell us that there is a fair amount of rights awareness in China, they also suggest that there is a wide gap between "cognitive" and "behavioural" levels of political culture. As Zhong *et al.* have argued, such words as "democracy" and "liberty" are widely approved, yet "much longer terms of socialisation and experience are needed to change people's behaviour".[30] Still, that is not to suggest that this transformation need be too protracted. After all, rights talk is still very recent in China, so that the speed of attitudinal change has already been very fast.[31]

Once again it is necessary to avoid attributing any determining force to such political-cultural factors; the very proliferation of rights talk shows that large parts of the Chinese population have been able to overcome political-cultural limitations of "rights consciousness". Chinese people have become accustomed to framing their wishes and interests in terms of "rights" in many areas. Some of the rights talk has gone along the legal channels that the regime suggests. To take a main example, there was fairly consistent rise in Administrative Litigation Law cases from 1990 (with the exception of a dip in 2000) up to over 100,000 in 2001[32]. In about 40% of these cases plaintiffs may have been successful.[33] As another important example, industrial workers have made much use of the "rights and interests" provisions of the Labour Law - by 2002 there were over 180,000 such disputes[34]. As Mary Gallagher shows, there has been a decline in use of local-level mediation and greater recourse to state involvement through arbitration, with a further trend to appeal arbitration decisions to the courts. She identifies greater "rights consciousness" among workers and suggests that they are "mimicking the state's own recourse to legality, and using these laws to press for their own rights and interests".[35] As Chin Kwan Lee remarks, "Workers' seizure of the rights rhetoric ironically means that their activism is at least partially channelled into, and restrained by, the state's new regulatory machinery and its discourse of legality."[36]

The political significance of popular uptake of rights talk is best demonstrated in Kevin O'Brien's notion of "rightful resistance":

Rightful resistance is a form of popular contention that (1) operates near the boundary of an authorized channel, (2) employs the rhetoric and commitments of the powerful to curb political or economic power, and (3) hinges on locating and exploiting divisions among the powerful. In particular, rightful resistance entails the innovative use of laws, policies, and other officially promoted values to defy "disloyal" political and economic elites; it is a kind of partially sanctioned resistance that uses influential advocates and recognized principles to apply pressure on those in power who have failed to live up to some professed ideal or who have not implemented some beneficial measure.[37]

The operation of "rightful resistance" has been demonstrated richly in studies of political processes, most notably in works by O'Brien and Lianjiang Li but also confirmed by many others. As outlined by O'Brien, "rightful resistance" appears to be broadly consistent with regime strategy of managing rights talk. Most importantly, it does not pit citizens against the regime. Rather, it is licensed by the Party-state (although O'Brien does say "near the boundary"), referring to the frameworks of rights protection set by the regime itself. The appeal to rights is restricted to particular and local issues and directs complaint against lower-level officials while affirming adherence to the regime.

Another main form of popular uptake of rights talk, however, is in much of the social unrest which has so agitated the regime. Here rights talk can go beyond the regime framework by both mobilising notions of rights beyond the regime's preferred interpretation and using forms of political action beyond the regime's prescribed channels. Such actions can be considered in the context of a range of potential threats the regime faces in managing rights talk.

Threats of Rights Talk

To sum up, while the Chinese regime remains guilty of sometimes horrendous rights abuses, according to standards which it has formally accepted, and its efforts to counter criticism have been disingenuous and deceptive, it's main approach has been not to repudiate rights talk but to try to control it. And this is not only for defensive reasons but also to channel rights talk to its own purposes. Key elements of a strategy for managing rights talk are understanding rights as interests, avoiding reference to universal abstract conceptions of rights as moral claims, insisting that rights are grants of the state and that they are expressed through law. This strategy has allowed some direct consideration of the relationship between the individual and Party-state, but in heavily circumscribed ways, restricted to protection from abuse in terms of specific laws and at lower administrative levels. The regime has sought to project itself as the protector of citizens' rights, again as expressed through law. This strategy was developed throughout the 1990s and has been continued by Hu-Wen. The Hu-Wen regime has sought to present itself as giving more emphasis and greater specificity in protecting rights. It has also given some attention to social and economic rights, for which its predecessors had largely abandoned responsibilities.

While there are many signs of success of this regime strategy, there are also many potential threats, of which the upsurge of rights-claiming "mass incidents" is the most obvious. Among the most important challenges the regime faces in effective, or even plausible, management of rights talk are:

1. Weakness of the legalised view of rights
2. Loss of the regime's ability to claim to protect interests expressed as rights and
3. Change in the political forms of rights claims.

Legal Weaknesses

As noted above, there has been considerable increase in the numbers of people seeking to defend rights and interests according to the legal forms prescribed by the regime. At the same time, of course, there can be no doubt that such procedures do not come close to dealing with all of the possible cases of rights abuses, even in terms of formal legal provisions. The regime's emphasis on the regulation of society by law is undermined by the still evident gaps and weaknesses in that legal system. As Yinqiu Zhang notes:

> Workers gradually developed the awareness of the rule of law and the willingness to use legal means in handling their disputes with management and, in so doing, they often succeeded. On the other hand, however, the legal weapon proved too heavy for ordinary workers to wield – they had to encounter enormous and often insurmountable barriers in lodging and winning lawsuits.[38]

And as summarised by Peerenboom with reference to the Administrative Litigation Law:

> The biggest obstacles to a law-based administrative system in China are institutional and systemic in nature: a legislative system in disarray; a weak judiciary; poorly trained judges and lawyers; the absence of a robust civil society populated by interests groups; a low level of legal consciousness; the persistent influence of paternalistic traditions and a culture of deference to government authority; rampant corruption; and the fallout from the unfinished transition from a centrally planned economy to a market economy, which has exacerbated central-local tensions and resulted in fragmentation of authority.[39]

To add to this formidable list there is the cost of pursuing legal avenues (which the regime claims to be dealing with in provision of greater levels of legal aid). Further, people may need considerable courage to pursue rights claims legally. A decision in their favour may simply be ignored by the authorities concerned, and successful applicants can suffer retaliation. They can certainly be subjected to intimidation, which is a reason why cases might be withdrawn and why many more are not started. One of the means for litigants to gain more purchase in the legal system is to gain press coverage, but that can hardly apply universally and still does not prevent retaliation.[40] There have been many well-publicised cases of activists and lawyers who have been harassed and punished. This can also be through "legal" means, as local authorities can find some real or imagined illegality in their actions, but an alternative or supplement to such official suppression is the use of thugs and violence.

The Regime and Interests

There are many potential challenges to one of the main planks of the regime's treatment of rights – that the scope and definition of rights is conditioned by the state's supposedly more synoptic and authentic/enlightened view of collective interests. First, there are bound to be many Chinese for whom this is not going to be persuasive in that they will have a notion of their interests which they are unwilling to subsume within a Party-state defined collective interest. For some ethnic groups, for example, a more particularistic ethnic identity is not satisfied by Party-state aggregations. Other forms of identities, such as religion, can have the same effect.

There are more general challenges to the credibility of the regime's claim to express collective interest. Pervasive corruption obviously undermines that claim. This can be linked to the issue of trust in the regime. As suggested above, one tactic of the regime has been to localise and isolate discontent, to treat all expressions of discontent as related to particular matters in a particular local area. Much field research suggests that this tactic has had considerable success, that people who are discontented do distinguish between the reliable Centre or higher levels and the corrupt or unreliable local authorities. As Li says on the basis of a survey of villagers 1999-2001,

> . . . while some villagers see a unified state that is either trustworthy or untrustworthy, more believe that there

are substantial differences between higher and lower
levels of government. Among those who perceive the
state as divided, most appear to feel that higher levels,
particularly the Centre, are more trustworthy than
lower levels.[41]

This perception is, of course, consistent with the "rightful
resistance" model and is useful to the regime, reinforcing its posture
as protector of rights and interests while harmful and unpopular
measures are supposedly inconsistent with regime intentions or
unlawful.

Central Party-state authorities constantly complain of the
failures of policy implementation and legal observance at lower
levels. While those complaints are no doubt often valid, in that local
implementation is inconsistent with Central directions, the regime's
efforts to distance itself from unfortunate effects are also often
disingenuous. As discussed in other chapters of this volume, a major
issue is the extent to which local officials have the resources to
comply with Central policies, especially taking into account the
fiscal limits they face. Local officials are subject to enormous
pressures to foster local economic growth, which can easily become
a higher priority than meeting rights obligations. Along these lines,
Maria Edin provides a counter to the notion of a well-meaning
regime frustrated by unruly or corrupt local officials:

> . . . the reason behind implementation failure is not so
> much the result of lack of central control but is rather
> an outcome of the centre's own policies.... this inability
> is not primarily because of the centre's lack of control
> over its local agents but because the centre's actions are
> constrained by its other policy priorities. The political
> will to reduce peasant burden becomes weaker when
> balanced against other, more important, policy goals. It
> will be very difficult for the party-state to reduce
> peasant burden as long as its primary goal is economic
> growth, a goal that is bolstered by the current regressive
> tax system.[42]

This depiction contrasts with the claim of local officials' self-interested or corrupt flouting of the regime's policies, but the two interpretations can both be valid. That is, the extent of wilful disobedience and of implicit higher-level pressures can vary from one place to another or can occur in different mixtures in different places. The regime has sought to position itself as the protector of interests, but it is questionable how long this shifting of blame to local officials can be plausibly sustained. And beyond that, even assuming complete good faith on the part of the higher levels, there are still questions about the extent to which they can avoid responsibility for lack of policy implementation at lower levels. Whether the causes are corruption or not, it is still not difficult to argue that higher levels bear overall responsibility for operation of political processes.

Politics of Rights

A principal concern of the regime is that rights talk can take threatening political forms. As suggested above, much rights talk is consistent with forms of political change which the regime finds acceptable or at least tolerable. It is, after all, the regime's intention that there should be new forms of expression of interests in accordance with economic changes. And there is some benefit in licensing people to keep a check on recalcitrant or wayward local officials. To some extent this can be linked to notions of political rights. Thus, the regime does not find threatening villagers' appeal to their "democratic rights"[43], as these are rights prescribed (and limited) by the laws on village-level elections and do not necessarily imply any wider demands for "democratic" reforms in the political system.

Pursuit of rights claims can also encourage further changes in the scope and means of political participation. Again O'Brien suggests mechanisms of gradual political change consistent with adaptation of rights talk. Thus he refers to "boundary-spanning contention", through which villagers "become polity members."[44]

> When villagers come to view state promises as a source
> of entitlement and inclusion, they are acting like citizens
> before they are citizens. Certain citizenship practices . . .
> are preceding the appearance of citizenship as a secure,
> universally recognized status. In fact, practice may be
> creating status, as local struggles begin in enclaves of
> tolerance, spread when conditions are auspicious, and
> evolve into inclusion in the broader polity.[45]

The regime emphasises citizens' rights as a legal form, and the actual pursuit of those rights allows citizenship to assume more substantial content. This may not be inherently threatening to the regime, although it may be unwelcome to lower levels of the Party-state where these new forms of political participation apply.

Of far greater concern to the regime is movement away from officially-sanctioned rights talk to the establishment of wider rights-based organisation. Reports of "mass incidents" often cite participants as emphasising the lack of organisation and claiming spontaneous outbreak. To a large extent this is prudential, as it is dangerous to be identified as a leader should there be retaliation and punishment for any incidents. Nevertheless, there are increasing numbers of individuals who do not shirk that responsibility but, in fact, have won considerable fame as rights proponents and organisers of rights-based activities. The regime has been intent on restricting forms of organisation which can be regarded as politically significant. That involves both discouraging durable organisations among particular rights claimants and also, more importantly, preventing linkages among separate groups. But these restrictions appear to be breaking down, as rights activists are building both horizontal and vertical links. The regime is most fearful of these trends among industrial workers[46] but has also been concerned with ethnic organisations and religious/spiritual bodies. Formerly peasants may have been regarded as less likely to spawn such organisations, but this appears to be changing. Provincial authorities have been forced to forbid the establishment peasant associations.

The other, often complementary, threatening change in political activity is the recourse to direct action and "mass incidents". This is at least implicitly a rejection of the forms of regime-sanctioned rights talk. O'Brien and Li suggest that much rural contention has grown impatient with the process and results of rightful resistance. As well as encouraging new forms of organisation, "Some protest leaders have concluded that because polite forms of contention, such as lodging complaints and filing administrative lawsuits, are ineffective, more attention-grabbing tactics (like blocking roads, sit-ins, or even riots) are needed to ratchet up the pressure on higher levels to intercede"[47].

Especially worrying to the regime is that the trends towards more extensive organisation and popular disturbance, are combined. According to a 2001 document of the Central Committee Organisation Department:

> What is especially worthy of attention is that at present the frequency of collective incidents (*quntixing shijian*) is rising more and more, their scope is broadening more and more, the feelings expressed are becoming fiercer and fiercer, and the harm they do is becoming greater and greater . . . The organisational level is visibly becoming higher. Formerly, incidents were mostly spontaneous and fairly loose (*songsan*). Now, many have leaders, are organized, and behind the participants there are core elements who exert influence and control. Some even hire lawyers and seek media support.[48]

Concluding Comments

A general potential threat to the regime is the mobilisation of other notions of rights, apart from those which are confined within Party-state-defined processes. As noted above, Chinese rights talk is diverse and there are competing conceptions of rights which are implicitly inconsistent with the notion that rights are grants of the state. The regime has shown sensitivity to the danger that these might be reinforced by external influences. Further, the regime itself has given some partial or rhetorical recognition of more abstract rights conceptions, as in its claims to protect "human rights". Within that, claimed citizens' rights, such as freedom of speech and association, are clearly open to interpretations differing greatly from the regime's. As Hu Jintao remarked: "Independent thinking of the general public, their newly-developed penchant for independent choices and thus the widening gap of ideas among different social strata will pose further challenges to China's policy makers"[49]. A tantalising, if still unlikely, prospect is that of movement away from rights talk to other concepts for framing social discontents which are potentially more threatening to the regime. Rights may be construed as interests, but it is possible to urge interests in another way. The obvious framework to emerge is that of class.[50]

As the Hu-Wen regime expresses greater sensitivity to issues of collective interests reflected in social inequalities, this can easily raise the question of whose interests are really being protected. The "harmonious society" framework is a two-pronged response to this. On the one hand, "harmony is not unification (*heyi*)"[51] - it does recognise the existence of differing interests. Accordingly, the Hu-Wen regime acknowledges the legitimacy of complaints that the interests of some have been neglected in the process of economic growth, and has indicated programmes to ameliorate the conditions of the disadvantaged. On the other hand, while competing interests are recognised, "harmony" necessarily means that they can be reconciled. In the process of reconciliation, particular interests must be fitted with a collective interest – and for some "fitted with" must mean "subordinated to". "Harmony" as a prime political virtue implies that people will be willing to subordinate their interests in this way – or, from the regime's perspective, at least not create disorder.

Rights talk is useful for "harmony" because it asserts the entitlements of all citizens in an apparently neutral process, as formally established by the regime. Even more useful is that rights typically refer to minima – that is, to standards which all citizens are supposedly guaranteed. As stated in Wen Jiabao's 2005 Work Report:

> We must truly protect the people's economic, political and cultural rights and interests, pay particular attention to solving acute problems affecting their vital interests, and ensure that poor urban and rural residents have the basic necessities of life.[52]

Notions of equity have restricted play in rights talk. Rights can be related to issues such as gender equality, or treatment of the disabled, where the issue is largely the extent to which designated groups enjoy supposedly universal entitlements. But rights are not typically linked to issues of distributional fairness. And, so long as supposed minimum standards of labour practices are observed, rights do not raise issues such as exploitation. The management of rights talk within a "harmonious society" framework is a means of getting away from questions of distribution and equity. As Alvin So discusses in this volume, such questions are amenable to understanding in terms of class, and class conflict would be anathema to the Communist Party.

Notes and References

1. Hu Jintao, "On the Construction of a Socialist, Harmonious Society" ["*Lun goujian shehuizhuyi hexie shehui*"] (speech at the opening session of the Symposium on Enhancing the Ability to Construct a Socialist, Harmonious Society, held at the Central Party School for principal provincial leaders, 19 February, 2005), *Renmin ribao*, 27 June 2005. p. 1.

2. Jiang Zemin, "Speech at the Rally in Celebration of the 80th Anniversary of the Founding of the Communist Party of China" in *Jiang Zemin on the "Three Represents"*, Beijing, Foreign Languages Press, 2002, p. 182.

3. Shi Ting, "Acceptance of Rights Replacing Reflex Fear of Protests", *South China Morning Post*, 7 July 2005.

4. Li Xi, "'Ugly Woman' in Beijing fights for her right to human dignity" ["*Beijing 'chounu' zhuitao rengequan an shenjie*"], *Renmin ribao* (overseas edition), 8 Aug. 2001, p. 4.

5. "Is the Right to Kiss Acceptable to the Law?" ["*Falu nengfou jiena qinwenquan?*"], *Beijing Youth Daily*, 7 August 2001, p. 3.

6. Pan Suiming, "Women Have the Right to Sex" ["*Zhudong ye shi nuxing de xing quanli*"], *Renmin ribao* (overseas edition), 24 Sept. 2001, p. 11.

7. The major sources for this summary are: Marina Svensson, *Debating Human Rights in China: A Conceptual and Political History*, Rowman and Littlefield, Lanham, 2002; Stephen C. Angle, *Human Rights and Chinese Though: A Cross-Cultural Inquiry*, Cambridge, Cambridge University Press, 2002. See also Angle and Svensson (eds), *The Chinese Human Rights Reader: Documents and Commentary 1900–2000*, M.E. Sharpe, Armonk, 2001; Randall Peerenboom, "Human Rights, China, and Cross-Cultural Inquiry: Philosophy, History, and Power Politics", *Philosophy East and West*, vol. 55, no. 2, 2005, especially the summary on pp. 291–292; Andrew J. Nathan, "Sources of Chinese Rights Thinking" in R. Randle Edwards, Louis Henkin and Andrew J. Nathan, *Human Rights in Contemporary China*, New York, Columbia University Press, 1986, ch.4; Robert Weatherley, *The Discourse of Human Rights in China: Historical and Ideological Perspectives*, Basingstoke, Macmillan, 1999.

8. Wang Gungwu, "Power, Rights and Duties in Chinese History", *Australian Journal of Chinese Affairs*, no.3, January 1980, pp.11–12.

9. Randall Peerenboom, "Rights, Interests, and the Interest in Rights in China", *Stanford Journal of International Law*, vol.31, Summer, 1995, p. 376.

10. *Debating Human Rights, op. cit.*, p. 82.

11. For insightful analyses of the relationship between rights and interests, see Peerenboom, "Rights, Interests, and the Interest in Rights in China", *op.cit.*, pp.359–386; and the debate between Angle, *Human Rights and Chinese Though, op. cit.*, pp. 208–225 and Peerenboom, "Human Rights, China, and Cross-Cultural Inquiry", *op. cit.*, pp. 292–297.

12. Ronald Keith, "The New Relevance of 'Rights and Interests': China's Changing Human Rights Theories", *China Information*, vol. X, no. 2, 1995, pp. 38–61.

13. *ibid.*, p. 60.

14. Yongding (pseud.), "China's Color-Coded Crackdown", *Foreign Policy*, October 2005 http://www.foreignpolicy.com/story/cms.php?story_id=3251.

15. Brantly Womack, "Modernization and Democratic Reform in China", *Journal of Asian Studies*, vol. XLIII, no. 3, May 1984, pp. 424. Womack adapts the distinction from Tang Tsou, *The Cultural Revolution and Post-Mao Reforms: A Historical Perspective*, University of Chicago Press, Chicago & London, 1986, p. xxiv.

16. For a summary of the debate, see Tong Shuquan, "Parent-Child Connect Is Launched in Beijing, and SMS Service Provokes Controversy" [*"Jingcheng tuichu "qinzitiong", shouji duanxin genzong haizi re zhengyi"*], *Beijing ribao*, 6 January 2005, p. 4.

17. See the comprehensive analysis in Hatla Thelle, *Better to Rely on Ourselves: Changing Social Rights in Urban China since 1979*, NIAS Press, Copenhagen, 2004. See also Zhaohui Hong, "The Poverty of Social Rights and Dilemmas of Urban Poverty in China", *Journal of Contemporary China*, vol. 14, no. 45, 2005, pp. 721–734.

18. "Report submitted by the Special Rapporteur on the Right to Education, Katarina Tomasevski, Mission to the People's Republic of China, 10–19 September 2003", 1 November 2003, http://www.right-to-education.org/content/unreports/unreport11prt1.html#contents. As Tomasevski nicely notes: ". . . the formal enactment of legal guarantees is routinely mistaken for the end rather than merely a means of human rights protection."

19. Beverley Hooper, "Consumer Voices: Asserting Rights in Post-Mao China", *China Information*, vol. XIV, no. 2, 2000, pp. 92–128.

20. Amendment to the Constitution, adopted at the Second Session of the Tenth National People's Congress, 14 March 2004. http//:law.people.com.cn/bike/viewnews.btml?=73475>. After the Session, Feng Jiancang, Director of a Human Rights Research Centre under the Ministry of Justice, said that the NPC would enact the Law of Human Rights as soon as possible. He suggested that a "pyramid-structured legal system for human rights protection" should be created, with the Constitution at the top, the Law of Human Rights at the upper middle, other laws such as the Law on the Protection of Women's Interests, the Law on the Protection of Teenagers and the Law on the Disabled at the lower middle, and regulations on citizens' rights protection at the bottom. (cited in "Chinese Experts Call for Enacting Law on Human Rights", Xinhuanet, 26 March 2004. http://humanrights.cn/zt/03102401/2004020041111153825.htm).

21. This included prohibition of sexual harassment – a timely provision according to the results of a survey claiming that 71% of Chinese women had suffered such harassment: *China Daily*, 31 March 2005, http://www.chinadaily.com.cn/english/doc/2005-03/31/content_429924.htm.

22. "Hotlines Hear Human Rights Complaints", *China Daily*, 27 June 2004 http://www.chinadaily.com.cn/english/doc/2004-06/27/content_343141.htm.

23. Administrative Litigation Law, Article 2. "A concrete administrative act in PRC administrative law is an administrative act which is addressed to, or has a legal effect on, a specific natural or legal person, and directly affect(s) the rights or interests of the addressee." Karin Buhmann, *Implementing Human Rights Through Administrative Law Reforms: The Potential in China and Vietnam*, Copenhagen, Jurist-og Økonomforbundets Forlag, 2001, p. 326.

24. On administrative law see Buhmann, *Implementing Human Rights Through Administrative Law Reforms, op.cit.*, especially ch.7; Randall Peerenboom, "Globalization, Path Dependency and the Limits of Law: Administrative Law Reform and Rule of Law in the People's Republic of China", *Berkeley Journal of International Law*, vol.19, 2001. But see Liebman, for the use of some "class action" procedures under Administrative Litigation Law; Benjamin Liebman, "Class Action Litigation in China", *Harvard Law Review*, vol. 111, no. 6, 1998, pp. 1530–1531.

25. Information Office State Council of People's Republic of China, "The Progress of Human Rights in China", December 1995. http://www.china.org.cn/e-white/phumanrights19/p-3.htm.

26. On the need to move away from a simple dichotomy of Party-state/society, to "unpack" the Party-state and to take account of its fragmented character, see several contributions in Peter Hays Gries and Stanley Rosen (eds), *State and Society in 21st Century China: Crisis, Contention, and Legitimation*, New York & London, Routledge Curzon, 2004. This collection also provides a useful overview of a range of forms of recent popular contention in China.

27. Kevin J. O'Brien and Lianjiang Li, "Popular Contention and its Impact in Rural China", *Comparative Political Studies*, vol. 38 No. 3, April 2005, pp.240–244. For another argument on the utility of promoting rights-talk for the regime, see also Sally Sargeson: "Media pronouncements popularized the central government-designed land rights regime through promises that rights-bearing villagers would be better equipped to protect their interests against the predatory lower echelons of the government bureaucracy. In encouraging and organizing villagers to report on infringements of their land rights, central leaders reconfigured the distribution of power and resources within government and between governments and the governed. But the land reforms also began to dismantle the collective property institutions that provided sustenance, income, and security to villagers, facilitated the transfer of vast tracts of farmland onto urban markets and transformed landless villagers into contingent workers." "Full Circle? Rural Land Reforms in Globalizing China", *Critical Asian Studies*, vol. 36, no. 4, 2004, pp. 639–40.

28. The most instructive, although now dated, collection of such data is Xia Yong (ed.) *Toward a Time of Rights* [*Zou xiang quanli de shidai*], Beijing: Zhongguo zhengfa daxue chubanshe, 1995. See also Andrew J.Nathan and Tianjian Shi, "Cultural Requisites for Democracy in China: Findings from a Survey", *Daedalus*, vol. 122, no. 2, 1993, pp. 95–123; Ming Wan, "Chinese Opinion on Human Rights", *Orbis*, vol. 42, 1998, pp. 361–374; Yang Zhong, Chen Jie and John M. Scheb II, "Political Views from Below: A Survey of Beijing Residents", *Political Science & Politics*, vol.30, 1997, pp. 474–482; Suzanne Ogden, *Inklings of Democracy in China*, Harvard

University Press, Cambridge, 2002, especially ch. 5. Many of the surveys cited focus on attitudes towards democracy rather than rights, but *mutatis mutandis* are often suggestive of levels of "rights consciousness".

29. Gao Hongjun, "The Awakening of Consciousness of Rights among Chinese Citizens" (*"Zhongguo gongmin quanli yishi de yanjin"*), in Xia Yong, *Toward a Time of Rights, op. cit.*, pp. 46–47.

30. Zhong, Chen and Scheb, "Political Views from Below", *op. cit.*, p. 476.

31. One sign of change in political attitudes is suggested by Wang *et al*, who adapted a 1990 opinion survey (Nathan and Shi, "Cultural Requisites for Democracy in China", *op.cit.*) in 2000. They detect significant change in areas such as tolerance (although there are some problems with comparability of the data over the two dates). Yanlai Wang *et al.*, "Economic Change and Political Development in China: Findings from a Public Opinion Survey", *Journal of Contemporary China* vol. 13, no. 39, 2004, pp. 203–222.

32. See Table 2.1 in Kevin J. O'Brien and Lianjiang Li, "Suing the Local State Administration: Litigation in Rural China" in Neil J. Diamant, Stanley B. Lubman and Kevin J. O'Brien (eds), *Engaging the Law in China: State, Society, and Possibilities for Justice*, Stanford University Press, Stanford, 2005, p. 32.

33. The figure is taken from Randall Peerenboom, "Globalization, Path Dependency and the Limits of Law", *op.cit.*, p.217. See also Minxin Pei, "Citizens v. Mandarins: Administrative Litigation in China", *China Quarterly*, no. 152, 1997, pp. 842–844, for some useful explanation on these data up until the mid-1990s.

34. Mary E. Gallagher, "'Use The Law as Your Weapon': Institutional Change and Legal Mobilization in China" in Diamant *et al.* (eds), *Engaging the Law in China, op. cit.*, p.54. For a specific study of workers' use of the Labour Law, see Yinqiu Zhang, "Law and Labour in Post-Mao China", *Journal of Contemporary China*, vol. 14, no. 4, August 2005, pp. 525–542.

35. Gallagher, "'Use The Law as Your Weapon'", *op. cit.*, p. 75.

36. Chin Kwan Lee, "From the Specter of Mao to the Spirit of the Law: Labor Insurgency in China", *Theory and Society*, vol. 31, 2002, p. 192.

37. Kevin J. O'Brien, "Rightful Resistance", *World Politics*, vol. 49, no. 1, 1996, p. 33.

38. "Law and Labour in Post-Mao China", *op. cit.*, p. 526.

39. "Globalization, Path Dependency and the Limits of Law", *op. cit.*, pp. 168–9. See also O'Brien and Li, "Suing the Local State Administration", *op. cit.*

40. For a detailed analysis of the role of the mass media in operation of the

Chinese court system, see Benjamin J. Liebman, "Watchdog or Demagogue? The Media in the Chinese Legal System", *Columbia Law Review*, vol.105, no.1, 2005, pp.1–157. As the title indicates, Liebman's analysis suggests that media involvement is not necessarily always conducive to greater fairness and transparency in the legal system.

41. Lianjiang Li, "Political Trust in Rural China", *Modern China*, vol. 30, no. 2, 2004, p. 229.

42. Maria Edin, "State Capacity and Local Agent Control in China: CCP Cadre Management from a Township Perspective", *China Quarterly*, no. 173, 2003. p. 51.

43. For example, Sylvia Chan reports the comments of peasant women defending their exercise of "democratic rights": "Research Note on Villagers' Committee Elections: Chinese-Style Democracy", *Journal of Contemporary China*, vol.7, issue 19, 1998, p.519.

44. Kevin J. O'Brien, "Neither Transgressive nor Contained: Boundary-Spanning Contention in China" in Gries and Rosen (eds), *State and Society in 21st Century China*, *op cit.*, p.114.

45. Kevin J. O'Brien, "Villages, Elections and Citizenship in Contemporary China", *Modern China*, vol.27, no. 4, 2001, p. 425.

46. For an excellent overview see Ching Kwan Lee, "Pathways of Labour Insurgency" in Elizabeth J. Perry and Mark Selden (eds), *Chinese Society: Change, Conflict and Resistance*, 2nd ed., London & New York, RoutledgeCurzon, 2003, ch. 3. Cf. Feng Chen, "Subsistence Crises, Managerial Corruption and Labour Protests in China", *China Journal*, no. 44, July 2000, pp. 41–63.

47. "Popular Contention", *op.cit.*, p. 426.

48. Cited in Thomas P. Bernstein, "Unrest in Rural China: A 2003 Assessment", Center for the Study of Democracy (University of California, Irvine), 2004 Paper 04–13 http://repositories.cdlib.org/csd/04-13/, p. 2. See also Murray Scot Tanner, "China Rethinks Unrest", *The Washington Quarterly*, vol.27, no. 3, 2004, p. 142. Zhou Yongkang is quoted: "Some people are organizing illegal multi-regional unions and gatherings under the banner of a petition, and some are demanding excessive and unreasonable requests with the excuse of defending rights." *South China Morning Post*, 1 August 2005.

49. *China Daily*, 28 June 2005.

50. See the contrast made by Lee: "Workers' historical experiences of state socialism, and the discursive and ideological frameworks constitutive of that political economy, form the basis for interpreting the institutional changes brought about by market reform as class exploitation. The effects of such former experiences of state socialism can be best illustrated by the different reactions of migrant workers. Migrant peasant workers'

encounter with market and capitalist forces bring about a critique alluding to 'alienation,' grounded more in terms of denial of human dignity, loss of personal autonomy, and dishonesty, not in terms of 'exploitation.'" "From the Specter of Mao to the Spirit of the Law", *op. cit.*, p. 204. But Lee also argues that, for state workers: ". . . the state has been and should be the guardian of national and collective interest, justice, basic needs and development. Such envisioning is empowering to the extent that workers hold the state responsible and are emboldened morally and politically to appeal to it – based on their contributions in the past – when state policies are violated at the local level. The same collective subjectivity, however, also imposes limits on how far workers go in claiming their interests and rights: state policies and the law are the limits beyond which they do not want or dare to tread. Hence, insurgency and its containment by the state's discourse of legality." (p. 216)

51. Xia Yong, "Human Rights and Chinese Tradition" in Angle and Svensson (eds), *The Chinese Human Rights Reader, op. cit.*, p. 388.

52. Wen Jiabao, "Report on the Work of the Government", Third Session, Tenth National People's Congress, 5 March 2005 http://english.peopledaily.com.cn/200503/14/eng20050314_176792.html.

5

The State and Labour Insurgency in Post-socialist China: Implication for Development

Alvin Y. SO

Recent economic reforms have led Blecher to proclaim that "China's workers have lost their world."[1] In the Maoist era of socialism, the working class as a whole made great strides in wages, welfare, employment security, and social status. The Chinese workers could enjoy stable, secure income; socially provided housing, medical care and children education; guaranteed lifetime employment; a work environment that often involved considerable workers' power, and social and political prestige. Starting in the 1950s, Chinese workers benefited from a way of life and a standard of living to be envied by their fellow workers in other countries.[2]

However, the economic reforms since the late 1970s have gradually deprived the Chinese workers of the above prerogatives. First of all, the dismantling of the state sector has led to severe problems of unemployment. From 1995 through 1999, the number of state-owned industrial enterprises fell from approximately 100,000 to 60,000. This decline translated into massive layoffs of state-sector workers. From 1996 to 2001, some 36 million state-enterprise workers were laid off; over the same period, collective firms laid off 17 million workers.[3]

Second, economic reforms led to the worsening of income

inequalities. The Gini coefficient for household income in China rose from 0.33 in 1980 to 0.40 in 1994 and to 0.46 in 2000. The last figure surpasses the degree of inequality in Thailand, India, and Indonesia. Most observers suspect that China's Gini coefficient now exceeds 0.50, placing its income inequality near Brazilian and South African levels.[4]

Third, there is the growing deterioration of working condition for the Chinese workers. Tim Pringle observes: "Abuses of Chinese workers' rights have been widely documented both inside and outside China over the past five years. Forced overtime, illegal working hours, unpaid wages, and dreadful health and safety conditions are commonplace. The general pace of work has increased dramatically as competition forces the prioritizing of order deadlines and production targets over safe and dignified working environments. 'There is no such thing as an eight-hour day in China anymore,' explained a private employment agency in Shulan, northeast China."[5]

Finally, the transformation of state enterprises have also meant that most workers have now lost their social safety net, including pensions, housing, health care, and increasingly even primarily and secondary education for their children. For example, state-owned enterprise (SOE) no longer provided pension benefits. Individual workers are now supposed to be served by a nationally organised system funded by worker, state, and employer contributions. Tragically, the state does not have sufficient funds to ensure adequate pensions.[6]

These destructive dynamics of the reform process has led to the growing misery of the working class. Dorothy Solinger points out that unemployment are incalculable but massive. She documents the dire straits in which Chinese laid-off workers find themselves. For those fortunate enough to have dodged the axe, their wages have not kept ace with other sectors or with inflation, and poverty is skyrocketing.[7]

Chinese working people have responded to the above reform policies by a new wave of labour protests. *China Labour Bulletin* reports that "almost every week in Hong Kong and mainland China, newspapers bring reports of some kind of labour action: a demonstration demanding pensions; a railway line being blocked by angry, unpaid workers; or collective legal action against illegal employer behaviour such as body searches or forced overtime."[8]

According to the official statistics, in 1998 there were 6,767 collective actions (usually strikes or go-slows with a minimum of three people taking part) involving 251,268 people. This represented an increase in collective actions of 900 percent from 1990s. In 2000, this figure further jumped to 8,247 collective actions involving 259,445 workers.[9] Given such widespread labour protests, no wonder that the Chinese government has identified labour problem as the biggest threat to social and political stability.[10]

The above figures represent a significant increase in labour protests that began in the early 1990s. Observing this trend of protest, labour activists and Marxists are generally optimistic in predicting that "labour protests look set to grow at a faster rate and with greater strength than in previous years."[11]

However, it must be pointed out that the above growing incidence of labour protests has not lead to the rise of labour movement. In general, the labour protest in post-socialist China Labour bears the following characteristics:[12]

- *Short duration*: less than 10 days
- *Small size*: less than 500 people
- *Compartmentalised*: the protests are isolated from one another, without spreading from one region/industry to another
- *Economistic*: mostly bread-and-butter issues, seldom raises political issues or structural issues
- *Legalistic*: mostly petitions, go through the existing legal laws and procedures, appeal to local authorities, and stay within legal limits.

The following cases reported by Feng Chen aptly illustrate the pattern of labour protests:[13]

- On 8 August 1994, more than 300 miners in a molybdenum mine at Yangjiazhangzi, Liaoning province, protested against wage arrears by blocking the local highway.

- On 13 April 1998, about 200 retired workers from a large plant in Wuhan city sat at an intersection of a main street and displayed banners that demanded the payment of their pensions, which had been delayed over six months.
- In March 1999, 500 laid-off coal miners demonstrated in front of the city government headquarters in Chengdu, the capital of Sichuan province, after being unpaid for three months. They displayed banners asking for food. The protest lasted for three days.

In short, labour protest in China tends to be "spontaneous, small-scale, short-lived, compartmentalised, economistic, and stayed within legal bounds." In the literature, labour protests are also characterised as "short-lived, economically motivated episodes,[14] "spasmodic, spontaneous and uncoordinated,"[15] and "spontaneous, leaderless."[16] Obviously, these small-scale, short-lived, spontaneous labour protests have failed to generate a national labour movement.

As such, the aim of this chapter is to study the puzzle: Why there is no labour movement in post-socialist China? Despite the economic reforms have intensified the structural contradictions against the Chinese workers, and despite labour protests were widespread over the past few years, why did they fail to produce significant strike waves and protest movements all over China? In other words, despite the Chinese workers engage in labour protests and class struggles, why they fail to form a class to protect its class interests?

This chapter argues that the state has played a decisive role in the shaping of the contour of labour protests in post-socialist China. To highlight the role of the state, this paper will first sketch the emergence of a strong party-state in socialist China. Then it will examine how this strong state carries out policies to divide, to disorganise, and to de-mobilise the working class. At the end, this paper will examine the future of labour protests and discuss its implication for the China's development.

The Strong Party-State in
Socialist and Post-socialist China

Before the Communist Revolution in 1949, China had a weak state but a strong class-divided society. In the first half of the twentieth century, the breaking up of the imperial state into warlord regions, the incorporation of China into the capitalist world-economy, the march toward capitalist industrialisation, and the two World Wars had generated new forms of class conflict in Chinese society. Of course, class conflict, by itself, is insufficient to start a revolution. However, class conflict had laid the foundation of the communist revolution when the Chinese Communist Party of China (CPC) seized this golden opportunity to wage political struggles against the ruling Guomindang government, the Japanese invaders, and the Chinese landlords during the World War II.

A totally new statist society emerged after the 1949 Communist Revolution. The CPC built up a Leninist-state that had the capacity to impose state policies onto the Chinese society. In addition, the CPC carried out a socialist project to eliminate the economic foundation of classes, so societal forces could be directly under the control of the state. The hostility from the U.S. during the Cold War, the forced withdrawal from the capitalist world-economy, and the constant threat of counter-revolutionaries had made the CPC determined to create a new statist society.[17]

In the statist society, the party-state monopolised the economic, political, and social resources in the society. Workers and peasants were completely dependent on the state not only for job and income but also for services, status, and influence in the community. The formation of a statist society exerted a profound impact on state-society relations. When class (and other political) organisations were either eliminated or absorbed in the state structure, there was no intermediation between the state and society. The state could directly control society and impose its policies on the society.

Thus, the party-state in socialist China was all-powerful in terms of its capacity and autonomy. It penetrated deep into society, was able to mobilise social forces and the capacity to carry out revolutionary projects and imposed its wishes onto the society. In addition, it was highly autonomous. Its policies and actions were not constraint by the economy and society.

Although the party-state has dropped it revolutionary project and adopted the "capitalist" economic reforms, and although Chinese society has been transformed form a statist to a class-divided society since the late 1970s, the structure and the authority of the party-state has not been undermined. It still has the capacity and the autonomy to shape the contour of working class in the following ways: Create social divisions within the working class, impose political repression to disorganise the working class, set up labour legislations to pre-empt labour protests, adopt the tactics of accommodation to diffuse labour protests, and maintain a moral high ground by shifting the blames to lower-level officials.

Create Social Divisions within the Working Class

In the Maoist era, there was little significant division among the Chinese workers. In general, they all enjoy stable, secure income, socially provided housing, health care and education, and guarantee lifetime employment. However, in the reform era, several state policies that resulted in creating deep social division in the working class.

First, there is the division between the employed and the unemployed workers. In order to ease the pain of unemployment for state workers, the state adopted a policy called "off-duty" (*xiagang*). "Off-duty" workers are those who maintain "employment relations" with the state enterprises, potentially re-employable if business improves, and who receive livelihood allowances amounting to only a tiny fraction of regular income. Also, "off-duty" workers are still allowed to receive certain fringe benefits like housing, and health services. "Off-duty" workers are entitled to the above arrangements for three years. Only after that will the social security departments of local governments become responsible for the laid-off workers. This "off-duty" scheme has helped to cushion the shock of unemployment and the class antagonism of state workers against the state. Cai Yongshun points out that labour protests are mostly carried out by laid-off workers in the state-owned enterprises, while the employed workers seldom offer any support.[18]

Second, there is the division between urban workers and migrant workers. The state allows the peasants to leave their farms but not their villages. Thus, the peasants are allowed to work in market towns and urban cities only as temporary migrant workers. They have no right to settle down permanently in these territories. A new class of temporary migrant workers, many of them young women known as *dagong mei* (maiden workers), has emerged in response to the employment opportunities and an estimated 100 million temporary migrant workers have left the countryside to enter towns and cities in search of non-agricultural jobs.

This state household registration system has created a *segmented labour market*. Urbanites work as permanent workers in the state sector or in high-paying primary labour markets which provided health care and other benefits. On the other hand, rural temporary migrants could only get jobs in the secondary labour market in the private and collective sectors, and pick up jobs that pay low salary and provide few benefits.[19]

Such labour market conditions have led to a divided working class, for it is reinforced by the pattern of residential segregation and ethnic stereotyping. Temporary migrant workers tend to live in very poor quality housing in the urban fringe. Migrant housing generally lacks such facilities as electricity, water supply, drainage and sewage systems, and fire prevention lanes. In addition, temporary migrant workers are regarded as outsiders and excluded form the local society. Local urban workers have assigned many negative ethnic labels to migrant enclaves, including "paradise of thieves and robbers," "camps for prostitutes," "retreats of hunted criminals," etc. Tensions have been growing between urban workers and temporary migrant workers.[20]

As Lee Ching Kwan remarks, "local urban workers and migrant workers are not ready allies in forming any class-based movement. Divided by localistic origins (local workers versus outside workers), sociocultural backgrounds (country folk versus urbanites), and age (young versus middle-aged and older), the two groups of workers often find themselves in competition for the same unskilled and low paid manufacturing jobs in both the state and the non-state sectors. . . . Even when they labour side by side within state-owned factories, conflict regarding wage rates and work allocation are common."[21]

Impose Political Repression to Disorganise the Working Class

In order for the working class to form a class, it needs its own organisation and its own leaders to concentrate its resources, to disseminate information, to articulate its interests and discourse, to plan strategy and tactics, etc. However, a fundamental problem for the Chinese working class is that they are disorganised, and their protests are often leaderless. Why is that so? What explains the lack of its own class organisation and leaders for the Chinese working class?

First of all, although enterprises are supposedly to form labour union to protect the interests of workers, unions formed in foreign-invested enterprises were mostly "company unions", i.e., they were led and staffed by management personnel who were mainly responsible for collecting union fees, organizing birthday parties and recreational events. These union leaders were also salaried shop floor supervisors or section heads in the factory administration.[22] Thus, they were on the side of management rather than on the side of workers when labour conflict broke out.

Similarly, although the All-China Federation of Trade Unions (ACFTU) are supposedly to take care of the interests of the workers in state-owned enterprises, Lee Ching Kwan reports that the ACFTU has proved to be too weak to protect workers rights. In fact, there is widespread illusion among rank-and-file workers towards the ACFTU, as most workers turn not to the ACFTU but to informal networks for support when their rights are encroached upon. [23] More often than not, official unions are controlled directly by management.

In 1989, taking advantage of the rebellious climate in the Tiananmen Square, Beijing workers attempted to form a Beijing Workers' Autonomous Federation (BWAF). This attempt greatly frightened the communist party leaders, as this BWAF has the potential for the workers to form an alliance with intellectual and human rights dissidents. Subsequently, this BWAF was met with ruthless suppression by the party-state.

In November 1999, the government announced new rules for public gatherings, requiring assemblies larger than 200 to obtain approval from local public security authorities. Gatherings larger than 3,000 will require the approval of security offices at a higher level. Since then, the communist party leaders continue to arrest, convict, and imprison any labour activists who try to form an independent labour organisation and start a violent protest, and just to make their intentions clear the party leaders "ordered cities across the country to augment their anti-riot police" in January 2001. [24]

Under this repressive environment, Choi Yongshun reports that workers in labour protests tend not resort to violent or dramatic forms of action because such action would increase the hostility around it and invite the suppression by the party-state. Such repressive environment also leads to a pattern of "leaderless protest" because being an organiser does not bring a person more benefits but put the person in a risky situation because of state repression. If individuals anticipate a risk of violence, they may refuse to assume a leadership role. As some labour activists admit: "We only work as consultants, because organizing is too sensitive. . . . We research the workers' situation; find out what ways work best. We only help workers who requests help. If they don't request help it's best to keep a distance from them." [25]

Without organisation and leadership, it is difficult to wage large-scale protest over a long period of time. As a result, Chinese labour protests tend to be small-scale, unplanned (spontaneous), and short-lived.

Set Up Labour Legislations
to Pre-empt Labour Protests

In addition to bolstering its coercive means of repression, the Chinese state also tried to institutionalise labour conflict through setting up a national labour dispute arbitration system. By 1997, some 270,000 labour dispute mediation committees at the enterprise level, and 3,159 labour dispute arbitration committees at county, city, provincial levels have been established. These committees are constituted by a "tripartite principle," which representatives from the state, labour, and the employer. In the last decade, enterprise mediation cases amounted to 820,000, while 450,000 cases of labour arbitration were processed. [26] The national hierarchy of labour dispute arbitration mechanism attests to the state's attempt to provide institutional channels for the resolution of labour conflicts during economic reforms. The emphasis is on pre-emption and mediation at the enterprise level, with arbitration at the local committee level. Submission of labour disputes to the civil court is the last resort.

Workers have seized this institutional space to redress grievances and defend their rights. Most disputes are economic in nature, with wages, welfare and social insurance payments being the most common causes of conflicts. Wage arrears are particularly pronounced in private and foreign-invested firms.

Thus, most workers have tried the labour dispute system first to express their grievances; only they fail to get what they want that they engage in labour protests publicly. In this respect, the national dispute system has pre-empted workers from engaging in labour protest and public demonstrations. Had the labour dispute system not instilled in the 1990s, labour protests should be more widespread and the possibility of it growing into a massive labour movement more likely.

Adopt the Tactics of Accommodation to Diffuse Working Class Protest

Although the state makes it clear that it is determined to suppress any labour protest organised by independent unions turned violent or politically oriented, the state is also quite willing to accommodate the requests of the labour protests if they are economistic, if they do not engage in any violent behavior, or if they stay within legal bounds. This accommodation policy of the state has greatly influenced the nature of labour protests emerged in the last decade: Labour protests are narrowly confined to be the type that is tolerated by the state and they have a chance to win some concessions.

Feng Chen reports that most of the labour protests could be labeled as "subsistence struggles"[27] It is when the workers are plunged into a subsistence crisis, as their wages go unpaid for months, their medical reimbursements are denied and jobs disappear, that they participated in protests. These workers did not demand to have their previous economic status back, but rather shouted slogans and displaced banners that declared the following:[28]

- "We Want Jobs."
- "We Want Food."
- "We don't demand Fish or Meat, Just Some Porridge."
- "Not a Yuan in Six Months, We Want Rice to Eat."
- "We Need to Eat, We Need to Survive."

These slogans and banners conveyed the desperation and outrage of the retired or unemployed workers, and also showed that their claims focused on demands for subsistence.

The government generally adopted a policy of conciliation and emphasised the use of "persuasion" and "education" to resolve the conflicts. Unless the protests turn into riots, local authorities usually disperse workers not by force but by promises to redress their concern about their subsistence. On the other hand, since this kind of "subsistence struggles" have only local, economistic demands (such as the need of emergency relief fund, or postponing and revising plant closure or relocation decisions), they are not that difficult to meet. A temporary stop-gap measure by the state is usually what is needed to silence the protest.

The willingness of the state to accommodate the demand of "subsistence struggle" explains why the labour protests were usually short-lived, confined to local areas, and failed to escalate into a large-scale social movement that involves workers from other areas or other industries.

Maintain a Moral High Ground
by Shifting the Blames to
the Lower-level Officials

In China's labour protest, local enterprises managers and local government officials, not central government officials, are often the target of attack. In fact, the higher-level government officials often punish the local officials (or overturn the lower-level officials' decision) in order to silence the disgruntled workers.

As a result, despite of widespread labour protests, the party-state is able to maintain moral grounds and is immune from the attack of workers. Corruptions and poor management decisions are located at the individual level. It was the local officials and enterprise managers who are corrupted and carried out the wrong decisions that threaten the subsistence level of the workers, and the higher-level officials in the central state have made it clear that they will not tolerate the mistakes committed by lower level officials. The central state and the higher-level officials claim that they and their economic reforms have done nothing wrong to cause the falling living standard and poverty of the workers.

In post-socialist China, Marc J. Blecher reports that since workers generally accepted the hegemony of the state and of the market reforms, they blamed their enterprise managers (rather than the state or the system) for their bad luck and poverty. A worker has the following to say during Blecher's interview[29]

> "Yes, of course it's unfair that my wages are lower and I have to endure wage arrears just because I happen to work in a plant that is not doing well. Does the state have responsibility? The state's policies are good. It's the implementation that is no good. Sometimes middle-level officials mess things up . . . Some people just turn bad after becoming officials."

By accepting the discourse that it is the local or the middle-level officials who are at fault, the Chinese workers appeal to the Central government to solve the problem of corruption or bad management in local government and local enterprises. By taking the moral high ground of the central government for granted, the workers thus want to seek help from the central state rather than to challenge its legitimacy. In this respect, labour protests could at most lead to the firing of some local or middle-level officials, but could not result in the development of a highly conscious working class who want to transform of the existing system.

Rapid Economic Development and Market Hegemony

The state's policies to divide and de-mobilise the workers are greatly assisted by the rapid economic development of China over the past two decades, which recorded an amazing growth of 9 percent per year. A booming economy is not conducive to labour movement for the following reasons.

A booming economy will provide more resources for the state to grant concession to the workers to satisfy their "subsistence struggles." In addition, a booming economy will also divert away from politics the energies of lively, smart people with leadership potential. In Cai's study, the leaders who emerged in the spontaneous labour protest were mostly elite workers who had good social networks. These kind of elite workers are likely to find employment elsewhere in a booming economy, thus they will not put a risk on their careers by participation in labour protests.

Furthermore, a booming economy will lend further support to the market hegemony, i.e., the economic reforms are good and there could be no return to the Maoist period; if the worker is not doing well, it is due either to bad luck or to lousy enterprise managers. The worker should try to think of a better way to make more money in the booming economy rather than in participate in labour protests.

In sum, a booming economy lends support to the ideology of market; it is not conducive to promote a national labour movement aims to achieve systemic transformation.

The Future of Labour Insurgency in China

In this paper, I argue that economic reforms have done great harms to the Chinese working class in terms of job security, wages, and entitlements (such as housing, health care, and education). Subsequently, the Chinese working class responded by engaging in protests, and the number of labour protests have significantly increased over the past decades. However, all these massive labour protests have failed to produce a nation-wide labour movement. The aim of this paper is to show that the state has played a decisive role in shaping the contour of labour insurgency in China.

The state has created deep social divisions in the working class, has prevented the working class forming its own organisation, has set up labour legislations to pre-empt labour protests, has pushed the protest towards the direction of "subsistence struggles", has punished middle-level officials in order to maintain a moral ground.

In addition, a booming economy has greatly facilitated the state to impose an ideological hegemony over the workers, making the workers to blame themselves rather than making claims on systemic change.

If the suppression, the diffusion, and the containment of labour insurgency by the state are so successful, what is the prospect for labour insurgency in China? Does the labour movement have any future in China? Given the fact that labour insurgency is a product of the structural contradictions of the economic reforms, labour insurgency could never be completely eliminated if the economic reforms are continued. Like an active volcano, labour protests could be intensified and exploded when the following two facilitating conditions are present.

First of all, labour insurgency could be intensified if there is a downturn in the economy, leading to massive unemployment. If an economic boom like the present helps the state to contain and to diffuse the labour protests, then an economic recession in the future may help to intensify the labour protests into a large-scale labour movement. During an economic downturn, not only labour protest would gain more support from the workers, but the state would be deprived of the vital resource to make concessions to protest workers.

In addition, labour insurgency could be intensified if there is a political crisis created by elite cleavages. Changes in ruling alignments create an opportunity structure for the growth of the labour protests and the expansion of social movements. As Andrew Walder points out, "'Tiananmen' is a classic case in which nascent protests interact with a divided elite and party-state apparatus . . . with impulses for protests from below."[30] If there is another elite division and power struggle during the regime transition, it is possible that labour protests – in conjuncture with democracy movements and other social movements – could be powerful enough to challenge the party-state's monopoly of power.

In short, although labour insurgency is at present confined to economistic, localised, and peaceful resistance, it does have the potential of becoming a revolutionary movement if the conditions of economic downfall and political crisis are present. As such, what is the implication of the above conclusion for China's development?

Implication for China's Development

China's model of development belongs to the type that relies heavily on foreign investment and export-led industrialisation. The success of this developmental model is dependent on cheap and docile labour. Foreign corporations set up branch factories in China because of cheap, docile Chinese labourers. Chinese exports out-compete other products in the global market mostly because of their low prices. Therefore, if the Chinese state is able to continue its suppression, containment, and diffusion of labour protest, China's should be able to continue its economic expansion. In the near future, China should be able to transform itself as a global economic power and exert its influence on the world.

Nevertheless, the widespread labour protest over the past few years has sent a warning signal to the Chinese party-state. A signal that there are indeed some deep-rooted structural problems caused by economic reforms; a signal that the Chinese state had better do something about the structural problems before they grow into a social movement. Learning from the 1989 Tiananmen Incident, the Chinese state leaders know very well that if the labour protests are linked with other kinds of social movement, they could threaten the survival of the regime.

The pressures exert by the labour protests, therefore, should prompt the state to take a path of "reform from the above" to deal with the structural problems. The present timing is very favorable to institute "reform from the above" because the state is not under any threat of survival and the booming economy has provided opportunities and resources to solve the deep-rooted structural problems. For example, the state could try to institutionalise a new social security net (welfare, health care, unemployment insurance, pension, etc.) to guarantee the economic survival of the weak (the unemployed, the sick, the elderly, the widowed, etc.). The state can also put forward a system of labour arbitration that is based on genuine tripartite representation which genuinely represents the interests of labour. These welfare and arbitration reforms should go a long way to undermine the structural grievances of the workers and to dampen the motivation of the worker rebels. Should that reform route be taken, the Chinese communist regime shall receive widespread support from the Chinese working class.

Notes and References

1. Marc J. Blecher. "Hegemony and Worker's Politics in China" *The China Quarterly* No. 170 (2002), pp. 283.

2. *Ibid.*, p. 283.

3. Martin Hart-Landsberg and Paul Burkett. "China and Socialism: Market Reforms and Class Struggle." *Monthly Review* Vol. 56 (No. 3), 2004, p. 58.

4. *Ibid.*, p. 59.

5. Tim Pringle, "The Path of Globalization: Implication for Chinese Workers." *Asian Labour Update*, No. 41 (Oct–Dec 2001).

6. Martin Hart-Landsberg, p. 61.

7. Dorothy Solinger, "Why we cannot count the unemployed." *The China Quarterly*, No. 167 (Sept 2001), p. 671.

8. Tim Pringle "Industrial Unrest in China – A Labour Movement in the Making?" *China Labour Bulletin*, 31 January 2002. Accessed through http://www.hartford-hwp.com/archives/55/294.html on 13 April 2003, p. 1.

9. *Ibid.*, p. 2.

10. Chen Feng, "Subsistence Crises, Managerial Corruption, and Labour Protests in China," *The China Journal*, No. 44 (July 2000), p. 41. Lee Ching Kwan, "Pathways of Labour Insurgency," in Elizabeth Perry and Mark Selden (eds.), *Chinese Society: Change, Conflict and Resistance* (Routledge, 2000), p. 41.

11. Trini Leung "The Third Wave of the Chinese Labour Movement in the Post-Mao Era" *China Labour Bulletin* 2 June 2002. Accessed "http:

www.hartford-hwp.com/archives/55/297.html" on 13 April 2003, p. 7. See also Martin Hart-Lansberg and Paul Burkett, "China and Socialism: Market Reforms and Class Struggle." *Monthly Review*, Vol. 56, No. 3, (July-August 2004), p. 76.

12. See Alvin Y. So, "Class Struggle Without Class? Labour Insurgency in Post-Socialist China." Paper presented to the conference "Social Movements and Social Change in East Asia" at Sungyunkwan University, Seoul, 1 December 2003.

13. Chen Feng, "Subsistence crises, managerial corruption, and labour protests in China," *The China Journal*, Vol. 44 (2000), p. 49.

14. Ching Kwan Lee, "Pathways of Labour Insurgency," in *Chinese Society: Change, Conflict, and Resistance*, p. 50.

15. Marc J. Blecher, "Hegemony and Workers' Politics in China," *The China Quarterly*, (2002), p. 285.

16. Chen Feng, "Subsistence Crisis, Managerial Corruption, and Labour Protests in China," p. 62.

17. Alvin Y. So, "Beyond the Logic of Capital and the Polarization Model: The State, Market Reforms, and the Plurality of Class Conflict in China," *Critical Asian Studies*, Vol. 37 (2005), pp. 481–484.

18. Cai Yongshun, "The Resistance of Chinese Laid-off Workers in the Reform Period," *The China Quarterly*, Vol. 170 (2002), p. 327–344.

19. Fan, Cindy. "Migration and Labour Market in Transitional China." Paper presented to the "International Workshop on Resource Management, Urbanization, and Governance in Hong Kong and the Zhujiang Delta," The Chinese University of Hong Kong, May 23–24, 2000.

20. Taubmann, Wolfang. "Urban Administration, Urban Development, and Migrant Enclaves." Paper presented to the "International Workshop on Resource Management, Urbanization, and Governance in Hong Kong and the Zhujiang Delta," The Chinese University of Hong Kong, May 23–24, 2000.

21. Lee Ching Kwan, "Pathways of Labour Insurgency," p. 58.

22. *Ibid.*, p. 51.

23. *Ibid.*, p. 55.

24. Erik Eckholm, "Chinese Officials Order Cities to Bolster Riot Police Forces," *New York Times*, January 30, 2001.

25. Cai Yongshun "The Resistance of Chinese Laid-off Workers in the Reform Period," pp. 336–337.

26. Lee Ching Kwan, "Pathways of Labour Insurgency," p. 47.

27. Chen Feng, "Subsistence Crises, Managerial Corruption, and Labour Protests in China," pp. 41–63.

28. *Ibid.*, p. 50.

29. Marc Blecher, "Hegemony and Workers' Politics in China," p. 291.

30. Andrew Walder, "Does China Face an Unstable Future?" in Maurice Brosseau, Kuan Hsin-chi and Y.Y. Kueh (ed.), *China Review 1997* (Hong Kong: Chinese University Press, 1997), pp. 344–45.

6

Conditionality for
China's Peaceful Rise

Guiguo WANG

The Chinese government declared its ambitious programme of peaceful rise at the beginning of this century. Although no specific definition of peaceful rise has been given, it is generally understood that the peaceful rise emphasises on the means for achieving the aim of making China an economically strong country and that in the process of developing China into a strong economic power, a peaceful world environment is required. It is equally important that China's bid for peaceful rise must be commensurate with the world trend of globalisation. With the world increasingly integrated, international organisations and international norms are playing a more and more important role. Against the above background, this article examines the characteristics of the world today and the policy alternatives China may adopt in its effort at peaceful rise.

Interweaving of International
Politics and Economy

In history, cooperation and disputes among countries began and ended in economic interests. The same also holds true for the case of national matters. As to how to achieve the desired objectives, it can take peaceful and non-peaceful means or by using military force. The kind of measures to be taken depends to a large extent on the nature of the issues involved, the interests at stake, the balance of power among the parties, the international and internal environment, etc.

At present, globalisation has become the mainstream of the world economy. The manifestation of globalisation in the economic plane has far exceeded the traditional international interdependence. Against the background of globalisation, the characteristic of interdependence in the contemporary world is stereoscopic. That is the interdependence not only exists among countries, among the developed countries, among the developing countries, but also between the developed and developing countries. Its manifestation is high frequency and large scale economic transactions and exchanges between the nations and private enterprises, among the enterprises themselves, between enterprises and individuals as well as between nations and individuals. Under such circumstance, any action or inaction by a nation or an enterprise may have direct effects on the economic environment or lives of other regions in the world. At the same time, nearly all economic activities more or less involve more than one economic sector. For example, transactions in non-ferrous metals and sale and purchase of special steels are ordinary commercial transactions. Yet, as information technology is highly developed today, from the quantity of import of non-ferrous metals and special steels, people may be able to ascertain the stage of development and the amount of storage of advanced weapons of and even the tactics and strategies to be adopted in war by the importing country. In order to restrict the ability of certain countries from developing the state-of-art weapons, those which have the ability to control the export of non-ferrous metals and special steels may impose export restrictions on the same. In a way, such kind of restrictions may achieve far more profound impact than restrictions on the export of weapons. If used with restrictions on export of weapons, half the work may achieve double results.

Trade in energy products such as oil also demonstrates to what extent the world interdependence has linked together economics with politics. One of the effects of industrialisation is the continued rise of dependence on energy. As a result, both oil-producing countries and oil-importing countries can exert certain influence on the price of oil, which in turn affects the economic environment of the countries concerned. In the past two years, the rise in oil prices was directly related to the skyrocketing demand by China and India for oil. The increasing reliance on imported oil not only entails the use of foreign exchange, more importantly, it involves foreign policies and energy strategies of the countries concerned. At least one of the reasons for the United States to invade Iraq was oil. Its sending troops to the Middle East and spending a lot of money in the colour revolution in Central Asia are also partially for energy resources. As the United States is in control of the oil producing countries in the Middle East, including Iraq, to diversify the energy sources has become an urgent issue for China. Iran which is with the world second largest oil reserve is a natural choice of energy resources for China. Iran on the other hand facing the threat of attack from the United States also needs a country like China to be its friend. In the end, out of different needs, the two countries' essential national interests have made them stand together and cooperate with each other.

As energy products such as oil is indispensable to the economic development, it can lead to diplomatic disputes or even armed conflicts. The recent disputes between China and Japan are an example. Toward the end of the last century, China and Russia started the negotiation for building a 2400 kilometre-long oil pipeline from Russia's Angarsk to Daqing in China. In May, 2003, China National Petroleum Corporation and Yukos from Russia agreed on the "YUKOS-CNPC General Agreement on Basic Principles and Agreement, Related to Long-Term Contract on Crude Oil Supply by Sino-Russian Pipeline". However, less than 4 months before the signing of the Agreement, Japan proposed the so-called "Nakhodka Line Proposal", i.e. to construct a pipeline from Angarsk to Nakhodka in Vladivostok, so as to enable Japan to get oil directly from that harbour. As the old English saying goes, there is no free lunch. In order to convince Russia, Japan first proposed to provide US$7.5 billion to Russia for developing a new oil base in Siberia, together with an additional US$1 billion for protecting the ecological environment of the area along the pipeline. This issue seems to be resolved when Hu Jintao, General Secretary of the Chinese Communist Party and President of China, visited Russia in 2005. On 8 July of the same year, Russian President Vladimir Putin expressed that Russia prioritised China's interests in the construction of the Siberian oil pipeline. The reason why the issue of how to construct the Siberian oil pipeline is regarded as "seems to be resolved" is because Japan later increased its offer by agreeing to pay US$9 billion in exchange for Russia's prior consideration of Japanese interests in lieu of others.

The United States also attempts to force the energy policy of other countries to serve its interests. On 26 July 2005, the U.S. Senate Foreign Relations Committee held a public hearing on the energy policies of China and India. Richard Lugar, chairman of the committee, in his opening speech, explicitly stated that the energy policy of and foreign investment by China and India in the energy sector were directly related to the national security of the United States.[1] As the world second largest energy consuming country and the third energy producing country, China's energy policy can affect the world energy market. Also both China and India have important investments in the Iranian energy industry, while the United States regards Iran as the axis of evil and the object of transformation of the 21st century. The economic and trade relationship between China and India with Iran, which is situated between Iraq and Afghanistan, will affect the American isolationist policy towards Iran, thus the United States is very concerned about every move of China and India in the region.[2] On 7 September 2005, Robert Zoellick, Deputy Secretary of State of the United States said that he was not sure how much China's energy policy was influenced by oil companies. Yet, he warned China that if it continued to pursue its energy deals with countries like Iran, it was "going to have repercussions elsewhere" and the Chinese government would have to decide if they wanted to pay the price.[3] The threat was obvious in the tone of Zoellick.

The dispute between China and Japan over the sovereignty and exploration right of the oil-gas fields in East China Sea also has far-reaching effect. Recently, ignoring the protest of the Chinese government, Japan renamed the three Chinese oil-gas fields in the East China Sea, namely "Chunxiao", "Duanqiao" and "Lengquan" into "Baihua", "Nan" and "Jiegeng" respectively.[4] It has not only resulted in fierce protest from the Chinese government, but also provoked anger of the Chinese people. If it is not dealt with appropriately, an armed conflict may break out.

China National Offshore Oil Corporation's (CNOOC) bid to acquire the Union Oil Company of California (UNOCAL), an American corporation, is another case of politicisation of economic and trade affairs. Acquisition and merger are a normal commercial activity. However, as one of the parties is a Chinese company, it became an ideology and international issue. The U.S. media and congressmen were concerned that the CNOOC's bid might affect the essential national security of the United States. It was in part due to the fact that UNOCAL is an oil company, but was also because the seabed exploration technology of UNOCAL might enhance the capability of China in exploring the seabed, which would in turn benefit the submarines of China. On 26 July 2005, the United States Congress passed a decision to extend the period for the U.S. Committee on Foreign Investment to examine the CNOOC's bid. Pursuant to the decision, the United States Department of Energy, Department of Homeland Security and Department of Defense would first conduct a 120-day long investigation, assessing the impact of the increase in energy demand of China on the economy and national security of the United States; the amount of American energy assets which had been acquired by China; whether the acquisition involved funding by the Chinese government; whether China allowed American enterprises to acquire Chinese enterprises, the differences between the investment laws of China and the United States. After the above Departments having completed their investigation with positive results, the Committee on Foreign Investment would initiate a 21-day long investigation.[5] Under the pressure of the U.S. government and politics, CNOOC was finally forced to withdraw its acquisition plan.[6] The United States always boasts that it is the freest market in the world. Yet, it doesn't even allow an acquisition by a Chinese company of an American company. This is obviously an irony, though not the first time for the United States which advocates globalisation to prevent others to have access to its markets. It also shows that international economic affairs and politics are inseparable.

It was reported that the United States levied a fine of US$47 million on the Boeing Company for selling nine airplanes equipped with gyroscopic microchips which are prohibited from being exported by the United States.[7] Gyroscopic microchip is a core orientation equipment of airplanes, which can ensure that airplanes fly stably to the accurate destination. If this technology is used in steering guided missiles, they will be able to hit the target with more accuracy. During the cold war, the United States was very sensitive about the transfer of such technology and equipment to the former Soviet Union. Yet the airplanes sold by the Boeing Company are always equipped with gyroscopic microchips. The issue is why the United States did not punish Boeing until now. Some claimed that it is the effect of "China Shock".[8] The so-called "China Shock" refers to the United States' startle, inconceivability and unacceptability of China's rapid economic development. From the perspective of the United States, for instance, it is utterly unthinkable that a Chinese company could compete with the second largest oil company in the United States for acquiring an American company.

There is another case which is more bizarre. The Republicans in the U.S. Congress proposed in mid July 2005 to impose countervailing duties on the products imported from China. The United States has always treated China as a non-market economy country, thus it has never imposed countervailing duties on products originating from China, as the existence of subsidy and the amount of subsidy can only be ascertained under the market environment. As the United States regards China as a non-market economy country, it should not levy countervailing duties on Chinese products. As a matter of fact, it is also impossible to determine the existence and amount of subsidy. The reason behind the move is that the Republican controlled government wanted the Dominican Republic-Central America Free Trade Agreement (DR-CAFTA) to be approved by the Congress.[9] Perhaps very few people can relate the imposition of countervailing duties on Chinese products to the passing of DR-CAFTA. The fact is that once the DR-CAFTA was approved, the agriculture and textile industry in central and southern part of the Untied States would be affected. In order to pacify the discontent of the society and those which may be affected, the Republican Congressmen attempted to push the DR-CAFTA through by attacking China.[10]

The above cases show that today with the globalisation prevailing, any commercial transactions may involve international politics, diplomacy and world strategies. In other words, under the trend of globalisation, non-commercial risks for commercial transactions and enterprises have increased. It not only adds an international dimension to commercial transactions, more importantly, along with the changes in international relations and international politics, the non-commercial risks pertinent to each transaction will change accordingly, although not all such changes can be adapted or managed by all the businesses. The aforesaid acquisition bid by CNOOC is a case in point. The development in globalisation also poses new challenges to policy makers of all the nations concerned. Some matters which were domestic in nature before now have an international character, when making decisions on such matters, account must be taken of the international impact; in other words, the decision-making will unavoidably be influenced by the international balance of powers, including non-governmental organisations.[11] Under such circumstances, each country, regardless its size, possesses some power in sanctioning other countries. For example, one of the characteristics of globalisation is the technologicalisation of the economy i.e. the technical content of commodities and the information value of transactions keep on rising. As such, in cases where a strong country refuses to abide by international obligations, other countries that are unable to adopt positive measures to impose sanctions may take passive measures such as refusing to accord protection to the intellectual properties from the former. This has been proved by far the most effective means in dealing with economically strong countries for violations.

Supremacy of International Norms

As a result of globalisation, international organisations serve as network of various economic and other activities which in turn directly impact on the lives of the members of the international community. One of the manifestations of globalisation is strengthened cooperation among international organisations themselves. Traditionally, as part of the Bretton Woods System, the World Bank and the International Monetary Fund ("IMF") have been regarded as "sister organisations". In their history for more than half a century, they played distinct roles and responsibilities. With globalisation proceeding, the World Bank and IMF signed a cooperation agreement at the dawn of the century, putting development issues at the top of the agenda of both organisations.

IMF has also concluded Trade Integration Mechanism Agreement with the WTO.[12] Pursuant to the Agreement, the IMF will provide assistance to the countries experiencing balance of payment difficulties as a result of trade liberalisation. Although it is still premature to make any conclusions as to the effect of Trade Integration Mechanism on trade liberalisation or globalisation, the fact that the agreement with the aim of promoting trade liberalisation is signed by the two international organisations which monitor monetary and trade policies is significant enough. The existence of Trade Integration Mechanism sends a clear message that trade liberalisation is the trend recognised by the international community, at least by the two international organisations. Any country which experiences balance-of-payments difficulties as a result of trade liberalisation can expect support from the IMF. The predictability of the availability of such assistance will enable the countries to undertake more risks in the process of trade liberalisation.

Apart from cooperation in policies and strategies, the cooperation and coordination among international organisations in specific matters have also been strengthened. In this respect, a prominent example is the cooperative relationship between the WTO and World Customs Organisation (WCO). For example, in *EU – Computer Equipment case*,[13] the Appellate Body of the WTO stressed that the implementation of the Harmonised System should not only take into account the need for harmonisation of the standard but also the views of the WCO Harmonised System Committee. In other words, the interpretation of the trade agreements under the WTO will be affected by the WCO through its classification of products. Taking into account the binding effect of the WTO dispute settlement mechanism on its Members, under such arrangement, the harmonised system adopted by the WCO and the decision of its Harmonised System Committee will in effect be binding on the WTO Members. This would not be conceivable when the extent of globalisation was less prevalent.

Certainly, the cooperation between the WTO and WCO did not start recently. During the GATT era, the then Customs Cooperation Council assisted, to a certain extent, the activities of the GATT. After the establishment of the WTO, the relationship between the two has become clearer than before. For example, the Agreement on Customs Valuation is part of the WTO system on trade in goods. Its enforcement depends on WCO. Besides, the rules of origin designed by WCO are primarily implemented by the WTO through the Agreement on Rules of Origin.

The WTO and UN have also engaged in significant cooperation. First, starting from the GATT period, the definition of developing countries and the implementation of the General System of Preferences is closely related to the UN. Secondly, the UN Harmonised System and Central Product Classification have tremendous effect on the WTO. This can be seen from the interpretation of *U.S. – Gambling case*[14] on the specific commitments of the United States. Thirdly, the International Trade Centre established between the WTO and UNCTAD is responsible for researching and analyzing international trade issues. It thus blurs the distinction of the traditional nature of these two international organisations.[15] International organisations such as the World Bank have sent observers to the WTO with the aim of strengthening cooperation among the international organisations. Under this general atmosphere, the mutual penetration, mutual effect and cooperation among international organisations are a feature of the contemporary world.[16]

Cooperation can to a certain extent strengthen the function of the international organisations. As a result of the participation of other international organisations, missions once impossible have become possible. Functions once impossible for a single international organisation to perform can now be carried out effectively with joint efforts of international organisations. Through this broad scope of cooperation, international organisations have formed a network world wide. Many matters which have traditionally been regarded as domestic are now dealt with in this framework. Some matters require the assistance of international organisations to be resolved effectively. Some matters can only be resolved within this framework. Hence, under the grand trend of globalisation, countries must pay adequate attention to the weight of international organisations in both economic and political matters which are mutually affecting each other. As that is the case, any country that is in control or is able to influence the decision-making of international organisations can carry out its national policies through the operation of international organisations. For example, in order to implement unilateralist policy and export American democracy, the President of the World Bank nominated by the United States and the American Ambassador to the United Nations are all with clear and strong political stands. Paul Wolfowitz, the former Deputy Defense Secretary of the United States, upon being appointed as the President of the World Bank publicly announced his intention of using the World Bank to assist the United States in promoting global democracy.[17] Put it simply, the United States will exercise its influence in the World Bank through lending loans by the latter to change the political structure of other countries. Looking back, perhaps without the support of international organisations such as the World Bank, the U.S. efforts in colour revolution in Central Asia might not have been so effective.

With the increasing influence of international organisations, NGOs have also moved gradually from the national to the international platform. The fast development of information technology and communication technology has greatly enhanced the strength of NGOs. The failure of the Seattle and Cancun WTO Ministerial Conference is fact proving. The abortion of negotiations on Multilateral Investment Agreement among the developed countries is also attributable to the efforts of NGOs. The attempts made by NGOs in the WTO dispute settlement are no longer any news.

Globalisation, especially the perfection and increasing influence of international organisations, leads to a decreasing role played by transnational corporations in international affairs. The fast paced development of science and technology has enabled medium and small enterprises to demonstrate their strength in international matters and more importantly to engage in transnational transactions. For instance, international investment and finance which were once the monopoly of giant transnational corporations are no longer their privilege. With the liberalisation of information and remarkable reduction in transaction costs, the relatively free transfer of capital and resources and quickened pace of cultural exchanges, medium and small enterprises can easily conduct business anywhere and in direct competition with traditional multilateral corporations. Now it is difficult to distinguish a multilateral company from a purely domestic concern. As a result, the network formed among the medium and small enterprises and traditional multilateral corporations serves as a unique political and economic platform at the international level. The decision-making by almost all the countries is unavoidably affected by this platform, the difference, if any, is in the degree of such influence.

Globalisation also has an important effect on the legislative, judicial and administrative organs of the nations. The Articles of Agreement of the IMF entered into after the Second World War has provisions requiring that exchange contracts in violation of the exchange regulations of any member shall not be enforced by any other member.[18] During the Asian financial crisis, in approving the drawing rights by the IMF members demanded the countries concerned to make economic adjustment and in some instances even changes in the domestic political structure. That was the reason why Korea called the day for its drawing funds from the IMF as the "Day of National Humiliation".[19] In practice, the World Bank also imposes conditions for lending which have direct impact on the political and economic lives of the borrowers. Such conditions include effort to combat corruption, adoption of anti-corruption measures, protection of minority groups, provision of opportunities for women in participating in politics and carrying out social reforms. These conditions have far reaching effect on borrowing members.

The influence of the WTO on the laws and legal systems of its Members is more direct, more concrete and more widespread. One of the distinctive characteristics of the WTO is the single undertaking whereby no member is allowed to make reservations to any agreement. Under the system, the minimum standards stipulated in various agreements as well as the specific and special commitments of the Members at the entry of the WTO have also become part of the laws of each Member, although each Member retains the choice of direct or indirect application of the WTO Agreement. The U.S. Antidumping Act of 1916, [20] U.S. Foreign Sales Corporation Act,[21] Japanese tax law,[22] European Union's import licensing system and regulations on wholesale and retail system of bananas[23] and the Canadian Patent Act[24] were found by the WTO DSU as violating the WTO Agreement and should be amended. Some of these laws had been in force for many years. However, upon joining the WTO, such laws had to be amended in accordance with the international standards. Another difference between the WTO Agreement and traditional international treaties is that it directly regulates the private rights. A case in point is the TRIPS.

TRIPS includes the basic WTO principles of the most-favoured nation treatment, national treatment and transparency. It also has specific provisions on granting patents and trademarks, the terms and conditions for granting intellectual property rights, the system and measures for protecting intellectual properties, and the standards relating to penalties for infringement.[25] There are also specific provisions on the power of the customs authorities and judicial review by the court of administrative decisions.[26] It is worthy to note that all these provisions are part of the law of each Member.

As the provisions of the WTO Agreement are part of the law of the Members, the ways and means for implementing such laws are inevitably monitored by the WTO. In the last ten years, the WTO has ruled many times that the decisions of the administrative organs were in violation of the WTO Agreement. More remarkable are cases involving the investigation of antidumping, countervailing duties and safeguards. *Argentina – Poultry case*[27] involved the standards for antidumping investigation; *U.S. – Softwood case*[28] concerned the Subsidies and Countervailing Measures Agreement; *U.S. – Steel case*[29] was related to the Agreement on Safeguards and *India – Patent case*[30] was under the TRIPS.

All the WTO agreements relating to trade in goods, services and intellectual property include standards of enforcement. More specifically, in enforcement, both the administrative and judicial organs must observe the principles of fairness and reasonableness, objectiveness and transparency, unless the matters concerned are unrelated to the WTO. As the WTO covers a broad scope, almost all the matters may involve trade in goods, services or intellectual property. It thus effectively incorporates the law enforcement organs under the WTO. Any judicial decision in violation of the WTO Agreement will constitute a breach of international obligations by the Member concerned. In *U.S. – Shrimp case*,[31] the DSU overturned the decision of the U.S. Court of International Trade. An overview of the decisions of the WTO DSU shows that most of its interpretations involved analysis of specific provisions of the agreements, sometimes interpretation of specific words or the use of punctuations. The laws of many countries relating to international trade and intellectual property protection have adopted the provisions of the WTO Agreement. Its result is that the power of autonomy of the national courts in interpreting its national laws has in fact been constrained – interpretation of domestic laws must now take into account the interpretation by the international community of the relevant words and phrases and relevant international standards.

Other international treaties, such as the Energy Charter Treaty[32] also has compulsory provisions and requirements on the contracting parties. For example, the Energy Charter Treaty on the one hand provides that the contracting parties should accord MFN treatment and national treatment to foreign investors, on the other hand, it requires each contracting party to agree to accept foreign arbitration in investment related disputes. In the applicability of the principles and standards of investment treatment, international arbitration bodies serve in effect as bodies above the national courts of the host countries parties to the Treaty.[33]

The development of globalisation leads to gradual convergence of the national laws of the members of the international community. This is first reflected in the laws relating to international trade, international finance, international investment, international taxation and intellectual property protection, followed by those relating to environment protection, development, human rights, competition, trade facilitation and government procurement. Such convergence is not simply a transplant of the laws of one country to another, or incorporation of the provisions of international treaties into the national laws, it is directly related to the legal culture, legal concept, legal value, legal spirit, legal policy and legal environment of the countries concerned. It is not restricted to similarity in general legal provisions, but more importantly, the methods, rules and standards of law interpretation. Needless to say, at present, such convergence of law is happening mainly in commercial sectors. With further development of globalisation, the laws relating to government governance and rule of law will be included. Eventually, any country facing international and national issues must inevitably consider the effect of international politics and economies as well as the restraints to be imposed by international organisations and international treaties.

Policy Alternatives

Facing the globalisation, every country has to take appropriate means to maximise the positive effects and avoid the adverse effects thereof. In order to achieve the aim of peaceful rise, China must also adopt the measures commensurate with the international trend of globalisation. This may involve the reconsideration of China's policies at multilateral, regional and bilateral levels. At multilateral level, in addition to its permanent membership at the UN Securities Council, China is member of the International Monetary Fund,[34] the World Bank, the World Trade Organisation,[35] the World Customs Organisation, the World Intellectual Property Organisation,[36] etc. In a word, China has participated in almost all the important multilateral organisations covering the areas from international politics, international peace, international trade and finance, to the protection of human, animal and plant health. What China could do is to increase the degree of its participation in the operation of such organisations.

China for a long time practised the low profile foreign policy and did not actively participate in international organisations such as the UN, World Bank and IMF. Even in WTO, it is only until the Cancun Ministerial Conference did it take an active part in the Group of 21. The effect of this policy on economic sectors is lack of interest in the regional arrangements. For example, in 1990s, China participated in the APEC, but it mainly displayed interests in non-economic issues. It did not exercise its influence as an important country in promoting regional economic integration. Even in the Shanghai Cooperation Organisation (SCO) which was initiated by China, the Chinese government has not fully stressed the importance of economic cooperation. Such situation is neither compatible with the status of China in this highly globalised contemporary world nor commensurate with its bit of peaceful rise. China must now pay more attention to the quantity and quality of its involvement in such organisations so that its foreign policies, political and economic, will be reflected in the decisions and actions of the international organisations.

What happened at the Fifth Ministerial Conference of the WTO held in Cancun, Mexico may be inductive for China to reconsider or even change its policies. At the Cancun Ministerial, China together with India, Brazil and other developing countries formed the Group of 21 to coordinate the positions of the developing countries.[37] The success of the Group of 21 in demonstrating the strength of the developing countries in the WTO may encourage China to take a more pro-active approach in multilateral organisations. From the experience of other countries, what China should concentrate is the procedural rules of the various organisations. A distinct feature of the Chinese legal culture is emphasis on the substantive provisions and substantive fairness. An important aspect of the rule of law, however, is due process and procedures which have already become an integral part of the international organisations. To play a significant role in any international organisation requires familiarity with and skillful use of the procedures, a challenge that China must conquer.

With the ever deepening of globalisation, multilateral organisations now manage various affairs which used to be handled by the states. It is fair to say that nowadays a lot of things cannot be done without the involvement of international organisations and still a lot of matters that could only be dealt with by international organisations. As a consequence of the growth in power by multilateral organisations, members of the international community try to find ways to preserve their own traditional rights and authorities whilst pushing the majority of others to be subject to international norms. One of the methods adopted by many countries is establishment of regional arrangements such as custom unions and free trade areas, which are considered as exceptions to the multilateral system. This is being done whilst almost all countries acclaim the superiority of the multilateral system. Another interesting development is that all countries support trade liberalisation and at the same time, try to slow down the speed of market opening and the scope of market access, to create trade barriers with or without legitimate objectives and justifications.

Against such international environment, China must adjust its strategy such that it can rise peacefully.

Compared with the developed countries such as the United States and the EU, China still lags behind in making good use of the international environment and international treaties. For example, the United States, the EU and Japan all play an important role in the WTO. Nevertheless, these countries still try hard to establish regional arrangements. The eastward movement of the EU and the southward advancement by the United States are cases in point. As a matter of fact, the developed countries in particular the United States always give priority to international politics over economic benefits in establishing regional arrangements. This shows that the current regional arrangements are no longer cooperation among a small group of countries which are geographically proximate. Many free trade arrangements are established across the continents to serve the purpose of international politics. Free trade agreements between the Untied States and Morocco, Chile and Singapore fall into this category.[38] Such trend has intrinsic reasons. Membership of international organisations like the WTO, the World Bank and IMF covers almost all the countries in the world. According to the MFN principle, all contracting parties should receive non-discrimination treatment. In order to maintain special political and military relations, they have to find other ways to provide more favourable treatment to their allies. Regional arrangement as an exception to the principle of MFN treatment thus emerged. It also explains why regional arrangements become all the more popular after the establishment of the WTO and with the world trade system continuing to improve and its scope continuing to expand.

It should be pointed out though that China has begun to pay attention to regional arrangements. One of such efforts is establishing a free trade area with the Association of Southeast Asian Nations (ASEAN) countries. In 2002, China and ASEAN signed the "Framework Agreement on Comprehensive Economic Co-Operation Between ASEAN and the People's Republic of China", with the objective of establishing a free trade area by 2020. In October 2003, according to "China-Thailand Zero Tariff Fruit and

Vegetable Agreement", China and Thailand began to accord each other zero tariff treatment to their respective fruits and vegetables.[39] In 2004, Chinese Premier Wen Jiabao and the leaders of ASEAN countries signed "Agreement on Trade in Goods of the Framework Agreement on Comprehensive Economic Co-operation between ASEAN and China" in Vientiane, capital of Laos. The Agreement stipulates that starting from 1 July 2005, China and ASEAN will gradually reduce or eliminate tariffs of 7,000 products. By 2010, China and ASEAN members such as Brunei, Indonesia, Malaysia, the Philippines, Singapore and Thailand will mutually reduce tariff of most products to zero, while for Burma, Cambodia, Laos and Vietnam, it should be 2015. In other words, by 2010, China – ASEAN Free Trade Area will be basically established.[40] This is by far the most significant achievement by China in regional arrangements. Needless to say, the Closer Economic Partnership Arrangements (CEPA) entered into between China and Hong Kong and Macao respectively are also achievements of China in regional arrangement. Nevertheless, taking into the uniqueness in background, framework and contents of the two CEPAs, they differ from other regional arrangements.[41]

Then, how to appraise the effectiveness of the Chinese policy? It should be assessed against the economic development needs of China. The trend and features of globalisation have been discussed above. The objective of China in economic development is to become an economically powerful country through peaceful means, i.e., peaceful rise. The accomplishment of peaceful rise needs a peaceful environment, which in turn requires mutual understanding of all the parties concerned. From the perspective of China, its primary task is to make the United States, Japan and other countries understand that an economically strong China will not impair their interests.[42] Out of their own strategic interests, the United States and Japan may not support the peaceful rise of China. For these countries, the best China can do is to make them used to the fact of a rising China. As stated by a commentator, "What should China do in face of the 'China Shock'? First, it should spend more effort in explaining its acts to the American public. Not all American politicians are honourable gentlemen or look after the interests of the whole world. If China does not want to become a political football, it should be cautious in public speeches, publicly admit its own flaws and explains its own intentions." [43] At the same time, "China should be careful in selecting its target. From an Asian perspective, it seems appropriate for China to criticise the atrocities inflicted by Japan during the Second World War, the fact that Japanese Prime Minister paid respect to Yasukuni Shrine and other Sino-Japanese disputes. However, Beijing should bear in mind that Tokyo is a close ally of the United States in Asia. If China always chooses Japan as the target, it will also worsen its relationship with Washington. If that is a new strategy of Hu Jintao, the president of China, it will be a laughing stock, a very bad one."[44]

From a strategic point of view, however, the United States and Japan differ from each other. Out of its own interest, the United States benefits most from a soar relationship between China and Japan. Suppose China and Japan become allies, say by forming a free trade area, the country that is mostly affected will be the United States. Some may think it is impossible for China and Japan to form an alliance. Yet, politics are always unpredictable. Shared interests may lead China and Japan to the same destination. This of course requires the leadership of both countries to have far-sighted views. With globalisation continues to develop and international environment keeps to change, formation of a Chinese and Japanese alliance certainly should be a choice for both countries.

Whilst forming a workable strategy towards the strong powers, China must also handle well its relations with the neighbouring countries. China should comprehend the possible misunderstanding of its neighbours and try to convince the latter that an economically powerful China will not injure their interests but will enhance the cooperation with them. The ASEAN free trade area can serve as a platform. China should also consider setting up free trade areas with other neighbouring countries like India, Pakistan and South Korea. At the same time, China should work hard to transform SCO into an organisation of economic cooperation. This is quite possible as Russia and Central Asian countries and China have great potential in supplementing each other economically. Cooperation in the energy sector will be the starting point.

To form free trade areas between China and its neighbouring countries is also an economic necessity. China assumed a number of distinctive obligations upon joining the WTO. Such special arrangements which were made by basing on the argument that China was not a market economy are mainly related to textile trade, antidumping, countervailing measures and safeguard measures. They will have significant impact on China's export and will effectively make China a "second-class citizen" in the multilateral trading system for many years to come. The aforesaid U.S. bill on subsidies against Chinese imports is an example.[45] It should be pointed out that although the Democrats accused the Republicans of tying the DR-CAFTA to the China issue, it agreed that actions should be taken against the trade practice of China. In fact, the Democrats believed their version could be more effective in dealing with China's US$162 billion in trade surplus with the United States. Hence, the Democrats and Republicans have no disagreement in adopting stringent measures against China. Phil English, the proposer of the bill, frankly commented that, the purpose of the bill was "to send a strong message to Beijing that the U.S. Congress will not sit idly by while China's mercantilist policy injures U.S. employers and costs us jobs."[46] Once the bill is passed, Chinese products exported to the United States may face endless countervailing duty investigations as one of its goals is to facilitate the enforcement of countervailing measures against non-market economy countries. Another objective of the bill is to monitor whether China has observed its commitments in intellectual property rights protection and market access. In addition, the U.S. Ministry of Finance will be required to submit biannual reports to the Congress analyzing the implementation and effect of the newly enforced exchange policy of China. The establishment of regional arrangements will also serve as the best possible means in breaking through the political and economic encirclement of the Untied States.

At the bilateral level, it was reported that on 28 October 2005, China and Chile reached an Agreement on Goods Trade under

Bilateral FTA.[47] It was first time ever that China signed a bilateral free trade agreement. The reason why Chile was chosen might be that the country has a lot of experience in setting up bilateral economic areas. As a result, Japan and Korea also chose Chile as the first partner of bilateral FTAs. It is expected that with the experience gained and the growing needs in its peaceful rise such as energy and raw materials, China will establish more such FTAs with both the neighbouring countries and those which are situated in other continents.

All in all, an important feature of this globalised world is that multilateral trade mechanisms such as the WTO continue to expand their coverage by moving to the investment and other areas and that at the same time, the number of regional arrangements is also growing fast. Economic activities of any country, region or enterprise are bound to interweave with the international politics in different degrees. Thus, any decision-making by governments and enterprises must take into account international political factors involved. Any move by the government of any country must be considered in line with its international strategies. In China's efforts of peaceful rise, any action and omission of action must be carefully planned by taking into account of the general trend of globalisation and their impact on the international community.

Notes and References

1. See <http://www.foreign.senate.gov/hearings/2005/hrg050726p.html>.

2. From the angle of geographical strategy, the relation between China and India is supplementary rather than competitive with each other. The geographical dividing line between China and India is the Himalaya Mountain. North of the mountain belongs to China, which is with high latitude, cold weather, thin air, barren land and is thus uninhabitable. South of the mountain belongs to India which enjoys warm southward ocean wind and with fertile soil. It thus determines that the strategic interests of India lie at the entrance of the Indian Ocean but not the northern mountainous region.

3. "China Warned on Energy Ties to Iran", *South China Mourning Post*, 8 September 2005, p. 8.

4. Ministry of Economy, Trade and Industry of Japan renamed the three oil-gas fields as Shirakaba, Kusunoki and Kikyo.

5. 27 July 2005, www.wenweipo.com.

6. 3 August 2005, www.wenweipo.com.

7. "Boeing May Be Fined for Exported Technology" Washington Post, 7 July 2005, Page D01, <http://www.washingtonpost.com/wp-dyn/content/article/2005/07/06/AR2005070602262.html>

8. "Why does "China Shock" Attack US Suddenly?" 18 July 2005, <http://news.chinatimes.com>

9. Dominican Republic – Central America Free Trade Agreement was signed between the United States, Costa Rica, Guatemala, Ecuador, Honduras, Nicaragua and Dominica on 5 August, 2004, which covers investment, trade, environment protection and labour treatment.

10. It was passed by the United States Senate on 30 June 2005 and then voted in the House of Representatives. After obtaining the approval of the Senate, anti-liberalization groups in the United States criticized it fiercely. On 27 July 2005, the House of Representatives approved the Dominican Republic - Central America Free Trade Agreement by a narrow majority of two votes.

11. It can be seen from the colour revolution carried out by the United States in Central Asian countries that the strategy of the United States in promoting "global democracy" is through backstage support from the government, NGOs act actively on the stage, while the local NGOs take the frontline.

12. http://www.imf.org/external/np/exr/facts/tim.htm.

13. European Communities – Customs Classification of Certain Computer Equipment (Complainant: United States), WT/DS62/R.

14. United States – Measures Affecting the Cross-Border Supply of Gambling and Betting Services (Complainant: Antigua and Barbuda), WT/DS285.

15. For more information about International Trade Centre, see <http://www.intracen.org/index.htm>

16. With the ever-increasing degree of globalization, cooperation among international organizations in specific matters is inevitable. An example is the container control programme between the UN Office on Drugs and Crime and World Customs Organization on combating drug trafficking and organized crime in Ecuador.

17. "The effect of U.S. macro-democarcy strategy on China" > *Hong Kong Economic Journal*, 3 May 2005, p. 18.

18. Article VIII:2(b) of Articles of Agreement of the IMF.

19. The drawing conditions for Korea included cutting off the relationship between the enterprises and government, and restructuring of big enterprises.

20. United States – Anti-Dumping Act of 1916 (Complainant: Japan), WT/DS162/R

21. United States – Tax Treatment for "Foreign Sales Corporations" (Complainant: European Communities), WT/DS108/R

22. Japan - Taxes on Alcoholic Beverages - Report of the Panel, WT/DS10/R, WT/DS11/R, WT/DS8/R

23. European Communities – Regime for the Importation, Sale and Distribution of Bananas (Complainants: Guatemala, Honduras, Mexico, Panama, United States), WT/DS158/R

24. Canada – Term of Patent Protection (Complainant: United States), WT/DS170/R

25. See Part 2 of the TRIPS.

26. *Ibid.*, sections 3 and 4 of Part 3.

27. Argentina – Definitive Anti-Dumping Duties on Poultry from Brazil (Complainant: Brazil), WT/DS241/R.

28. United States – Preliminary Determinations with Respect to Certain Softwood Lumber from Canada (Complainant: Canada), WT/DS236/R.

29. United States – Definitive Safeguard Measures on Imports of Steel Wire Rod and Circular Welded Quality Line Pipe (Complainant: European Communities), WT/DS214/R.

30. India – Patent Protection for Pharmaceutical and Agricultural Chemical Products (Complainant: European Communities), WT/DS79/R.

31. United States – Import Prohibition of Certain Shrimp and Shrimp Products, WT/DS58/R.

32. The Energy Charter Treaty was signed in Lisbon on 17 December 1994. For the full text of the treaty, please visit the official website: http://www.encharter.org/.

33. One of the reasons listed under the Energy Charter Treaty for referring investment disputes to arbitration is to evade the jurisdiction of the courts of the host country. Another reason is that enforcement of arbitral awards can be done in accordance with the United Nations Convention on the Recognition and Enforcement of Foreign Arbitral Awards. See Article 26 of the Energy Charter Treaty.

34. For discussions on the International Monetary Fund and the World Bank, see Guiguo Wang, *International Monetary and Financial Law* (2nd Ed.) (Beijing: Peking University Press, 2002).

35. For discussions on the system and operation of the World Trade Organization and the impact of the WTO on China, see Guiguo Wang, *The Law of the WTO: China and the Future of Free Trade* (Sweet & Maxwell Asia, 2005).

36. For discussions on the features and function of the World Intellectual Property Organization, see Guiguo Wang, *International Investment Law* (Beijing: Peking University Press, 2001), chapter 11.

37. For discussion on the Cancun Ministerial Conference and the reasons for its failure, see Guiguo Wang, "WTO in post-Cancun era", *Journal of International Economic Law*, Vol. 10 (2004), pp. 69–82.

38. It is reported that in early August 2005, Japan and Thailand reached a basic agreement on free trade. It is part of the plan of Japan in entering ASEAN. See Daniel Ten Kate, ThaiDay , "Japan, Thailand Closer to Free Trade Deal' Asia Times, 3 August 2005, http://www.atimes.com/atimes/Southeast_Asia/GH03Ae01.html.

39. In the first quarter of the year after the implementation of tax free measures, the import of vegetables from Thailand to China amounted to RMB556 million with a tax reduction of RMB31.48 million; the amount of imported fruit is RMB240 million while the amount of tax reduction is RMB38.88 million. See *Hong Kong Economic Journal*, 30 June 2005, p. 31.

40. At that time, it may be the third largest free trade area in the world, with a total value of production amounting to US$2000 billion, volume of trade amounting to US$1,200 billion. See *Hong Kong Economic Journal*, 30 June 2005, p31.

41. For discussions on the CEPA, see Guiguo Wang, "The China-Hong Kong Closer Economic Partnership Arrangement revisited", *The Journal of World Investment & Trade*, Vol. 5 (2004), No. 1, pp. 177–185.

42. Since China's entry into the WTO, the volume of export from the United States to China rose by 80%, while the U.S. world export increased by 11%. See the speech of Christopher R. Hill, the U.S. Assistant Secretary of State for East Asian and Pacific Affairs, in the public hearing of the United States Congress on 26 May 2005 regarding the issue of Northeastern Asian countries.

43. "Why does 'China Shock' shock the United States suddenly?" 18 July 2005, http://news.chinatimes.com.

44. *Ibid.*

45. On 26 July 2005, the U.S. House of Representatives voted on the bill proposed by the Republicans, 240 voted for it and 186 against. As the bill was voted through the simple procedure, it required two-thirds majority votes, thus the bill was not passed.

46. "Democrats Block CAFTA-Related China Trade Bill" 26 July 2005, http://today.reuters.com/News/NewsArticle.aspx?type=politicsNews&storyID= uri:2005-07-26T215003Z_01_N26322424_RTRIDST_0_POLITICS-TRADE-CONGRESS-USA-DC.XML&pageNumber=1&summit=.

47. http://english.mofcom.gov.cn/aarticle/photogallery/yixiaozhun/200511/ 20051100697415.html.180

7

Foreign Policy of a Rising Power: Is China a Threat or Is It a Responsible State?

Gerald CHAN

What is new about China's foreign policy under its fourth generation of leaders led by Hu Jintao and Wen Jiabao, in terms of its decision making, its global behaviour, and its behaviour in Asia? By casting China's "new" policy against the pattern of its past foreign-policy behaviour, this chapter aims to ascertain whether China has embarked on a completely new foreign-policy path, or whether things have stayed more or less the same as in the recent past, or whether recent changes in foreign policy constitute a kind of incremental adjustments that, taken together, make a fresh start in its foreign policy and relations. The chapter suggests that the third trajectory seems to be closer to reality: that is, China is on a path of renewing the way in which it conducts its foreign affairs. In analysing new developments in Chinese foreign policy, the chapter attempts to make a preliminary assessment as to whether the country has become a threat to the security of others or whether it has become a responsible member of the "international community."[1]

Foreign-policy Decision-making

Of the three areas to be investigated here, namely: decision making, global behaviour, and regional behaviour, the most difficult one to do is the task of identifying any new features of China's decision-making. This is because the decision-making process in China is largely opaque. So this area will receive comparatively little attention here.[2] Never the less, it is clear that China now has a fourth generation of leaders led by Hu Jintao,[3] who succeeded Jiang Zemin as the General Secretary of the Chinese Communist Party in November 2002, President of the State in March 2003, and Chairman of the Central Military Commission in September 2004. (The first generation of leaders was led by Mao Zedong, the second by Deng Xiaoping, and the third by Jiang Zemin.)

Premier Wen Jiabao is said to have sided with Jiang at the early stage of top leadership change from the third to the current fourth generation. However, there is no evidence to suggest that Hu and Wen do not see things eye-to-eye with each other, and it would be prudent to assume that they work together well, especially after the experiences in battling against SARS (Severe Acute Respiratory Syndrome or atypical pneumonia) and in handling the impact of the U.S. led war in Iraq. Both events took place in the first half of 2003. This assumption will of course be put to the test as time goes by. It is also possible that as Jiang's personal power dwindles, Hu and Wen may forge some sort of strong working relationship. Of greater constraint to Hu's exercise of power is the composition of the Politburo Standing Committee (the top decision-making body). The majority of its nine members are said to be siding with Jiang, including another prominent leader, Vice President Zeng Qinghong.[4]

Li Chang, an American university professor of Chinese origin, has been keeping a very close watch over the rise and fall of top Chinese leaders for a considerable period of time. Recently he suggests that the Chinese Communist Party is adopting some kind of intra-Party democracy: a new bipartisanship.[5] Two factions have started to appear. One, coined by Li as the "elitist coalition" led by former Party chief Jiang and his protégé, Zeng. The other, dubbed "populist coalition", is led by Hu and Wen. These two factions represent different regional and socioeconomic interests and divergent priorities. Their diversity goes beyond the conventional labelling of conservatives versus the reformists. Both factions agree on the preservation of the supreme power of the Party, but each acts as a check against the other to maintain some sort of uneasy balance in governing China. Apart from the Politburo, Li also finds that this kind of bipartisanship exists in other institutions such as the Presidency, the State Military Commission, the State Council, the National People's Congress, and the Chinese People's Political Consultative Conference. The impact of such bipartisan arrangement on Chinese foreign policy is not yet clear, but there seems to be a divide between the two, with the "populist coalition" favouring the "peaceful rise of China" whereas the "elitist coalition" cautioning that such a concept may hamstring China's possible use of force against Taiwan.

Hu Juntao did two things that broke with tradition. First, he scrapped the pompous ceremonies held at airports to farewell senior leaders embarking on official overseas trips. Secondly, he cancelled the 2003 summer retreat of the Party's top leaders to Beidahe, a seaside resort on the outskirt of Beijing. This annual retreat used to provide an opportunity for top leaders to trade deals, to iron out policy differences, to make important decisions, and to draw up guidelines for the work of government bureaucracies. Hu's decision to suspend these activities, either as a cost-cutting measure or as a way to allow important decisions to be made in a more formal setting,[6] surprised but won the praise of many observers.

Hu has assumed top positions in many Small Leading Groups within the Politburo which oversee various policy-making areas, such as foreign policy, economic policy, and relations with Taiwan. He will certainly find the exercise of supreme power has its limits in China's political system. Somehow he has to strike a delicate balance between what he wants to do, such as eliminating corruption, liberalising the press,[7] and making the work of the Politburo more transparent on the one hand and, on the other,[8] the constraints he has to face when exercising power. In an important Party speech made on 1 July 2003 to commemorate the anniversary of the founding of the Chinese Communist Party, he found it necessary to stress the importance of the Three Representatives.

These are ideas promoted by Jiang Zemin and his close associates in order to put Jiang's personal stamp on China's development. The purpose of the Three Representatives – that the Party must always represent China's advanced productive forces (now interpreted as to include the capitalist class), China's advanced culture, and the fundamental interests of the overwhelming majority of the Chinese people[9] – is to legitimise the contributions made by the once-despised bourgeoisie to China's economic development. Whether the idea of the Three Representatives is new or not, or whether it is of great significance or not to China's development are of secondary importance, as it is very much up to the top Party leaders to interpret the meaning of the Three Representatives. What is more important is the fact that the idea is the brainchild of Jiang Zemin, which means that, if Jiang has his way, his influence on China's development in the foreseeable future will be assured, and his personal standing in the history of contemporary China secured.

A new crop of young professionals have begun to take over key positions in the foreign-affairs ministry. Li Shaoxing, said to be groomed by former Foreign Minister and Vice Premier Qian Qichen, is now China's foreign minister, having served previously as ambassador to the United Nations and ambassador to the United States. Also, Vice Foreign Minister Wang Yi has made himself popular by the media for organising the six-party talks in Beijing in August 2003 to defuse North Korea's nuclear threat. Fu Ying, Director-General of the Department of Asian Affairs of the ministry, is actively involved in policy issues relating to Asia, including Northeast Asia as well as the Association of Southeast Asian Nations.[10]

In addition, a reshuffle of senior officials at municipal, provincial and central government ministry levels, which began in December 2004, is likely to bring in a new generation of more than three hundred technocrats in their forties and fifties in the coming years.[11] These officials have the opportunities to acquire new learning and new thinking, thanks to the reforms and opening up in the past twenty-five years or so. Large numbers of students as well as middle-ranking cadres go overseas each year to receive higher education or training. Professional and educational institutions overseas help to set up training courses of various kinds to assist China in building up its capacity to manage problems in various fields. These overseas efforts, extended by countries such as the U.S. and those in the EU and international institutions such as the World Bank, the Asian Development Bank, and the United Nations Development Programme, form part of a larger foreign assistance programme or exchange programme with China. Trainings in the areas of law and trade are particularly popular. The ideational change brought about by these activities in China is subtle but profound, with flow-on effects reaching upwards to senior leaders, sideways to peer groups, and downwards to the general public. Seen in a long-term perspective, this kind of systemic change taking place at the basic, working level is arguably no less important than the leadership change at the top. Furthermore, the development of civil society in China, helped by the growth of NGOs and the exponential increase in the use of information technology,[12] adds another new dimension to the influence put on the formulation of Chinese foreign policy.[13]

While changes in the top decision-making structure and process are difficult to fathom, changes in China's global and regional behaviour are by comparison easier to observe. The sources and implications of such behavioural changes are, nonetheless, difficult to delineate and evaluate.

China's Global Behaviour: "Living with the Hegemon"[14]

China's diplomacy these days can be described as pragmatic, nuanced, and constructive.[15] It is pragmatic in the sense that it is much less swayed by ideological considerations than before. It is now driven by a need to enhance its national interests in a more rational way. This kind of pragmatism has been in the making since the end of the Cultural Revolution, with increasing intensity over time, although it had suffered a major setback due to the Tiananmen Incident in 1989. China's style of pragmatic diplomacy, however, is different from many other countries because of its unique historical baggage and its designated national goals. Historically, it was once the strongest and richest civilisation on earth, but had suffered extreme humiliation at the hands of Western imperial powers for a hundred years just before 1949. China today still bears the scars of such humiliation, psychologically if not physically. It is difficult for the collective mind of China to forget this historical episode, as generations after generations of Chinese are being taught the lessons to be learnt. Children are inculcated at an early age with the dream of reviving China's former glory. Thus catching up with the outside world, especially with the West, has become an obsession of political leaders and intellectuals since China was prised open by Western gunboat diplomacy in the mid-nineteenth century. Extreme socialism had been tried with disastrous results, causing the death of some thirty million people from famine and epidemics in a blind pursuit to catch up with the West through a mass movement called the Great Leap Forward in the late 1950s.[16]

The goal to become rich and strong has not changed over the decades, as a rich and strong China will ensure that it will not be bullied again. To achieve this, China has to modernise, and the Four Modernisation programmes of Agriculture, Industry, Science and Technology, and Military, initiated by Deng Xiaoping's under the reform and opening-up policy in the late 1970s, are still ongoing. China's diplomacy is geared towards achieving these goals, although under a new label called "peace and development' since the 1990s. A peaceful environment – internationally, regionally, and domestically – would be conducive to China's effort to develop. China cannot go back to the days of making revolutions at home and exporting them overseas. At present the country pursues a peaceful and independent foreign policy that is multi-dimensional, multi-faceted, and multi-layered. Independence carries a special historical ring: Chinese leaders do not want to side again totally with either Russia or the United States, as they have learned some hard lessons from the 1950s to the 1970s. Multi-dimensional means that China wants to develop friendly relationships, in bilateral as well as multilateral ways, with all countries in the world, big or small, rich or poor, near or afar, irrespective of their ideological beliefs. Multi-faceted refers to a comprehensive improvement in relations, embracing not only economics and politics, but also science and technology, culture and friendship, and so on. And multi-layered refers to multiple levels of diplomacy: international, regional, Track I (governmental), Track II (semi-governmental), and Track III (people-to-people).

China is growing strong, economically, politically, and militarily. Since the 1980s its economy has been growing at an average rate close to ten per cent per annum. Despite the outbreak of SARS in the first half of 2003, its growth rate in the year reached a seven-year high of 9.1%,[17] much to the surprise of many observers.[18] The rate registered in the first half of 2005 was 9.5%.[19] China is the fourth largest trading nation after the United States, Japan, and Germany.[20] *Financial Times* of London reports that in the first quarter of 2003, China accounted for about 50% of the world's economic growth,[21] its exports enjoying 35% increase,[22] and its fiscal reserve stood at US$364.7 billion as of August 2003,[23] rising to a staggering amount of US$609.9 billion by the end of 2004.[24] According to the International Monetary Fund, China's share of the world's output of goods and services has nearly doubled since 1991, to 12.7%, closing in on the EU's 15.7% and approaching America's 21%.[25] Using purchasing-power-parity method of calculation, China's GDP in 2005 ranks second in the world, about 62% of the U.S., and 1.94 times Japan's, the third largest.[26] It has been projected that by 2020 China's growth in purchasing-power-parity terms would be equal to that of the United States,[27] although its GDP per capita would still lag far behind that of America.[28] Chinese statistics may not be very reliable but those who have seen the fast economic growth and development in many major Chinese cities within a short period of time, in terms of huge infrastructure projects, the rising standard of living in the urban areas, and the lavishness of the newly rich, will hardly fail to be stunned. It is in the end the perception of business executives around the world that matters in driving economic growth, and, in this respect, foreign direct investments keep pouring into the country to exploit its cheap labour. The amount jumped from US$47 billion in 2001 to US$53 billion in 2002, making an accumulated total of US$448 billion as of 2002.[29] The average annual FDI to China surpassed that of the U.S. in mid-2002. So much so China is said to be the traders' paradise for the rest of this century,[30] although there are no lack of speculations about its forthcoming collapse as a result of financial, banking and other socioeconomic problems.[31]

History has shown that a country that grows economically strong will find itself having more interests to protect and promote. It happens to the U.S. now, and has happened before to the U.K., Spain, and Portugal. China has to maintain its growth momentum and to strike a balance between economic growth and social development, including environmental sustainability and an even distribution of wealth; it has to ensure that its energy sources such as oil supplies are secured; it has to ensure that its sea lanes of communication are safe; it has to ensure that its overseas interests, commercial and political, are adequately looked after; and so on. All these conditions help to stimulate, in one way or another, to the growth of China's political assertiveness and its military modernisation.

China has become a full member of the international community, maintaining diplomatic relations with 163 countries (as of end 2003),[32] and membership of nearly all the important intergovernmental organisations of the world as well as a growing number of major international non-governmental organisations (46 and 1,567 respectively as of 2004).[33] Its single most important bilateral relationship is with the United States. This relationship between the world's sole superpower and the world's rising power is interesting and important because it defines the peace-and-war situation of the world, at least according to theorists of hegemonic stability.[34] The superpower tries to stay on top of the power hierarchy of states to continue to give directions, if not orders, to all others, while the rising power disgruntles in silence most of the time but cries foul sometimes. The latter is fully aware, however, that it has to live and deal with the hegemon.[35] Interestingly, Zbigniew Brzezinski, former National Security Adviser to President Jimmy Carter, admonishes the need to live with China and to recognise "an obvious but fundamental reality: China is too big to be ignored, too old to be slighted, too weak to be appeased, and too ambitious to be taken for granted."[36]

Sino-U.S. relations in the past decades have been marked by a pattern of love-hate relationship. When George W. Bush assumed Presidency in January 2001, he promised to make a difference by taking whatever measures necessary to defend Taiwan against military attacks by China. However, the campaign against global terrorism since late 2001 seems to have brought China and the U.S. working closer together, despite the American bombing of the Chinese embassy in Belgrade in May 1999 and the collision of an American spy plane with a Chinese jet fighter near Hainan Island in March 2001, resulting in the death of a Chinese pilot.

America's interests in Asia in general and in China in particular consist of a mix of strategic and commercial components. The U.S. is deeply concerned with its increasingly huge trade deficit with China, some US$162 billion in 2004 according to the U.S.[37] It has been exerting pressure on China to appreciate its currency in the belief that such a revaluation would reduce the trade imbalance and save jobs. In July 2005 China did appreciate its currency by about 2.1 per cent against the U.S. dollar, a decision that has been welcomed by the U.S. as a small step in the right direction. Meanwhile China, together with other fast developing countries like India and Brazil, and the Cairns Group of agricultural producers, voice objections to the huge subsidies that the U.S. government gives to its farmers, dumping subsidised agricultural produce at low prices and hurting the livelihoods of farmers in the poor developing South and other efficient farm producers. The world's wealthiest countries, including the U.S. and some in the European Union, give more than US$300 billion of subsidies a year to their farmers, more than the gross national product of Sub-Saharan Africa.[38] The failure of the WTO talks at Cancun in Mexico in September 2003 between the world's poor countries and the world's rich over trade and investments has highlighted the increasingly pivotal role that China plays in North-South relations.

How to deal with the U.S. remains the primary foreign-policy task for China. In the Group of Eight meeting in France in May 2003, Hu Jintao managed to obtain an assurance from George Bush that the U.S. would honour its three communiqués with China,[39] maintain the one-China policy, and discourage Taiwan's independence. In return Hu gave Bush his assurance to help resolve the North Korean nuclear issue. How Bush's assurance affects cross-Strait relations has yet to be worked out, although it represents a significant climb-down from his 2001 statement that he would do whatever necessary to defend Taiwan. Despite the ups and downs in bilateral relations, at present China and the United States enjoy warm relations because of their harmony of strategic interests in combating terrorism and in dealing with the North Korean nuclear issue. In their summit in France, Bush invited Hu to visit the United States. Hu was scheduled to do so in September 2005, his first official visit to the U.S. as President.[40] Premier Wen Jiabao was warmly received when he visited the U.S. in December 2003. Bush reiterated America's one-China policy and warned Taiwan's President Chen Shui-bian for proposing to hold a referendum to gauge the view of the people of Taiwan on the issue of independence. In a significant departure from the past, Beijing dispatched a mission to Washington DC in February 2004 to seek help from the Bush administration to stop Taiwan from holding such a referendum to coincide with its presidential election in March.[41] Despite the seemingly warm relationship between the two powers, the U.S. Department of Defense issued a report to Congress, released in July 2005, pointing out that the military buildup of China posed a threat to countries in Asia and beyond.[42] To be expected, China rebuked the report for suggesting a "China threat".[43] This incident serves to highlight the potentially tense rivalry underlying their apparently warm relationship.

China's thirst for oil and other minerals adds a new dimension, not only to its foreign-policy behaviour but also to a heightened tension in its relations with other countries, in particular the United States.[44] In recent times, Chinese top leaders not only visited rich countries in the West, but also source-rich countries in Africa and Latin America. Their visits were accompanied with an entourage of businesspeople looking for trade and investments in these countries, the policies of some of which are at odds with the U.S., including, for example, Iran. China's quest for oil security will intensify the competition for resources between itself and the U.S., the two largest oil consumers in the world. The quest will also push China to explore the oil reserves in Asia, thus intensifying the conflict between itself and Japan and other Southeast Asian countries over disputed territories in the East China Sea and the South China Sea.[45] The containment policy of the U.S. towards China, started since the 1950s, has been loosened by engagement from time to time since the 1980s subsequent to domestic and international circumstances, but is firmly in place when the U.S. needs to strengthen it.

In January 2004 Hu Juntao made his first official trip to the West, to France to mark the fortieth anniversary of the establishment of diplomatic relations between the two countries. Hu was accorded with the highest honour, being given the rare opportunity to address a joint session of the two Houses of the French Parliament, although there were boycotts imposed by some of its members over China's human rights and other records. Officially France marked the occasion of the visit by declaring 2004 The Year of China. Hu's visit was greeted with a lot of festive and cultural activities coinciding with the Chinese Lunar New Year celebrations in Paris. French President Jacque Chirac welcomed Hu at the airport and warned Taiwan not to hold a referendum in March 2004 in parallel with its presidential elections, pointing out that such an action would destabilise regional peace and security. In addition, Foreign Minister Dominique de Villepin called on the European Union to lift its embargo on the sale of military weapons to China imposed since the Tiananmen Incident of 1989. The French have good reasons to celebrate the strengthening of bilateral ties as China looms large in the global political economy and as both countries would like to see the formation of a multipolar world, which could serve as a check against America's unilateralism. Bilateral trade between China and France rose by sixty-one per cent in 2003 over the previous year, although the amount of trade represented less than two per cent of France's total trade with the rest of the world. Germany, whose trade with China also rises rapidly, shares a similar worldview with France. Although the U.K. sides more with the U.S. than with France and Germany in the global order, the U.K. also realises the growing importance of its relations with China. On his visit to Beijing in July 2003, British Prime Minister Tony Blair said that "China . . . is an absolutely central relationship for Britain," while Premier Wen Jiabao said that China "wanted the U.K. to be China's 'leading European partner.'"[46] On the whole, relations between China and the EU have improved steadily, boosted by bilateral trade and strategic expediencies, despite differences over the issue of human rights and the timing of the lifting of arms embargo amongst EU members.

China is a latecomer to the world of international organisations. It was not until 1971 when the People's Republic of China (PRC) entered the United Nations that the country subsequently gained entry to a host of other specialised agencies associated with the United Nations system, such as the United Nations Education, Scientific and Cultural Organisation, the World Health Organisation, the Food and Agriculture Organisation, and so on. Many other major intergovernmental organisations outside the UN framework too began to recognise Beijing. Subsequent to its adoption of the reform and opening-up policy in late 1978, China began to increase substantially its participation in international non-governmental organisations (INGOs). [47] Considering the geographical and population size of China, its current membership of INGOs is still very small,[48] partly because of its low level of civic awareness and its relatively small number of local NGOs,[49] and partly related to its stage of economic development and technological advancement.[50] China's entry into the World Trade Organisation in December 2002 completes its nominal membership of the Bretton Woods system, it was being admitted to the World Bank and the International Monetary Fund in 1980. China became a member of the International Olympic Committee in 1979, an important INGO in which Taiwan was also simultaneously admitted under the name of Chinese Taipei. In 1985 both China and Taiwan participated in the Los Angeles Games, for the first time in history. And in 2008 Beijing is going to host the summer Olympic Games, an opportunity for the country to showcase its developmental achievements and its global friendship, and for improving its relations with Taiwan.[51]

Running in parallel with China's participation in the major intergovernmental organisations is its accession to major international treaties. When the PRC was established in 1949, it was eager to gain international recognition and legitimacy. But because of its communist credentials, its involvement in the Korea War (1950-53), and its animosity with the United States, which controlled in large part the functioning of many major international organisations, China was denied entry to the United Nations. Domestic turmoil during the Great Leap Forward (1958–1960) and the Cultural Revolution (especially in the late 1960s) meant that China was excluded from the world of international treaties and organisations. Before China's entry into the United Nations in 1971, it had only entered into five major international treaties (one dealing with international aviation and the other four dealing with the Geneva Conventions relating to war). Subsequently China entered into a number of treaties in connection with its newly acquired membership of the specialised agencies of United Nations. The bulk of China's accession to international treaties, however, occurred only after the country had adopted its reform and opening-up policy. Some eighty-seven per cent of China's 266 treaty memberships as of end-2003 were entered into after 1978.[52] The decision to end its isolation at the end of the Maoist era and to engage with the outside world is a critical factor in China's improving relations with global norm. It has been found that China's compliance record with international treaties in terms of abiding by their rules and norms over the past twenty-five years or so has been good. However, a lot of work remains to be done if the country is to improve its record, partly because of its existing weak state capacity (for example, its rudimentary legal system) and partly because of the high expectations and demands of the outside world, especially the United States.[53]

China in Asia: A Threat or an Opportunity?

It is in the Asia-Pacific region that China finds itself more comfortable with its neighbours. It is also in this region that its influence is more profound, its security more at risk, and its diplomatic approach coming under greater challenge. Traditionally, the Han Chinese have been inwardly looking, but China's long history and civilisation, together with its pattern of intermittent but mass migration to neighbouring countries, mean that these countries have for a long time felt its presence. To many, China has been and is likely to remain, in the foreseeable future, the Middle Kingdom or the region's "central heart".[54] When it is strong, it finds peace with its neighbours. Only when it is weak would its security come under threat from its then relatively stronger neighbours.

China occupies a huge landmass in Asia. It shares land borders with fourteen countries and sea borders with seven. Since 1949, it has engaged in wars with no less than four major countries: the United States, the former Soviet Union, India, and Vietnam. Although it has enjoyed relative peace since the 1970s, it has three nuclear neighbours (Russia, India, and Pakistan), one suspected nuclear state (North Korea), and at least three countries with the potentials to produce nuclear weapons at short notice (South Korea, Japan, and Taiwan). Its current good-neighbourly policy is borne out of necessity, since a peaceful environment, globally and regionally, is conducive to its development and to its effort to catch up with the West.

In pursuit of such a policy, it has been reaching out to its neighbours both bilaterally and multilaterally. It has established diplomatic relations with virtually all of them and has joined most of the important regional organisations, including the Asia

Development Bank, the Asia-Pacific Economic Cooperation forum, the ASEAN Regional Forum, and the Council for Security Cooperation in the Asia-Pacific. Apart from joining these and other regional organisations in Asia and elsewhere, it has taken the lead to establish regional organisations, such as the Shanghai Cooperation Organisation (known formerly as the Shanghai Five) and the Boao Economic Forum, both in 2001. The Shanghai Cooperation Organisation, which now brings together six countries in Central Asia,[55] aims to deal with common security problems such as ethnic violence, smuggling, and terrorism and to promote regional economic cooperation. A secretariat was set up in Beijing on 15 January 2004, with a former Chinese ambassador, Zhang Deguang, serving as its first secretary-general.[56] In 2005 Iran, India, and Pakistan joined as observers and, at its summit meeting in July, the group called on Washington to set a date for withdrawing its troops from Central Asia, deployed since late 2001.[57] The Boao Economic Forum is China's answer to the World Economic Forum at Davos, Switzerland, the latter running annually by developed countries in the West. The Davos forum held in early 2004 was described by some observers as a forum about "China, China, and China",[58] indicating the impact of a rising China on the global economy.

Southeast Asia provides a primary testing ground for China's new diplomatic approach. The Association of Southeast Asian Nations (ASEAN) grouping is the most active regional organisation in Asia. On the one hand, China has a strong interest in developing good relationship with this group of countries. On the other, it has territorial disputes over the Spratly and Paracel Islands with some of its members – including Malaysia, the Philippines, and Vietnam. In the past China adopted a bilateral approach to negotiate with them, but in recent years it has changed its approach to embrace a multilateral approach as well, especially in promoting a cooperative way to deal with what it calls "new security issues", which include social, cultural, ecological, crimes and public health issues, apart from the traditional issues of political security and economics.[59]

China's relationship with ASEAN has entered a new phase, having signed in 2003 the treaty of Amity and Cooperation with the grouping to keep a code of conduct of good behaviour towards each other. This non-aggression treaty may serve as a blueprint for solving the long-standing territorial dispute between China and some Southeast Asian countries. On the trade front, China is prepared to enter into a so-called "early harvest" agreement, allowing some ASEAN countries to receive beneficial treatment from it over some goods. This agreement forms a first step in putting in practice a free trade agreement signed between China and ASEAN in 2002. At the opening summit meeting of the ASEAN countries on 7 October 2003 in Bali, Indonesia, Wen Jiabao said that bilateral trade between China and ASEAN rose by 55.5% in the first half of 2003 over the same period in the previous year. (Bilateral trade for the whole year hit US$78.2 billion, up 42.8% from the previous year.)[60] He expressed the hope that the trade volume between China and ASEAN would surpass US$100 billion by 2005, edging close to the trade volume valued at US$120 billion between ten ASEAN countries and the U.S. in 2002.[61] That target was achieved in late 2004. In fact China's trade with the rest of Asia, including ASEAN, topped US$495 billion in 2003, up 36.5% over 2002, according to Chinese statistics. [62] At present China's investment in Southeast Asian countries grows at an annual rate of more than 20% in some countries and, more than 40% in others.[63] The initial fear harboured by Southeast Asian countries that China's competitiveness might eat into ASEAN's economic growth has proved to be unfounded. Quite the contrary, China has become the engine of growth in the region, replacing in some respects the role played previously by Japan. Interestingly, the China boom also plays a key role in fuelling Japan's recovery. In 2003 Japan's exports to China increased by 33.2% to reach a record total of US$62.9 billion, a figure more than doubled since 2000.[64] And in 2004 bilateral trade between the two countries grew to US$168 billion, a 26% rise from a year earlier.[65] So much so, China has become the number one export market not only for Japan, but also for South Korea and Taiwan. The orientation of Asian countries towards China is shown by the fact that out of the thirty-five important meetings of ASEAN in a three-month of 2004, nineteen were conducted with China.[66]

China certainly enjoys unprecedented good relationships with its neighbours. Recent polls conducted across many Asian countries have reflected a rather dramatic change in public opinion in favour of China. Of the 78,000 foreign students studying in Chinese universities in 2004, 80% came from other Asian nations.[67] The developments of ASEAN + 3 (China, Japan, and South Korea), the East Asian Summit, and China's free trade arrangements with East Asian and with ASEAN (the latter by 2010) augur well for China's relations with its Asian neighbours.

Of all the recent Chinese efforts to combat the outbreak of inter-state conflicts, its initiation to bring North Korea to the negotiation table with four other countries – South Korea, the United States, Russia, and Japan – to a six-party talk held in Beijing in August 2003 to defuse the nuclear threat posed by North Korea is the most prominent one. Whether it is out of self interests or regional or global concerns for peace, the talk has won the appreciation of other countries and has helped to uplift Sino-U.S. ties to an unprecedented level during the Bush administration. The South Korean delegates described the talks as cordial. The Japanese delegates, however, stated that North Korea's nuclear weapons programme was unacceptable and that it should release all kidnapped Japanese. The United States insisted that North Korea should scrap its nuclear weapons programme in a complete, permanent, and verifiable way, while North Korea asked the U.S. to change its hostile stand and to provide a security guarantee for North Korea. Russia hoped that the meetings would help to promote dialogues and to build trust and confidence. The Chinese host hoped that some tangible results could ensure peace and security in Northeast Asia. The fact that the six-party talks took place at all in Beijing, despite the absence of a communiqué after four rounds of negotiations as of mid-2005, means that China has earned at least some diplomatic laurels. The crux of the problem seems to lie in procedural matters relating to sovereignty, aid, and disarmament (who does what first and followed by what) amidst a long-standing absence of trust.

The political situation in South Asia presents a case of classical balance of power at work. While China has for a long time made use of the animosity between India and Pakistan by allying the later against the former, with whom China fought a bitter war in 1962 along their disputed border, it has recently developed warm relations with India to ease border tensions, to boost bilateral trade,[68] and to forge a common front in world trade negotiations based on a shared history of non-alignment and solidarity with the developing world. The United States, on the other hand, has had cold relations with both India and Pakistan, warning both nuclear powers (since 1998 when both tested their nuclear weapons for the first time) not to raise their tensions. The event of 9/11 has led the U.S. to draw Pakistan closer to its side in its war against terror in Afghanistan. However, Pakistan is an Islamic state and has schooled some of the terrorists in the West. While India snubs the International Atomic Energy Agency and refuses to sign the Comprehensive Test Ban Treaty and the Nuclear Non-Proliferation Treaty. Recently the U.S. finds that this "largest democracy" share some common interests with it and can be groomed to balance the rise of China, apart from using the U.S-Japan alliance. While India is happy to improve relations with the U.S., it has come to some sort of rapprochement with Pakistan and to forge a strategic relationship with China and Russia.[69] The three countries – China, India, and Russia – hold 40% of the world's population and 20% of its economy.[70] China and India together receive 75 to 80% of all Russia arms exports.[71] India and China held their first joint naval exercise in the East China Sea near Shanghai in November 2003,[72] which followed immediately another one between China and Pakistan in the same area a month earlier – the first time ever for China with any country since 1949.[73] And in August 2005 China and Russia held a large scale military exercise involving 10,000 troops and an array of modern military technology near Vladivostok and China's Shandong province.[74] Both China and India take measures to improve their respective relations with ASEAN, and both join the U.S., Australia, Japan, and South Korea in promoting a wider use of modern technology to tackle air pollution but without however setting targets on gas emissions, much to the disappointment of many Kyoto Protocol signatory states and green groups, as the American led collective effort is likely to undermine the Protocol. International relations amongst the major states in South Asia are so fluid and changeable – nearly all are partners and competitors with each other at the same time – that it is difficult to see any clear-cut trend from developing.

China is certainly a regional power to be reckoned with, partly because of its traditional influence in the region and partly because of its present good-neighbourly policy directed at its neighbours. Its regional influence is buttressed by its growing economic strength, relative to the decline of Japan's influence. Some twenty years ago, American academic Steven I. Levine remarked that China was a regional power on the verge of reaching out to the world.[75] Now it would be fair to say that China is an established regional power in a rapid transition to become a global player. The exact juncture at which this transition takes place is not clear. Apparently China has begun to throw its weight around the Asia-Pacific region, led by increasing volumes of trade and investment. Its rising economic interests in the world have led to its greater political involvement beyond its immediate neighbourhood, thereby creating a lot of uncertainties and turbulence for its own domestic development as well as its international relations. (See Table 1 for a summary of the main sources of China's threat and responsibility.)

Table 1
Main Sources of China's Threat and Responsibility

	Decision-making process	Global behaviour	Regional behaviour
Threat	Opaqueness	Military build-up	Impact of war against Taiwan
Responsibility	Transparency	Rule compliance; UN peacekeeping	Six-party talks; Free trade zones

Conclusion

China is an old civilisation, and the PRC is only a relatively new state. Established in 1949, the PRC government often referred to itself as the new China. Like many newly established dynasties in the past, it wanted to discard or even destroy the past in order to establish its legitimacy in a new order. A new China trying to rebuild itself while bearing the historical burdens of the past has never been easy. Mao's experimentation with an extreme form of socialism inflicted heavy human casualties and economic costs to the country. Deng brought some semblance of normality to the country. Following Deng's initiatives, Jiang pushed the country forward along the path of modernisation and economic development. The current fourth generation of leadership under Hu has a huge task of (re)building the state ahead. Deng, Jiang and Hu have successively and steadily steered and strengthened China's engagement with the outside world. Although we do not know what sort of future will hold for the Hu administration, the trend over the last twenty-five years of reform has shown that China has sought to increase its participation in international organisations and has made a lot of effort to comply with international treaties and norms. This situation leads scholars such as Alastair Iain Johnston, Robert Ross, and others to conclude that China is a status-quo power rather than a serious challenger to the existing world order.[76]

From an official U.S. perspective, if China is a status-quo power, identifying with the terms and conditions of the global order established and maintained by the U.S. and the West, then it would pose little threat to American and Western interests. Consequently, the China Threat theory, at least in its extreme form in which China is portrayed as a major military threat, fails to hold. The ensuing situation would consequently carry important implications for American foreign policy and for global peace and security.

China's current diplomacy is guided by its modernisation goal, which entails the development of peaceful relationships with its neighbours, ensures a stable supply of oil and other commodities to sustain its economic growth, and lives in an ambivalent relationship with the world's hegemon – the United States – which tries to shape the political economic development of China by containing and engaging with it at the same time.

As China grows strong, will it become a responsible member of the international community, complying with the rules, norms, and principles of the existing politico-legal system? This question opens up a huge area for investigation because it deals with an area of soft law in which values and cultures play an important part. It is an area in which debates about what constitutes responsibility and compliance abound and are unlikely to be settled easily. Decisions as to whether or not a country is responsible and whether or not a country is compliant with international law depend on different perspectives, interests, the issues involved, timing, conditions, and power play. In a broad brush and as a hypothesis for further testing, one can perhaps see that in the past twenty-five years or so China has become more responsible, both internationally and domestically, in the areas of arms control and disarmament, global trade, the observance of human rights, the protection of the environment,[77] and more recently, in the management of public health. The general view seems to be that China has achieved quite a lot, but more remains to be done if it is to meet the standards demanded by the outside world, especially by the United States and the West.

Acknowledgments

An early version of this chapter was presented as a paper in a Joint Conference organised by the National Policy Foundation in Taipei and the Centre of International Studies at Cambridge University, held in Churchill College, Cambridge, on 12–14 October 2003. I'm grateful to Dr Philip Towle of the Centre for inviting me to present the paper and Dr Peter Ferdinand of the University of Warwick for discussing it. I have benefited from the comments and criticisms made by conference participants. Dr P.K. Lee of the University of Kent, U.K. (formerly of the Open University of Hong Kong) has consistently kept me informed of developments in Chinese foreign policy, for which I am most thankful.

Notes and References

1. The term "international community" needs some clarification as it has been used by different politicians and academics in different ways. For example, when President George Bush said that the international community would not tolerate Iraq's weapons of mass destruction, he apparently referred to the international community dominated by American values or the American view of a desirable world order. The different usage of the term led the *Foreign Policy* magazine of the Carnegie Endowment for International Peace in Washington DC to publish a special issue on "What is the international community?" in its September/October 2002 issue. The magazine invited nine notable thinkers, activists, journalists and policy makers from across the ideological spectrum to scrutinise the idea of international community and to offer their views.

2. Some useful works have been published in this area, including David Lampton (ed), *The making of Chinese foreign and security policy in the era of reform, 1978–2000* (Stanford: Stanford University Press, 2001); Lu Ning, *The dynamics of foreign-policy decisionmaking in China* (Boulder, CO: Westview Press, 1997); Carol Lee Hamrin and Zhao Suisheng (eds), *Decision-making in Deng's China: perspectives from insiders* (Armonk, NY; London: M.E. Sharpe, 1995); Kenneth Lieberthal and Michel Oksenberg, *Policy making in China: leaders, structures, and processes* (Princeton, N.J.: Princeton University Press, 1988); and A. Doak Barnett, *The making of foreign policy in China: structure and process* (London: I.B. Tauris & Co. Ltd., 1985).

3. For a biography of Hu, see http://english.peopledaily.com.cn/data/people/hujintao.shtml (accessed 16 August 2005).

4. Zeng is regarded as a potential challenger to Hu. See Wen Yu, "Zeng Qinghong: a potential challenger to China's heir apparent," *China Brief*, the Jamestown Foundation, Vol. 1, Issue 10 (21 November 2001).

5. Li Chang, "The new bipartisanship within the Chinese Communist Party," *Orbis*, Vol. 49, No. 3 (Summer 2005), pp. 387–400.

6. Some observers also speculated that the cancellation of the Beidahe retreat might have to do with the SARS outbreak.

7. It seems that the issue of press freedom or otherwise in contemporary China offers a classic case of chequered development, characterised by two steps forward and one step back.

8. Nailene Chou West, "At the crossroads," *South China Morning Post*, China National Day special supplement, 1 October 2003, p. S1.

9. "To include 'Three Representatives' in CPC Constitution reflects common aspiration," Xinhua News Agency, Internet ed., 11 November 2002.

10. Fu obtained her M.A. in International Relations from the University of Kent, U.K. She is the author of "China and Asia in a new era," *China: An International Journal*, Vol. 1, No. 2 (September 2003), pp. 304–12.

11. Wang Xiangwei, "Hu presides over massive reshuffle to cement power," *South China Morning Post*, Internet ed., 31 January 2005.

12. China is the world's second largest Internet market after the U.S. The number of people in China using the Internet grew by 9 million in the first half of 2005 to reach 103 million. See *Weekend Herald*, Auckland, New Zealand, 23 July 2005, p. B9.

13. I'm grateful to Peter Ferdinand of the University of Warwick for pointing this out to me. For some useful discussions about the impact of the Internet on China's politics and society, see the review essay on four books by Christopher R. Hughes, "China and the Internet: a question of politics or management," *The China Quarterly*, No. 175 (September 2003), pp. 818–24. See also Shanthi Kalathil, "China's new media sector: keeping the state in," *The Pacific Review*, Vol. 16, No. 4 (December 2003), pp. 489–501.

14. The subtitle is in a way borrowed from Jia Qingguo, "Learning to live with the hegemon: evolution of China's policy toward the U.S. since the end of the Cold War," *Journal of Contemporary China*, Vol. 14, No. 44 (August 2005), pp. 395–407.

15. The fact that Chinese diplomacy these days is nuanced and constructive is the editorial opinion of *International Herald Tribune*, see its editorial, 15 October 2003, p. 8. Wang Gungwu, Director of the East Asian Institute at the National University of Singapore, says that "the new leadership has displayed populism, decisiveness, openness and flexibility...." See *EAI Bulletin*, East Asian Institute, National University of Singapore, September 2003, p. 2.

16. Judith Shapiro, *Mao's war against nature: politics and the environment in revolutionary China* (Cambridge: Cambridge University Press, 2001), p. 86; Jasper Becker, *Hungry ghosts: China's secret famine* (London: John Murray, 1996), p. xi. Chang Jung, in her latest book with Jon Halliday entitled *Mao: the unknown story* (London: Random House, 2005), points out that 70 million people died under Mao's rule, of which 38 million died during the Great Leap Forward (cover jacket).

17. *People's Daily*, Internet ed., 21 January 2004.

18. For example, the 18 October 2003 issue of *The Guardian* (p. 3) reported a forecast of 8.5%.

19. Richard McGregor and Andrew Yeh, "China's economy grows 9.5%," *Financial Times*, Internet ed., 20 July 2005.

20. According to the World Trade Organisation's 2001 statistics, quoted by David Lague, "China bids to rule the waves," *Far Eastern Economic Review*, Internet ed., 18 September 2003.

21. *Financial Times*, 11 August 2003, p. 15.

22. *Financial Times*, 29 August 2003, p. 17.

23. *Financial Times*, 1 September 2003, p 16; 30 September 2003, p. 14. This amount pales, however, in per capita terms.

24. *The Standard*, Hong Kong, 12 January 2005, p. A9.

25. *International Herald Tribune*, 16 December 2003, p. 13.

26. Wang Fei-Ling, "Lots of wealth, lots of people, lots of flaws," *International Herald Tribune*, Internet ed., 21 July 2005.

27. See, for example, Jeffrey D. Sachs, "Welcome to the Asian century," *Fortune*, 26 January 2004, pp. 32-3. Interestingly, India's GDP, in purchasing-power-parity, will also surpass that of the U.S. in about 2045.

28. According to Zheng Bijian, China's per capita income ranks about 100th in the world. See Zheng Bijian, "China's 'peaceful rise' to great-power status," *Foreign Affairs*, Vol. 84, No. 5 (September/October 2005).

29. *The Guardian*, 5 September 2003, p. 21; *Financial Times*, 8 October 2003, p. 21.

30. John Thornton, former president and co-chief operating officer of Goldman Sachs, who was due to take up a chair professorship in the School of Management and Economics at Tsinghua University, Beijing, said that one of the four big themes in the early 21st century was the emergence of China. According to him, the single greatest need, certainly in the U.S., and probably in the world, was education for the elites about China. The other three themes were the turmoil in the Islamic world, the disgraceful way in which the world treats Africa, and the denigration of the environment. See *Financial Times*, 22 August 2003, p. 10.

31. Gordon Chang, *The coming collapse of China* (New York: Random House, 2002); and Joe Studwell, *China dream: the elusive quest for the greatest untapped market* (New York: Atlantic Monthly Press, 2002).

32. China's Ministry of Foreign Affairs website, www.fmprc.gov.cn/chn/ziliao/2193/t9650.htm (accessed 15 August 2005).

33. These major organisations include federations of international organisations (type A), universal organisations (type B), inter-continental organisations (type C), and regional organisations (type D). *Yearbook of international organizations 2004/2005* (Munich: K.S. Saur, 2004), Volume 2, p. 1,702.

34. For a recent application of this theory to an analysis of Sino-U.S. relations, see Evelyn Goh and Amitav Acharya, "The ASEAN Regional Forum and US-China relations: comparing Chinese and American positions," Draft paper prepared for the Fifth China-ASEAN Research Institutes Roundtable, "Regionalism and community building in East Asia," University of Hong Kong, 17–19 October 2002.

35. Jia, "Learning to live with the hegemon: evolution of China's policy toward the US since the end of the Cold War." Wang Jisi, "China's search for stability with America," *Foreign Affairs*, Vol. 84, No. 5 (September/October 2005).

36. Zbigniew Brzezinski, "Living with China," *The National Interest*, Spring 2000, pp. 6–7.

37. *International Herald Tribune*, 23–24 April 2005, p. 16. The total amount of U.S. trade deficit with the world in 2004 was US$617 billion. According to China's customs statistics, it trade surplus with the U.S. is about half the amount of the U.S. count. See *Financial Times*, 23 April 2004, p. 6.

38. *International Herald Tribune*, 10 September 2003, p. 1.

39. The first was called the Shanghai Communiqué of 1972 signed towards the end of U.S. President Richard Nixon's visit to China in February. The second communiqué was signed in December 1978 to establish bilateral diplomatic relations on 1 January 1979. The third, signed in August 1982, made specific reference to the American sales of arms to Taiwan.

40. Although Hu visited the country in May 2002 as Vice President.

41. *International Herald Tribune*, 6 February 2004, p. 2.

42. "The military power of the People's Republic of China 2005," Annual report to Congress by the Office of the Secretary of Defense, U.S. Department of Defense.

43. Chinese Vice Foreign Minister Yang Jiechi said that China's increase in defense expenditure must be seen against the country's effort to improve the living conditions of its servicemen amidst its economic development. He said that China's military payout in 2004 totaled US$25.579 billion (against the U.S. estimate which was about three times as much). Yang said that "the U.S. defense expenditure hit 455.9 billion US dollars [in 2004], or 17.8 times more than that of China in total payout and 77 times more than that of China in term[s] of per-capita defense expenditure." See "China refutes US report on Chinese military power," www.chinaview.cn, 20 July 2005.

44. David Zweig and Bi Jianhai, "China's global hunt for energy," *Foreign Affairs*, Vol. 84, No. 5 (September/October 2005).

45. For an in-depth analysis of this area, see Pak K. Lee, "China's quest for oil security: oil (wars) in the pipeline?" *The Pacific Review*, Vol. 18, No. 2 (June 2005), especially pp. 279 and 283.

46. *The Independent*, London, 22 July 2003, p. 5.

47. For a full-blown analysis of China's relations with INGOs, see Gerald Chan, *China and international organisations: participation in non-governmental organisations since 1971* (Hong Kong: Oxford University Press, 1989).

48. In membership counts, China is still way behind Japan and India, and is about at par with South Korea. *Yearbook of International Organizations 2004/2005*, Vol. 2, p. 53, Figure 2.1.3.(c). See also Gerald Chan, "Is China a "responsible" state? An assessment from the point of view of its multilateral engagements," in Joseph Y.S. Cheng (ed), *China's challenges in the twenty-first century* (Hong Kong: City University of Hong Kong Press, 2003), pp. 221–30.

49. In 1997 there were only a handful of NGOs, mostly based in Beijing. By August 2002, the number had reached some 250 across the country. See *South China Morning Post*, Internet ed., 21 August 2002. This number seems to be small, probably due to a strict definition of NGO used by the source, thereby excluding a large number of government sponsored NGOs. *The law yearbook of China* indicates that there were 142,121 *shehui tuanti* (or social organisations) and 124,491 *minban feiqiye danwei* (private non-enterprise units, such as research and educational institutes and foundations). See *Zhongguo falue nianjian* [*The law yearbook of China*] (Beijing: Press of Law Yearbook of China, 2004), p. 1,073. Zhuang Ailing, founder of Shanghai-based Non-Profit Organisation Development Centre, estimates that China at present has approximately 700,000 to 800,000 NGOs. See *Shanghai Daily*, 23 August 2004, p. 12.

50. Kjell Skjelsbaek, "The growth of international nongovernmental organization[s] in the twentieth century," in Robert O. Keohane and Joseph S. Nye, Jr. (eds), *Transnational relations and world politics* (Cambridge, Mass.: Harvard University Press, 1972), pp. 83–4.

51. Gerald Chan, "From the "Olympic formula" to the Beijing Games: towards greater integration across the Taiwan Strait?" *Cambridge Review of International Affairs*, Vol. 15, No. 1 (April 2002), pp. 141–8.

52. Gerald Chan, *China's compliance in global affairs: trade, arms control, environmental protection, human rights* (Singapore: World Scientific, 2006), chapter 3.

53. *Ibid.* and Gerald Chan, "Globalization rules and China's compliance," *China Report*, Vol. 41, No. 1 (January-March 2005), pp. 59–67.

54. A term used by Eric Teo Chu Cheow, "An ancient model for China's new power," *International Herald Tribune*, 21 January 2004. Cheow compares China's current relationship with its neighbouring countries with the tributary system of the Chinese empire in the Ming and Qing dynasties.

55. These are China, Russia, Kazakhstan, Kyrgyzstan, Tajikistan and Uzbekistan. See http://www.fmprc.gov.cn/eng/topics/sco/t57970.htm (accessed 16 August 2005).

56. The organisation had a small budget of US$3.5 million in 2004, with

China and Russia each contributing 24% to this total. See *South China Morning Post*, 16 January 2004, p. A7.

57. Burt Herman, "Russia, China kick off military exercises," *Associated Press*, Internet ed., 18 August 2005.

58. A remark made by Lourdes Casanova, a professor at the Insead business school near Paris, reported by Eric Pfanner, "The talk of the town at Davos: China," *International Herald Tribune*, Internet ed., 25 January 2004.

59. According to Michael Yahuda, China tries to build new regional security architecture in Asia, but not without difficulties. See his "Chinese dilemma in thinking about regional security architecture," *The Pacific Review*, Vol. 16, No. 2 (June 2003), pp. 189-206.

60. Edward Cody, "China's quiet rise casts wide shadow," *Washington Post*, Internet ed., 25 February 2005.

61. *International Herald Tribune*, 8 October 2003, p. 12.

62. David Shambaugh, "Rising Dragon and the American Eagle – Part I," YaleGlobal online, 20 April 2005.

63. *Ibid.*

64. "Japanese business ties with China explode," *The Associated Press*, Internet ed., 8 February 2004.

65. *International Herald Tribune*, 7 April 2005, p. 3.

66. Jane Perlez, "As U.S. influence wanes, a new Asian community," *International Herald Tribune*, 4 November 2004, p. 2.

67. Shambaugh, "Rising Dragon and the American Eagle – Part I."

68. For a detailed analysis of China's economic and strategic interests in South Asia, see Tarique Niazi, "China, India and the future of South Asia," JapanFocus.org (posted 21 August 2005, assessed 26 August 2005).

69. India and Pakistan have agreed to set up a hotline and to notify each other of missile tests. See *Daily Times*, Pakistan, Internet ed., 31 August 2005.

70. "A strategic triangle," *Beijing Review*, Internet ed., 31 May 2005.

71. Igor Khripunov and Anupam Srivastava, "Russia-Indian relations: alliance, partnership, or?" *Comparative Strategy*, Vol. 18, Issue 2 (April-June 1999), pp. 153–72.

72. *BBC news*, 14 November 2003.

73. *China Daily*, Internet ed., 25 September 2004.

74. *The Dominion Post*, Wellington, 20 August 2005, p. B3; *Weekend Herald*, Auckland, 20 August 2005, p. B10.

75. Steven I. Levine, "China in Asia: the PRC as a regional power," in Harry Harding (ed), *China's foreign policy in the 1980s* (New Haven: Yale University Press, 1984), pp. 107–45.

76. Alastair Iain Johnston, "Is China a status quo power?" *International Security*, Vol. 27, No. 4 (Spring 2003), pp. 5-56. Robert S. Ross, "China II: Beijing as a conservative power," *Foreign Affairs*, March/April 1997. Dennis V. Hickey says China is a "status-quo power" in East Asia. See Hickey, "China's relations with Japan, the Koreas, and Taiwan: progress with problems," Woodrow Wilson International Center for Scholars, Washington DC, Asia Program Special Report, No. 126 (January 2005), pp. 9–15. Interestingly, Wang Jisi, Dean of the School of International Studies at Peking University and Director of the Institute of International Strategic Studies at the Central Party School of the Communist Party of China, is adamant that "a cooperative partnership with Washington is of primary importance to Beijing" and that "it would be foolhardy . . . for Beijing to challenge directly the international order and the institutions favored by the Western world." See Wang, "China's search for stability with America."

77. For some preliminary analyses, see Chan, *China's compliance in global affairs*.

8

How China Deals with
the "China Threat" Perception

Joseph Y. S. CHENG

Introduction

From the Korean War in 1950 to the emergence of the Sino-American *rapprochement* in 1969, China was "in the forefront of the Cold War in Asia and the main target for American isolation and containment".[1] In order to break the American arc of containment, China supported Communist insurgent movements in Southeast Asia, whose aim was the overthrow of national governments by force and the establishment of revolutionary regimes.[2] In the Cold War context, China was perceived by its anti-Communist neighbours as a power dissatisfied with the *status quo* and intent on exporting revolution, Chinese style. China's influence to a considerable extent depended on its "soft power",[3] ranging from Mao Zedong's charisma, to the Chinese Communists' ideological appeal and their attempt to present an attractive model of socio-economic progress offering a successful alternative to the Third World.

China's entry into the United Nations in 1971 and its securing of a permanent seat in the Security Council with a veto, together with President Richard Nixon's visit in February 1972, restored China's status as a respectable member of the international community, a fact well demonstrated by the large number of countries establishing diplomatic relations with China in the first half of the 1970s. The end of the Cultural Revolution and the return to power of Deng Xiaoping laid the foundation for China's economic reforms and opening to the outside world which began at the end of 1978. Since then, China's economic development strategy has been similar to that of other developing countries in East and Southeast Asia. It has also been competing with other Third World countries for aid and loans from international organisations such as the World Bank, as well as from Western countries and Japan. After China joined the Multi-Fibre Arrangement and indicated its intention to participate in the General Agreement on Tariffs and Trade (GATT), it too entered into hard bargaining for export quotas from the developed countries in competition with the developing countries, particularly those from East and Southeast Asia.

All these actions demonstrated that China was gradually freeing itself from various ideological restrictions and trying to compete with other Third World countries within the existing international financial and trade framework. Such competition might have initially aroused jealousy and suspicion from the members of the Association of Southeast Asian Nations (ASEAN) and other developing countries, but in the longer term, only through this means would China be accepted by them. In some ways, China was probably quite accommodating in supporting the Third World's demands. For example, China was the first country to endorse Sri Lanka's proposal for turning the Indian Ocean into a zone of peace, and the Malaysian proposal for the neutralisation of Southeast Asia. Distinguishing itself from the two superpowers, while fully realizing its limited military and economic capabilities, China's support for non-alignment and neutralisation served its objectives well. In the field of arms control and disarmament, China's declaration, neither to be the first to use nuclear weapons nor to use them against non-nuclear countries, won support from the Third World.[4]

China's initial years of economic reforms and opening to the outside world coincided with a short period of pseudo-alliance between China on one hand and the United States as well as Japan on the other. At that time, Soviet expansion reached its peak and there were some indications that it might have been able to gain an upper hand in the strategic balance while continuing to extend its lead in conventional forces. The domination of Indochina by Vietnam, the limited war with Vietnam in February and March 1979, the Soviet occupation of Afghanistan at the end of 1979 and the increasing Soviet arms supply to India all threatened China's security. The Chinese leaders then believed that in its relations with the two superpowers, a tipping of the scale against the Soviet Union was necessary.

In 1982-83, Chinese commentaries and analyses, through the country's official mass media and major publications, revealed a changing perception of Soviet-American balance. They tended to judge that Soviet influence had hit its peak in the middle and late 1970s, and had begun to decline at the end of the same decade. The Chinese leadership's assessment was that the Soviet-American military balance would remain unchanged for some time. It also believed that the conservative forces in the United States insisting on a hard line towards the Soviet Union had the upper hand.

China's relations with the two superpowers then differed from those in any period since 1949. On one hand, Chinese leaders attempted to distance themselves from the United States and avoid any situation that would suggest the formation of a pseudo-alliance, while stressing the independence of Chinese foreign policy. On the other hand, China did not engage in radical opposition to the two superpowers as it had in the early 1960s. The Chinese leadership wanted a dialogue with both superpowers, sharing the same stand or even co-operating with either of them in certain regions or on certain issues depending on circumstances. China would oppose the hegemonism of either or both of the superpowers. The Chinese leaders recognised that the outbreak of a new world war could be delayed or even prevented as a result of the mutual containment and equilibrium between the two superpowers, which would remain unchanged for some time. This situation increased the freedom of the developed and Third World countries, for they could often resist one superpower with the aid of another.

In line with this analysis of the world situation, it was announced in May 1985 that a million soldiers and officers from the People's Liberation Army (PLA) would be demobilised in about two years.[5] China's 1985 military budget amounted to slightly over 18 million yuan and was still below the level of 1980.[6] Hence round about 1982 and 1983, Chinese leaders for the first time since the founding of the People's Republic of China (PRC) believed that China was not under any serious threat. They were confident that China could secure a peaceful international environment to concentrate on its modernisation. Up to this time, Chinese leaders from Mao Zedong to Deng Xiaoping were not aware that China could be perceived as a threat. At least from an ideological point of view, they could not admit it, but simply treated such a perception as propaganda against China by countries hostile to it.

China's modernisation also demanded its acceptance of, and adaptation to, the existing international system, especially the international financial and trade institutional framework dominated by Western countries. In the mid-1980s, China joined the International Monetary Fund and the World Bank, and it also sought to participate in the General Agreement on Tariffs and Trade.[7]

Professor Tsou Tang suggested in *World Politics* in April 1974 two preconditions for the deradicalisation of the foreign policy of a revolutionary state such as China.[8] First, it would have to come to perceive the existing international order as strong and enduring; and second, it would have to believe that it had acquired a "fair stake and a proper place" in that order. These two preconditions seem to exist in the case of China since the early 1980s.

Since the fall of the Gang of Four, China's modernisation programme and its leaders' pragmatic attitude regarding foreign trade, loans, economic co-operation and joint ventures have opened up an enormous market with a huge potential for Western and Japanese capital and advanced technology. The Chinese government not only accepts long-term commercial credits, but since 1979 it has also requested for long-term low-interest loans from Japan's Overseas Economic Co-operation Fund, which actually amount to foreign aid. Regarding trade, investment and economic co-operation, China began to offer various forms of compensation trade and joint ventures, as well as accepting completely foreign-owned enterprises. It also imitated the "export processing zones" of Taiwan and South Korea and established "special economic zones" in the provinces of Guangdong and Fujian. Western oil companies were invited to take part in the exploration and exploitation of China's energy resources too. This pragmatism substantially enhanced China's ability to trade and accelerated the development of China's resources, especially labour resources. China's heavy involvement in the international trade network meant that it appreciated the value of a good image.

In most Western countries, about 70% of foreign affairs are related to the economy. As China's foreign economic relations multiplied, China's diplomacy began to approximate this pattern. Since the mid-1980s, China's relations with the Third World have usually involved agreements on trade, scientific and technological co-operation, aid projects, loans and so on; trade, tariffs, protection of investment and various forms of economic, scientific and technological co-operation have been dominating China's relations and negotiations with developed countries. Even in the case of Sino-American relations, with the exception of the Taiwan question, recent disputes between the two countries are predominantly over economic issues. The initial concrete achievements in the improvement of Sino-Soviet relations in the early 1980s were an increase in trade and the resumption of border trade.

In sum, the emergence of the handling of the "China threat" issue in China's foreign policy-making process took place after Chinese leaders had considered that China was no longer under serious threat, that China required a peaceful international environment to concentrate on its modernisation, and that China needed a good image to facilitate its heavy involvement in the international trade network.

Multipolarity, the "China Threat" and Partnerships

With the disintegration of the Soviet Union and the dissolution of the Warsaw Pact, Chinese leaders perceived the early 1990s as a transitional period between bipolarity and multipolarity, and they considered that such a transition would last for a considerable length of time. The United States was the ultimate winner of the Cold War, and it became the only superpower in the world, thus the "strategic triangle" could no longer be exploited by China.[9] In the post-Cold War era, however, China has been relieved of the direct military threat from Russia. Both Russia and the United States have a military capability far superior to that of China, but they would not have any motivation to attack China in the foreseeable future.

The Chinese leadership was convinced that a fundamental factor for the termination of bipolarity had been the backwardness of the Soviet economy and its scientific and technological developments. The multipolar world was still in its very early stages, and the emergence of a new balance of power would ultimately depend on the competition in "comprehensive national power", the main components of which are economic and technological power. China would need to concentrate on the intermediate and long-term competition in building "comprehensive national power", otherwise it would fall behind in this competition.

Hence China needed a peaceful international environment to concentrate on economic modernisation, and it would try its best to secure such an environment in the foreseeable future. Striving for a peaceful international environment certainly involves establishing friendly relations with neighbouring countries and avoiding conflicts with them. This has probably been China's most important foreign policy objective since 1983, and it has achieved results in the past two decades and more. This policy means that advancing China's national interests by force or the threat of force would be very costly.

China's economic development achieved remarkable success in the 1980s; and despite the Tiananmen Incident in 1989, its economic growth again picked up significant momentum after Deng Xiaoping's southern tour in early 1992. China was generally recognised as an emerging major power, and Chinese leaders had to deal with this perception. In the mid-1990s, China's official media often attacked the United States for trying to block China's economic development. A *Renmin Ribao* commentary, for example, stated: "The United States will not allow the emergence of a great country on the European or Asian continent that threatens its power to dominate."[10] Chinese leaders appreciated that China's neighbours were concerned that its rapid economic growth might be translated into an expansion of military strength. China's flexing of its muscles in the South China Sea in early 1995 was a case in point. Chinese leaders feared that such a perception of a China threat would offer support to the renewal of a strategy to "contain" China. The deterioration of Sino-American relations in 1995-96 and the establishment of formal diplomatic relations between the United States and Vietnam also generated speculation of a possible "containment" strategy against China initiated by the United States and supported by Japan, ASEAN, and Vietnam.

Jiefangjun Bao (*Liberation Army Daily*), for example, accused the proponents of the "China threat" theory of aiming to sow discord between China and its Asian neighbours in view of Washington's waning influence in the region. It was said that countries against China wanted a bigger share of the Asian arms trade, and they also called for the containment of China.[11] Nevertheless, Chinese leaders were still eager to cultivate cordial relations with the Western countries, and especially the United States. This is why the then Premier Li Peng considered the Sino-American summit the most important event in China's foreign relations in 1997, and he acknowledged that Jiang Zemin's successful visit marked the termination of the Western countries' unjust sanctions against China.[12] At the end of 1998, China also rejected the Russian proposal to establish a "strategic triangle" of Russia, China, and India to contain American influence in global affairs.[13]

The Chinese leadership obviously prefers a multipolar world in which the major powers can develop friendly ties with each other and in which non-zero-sum games are the norm. Power blocs and security alliances tend to exacerbate tension and eventually limit the options of the major powers involved. Diversified sources of capital, technology, and management know-how, as well as a broad spectrum of partners for economic co-operation, also constitute part of the Chinese leaders' preferred scenario.

China's strategic partnerships provide the standard mode of behaviour governing relations among the major powers in a multipolar world. While adhering to an independent foreign policy line and emphasizing the Five Principles of Peaceful Co-existence,[14] the concept of strategic partnership reflects the importance attached to relations with major powers on the part of the Chinese leadership. In contrast to the Five Principles of Peaceful Co-existence, strategic partnerships imply that China looks upon itself as a major power and pursues the legitimate interests of one in a multipolar world.

On the basis of the speeches and statements from Chinese leaders and spokesmen of the Chinese foreign ministry, the kind of partnership relationship that China has been promoting since the mid-1990s is one of equality, friendly co-operation and lack of confrontation. The Chinese leadership has been emphasizing the "three nos" principles in the Sino-Russian strategic, co-operative partnership, meaning that the relationship involves no alliance nor confrontation, and is not directed against or at the expense of a third party.[15] It also reiterates, in the building of a constructive strategic partnership between China and the United States, that "China is not a potential adversary of the United States, much less an enemy of the United States, instead it is a trustworthy partner for co-operation".[16]

An analysis of Chinese foreign policy documents reveals that the partnership relationships promoted by the Chinese leadership share a number of characteristics. In the first place, as indicated by the former Chinese foreign minister, Qian Qichen, at the end of 1997, states of the world should respect each other in a multipolar power configuration. They should treat each other as equals, promote mutual benefit, seek to establish consensus and tolerate differences among them. They should engage in friendly co-operation, not engage in confrontation, not form an alliance, and not act against the interests of a third state. Chinese leaders believe that the above constitutes the foundation of the new relationship among states in the twenty-first century.[17]

In the Sino-Russian joint communiqué released during Boris Yeltsin's visit to China in April 1996, it was stated: "The trend towards global multipolarity is developing. The quest for peace, stability, co-operation and development has already become the mainstream of contemporary international life. ... Both sides reaffirm that mutual respect and equality are the important principles of maintaining and developing normal, healthy state relations. Countries irrespective of being large or small, developed or developing, or whose economies are in transition, are equal members of the international community. People of every country have the right to choose independently their social system, developmental path and model, based on their respective national conditions, in the absence of foreign interferences."[18]

Chinese leaders appeal to their counterparts of major countries to actively identify common interests. They hope that differences and contradictions in social systems and values will not affect the healthy development of state-to-state relations. The use of phrases such as "facing the twenty-first century" and "straddling over the present and the next centuries" in the partnership relationships between China and other major powers signified Chinese leaders hoped to maintain such relationships among major powers on a long-term, stable basis. Chinese leaders apparently consider state-to-state relations in terms of non-zero-sum games, and they appeal for the abandonment of the Cold War mentality.

Mutual co-operation should cover all sectors, especially economic, trade, and scientific and technological exchanges. This is in line with the Chinese leadership's position that peace and development constitute the main themes of the post-Cold War era, and that China would concentrate on its objective of modernisation. Strengthening of communications is another important aspect of partnership relationships. Exchanges of visits at the heads of state level, scheduled meetings between premiers, joint commissions involving senior officials, hot-lines and various channels of communications are typical provisions in China's partnerships with other major powers.[19]

These high-sounding principles are apparently sincere, as they are in accord with China's strategic objectives: (a) to maintain a peaceful international environment to concentrate on economic development; (b) to improve China's dialogue with all major powers and regional organisations to ensure recognition of China's major power status and enhance China's influence in international affairs; (c) to push for multipolarity and to prevent the United States from dominating international affairs; (d) to facilitate progress in China's economic diplomacy to open up markets and attract investment, advanced technology and management expertise from diverse sources; and (e) to improve China's image in the international community.

Obviously China's relations with the major powers have not been without problems, particularly with regard to the United States and Japan. China has yet to convince its neighbours that it does not constitute a threat to them, and will not do so even when its national power will be considerably improved in several decades' time. Chinese leaders have to exercise restraint to prevent China's territorial disputes with its neighbours and the Taiwan question from escalating into military conflicts. They also have to show that their advocacy for a new international political and economic order remains constructive, and that China's experts have meaningful proposals to offer. All these are formidable challenges for Chinese strategic planners in the twenty-first century.

To ensure that China will not be perceived as adopting an alliance strategy to facilitate its emergence as a major power, Chinese leaders have been at pains to emphasise that the concept of partnership is related to the Chinese diplomatic principle of "not establishing an alliance or strategic relationship with any major power". In his opening address to the Twelfth Party Congress in 1982, Deng Xiaoping stated: "China's affairs have to be handled in accordance with China's conditions; their handling has to depend on Chinese people's strength. Independence and self-reliance, in the past, present and future, remain our standpoint."[20] In May 1984, in his meeting with the then Brazilian President, João Baptista de Oliveira Figueiredo, Deng Xiaoping's statements were more straightforward: "China's foreign policy is a policy of independence, of genuine non-alignment. China has no alliance relationship with any country; it adopts a completely independent policy. China doesn't play the United States card, nor does it play the Soviet Union card. China does not allow others to play the China card too."[21] China's position of never establishing an alliance or a strategic relationship with any big power was one of the ten principles guiding Chinese foreign policy as presented in Zhao Ziyang's report to the National People's Congress in March 1986.[22] Indeed this was a core principle of China's foreign policy of independence and peace in the 1980s.

It appears that China's rationale for the promotion of bilateral partnerships among major powers includes the following elements. In the first place, China wants to secure a peaceful, stable international environment to pursue its modernisation. On August 28, 1998, Jiang Zemin, in his speech at the ninth ambassadorial conference held by the Ministry of Foreign Affairs, indicated that Chinese foreign policy straddling across the next century "should work hard to generate a better environment along China's periphery and internationally to realise the strategic objective of China's socialist modernisation construction".[23] A stable international environment includes the global environment, the regional environment and the environment along one's borders. In the case of China, Chinese leaders believe that geopolitical factors dictate that the stabilisation of China's relations with the major powers is crucial to its securing a stable international environment.

Secondly, Chinese leaders want to promote global multipolarisation and seek due recognition of China's status as an important pole in a mulitpolar world. In March 1990, Deng Xiaoping made the following observation in his discussions with some leading cadres: "The situation in which the United States and the Soviet Union dominated all international affairs is changing. Nevertheless, in future when the world becomes three-polar, four-polar or five-polar, the Soviet Union, no matter how weakened it may be and even if some of its republics withdraw from it, will still be one pole. In the so-called multi-polar world, China will be counted as a pole."[24] Chinese leaders believe that China's pursuit of multipolarity in the international political and economic order is only natural in view of its position as a major power with considerable influence, as the largest developing country and as a member of the Third World.[25]

Finally, the Chinese leadership has been engaging in developing new strategic thinking and ideological positions in support of China's emergence as a major power in the twenty-first century. The emergence of a major power relies not only on "hardware" such as economic power, military force, etc., it also depends on "software" including an international strategy, values, and so on.[26] As argued by Paul Kennedy, the wisdom of the governments concerned will be a crucial factor determining the outcome of the competition among the United States, Russia, China, Japan and the European Union.[27] Some Chinese scholars consider that the correctness of the international strategy is a fundamental factor contributing to the rise and fall of a country.[28]

Chinese leaders anticipate that China's emergence as a major power may attract a strong negative response, especially from other major powers. The "China threat" theory is obviously one type of response. Hence, Chinese leaders consider the handling of China's relations with its neighbours and other major powers a serious challenge. The partnerships that China has developed with various major powers since the mid-1990s reflect the strategic thinking of the Chinese leadership in preparing China for the next century. By now, China's network of partnerships is more or less in shape. Within this network, China hopes to forge a pattern of relations among major powers based on equality, co-operation, mutual respect and mutual checks and balances. This, to some extent, also reflects the changing values of Chinese foreign policy from classical realism to legalism.[29] There is a recognition among Chinese scholars that international law is not a strong point among Chinese diplomats, and China must work hard to enhance its influence in international organisations.

Though China's network of partnerships is more or less in shape, and in fact this model has become a significant trend in the post-Cold War era, yet China still encounters many restrictions. In the first place, China's capabilities are limited; it is not strong enough to direct other major powers to act in accordance with its strategic principles. More important still, the United States remains the sole superpower, and a genuine multipolar world is at best a distant goal. The United States' attempt to maintain its superior status in a unipolar world constitutes the major obstacle to China's promotion of its new model of relations among major powers.

Multilateral Diplomacy, Regionalism and the "China Threat" Perception

The Chinese leadership hopes that the emergence of regional powers and regional organisations in the developing world will help to bring about a multipolarity different from the traditional one dominated by a small number of major powers. It is envisaged that this new type of multipolarity will better preserve peace and democratise international relations, thus contributing to the establishment of a new international political and economic order. In this context, the Latin American countries' boycott of U.S. sanctions against Cuba, ASEAN's admission of Myanmar against the objections of the West, and the Arab countries' opposition to U.S. military action against Iraq are some international issues that are seen as enhancing the evolution towards multipolarity. Jiang Zemin, in a speech in Pakistan on December 2, 1996, stated: "The trend towards multipolarity, with the widespread emergence of the developing countries as its important characteristic, is like a torrential river which cannot be blocked."[30]

In the era of economic reforms and opening up to the external world, China wants to secure a peaceful international environment to concentrate on economic development. Its strategy in the Asia-Pacific region has been consistent: to stabilise China's periphery, and treat the region as China's base. Naturally these objectives can only be realised if the countries in the region do not perceive China as a threat.

Chinese leaders accept that regional co-operation is an irreversible trend in global economic development and in the evolution of the contemporary international power configuration. As the largest developing country in the Asia-Pacific region, China has to participate in and promote regional economic co-operation enthusiastically in order to strengthen its influence in the region. This activism since the 1990s has been in sharp contrast to the aloofness and the lack of a regional policy in the 1970s. The Chinese authorities understand that only through active participation will China then be able to benefit from the regional economic co-operation process, and direct the flows of capital, technology and commodities in directions favourable to China's development. They certainly hope to influence the orientation and development of the organisations for regional co-operation, and at the same time enhance China's position to oppose hostile blocs and organisations. It has been with such intentions that China has participated in the Asia-Pacific Economic Co-operation (APEC), Pacific Economic Co-operation Council (PECC), ASEAN Regional Forum (ARF), and so on. It is hoped that such participation would promote common interests and indirectly reduce the perception of the "China threat".

In the past two decades and more, China and the countries of Southeast Asia have been concentrating on strengthening their economic base. In their pursuit of economic development and prosperity, economic linkages between them in the areas of trade, investment, finance and technology have been strengthening. At the same time, China and ASEAN share very similar stands on issues like Asian values. The discourse on Asian values which emerged in the early 1990s was articulated most conspicuously by the then Prime Minister of Singapore, Lee Kuan Yew, and the then Prime Minister Mahathir Mohamad of Malaysia.[31] They argued that the ethical foundations of Asian societies rest on values that emphasise consensus and harmony, loyalty to family and community, hierarchy and deference to authority, as opposed to Western ideals which stress individual rights, civil liberties, and competitive politics. The consensus on Asian values between China and ASEAN was best symbolised by the Bangkok Declaration, which embodied their agreement on the common human rights position to be articulated at the World Conference on Human Rights held in June 1993 in Vienna. The Bangkok Declaration emphasised economic growth, community interests, non-interference in other countries' domestic affairs, and respect for each other's different socio-economic, historical and cultural backgrounds.[32]

The Chinese leadership and China's Southeast Asian experts are aware that serious problems face the development of Sino-ASEAN relations in the future. They acknowledge that the regional dynamics among the ASEAN states still take priority over their relations with China. In the early 1990s, when China was attempting to improve relations with its neighbours to ensure that it would enjoy a peaceful international environment, the ASEAN states were also considering how to meet the challenge of integrating China into the Asia-Pacific community by offering it a reasonable stake and a constructive role in the region.

In this mutual engagement process, both parties broadened their respective concepts of security to include not only the military, but also the political and economic aspects as well. Chinese leaders were also aware that China's ambition to become a global power would mean that its Southeast Asian neighbours would be carefully analyzing the intent and meaning of every move on its part. China's contribution or threat to the overall peace and stability of the Asia-Pacific region would be the key variable determining the ASEAN states' support, or at least tolerance, of China's ambition.

Chinese leaders appreciated that they had to demonstrate an awareness of the needs of the ASEAN states, and endorse their idea of security equilibrium and the promotion of regional economic integration. The strengthening of Sino-ASEAN relations in the early 1990s was partly a result of China's active responses to the ASEAN proposals on confidence-building measures and preventive diplomacy in the region. Both parties were eager to establish multi-layered channels of consultation on a bilateral and multilateral basis, as they realised that security co-operation would conform to their mutual interests.

The peaceful resolution of the Cambodian issue through the Paris Peace Conference of 1989-91 reinforced Sino-ASEAN trust at the end of the Cold War. The strengthening of dialogue and mutual trust between China and the ASEAN states established a good foundation for the parties concerned to avoid the subsequent territorial disputes over the Spratly Islands from seriously damaging their relations.[33] Chinese leaders quickly attempted to defuse the Mischief Reef incident in early 1995. In March 1996, China and the Philippines held their first annual vice-ministerial talks to resolve problems caused by the conflicting claims to the Spratlys.[34] Earlier at the ARF meeting in August 1995 in Brunei, the Chinese government indicated for the first time that it would abide by international law in sovereignty negotiations with the claimants to the Spratlys. This was a significant concession on the part of Beijing which had hitherto simply insisted that the Spratlys were Chinese territory. The fact that the Chinese government allowed the issue to be brought up in a multilateral forum, though only in an informal consultative session, was another notable concession because previously it had insisted on tackling the territorial dispute on a bilateral basis.[35]

Both China and the concerned ASEAN states do not expect their territorial disputes over the Spratly Islands to be resolved in the foreseeable future. However, they believe that they share a common interest in maintaining a peaceful, stable environment in the region so that they can all concentrate on economic development. The Chinese government's limited concessions, however, have not been able to put the ASEAN states entirely at ease. There is still a serious concern with what is perceived as China's policy of gradual expansion in the South China Sea. This policy has been depicted as "creeping assertiveness", and as "talk and take" by the then Philippine Defence Secretary.[36] "Creeping assertiveness" is a gradual policy of establishing a greater physical presence in the South China Sea without recourse to military confrontation.[37] The perception of "creeping assertiveness" is related to that of the China threat.

Subscribers to the view of "creeping assertiveness" believe that the Chinese military does not have the capabilities to dominate the

South China Sea yet, and that China at this stage does not want to provoke the United States into adopting a more assertive stand in Southeast Asia and push ASEAN closer to the latter. Those who are concerned with the China threat also consider that at present China is not yet a serious threat to ASEAN because of its limited military projection capabilities, but the threat will become significant in two to three decades when China becomes much stronger economically and militarily, and when China's economic development generates a huge demand for resources, especially energy resources, pushing China onto the road of expansionism. Those in ASEAN who are concerned with China's "creeping assertiveness" and the China threat naturally welcome the renewed American efforts to revitalise bilateral security ties with Japan, South Korea, Australia, Thailand and the Philippines, as well as a more conspicuous forward deployment of U.S. forces in the Asia-Pacific region. Many in the Philippines and the hardliners in the United States have urged both the Clinton and Bush Administrations to strengthen the U.S.-Philippines military alliance, as the Philippines is the ASEAN state with the most recent record of active maritime clashes with China. They propose this as part of a comprehensive campaign to deter China's increasing regional influence.

China's support for ASEAN during the Asian financial crisis in 1997-98 has also enhanced mutual trust between them. China's relative economic health has won considerable admiration in ASEAN. In August 1997, China offered Thailand US$1 billion to help it overcome its financial difficulties. Similarly, it provided assistance to Indonesia. In December 1997, at the summit among ASEAN, China, Japan and South Korea in Kuala Lumpur, the then President Jiang Zemin pledged US$4-6 billion for the International Monetary Fund's programme to support Southeast Asia, and to take part in other assistance programmes. Chinese leaders also promised not to devalue the *renminbi* so as to avoid another round of competitive devaluations among Asian currencies. They considered this an important contribution to stabilise the financial markets in Asia and a sacrifice on China's part, a view that is shared within ASEAN.[38]

In the 1990s, the ASEAN states were able to maintain a security equilibrium in Southeast Asia and promote security co-operation in the region because all the major powers involved had no intention nor the capabilities to dominate the region. Those powers were willing to allow ASEAN to take the initiative in the ARF and other regional organisations. ASEAN's significant role was therefore premised on the common interest among the major powers in maintaining the regional security equilibrium.

The launching of the ARF in Bangkok in 1994 gradually won China's firm support. It was conceived as a new security framework for Asia and the Pacific in the post-Cold War era. Initially, Chinese leaders had some concerns that the West might try to use the ARF to "contain" China. Similarly, China appreciated ASEAN's important role in initiating the Asia-Europe Meeting (ASEM), first held in Bangkok in March 1996. This is a dialogue between the European Union and the countries of East and Southeast Asia. Singapore, its main initiator, and Thailand, the first host of the meeting, are both ASEAN members. Tension among the major powers, however, will limit the role of ASEAN; and confrontation among the major powers will disrupt the regional security equilibrium and force the ASEAN states to take sides, a scenario which the latter will try their best to avoid.

In this connection, the difficulties and tensions in Sino-American relations during the first months of the second Bush administration caused considerable concern among the ASEAN states. Since the disintegration of the Soviet Union, the ASEAN states have been applying a policy of linkage to ensure a continued American military involvement in regional security affairs. They have offered access to military facilities in their countries to U.S. forces to enable them to maintain a strong military presence in East and Southeast Asia to balance off China, and to prevent possible rivalry developing among the region's middle powers.[39]

If China and the United States perceived each other as "strategic partners" or at least worked to ensure that their bilateral relationship is a "constructive and co-operative" one, the American military presence in Southeast Asia would not be seen as a threat to

China. If both countries treated each other as competitors, then Beijing's tolerance would be much reduced. When the two countries engage in confrontation, the forward deployment of the United States forces in the region would become a source of friction involving the ASEAN states. An early indicator emerged on April 17, 2001 when a People's Liberation Army (PLA) naval patrol vessel intercepted three Australian warships sailing through the Taiwan Straits. The key allies of the United States in East and Southeast Asia generally interpreted this as a disturbing signal that would likely make them come under pressure from the Chinese leadership as China and the United States moved towards strategic competition.

Tension in the Taiwan Straits area in 1995-96 contributed to the strengthening of the U.S.-Japan defence co-operation, Japan's rapid growth in its military capabilities, and the incorporation of Taiwan into Japan's area of security vigilance, under the pretext of the "situation in areas surrounding Japan that have an influence on Japanese peace and stability".[40] In early 2005, the U.S.-Japan Security Consultative Committee further announced that the peaceful settlement of the Taiwan question had been included in the "common strategic objectives" of the two countries. In the eyes of Beijing, the security alliance system of the United States, including the U.S.-Japan security alliance, not only aims at a common enemy, but also goes against a specific ideology or civilisation, especially when a Sino-American "strategic partnership" becomes impossible. Furthermore, in the case of Japan, South Korea and Taiwan, military alliance and defence co-operation are more than a common defence arrangement; they also serve as mechanisms for Western values and ideas to penetrate into regional societies.[41]

Competition between China and Japan may well become more intense in the years to come, given the difficult bilateral relations at this stage. Japan is already a political power with formidable military strength. China's economy and military capabilities will continue to develop. How a powerful China lives with a powerful Japan poses a question never experienced by the two countries in their modern history. This adjustment process will be made all the more difficult in the event of a serious setback in Sino-American relations because Japan will then be forced into the awkward position of having to choose between the United States and China. The rising sense of nationalism in both China and Japan is also a negative factor to be reckoned with. How Japan responds to such an awkward position will certainly have a significant demonstration effect on the ASEAN states.

Chinese leaders' worry about the deterioration in Sino-American relations and the potential danger of the "containment" of China by Western countries has been an important motivation for their promotion of East Asian regionalism through the "ASEAN plus China" and the "ASEAN plus 3" routes. On the part of the ASEAN states, they hope that this regionalism may enable them to deal with Western countries from a position of strength on issues such as protectionism, in contrast to their impotence during the Asian financial crisis. They share Beijing's resentment against Washington's arrogance and unilateralism, as well as China's promotion of a more multipolar world. They are disappointed with APEC's failure to serve as an engine to push the World Trade Organisation (WTO) to launch a new round of global trade negotiations; they have also become more cautious about globalisation.[42] As long as the Chinese leadership is aware of the limitations of the "ASEAN plus 3" process and does not overplay its desire to exclude the United States, it should be satisfied with the present achievements.

Beijing understands that China's economic growth has generated increasing concern regarding competition from China among ASEAN members. Experts in China tend to argue that foreign direct investment flows to China and to the rest of Asia have been complementary and not competitive. It seems that ASEAN will benefit disproportionately from China's entry into the WTO. It has also been observed that servicing China's expanding middle class is likely to become an increasingly important source of revenue for the ASEAN states, especially Thailand and Singapore. Chinese tourists in the ASEAN states have been increasing rapidly; Asian companies which can capitalise on exporting agricultural goods to China's more discerning middle classes will also do well. Such development trends are predicated on the maintenance of healthy economic growth in China. There is a more pessimistic view, however, that competition from China may hurt countries like Thailand, Indonesia, and the Philippines, because their economies are at a similar stage of development as that of China. Owing to the diversity in China, it may be simultaneously developing its agricultural, industrial and technological sectors, and hence there may not be much room to absorb more agricultural imports from the ASEAN states. Freer trade, however, should definitely offer a more optimistic outlook.

Economic contacts would help to enhance mutual understanding between China and ASEAN, especially at the people-to-people level. The strengthening of common economic interests will provide a better foundation for confidence-building measures, preventive diplomacy and eventually conflict resolution. China realises that it has to be more active in multilateral diplomacy, especially at the regional level, and some efforts, though still far from adequate, have been made. The Boao Forum for Asia is a good example of such initiatives and their limited success. The Chinese government's enthusiastic support for a non-governmental, non-political and private-sector driven organisation is indeed a sign of the times. Obviously Chinese leaders are now ready to play a more active part in Track-2 processes.

ASEAN is probably the best example of China engaging in regional organisations and multilateral diplomacy to deal with the "China threat" perception on the part of its neighbours. The Shanghai Co-operation Organisation (SCO) is another useful case study; and China's policy towards this regional organisation will be briefly analyzed in this section too.

When the Soviet Union disintegrated at the end of 1991, the Chinese government promptly recognised the Russian Federation and the other eleven republics. Diplomatic relations with them were established rapidly. The Chinese government actively cultivated good relations with these countries and offered them government loans and commodity credits. Leaders from these countries were invited to visit China and, in 1992-93, there were top leaders from these countries visiting Beijing almost monthly.[43] In 1994, the then

Premier Li Peng visited Uzbekistan, Turkmenistan, Kyrgyzstan, Kazakhstan and Mongolia. During the visits, he enunciated the four major principles governing China's relations with the Central Asian republics. They were to maintain good-neighbourly relations and peaceful co-existence; to promote equality and mutually beneficial co-operation in pursuit of common prosperity; to respect the sovereignty and independence of the peoples of Central Asia through a policy of non-interference in their internal affairs; and to seek and preserve stability in the region.[44]

Friendly relations and expanding economic ties with these Central Asian neighbours were expected to help China contain the troubles from the national minorities in the provinces and autonomous regions in the Northwest. Negotiations at the expert level were held between China on one side and Russia, Kazakhstan, Kyrgyzstan and Tajikistan on the other on the reduction of military forces along the border regions and confidence-building measures. These negotiations led to an agreement among the five countries in April 1997 on reducing troop levels along their common border of over 7,000 km to about 260,000. Tanks, armoured personnel carriers, and artillery would be cut substantially too.[45]

This approach to Central Asia was in line with the belief of Chinese leaders that the end of the Cold War would enhance instability and facilitate the re-emergence of various territorial disputes, ethnic contradictions and religious conflicts. Some of these troubles would have an adverse impact on China too, such as the demonstration effects of the rise of ethnic-nationalism and Islamic fundamentalism in the newly-independent Central Asian republics on the national minorities in Xinjiang and Inner Mongolia.

On the basis of the achievements in the 1990s, China was able to take the lead in June 2001 to formally establish the SCO involving China, Russia, Kazakhstan, Kyrgyzstan, Tajikistan and Uzbekistan. Since then, the SCO has evolved into an economic, energy and security forum. In contrast to the ARF, the SCO has been more ready to engage in institutionalisation. In the third heads of state meeting held in Moscow in May 2003, agreement was reached on the establishment of a general secretariat (with a budget and a secretary-general) in Beijing and an anti-terrorism centre in Tashkent. There are regular meetings at the foreign minister, prime minister and head of state level. In the July 2005 meeting, Iran, Pakistan, India and Mongolia were invited to take part as observers, a possible sign of ambitious expansion plans for the organisation.

A few months after the founding of the SCO, the September 11 Incident prompted the establishment of an American military presence in Central Asia. This military presence was welcomed by the Central Asian republics concerned which were eager to attract American economic assistance and interested in exploiting the American influence to achieve a new balance of power equilibrium allowing them more room of manoeuvre. This military presence was facilitated by the Putin administration too.

SCO members share the common interest of combating terrorism, religious extremism and separatism. After the "rose revolution" in Georgia in 2003, followed in turn by the "coloured revolutions" in Ukraine and Kyrgyzstan, as well as a rebellion in Uzbekistan, there are now strong suspicions that the Bush administration, supported by some Western governments, have been trying to overthrow the region's traditional authoritarian and pro-Russian regimes. Chinese leaders were certainly pleased that in the joint declaration released after the SCO summit in July 2005, it was demanded that the international coalition against terrorism led by the United States should "decide on the deadline for the use of the temporary infrastructure and for their military contingents' presence" in the Central Asian countries.[46]

China, as well as Russia, have been exploiting the anti-American sentiments in Central Asia. In August 2005, when China and Russia held a large-scale joint military exercise, the other four SCO members also despatched military observers. Oil has been another important factor; in reducing American influence in the region, China hopes that it will have a better chance in its competition with the United States for the region's energy resources. Soon after a violent suppression in eastern Uzbekistan in May 2005 by President Islam Karimov which caused the United States and other Western countries to call for an independent inquiry, Karimov visited Beijing. He was offered political support by the Chinese leadership, as well as a contract for a US$600 million oil and gas joint venture.[47]

The SCO therefore has been a useful vehicle for China to promote common interests with the Central Asian republics as well as Russia. It has served to maintain political stability in China's border provinces and limit the influence of hostile forces. Trade and investment activities have only been stepped up in recent years. But China has to bear the risk of supporting unstable authoritarian regimes, whose collapse may severely undermine its influence in the region.

Responsibility, Reform and the "China Threat"

In the recent decade or so, Chinese leaders often emphasise that China has been a responsible member of the international community on issues ranging from arms control to environmental protection, international trade exchange rate of the yuan, etc. As the country with the largest population in the world, China's behaviour naturally has a major global impact. As an emerging major power seeking international recognition and acceptance, as well as the removal of the "China threat" perception, responsible international behaviour is of special importance to China.

In the 1960s, soon after China's first successful nuclear test, Chinese leaders pledged not to use nuclear weapons first and not to use nuclear weapons against non-nuclear states. In the 1970s and 1980s, China was probably the most enthusiastic major country endorsing various nuclear-weapons-free zone proposals from Third World countries.[48] As indicated above, Chinese leaders' promise of not devaluing the yuan so as to avoid another around of competitive devaluations of currencies among neighbouring Asian countries has been broadly praised internationally.[49] In foreign relations, China has been exercising restraint so that its emergence as a major power will not be seen as a threat.

China's weaknesses, however, can be perceived as threats too. If China's economic collapse leads to an exodus of refugees, China's neighbours will feel threatened. If China's lack of political reforms, government incompetence and corruption finally lead to political and social instability, peace and stability in the Asia-Pacific region will be adversely affected. China's environmental pollution spreads to its neighbours. Its inefficient use of natural resources resulting from rapid economic growth adds a lot of pressure to international commodity markets and the balances in demand and supply regarding raw materials. Hence domestic reforms constitute an important part of China's responsible behaviour, re-assuring the international community that China's development should not be perceived as a threat.

By 1988, even before the Tiananmen Incident, Deng Xiaoping already realised the urgent need for the deepening of reforms. He stated: "China is conducting a deep reform in order to create better conditions for future development. We do not just set our sight on the twentieth century, but also think about the new century. The problem is that if we do not move ahead, we have to retreat. Only deep and comprehensive reform can guarantee that we can build a relatively well-to-do (*xiaokang*) society by the end of the twentieth century and make more progress in the next century."[50] In the third plenary session of the Thirteenth Central Committee of the Communist Party of China (CPC), deep and comprehensive reform became the Party line.

The Tiananmen Incident was a severe setback to China's foreign relations.[51] But Deng Xiaoping's famous southern tour in early 1992 renewed the country's momentum of reforms and economic growth. The Fourteenth National Congress of the CPC in the following September decided to establish a "socialist market economy with Chinese characteristics". The Fifteenth National Congress of the CPC in 1997 put forward the objective of building "a state based on the rule of law". These two important goals have defined the parameters of China's reform programme at this stage.

The establishment of a complete market economy coincides with China's intention to integrate into the international economy in accordance with capitalist principles and rules of the game defined by the developed countries in the West. Domestically, the Chinese leadership accepts the objective of "small government, big society" in its attempt to reform the government's functions. The relative size of the state-owned sector has been in decline, while the private sector and the foreign-invested sectors have been expanding rapidly. Practice of the principles of the market economy has led to imbalances and widening of the gap between the rich and poor. The new leadership under Hu Jintao and Wen Jiabao has recognised such imbalances and pledges to achieve more co-ordinated development minimizing the differences between urban and rural areas, between regions and between social and economic development, and securing a better balance between human development and environmental protection as well as that between exported-oriented growth and that based on domestic demand.

These imbalances are sources of potential political and social instability. Chinese leaders believe that they have to maintain an annual economic growth rate of about 7% in order to contain unemployment and generate resources for the central government to re-distribute incomes to minimise the socio-economic contradictions. Given China's increasing integration into the international economy, it will be more and more affected by international business cycles. There is a concern that an economic slowdown may sharpen all the socio-economic contradictions threatening political and social stability.

The impressive economic development in China has become an engine of growth for its neighbours' economies. An economic slowdown in China will adversely affect them too. In recent years, China's demand for natural resources has led to sharp rises in prices in international commodity markets. Its forest conservation programmes and demand for hard timber due to the construction boom have meant an expansion of imports from Indonesia, Myanmar, Cambodia and other countries, resulting in an acceleration of deforestation in them. As an international workshop, China's manufacturing industries remain inefficient. According to a study, labour productivity in its traditional industries is only one third of the world average and one tenth of that in developed countries. Energy consumption of the manufacture of China's major industrial products far exceeds that of developed countries; energy consumption of the manufacture of per ton of steel in the key plants of China's metallurgical industrial sector is 20% to 40% higher than that of developed countries.[52]

Herein lies the challenge and potential. There is keen competition for new sources of energy between China on one hand, and the United States, Japan and India on the other in Russia, the Central Asian republics, Africa and Latin America. Failure by a subsidiary of the state-owned China National Offshore Oil Corporation (CNOOC) to acquire Unocal in the United States was related to the perception of the "China threat" and generated some ill will in Sino-American relations. Yet technology transfer from the United States and other Western countries ranging from energy-saving devices to the peaceful use of nuclear energy will help China considerably reduce its energy consumption and dampen the rise in demand for energy in the international market. This is the United States' strategic choice: to encourage responsible behaviour on the part of China in the international community.

Concern with China's political and social stability is related to the human rights condition, political reforms and corruption in China. Chinese leaders are obviously determined to combat corruption; there has been improvement in the human rights condition in the country, but the CPC has no intention of compromising its monopoly of political power. The so-called political reforms have largely been limited to administrative reforms and intra-Party democratic reforms without allowing the leadership of the Party to be challenged. The Chinese authorities have been working hard to seek recognition of China's market-economy status by the European Union and the United States. They have released a number of White Papers on human rights and arms control; they have also been taking part in many bilateral and multilateral dialogues on these two issues. Obviously China's participation in the international economy demands a good image which Chinese leaders have been eager to cultivate.

The fact that China is not a democracy and makes little efforts in democratisation remains a handicap in China's foreign relations. It has often been suggested that the neo-conservatives in the American political establishment favour closer ties with Russia than with China because they consider Russia a democracy. Similarly they prefer the cultivation of India to balance against China for the same reason. In the eyes of the Western world, an authoritarian regime opposing democracy rejects many universal values it cherishes; and democratic governments find it difficult to develop close relations with non-democratic ones. In this connection, Taiwan attracts a lot of sympathy in the international community. Authoritarianism also gives rise to concern for the danger of the collapse of the Chinese Communist regime.

Acceptance of the principles of a market economy implies accepting the existing international division of labour and exploiting China's comparative advantage in the international economy. This position in turn supports the policy of opening up to the external world. China's joining the WTO in 2001 symbolises its embrace of globalisation. Its full integration into the international economy promotes its foreign trade, which grew from US$135.7 billion in 1991 to more than US$1.1 trillion in 2004. China has now become the world's third largest trading country, only after the United States and Germany.

China's opening up to the external world also means convergence with international norms. It is not clear whether Chinese leaders were aware of the "convergence theory" during the prescribed convergence with international norms in the 1990s.[53] Obviously this convergence dampens China's threat to establish a new international political and economic order, and indicates that China is ready to compete according to the prevailing rules of the game. Opening up to the external world and integration into the international economy also demand the rule of law in the domestic scene, i.e., institutionalisation and predictability. Promoting the rule of law in turn will contribute to political and social stability in China.

The promotion of the rule of law raises the question of the

source of legitimacy of the Chinese Communist regime. In the modernisation era, Chinese leaders considered that the regime's performance in raising the people's living standard would be the foundation of its legitimacy. But rapid development has generated imbalances and contradictions, and the Chinese leadership is acutely aware of the problem of an ideological vacuum. Nationalism has been cultivated by the Chinese authorities to fill this vacuum, but the promotion of the official version of nationalism often gives rise to spontaneous unofficial versions of nationalism as well. The latter may tarnish China's international image; and in the case of Sino-Japanese relations, they are a serious problem. In the end, there is no substitute for democracy.

Conclusion: China's Peaceful Rise

In view of China's still limited military and economic capacities, a multipolar world in the twenty-first century would provide the most favourable environment for it to exert its influence in international and regional affairs as a major power. The Chinese leadership certainly sees the predominance of the United States as the sole superpower in the world as unacceptable, both from an ideological and national interest point of view. The perception that the United States does not want to see a strong China and that it wants to "contain" China has reinforced the above view. But Chinese leaders want to highlight the common interest between the two countries, and persuade the United States to see the benefits of maintaining good relations with China, or at least to avoid a sharp deterioration in the bilateral relationship. In the longer term, Chinese leaders would like to work to facilitate the emergence and consolidation of multipolarity in the global power transfiguration.

The Chinese leadership prefers a multipolar world in which the major powers can develop friendly ties with each other based on partnerships and in which non-zero-sum games are the norm. The Asia-Pacific financial crisis in 1997-1998 and China's increasing dependence on international trade have highlighted the significance of China's "economic security". The Chinese leadership considers that because of the keen competition for markets and resources in the context of globalisation as well as the enhancement of regionalism, the economic development of one individual country will be more vulnerable to the influence of external factors. Hence the strengthening of co-ordination among governments concerned will become all the more essential. This implies that Chinese leaders will attempt to further develop China's dialogue and multilateral co-operation first with the major powers, its Asian neighbours, and eventually with all countries in the world, including those in Latin America and Africa.[54]

China's joining the WTO symbolises China's response to globalisation. It appreciates that if it does not open its doors, isolation will only exacerbate its backwardness. Despite the economic and political costs, China has no alternatives but to accept world-wide competition according to the rules defined by the developed countries. China can only catch up with the latter through global competition. The ultimate challenge to the CPC's monopoly of power is not to be under-estimated; and multilateral economic diplomacy will be more significant in China's foreign relations in the future.

Globalisation and China's deepening integration into the international economy mean that the management of its international financial and trade risks has become a much more important and difficult task. This task has its foreign policy and domestic reform aspects. China's impressive economic growth has increased its weight in the Asia-Pacific region, and to a lesser extent, in the global economy. This implies influence as well as responsibilities. In this connection, Chinese foreign policy researchers have been engaging in discussions of interdependence in international relations as well as the relationship among interdependence, international organisations and state sovereignty since the early 1990s.

At the end of 2003, the new Chinese leadership began to articulate the concept of China's peaceful rise publicly. On

December 26, 2003, in commemoration of the one hundred and tenth anniversary of Mao Zedong's birthday, Hu Jintao, General Secretary of the CPC Central Committee, stated that China had to "insist on following the development path of a peaceful rise".[55] About two weeks earlier, in a speech delivered at Harvard University in the United States, Premier Wen Jiabao elaborated on the concept as follows: "In expanding our opening up to the external world, we, at the same time, have to adequately and more self-consciously rely on our own institutional innovations; rely on our developing and expanding domestic market; rely on transforming the huge savings of the residents into investment; and rely on the raising of the nation's quality and the progress of science and technology to resolve our resources and environmental problems. The gist of China's development path of a peaceful rise lies in the above."[56]

The concept "peaceful rise" soon attracted some criticisms. Those in favour of a strong military were not comfortable with too much emphasis on a "peaceful" foreign policy, especially when the military option had to be retained regarding the Taiwan issue. There were critics who argued that the word "rise" should be avoided. There was also speculation that Jiang Zemin at that time was unhappy with Hu Jintao's over-eagerness to present the major foreign policy innovation to build his own political stature. By April 2004, the term "peaceful development" began to replace "peaceful rise" in the official discourse, though the latter's central arguments remain in force.[57]

Chinese academics in the international relations field consider China's peaceful rise to be a long-term process in motion at this stage. The approach focusses on the status and function of China in the international system and world market, including its adaptability, integration, influence and creativity.[58] Through active participation in the processes of economic globalisation, China has captured the opportunity to rise as a major power. The contribution of China's economic growth to the world economy lies in the following areas: first, it leads to the stable improvement of the living standards of China's 1.3 billion population; second, it constitutes important momentum pushing for Asia's economic development, and in turn serves as a positive factor in the global economic development; third, it facilitates the achievement of the optimal allocation of resources in the world market through China's participation in the international division of labour; and finally, it helps China assume a constructive role in the international economic mechanisms, and as a linkage between developed countries and developing countries.

The rapid increase of the weight of China's economy in the world market has generated some maladjustment between the external world and the China market, including the valuation of the yuan, China's huge trade surpluses, large-scale re-location of industries to China, global deflation, and so on. Chinese leaders have pledged to tackle these issues when China's economic structure stabilises and when China can absorb the shock of these adjustments. They also indicate that investment outflow from China will gradually accelerate.

The Chinese leadership is acutely aware of the danger of the spread of the "China threat" perception. They understand that the rise of a new major power will probably be perceived as a challenge and threat by the existing major powers. Chinese leaders are concerned that such perception will lead to the "containment" of China. In fact, they believe that the United States has been engaging in such "containment", which in fact is the main cause of the conflicts in Sino-American relations. Chinese academics attempt to explain that China's peaceful rise involves a re-definition of national interest and national security by the Chinese authorities as common interest and a new concept of security.

According to this new concept of security, China's security is not an isolated issue; it is mutually interdependent with that of the Asia-Pacific region and indeed of the entire global community. This new concept of security involves non-traditional security and human security, and in fact can serve as the basis for co-operation between China and the other major powers. In this connection, Chinese leaders will attempt to establish a new framework for international relations, but they understand that they only have limited support. It is hoped that this new framework will expand the strategic space for China's peaceful rise. To secure another twenty to fifty years' time for China to develop its economy and to catch up with the advanced countries in the world is the most important strategic objective in accord with China's core national interest; such an objective is to facilitate China's peaceful rise. China therefore is willing to make concessions to secure this strategic space. This is probably most conspicuous in Sino-American and Sino-Japanese relations; indeed, Chinese leaders have often been criticised by the domestic intelligentsia for being weak in dealing with these two countries.

This approach arguably is the strategy of the weak, and is in line with the Chinese leadership's objective of gaining time. Chinese leaders typically appeal for overcoming differences through dialogue and negotiation. As an implicit critique against U.S. unilateralism and Samuel P. Huntington's thesis of "the clash of civilisations",[59] the Chinese public information machinery preaches mutual respect, mutual exchange and mutual learning among various civilisations, different social systems and development paths while engaging in peaceful competition. In line with China's relative weakness, Chinese leaders have been eager to promote multipolarity as the new global power transfiguration, the democratisation of international relations, the strengthening of the role of the United Nations, and respect for the diversity of development models. Within this framework, the Chinese leadership considers that priority should go to China's neighbours, while the major powers are the key, and the developing countries are the foundation.

Up till now, Chinese leaders have largely been successful in avoiding provocations leading to active policies on the part of the United States and other major powers to contain China. China's smaller neighbours clearly indicate a preference to engage China too. But China's rapid development generates domestic imbalances and contradictions, which in turn threaten political and social stability. While the Chinese authorities are aware of the problems, they are yet reluctant to give up the CPC's monopoly of political power. Hence authoritarianism will continue to cause speculation of political instability in the future, and constitute an obstacle in strengthening relations with the United States and the Western world.

Notes and References

1. Michael Yahuda, *The International Politics of the Asia-Pacific, 1945–1995* (London: Routledge, 1996), p. 193.

2. Harold C. Hinton, China's Turbulent Quest: *An Analysis of China's Foreign Relations Since 1949* (Bloomington: Indiana University Press, 1972), p. 86.

3. Joseph S. Nye, Jr., *Soft Power: the Means to Success in World Politics*, (New York: PublicAffairs, 2004).

4. See Joseph Y.S. Cheng, "The Evolution of China's Foreign Policy in the Post-Mao Era: From Anti-Hegemony to Modernization Diplomacy", in Joseph Y.S. Cheng (ed.), *China: Modernization in the 1980s* (Hong Kong: The Chinese University Press, 1989), pp. 161–201.

5. *South China Morning Post* (an English language newspaper in Hong Kong), 15 April 1986.

6. *Ming Pao* (a Chinese language newspaper in Hong Kong), 8 February 1986.

7. Zhang Zeyu, "China Positions Itself to Rejoin GATT", *Beijing Review*, Vol. 29, No. 10, 10 March 1986, pp. 4–5.

8. Tsou Tang, "Statesmanship and Scholarship", *World Politics*, Vol. 26, No. 3, (April 1974), pp. 428–450.

9. See, for example, Chen Qimao, "New Approaches in China's Foreign Policy", *Asian Survey*, Vol. 33, No. 3, (March 1993), pp. 237–251; and Yan Xuetong, "China's Post-Cold War Security Strategy", *Contemporary International Relations*, Vol. 5, No. 5, (Beijing: China Institute of Contemporary International Relations, May 1995), pp. 1–16.

10. Lu Jianren, "China's Diplomatic Strategy Towards ASEAN at the Turn of the Century" (speech delivered at the Contemporary China Research Centre, City University of Hong Kong on December 15, 1997). At that time, Dr. Lu was Secretary-General, APEC Policy Research Centre, and Assistant Director, Institute of Asia-Pacific Studies, Chinese Academy of Social Sciences.

11. *Jiefangjun Bao* (*Liberation Army Daily*, Beijing), 3 November 1995; and *South China Morning Post*, 4 November 1995.

12. In January 1998, the then Premier Li Peng was interviewed by the U.S.-based monthly *China Information*. See *Ming Pao*, 5 February 1998.

13. *Ibid.*, 23 December 1998.

14. The Five Principles of Peaceful Co-existence were jointly initiated by China, India and Burma in 1953–54; they were initially to apply to relations among countries with different social systems. They are: respect for territorial integrity and sovereignty, non-interference in domestic affairs, equality and mutual benefit, mutual non-aggression, and peaceful co-existence. They are still presented by the Chinese leadership as guidelines for China's foreign policy today.

15. The "no alliance" and "not directed against or at the expense of a third party" principles were first raised in the Sino-Soviet Joint Declaration in 1989; see *Renmin Ribao* (Beijing), 19 May 1989. The "no confrontation" principle was first proposed in connection with Sino-American relations in the post-Cold War era; see *ibid.*, 1 December 1992.

16. The then Chinese Premier Zhu Rongji mentioned this in his speech at the Massachusetts Institute of Technology during his trip to the United States in April 1999; see *ibid.*, 16 April 1999.

17. *Ibid.*, 18 December 1997.

18. *Ibid.*, 26 April 1997.

19. "Goujian Xinshiji de Xinxing Guojia Guanxi (Constructing a New Model of State-to-State Relationship for the New Century)", *Renmin Ribao* editorial, 8 December 1997.

20. Deng Xiaoping, "Opening speech at the Twelfth National Congress of the Communist Party of China (September 1, 1982)", in *Selected Works of Deng Xiaoping (1982–1992)* (Beijing: Foreign Languages Press, 1994), p. 14.

21. Deng Xiaoping, "We must safeguard world peace and ensure domestic development (May 29, 1984)", in *ibid.*, pp. 66–67.

22. Han Nianlong (ed.), *Dangdai Zhongguo Waijao (The Foreign Policy of Contemporary China)* (Beijing: Chinese Social Science Press, 1990), pp. 472–475.

23. *Renmin Ribao*, 29 August 1998.

24. Deng Xiaoping, "The international situation and economic problems (March 3, 1990)", in *op. cit.*, p. 341.

25. See, for example, Yan Xuetong, "Study report on China's foreign relations in 1997–98: international security environment for China's rise", in China Society for Strategy and Management Research (ed.), *Study Reports on International Situation 1997–1998 (Beijing: China Society for Strategy and Management Research, 1998), pp. 81–91.

26. Joseph S. Nye, Jr., *Bound to Lead: The Changing Nature of American Power* (New York: Basic Books, 1990); and Andrew Nathan and Robert Ross, *The Great Wall and The Empty Fortress: China's Search for Security* (New York: W.W. Norton, 1997), p. 18.

27. Paul Kennedy, *The Rise and Fall of the Great Powers: Economic Change and Military Conflict from 1500 to 2000* (New York: Random House, 1987), p. 540.

28. Huang Shuofeng, *Guojia Shengshuai Lun* (*On the Rise and Fall of States*) (Changsha: Hunan Press, 1996), pp.1–5; and Bo Guili, *Guojia Zhanlue Lun* (*On National Strategy*) (Beijing: China Economic Press, 1994), pp. 8–9.

29. Li Baojun, "Zhanlue Huoban Guanxi Yu Zhongguo Waijao de Lishi Jueze (Strategic Partnerships and the Historical Choice for Chinese Foreign Policy)", in Joseph Y.S. Cheng (ed.), *Houlengzhan Shiqi de Zhongguo Waijao* (*Chinese Foreign Policy in the Post-Cold War Era*) (Hong Kong: Cosmos Books Ltd., 1999), pp.75–99.

30. See He Fang, "Yinian lai Nanbai Guanxi de Bianhua yu Fazhan" ("Changes and Developments in North-South Relations in the Past Year"), *Remin Ribao*, 28 December 1997.

31. See Fareed Zakaria, "Culture is Destiny: A Conversation with Lee Kuan Yew", *Foreign Affairs*, Vol. 73, No. 2, (March/April 1994), pp. 109–126; and Mahathir Mohamad, *A New Deal for Asia* (Kuala Lumpur: Pelanduk Publications, 1999).

32. See Leonard C. Sebastian, "Southeast Asian Perceptions of China: The Challenge of Achieving a New Strategic Accommodation", in Derek da Cunha (ed.), *Southeast Asian Perspectives on Security* (Singapore: Institute of Southeast Asian Studies, 2000), p. 174.

33. See Joseph Y.S. Cheng, "China's ASEAN Policy in the 1990s: Pushing for Regional Multipolarity", *Contemporary Southeast Asia*, Vol. 21, No. 2, (August 1999), pp. 189–193.

34. *South China Morning Post*, 5 and 16 March 1996.

35. *Ibid.*, 3 August 1995.

36. "Erap orders blockade of Mischief Reef ", *Philippine Daily Inquirer* (Manila), 11 November 1998.

37. See Ian James Storey, "ASEAN and the Rise of China: The Search for Security in the 1990s" (Ph.D. thesis submitted to the Department of Public and Social Administration, City University of Hong Kong), (March 2001), pp. 150–153.

38. *Ming Pao*, 18 April 1998.

39. See Renato Cruz De Castro, "Managing 'Strategic Unipolarity': The ASEAN States' Responses to the Post-Cold War Regional Environment", in Derek da Cunha (ed.), *op. cit.*, pp. 60–80.

40. Wang Yunlang, "Zhoubian Guojia Haijun Liliang de Fazhan ji dui Woguo de Yingxiang (The Naval Development of Our Periphery Countries and Its Impact)", *Junshi Xueshu* (Military Studies), No. 10, (1995), pp. 7–10.

41. You Ji, "The Chinese Perception on the Changing Security Situation in East Asia", *China Studies* (Hong Kong), No. 6, (2000), p. 140.

42. Daljit Singh, "Southeast Asia In 2000: Many Roads, No Destination?", in Daljit Singh and Anthony Smith (eds.), *Southeast Asian Affairs 2001* (Singapore: Institute of Southeast Asian Studies, 2001), pp. 10–13.

43. See Qu Xing, "Shilun Dong'ou Jubian he Suliau Jieti Hou de Zhongguo Duiwai Zhengce" ("Discussion of China's Foreign Policy Since the Radical Changes in Eastern Europe and the Disintegration of the Soviet Union"), *Journal of Foreign Affairs College*, No. 37, 25 December 1994, p. 21.

44. Qian Qichen, "Shizhong Buyu de Fengxing Duli Zhizhu de Heping Waijiao Zhengce" ("Forever Implementing a Peaceful Foreign Policy of Independence and Self-reliance"), *Qiushi Zhazhi (Seeking Truth)*, No. 12, (June 1995), p. 5.

45. See Joseph Y.S. Cheng and Shi Zhifu, "Zhongguo yu Dulianti Guojia, Dongou Guojia Guanxi de Queli he Fazhan" ("The Establishment of Relations and Subsequent Developments Between China and the CIS States and Eastern European Countries"), Chapter 4, in Joseph Y.S. Cheng and Shi Zhifu (eds.), *Zhonghua Renmin Gonghegou Duiwai Guanxi Shigao (A Draft History of the Foreign Relations of the People's Republic of China)*, Vol. 4, 1989–1999 (Hong Kong: Cosmos Books Ltd., 2000), pp. 133–172.

46. *South China Morning Post*, 8 July 2005.

47. *Ibid.*

48. See Joseph Y.S. Cheng, "The Evolution of China's Foreign Policy in the Post-Mao Era: From Anti-Hegemony to Modernization Diplomacy", Chapter 6, in Joseph Y.S. Cheng (ed.), *China: Modernization in the 1980s* (Hong Kong: The Chinese University Press, 1989), pp. 191–192.

49. See Avery Goldstein, *Rising to the Challenge: China's Grand Strategy and International Security* (Stanford, California: Stanford University Press, 2005), p. 129.

50. Deng Xiaoping, *Deng Xiaoping Wenxuan*, Vol. III (*Selected Works of Deng Xiaoping*, Vol. III) (Beijing: Renmin Chubanshe, 1993), p. 268.

51. See Joseph Y.S. Cheng, "China's Post-Tiananmen Diplomacy", in George

Hicks (ed.), *The Broken Mirror: China After Tiananmen* (Essex, United Kingdom: Longman Group, 1990), pp. 401–416.

52. Chapter 8 "Zhongguo Yinqing: Shijie Jinyicun, Zhangxian Huaxia Gongxian (The China Engine: Highlighting China's Contributions in a Closely Inter-dependent World)", in Zhang Youwen, Huang Renwei, et al., 2004 *Zhongguo Guoji Diwei Baogao* (*China's International Status Report 2004*) (Beijing: Renmin Chubanshe, 2004), p. 213.

53. See Samuel P. Huntington, *Political Order in Changing Societies* (New Haven, Connecticut: Yale University Press), 1968.

54. Ma Zhongyuan, "Zhongguo Zuochu 'Jingji Anquan' Zhanlue Juece" ("China Has Developed a Policy Concerning an 'Economic Security' Strategy"), *The Mirror* (a Hong Kong Chinese monthly), No. 255, (October 1998), pp.32–34.

55. For the text of Hu's speech, see *Renmin Ribao* (Beijing), 27 December 2003.

56. See *ibid*. (overseas edition), 12 December 2003.

57. See Avery Goldstein, *op. cit.*, pp. 191–192; see also Joseph Kahn, "Former Leader Is Still a Power in China's Life", *New York Times*, 16 July 2004.

58. See, for example, "Daolun: Heping Jueqi – Qiangguo Ding Mubiao Tuidong Shijie Gongying" ("Introduction: Peaceful Rise – Major Power Sets the Objective Pushing for a Global Win-Win Scenario"), in Zhang Youwen, Huang Renwei, et al., *op.cit.* (Beijing: Renmin Chubanshe, 2004), pp. 1–15.

59. Samuel P. Huntington, *The Clash of Civilizations and the Remaking of World Order* (New York: Simon and Schuster, 1996).

9

The Challenges of China's Peaceful Development

Guoli LIU

This chapter examines the theoretical and policy challenges for China's peaceful development in an uncertain and increasingly complicated international environment. Zheng Bijian, one of China's leading strategists, argues that there are three big challenges facing China today. China's shortage of resources poses the first problem. The second is environmental: pollution, waste, and a low rate of recycling together present a major obstacle to sustainable development. The third is a lack of coordination between economic and social development. [1] China's deep reform, i.e., profound political and socio-economic changes, requires a peaceful international environment while largely peaceful environment has contributed to China's successful economic reform. However, without meaningful political reform, China's growth may not be sustainable. When socio-economic development runs into deep trouble, China might not be able to maintain its peaceful orientation in foreign policy. Thus, the relationship between peaceful development and China's deep reform is dialectic. Success in one will strengthen the other. On the other hand, failure or crisis in one aspect will certainly have serious consequences on the other.

By examining the above-mentioned major challenges, we will also address the following key the following key questions: Is domestic reform driving Chinese peaceful foreign policy, or is the opening and peaceful foreign policy driving the deep reforms inside China? What are the most important domestic political and socioeconomic issues that affect Hu Jintao's foreign policy? What international challenges will shape China's reforms in return? This chapter is divided into three sections. The first section examines the emerging patterns of China's peaceful development. The second section highlights the internal challenges of sustainable development. The last section examines the external challenges of China's peaceful rise.

The Emerging Pattern of China's Peaceful Development

A peaceful international environment is essential for achieving sustained economic development. In a centralised political system, domestic factors including elite politics tend to play a more significant role in foreign policy than in a pluralist system. In the era of Mao Zedong, Mao played a dominant role in China's key foreign policy decisions. One of Mao's key assumptions in the 1960s and early 1970s was that war was inevitable and China must be prepared against wars.[2] When Deng Xiaoping emerged as China's paramount leader in 1978, he made a fundamentally different assumption that world war would not break out in the foreseeable future. Thus, China should stop its "class struggle" and end its active preparation for armed conflict. Instead, the core task should shift to economic development aimed at "the four modernisations" – modernisation of industry, agriculture, national defence, and science and technology. Since then, economic development has been a core objective for the Chinese leadership. As a result, domestic economic consideration has played a greater role in China's foreign policy. In pursuit of economic goals, China moved to improve relations with the broadest possible range of countries. Ideological obstacles to better relations were largely eliminated, and a pragmatic approach helped in general to resolve problems with foreign powers. Economic considerations accelerated the normalisation of diplomatic relations with the United States in 1979 and led to a gradual expansion of the circle of normal relations.[3]

China has truly enjoyed the benefit of dynamic growth in a peaceful environment for more than a quarter century. Chinese GDP and per capita GDP have both experienced continuous high growth rates. In aggregated terms China is an economic power whose rapid growth is felt by the whole world. From 1979 to 2004, China's average annual growth rate was over 9%. According to the World Bank, China saw a 6-fold increase in GDP from 1984 through 2004. China contributed one-third of global economic growth in 2004.[4]

Having suffered a scourge of wars and civil conflicts, the Chinese people know full well that peace is precious and that development is important. Modern history has taught the Chinese a very clear lesson, i.e., China cannot develop well without a peaceful environment. Since Deng Xiaoping's "independent peaceful foreign policy" came into being in the early 1980s, China has followed a peaceful foreign policy. China's most fundamental policy since Deng era has been "reform and opening" aimed at building a strong and prosperous country. As Table 1 indicates, this policy has led to an extraordinary GDP growth rate almost four times higher than the world average rate between 1990 and 2001.

Table 1
China's GDP Growth Rate
in Comparative Perspective, 1990–2001

Country	Average Annual Growth Rate (%)
China	10.0
Singapore	7.8
India	5.9
South Korea	5.7
United States	3.5
France	1.8
Germany	1.5
Japan	1.3
Russia	–3.7
World Average	2.7

Sources: Adapted from World Bank, *World Development Report 2003* (New York: Oxford University Press, 2003), Table 3, pp. 238–239.

China's development requires several key factors. Social and political stability is crucial for development. Development and stability should be achieved through continuous reform of economic and political system. Development can only be achieved by further promoting opening up policy and fully integrating China into the globalisation trend. These factors are interrelated. The international system today contains a lot of uncertainty. Thus, peaceful environment cannot be realised without hard work.[5] Creating and maintaining a peaceful environment requires a consistent grand strategy. It is reasonable to argue that China has followed such a grand strategy of peaceful development. As Avery Goldstein points out: China's emerging grand strategy links political, economic and military means in an effort to advance the PRC's twin goals of security and great-power status.[6]

This is a new grand strategy for the "peaceful rise" (*heping jueqi*) of China. Deng Xiaoping initiated China's "peace and development" line in the 1980s, and since that time China has been one of the biggest beneficiaries of the post-Cold War reduction of inter-state violence.[7] On the other hand, China's deep reform and rapid growth have made a growing contribution to regional and world economic vitality. Whereas the rise and fall of nations has often been accompanied by crisis and instability (as in the cases of Germany and Japan in the first half of the 20th century), China's deep reform is based on the premise of a peaceful rise. It remains to be seen whether this paradigm shift will materialise.

Chinese cultural tradition, featuring "unity in diversity" (*he er butong*) and "priority to peace" (*he wei gui*), goes a long way toward facilitating China's harmonious coexistence and sharing of prosperity with the Asia-Pacific region and the world at large. China's peaceful rise brings to the Asia-Pacific region opportunities for development, conditions for peace, and space for cooperation.[8] In the process of its peaceful rise, according to Zheng Bijian, "China has formed a new security concept that differs from any traditional concept. With mutual trust, mutual benefit, equality, and cooperation as its core notions, our new paradigm firmly abandons the strategic framework in which big powers in the past vied for spheres of influence, engaged in military confrontation, or exported ideologies. Ours is a comprehensive and strategic concept with peaceful existence as its precondition, common interests as its basis, strategic cooperation as its bond, and common development as its objective. History and experience have repeatedly proved that armed forces cannot make peace, and that power politics cannot ensure security. The collective security achieved through cooperation among the Asia-Pacific countries will surely lead to universal, lasting peace and rapid, sustained development."[9]

China's peaceful development requires not only a peaceful international environment but also "deep reform." China's reform since 1989 and especially since 1992 has been quite different from the previous reforms. The most appropriate term to define this recent stage of China's reform is "deep reform." Deep reform has been transforming the nature of Chinese politics, economics, and society. Thus it is important to ask the following questions: What is deep reform? Where does it come from? What is distinctive about reform since 1989? Since 1978, reform has been a key theme of China's economic and political development.[10] After one decade of rapid economic growth, China's reforms encountered serious obstacles. By 1988 Deng Xiaoping himself had realised the urgent need for deeper reform: "China is conducting a deep reform in order to create better conditions for future development. We do not just set our sight on the twentieth century but also think about the new century. The problem is that if we do not move ahead we have to retreat. Only deep and comprehensive reform can guarantee that we can build a well-to-do (*xiaokang*) society by the end the twentieth century and make more progress in the next century."[11] The third plenary session of the 13th Congress of the Communist Party of China (CPC) in September 1988 first proposed "comprehensive deep reform."

Deep reform has multiple international and domestic causes, preeminently including the need to reconcile the contradictions and conflicts of earlier reforms. The 1989 Tiananmen crisis and the collapse of the Soviet bloc forced the Chinese leaders to carefully consider their options. Some conservative officials in Beijing thought all the domestic and international crises were results of too much reform, too soon. But Deng and other reformers drew a totally different conclusion. They saw the collapse of the USSR as a result of not having had effective reforms soon enough. Deng clearly realised that it was a dead end not to reform. Only fundamental and comprehensive reform could save China from a Soviet type train wreck. After the 1989 crisis in Beijing, Deng strongly urged Jiang Zemin and other Chinese leaders to uphold the policy of reform and opening.

As he became increasingly impatient with the slow and cautious pace of reform pursued by his successors in 1990–1991, Deng made the famous southern tour in 1992 to publicly promote further opening and reform. He emphasised that whoever did not firmly support reform and opening should be removed from power. Jiang Zemin, Li Peng, and the rest of the Politburo leadership promptly and publicly agreed. Since then, deep reform has been the phrase that best catches the spirit and substance of political change and economic development in China. The 14th CPC Congress in September 1992 decided to establish a "socialist market economy with Chinese characteristics." The 15th CPC Congress in 1997 set the goal of building "a state based on the rule of law." Building a market economy and a "rule of law" state are two fundamental goals of China's deep reform, which includes the following core features.

First, the most fundamental development is to build a complete market economy instead of a halfway economy between plan and market. Marketisation has become a clear goal and the growth of mixed ownership has been encouraged. Unlike the earlier stage of experimental reform aptly described as "crossing the river by feeling the stones under feet," since 1992 Chinese reformers have set a clear goal of establishing a socialist market economy. In addition to lifting state control and allowing prices to float, the rapid growth of private economy, joint ventures, solely foreign owned enterprises, and reorganisation of state-owned assets have led to a truly "mixed ownership economy." The range of the economic reform has been much broader. Initially, the economic system was reformed incrementally to improve incentives and increase the scope of the market. The new reform has penetrated much more deeply into fiscal, financial, administrative, property rights, and other key aspects of the Chinese economy. Many formerly forbidden rules were broken and many closed areas were opened up. The reformers initiated a financial reform in 1994 in order to increase state capacity. Since then, there has been more centralisation of financial power and a shift from central planning to market regulation. State revenue has increased significantly as a result of the nation-wide collection of the value added tax. The reformers have aimed at more centrally controlled, managed growth and left behind the boom and bust cycles of the 1980s. State capacity has grown as a result of these financial reforms. Such deep reform has allowed China to sustain high growth rates despite the Asian financial crisis in 1997 (true, it also helped that China's currency is not yet directly exchangeable on world markets). Market reform has both positive and negative consequences. On the one hand, reform has led to greater efficiency and higher productivity. On the negative side, incomplete market reform has resulted in widespread corruption and a growing disparity between the rich and the poor.

Second, the open-door policy has progressed to comprehensive opening in the context of globalisation. Having learned the tough lessons of Mao Zedong's self-reliance policy, which went to extremes during the Cultural Revolution (1966–76), and then tasted the first sweet fruits of Deng's opening policy after 1978, Chinese reformers realised that isolationism was a dead end and that comprehensive opening provided the best opportunity for socioeconomic development. After a temporary retrenchment from opening to the outside world in 1989–1991, China began a bold new phase of opening to all countries in the world in 1992. Such dramatic and decisive opening has led to a sharp rise in both foreign trade and direct foreign investment. China's open door policy is not a short a short term tactics but a long term strategy. This strategy is best demonstrated by China's firm commitment to comprehensive opening beginning with the Special Economic Zones in the southern costal areas in the late 1970s and extending to 14 open cities in

1984. The opening was expanded to Shanghai Pudong in early 1990s and then further expanded to inland areas. Such SEZs and open cities have played important roles in promoting foreign trade, opening up markets, and attracting FDI.[12] Foreign trade and foreign investment have played very important roles in China's economic development. China's dynamic and fruitful participation in the world economy is the result of peaceful and relatively stable global trading and financial systems. There is no doubt that China cannot enjoy such sweet fruits of globalisation without the reform and opening policy. The opening policy is dependent on a peaceful international environment. China's open door policy is based on the strategic assumption that there will be no major wars in the foreseeable future. Foreign trade and FDI will both be disrupted or even completely stopped if major armed conflict involving China occurs. The rapidly growing connections between China and the outside world have had a profound impact on all major institutions and aspects of social behaviour. The scope and speed of China's opening to the outside world has accelerated since 1992, leading to China's entry into the World Trade Organisation (WTO) in 2001. Comprehensive opening is reflected in the growing volume of trade, financial transactions, travel, and other exchanges between China and all major regions of the world. China's total imports and exports have increased from US$135.7 billion in 1991 to more than US$1.1 trillion in 2004 and US$1.4 trillion in 2005. China has become the world's third largest foreign trader behind the U.S. and Germany. This is truly extraordinary considering the fact that China ranked 32nd with a small trade volume of $20 billion in 1978. China has also become the largest recipient of direct foreign investment in the world, receiving a total of more than $570 billion. The degree of interdependence between China and the world economy has grown to an unprecedented level. As a consequence, China has gained multiple benefits, chiefly an accelerated economic growth rate. On the other hand, China has also been exposed to the growing pressure and risks of globalisation. The 1997 Asian financial crisis and the 2003 SARS epidemic were two examples of the new challenges confronting the Chinese.

Third, "the rule of law" has been transformed from a governing instrument to a fundamental goal of reform. Chinese reformers have taken the legal system more seriously than ever before. They realised that their legitimacy and governance must have a legal and constitutional foundation. Numerous new laws have been enacted and put into practice. But China still has a long way to go before solidly establishing the rule of law. Although the Constitution has been amended several times, many parts of the 1982 Constitution (written under the context of highly centralised political power and command economy) have become outdated. The next stage of deep reform may require more fundamental constitutional change.

Fourth, meaningful political reforms including political institutionalisation and systemic leadership transition have taken place. Tiananmen destroyed forever the myth that China could engage in economic reform without touching the political system. In reaction to that traumatic event, the leadership not only emphasised a certain amount of recentralisation and popular control but a renewed focus on political reform and improved governance. Indeed, any significant economic reform would be impossible without some political change of the formerly highly centralised Chinese political system. Deng Xiaoping initiated the first round of political change in 1978–1981, and after temporary setbacks in 1986 Zhao Ziyang unleashed new initiatives at the 13th Party Congress in 1987. In the 1990s, political reform has adjusted its direction, now focusing on: (1) relatively smooth leadership transition from the third generation to the fourth generation, (2) institutionalisation of political elite selection from the top to the basic levels, (3) further separation of political and administrative functions of the party-state, (4) gradual expansion of the range of political discourse associated with information revolution, (5) village elections and experiment of self-governance in residential communities, and (6) reformulation of official ideology including the emergence of the "three represents." Thus deep reform has led to a new level of ideological pragmatism and re-legitimisation through development. Productivity and prosperity have become the ultimate criteria for economic and political success. Jiang Zemin formalised this in his contribution to official ideology, the "three represents." This formulation stresses that the CPC's mission is to represent the most advanced productive forces, the most advanced culture, and the fundamental interests of the overwhelming majority of the Chinese people. Though apparently bland and innocuous, this dramatic departure from proletarian revolution and class warfare has allowed the leadership to refocus its tasks on modernisation without institutional breakdown. As a result, Chinese politics today is more institutionalised, more predictable, and more performance oriented. In contrast to deep reform in financial and trading sectors, China's political change, though extensive, has been relatively slow. The contradiction between deep economic reform and slow political reform has become a bottleneck for the next stage of China's reform. And there are some indications that the "fourth generation" leadership will make political reform a higher priority. For instance, fighting against corruption is one of the biggest challenges facing the CPC leadership, threatening to undermine the legitimacy of the government and erode the basis of the ruling party. And Hu Jintao said that in order to resolve the corruption issue, the CPC must "deepen reform to create a new system."[13] This would be a further step in the direction of deep reform.

Deep reform also implies that China will be fully integrated into the international system. Liu Jie systematically studied China's participation in international regimes as an essential part of peaceful rise.[14] International regimes refer to the norms, procedures, and standards of decision making in various issue areas. The regimes have played constructive roles in stabilizing and facilitating international economic interaction, human rights protection, and even peace and security. Participation in international regimes is an indicator of a country's openness. For a long time, China was an "outsider" of international regimes. As China's reform deepens and opening expands, Beijing has adopted much more positive attitudes toward international regimes. China today has joined most international organisations and their related regimes. The current international regimes are dominated by Western countries. The core values, systemic structure, standards of behaviour and decision making procedures are not necessarily consistent with China's strategic goals. Nevertheless, the Chinese leaders have realised that there is no viable alternative than participating in the international regimes. Although China is under the influence and restraint of the current international regimes, it will make necessary reform and adjustment and might have some impact on the evolution of the international regimes. From another perspective, joining international regimes such as following WTO rules will provide powerful incentives for China to deepen its domestic reforms. The following section examines internal challenges of sustainable development.

Internal Challenges of Sustainable Development

China faces multiple internal challenges to its development. It is undisputable that China has enjoyed extraordinary high growth rate over a quarter century. The key question is whether China's strong growth is sustainable. As Zheng Bijian points out, China faces three big challenges. The first is that of natural resources. Currently, China's exploitable oil and natural gas reserves, water resources, and arable land are all well below world average in per capita terms. The second challenge is the environment. Serious pollution, the wasteful use of resources, and low rates of recycling are bottlenecks for sustainable economic development. The third is the lack of coordination between economic and social development. These major challenges, alongside rapid growth, mean that China is facing both a period of development and a period of tough choices.[15]

Energy shortages and especially low energy efficiency have become serious bottlenecks of Chinese growth. In 1990, China net exported 24 million tons of crude oil. Very soon China became an oil importer rather than exporter. The country net imported 80 million tons of crude oil by 2002. In 2003, oil only account for 23% of China's total energy consumption. In the same year, coal accounted for 67% of China's energy consumption. China produced and consumed close to 1.3 billion metric tons of coal in 2003. That is about 1 ton of coal for every Chinese. The heavy reliance on coal has very serious environmental and health consequences. Air pollution alone, primarily from coal burning, is responsible for over 300,000 premature deaths each year. Chinese electricity consumption jumped from 623 billion kwh in 1990 to 1633 billion kwh in 2002. When more and more manufacturing facilities are moving to China, energy consumption is also increasing rapidly. China has become the second largest consumer of energy resources in the world only behind the United States. In 2004, each U.S. citizen consumed about 25 barrels of oil while each Chinese citizen used about 1 and a half barrel of oil. It is not hard to imagine what kind of a global oil crisis will occur if the Chinese per capita oil consumption getting closer to the U.S. level. Obviously, China cannot and should not blindly follow the U.S. pattern of heavy consumption of oil. China must find a new pattern of growth that relies on less energy. However, China's energy efficiency is far behind that of the United States and even further behind that of Japan. China has tremendous troubles with extensive growth. It is difficult but absolutely necessary to make a transition to intensive growth. According to the China's top statistician Li Deshui, China only produced 4.4% of the world's total GDP in 2004, yet the crude oil it devoured accounted for 7.4% of the world's total; coal, 31%; iron ore, 30%; rolled steel, 27%; and cement, 40%.[16]

A closely related issue is ecological and environmental challenge. Environmental pollution in China is very serious. Ecological situation is deteriorating. Enormous energy consumption with low returns has become a severe problem. Ecological and environmental challenge has become a serious bottleneck for Chinese sustainable economic development.[17] China has witnessed numerous environmental disasters including flooding, desertification, water scarcity, and dwindling forest resources. The economic costs of environmental degradation and pollution are dramatic. Environmental degradation and pollution constrain economic growth, contribute to large-scale migration, harm public health, and engender social unrest. Moreover, there is the potential for the environment to serve as a locus for broader political discontent and further political reforms.[18]

With the structural transition of the Chinese economy and especially the reform of state-owned enterprises, millions of workers have been laid off. China has been experiencing a paradoxical phenomenon: on the one hand there is a growing demand of skilled workers, on the other hand there are increasing number of "surplus labors." At the same time, labour migration is natural. But China is experiencing the largest movement of rural labour in history. In recent years, Chinese cities have absorbed more than 100 million rural workers, and they are expected to see an influx of another 250 to 300 million in the next two or three decades. Under the circumstances, it's hardly surprising that China's effort to establish a new social safety net has fallen short, especially given its socialist roots. The lack of social safety net for large sectors of the population has become a source of social instability.

At a time of rapid growth and growing prosperity, the issues of income disparity become more conspicuous. One of the world's most egalitarian societies in the 1970s, China in the 1980s and 1990s became one of the more unequal countries among developing countries. The Gini coefficient of inequality in household income rose by 7 percentage points (18%) between 1988 and 1995. Inequality of rural household per capita income rose an estimated 23% over the same seven years; urban inequality increased even faster – by 42%. [19] Data on household consumption clearly demonstrates the growing disparity of income between urban and rural households and severe disparity among regions. For instance, the consumption gap between rural households and urban households jumped from 227 yuan in 1978 to 5365 yuan in 2000 and 6110 yuan in 2003. The household consumption gap between the wealthiest cities (Beijing 10584 yuan, Shanghai 15866 yuan) and the poorest provinces (Guizhou 1770 yuan, Gansu 2171 yuan) are extraordinarily large. [20] Such gap far exceeds the disparity between the advanced cities and less developed states in the United States. Chinese leaders have realised the growing regional disparity and proposed a grand plan to develop the big West. There has been a lot of talk but not enough actions to adequately address the growing regional disparity. For many years, the reforms promoted the idea of "getting rich is glorious" and encouraged some people and some regions to become rich first. Such policies naturally favored the people with better education and greater skills. The opening policy especially favoured the costal areas with good infrastructure and strong entrepreneurial tradition.

As new leaders with working background in the poor provinces of Gansu, Guizhou and Tibet, Hu Jintao and Wen Jiabao formulated a new direction in China's development path away from blind pursuit of economic growth toward "scientific development," a variation on the idea of sustainable development. This new model stresses improving people's livelihood and protecting the environment. It remains to be seen whether the path will depart substantially from an economic development program that is based fundamentally on inequality and tends to further it.[21] "The most pressing challenges in the years to come may spring directly from the rising expectations created by the regime's own professions of belief in a more compassionate development model."[22] China needs sustained rapid growth of the economy, but it also needs speed up social development; it wants to maintain dynamic growth trend in East China, it also wants to achieve common development of the Eastern, Central, and Western China. Reformers must confront the dilemmas between equity and dynamic growth, between deepening of reform and maintaining social stability.

An emerging problem is the health crisis. A recent survey by Chinese Academy of Social Sciences indicates that 65% of the people in China do not have health insurance. About one quarter of the people surveyed do not seek medical treatment because of unaffordable health care costs.[23]

Zheng Bijian proposed three strategies to deal with the above challenges. The first grand strategy refers to a new pattern of industrialisation. China's development cannot rely on old pattern of industrialisation of high input, high energy consumption, and heavy pollution. Instead, China should take a new path of industrialisation with more high technology, higher economic efficiency, low resource consumption, less environmental pollution, and full utilisation of human resources advantages. The second grand strategy is to actively participate in economic globalisation by transcending the path of modern latecomers of great powers and the Cold War mentality. China will not repeat the German road of World War I, and the German and Japanese road of World War II. Both Germany and Japan resorted to seeking world hegemony via violent struggle over resources. China will also not repeat the old path of Cold War confrontation and struggle for hegemony after World War II. The third grand strategy is to build a socialist harmonious society by transcending the outdated model of social governance. In sum, China's strategy is aimed at peace and harmony, i.e., internal harmony and external peace.[24]

This peaceful strategy has affected Beijing's policy of "one country, two systems," and peaceful unification with Taiwan. Beijing's focus has been on peaceful means. In recent years, cross Taiwan Strait economic relations have expanded very drastically. Economic interdependence between Taiwan and the mainland has become a fact of life. Leaders of the Taiwan opposition parties including the Nationalist Party, People First Party, and the New Party have conducted historic visits to the mainland and held fruitful talks with the top CPC leaders in 2005. However, serious differences remain between the CPC and the ruling Democratic Progressive Party (DPP). The issue of Taiwan continues to be potentially explosive and very dangerous. If Taiwan declares independence, Chinese leaders cannot afford to stand idle. Pro-independence forces in Taiwan constitute serious threat to peace and stability in the Taiwan Strait. If Beijing has to respond with military means to Taiwan independence, the peaceful environment in the Taiwan Straits and East Asia will be seriously affected.

China's peaceful development requires a deep reform that will provide both institutional and technological innovations. In more than 20 years, China has made enormous progress and built a firm foundation for the development of a great power in the future. At the same time, China has accumulated a large number of domestic problems while going through a series of profound changes. As we discussed above, many urgent problems needed to be solved in Chinas. These problems include rising unemployment, rampant official corruption, weak legal system, growing regional disparity, growing gap between the rich and the poor, unequal access to education, population problems, energy bottlenecks, and severe environmental problems. If the critical problems cannot be solved or alleviated effectively, they may cause crisis and lead to calamitous impact on political and social stability. In recent times, Chinese citizens often put corruption, bureaucratism, increase in unemployment and laid-off workers, and widening gap between the rich and the poor as the four main factors affecting social stability in China.

The tough problems that China is confronting today can only be resolved through the deepening of reform. The achievements of reform and opening-up have alleviated social contradictions, the psychology of social members is gradually tend to be moderate. Radical liberals and dogmatic conservatives have both been marginalised in the 1990s. In the political centre with the upper level political leaders and technocrats of China, political attitude has moved toward the middle. There are no strong ideology conflicts, unlike in the mid- and late-1980s when the opinions of leaders varied sharply which led to the spilt of the senior leaders. The young students who have played radical role in the history have been to some extent depoliticised in the market environment. Widespread corruption has in fact weakened the Chinese government's managerial ability, but the Chinese political system still retains certain mobilisation power. China may prevent the social crisis if it properly manages politics, implements system innovation, overcomes corruption and polarisation, and distributes the fruits of the economic growth more rationally among all social members. If the reformers improve the supervising system effectively, via the democratic construction at the basic level, pursue inner-party power check and balance mechanism, China will move in the direction of democratisation with Chinese characteristics.[25] "China's political future depends on conducting reform in development, and seeking stability through change."[26] Brantly Womack provides an insightful analysis of the theoretical and practical issues in regard with the "party-state democracy." It is important to examine the transition from a revolutionary party to a "governing party" and "democracy" under the new leadership.[27]

In China today, fundamental political change could start from the grassroots creeping democratisation and the intra-party democracy and move to a more open and free election at higher levels of the government while allowing Chinese government to maintain the stability for economic development. There will be no real "check and balance" without democracy. Without check and balance, there will be no real solution to corruption, and there will be no real peace and stability in China in the long term. Suppression works temporarily, but not in a long-term, and the cost is too high and it undermines the credibility and legitimacy of the government. That is why "deep reform" is necessary. The "deep reform" is not simply "rectification of party discipline," "mass line," "people-oriented" etc. propaganda, but real political reform, which is not simply "administrative" in nature, but "political" in nature – transforming the relationship between the party and the government, between the party leaders and the rank-file members, and between the government and the citizens. Such fundamental political reform will continue to affect the international environment of China. As China becomes more democratic and provides better protection of human rights, it will be more conducive for the Chinese leadership to achieve its strategic goals (such as high tech imports and transfer, a long-term "strategic relationship" with the US and the West, and energy supplies) and create a favourable international environment for China's "peaceful development." The above analysis indicates that domestic reform and external environment are dialectic and interrelated with each other. Although the U.S. and EU may recognise that China has no intention to change the existing world order, but, in order for them to have trust in China and to incorporate China into the international system without containing her, they will have to pay attention to the domestic political reform and how China plays the role in the system – to what extent China can be cooperative with them. Therefore, democratic reform is essential both for maintaining a long-term domestic stability and for maintaining a peaceful international environment that would allow China to achieve its foreign policy strategic goals.[28]

External Challenges to China's Peaceful Rise

In the post-Cold War era and especially since the mid-1990s, the rise of China has become a very controversial topic in international studies. With the world's fastest economic growth in the last two decades, rising China has sired many debates in the world.[29] According to Joseph S. Nye, the "rise of China" is a misnomer: "re-emergence" is more accurate.[30] Inside China, both "rise" (*jueqi*) and "national rejuvenation" (*minzu fuxing*) have been hotly discussed.[31]

"China's peaceful rise" is a relatively new concept in Chinese public discourse. On 3 November 2003, Zheng Bijian, the former vice president of the CPC Central Party School and now Chair of the China Reform Forum, addressed a plenary session of the Bo'ao Forum for Asia. In his speech, titled "A New Path for China's Peaceful Rise and the Future of Asia," Zheng introduced the concept of China's "peaceful rise" (*heping jueqi*): "In the 25 years since the inception of its reform and opening up, China has blazed a new strategic path that only suites its national conditions but also conforms to the tide of the times. This new strategic path is China's peaceful rise through independently building socialism with Chinese characteristics, while participating in rather than detaching from economic globalisation."[32]

Zheng insisted that although China would rely mainly on its own strength, it needed a peaceful international environment to accomplish the task of lifting its enormous population out of a condition of underdevelopment. He also pledged that China would rise to the status of a great power without destabilizing the international order or oppressing its neighbours: "The rise of a major power often results in drastic change in international configuration and world order, even triggers a world war. An important reason behind this is that these major powers followed a path of aggressive war and external expansion. Such a path is doomed to failure. It today's world, how can we follow such a totally erroneous path that is injurious to all, China included? China's only choice is to strive for rise, more importantly strive for a peaceful rise."[33]

Premier Wen Jiabao took the initiative to push the concept of peaceful rise further toward a policy formulation when he used the term in a speech at Harvard University on 10 December 2003.

> There are many challenges to China's peaceful rise. It is neither proper nor possible for us to rely on foreign countries for development. . . . While opening still wider to the outside world, we must more fully and more consciously depend on our own structural innovation, on constantly expanding the domestic market, on converting the huge savings of the citizens into investment, and on improving the quality of the population and scientific and technological progress to solve the problems of resources and the environment. Here lies the essence of China's road of peaceful rise and development.[34]

China has followed a good neighbour policy and built friendly relations with almost all of its neighbours. The only major neighbouring country that has serious political differences with China is Japan. Militarism and right-wing political extremism are growing in Japan. China is surrounded by a number of countries with troubled bilateral or multilateral relations. For instance, India and Pakistan have long been in territorial and religious disputes. The fact that both India and Pakistan are armed with nuclear weapons now makes the situation more intense. North Korea has been developing a nuclear programme. It's difficult to tell whether the six-party talk can achieve positive result in the near future. A nuclear North Korea will seriously disrupt the regional security order and have negative consequences for Beijing's peaceful foreign policy. China and Russia are enjoying their best relations in decades. However, there is no certainty that Sino-Russo relations will always remain trouble free. In fact, both sides have some deeply rooted mistrust and mutual suspicion. Russia is also concerned of China's growing emigrants to the Russian Far East. Nevertheless, it seems that common interests between Russia and China exceed their differences. China and Russia will conduct a joint military exercise in 2005. The two countries share some strategic concerns especially on the common fight against terrorism, Islamic fundamentalism, and separationism in Chechnya and Taiwan.

The concept of a peaceful rise does not depend on China alone. It also demands that the rest of the world help China create an international environment where this sort of rise can take place. Internationally, China faces a host of established powers, most notably the United States, with their own economic and political concerns.

The most important bilateral relationship for China is Sino-American relations. A healthy relationship with the United States is critical for creating a favourable international environment for reform and opening, for defending China's national security, and for achieving China's modernisation with assistance of U.S. capital, technology, and management experience.

Sino-American relations has entered a new period of stability due to the following factors. First, U.S. strategy of anti-terrorism has broadened the foundation of Sino-American cooperation. In the near future, the U.S. is not likely to treat China as a main competitor. Second, both China and United States are seriously concerned of the proliferation of weapons of mass destruction. Both sides do not want to see nuclear weapons in Korean peninsula. Beijing has played a critical role in making the six party talk about North Korea's nuclear issue. Third, both Beijing and Washington have realised the sensitivity of the Taiwan issue. The Bush administration has reemphasised the One China policy. Beijing has demonstrated greater determination against Taiwan independence on the one hand and greater flexibility in exploring peaceful means to solve the Taiwan issue on the other hand. Fourth, rapid development of trade relations between China and the United States has created a broad and strong economic foundation for the bilateral relations. At the same time, a lot of tensions have intensified because of the growing frictions of trade deficits, and Chinese proposed purchase of sensitive companies such as UNOCOL. Managing Sino-American relations is a priority of Chinese diplomacy. In the view of Gong Li, a professor at the CPC Central Party School, "the fundamental interests of China in the 21st century include peaceful rise, modernisation, and national unification. None of these strategic issues can be resolved by getting around (*raokai*) the Untied States."[35] If Gong's view is right, success of failure in managing Sino-American relations might affect the fate of China's development and peaceful rise. A similar argument can be made that the United States cannot resolve many important regional especially East Asian and global issues without actively engaging China.

Can the new stability in Sino-American relations last? According David Shambaugh's analysis, neither the U.S. or China seeks a deterioration of relations. Indeed, both countries are otherwise preoccupied. The United States is committed to the war against terrorism and improving the domestic economy. China faces the tough challenges of deep reform and is in the early stages of a prolonged and wrenching process of implementing the terms of its accession to the World Trade Organisation. Shambaugh concludes: "If wisely managed by both sides – and if the key sensitivities of each are respected rather than provoked – the new stability in Sino-American relations may endure."[36] But Shambaugh's optimistic vision is rejected by the "offensive realist" John J. Mearsheimer, who believes that the United States will not tolerate the rise of China as the dominant power in Asia.[37]

Zbigniew Brzezinski provided an insightful analysis of the connections between peace and China's development. Chinese leaders fully understand that a confrontational foreign policy could disrupt that growth, harm hundreds of millions of Chinese, and threaten the CPC's hold on power. China's leadership appears rational, calculating, and conscious not only of China's rise but also of its continued weakness. "Even beyond the realm of strategic warfare, a country must have the capacity to attain its political objectives before it will engage in limited war. It is hard to envisage how China could promote its objectives when it is acutely vulnerable to a blockade and isolation enforced by the United States. In a conflict, Chinese maritime trade would stop entirely. The flow of oil would cease, and the Chinese economy would be paralyzed."[38] Fundamentally speaking, a peaceful diplomacy is the only correct choice for China in the era of globalisation.

The strategy of peaceful development is not only a logical extension of domestic reform, but also a result of historical learning. Wang Jisi, Dean of the School of International Studies at Peking University, examined the historical lessons of Soviet-American struggle for hegemony and concluded that China must not engage in a new Cold War with the United States.[39] Unlike the former Soviet Union, China has neither desire nor ability to contend for hegemony with the United States. The U.S. also does not treat China as a main strategic threat. The Soviet Union followed the command economy. China has completely abandoned the command economy and moved toward a market economy. Having tasted the sweet fruits of marketisation and globalisation, there is no reason for China to return to the command economy. This is a powerful reason that China will not be a Soviet type competitor against the United States. The former Soviet Union committed a fatal mistake by engaging in an extraordinarily costly arms race against the United States. Although Soviet GDP was only about half of that of the U.S., Soviet military spending of $175 billion actually exceeded U.S. military spending of $115 in 1980. Extremely high level of military spending and a stagnant economy contributed to Soviet decline and final collapse. Wang's key conclusions are: First, Chinese leaders have a sober understanding of the China's condition. They define China as an "economically and culturally backward developing country." The gap between the Chinese economy and U.S. economy today is greater than that between the Soviet Union and the U.S. during the Cold War. Militarily, in terms of defense spending, strategic nuclear missile, Naval and Air forces, etc, the U.S. currently enjoys absolute advantage. China has a realistic goal of becoming a country with middle level per capita income by the mid 21st century. This formed a sharp contrast with the former Soviet Union that claimed to have achieved "developed socialism" and aimed at overtaking the U.S. both economically and militarily. Second, China has a clear understanding of economic globalisation and international strategic balance. As a result, it actively participates in globalisation and advocates "win-win" in international cooperation and competition. China has jointed almost all major international organisations and regimes. Third, while the fundamental goal of Soviet foreign policy was to "bury world capitalism," Chinese foreign policy is aimed at creating a favourable international environment for development, defending territorial sovereignty, and facilitating national unification. Thus, China truly appreciates the strategic opportunity for peace and development. It does not wish to lead any international effort against any great power. China is against U.S. hegemonism and unilateralism. Unlike the former Soviet Union, however, China does not base its foreign policy on ideology, nor does it build bloc or sphere of influence, form exclusive trading bloc, or form any military alliance. Furthermore, China pays special attention to strategic dialogue, communication and mutual understanding with the United States and other great powers. In the early 1990s, Chinese leaders proposed to U.S. leaders to use "increase mutual trust, reduce troubles, develop cooperation, and avoid confrontation" as principles for managing Sino-American relations. In the post-Cold War era, Sino-American relations have experienced several twists and turns. Fortunately, the two sides have been able to prevent the crises from getting out of control because leaders on both sides have put common interests above their differences. Since the end of the Cold War, China's national strength has increased significant. At the same time, the position of the U.S. as the only superpower is not weakened but strengthened in some aspects. Such development indicates that China and the U.S. not only can enjoy win-win in economic relations, but also have win-win situation in global security and political relations rather than engaging in "zero-sum game."[40]

Despite the recent high speed of economic growth," China's economy in 2004 was just one-seventh the size of the U.S. economy, and one-third the size of Japan's. In per capita terms, China is still a low-income developing country, ranking below one-hundredth in the world. China's development is a long-term project.

Paul Kennedy's careful examination of long-term historical trends suggests that the rise and fall of great powers has been a significant part of world history.[41] If China seizes the unique historic opportunity, it might achieve the ambitious goal of "peaceful rising." The ultimate success of this grand strategy of peaceful development demands not only persistent hard work of many generations of Chinese people but also a true spirit of cooperation of other great powers. It remains to be seen whether Chinese leaders can maintain a delicate balance between rapid domestic growth and a peaceful foreign policy. As U.S. Deputy Secretary of State Robert Zoellick recently points out, "we now need to encourage China to become a responsible stakeholder in the international system. As a responsible stakeholder, China would be more than just a member – it would work with us to sustain the international system that has enabled its success."[42] As China continues its rapid development, its stakes in world will not doubt rise accordingly. Whether they can successfully meet the challenges of peaceful development will affect not only the wellbeing of the Chinese people but also the whole global community.

Notes and References

1. Zheng Bijian, "China's `Peaceful Rise' to Great Power Status," *Foreign Affairs* (September/October 2005): 18–24.

2. One of the most widely publicised slogans during the Cultural Revolution was Mao's saying of "*Beizhan, beihuang, wei renmin*" (Be prepared against war, be prepared against natural disaster, and do everything for the people). In contrast, one of Deng Xiaoping's most famous statements is "taking economic development as the central task."

3. See Barry Naughton, "The Foreign Policy Implications of China's Economic Development Strategy," in *Chinese Foreign Policy: Theory and Practice*, edited by Thomas W. Robinson and David Shambaugh (New York: Oxford University Press, 1995), pp. 47–69.

4. See http://web.worldbank.org/WBSITE/EXTERNAL/COUNTRIES/EAST ASIAPACIFICEXT/CHINAEXTN/0,,contentMDK:20680895~menuPK:3 18976~pagePK:1497618~piPK:217854~theSitePK:318950,00.html#Facts (Accessed on December 7, 2005). All the data in this chapter come from *China Statistical Yearbook 2004* (Beijing: China Statistics Press, 2004) unless otherwise noted.

5. Liu Jianfei, "Heping waijiao shi Zhongguo de changqi guoce," (Peace Diplomacy is China's Longterm National Policy), in *Zhongguo Heping Jueqi Xindaolu* (*New Path of China's Peaceful Rise*), Institute of International Strategic Studies, CCP Central Party School (Beijing: CPC Central Party School Press, 2004), pp. 102–117.

6. Avery Goldstein, "An Emerging China's Emerging Grand Strategy: A Neo-Bismarckian Turn?" in *International Relations Theory and the Asia-Pacific*, edited by G. John Ikenberry and Michael Mastanduno (New York: Columbia University Press, 2003), p. 83.

7. For various perspectives on this issue, see Guoli Liu ed., *Chinese Foreign Policy in Transition* (New York: Aldine de Gruyter, 2004).

8. Zheng Bijian, "China's Peaceful Rise and Opportunity for the Asia-Pacific Region," Roundtable Meeting between the Bo'ao Forum for Asia and the China Reform Forum (April 18, 2004). http://www.brook.edu/ dybdocroot/FP/events/20050616bijianlunch.pdf#search=`china's%20peac eful%rise'.

9. Zheng Bijian, "China's Peaceful Rise and Opportunity for the Asia-Pacific Region," Roundtable Meeting between the Bo'ao Forum for Asia and the China Reform Forum (18 April 2004). http://www.brook.edu/ dybdocroot/FP/events/20050616bijianlunch.pdf#search="china's%20peac eful%rise".

10. Lowell Dittmer, *China under Reform* (Boulder, CO: Westview Press, 1994).

11. Deng Xiaoping, *Deng Xiaoping wenxuan*, vol. III (*Selected Works of Deng Xiaoping, Vol. III*), (Beijing: Renmin chubanshe, 1993), p. 268.

12. See Sujian Guo and Han Gyu Lheem "Political Economy of FDI and Economic Growth in China: A Longitudinal Test at Provincial Level," *Journal of Chinese Political Science*, vol. 9, no. 1, (2004), pp. 43–62.

13. *Remin Ribao*, January 12, 2005, 1.

14. Liu Jie, *Jizhihua Shengcun: Zhongguo heping jueqi de zhanlue juece* (Living under Regimes: The Strategic Choice in the Course of China's Peaceful Rise), (Beijing: Shishi chubashe, 2004).

15. Zheng Bijian, "China's Development and Her New Path to a Peaceful Rise," Villa d'Este Forum (September 2004). http://www.brook.edu/ dybdocroot/FP/events/20050616bijianlunch.pdf #search="china's%20peaceful%rise".

16. See http://news.xinhuanet.com/english/2005–12/20/content_3947262.htm (Viewed on 20 December 2005).

17. Elizabeth C. Economy, *The River Runs Black* (Ithca: Cornell University Press, 2004). One city after the next is offloading its polluting industries outside its city limits, and polluting industries themselves are seeking poorer areas. Heavy air pollution contributes to respiratory illnesses that kill up to 300,000 people a year. "Over the past 20 years in China, there has been a single-minded focus on economic growth with the belief that economic growth can solve all problems," said Pan Yue, the outspoken deputy director of China's State Environmental Protection Administration. "But this has left environmental protection badly behind." Quoted in Jim Yardley's "Rivers Run Black, and Chinese Die of Cancer," *New York Times*, September 12, 2004, pp. A1, 8.

18. Elizabeth Economy, "China's Environmental Challenge," *Current History* (September 2005), 278–283.

19. Carl Riskin, Zhao Renwei, and Li Shi eds., *China's Retreat from Equality: Income Distribution and Economic Transition* (Armonk: M. E. Sharpe, 2001), p.3.

20. *China Statistical Yearbook 2004*. Beijing: China Statistics Press, 2004.

21. Mary E. Gallagher, "China in 2004: Stability above All," *Asian Survey 45*: 1 (2005), p. 28.

22. Gallagher, "China in 2004: Stability above All," p. 32.

23. See http://zaobao.com.sg/special/realtime/2005/12/051221_33.html (Viewed on 21 December 2005).

24. Zheng Bijian, "Using `Three Strategies' to Meet `Three Challenges'," *Renmin Ribao*, 22 June 2005, p. 1.

25. For more in depth analysis along this line of thinking, see Ye Zicheng, *Zhongguo da Zhanlue: Zhongguo chengwei shijie daguo de zhuyao weiti ji zhanlue xuanze* (*China's Grand Strategy: Key Issues and Strategic Choices in China's Development as a World Power*) (Beijing: China Social Science Press, 2003).

26. Xiao Gongqin, "China is not likely to have political turmoil," *Strategy and Management*, 2003, no. 6.

27. Brantly Womack, "Democracy and the Governing Party: A Theoretical Perspective," *Journal of Chinese Political Science*, vol. 10, no. 1, (2004), pp. 23–42.

28. Sujian Guo contributed to this critical argument.

29. For contending views on the rise of China, see Samuel S. Kim, "China's Path to Great Power Status in the Globalization Era," *Asian Perspective*, 27: 1 (2003): 35–75; Stuart Harris and Gary Klintworth, eds., *China as a*

Great Power: Myths, Realities and Challenges in the Asia-Pacific Region (New York: St. Martin's Press, 1995); Avery Goldstein, "Great Expectations: Interpreting China's Arrival," *International Security* 22: 3 (Winter 1997–98): 36–73; Michael Brown et al., eds., *The Rise of China* (Cambridge, MA: MIT Press, 2000); and Gordon G. Chang, *The Coming Collapse of China* (New York: Random House, 2001). It is interesting that *Newsweek*, *U.S. New & World Report,* and *Time* had cover stories and special reports respectively on "China's Century," "China Challenge," and "China's New Revolution" in May and June 2005. For a Chinese view, see Peng Peng ed., *Heping Jueqi lun* (*Peaceful Rising Theory: The Path of China Becoming a Great Power*), (Guangzhou: Guangdong renmin chubanshe, 2005).

30. Joseph S. Nye, "China's Re-emergence and the Future of the Asia-Pacific," *Survival* 39 (1997–1998): 65–79. Historian Jonathan Spence also prefers to call China's recent development as "reemergence." In a series of essays published in *Foreign Policy* (Jan-Feb 2005, pp. 44–58), Jonathan Spence, Martin Wolf, Minxin Pei, Zbigniew Brezezinski, and John J. Mearsheimer discuss how China is changing the world. They debate whether China is more interested in economic development than war, whether China can rise peacefully, and whether China needs to be "contained."

31. For instance, both Jiang Zemin and Hu Jintao frequently talk about *zhonghua minzu de weida fuxing* (great rejuvenation of the Chinese nation). The theme of the 2005 annual meeting of the Chinese Association of Diplomacy is "China's Peaceful Rise." The meeting is held on 13–14 August 2005 in Kunming, China.

32. Zheng Bijian, "A New Path for China's Peaceful Rise and the Future of Asia," 3 November 2003, http://hisotry.boaoforum.org/English/E2003nh/dhwj/t20031103_184101.btk.

33. *Ibid.* Quoted in Robert L. Suettinger, "The rise and descent of 'peaceful rise'," *Chinese Leadership Monitor,* no. 12 (2004).

34. "Turn Your Eyes to China," full text of Premier Wen's December 10, 2003, speech at Harvard University, *People's Daily* online, December 12, 2003.

35. Gong Li, "Zhongguo de duimei zhengce yu Zhonguo heping jueqi xindaolu," (China's Policy toward the United States and China's New Path of Peaceful Rise), in *Zhongguo Heping Jueqi Xindaolu* (*New Path of China's Peaceful Rise*), Institute of International Strategic Studies, CPC Central Party School (Beijing: CPC Central Party School Press, 2004), p. 252. See also Yasheng Huang, "Sino-U.S. Relations: The Economic Dimensions," in *In the Eyes of the Dragon: China Views the World*, edited by Yong Deng and Fei-Ling Wang (Lanham, MD: Rowman & Littlefield Publishers, 1999), pp. 159–181.

36. David Shambaugh, "Sino-American Relations since September 11," *Current History* (September 2002): 243–249.

37. This is the conclusion of Mearsheimer's book, *The Tragedy of Great Power Politics* (NewYork: Norton, 2001), pp. 401–402. Mearsheimer argues that the United States does not tolerate peer competitors. As it is demonstrated in the 20th century, it is determined to remain the world's only regional hegemon. Therefore, the United States will seek to contain China and ultimately weaken it to the point where it is no longer capable of dominating Asia.

38. Zbigniew Brzezinski, "Make Money, Not War," in Suzanne Ogden (ed.), *Global Studies: China*. Eleventh edition (Guilford, CT: McGraw-Hill/Dushkin, 2006), pp. 181–182.

39. Wang Jisi, "Sumei zhengba de lishi jiaoxun he Zhongguo de jueqi" (Historic Lessons of Soviet-U.S. Contending for Hegemony and the Path of China's Rise), in *Zhongguo Heping Jueqi Xindaolu* (*New Path of China's Peaceful Rise*), Institute of International Strategic Studies, CPC Central Party School (Beijing: CPC Central Party School Press, 2004), pp. 5–25.

40. *Ibid*. For an insightful analysis on U.S.-China relation, see Wang Jisi, "China's Search for Stability With America," *Foreign Affairs* (September/October 2005): 39–48.

41. Paul Kennedy, *The Rise and Fall of Great Powers* (New York: Vintage Books, 1987).

42. See Robert B. Zoellick's remarks to National Committee on U.S.-China Relations New York City, 21 September 2005, http://www.state.gov/s/d/rem/53682.htm (Viewed on 20 January 2006).

10

The PLA's Missile Force and Its Anti-NMD Initiatives

YOU Ji

The end of the Cold War resulted in a complex global nuclear situation that poses an increased challenge to China's strategic security. Around its territories a number of new nuclear powers have emerged: North Korea, India, Pakistan and Japan, which may be on the edge of nuclearisation. Most importantly, the U.S. *Nuclear Posture Review* promulgated in 2002 specifically identified the PRC as a potential target for a pre-emptive nuclear strike. In response China has stepped up its nuclear weapons programmes. In the last few years new generation nuclear missiles have been introduced to the Strategic Missile Force (SMF) of the People's Liberation Army (PLA). China has also achieved breakthroughs in the associated technologies such as satellite-based control and guidance systems for its intercontinental missiles. It seems that China has moved one step closer to real combat operations.[1] In PLA terminology, this means its nuclear units have set up full protocols to strike their designated targets, immediately after they receive orders from the Central Military Commission of the Party (CMC). In addition, the PLA Navy (PLAN) will acquired nine new prototype nuclear attack submarines, the 093, which are capable of firing nuclear tipped long-range cruise missiles. The 094 strategic nuclear submarines are also undergoing sea trials which have reached the final stages of development. With three multiple war heads in each of the 16 intercontinental ballistic missiles on board, China may soon truly

273

have a triad capability.[2] This sharpening of the nuclear sword is reflected by the Chinese efforts in transforming its nuclear deterrence from a "hiding force" to a "fighting force".

Another factor driving China's slow but steady nuclear modernisation is external, namely, the development of the U.S. missile defence system, either in the form of the National Missile Defence (NMD) or in the form of the Theatre Missile Defence (TMD). Although the Chinese are concerned about the U.S. deployment of anti-missile capabilities in recent years, their worry is more political and diplomatic at the moment due to the tremendous difficulties inherent in the research and development (R&D) of both the NMD and TMD systems. They are fearful that that missile defence systems may provide a new mechanism for the U.S. to forge closer military ties and develop alliances with regional countries as a way of deterring China. This is especially true if Taiwan is incorporated into the system. Moreover, because the PLA believes that technological progress may one day be such as to make the TMD work effectively, it sees the modernisation of its nuclear capability as a race against time. The TMD plans have generated a higher level of urgency for the PLA to achieve better readiness for action, develop new nuclear combat guidelines, deploy more launching units, and quicken the pace for deployment.

The Evolving Nuclear Strategy

The bulk of Chinese nuclear force is in the Strategic Missile Force (SMF), the smallest service in the PLA, with only 4.5% of its total manpower, and an allocation of about 5% of the country's defence budget.[3] Yet it assumes a disproportionate share of the burden of military deterrence through its capability to launch a second strike, nuclear or conventional, against the major powers. For a long time the Chinese nuclear strategy was based on the concept of *minimum deterrence*. It is defensive in nature and emphasises retaliation rather than pre-emption. The Chinese notion of deterrence is the belief that possessing a credible retaliatory capability will convince the enemy not to wage a war against China. The strategy is predicated upon China's ability to demonstrate that it can fight and not lose a nuclear war, and the high cost would convince the initiator that a nuclear exchange would be fruitless. Here the definition of victory is typical of the Chinese, as remarked by Major General Peng Guangqian, "In a nuclear war even if the U.S. could destroy us 100 times we would be victorious if we could destroy it once".[4]

From Minimum Deterrence to Limited Deterrence

Nuclear deterrence is a part of China's overall defence posture, which consists of three tiers of forces – (1) passive civil defence, in keeping with the Clausewitizian notion that the social and political dimensions of war must be coordinated; (2) active defence to help minimise the potential damage; and (3) offensive forces able to take the war to the enemy.[5] China maintains only a minimum nuclear arsenal due to financial constraints, shortage of key materials and technological inadequacies. The posture is closely linked to China's no-first use policy, which was formulated in the 1960s under the understanding that an insufficient nuclear capability could invite a surgical strike by more advanced nuclear powers rather than assuring the Chinese of a desirable level of national security.

To the current PLA commanders, minimum deterrence is an awkward nuclear strategy: it is too defensive, and basically only a diplomatic statement. It is awkward also because it is not applicable to any foreseeable scenarios of a nuclear or conventional war. Considering China's strong conventional forces vis-à-vis her Asian neighbours, it is unnecessary to employ nuclear deterrence. The political price would be too high. Neither is this kind of deterrence effective enough against the superpower, given its overwhelming nuclear superiority. What then, is the use of the PLA nuclear force, which receives great resources? This doctrine of minimum deterrence has fatal flaws but it is an unavoidable transitional guideline for deterring an all-out war. When the strategy was first formulated, the main goal of Chinese nuclear weapons was to deter a massive land invasion inside its own territories, the most acute security threat against which the PLA had no other effective means to deal with.[6] In essence it is a strategy to "buy-time". Only when the enemy was deterred from invading China, would the PLA develop more nuclear weapons that could be used against the targets of the adversaries in their home land. By then the level of deterrence could be upgraded and the nature of deterrence changed.

As the demise of the USSR removed the last potential of a large land invasion of China, the concept of minimum deterrence has become ill-fitted to the PLA's nuclear strategy. At the same time the SMF has made great strides in improving both the quality and the quantity of its nuclear forces. The numbers of missiles have increased and their survivability, strike accuracy and mobility have also improved. The quantitative and qualitative improvements have allowed the PLA to contemplate a more offensive war-fighting doctrine as a guide for its transformation. As a result, the SMF has gradually focused on external targets for a second strike. More importantly, the retaliatory principle has also been gradually revised from that of a counter-value to one of counter-force, in tandem with Chinese technological achievements. In a way, the process of Chinese nuclear modernisation is one that is driven by technological progress rather than by a doctrinal concept. Certainly this is in line with the general trend of nuclear modernisation of any other country, that is, with improvements in the range and accuracy of missiles, targeting choices have become more abundant. The combat strategy and models have been consequently updated as a result.

For the PLA, technological progress has resulted in her updating its strategic thinking on the combat use of nuclear weapons. The outcome is the embrace of a new nuclear doctrine of limited deterrence.[7] In PLA terminology this is about a transition from "hide" to "fight" in war preparation, reflecting its changing attitudes toward nuclear weapons, from viewing them as an unusable means of mass destruction to recognising their practical use for battlefield conflict.[8] With the improvement of China's nuclear technology, particularly those that relate to accuracy, longer range and mobility, the PLA's confidence in its ability to successfully wage nuclear warfare has been enhanced. Indeed, younger PLA generals have gradually broken the psychological shackles imposed by the long-lasting strategy of minimum deterrence, which was the logical root-cause for the mentality of hiding. When designing "war game" plans, these younger generals are tempted to formulate scenarios in which they fire nuclear missiles in high-tech wars.[9]

What is interesting though is that Beijing's official policy is still minimum deterrence. Accelerated modernisation of nuclear arsenals by any country has become taboo in the post-Cold War world and is especially applicable to China who has proclaimed the goal of a peaceful rise. More importantly the Chinese effort to increase nuclear capability in terms of longer range and better accuracy at a time when the Soviet nuclear threat has diminished can easily be interpreted as targeting America and is diplomatically unwise. Therefore, limited deterrence does not appear in official vocabulary, and is basically a PLA conceptual discussion. However, whatever the official rhetoric, the fact is that the Chinese nuclear force is not, and it has never been, guided by minimum deterrence.

Contemplating Tactical Nuclear Warfare

Despite an element of offensiveness in the doctrine of limited deterrence, the overall posture of the Chinese nuclear force has remained defensive. This can be seen from the fact that the numbers of inter-continental ballistic missiles (ICBMs) have remained the same for several decades, although their quality has been continuously improved.[10] Furthermore, the number of PLAN's nuclear ballistic missile submarines will be small, probably ranging from six to eight. This may be due less to China's financial constraints on maintaining a large nuclear stock than to its concern of the U.S. response. It is well within China's economic affordability to create a kind of MAD (mutually assured destruction) capability, which in the minds of China's strategists, is measured by about 200 ICBMs. The attainment of this MAD capability would only cost an incremental US$ 2 billion.[11] Yet, if Beijing embarks on this path, Washington would immediately view Beijing as a strategic competitor and the associated political and economic costs, that is, in terms of trade with the U.S. would be very high. Unless the PRC is backed into a corner, that is to mean fighting a Taiwan war with US involvement, it would not choose this option. On the other hand, if Beijing feels that it is under an acute security threat, it will be relatively easy for the PLA to acquire a MAD capability, and this within a relatively short period of time. According to Johnston, at least a limited deterrence capability is within the reach of the PLA.[12]

Indeed the limited deterrence doctrine adds new dimensions to China's nuclear strategy: war game plans should be formulated on the premise of retaliation without being first hit by a nuclear bomb. Although Beijing is still politically bound by its pledge of non-first-use, the military has long explored scenarios of first use, as it believes that the lethality of new high-tech conventional weapons has matched that of tactical nuclear ones. If China is subjected to the Kosovo type of mass destruction, it may be left with no other choice but to contemplate using something dramatic as a counter-measure. After achieving a second strike capability some military planners are now tempted to contemplate the use of nuclear weapons in an escalation of conventional war, which they believe may place a nation's survival at stake just as much as nuclear attack.[13] PLA researchers often cite the example of the USSR's plan to initiate a nuclear attack against China to illustrate that the use of nuclear weapons is not inconceivable. They are particularly impressed by Russia's new national defence doctrine, which has deleted the provision of not employing nuclear weapons first in an all-out war.[14]

China's nuclear war-fighting preparation begins with its efforts to grasp the nature, process and consequences of a tactical nuclear war. According to the interpretation of PLA researchers, tactical nuclear war means attack on the opponents' military targets in general, and nuclear facilities in particular. Such an exchange is tactical because it is limited in nature, meaning there is still room for both sides to negotiate a cease-fire before it is escalated to engulf urban centres. In the last decade or so the PLA has accorded new emphasis to developing small-yield and highly accurate nuclear and conventional missiles for counter-force purpose only, in a hope that the Chinese population can be spared from nuclear disaster. In terms of doctrinal evolution the PLA has accepted the idea that even in an all-out war in the future, tactical nuclear weapons aimed at military facilities would be preferred to strategic ones aimed at urban centres. This has led PLA strategists to embrace the concept of a theatre nuclear war with missiles launched only against the intruding forces in a limited geographical area, although this area can be physically large. This is in sharp contrast to their old mentality that any nuclear fight was for mass destruction. They would argue that if a missile landed on the Bolshoi Theatre instead of the Kremlin, it would be equally effective and that, even if every missile had pinpoint accuracy, the limited number in the PRC's small arsenal could destroy only a small fraction of the enemy's silos, leaving China disarmed before the enemy's remaining missiles.[15]

PLA strategists now agree with their western colleagues that nuclear missiles would most likely be used at the theatre level and against defence assets. PLA war games are then played for achieving battlefield victory rather than the destruction of the world.[16] While ICBMs hold urban centres hostage at the strategic deterrence level, short-to-medium ranged, low-yield tactical nuclear weapons and land attack cruise missiles (LACMs) can be deployed to offer the second tier deterrence against the enemy's key defence sites. This is of particular value for a force inferior in conventional means. A weak navy, for instance, might be left with little choice but to use tactical nuclear means to deal with the superpower's nuclear aircraft carrier battle groups. In September 1988 when the PLA tested China's first neutron bomb, Western intelligence agencies discovered that China has possessed tactical nuclear weapons with a yield of below 30,000 tons from as early as the beginning of the 1970s.[17]

The fundamental reason for PLA planners to contemplate the

use of tactical nuclear weapons is to fill a gap in China's nuclear deterrence strategy. As a weak nuclear power, China was long subject to nuclear blackmail by the superpowers, which could choose whether to wage a nuclear war, the kind of nuclear war to wage, and when to start such a war. China's deterrence can only be effective when it has the means to deal with all kinds of nuclear threats. By the PLA's assessment, if China were forced into a nuclear war, it is most likely a tactical one, such as a nuclear surgical strike. This would make it very difficult for the PLA to respond with strategic nuclear weapons that target only urban centres. So if China did not possess effective tactical nuclear weapons, it would be deprived of a crucial means for deterrence, both politically and militarily.[18] According to the PLA joint campaign guidelines, the function of tactical nuclear missiles parallels that of the Air Force and the Navy, although the use of missiles is under much tighter central control.[19] A maritime scenario has been postulated as one of a range of scenarios where the PLA might use nuclear weapons.[20]

Getting Ready to Fight

China's nuclear strategy designated a two-stage development process to attain readiness for a nuclear war. The first stage aimed to resolve the problem of survivability, or how to hide, under a PLA slogan of "force consolidation"; and the second, the problems of missile range and accuracy, or how to fight, under another PLA slogan of "practical operation".[21] The improvement of survivability, and of launching range and accuracy have been the primary objectives of the PLA SMF since the outset of its nuclear programme. After 40 years of development, the SMF has accomplished these goals. Its ICBMs can target key American cities, and the technology of its sea-based missiles has gradually become mature. As a result, the PLA has now reached a relatively high level of nuclear readiness.

The emphasis of China's nuclear force had been placed on "force consolidation" which in actual terms means survivability. It is dependent on two crucial factors: (1) the survivability of launching sites, and (2) the mobility of the launching units. China's non- first use (NFU) policy puts great demands on the SMF, as it must be able to perform its mission after absorbing a nuclear strike. As the PLA had to rely exclusively on land-based ICBMs for a second strike before the 094 submarine becomes fully operational, the "consolidation" of the silos of DF-5 missiles is the key for China to hit back at a target 10,000 km away.[22] Long-range capabilities are regarded as another key factor of deterrence value. Without long-range missiles the PLA cannot target potential enemies beyond a certain distance, and without them China's deterrence is neither reliable nor credible. From the very beginning, goals for increasing the missile reach was set stage by stage, starting with the targeting of U.S. bases in Japan and Korea, and then to the U.S. bases in the Philippines, Guam, then Moscow, and finally, continental America. Currently, about 14 percent of China's strategic missiles can reach the U.S. In the long run, the PLA will proportionally augment this percentage as a key goal of force development. According to one PLA calculation, if this ratio can be raised to 70%, it will effectively strengthen China's national security. Therefore, a key task of adjusting the PLA nuclear force structure concerns the increase of ICBMs in comparison with short-range missiles.[23]

Mobility is about a strategy of nuclear "guerrilla warfare".[24] To this end, the PLA has tested various methods in the last two decades to improve the rapid response capabilities of its inter-continental (ICBMs) and intermediate range ballistic missiles (IRBMs). The launching units and facilities are put on the move all the time. Thousands of miles of roads have been constructed to link a great number of launching sites with the central command, control, communications, computerisation, intelligence, surveillance, and reconnaissance (C4ISR) networks. Every launching unit has several reusable launching sites. In each of these sites, launching data for fixed targets are continuously updated and different launching protocols are practised regularly. In war, the constant updating of data and the continuous training will save precious response time.

In order to raise survivability and mobility levels, the R&D of solid fuel propellants, miniaturised warheads, and the development of a sophisticated command, control, communications, and intelligence (C3I) systems are given top priorities. The solid fuels are of particular importance because most of China's mobile missiles (mainly the DF-3 IRBMs) are propelled by liquid fuel, which requires two hours to be prepared for launch, a time considered too long for the demands of a high-tech war.[25] Solid fuel is viewed as the key to improvements in response times and is especially crucial for the submarine-based missiles. Since 1985, when the PLA launched its first solid-fuelled mobile missile, China has invested heavily in its missile transportation vehicles and launching platforms.[26]

China's high-tech defence strategy has moved the PLA nuclear force from the stage of "force consolidation" to that of "practical operation". The PLA has since broken away from its traditional passive nuclear posture. In 1984, the CMC officially ordered the SMF to assume offensive retaliatory missions.[27] During the mid-1980s the SMF conducted 120 exercises. The majority of these were designed to assist the army's campaign operations at the divisional level or above.[28] By 1991, the SMF had acquired all-weather and all-situation operational capabilities. Every launching brigade has been put on strategic duty and is able to carry out combat missions assigned by the CMC. This meant that the SMF had transcended a historical developmental stage.[29]

Simulation and live ammunition launches in remote areas aim at specific targets and proceed in pre-determined circumstances of nuclear exchange. When China staged its "war games" in 1995 and 1996, group launch became the standard exercise. It is believed that group launches will be one of the chief means to affect a blockade of Taiwan's waterways. Since the Gulf War in 1991, the SMF has been trained to respond quickly in situations including retaliation after a nuclear surgical strike, bio-chemical warfare, and maritime warfare. Most of these are mobile launches. Reducing pre-launch time is one of the key aims in training. In addition to emergency launching plans, one indicator of the SMF's conceptual shift towards "how to fight" has been its troop redeployment and battle-field construction, mainly from the three "norths" (north China, northeast China and northwest China) to the east (the Taiwan Straits). It is part of the PLA's shift of security gravity: taking a strategically defensive posture in the north but preparing for an offensive posture in the east.[30]

New Modernisation Programmes

The modernisation of the SMF has speeded up in the last decade. One realistic but unpleasant prospect for the SMF is that the rapid high-tech advance of the U.S. may translate the "Star Wars" initiative into reality. Once an effective missile defence system consisting of both strategic and theatre capabilities is established, the bulk of China's nuclear arsenal may be rendered impotent. The PLA has no other choice but to improve the penetrability and accuracy of its ICBMs. This sense of vulnerability underlies China's tenacious efforts to continue with nuclear testing in order to reduce the size of the DF-31 (ICBMs with a range of 8000 km) and the JL-2 (6000 km range) warheads (about 700 kg), so that they can be made multiple, independently targetable, re-entry vehicle (MIRV) capable and thus be able to better fit into mobile and submarine launching platforms. The weaker throw weight of their solid-propellant also highlights the need to lighten the warheads of DF-31 and JL-2. The DF-31 has become operational ahead of expectations and the JL-2 is near deployable status.[31] The first decade of this century will prove to be crucial for China's nuclear development.

At the same time, design and development is under way for an even more advanced second-generation nuclear weapon, the DF-41 mobile, three-stage solid-propellant ICBMs. With a range of 12,000 kilometres, it can reach almost any city in the world. As the largest missile in the SMF's inventory, this system will replace the DF-5A in the next five years.[32] Once deployed, the missile will represent a leap forward for China's war-fighting readiness. There have been reports that the Chinese are incorporating advanced Russian rocket technology into the design of the DF-41. For instance, China is learning how to improve cryogenic rocket engines from Russian technology associated with the Kosmos, Tsyklon, and heavy-lift Zenit rockets, and also learning indirectly from the technology associated with the SS-18/19 ICBMs.[33]

The Naval Nuclear Connection

All of China's inter-continental nuclear missiles are land-based, which means that they are vulnerable to an enemy first strike. Although these weapons are well hidden, the PLA is fully aware that advanced satellite technology will enable China's potential opponents to identify the whereabouts of the silos and mobile missiles by following the tracks of the vehicles that travel to and from those otherwise inaccessible areas. One counter-measure adopted by the PLA is to put up as many fake launching sites as possible. However, Western analysts quoted Admiral Liu Huaqing as saying that after a first strike, only about ten per cent of China's nuclear arsenal would survive.[34] By other PLA estimates, up to two thirds of the SMF's nuclear weapons might survive, leaving a sufficient number of warheads for a counter strike.[35] However, PLA leaders cannot be sure how many land-based nuclear weapons would actually survive a precision first strike and the numbers that will be available for subsequent attacks. Emulating the U.S. approach to countering the USSR's nuclear threat, the Chinese has placed increasing importance on sea-based nuclear launching platforms, which were among China's three top R&D projects in the 1970s.[36] (The other two projects concerned inter-continental nuclear missiles and communications satellites). Chinese strategists have studied and accepted the U.S.'s nuclear strategy, which relies on nuclear submarines as the basis for a second-strike capability. Admiral Liu summarised the new thinking in China's nuclear strategy as follows:

> "In the face of a large-scale nuclear attack, only less than ten percent of the coastal launching silos will

survive, whereas submarines armed with ballistic missiles can use the surface of the sea to protect and cover themselves, preserve the nuclear offensive force, and play a deterrent and containment role".[37]

Therefore, the top priority of China's nuclear modernisation has been to gradually move a significant proportion of its land-based nuclear capabilities onto submarines.[38]

By 2007 China will have developed a relatively reliable nuclear submarine fleet. Nicknamed the 09 Unit and with a ranking equivalent to a group army in military bureaucratic ranking, the PLA Navy's nuclear submarine fleet is gradually expanding. In the next five to seven years it may comprise over a dozen nuclear-powered submarines. At the moment, however, most of these nuclear submarines consist of the *Han* class tactical attack boats, which have a displacement of 5,000 tons and a crew of 73. Numbering five or six, each of these tactical submarines can launch 12 C-802 cruise missiles with a range of about 50 kilometres. The C-802 is fairly accurate with terminal guidance measures. The missile is conventional but it can be equipped with a nuclear warhead. The only strategic missile submarine, *Xia* class SSBN, is more of an experimental boat. Manned by 104 officers and sailors, it is 120 metres in length, with a displacement of 8,000 tons. It is said to carry 12 HL-1 nuclear missiles, each propelled by solid fuel and deployed with a single two megaton nuclear warhead. Although its everyday running is the responsibility of the Navy, the control over the nuclear bottom is certainly not under the control of the Navy but higher up the chain of command. However, no detailed accounts are available for how the command, control and communications are channelled between the CMC, the Naval Headquarters, and the '09' Fleet.

The PLA high command is well aware that a single nuclear submarine will not make China's second strike capability robust. To achieve this goal, the PLA has undertaken two programmes to simultaneously transform the navy. The first is to develop a new, much-improved nuclear attack submarine, nicknamed the 093, with technology similar to the Russia's Victor III SSN. Indeed, the PLA has reportedly received Russian help in coating the 093's hulls to improve noise insulation. It is said that at least two of them have entered service. The noise level of the 093 submarines may have reached about 115 decibels, similar to that of the U.S.'s in the early 1990s. This is a remarkable progress. The second programme is the construction of a second but modified version of the *Xia* class submarine (094 type SSBN) in the Huludao Naval Ship Plant. This boat has an enlarged displacement of over 10,000 tons and carries the HL-2 nuclear missiles with multiple, independently targetable, re-entry vehicle nuclear warheads. With a much more sophisticated terminal guidance system and enlarged range of 8,000 kilometres, this new type of submarine will be of a greater deterrence to China's potential opponents. Despite this, Western analysts have raised their doubts regarding the technological sophistication of these new SSBNs, and funding difficulties have slowed down the development considerably.

Indeed the huge cost and complex technological requirements for developing new nuclear submarines have greatly slowed the realisation of the PLA plan to base its nuclear retaliatory capability in submarines. Rapid industrial development has compelled the civilian sectors to compete with the PLA for nuclear facilities that supply energy and other economic purposes. Moreover, the PLA has been confronted with serious accuracy problems of missiles launched from under water. Despite all the difficulties, the PLA will continue to give top priority to the development of submarine-based missile launching platforms that helped the Chinese to achieve breakthroughs in the late 1990s, as the first ship of 094 submarines was launched for sea trial. Its JL-2 missile, a sea-based version of the DF-31, is a huge improvement on the JL-1 with a range three times the latter (about 6000 nm). Both the ship and its missiles were scheduled to enter service in 2003 and series production could follow. The significance of this new fleet lies in its MAD (mutually assured destruction) capabilities. If the PLAN constructs at least six of them, each with 16 launchers, and each missile with three multiple warheads, there will be a total of 288 ICBMs that can reach North America. The deterrence equation will be significantly altered. Therefore, the completion of a strategic nuclear submarine fleet is well worth the money in the minds of top Chinese leaders despite its lengthy development process.

China's Effort to Break the U.S. Missile Defence

As mentioned earlier, U.S. missile defence systems, the ballistic missile defence (BMD), and the theatre missile defence (TMD) have constituted a driver for China's nuclear modernisation. For instance, Chinese military establishment is using BMD as a pretext to secure more funding for developing new missiles, such as manoeuvrable re-entry vehicles (MARVs), as a way to deal with BMD.[39] The National Missile Defence (NMD) of the U.S. has set as a goal the interception of 20 ICBMs for the first phase of development. Logically, this clearly targets China's inventory of some 20 ICBMs.[40] Also, as the TMD gradually unfolds, the PLA is working out measures to counter its effect. The design of China's first generation of land attack cruise missiles (LACMs) has specifically configured into it an anti-TMD element.[41]

A New Arms Race in the Making?

Some Western security experts point out that U.S. missile defence represents the security hazard that would cause an action-reaction arms race in the region.[42] Many Chinese strategists are eager to agree. To avoid a situation where China's limited ICBMs will be neutralised when NMD becomes operational, the PLA may have already augmented the effort to add more ICBMs to its arsenal. The U.S. Department of Defence released a report asserting that the number of China's ICBMs could have more than doubled by the end of this decade.[43] What would be response of Japan or India? Certainly this not the concern of the Chinese who believe that maintaining a credible nuclear deterrence is crucial to make the U.S. balk at intervening in a Taiwan war and that it is the U.S. that has initiated the missile race in the first place.

This means that psychologically at least, the NMD/TMD initiatives may intensify the regional arms build-up. When missile defence widens the gap of military balance by one side, the other side will feel more threatened. Its impulsive reaction will be to increase its arsenal of attack missiles to overwhelm the system. A few rounds of this action/reaction race will pave the way for the qualitative improvement of missile technology. In fact the upgrading and enlarging of its missile inventory has become a strategic imperative for the PLA. Missiles are seen as one viable means to compensate China's inferior attack capabilities.[44] As the PLA's other punches are relatively weak and short, employment of missiles becomes one of its few asymmetrical measures in RMA warfare.[45]

Japanese military experts argue that because Japan has not had long-punch capabilities, it has to have a more sophisticated shield to cover itself from the enemy's attack.[46] But the PLA construes this as, "When one side in the conflict is safely protected by a shield, he would be emboldened to hit his enemy even with short punches".[47] Moreover, the missile defence technology can easily be used to augment the offensive systems capable of long punches. This is probably one of the reasons that Japan is participating in research involving the development of the missile defence system.

Regional Implications

In the foreseeable future, Chinese concerns about the missile defence system is less about its military value than its geo-political implications. The TMD programme is behind the U.S.'s alliance-enhancing effort in the region and its real effect on China's military security is still debated in Beijing. Some analysts question the ability of the system in dealing with a saturated missile attack. The Patriot PAC-2 has a poor performance record, and the PAC-3 is not only too expensive for the user to fire in large numbers but also not fully reliable in combat.[48] For instance, normally three PAC-3 missiles would be launched to intercept one incoming ballistic missile. Now the PLA has deployed about 700 M-series missiles close to the Taiwan Straits. This requires over 2000 PAC-3s to achieve a successful destruction rate of 85%. In terms of the cost/effectiveness ratio, each M-missile is priced at about US$ 300,000 versus US$ 3 million for each PAC-3, a ratio of 10. For the defensive side, how would it plan a war of TMD? The interceptor of NMD can make only one manoeuvring move before its fuel runs out. More importantly, according to estimates by U.S. scientists, for every dollar spent on developing attack missiles it has to be matched by seven in designing the defence system. This is the figure often cited by PLA specialists on missile defence. It is interesting to note that while China's IR generalists still insist on the driving effect of the missile defence for an arms race, the arms control experts have already disputed such a view and see the missile defence system as lacking real teeth.[49]

Yet politically, the TMD is seen as a major threat to China's security. Basically, it is a form of collective defence that connects the U.S. and its allies more closely through an advanced technological network, that is, via an integrated command and control system. Taiwan, for instance, seeks to be part of the TMD exactly because it is in great need to be politically linked to such a network, even though from a military point of view, the TMD will not meet the requirements for the Island's air and missile defence needs.

Therefore, the TMD will, in the coming decade, be seen more as a U.S.-centred regional defence system against China than an operational weapons system, given its current technological inadequacies. In this light TMD is an expression of U.S. security commitment to its allies and signals a redefined power relationship in the Far East. An effective TMD cannot leave many geographic holes in its network and has to allow the participants to share top U.S. C4ISR information and facilities. If Taiwan is brought into the system, it would embolden its leaders to pursue independence in a more forceful way, under the assumption that American assistance is guaranteed.[50] Therefore, the TMD works like a powerful magnet drawing the U.S. and its allies together more closely.

Conclusion

China continues to press ahead with its nuclear modernisation as a way to obtain credible deterrence against any war scenario involving the U.S., and potentially Japan. To the PLA the need to enhance its nuclear forces stem from the concern over backward conventional capability. A reliable second-strike capability may provide it with a level of confidence that no other weapons can, although the PLA's nuclear arsenal is one generation behind the major powers. The development of nuclear weapons is also relatively cheap compared with the development of high-tech conventional arms in order to achieve the same level of deterrence.

In the last decade the world has witnessed the transition of the PLA Strategic Missile Force from a "hiding power" to a "fighting power", as both its hardware and software achieved qualitative progress. With a primitive retaliatory capability there is a sea-change in the mentality of PLA generals who are ready to discard the concept of *minimum deterrence*. In its place, a doctrine of *limited deterrence* is being developed to guide the preparation for future wars. Although still defensive in nature, the concept emphasises the adroit response to any nuclear threat confronting the Chinese. Diplomatically, Beijing may continue to stick to the non-first-use policy, which is a principal tenet of *minimum deterrence*. In military terms unpredictable combat situations may lead PLA commanders to contemplate the possibility of pre-emptive strikes. PLA Commanders have been alarmed by the U.S. Nuclear Posture Review and renouncement of the non-first-use policy by Russia.

One important item of China's nuclear modernisation is the enhancement of its nuclear submarine force. With weak sea-based launching capabilities, China's nuclear triad exists only in theory. Under the acute threat of U.S. precision strike, the survivability of China's land-based missiles is questionable. The PLA has no choice but to strengthen its nuclear submarine fleet. The end result of this effort would be a Chinese de facto MAD capability. Finally, the missile defence initiatives by the U.S. have generated new impetus for the PLA to enlarge its nuclear arsenal. Although for the time being, neither the NMD nor the TMD poses a real threat to Chinese missile attack capability, the PLA has taken no chances, given that technological breakthroughs cannot be discounted, a phenomenon which China herself has benefited from over the last several decades. Working on the presumption that the missile defence may eventually work, the Chinese are devoting more resources in modernising its missile inventory by increasing the number of higher quality delivery vehicles in its force.

The Chinese nuclear force is looking visibly more mature than at any time in the last three decades, with a set of more practical combat doctrines from the strategic to the tactical levels, and more reliable second-strike capabilities. This development will certainly exert an enormous impact on the regional military balance in the years to come.

Notes and References

1. SMF has a nick name Dier Paobing (the Second Artillery), given by Zhou Enlai, China's first premier, in 1965. It was used then for the purpose of keeping China's nuclear forces in secret to both domestic and international watchers.

2. See western analysis on China's nuclear triad, Bradley Hahn, "China: Nuclear Capability - Small but Growing", *Pacific Defence Reporter*, May 1989, p. 42; and Chong-pin Lin, *China's Nuclear Weapons Strategy: Tradition within Evolution,* (Massachusetts: Lexington Books, 1988). Although China was successful in developing a strategic nuclear submarine in the 1980s, only one was commissioned as a test boat. The range of its missile is short, and the level of its combat readiness is low. Therefore, the much talked about triad capability of the PLA has been theoretical

3. Alastair Iain Johnston, "The Prospects for Chinese Nuclear Force Modernisation: Limited Deterrence versus Multilateral Arms Control", *The China Quarterly*, No. 146, June 1996, pp. 548–576.

4. Peng's talk to *Across the Strait*, a current affairs programme of CCTV, 25 June 2004.

5. Gerald Segal, "Nuclear Forces", in Gerald Segal and Bill Tow (eds.), *Chinese Defence Policy* (London: Macmillan, 1984), p. 104.

6. The initial proposal for the PLA to develop tactical nuclear weapons originated from the calculation of the PLA high command in the 1970s that they had no conventional weapons effective enough to hold back a large-scale Soviet tank invasion in the north and northeast China, where the land is flat and the distance between Beijing and Mongolia is only 600 kilometres. Against such an invasion no weapons other than neutron bombs or 105 mm nuclear shells would be more effective in putting up a desperate defence. Xu Guangyu, Yang Yufeng and Sang Zhonglin, "Zhanqiu He Zhanzheng De Kenenxin Jidui Wojun Zhanyi Zuo De Yingxiang (The possibility of theatre nuclear warfare and its impact on our army's campaign operations)", in Editor Group (eds.), *Toxiang Shengli De Tansuo (Exploration of the path toward victory)* (Beijing: the PLA Publishing House, 1988), pp. 1086–1106.

7. Alastair I. Johnston, pp. 548–576.

8. Zhang Baotang, "Dui Xingshiqi Zhanlie Daodan Budui Zhanbei Jianshe Jige Wenti De Chutan (On a few questions concerning the development of the SMF in the new era)", in the PLA NDU (ed.), *Jundui xiandaihua jianshe de sikao* (The study of the modernization programmes for the PLA), Beijing: the PLA NDU Press, 1988, pp. 411–420.

9. Xu Jian, *Daguo Changjian (The large country and long sword: the evolution of the SMF)* (Beijing: Zuojia Chubanshe, 1995).

10. There is not much change at all if we compare the figures presented in The International Institute for Strategic Studies' annual book on *Military Balance* between the mid-1980s and 2004.

11. Discussion with Shen in Beijing, November 2003. Also, Kori Urayama, "China Debates Missile Defence", *Survival*, Vol. 46, No. 2, 2004, p. 132. Also, discussions with Shen Dingli of Shanghai Fudan University in January 2004, Beijing.

12. See the analysis of Alastair I. Johnston, pp. 562–564.

13. Xu Zhongde & He Lizhu, "Yuce Weilai Zhanzheng Buke Hushi Hewuqi De Weixie (The nuclear threat should not be ruled out in study of the future wars)", in the PLA Academy of Military Science (ed.) *Junshi Lilun Yu Guofangjianshe (Military theory and development of national defence)*, (Beijing: the PLA Academy of Military Science, 1988), p. 192.

14. In private conversations with a number of senior Chinese researchers immediately after the Gulf War, I asked them whether the PLA would consider the use of nuclear weapons as the last resort if it were in the Iraqi's position and deemed that nothing could stop the enemy's advance. They agreed that it would probably be the only option left to the PLA. Some of them cited the Russian example to make the point.

15. Lewis, John Wilson, and Hua Di, "China's Ballistic Missile Programmes: Technologies, Strategies, Goals", *International Security,* Vol. 17, no. 2, Fall 1992, p. 21.

16. Xu Guangyu, Yang Yufeng and Sang Zhonglin, pp. 1086–1106.

17. The U.S. Defence Intelligence Agency, *Soviet and People's Republic of China: Nuclear Weapons Employment Policy and Strategy*, Part II, March 1972, p. 25.

18. Xu Guanyu, Yang Yufeng and Sang Zhonglin, p. 1091.

19. Huang Bin, *Zhanqiu Yu Zhanqiuzhanyi (War zones and war zone campaigns)* (Beijing: the PLA NDU Press, 1990), p. 158.

20. Editor group, "Zhanlie Daodan Budui Zhai Chengzhang (The development of the SMF)", in the CCTV Press (ed.), *Junwei jinxingqu* (The marching song for the PLA), Beijing, 1987, pp. 97–98.

21. Zhang Baotang, p. 412.

23. Zhang Jingxi and Zhang Mengliang, "Shilun Zhanlicxing Zhanyi Heliliang De Yunyong He Zhujunbingzhong De Xietog (On the use of nuclear force in strategic campaigns and the coordination of the SMF with other services)", in Editor Group (eds), *Tongxiang Shengli De Tansuo (Exploring the ways towards victory)* (Beijing: the PLA Publishing House, 1987), p. 1018.

23. Quoted from "China's Nuclear Missile Strategy", *Independent (Russian)*, 14 December 1995. However, China's focus on the Taiwan situation may have changed this plan.

24. Xu Jian, 1995, p. 378.

25. Liu Zhongyi, "Taiyuan Weixing Fashe Zhongxin Ceji (The brief look at the Taiyuan satillite launching centre)", *Jingyang Wenyi*, No. 2, 1992, p. 26.

26. Yu Hao, et al, *Dangdai Zhongguo: Zhongguo Renmin Jiefajun* (Contemporary China: the PLA) (Beijing: Renmin Chubanshe, 1994), p. 528.

27. Ling Yu, "Zhingguo Daodan Yanxi He Dier Paobin (The Chinese missile exercises and the SMF)", *Guangjiaojing*, No. 8, 1995, p. 22.

28. Ling Yu, 1989, p. 69.

29. Wang Huangping and Xu Jian, "Ai, Zhuzao Daodan Bulou De Junhun (Love constitutes the soul of missile troops)", *Laiowang*, No. 25, 1993, p. 12.

30. Xu Fangting and Liu Hongji, "Xinshiqi junshi douzhan zhunbei juyao" (Some major points on war preparation in the new era), *The Journal of the PLA National Defence University,* no. 10, 1995, p. 23.

31. "Chinese Nuclear Forces 1993", Supplement (8 November 1993) to *The Bulletin of the Atomic Scientists*, Vol. 49, no. 9, November 1993, p. 24. See also *Trends,* supplement to *Business Times (Singapore)*, 27-28 November 1993.

32. John Wilson Lewis and Hua Di, 1992, p. 29.

33. IISS, *Strategic Survey 1997/1998* (London: Oxford University Press, 1998), p. 170.

34. John Downing, "China's Maritime Strategy", *Jane's Intelligence Review*, April 1996, p. 189.

35. Zhao Yunshan, "Zhonggong Hedaodan Zhanlie Sixiang De Guoqu, Xianzhai Yu Weilai (The past, present and future of the CCP's nuclear strategy)", *Zhonggong Yanqiu*, Vol. 31, No. 5, 1997, p. 95.

36. Yu Hao, et al, p. 527.

37. *Liaowang*, No. 33, August 1984, cited from Mohan Malik, "Chinese Debate on Military Strategy", *Journal of Northeast Asian Studies*, Summer 1990, p. 18.

38. Bao Zhongxing, "Jianshe Tianjun Gguoxiang (The initial design for the creation of a space army)", in the PLA NDU (ed.), *Jundui xiandaihua jianshe de sikao* (The study of the modernization programmes for the PLA), Beijing: the PLA NDU Press, 1988, pp. 420–443.

39. Kori Urayama, p. 133.

40. The view of European participants at an IISS workshop on transatlantic dialogue on NMD in UK, 12–13 December 2000, *IISS Newsletter*, Spring, 2001, p. 11. Also Philip Gordon, "Bush, Missile Defence and the Atlantic Alliance", *Survival*, Vol. 43, No. 1, 2001, pp. 17–36.

41. This refers to the Hong Niao (Red Bird) LACM system consisting of four classes. HN-1 and HN-2 have become operational; the former with a range of 400–600 km and the latter 1500–2000 km. HN-3 with a range over 2500 km is still under development.

42. Desmond Ball's remark to the *15th Regional Security Roundtable*, Kuala Lumpur, 1 June 2000.

43. Its 2003 annual report on China's military power, p. 31.

44. Dennis Gormley, "Dealing with the Threat of Cruise Missiles", *Adelphi*

Paper 339, 2001, p. 51.

45. You Ji, "Learning and Catching Up: China's RMA Initiative", in Emily Goldman and Thomas Mahnken (eds.), *The Information Revolution in Asia* (New York: Palgrave Macmillan, 2004), pp. 97–124.

46. William Tow's speech to the conference *Strategic Update*, Canberra, 29 September 1999.

47. Yu Juliang, "A Review of U.S.-Japan Joint Security Communique One Year after its Announcement", *The Journal of the PLA National Defence University*, No. 6, 1997.

48. In the second Iraqi War some Iraq's Chinese-made HY-2 missiles came dangerously close to their targets before they were engaged by PAC-3, revealing the defects of the system. HY-2 is a primitive version of cruise missiles. Dennis Gormley, "Missile Defence Myopia: Lessons from the Iraq War", *Survival*, Vol. 45, No. 4, 2003/2004, p. 66.

49. When I presented the view that TMD/NMD may cause an arms race in a regional security conference jointly organised by Pugwash and Institute of Applied Physics and Computational Mathematics in Beijing in October 2003, a number of Chinese arms control specialists challenged me, saying the NMD/TMD initiatives would not lead to an arms race in the region.

50. Robert Manning and James Pryzstup, "Asia's Transition Diplomacy: Hedging against Futureshock", *Survival*, Vol. 41, No. 3, 1999, p. 59.

11

Non-traditional Security Threats in China: Challenges of Energy Shortage and Infectious Diseases

Pak K. LEE
Lai-Ha CHAN

Security debate in the past two decades has shifted dramatically away from a state-centric perspective to a position that embraces human-centric viewpoint. Stimulated by the end of the Cold war, similar to its counterparts in the West, albeit with a time lag, security studies in China began to undergo a paradigm shift with scholars and policymakers paying increasing attention to non-traditional security threats. The way whereby China changes its perception of security concerns can directly affect its policy and external behaviour about coping with the existential threats. This paper is going to examine how the new security concerns arise in China. Using energy (crude oil) and infectious diseases (HIV/AIDS) as case studies, it will analyse to what extent and how China broadens its concept of security. Towards the end of this essay, we will address how this study of new security concern advances our understanding of China's foreign-policy behaviour.

Changing Concept of Security

An essentially contested concept notwithstanding, security has long been a key research topic in International Relations (IR). A standard definition of security is "the absence of existential threats to the state emerging from another state".[1] During the Cold War era, this concept was largely understood as military security against invasion by other states. This traditional understanding of security is rooted in realism or its modern variant, neorealism. According to realists, security can best be understood in terms of threats to state sovereignty and territory, and hence, security studies have mainly been concerned with "high politics", relating to war and peace, diplomatic alliances, or the balance of power in inter-state relations.[2] The referent object in traditional security studies, or the thing that needs to be secured or protected, is the state, and the main sources of threat to the state are other states that have the capabilities and intention to use force to achieve their goals. Therefore, the only means for a state to counter such threats is military deterrence.[3] Han Morgenthau argued that the fundamental aim of foreign policy must be to ensure "the integrity of the nation's territory, of its political institutions and of its culture."[4] Stephen Walt echoes in contending that security studies must be about the study of the threat, use, and control of military force.[5]

This traditional, realist understanding of security, however, comes under criticism from two fronts – the unit of analysis of security and the source of insecurity – in the post-Cold War period. The first is concerned with the referent object of security. Apart from the state, should society, human beings or even the world also be given equal consideration in the discussion of security needs? Second, the traditional definition gives an exclusive attention to physical dimension of security or territorial integrity. Critics argue that as a consequence of globalisation and the end of the Cold War, state survival, which realists stress, is no longer at high stake whereas the prominence of other dimensions of security, such as economic security, information security and environmental security, is on the rise.[6]

An advance of a human security approach, which attaches significance to the protection of people from critical and life-threatening dangers, is to address the first critique. A response to the second criticism is to acknowledge that security is not simply a military issue and to advocate a broader, multisectoral approach to security by addressing non-military (or non-traditional) sources of security threats.[7] The broadening approach emphasises that the notion of security should no longer be limited to the military domain. As long as an issue poses an "existential threat" to the society and needs extraordinary measures to handle it, it can be deemed as a security issue. There are different dimensions of security that could pose direct threat to a state and, therefore, the security agenda should be open to many different types of threats.[8] Nevertheless, the securitizing power under the 'broadening' approach may still reside within the state.

It is against this backdrop that non-traditional security issues are given attention. Neoliberals, the archrivals of neorealists, have long argued that security is not only concerned with the protection of the state against external military threats. In addition to sovereignty, territorial integrity and political independence, there are other types of values that are also under threat. These values include material well-being of the citizens, individual and communal identity, public health and sustainable development. The sources of the threat are also different from those for traditional, military-oriented security. The tangible threats to human life, however, ought to originate from human agency rather than from natural environment or the natural process of life. In security discourse, the protection of the non-military, non-state-centric values is regarded as non-traditional security.[9]

In short, the dichotomy between traditional and non-traditional security is concerned with that between neorealism and neoliberalism about what values are to be protected from threats and what factors shape the security landscape. Terrorism, organised crime, drug trafficking, illegal migration, spread of contagious diseases, shortage of natural resources, and environmental degradation are generally considered the most serious non-traditional security issues. Given that these issues transcend national borders, effective resolution calls for multilateral cooperation among a wide array of state and non-state actors in the framework of global or regional governance. A caveat here is in order. While it is widely believed that the traditional concept of security needs an overhaul, the proponents of expanding the scope of security studies fail to arrive a consensus over where the boundaries of the broader definition should be. So, in the words of constructivists, the concept of security *per se* is an intersubjective understanding. Securitisation is the process of "constructing a shared understanding of what are to be considered security issues, and what should be seen as threats." While there is little dispute that security refers to survival in the face of existential threats, there is wide disagreement between different societies as to what constitutes an existential threat.[10]

Overall, this paper focuses on how the Chinese government deals with the non-traditional security issues of energy shortage and the spread of infectious diseases. Key questions are: Does China attempt to address these two identified non-traditional security issues through multilateral cooperative arrangements? Why does China behave as it is observed? What are the hurdles to and the prospects of China's participation in multilateralism? In addressing these questions, however, we need to examine, in the first place, the peculiarities of China's notion of non-traditional security. Questions to be address are: Which sectors or issues should be securitised and why?

China's Conception of Non-traditional Security

In Western literature on security studies, non-traditional security threats are characterised by four common features. First, they originate with substate or trans-state actors or factors. In other words, they are not state-centred. Second, they are multidimensional and multidirectional without any geographical boundary. Third, they are not amendable to traditional military solutions. Finally, they endanger both human beings as well as the state.[11]

Whereas students of security studies in the West, as said before, started to re-visit the traditional model of security in the early 1980s,

China did not re-visit the concept until 1996 when a new security concept began to evolve. Since then, leaders and scholars in the country have increasingly used this new security terminology in their speeches and writings. An official statement was first presented to the ASEAN Regional Forum in July 2002. With American hegemony as its target, the new security concept calls for using cooperative means to deal with security issues. It stresses the importance of "common security" as well as multilateral approach to manage security threats such as economic security, food security, energy security, financial security, and environmental security. With this new security concept, China began to advocate a multilateral approach to participating in international affairs. It takes an active part in international forums and works with various international governmental organisations and non-governmental organisations. According to some China scholars, the acceptance and adoption of international regulations can not only undermine the "China threat" argument, but also improve the international security environment as well as its international status.[12]

As a separate and yet related development, in the wake of the Asian financial crisis in 1997–98, the Chinese government started to be concerned about economic and financial security. However, the term of non-traditional security did not enter official discourse until 2001 after the September 11 terrorist attacks on the U.S.. The first multilateral agreement on non-traditional security issues that China inked was the one with the ASEAN in November 2002.[13] After the SARS outbreak in early 2003, discussions about non-traditional security among Chinese leaders and scholars have gradually sprouted up. The first research project on "China and non-traditional security issues" was undertaken in September 2003, followed by the first national academic conference on the issue held in Beijing in December 2003, under the auspices of the Institute of World Economics and Politics at the Chinese Academy of Social Sciences (CASS). In order to strengthen dialogues about how to address non-traditional security threats in the era of globalisation, *Shijie jingji yu zhengzhi* (*World Economics and Politics*), a monthly academic journal published by the Institute of World Economics and Politics, has run a special column on "non-traditional security studies" since 2003.[14]

Wang Yizhou, vice director of the Institute of World Economic and Politics and editor of *Shijie jingji yu zhengzhi*, argues that China should use an "Asian Way" approach to tackle non-traditional security challenges with its neighbouring countries. Key to the Asian Way perspective is consensus building through informal, non-legalistic and non-binding dialogues, discussions and consultations rather than majority voting, and the norms of respect for national sovereignty (formal equality) and non-interference in the internal affairs of other states.[15] In addition, Wang attaches significance to the role of China as a permanent member of the UN Security Council in promoting the Asian experience of handling non-traditional security issues in the global institution. So in essence, while China's conceptualisation of non-traditional security threats calls for multilateral cooperation and participation in global governance, it is in large measure a state-centric concept. The state has to take lead to address the non-traditional security challenges, which in turn, are seen as posing threats to the security of the state. The traditional concept of security in China undergoes a gradual process of transition, with lingering smell of the traditional static concept.[16]

On the issues that would not adversely affect its national sovereignty and security vis-à-vis the United States, China is willing to use multilateralism and tries to seek common ground while maintaining differences intact. Key non-traditional issues under examination include information security, terrorism, ethnic conflict, drug trafficking, illicit migration, money laundering, piracy, economic insecurity (particularly, financial crisis and energy shortage), environmental degradation, and epidemics. However, national sovereignty is still the most sensitive and thorny issue on the Chinese agenda. The role of state in managing non-traditional security issues is affirmed. Internal socio-political stability is still a major concern for the Party and the government. Although the Chinese government is now paying more attention to non-traditional security and tend to accept the idea of human security that protects people from threats, the government has never formally used the term "human security". Instead, "people's safety" is used. The major reason is its concern about the adverse effect on territorial integrity. In facing pro-independence activities in Taiwan, Tibet, and Xinjiang, Beijing always takes a strong position against the notion of "human rights overriding sovereignty".[17] Seen from this perspective, China, on the one hand, emphasises the five principles on peaceful co-existence and humanitarian assistance (not humanitarian intervention), on the other hand, it is also mindful of any infringement in its territorial integrity. Therefore, the Chinese government skilfully use the term "people's safety" rather than "human security" to address human security issues. Nevertheless, China's conception of non-traditional security and its understanding of "human security", as described by Paul Evans, is more flexible and sophisticated than many other outsiders have thought.[18] In a nutshell, there is a broadening without a deepening of the security concept in Chinese security studies.

The following two sections look at two non-traditional challenges to security, namely oil shortage and infectious disease. A principal reason for devoting the rest of the paper to these two issues is that there has been a meteoric rise in concern by the public as well as policymakers about the far-reaching impact of oil shortage since 1993 and of the spread of infectious disease since the early 21st century on national security and development.

Economic Security in China: A Study of Oil Security[19]

China, once a country self-sufficient in oil, began to pay serious attention to oil security in 1993 when it became a net oil-importing country. Since then China has become increasingly dependent on oil imports. The net imports increased sharply to 117 million tonnes, meeting 37.9% of China's domestic consumption of oil, in 2004. In contrast, the ratio was only 5.8% in 1993.[20]

The increasing dependence on foreign sources of oil is largely attributable to the sluggish growth of domestic production of oil and the rapidly rising consumption of the resource in the country. Although domestic output of crude oil rose to 160.74 million tons in 1997 from 138.31 million in 1990, since 1997 the production has stagnated in the range between 160 and 170 million tonnes per annum. The largest Daqing oilfield in Heilongjiang province began to reduce production in 2003, with the annual output falling below 50 million tonnes in the year.[21] At the same time, however, the spread of industrialisation, the growth of population, and the remarkable growth of personal wealth have produced a huge demand for automobiles, home appliances and other consumer goods. China's consumption of oil therefore rose rapidly to 308.6 million tonnes in 2004 from 140.5 million tonnes in 1993. The increase in 2004, a rise of 15.8% over 2003, was particularly striking. Chinese crude imports in 2004 soared 34.7% to 122.7 million tones. [22] China's domestic estimates of its gaps in oil production and consumption also indicate that the annual deficit in oil supplies would increase to 197 million tonnes in 2015 and 250 million tonnes five years later.[23] The inevitable reliance on imported oil has renewed Chinese long-standing concerns about energy security. Oil has become a source of vulnerability for China.

The sharp rise in crude oil price in 1999–2000 also led China to care about its oil security. The immediate effect of the price hike for China was a sharp rise in the net imports of oil in pecuniary terms in 1999 and 2000. China's net imports of oil soared from US$1.75 billion in 1998 to US$3.88 billion in 1999 and US$12.73 billion the following year. Since then the annual oil import bills have exceeded US$10 billion.[24] Given the continuous rise in crude oil price since 1999, prompted by disruptions in oil production in Iraq, Africa, and Russia as well as the rapid growth of oil demand by such populous countries as China and India, it is very unlikely that oil price would fall below the low levels in 1998.[25] Among oil-importing countries, China is particularly vulnerable to sustained high oil prices for two reasons. One is its high oil intensity. China is a heavily oil intensive economy, consuming 1.56 million barrels per US$1 billion of gross domestic product (measured in 1996 U.S. dollars) in 2003, nearly twice the world average. This is due to inefficiency in the production and consumption of oil in the country.[26] Another challenge facing China is that it would have to import an increasing amount of oil at relatively high prices. With a currency peg to the US dollar, in which global crude oil is traded, China suffers more than Japan and Europe from the rising oil price.[27]

These unfavourable developments led Hu Jintao, the general secretary of the ruling Chinese Communist Party and State President, to emphatically single out oil as an area of concerns in a central economic work conference in late November 2003, articulating it in security terms.[28] China's strategy to enhance its oil security is to expand *national* control over oil resources. However, this parochial, national approach escalates latent conflicts with two major Asian oil consuming countries, namely Japan and India, as well as with the United States, the largest oil-consuming state in the world.

Increasing Rivalry with Two Asian Giants: Japan and India

The Chinese effort to engage Russia in energy trade commenced as early as 1994 when China indicated that it would develop a pipeline from the Kovykta gas fields near Irkutsk.[29] During a Sino-Russian summit in July 2001, the two countries reached an agreement calling for formulating a plan for constructing a long-discussed US$1.7–1.8 billion oil pipeline from Angarsk (also near Irkutsk) in eastern Siberia to Daqing in Heilongjiang province. It was expected that the 2,400-km pipeline – the Daqing line – could be completed as early as 2005 and that an annual initial throughput of as many as 20 million tonnes (147 million barrels) would be shipped to China.[30]

However, since 2002 China has found that it has to compete severely with Japan over where the oil pipeline would run. In November 2002 the Russian Federal Security Commission, chaired by Vladimir Putin, reportedly favoured a port in Far East as the destination.[31] With an aim to reduce its heavy dependence on oil from the Gulf region, Japan's Prime Minister Junichiro Koizumi in his visit to Russia in January 2003 lobbied for a rival pipeline to the Pacific port of Nakhodka, near Vladivostok (the Pacific line, for short). Japan showed willingness to provide low-interest loans for the project that would cost US$5 billion. Japan was allegedly ready to purchase all the oil that would be shipped through the pipeline to the Pacific port and was willing to participate in the pipeline construction. The Japanese scheme was supported by Transneft, a Russian state-owned pipeline operator, and believed to be preferred by Moscow. With an annual throughout capacity of 50 million tonnes, the Pacific-bound pipeline would serve Russian interests by facilitating Russian exports of oil to multiple markets, including Japan, South Korea and even the U.S., and more importantly, by allowing it to retain control over the exports of oil, as the pipeline is built on Russian land. Russia also held that it would be inadvisable to rely solely on a pipeline running into an "enclosed market, that is, China".[32] Under strong lobbying from Japan, which sent delegations of energy officials and diplomats to Moscow in April 2003 with an offer to finance the entire Japan-bound pipeline project, Russia changed tack in one month's time.[33] It was initially expected that when Chinese President Hu Jintao visited Russia in late May 2003, the two countries would seal the deal.[34] But what China could achieve in the summit meeting was only that China National Petroleum Corporation and Yukos signed a 25-year oil deal worth US$150 billion. CNPC would buy up to 5.13 billion barrels of oil between 2005 and 2030, representing 10% of China's oil needs in the period. While the deal would help China revitalise the industrial economy of its northeastern provinces, Vladmir Putin was non-committal to the Daqing pipeline by saying that the routes needed to be further discussed by experts. The oil deal was only said to "pave the way" for the pipeline.[35] Putin said, however, in June that the Pacific pipeline "looks preferable because it allows broad access to markets".[36]

To regain the initiative from China, Japan dispatched a delegation, led by Iwao Okamoto, director-general of Natural Resources and Energy Agency, to Moscow in July 2003. The Japanese energy officials discussed with their Russian counterparts about providing financial and technical assistance to the construction of the Pacific pipeline and the development of oilfields in eastern Siberia. The Japan Bank for International Cooperation was said to be willing to finance the construction project even without any loan guarantees from the Russian government.[37] The state-owned Japan National Oil Corporation would also offer technical assistance to Russia to help develop Siberian oilfields. As a result, when then-Russian Prime Minister Mikhail Kasyanov visited Beijing in September, he openly declared that the Daqing pipeline had been postponed for several months. Prior to the visit by Kasyanov, Russia postponed meeting with Chinese officials on the pipeline and the Russian Ministry of Natural Resources, an ecological commission, rejected the two routes for environmental reasons.[38] The substance of the Japanese financial offer became more concrete in October 2003 when the Japanese Deputy Foreign Minister Hitoshi Tanaka visited Moscow. Japan revealed that it would provide US$5 billion in low-interest loans to support the construction of the Pacific pipeline and a further US$2 billion for the discovery and development of eastern Siberian oilfields.

The fate of the Daqing line was also clouded by the arrest of Mikhail Khodorkovsky, chief of Yukos, in October 2003. Yukos under Khodorkovsky had supported the building of the Daqing pipeline that would carry crude oil from its fields in the Tomsk region of western Siberia and would reduce its dependence on state-owned oil transport company. In contrast, both the state-owned pipeline operator Transneft and oil producer Rosneft favoured the Pacific route.

The rivalry between China and Japan and the standoff between Kremlin and Khodorkovsky led to a repeated delay to reach a final decision on the routing of the pipeline. Meanwhile, Russian officials were studying a compromise project that would construct a main pipeline to Nakhodka with a spur to Daqing. China was apparently not opposed to this compromise solution, but insisted that the Daqing line be built first.[39] Viktor Khristenko, then Russian Minister of Industry and Energy told Liu Guchang, China's ambassador to Russia, in late June 2004 in Moscow that Russia had already abandoned the Angarsk-Daqing and Angarsk-Nakhodka lines. Instead, according to Khristenko, the Taishet-Nakhodka route would be the most reasonable one. As soon as the routing of the pipeline could be finalised, Russia would start discussing with China about how branching off the pipeline to China.[40]

When Chinese Premier Wen Jiabao was in Moscow in September 2004 to push for the Kremlin to give priority to "the construction of a pipeline in the direction of China" by pledging to invest US$12 billion in Russian infrastructure and energy sector, he once again received a vague commitment from the Russian government that the latter would "actively consider" the option of the Daqing branch after the approval of the feasibility study of the Pacific route.[41] During Putin's visit to Beijing one month later, the two countries still failed to agree to the pipeline, despite that they signed a raft of agreements, including one on the demarcation of the border along the Ussuri river, a dispute that had lingered for 40 years. China had intended to concede in the border issue in return of a "reciprocal friendly gesture" on the part of Russia. However, with an emphasis on the eve of the visit that his country's national interests would come first in deciding where to build the pipeline, Putin hinted that the final decision would not favour China.[42] On December 31, 2004 the Kremlin announced that Transneft would construct a "system of pipelines" with an annual capacity of 80 million tonnes (1.6 million barrels per day) from Taishet to Perevoznaya near Vladivostok and Nakhodka. In the Russian statement there was no mention of a spur going to China.[43]

However, given that the oil rivalry is never simply a matter of commercial competition, geopolitical factors play a significant role in Russian re-examination of its energy relations with China and Japan. In addition to the subsequent failure to secure substantial economic commitments from Tokyo after the announcement of the system of pipelines from Taishet, Japan's attempts to tie the investment in the pipeline to the resolution of its territorial dispute with Russia over Kuril islands and more importantly, the American interventions in the general elections of a number of Central Asian countries have led Moscow to be convinced that it is imperative to consolidate its relations with Beijing. Accordingly, Russia revealed a short-term plan to build the Siberian pipeline up to Skovorodino only. From there, a branch line to China was said to be constructed in July 2006. Nevertheless, variables still remain. Russia has refused to sign an intergovernmental agreement with China on the construction of the oil pipeline to China. In contrast, Vladmir Putin promised in his visit to Japan in November 2005 that Russia would eventually bring Siberian oil to the Asia Pacific region, including Japan. The two countries signed preliminary accords on the pipeline.[44]

The competition over oil between China and Japan unfortunately renews tension and distrust between the two Asian powers. On the one hand, Japan feels threatened by China's ballooning growth of oil and gas imports, which would make it less able to find sufficient energy resources in the international market. In August 2004 Japan struck a cooperation agreement with four Central Asian nations – Kazakhstan, Kyrgyzstan, Uzbekistan and Tajikistan. Japan would provide economic aid to the Central Asia states in return for cooperation in a number of areas including energy.[45] The Japanese move was viewed as a strong sign that Japan has spared no effort to promote its economic and political presence in oil-producing areas. On the other hand, China is so paranoiac that it views the Japanese intrusion into the Sino-Russian oil deal as a means whereby Japan aims not only to strengthen its political clout in East Asia but also to contain China. Lu Nanquan, a vice director of the Russian Research Centre at the Chinese Academy of Social Sciences in Beijing, holds that Japan's move aims at weakening China's stable economic growth by threatening its energy security and at adversely affecting the strategic partnership between China and Russia.[46] The Japanese involvement in the construction of the pipeline intensifies the security dilemma facing China and Japan.[47] In response, China has actively competed with Japan over oil in China's offshore areas between the two nations.

The setback in Russia inevitably prompts China to pay increasing attention to the energy resources in the country's offshore areas. Conflicts between China and Japan over the exploitation of oilfields in the East China Sea have recently become intense. They hold competing views of how the boundary of its respective exclusive economic zone (EEZ) is to be drawn, though both allege that they abide by the rules laid down in the United Nations Convention on the Law of the Sea. China claims that its EEZ should extend to the edge of the continental shelf (i.e. close to Okinawa). Defining the boundary as a line equidistant from the coasts of the two countries, Japan expressed concerns about the construction of new Chinese natural-gas drilling rigs close to its EEZ in the East China Sea – just 4 km away from the median line between the two country's coasts. Japan contended that China could siphon off resources from Japan's EEZ, even though legally speaking the rigs are in the Chinese territory. It has been estimated that the East China Sea hold 6-7 billion tonnes of oil and gas, much of which lies in the west of the centre line.[48]

In June 2004, senior officials of Japan's Ministry of Economy, Trade and Industry and Foreign Ministry met their Chinese counterparts and expressed Japan's concern and asked China to present solid evidence that the gas fields do not encroach on Japan's EEZ, but the Chinese side was reportedly not committal or countered by arguing that Japan had no right to request the information, as China was exploring only its own areas of East China Sea.[49] Coinciding with the release of a revamped National Defence Programme Outline, covering the period April 2005 – March 2009, which singled out China and North Korea as potential threats to the country,[50] Japan was reported to start building a high-performance ocean survey vessel, estimated to cost 20–24 billion yen, to gauge the size of the underwater reserves in the Sea. Both countries have held to no avail rounds of talks in 2005 over the disputed oil and gas deposits in the East China Sea. Although China insists that the median line is a theory unilaterally developed by Japan rather than the result of bilateral negotiations, it cannot be formed as the basis for the talks, the bone of contention remains with the median line. China proposed in May 2005 a joint development of gas fields *inside* Japan's part of the median line. In response, Japan made a counterproposal in early October that covers four Chinese gas fields – Chunxiao, Tianwaitian, Duanqiao and Longjing – near the line.[51] The United States had urged the two countries to exercise restrain over the issue. Although the U.S. claims that it is non-partisan in the maritime dispute, it is rather generally believed by China that it is part of Japan's national strategy to side with the U.S. to contain China.[52]

China's voracious appetites for oil and its worldwide quest for oil security have also fuelled the concerns of India, another Asian fast-growing economy, about its own energy security. In recent years Indian domestic annual oil production has been stagnant at between 36 million tonnes and 38 million tonnes while its annual oil consumption had risen steadily to 119.3 million tonnes in 2004 from 67.4 million tonnes in 1994.[53] The South Asian country relies on overseas supplies for 70% of its crude-oil demand.

China and India have been engaged in talks about forming an energy synergy in securing oil and gas resources abroad. One option proposed by India is to jointly bid with China for oil and natural gas resources in Iran and Sudan where both countries have substantial investment. The two countries have been pondering constructing a single transportation route for Iranian gas to go to India via Pakistan. The pipeline could be extended to China's Yunnan province from India. Mani Shanker Aiyar, India's then Minister of Petroleum and National Gas, visited Beijing in January 2006 and the countries signed a memorandum of understanding on energy cooperation.

Nevertheless, in spite of the rhetoric of cooperation, fierce competition for oil between the two Asian giants is ongoing. Akin to the strategy used by China, India has strengthened its presence in oil-rich countries to secure its oil supplies. India's Oil and National Gas Corporation (ONGC) was reportedly in January 2005 in talks with Russia about investing in Yukos shortly after the auction for Yuganskneftegaz. ONGC could spend as much as US$2 billion for a 15% stake. Subir Raha, the Corporation's chairman and managing director, has said that India and China would be engaging in a fierce competition over energy sources. Mani Shanker Aiyar was touring Kazakhstan and Russia in February 2005. In Moscow he met

Rosneft's head, Sergei Bogdanchikov as well as his Russian counterpart, Viktor Khristenko, and reportedly expressed interest in acquiring stakes in Yuganskneftegaz. A subsidiary of ONGC also clinched in the same month a 25-year deal with National Iranian Oil Company to import liquefied natural gas and develop two Iranian oilfields, including Yadavaran, in which China has also invested, and a gas field. India shows an interest in importing gas from Myanmar through Bangladesh. While it battles with China for oil resources in West Africa, notably Angola, India is exploring the possibilities of investing in oil industry in Ecuador in South America and Saudi Arabia.[54]

As a sign of his worries about China's relative gains, Indian Prime Minister, Manmohan Singh, said in January 2005 that his government would restructure state-own oil firms to enable them to compete with China over oil.[55] State-owned oil companies in the two countries have confronted with each other in their purchases of overseas oil companies. In October 2004, China blocked a bid by ONGC to purchase a stake from Royal Dutch Shell in an offshore oil block in Angola by offering the African country a development aid worth US$2 billion. Another notable example is PetroKazakhstan, a Calgary-based Canadian company with oil fields in Kazakhstan. Eventually China National Petroleum Corporation won the auction. A less well-known case is the acquisition of Calgary-based EnCana Corporation's oil subsidiaries in Ecuador by Andes Petroleum Corporation, a consortium held mainly by both CNPC and China Petroleum and Chemical Corporation (Sinopec). India's Oil and Natural Gas Corporation had participated in the bidding before withdrawal. Another arena for mutual competition may be Russia where China is eyeing an investment in Yuganskneftegaz, the main production unit of Yukos brought by Rosneft while India has stakes in the Sakhalin gas project. Lukewarm feedback from Beijing on energy cooperation has also led India to seek alliance with Taiwanese oil companies in securing oil supplies in Latin America and Africa where lie more than two-thirds of the countries still recognising Taiwan. Even while Mani Shanker Aiyar was in Beijing and the ink was barely dry on the Sino-Indian mutual agreement, China was courting Myanmar prompting the latter to sell natural gas exclusively to China from a field partly owned by an Indian company.[56]

Fuelling U.S. Wariness

China's unilateral approach to enhancing its oil security also results in strengthening ties with non-U.S.-friendly oil-producing countries in the Gulf region, particularly Iran. In 2001 Sinopec struck a deal to explore oil in central Iran's Zavareh-Kashan and has discovered crude oil there. In April 2004 shortly after the visit by Iranian Vice-President Mohammad Sattarifar to Beijing, Sinopec was reportedly in talks with Iran to import annually at least 5 million tonnes of liquefied natural gas from Iran's largest Azadegan oilfield. Half a year later the two countries signed a preliminary accord whereby Sinopec was to buy 250 million tonnes of Iranian liquefied natural gas over 30 years and to develop Iran's Yadavaran oilfield in the southwest, close to the Iraqi border, which would sell 150,000 barrels per day to China, over 25 years. The deal as a whole is estimated to be worth US$70–100 billion. Iran also expressed its preference that China would replace Japan as its biggest oil and gas buyer.[57]

Growing Sino-Iranian relations have raised American eyebrows. The U.S. is never convinced that with rich oil resources, Iran has the need to develop civilian nuclear energy. Coupled with the fact that Abdul Qadeer Khan, founder of Pakistan's nuclear programme, admitted that under an underground nuclear smuggling operation managed by him, Iran was provided not only with equipment for enriching uranium, but also with actual designs for atomic weapons, the U.S. is concerned that a Sino-Iranian strategic alliance whereby China would transfer weapons and military technologies to Iran in return of oil from the latter would emerge. This could erode U.S.'s ability to put international pressure on Iran over its nuclear programme. Not only was China Iran's second largest military supplier between 1995 and 2002, providing the Persian state with nearly 29% of what it had acquired, China had also voiced until July 2006 its opposition to an American move to refer Iran to the UN Security Council over its nuclear programme. As late as November 2006 both China and Russia were opposed to imposing UN sanctions against Iran. In an apparent move to rush through the deal before the punitive measures took effect, Iran indicated in November 2006 that the contract for developing the Yadavaran oil field by Sinopec was complete and ready to be signed. In addition, China's CNPC was allegedly in talks with the Persian state for an agreement to invest up to US$3.6 billion in the Iranian South Pars gas field.[58]

China's engagement with Myanmar, owing to its voracious appetite for hydrocarbons in the Southeast Asian country and the plan for constructing an oil pipeline linking Sittwe in Myanmar and China's Yunnan province, has impeded American efforts to employ UN sanctions against the military junta.[59]

Robert Zoellick, U.S. Deputy Secretary of State, warned in early September 2005 that China could not achieve energy security by pursuing oil deals with countries that the U.S. considers troublesome. Rather, the approach would only result in conflicts with the U.S..[60] In a comprehensive statement about U.S. policy towards China delivered to the National Committee on U.S.-China Relations later in the month, he criticised China of locking up energy supplies in the world and of dealing with Sudan to achieve energy security, regardless of poor governance in the host country.[61]

Health Security in China: A Case Study of HIV/AIDS

Since its economic reform which started by the end of the 1970s, the Chinese government has placed economic development at the top of its policy agenda. People's access to public-funded health care in China has been declining progressively. During the Mao era, China's health policies emphasised wide entitlement and access to medical care. With the implementation of village medical practitioners or so-called "barefoot doctors", 94% of China's villages were covered by the cooperative medical scheme. [62] Alongside its economic reform, China's public health system has switched to a user-pay health system since the early 1980s. While it is true that technological skill has improved as a result of the market-oriented reform, China's medical reform has been a failure in terms of access to medical care. In a world health report entitled "Health Systems: Improving Performance", published by the World Health Organisation in 2000, China's health-care system was rated poorly. It was ranked 188th on the dimension of fairness of financial contribution, leading China to become one of the most unfair countries in the world.[63] More seriously, China's poor public health system has exposed its deficiencies to control emerging infectious diseases. Hepatitis, tuberculosis, HIV/AIDS, SARS and avian flu are cases in point. It has been argued that China is now facing a significant health security challenge and that security threats are largely domestic in nature.[64] However, the Chinese government has long treated public health as a domestic social issue. For more than twenty years, health issue has received limited attention on the government agenda and leaders have seldom referred to global health problems in their policy speeches. Infectious diseases could hardly play a role in country's security calculus.

We concentrated our study on the spread of HIV/AIDS in this paper, as it is one of the most concerned infectious diseases for many countries as well as China. Even though HIV/AIDS is a chronic and life-threatening disease that is largely preventable, its effects on an economy as well as socio-political stability could potentially be more destructive than the effects of war, which have been demonstrated in many African countries.[65] In China, as of the end of 2005, 650,000 people are living with HIV or AIDS, according to the government and the United Nations' figures released in early 2006.[66] The adult prevalence of HIV, although low, has recently been increasing by about 20–30% per year. With a population of 1.3 billion, China's total number of HIV carriers is much higher than all of the Southeast Asian countries combined. In addition, according to official figures, from 1985 to August 2005, only 132,545 people had been tested and confirmed as HIV carriers in China.[67] In other words, more than 80% of HIV carriers are probably not aware that they are HIV-positive. Owing to a lack of information and knowledge about the disease in rural China, the number of people who are infected will continue to grow rapidly. It is predicted that the number of infected Chinese will reach 10 million by 2010 if the government does not modify its existing policies. In describing the spread of HIV/AIDS, a UNAIDS report, published in June 2002, stated that "China is on the verge of a catastrophe that could result in unimaginable human suffering, economic loss and social devastation".[68] The Center for Strategic and International Studies in the United States also warned that China would be one of five countries which stand on the second wave of HIV/AIDS pandemic.[69] Akin to sub-Saharan African nations, China's HIV/AIDS has already leapt from marginal groups into the general population. Nevertheless, since the first case of AIDS in China was reported in 1985, the Chinese government had concealed or denied the existence of an AIDS crisis in the country until the turn of the century. With growing awareness of the threat of the infectious disease, China has taken multifaceted steps to combat HIV/AIDS.

A Proactive Multilateral Approach?

Since the beginning of this century, the Chinese central government has demonstrated an increasingly willingness to combat the diseases and engage with different countries and international organisations in managing public health, especially the HIV/AIDS, crisis. Beijing has proactively used multilateral approach to cooperate with a wide array of actors to tackle this imminent threat. It is now a participant in the Global Fund to Fight AIDS, Tuberculosis and Malaria, the ASEAN+3 on Enhancing Cooperation in the field of Non-traditional Security Issues, the International AIDS Conference and the

International Congress on AIDS in Asia and the Pacific. Chinese leaders have taken part in all of them and have reiterated their promise to play an active role in the regional and global fight against HIV/AIDS. In order to further scaling up its response to pandemic, China has also drawn a wide range of actors, including state, non-state and private actors, into a partnership relationship to combat the problem in China. Accordingly, China has cooperated with more than 20 international organisations and countries on the prevention and control of AIDS in China.[70] For example, China has cooperated with the United States through the U.S. Global AIDS Programme. Since 2002, the U.S. government has committed over US$35 million over five years for HIV/AIDS-related activities in China. Since 2003 the U.S. funding of HIV/AIDS prevention, care and treatment services has increased by 82%. Northeastern China's Heilongjiang province is one of the beneficiaries of the collaboration. Since June 2004, the U.S. Global AIDS Programme has helped set up 15 of the province's 21 HIV surveillance sites at disease control and prevention centres.[71]

As part of its cooperative programme with intergovernmental organisations (IGOs), China collaborates with the UNICEF in implementing a national AIDS policy known as "Four Frees and One Care". The policy calls for free schooling for orphans, free measures for preventing mother-to-child-transmission, free AIDS testing for all, free medicine for people living with AIDS, and care for AIDS patients as well as their family.[72] UNICEF began in October 2001 carrying out an experimental intervention scheme in the seven most seriously plagued villages in Shangcai county in Henan province. By June 2003, intervention had extended to all 25 villages in the county, and a supervisory group for the intervention work had been formed.[73] In the period 2006–2010, UNICEF will spend up to US$100 million on combating HIV/AIDS in China.[74]

China is also engaged in a partnership with the Global Fund to Fight AIDS, Tuberculosis and Malaria, an international non-governmental organisation (INGO). This INGO granted the Chinese Centre for Disease Control and Prevention (CDC) US$63 million by June 2004 to run the China Comprehensive AIDS Response

(CARES) Project.[75] This project is to finance a community-based HIV treatment, care and prevention programme in central China. The Ministry of Health has been undertaking pilot programmes to provide free, domestically produced antiretroviral drugs in 50 counties with high prevalence rates.[76] In addition, the Clinton HIV/AIDS Initiative signed a Memorandum of Understanding with China in April 2004 to jointly develop a nationwide care and treatment plan. Working with the Chinese Ministry of Health, the Initiative provides HIV/AIDS prevention educational programmes and drug treatment in Henan, Yunnan, and Anhui provinces.

More surprisingly, a jointed report issued in August 2005 by State Council's Development Research Centre and the World Bank pointed a finger at China's public health-care system for its failure to prevent and control both serious chronic diseases and infectious diseases. The fact that it might be the first time that an official body criticises public health-care system is widely regarded as path-breaking. The Minister of Health, Gao Qiang, on his ministry's website, even accused hospitals in China of being motivated by profit rather than the health of their patients. With exorbitant fees, the poor are denied access to proper medical care. In addition, China not only had failed to provide adequate health care to most of the citizens, but also the national health system was unable to properly cope with large-scale epidemics and diseases.[77] Shortly after the release of the report, Gao Qiang and his health officials visited Australia in September 2005. During the visit, they paid particular attention to the control and prevention of HIV/AIDS and the respective roles of state and federal governments in health provision.[78] It seems that the Chinese government is paying increasing attention to its health security and their response to the HIV/AIDS crisis is more promising. Strengthened cooperation with institutions of global health governance notwithstanding, whether China can successfully address the non-traditional security threat of infectious disease domestically is far from certain. According to the UNAIDS/WHO's AIDS Epidemic Update: December 2005, China has not done enough to stem the spread of the disease. Poor public awareness about the epidemic was one of the factors that hindered effective response.[79] So, in the final analysis, it depends largely on whether China has been socialised into the norms and rules of good governance, particularly in participation (i.e. inclusion of stakeholders to mobilise their support and cooperation) and transparency initiatives.[80]

Socialised into Good Governance?

Since the central government admitted in June 2001 the HIV/AIDS problem in the country, it has been increasingly concerned about the negative impact of the pandemic on the society as well as the economy. The campaign against HIV/AIDS has undergone an immense change. The government has increased its commitment to tackling HIV/AIDS inside the country and hence fighting the disease has gradually become a national issue. As a sign of its determination, Premier Wen Jiabao and President Hu Jintao paid high-profile visits to AIDS patients in 2003 and 2004, respectively, demonstrating to local governments and the international community that the central leaders would take the issue seriously. In order to transform its policy rhetoric into practice, the Chinese government has consecutively implemented a variety of activities inside China as well as drawn a wide range of actors, such as intergovernmental organisations, non-governmental organisations, civil society organisations to prevent and control its HIV/AIDS crisis.

A new State Council AIDS Working Committee was established in February 2004 under the leadership of Vice Premier Wu Yi in a bid to coordinate and promote collaboration among the government, agencies, the private sector and civil society.[81] In a National People's Congress (NPC) meeting in March 2005, Premier Wen Jiabao reiterated the central government's determination to improve China's public heath system, particularly in fighting HIV/AIDS. With regard to legislation, China revised its Law on the Prevention and Control of Infectious Diseases in August 2004. The new law became effective from 1 December 2004.[82] According to Xinhua News, this was the first time that HIV/AIDS had been specifically targeted in national legislation. Under this new law, all local governments must strengthen prevention and control measures to prevent the spread of HIV. It is intended to ensure that victims of the disease have access to treatment and are not discriminated against.[83] In addition, China's Ministry of Health has completed drafting regulations on AIDS prevention and control. The draft regulations outline the principles, roles and responsibilities of various government departments in the prevention and control of HIV/AIDS. They aim to protect the legal rights of the HIV infected and AIDS patients. All officials above county levels will be provided training on HIV/AIDS prevention and control and those irresponsible government officials, if found dereliction of duty on the control and prevention of HIV/AIDS, will be punished according to the regulations. The regulations were approved by the NPC in January 2006.[84]

The country's financial budget for annual AIDS control has been dramatically increased since 2003.[85] For example, to scaling up antiretroviral therapy, the government has committed an estimated US$27 million in 2004 and US$33 million in 2005.[86] In August 2004, a new program was announced whereby approximately US$30 million (240 million yuan) will be invested in building some 600 township and county hospitals in Henan province, the epicentre of the blood-related HIV/AIDS epidemic.[87] Other HIV/AIDS preventative measures include providing free HIV/AIDS tests for the general public as well as free treatment for infected people who cannot afford it, compulsory HIV/AIDS education in the secondary school curriculum and various education campaigns. A 100% condom use programme is already under way in 10 provinces, whereby through health and family planning networks, free condoms are distributed to the public.[88] In addition, with a target of keeping the number of people infected with HIV below 1.5 million by 2010, the central government has put aside 3.86 billion yuan between 2005 and 2007 for prevention work to fight against HIV/AIDS.[89]

China is now calling on the private sector to join in its combat against HIV/AIDS. Wu Yi urged in March 2005 that private businesses and non-governmental organisations should play a role in halting the spread of HIV/AIDS in China. In a summit on AIDS, jointly hosted by the Ministry of Health and the Global Business Coalition on HIV/AIDS in Beijing on 18 March 2005, Wu explicitly stated that combating AIDS is not just a government obligation, "but also the common responsibility of society as a whole, including business".[90] This is the first time that the Chinese government has called for public-private partnerships in managing its health crisis. In summary, China is now contributing to collective actions aimed at curbing the spread of HIV/AIDS inside China.

The Chinese government also cooperates with domestic civil society organisations (CSOs). An example is the Beijing AIZHI Action Health Education and Research Institute, which was established in 1994 but did not officially register with the Chinese government until October 2002. It is engaged in HIV/AIDS education, research and mobilizing attention to the problem of HIV/AIDS in children and orphans in China. Although its headquarters are located in Beijing, its activities mainly focus on HIV/AIDS patients in Henan province. Its relationship with the local government is shaky, however. While its activities were sometimes banned by the government, it has also assisted the province in tackling the thorny HIV/AIDS problem. The organisation has strong connection with Dr Gao Yaojie.[91] As will be discussed in detail below, Dr Gao was accused of being "anti-government" after unveiling negative information about the disease in Henan. However, in the wake of a three-hour private meeting between Wu Yi and her in December 2003, the local government began to be more tolerant of her activities in the province.[92] The national China Central Television (CCTV) honoured her with the "Touching China" award in 2004. In addition, she recently got her new books *Yiwan feng xin* (*Ten Thousand Letters*) (2004), and *Zhongguo aizibing diaocha* (*The Investigation of AIDS in China*) (2005) published. The books reveal her encounters in the AIDS villages in the province. Interestingly, the first book was published by the Chinese Academy of Social Sciences (CASS), a scholarly institution-cum-government think-tank in Beijing. At an international symposium, which was held in Beijing on 31 August 2005, Chinese

Vice Health Minister Wang Longde emphasised that Chinese NGOs have played an outstanding role in fight against HIV/AIDS, especially in the fields where the government cannot go deep, notably the homosexuals. He reiterated that the government would work closely with the international community and strengthen its support for the NGOs in China.[93]

On the other hand, China's transparency problem in revealing the real situation of HIV/AIDS has often been deemed problematic by various sources. Those brave enough to expose the HIV/AIDS epidemic in the localities are often vilified as unpatriotic and "anti-government". People who leaked any negative information about the disease would be penalised or kept in quarantine. One of the ample examples was Dr Gao Yaojie. Dr Gao, a 77-year old gynaecologist in Henan province, has been named an AIDS crusader and has fought the scourge of HIV/AIDS since 1996. After exposing the HIV/AIDS epidemic and the misconduct of health officials and private entrepreneurs in the collection and dissemination of blood in the province, Dr Gao was accused of being "anti-government". Another example was Li Qianji, a clinic worker at the Xingtai Blood Centre in Hebei province in Northern China. After appearing in a TV programme on 13 August 2004 about the dangerous practices of blood collection and the sale of tainted blood and plasma to Shanghai, Beijing and Hebei in the 1990s, Mr Li's monthly salary was cut from a normal 1,500 yuan to 2.75 yuan in February 2005. The Centre's director claimed that his salary cut was triggered by pressure from the provincial government.[94] In addition, Xingtai Blood Centre also tried to sue *China Pharmaceutical News* for defamation after it reported the Centre's mismanagement of HIV-tainted blood products. The report aroused the ire of the Ministry of Health, which then ordered the Hebei provincial health bureau to investigate blood supplies at Xingtai in December 2004 and January 2005. Although the Hebei provincial health bureau did not directly confirm the mismanagement accusations, they did ask the Centre to improve the supervision of blood supplies and to strengthen their crackdown on illegal blood sales.[95]

Furthermore, anecdotal evidence suggests that rifts exist

between the central government and local governments in containing HIV/AIDS. It is quite obvious that local governments are unwilling to let the central government be aware of the genuine situation of HIV/AIDS in their areas. In early February 2005, for instance, while Premier Wen Jiabao was paying a visit to an AIDS village in Shangcai county, Henan, the local government did not allow an AIDS orphan girl to make a direct appeal to Wen for redress of an injustice. The provincial authorities also impose a ban on Dr Gao's books.[96] The local governments in a sense are still at pains to cover up the crisis.

Having said that, in comparison with its previous denial and deliberate cover-up of the disease before 2001, China's current proactive attitude towards multilateralism in managing the pandemic marks an important milestone on the road towards good governance, especially towards providing global public good in health. Even though there is much room for improvement in the areas of participation and transparency, its recent more cooperative behaviour in the prevention and control of the HIV/AIDS serve as a good starting point for China to extend its role in global health governance, especially in handling the growing threat of avian flu.

Implications for Understanding China's External Behaviour: Unilateral or Multilateral?

This chapter has demonstrated that in dealing with oil security, China is adopting a unilateral and confrontational approach whereas using a multilateral and cooperative perspective in tackling public health challenges. China's behaviour is rather inconsistent. It embraces multilateralism selectively. How can we account for its behaviour?

A key argument we would like to advance here is that China utilises multilateralism or global governance instrumentally. It gives support to or is committed to multilateralism only if the process enhances its capability to handle non-traditional security challenges, helps it reduce its vulnerability and weakness or promotes a multipolar international system that would undermine the hegemony of the U.S.. We do not rule out the possibility that as a result of social learning that takes place when it participates in the activities of various international organisations, China is socialised into accepting international norms and rules of multilateralism.[97] However, we have so far not garnered substantial evidence to prove the claim.

China has been regarded as "the high church of *realpolitik*" and has resisted any international intervention into its domestic affairs, especially after an intrusion by Western powers for more than 100 years since the late Qing dynasty.[98] Its sensitivity on national sovereignty has made it resist all of the possibility to internationalise those it deems as domestic issues. It accepts multilateral approach to manage the HIV/AIDS crisis because China lacks human and material resources to deal with the deadly disease alone and therefore needs the participation of transnational actors. The cooperation with different actors could draw them to assist in and contribute to solving the transmission of HIV. With this rational interest, China is inclined to cooperate with various international organisations in tackling its HIV/AIDS problem. In addition, with a power to veto in the Security Council, China wants to strengthen the power of the United Nations and its subsidiary bodies in managing global issues. The aim to constrain the American predominance gives China an additional incentive to cooperate actively with the WHO in dealing with infectious diseases.

However, drawing in a multiplicity of actors to combat its domestic HIV/AIDS problem will inevitably internationalise the issue. In addition, international involvement would breed the growth of domestic NGOs, which would potentially attenuate the supremacy of the Chinese Communist Party in ruling the country or erode the autonomy of the state. With this consideration, why is China still willing to take the risk? To what extent, can we argue that China has been socialised into accepting international norms and rules promoted by transnational actors? It is possible that its accession to major international institutions in the last twenty years has been conducive to China's learning and acceptance of the norms of international community. Coupled with the bitter experience of being ostracised by the global community during the SARS outbreak in 2003, China has been increasingly aware that it has to shoulder responsibility to provide public goods such as public health to its own citizens as well as the global community. However, its embrace of the norms of participation and transparency is still open to dispute.

The Chinese approach of tackling energy security, in contrast, reflects largely the influence of realist thought. China still upholds that the state and state-owned oil companies are the sole actors. With painful experience of military confrontation with Japan and India, China tends to hold that Japan serves as a junior partner of the U.S. in the latter's attempt to contain the rise of China and that with the acquiescence of the U.S., India will eventually emerge as a competitor with it in Asia.[99] A multilateral approach in dealing with energy security contributes little to promoting a multipolar international system that could undermine U.S.'s dominance. Accordingly, it adopts a self-help strategy, skirting around the cooperative, multilateral approach. China may even harbour suspicions about the ultimate intent of U.S.-dominated multilateralism.[100] Robert Zoellick has indicated that the Bush administration encourages China to adopt a broader definition of energy security that would include cooperative efforts with the U.S. and others. While criticising China of locking up energy supplies in the world, he suggests that China work with the United States and others, including the International Energy Agency, to develop diverse sources of energy and advises China to cooperate with the United States and Japan on both regional and global challenges.[101] However, what lies behind the veil of multilateralism is apparent when the U.S. is urged to strengthen East Asian regional integration by working with such democratic nations in the region as Japan, Australia and South Korea. This multilateral approach, the argument goes, will contribute to regional peace and stability by spreading the values of democratic governance and transparency. An overriding aim of this regionalism is to nudge China towards good governance.[102]

In conclusion, there is no substantial and converging evidence that would back up the claim that as a result of globalisation and of China's increasing participation in global governance, China will necessarily embrace multilateralism as well as good governance. It varies, depending on which actors are involved, whether the issue concerned has geostrategic implications (i.e. whether it is on the borderline between traditional and non-traditional security threats), and perhaps more importantly, whether the process will put U.S. power under restraint or let the hegemon assume a predominant position.

Notes and References

1. Harald Müller, "Security Cooperation," in Walter Carlsnaes, Thomas Risse and Beth A. Simmons (eds), *Handbook of International Relations* (London: Sage Publications, 2002), p. 369.

2. Wong Yizhou, "Rethink Approach to Security Threats", *China Daily*, 29 May 2003, p. 6.

3. Pauline Kerr, *The Evolving Dialectic Between State-Centric and Human-Centric Security* (Canberra: Working Paper 2003/2, Department of International Relations, Australian National University, September 2003), p. 4.

4. Quoted in Peter Hough, *Understanding Global Security* (London: Routledge, 2004), p. 3.

5. Stephen Walt, "The Renaissance of Security Studies", *International Studies Quarterly*, 35(2), 1991, p. 212.

6. Strictly speaking, the re-assessment of the traditional approach to security took place well before the Cold War waned, as evidenced in the publication of Buzan (1983) and Ullman (1983). However, it is fair to argue that the end of the Cold War gave an added impetus for rethinking about the concept of security and the call was accepted by a wide array of scholars in the field. See Barry Buzan, *People, States and Fear: The National Security Problem in International Relations* (Brighton: Wheatsheaf, 1983) and Richard Ullman, "Redefining Security," *International Security*, 8, 1983, pp. 129–153.

7. The first response is also known as a "deepening" approach to security studies or a "critical" study of security. Key proponents include Ken Booth and Richard Wyn Jones. See, among others, Ken Booth, "Security and Emancipation," *Review of International Studies*, 17(4), 1991, pp. 313–326; Richard Wyn Jones, *Security, Strategy and Critical Theory* (Boulder, CO: Lynne Rienner Publishers, 1999); and Richard Wyn Jones

(ed), *Critical Theory and World Politics* (Boulder, CO: Lynne Rienner Publishers, 2001). The definition of human security is taken from Ramesh Thakur and Edward Newman, "Introduction: Non-traditional security in Asia," in Ramesh Thakur and Edward Newman (eds), *Broadening Asia's Security Discourse and Agenda: Political, Social, and Environmental Perspectives* (Tokyo: United Nations University Press, 2004), p. 4.

8. Michael Sheehan, *International Security: An Analytical Survey* (Boulder: Lynne Rienner Publishers, 2005), p.43.

9. Tsuneo Akaha, "Non-traditional Security Issues in Northeast Asia and Prospects for International Cooperation," a paper presented to "Thinking Outside the Security Box: Non-traditional Security in Asia: Governance, Globalisation, and the Environment," United Nations University Seminar, United Nations, New York, 15 March 2002, available at http://www.ony.unu.edu/seminars/securityinasia/akaha.pdf (accessed on 11 October 2005).

10. Michael Sheehan, *International Security: An Analytical Survey* (Boulder, CO: Lynne Rienner Publishers, 2005), p. 62.

11. Terry Terriff *et al.*, *Security Studies Today* (Cambridge: Polity Press, 1999), pp. 115–116.

12. Wang Yong, "Lun zhongguo di xin anquan guan" (On China's new security concept), *Shijie jingji yu zhengzhi* (*World Economics and Politics*), Issue 1, 1999, pp. 42–45; Wang Yizhou, *Tanxun quanqiu zhuyi guoji guanxi* (*International Relations in a Globalised Perspective*) (Beijing: Beijing daxue chubanshe, 2005), p. 126.

13. "The Joint Declaration of ASEAN and China on Cooperation in the Field of Non-Traditional Security Issues," available at http://www.aseansec.org/13186.htm (accessed on 22 November 2005).

14. Wang Yizhou, *China Facing Non-traditional Security: A Report on Capacity Building* (Ford foundation Program Report, 3 December 2004), pp. 3–4, available at http://www.iwep.org.cn/english/ford%20programm/table.htm (accessed on 22 November 2005); Lu Zhongwei (ed), *Fei chuantong anquan lun* (*On Non-traditional Security*) (Beijing: Shishi chubanshe, 2003), pp. 9–95.

15. Literature on "Asian Way" or "ASEAN Way" is rich. Representative ones include Michael Haas, *The Asian Way to Peace: A Story of Regional Cooperation* (New York: Praeger, 1989) and Amitav Acharya, *Constructing a Security Community in Southeast Asia: ASEAN and the Problem of Regional Order* (London: Routledge, 2001).

16. Wang Yizhou, *Tanxun quanqiu zhuyi guoji guanxi*, pp. 179–181. Although Wang (p. 185) argues for the importance of human security in non-traditional security, he admits that human security is often ignored in the discussion of the issue.

17. Shulong Chu, *China and Human Security* (North Pacific Policy Papers No.

8) (Vancouver: Program on Canada-Asia Policy Studies, Institute of Asian Research, University of British Columbia, 2002), pp. 4–5, available at http://www.iar.ubc.ca/Pcaps/pubs/nppp8_final.pdf (accessed on 22 November 2005).

18. Paul Evans, "Ren di anquan yu dongya: huigu yu zhanwang," (East Asia and Human Security: Review and Prospects), *World Economics and Politics (Shijie jingji yu zhengzhi)*, Issue 6, 2004, pp. 43–48.

19. This section draws on, with updates in various places, Pak K Lee, "China's Quest for Oil Security: Oil (War) in the Pipeline?" *Pacific Review*, 15(2), June 2005, pp. 265–301.

20. The data are drawn from *Almanac of China's Foreign Economic Relations and Trade 1994/95*, pp. 681, 700–701; *Zhongguo tongji nianjian 1996*, p. 206; and British Petroleum, *BP Statistical Review of World Energy 2005*, pp. 10, 19.

21. Its output fell to 48.4 million tonnes in 2003 and further to 46.4 million tonnes in 2004 (*Liaowang dongfang zhoukan* [Shanghai], April 1, 2004, 44 – 46).

22. British Petroleum, *BP Statistical Review of World Energy* 2004, p. 19; 2005, p. 19.

23. *Wen Wei Po* [Hong Kong], 28 July 2004, p. A6; *21 shiji jingji baodao* [Guangzhou], 2 September 2004, p. 3.

24. See Lee, "China's quest for oil security," Table 3 (p. 269).

25. The average spot prices of West Texas Intermediate crude oil rose to US$41.49 per barrel in 2004 from US$14.39 per barrel in 1998 (British Petroleum, *BP Statistical Review of World Energy* 2005, p. 14).

26. Economist Intelligence Unit, "Asia at risk from high oil prices," *EIU Viewswire*, 3 September 2004.

27. "The price of oil: not so bad", *The Economist*, 20–26 March 2004.

28. *Liaowang dongfang zhoukan*, 15 July 2004, pp. 60–61.

29. Andrews-Speed et al. *The Strategic Implication of China's Energy Needs*, Adelphi Paper 346 (London: International Institute for Strategic Studies, 2002), p. 62.

30. E. S. Downs, *China's Quest for Energy Security* (Santa Monica, CA: RAND, 2000), pp. 28–29; A. M. Jaffe and S. W. Lewis "Beijing's oil diplomacy", *Survival*, 44(1), 2002, pp. 115–134; "Beijing to buy Russian-made jet fighters", *South China Morning Post*, 19 July 2001; "Siberia focus of pact" *South China Morning Post*, 28 September 2001; *Wen Wei Po*, 28 September 2001, p. A2.

31. *Huanqiu shibao* [Beijing], 19 December 2002, p. 16.

32. I. Gorst, "Russia delays decision on routing Far East oil pipeline", *Platts Oilgram News*, 81(50), 14 March 2003.

33. Subsequent to Koizumi's visit to Russia in January 2003, major Japanese

political leaders, including Foreign Minister Yoriko Kawaguchi and former Prime Minister Yoshiro Mori, paid visits to Moscow to lobby for the Pacific route ("Government ups ante in Siberia oil race," *Daily Yomiuri*, 11 July 2003).

34. C. Hutzler, "China's Hu to meet G-8 leaders", *Asian Wall Street Journal*, 22 May 2003; *Wen Wei Po*, 27 May 2003, p. A5.

35. *21 shijie jingji baodao*, 2 June, 2003, p. 2; Q. Hu, "Nation wins oil pipeline agreement", *China Daily*, 29 May 2003; A. Raff, "Russia's Yukos signs big deals on oil for China", *Asian Wall Street Journal*, 29 May 2003; "Russia and China in pledge on oil projects", *South China Morning Post*, 28 May 2003; *Wen Wei Po*, 29 May 2003, p. A3.

36. *Oil and Gas Journal*, 7 July 2003, p. 9.

37. In early 2003, Japan attached a condition to the offer of the loan. It was that the Russian government would provide a guarantee for future repayment of the loan. But Russia, which had already had huge outstanding foreign debts, was reluctant to accept the condition-attached loan offer ("Japan proposes loaning full sum for Russian oil pipeline," *Kyodo News*, 16 April 2003).

38. *Liaowang*, 15 September 2003, pp. 58–60; N. C. Wiest, "Russia puts US$2.5b oil pipeline deal on hold", *South China Morning Post*, 25 September 2003; D. Zhdannikov, "Russia decision on China pipeline may take a year", *Reuters News*, 25 September 2003.

39. A. Bezlova, "China: Russia's second thoughts slow plans to vary oil sources", *Inter Press Service*, 26 September 2003; D. Hsieh, "Bad news for China's oil pipeline plans", *Strait Times*, 6 November 2003; "No decision on routing of Russia 1st east oil export line till 04", *Platts Commodity News*, 24 September 2003; D. Zhdannikov, "Russia decision on China pipeline may take a year", *Reuters News*, 25 September 2003.

40. Taishet is about 500 km northwest of Angarsk. *Huanqiu shibao*, 2 July 2004, p. 2; *21 shiji jingji baodao*, 5 July 2004, p. 9.

41. "Russia has decided on oil pipeline route to Pacific; Tokyo ambassador", *Agence France-Presse*, 24 September 2004; S. Blagov, "China's Russian pipe dream", *Asia Times Online*, 28 September 2004, available at http://www.atimes.com/atimes/Central_Asia/FI28Ag01.html; "Russia to Consider Daqing pipeline after Taishet-Nakhodka study", *Prime-TASS Energy Service*, 24 September 2004; T. Shi, "Wen returns with deals in pocket", *South China Morning Post*, 26 September 2004; *Wen Wei Po*, 21 September 2004, p. A8 and 26 September 2004, p. A4.

42. "China pressures Putin on pipeline", *BBC News*, 15 October 2004, available at http://news.bbc.co.uk/1/hi/world/asia-pacific/3746444.stm; and "Putin team hints Japan will get oil pipeline", *South China Morning Post*, 16 October 2004. The two countries also could not seal an agreement on a proposed gas pipeline that would deliver natural gas from the Kovykta field in eastern Siberia to China and South Korea. It was

expected that even if the discussion of the oil pipeline had been stalled, Russia would have given the gas pipeline the green light. See C. Buckley, "Siberia-China pipeline plan remains in talking stage", *New York Times*, 16 October 2004.

43. "Russia orders oil pipeline to Pacific", *Agence France-Presse*, 31 December 2004; "China shunned as Russia decides on Pacific oil pipeline", *South China Morning Post*, 1 January 2005. Transneft had reportedly proposed to the Russian government that a 4,368 km pipeline from Taishet to Nakhodka be constructed in two stages. Under the first stage, a pipeline would be built from Taishet to Skovorodino, which is only 70 km north from the border between Russia and China. From Skovorodino, a spur to China would be built. Under the second stage a pipeline would be constructed from Skovorodino to the Pacific coast. The two lines would be able to deliver 1.6 million barrels per day. See N. Sharushkina, "Putin orders decision on Pacific oil pipe", *International Oil Daily*, 3 November 2004.

44. J Helmer, "China beats Japan in Russian pipeline," *Asia Times Online*, 29 April 2005, available at http://www.atimes.com/atimes/Central_Asia/GD29Ag01.html; "King Soloman's pipes: Russian oil," *The Economist*, 1 – 7 May 2005; S Blagov, "Moscow hardens towards Tokyo," *Asia Times Online*, 17 August 2005, available at http://www.atimes.com/atimes/Central_Asia/GH17Ag01.html; *Huanqiu shibao*, 9 September 2005, p. 3; R Giragosian, "The Sino-Japanese pipeline struggle," *Asia Times Online*, 18 October 2005, available at http://www.atimes.com/atimes/China_Business/GJ18Cb02.html; "Russia, China talk energy," *International Oil Daily*, 2 November 2005; James Brooke, "Putin promises Japan pipeline," *International Herald Tribute*, Hong Kong edition, 22 November 2005; "Putin, Koizumi gloss over islands row," *South China Morning Post*, 22 November 2005.

45. "Expert: China should be cautious over Japan's moves in Central Asia, *AKIpress (Kyrgyzstan)*, 2 September 2004; S Blagov, "Russia tangles with Japan and China", *Asia Times Online*, 1 September 2004, available at http://www.atimes.com/atime/Central_Asia/FI01Ag01.html; *21 shiji jingji baodao*, 6 September 2004, p. 33.

46. *Shijie zhishi* [Beijing], 16 October 2003, pp. 44–46; *Huanqiu shibao*, 11 August 2004, p.7.

47. According to Robert Jervis, in an anarchic international system a security dilemma exists when "many of the means by which a state tries to increase its security decrease the security of others." Robert Jervis, "Cooperation under the security dilemma," *World Politics*, 30(2), 1978, p. 169.

48. *Huanqiu shibao*, 28 June 2004, p. 7; *Shijie zhishi*, 1 July 2004, pp. 34–35; K. Takahashi "Gas and oil rivalry in the East China Sea", *Asia Times Online*, 27 July 2004, available at http://www.atimes.com/atimes/

Japan/FG27Dh03.html.

49. "Arroyo strikes a Spratlys deal with China", *Far Eastern Economic Review*, 16 September 2004; "China refuses to share offshore natural gas exploration information with Japan", *Xinhua News Agency*, 7 September 2004; "Japan to build vessel to inspect gas fields in East China Sea," *Nikkei Report*, 13 December 2004.

50. J. Brooke, "Japan's new military focus: China and North Korea threats", *New York Times*, 11 December 2004; *Huanqiu shibao*, 13 December 2004, p. 16.

51. "China rejects gas field demand," *Daily Yomiuri*, 1 October 2005; "More talks this month on gas row with Japan," *South China Morning Post*, 2 October 2005.

52. K. Zhang, "China and Japan's oil rivalry unavoidable", *China Daily*, 13 July 2004.

53. British Petroleum, *BP Statistical Review of World Energy 2005*, pp. 7, 10.

54. "India chasing China in Asian superpower rivalry for West Africa oil stakes", *Agence France-Presse*, 15 October 2004; M. K. Bhadrakumar, "India finds a $40bn friend in Iran", *Asia Times Online*, 11 January 2005, available at http://www.atimes.com/atimes/South_Asia/AG11Df07.html; K. Bradsher, "Alert to gains by China, India is making energy deals", *New York Times*, 17 January 2005; N. Buckley, F. Gurrera, R. Marcelo and K. Morrison, "India looks to Russia and Iran for energy", *Financial Times*, 8 January 2005;; "Russia Welcomes India as possible oil partner", *International Herald Tribute*, online edition, 23 February 2005, available at http://www.iht.com/articles/2005/02/22/business/rusoil.html; E. Luce and K. Morrison, "India to open talks with Burma and Bangladesh on gas pipeline", *Financial Times*, 11 January 2005; "India eyes stakes in Russian oilfields", *South China Morning Post*, 21 February 2005; G. L. White, J. Larkin and J. Singer, "India seeks stake in Russia's Yugansk", *Asian Wall Street Journal*, 12 January 2005.

55. Manmohan Singh said, "I find China ahead of us in planning for the future in the field of energy security. We can no longer be complacent and must learn to think strategically, to think ahead and to act swiftly and decisively" (S. Ghosh, "PM cites China: oil PSUs can do with new look, compete abroad," *Indian Express*, 17 January 2005).

56. Jyoti Malhotra, "India, China: comrades in oil," *Asia Times Online*, 19 August 2005 (available at http://www.atimes.com/atimes/South_Asia/GH19Df04.html); Antoaneta Bezlova, "China's oil quest causes friction," *Asia Times Online*, 10 September 2005, available at http://www.atimes.com/atimes/China/GI10Ad04.html; "China's Andes signs EnCana deal," *Asia Times Online*, 17 September 2005, available at http://www.atimes.com/atimes/China_Business/GI17Cb01.html; Indrajit Basu, "India discreet, China bold in oil hunt," *Asia Times Online*, 29 September 2005, available at http://www.atimes.com/atimes/South_Asia/

GI29Df01.html; Anotoaneta Bezlova, "China oil rivalry pushes India, Taiwan closer," *Asia Times Online*, 5 October 2005, available at http://www.atimes.com/atimes/China_Business/GJ05Cb01.html; Jo Johnson, "Lesson for India from energy rivalry," *Financial Times*, 17 October 2005. Siddharth Srivastava, "India, China work out new energy synergies," *Asia Times Online*, 26 September 2006, available at http://www.atimes.com/atimes/South_Asia/HI26Df01.html.

57. See Lee, "China's quest for oil security," pp. 281–283.

58. Michael T. Klare, *Blood and Oil: The Dangers and Consequences of America's Growing Dependency on Imported Petroleum* (New York: Metropolitan Books, 2004), pp. 173–174; Michael Richardson, "An axis of energy?" *South China Morning Post*, 12 November 2004; Sharif Shuja, "Warming Sino-Iranian relations: Will China trade nuclear technology for oil?" Jamestown Foundation China Brief, 5(12), 24 May 2005, available at http://www.jamestown.org/publications_details.php?volume_id=408& issue_id=3344&article_id=2369793 (assessed on 18 September 2005); Helene Cooper *et al.*, "Russia and China, in shift, inch toward Iran sanctions," *New York Times*, 13 July 2006; Marc Wolfensberger, "Iran and China poised to sign pact on oil field," *International Herald Tribute*, 26 November 2006; "China close to deal on second Iranian gas field," *International Herald Tribute*, 11 January 2007.

59. Jane Perlez, "Myanmar is left in dark, an energy-rich orphan," *New York Times*, 17 November 2006; Colum Lynch, "Russia, China veto resolution on Burma," *Washington Post*, 13 January 2007.

60. The countries include Iran, Sudan, Venezuela and Burma (Carol Giacomo, "US warns China on energy ties to Iran," *Reuters News*, 7 September 2005).

61. Robert Zoellick, "Whither China: From membership to responsibility," a speech given to the National Committee on US-China Relations, 21 September 2005; released by the State Department in "United States urges China to be responsible world citizen," *States News Service*, 22 September 2005.

62. In 1969 a Rural Cooperative Medical System was initiated in villages in China. As a result of this medical schedule, there was a huge demand for medical practitioners but the supply was not enough. In order to solve this problem, 'production teams' in the villages could recommend some peasants' children to receive short-term medical training courses at medical schools at the provincial level. After the training, they were sent back to villages as medical practitioners and provided some basic medical services. Peasants called them as "barefoot doctors". Until 1974, there were roughly one million "barefoot doctors" in China. Although "barefoot doctors" only provided basic health services, life expectancy had increased to 68 years in 1985 from 35 years in 1952. Infant mortality dropped to 34 per 1000 from about 250 per 1000 live births during the same period (*Shijie zhishi*, 1 September 2005, p. 29; and Liu Yuanli,

"China's Public Health-care System: Facing the Challenges", *Bulletin of the World Health Organization*, 82(7), July 2004).

63. Poor people in China can hardly gain access to health-care system. According to a national health survey in 2003, about 64% of people in urban areas cannot afford to see a doctor who they should have been treated by a doctor. In rural areas, the figure was even up to 73%. See David Lague, "Chinese health care under fire: criticism, surprisingly harsh and public, signals acute crisis", *International Herald Tribune*, 20 August 2005, Internet Edition.

64. Andrew Thompson, "International Security Challenges Posed by HIV/AIDS: Implications for China", *China: An International Journal*, 2(2), September 2004, p. 295.

65. According to the WHO, a total of 308,000 people died in Africa in 1998 because of wars, but HIV/AIDS killed more than 2 million that year. See World Health Organisation, "Scaling Up the Response to Infectious Disease: A Way Out of Poverty", p. 13, available at www.who.int/infectious-disease-report/. In addition, one-quarter of the adult population in South Africa is HIV positive. As a result, its ability to participate in international peacekeeping is limited and more than two million orphans are without homes. Deaths from full-blown AIDS are not projected to peak until the period 2009–2012, and the number of HIV infections is still increasing. See Jennifer Brower and Peter Chalk, *The Global Threat of New and Reemerging Infectious Diseases: Reconciling U.S. National Security and Public Health Policy* (CA: RAND Corporation, 2003), p. xiv.

66. Ministry of Health, People's Republic of China, Joint United Nations Programme on HIV/AIDS, and the World Health Organisation, *2005 Update on the HIV/AIDS Epidemic and Response in China* (Beijing: National Center for AIDS/STD Prevention and Control, China CDC, 24 January 2006)..

67. "China reports 132, 545 reported cases of HIV infection", *Xinhua News Agency*, 7 November 2005.

68. *Report on the Global HIV/AIDS Epidemic* (UNAIDS, 2002).

69. In a symposium "The HIV/AIDS Pandemic: the Second Wave", hosted by the Center for Strategic and International Studies (CSIS) on 7 June 2005, five countries, China, India, Russia, Ethiopia and Nigeria, were identified as second-wave countries in the fight against HIV/AIDS. All of them would require new strategies for implementing prevention programs. See "Confronting the Second Wave of the HIV/AIDS Pandemic", http://www.csis.org/ (accessed on 14 June 2005).

70. "China outlines strategy to fight AIDS", *China Daily*, 10 July 2004.

71. "Sino-US programme targets HIV/AIDS", http://au.china-embassy.org/eng/xw/t199281.htm (accessed on 13 June 2005).

72. See http://www.unicef.org/china/hiv_aids_535.html and http://www.unicef.org/china/hiv_aids_536.html (accessed on 14 June 2005).

73. "Checking mother-to-child HIV transmission", *China Daily*, 15 January 2005.

74. Stephanie Hoo, "UNICEF chief lists AIDS, childhood injuries as fresh challenges facing a changing China", *Associated Press Newswires*, 24 February 2005.

75. David Murphy, "Red Alert", *Far Eastern Economic Review*, 15 July 2004, Internet Edition.

76. See http://www.chinacdc.net.cn/globalfund/eprojectoverview.asp (accessed on 14 June 2005).

77. "Gao Qiang: fazhan yiliao weisheng shiye, wei goujian shehuizhuyi hexieshehui zuo gongxian" (Gao Qiang: Developing a public health service, contributing to the construction of a socialist and harmonious society)", Ministry of Health, People's Republic of China, available at: http://www.moh.gov.cn (accessed on 27 October 2005).

78. Catherine Armitage and Zhang Yufei, "China looks our way for healthcare solutions", *The Australian*, 19 September 2005, Internet Edition.

79. The section on Asia is available at http://www.unaids.org/epi2005/doc/EPIupdate2005_pdf_en/Epi05_06_en.pdf (accessed on 23 November 2005); "Fight against HIV/Aids lags on the mainland, UN warns," *South China Morning Post*, 22 November 2005.

80. For studies of good governance and its application to containing HIV/AIDS, see World Bank, *Governance and Development* (Washington, D.C.: World Bank, 1992); World Bank, *Governance: The World Bank's Experience* (Washington, D.C.: World Bank, 1994); Asian Development Bank, Governance: Sound Development Management (Manila: Asian Development Bank, 1995); Lee-Nah Hsu, *Governance and HIV/AIDS* (Bangkok: UNDP South East Asia HIV and Development Project, 2000).

81. *A Joint Assessment of HIV/AIDS Prevention, Treatment and Care in China* (State Council AIDS Working Committee Office and the UN Theme Group on HIV/AIDS in China, December 2004).

82. "HBV victims face improved job chances", *China Daily*, 19 January 2005; "China acts to tackle AIDS spread", *BBC News*, 28 August 2004; and "Law spreads the load in AIDS battle", *Sunday Morning Post*, 29 August 2004, p. 6.

83. "Aids, Sars play role in revision of diseases law", *Financial Times*, 31 August 2004.

84. "New rules to combat AIDS spread", *China Daily*, 28 October 2005; "China to issue rules on AIDS control within the year: health official", *Xinhua News Agency*, 27 October 2005; and "China's fight against AIDS – vaccine in clinical test, regulations on prevention drafted",

Xinhua News Agency, 11 March 2005. Embassy of the People's Republic of China in the United States of America, "Statute shows greater resolve in AIDS control," 13 February 2006, available at http://www.china-embassy.org/eng/xw/t235120.htm.

85. "Human rights situation improved in China", *China Daily*, 12 December 2004, Internet Edition.

86. See www.who.int/3by5/cp_chn.pdf (accessed on 15 June 2005).

87. "Severe Atypical Respiratory Syndrome (SARS) and Workers in China: A Preliminary Analysis", *Solidarity Center*, July 2004; "Nation steps up efforts to contain HIV/AIDS", *China Daily*, 7 April 2004, Internet Edition.

88. See www.who.int/3by5/cp_chn.pdf (accessed on 15 June 2005).

89. Embassy of the People's Republic of China in the United States of America, "China earmarks $476 mln for AIDS/HIV control," 27 December 2005, available at http://www.china-embassy.org/eng/xw/t228326.htm.

90. Matt Pottinger, "China Urges Businesses to Stem AIDS", *The Asian Wall Street Journal*, 21 March 2005; Josephine Ma, "Lack of information hinders fight against Aids", *South China Morning Post*, 19 March 2005.

91. The Website of this organisation is: http://www.aizhi.net/.

92. "Top Chinese leader met with country's most famous AIDS activist", *Agence France Presse*, 18 February 2004.

93. "NGOs play 'outstanding' role in fight against HIV/AIDS: vice health minister", *Xinhua News Agency*, 31 August 2005.

94. Siu-sin Chan, "HIV whistle-blower still paying the price", *South China Morning Post*, 28 March 2005.

95. Siu-sin Chan, "Blood center sues newspaper over report it spread virus", *South China Morning Post*, 28 March 2005.

96. *Ming Pao Daily News* [Hong Kong], 10 February 2005, p. B2; "AIDS in China: blood tests," *The Economist*, 20–26 January 2007.

97. For studies of China's international socialization and learning, see Ann Kent, *China, the United Nations, and Human Rights: The Limits of Compliance* (Philadelphia: University of Pennsylvania Press, 1999) and idem, "China's international socialisation: The role of international organizations," *Global Governance*, 8(3), July – September, pp. 343 - 364.

98. Thomas Christensen, "Chinese Realpolitik", *Foreign Affairs*, 75(5), September–October 1996, pp. 37–52.

99. In July 2005 the U.S. reversed a decades-long policy against helping countries develop nuclear programmes by agreeing to grant India access to civilian nuclear technology while India has not been a signatory to the Nuclear Non-proliferation Treaty and the agreement does not cover

Indian military programmes. It has been argued that the U.S. uses this upgrade in its relations with India to counterbalance China. The U.S. prodded India to vote in a meeting of the International Atomic Energy Agency in September 2005 in favour of referring Iran to the Security Council because of the latter's nuclear programme. Indian leaders have vowed to continue supporting the American stance. China expressed concerns in October 2005 that the agreement would erode international controls on nuclear weapons (see Steven R. Weisman, "U.S. to broaden India's access to nuclear-power technology," *New York Times*, 19 July 2005; Dana Milbank and Dafna Linzer, "U.S., India may share nuclear technology," *Washington Post*, 19 July 2005; Howard LaFranchi, "Why US is shifting nuclear stand with India," *Christian Science Monitor*, 20 July 2005; *Renmin ribao*, 26 October 2005, p. 3; Joel Brinkley, "U.S. nuclear deal with India criticized by G.O.P. in Congress," *New York Times*, 31 October 2005; Siddharth Srivastava, "Beijing blusters over India's nuclear deal," *Asia Times Online*, 5 November 2005, available at http://www.atimes.com/atimes/South_Asia/GK05Df01.html). In late October 2005 the US and Japan reached an agreement to reshape their military alliance. A path-breaking measure is that nuclear-powered warship will be allowed to be based on Japan's territory. Shortly after the announcement of the deal, Junichiro Koizumi vowed that Japan would revise it pacifist constitution in order for its military force to play a more active role in international security (see "U.S. to base nuclear ship in Japan," *International Herald Tribute*, Hong Kong edition, 29–30 October 2005; "Koizumi advocates new military role," ibid., 31 October 2005).

100. Wang Jisi of Peking University argues that the United States should be excluded from the inaugural East Asia Summit scheduled for December 2005 (*Ta Kung Pao* [Hong Kong], 21 June 2005, p. A4). In addition to the 10 ASEAN member states, China, Japan, South Korea, Australia, New Zealand and India will participate in the Summit meeting in Kuala Lumpur.

101. Zoellick, "Whither China: From membership to responsibility."

102. Sherman Katz and Devin Stewart, "Hedging against the China challenge," *PacNet Newsletter* (Pacific Forum, Center for Strategic and International Studies), No. 43, 29 September 2005, available at http://www.csis.org/media/csis/pubs/pac0543.pdf.

12

Problems in Social Security Development: Challenges and Policy Reforms

Raymond NGAN

Have reforms in social security policies during the Hu Jintao and Wen Jiabao era helped bring about improvement in social protection schemes in China? This paper will focus on reforms in such policies, with a particular focus on the following domains: effectiveness of the "minimum living assistance scheme", reforms in unemployment insurance, reforms in old age pension schemes and an overall critique of the 3-tier social security protection system in Mainland China. Can these reform measures seek to enable the Hu-Wen leadership achieve its primary goal of creating a harmonious society? It is found that problems are still abound in unemployment insurance and old age pension reforms with an aggravating wealth gap and rising social unrest among farmers forced off their land to make way for development. The challenge of how to resolve uneven social development, particularly the rich-poor gap between cities and villages, is a fundamental social care challenge for the Hu-Wen government.

Introduction: The Need for a Harmonious Society amid Rising Wealth Gap and Social Unrest

Providing assistance to vulnerable groups and resolving social conflicts are key issues the Hu-Wen government has tried to address in the 11th Five-Year Programme covering the years 2006–2010[1]. President Hu Jintao aspires to build a harmonious society by narrowing the wealth gap and solving widespread political and social problems which threaten stability. Social policies reforms, especially changes in social security protection schemes on vulnerable social groups notably the unemployed, the destitute and the old, are receiving increasing attention from the Central government. One of the main goals in the 11th Five-Year Programme (2006–10) is the aim for an overall increase in income levels and living standards in urban and rural areas, maintain stable commodity prices, and significantly improve living conditions, education, health and hygiene.[2]

This chapter will examine changes made to China's social security measures in unemployment insurance, old age pension and the effectiveness of "minimum living assistance scheme" in urban cities, with an overall critique on the 3-tier social security protection system[3]. It is argued that, despite such reform measures, problems are still abound and gaps in social protection schemes are still obvious with migrant workers flooding from villages and western inner provinces to work in coastal cities. As noted by studies done in the 2006 Blue Book of Social Development,[4] social stability had worsened since 1990 amid widening wealth disparity among urban and rural areas, the rich coastal cities and the poorer inland provinces. A dramatic rise in land disputes and clashes between the public and government officials over environmental issues were noted especially during the years 2003-05.[5] The rural-urban gap remains large. In 2005, per capita disposable income in urban areas rose by 9.6% in real terms to 10,493 yuan. In the rural areas where three-fifths of the population resides, was a modest growth rate of 6.2%, taking average income to just 3,255 yuan.[6] What are the developmental lessons learnt? What are the challenges ahead in social care for the Hu-Wen leadership? A more balanced growth formula for China in economic and social development needs to be considered seriously. More concrete and effective social protection measures need to be worked out. Prime social care objectives need to be supported by concrete and detail social development implementation plans with resource support by the Central government.

Problems in Social Security Development

As a Socialist country geared to protect the livelihood of workers, social security schemes were introduced early in Communist China since 1951 with the enactment of the Labour Insurance Act.[7] However, it turned out to protect mostly salaried workers in state-owned and collective enterprises in urban areas.[8] The rural population was largely left out until 1991, when the State Council decided to introduce Old Age Insurance Protection schemes in rural areas. However, participation in these rural social insurance schemes are still largely voluntary, and is mostly confined to relatively well-off rural county areas along the coastal regions, and the level of benefits are still low and not attractive.[9] Chow (2000) commented that "experience has found that this kind of savings scheme in rural counties would be most useful to peasants who are neither rich nor poor."[10] The rich ones would find the protection offered insignificant while poorer rural areas are too poor to make regular monthly contribution. Since 1978, with more migrant young workers flooding to cities for open employment, there is an enlarging care gap in social protection for older people living in the countryside.[11]

Economic reforms since 1978 are changing the Socialist system of "iron-rice bowl" lifelong employment for workers to one of employment by contract.[12] A new group of contract workers have been employed by private and collective enterprises. In the 10th Five-Year Development Plan (2001–05), massive reforms had been introduced in order to make state-run enterprises become more competitive. These measures include the restructuring and amalgamation of enterprises, putting bankrupt enterprises on sale, the promotion of "responsibility" in management and the adoption of a "shareholding system".[13] However, this policy of reforming and revamping bankrupting state-owned enterprises (SOEs), has exacerbating the problems of unemployment with a huge increase in redundant workers.[14] The problem of how to provide adequate unemployment insurance benefits to unemployed and redundant workers in bankrupting SOEs is taking shape to be a major social protection problem affecting the move to promote a harmonious society. How to help these workers find jobs and not on the dole is a matter of overriding concern!

China's Labour Insurance system, before its massive reform changes in 1993, was largely an enterprise-based pension system with the sole contribution shouldered by workers' employing enterprises, with contribution rate as high as about 20% to 25% of workers' total wage payments. Besides, the benefit levels were very generous, with some pensioners collecting pensions of 80% of their final salary, along with housing quarters and subsidised health care.[15] With the implementation of the one-child policy, China is facing rapid population ageing as a result of falling fertility and increasing longevity in the past several decades. The population aged sixty and above increased from 76.6 million, or 7.6% of the total population, in 1982 to 127 million people in 2000, or 9.8% of the total population.[16] It is projected to increase further, to 15.2% of the total population by 2020.[17] It is thus understandable when the World Bank warned in 1997 that China's old age pension system is financially unsustainable in view of an ageing population with mounting cost of pension payments shouldered primarily by workers' employing enterprises, being mostly state-owned enterprises or collective enterprises.[18]

On the other hand, the benefit levels provided by the "Minimum Living Assistance scheme" (zuidi shenghuo baozhang) in urban cities are very low and meagre for a subsistence living for the urban poor. The average per capita assistance level (159 yuan) was only 14% of the average wage and 23% of the per capita disposable income of urban residents in 2004, with a wide range in assistance levels among the affluent and poor cities.[19] For example, the assistance scale rate in October 2005 was 330 yuan per month in the affluent city of Guangzhou in Guangdong Province in the South and 161 yuan per month in Urumqi city in the West inner province, reflecting a poverty-stricken scale rate of assistance in poor cities.

Correspondingly, the unemployment insurance is also faced with a low assistance benefit level. In average, it is as low as 30% to 40% of the average wages, compared with the standard rate of 50% of workers' former salary before unemployment as proposed by the International Labour Office.[20] With rising levels of unemployment, gaps in social protection in terms of adequacy over a maximum period of two years as provided by the unemployment insurance and the Minimum Living Assistance scheme are creating mounting social problems affecting the steady move towards a harmonious society.

Lastly, reforms in medical care are pushing hospitals to be market-driven and self-financing, with mounting increase on the level of fees and charges for surgical operations, medical scans, laboratory tests and examinations. Ordinary people without a medical insurance scheme by their employing enterprises are facing high cost of payments for these medical expenses. However, the cost of public expenditure on medical and hospital payments for insurance workers in state and collective enterprises are on an alarming increase. It rose from a level of 70 billion yuan in 1990 to 476.4 billion yuan in 2000, an increase of seven times in ten years. It had increased to 568.4 billion in 2002, a further increase of 24% when compared with that in 2000.[21] The Hu-Wen leadership is paying close attention to redress this unhealthy spending pattern.

Summing up, although the Hu-Wen government is calling for the strong need to develop a harmonious society for a stable government, old problems in social security protection schemes are still abound, with aggravating care gaps for an effective social care safety-net for rural farmers, unemployed worker, and a worrying inflation in medical and hospital expenses. How could the Hu-Wen leadership effectively tackle these problems in their social care agenda for the whole country?

Reforms in Social Security Provisions: What Next and How Effective?

Major Goals in Social Security Reforms

In the Fifth Plenum of the 16th Central Communist Party held in

October 2005, President Hu Jintao called for the need to build a harmonious society by narrowing the wealth gap and solving widespread political and social problems which threaten stability. As a result, major goals set in the 11th Five-Year Programme 2006–2010 are: maintaining social harmony, rapid and sustainable economic growth, further reducing poverty and integrating more with the world economy. Social security reforms especially in examining their further scope of extending effective coverage to include the rural population and in enabling more unemployed and redundant workers returning to work are heralded as important social policies. It has been reported by the media that "providing assistance to vulnerable groups and resolving social conflicts are the key issues the Hu-Wen government has tried to address in the 11th Five-Year Programme.[22] The provision of effective social care safety-nets through social security reforms is being adopted as a positive way to address social conflicts.[23] Main policy goals in the 11th Five Year Programme include notably:

  i)   how to strive for a more healthy and complete social security system so that the contribution load can be spread more evenly among the State, employing enterprises and workers,
  ii) further reduce the number of people living in poverty,
  iii) create more jobs in urban and rural areas,
  iv) significantly improve health and hygiene.

Approaches and Policies to Improve Unemployment Insurance

Following massive economic restructuring of bankrupting SOEs, there has been a marked increase in unemployed and redundant workers. The official unemployment rate has been on the increase from 2.39 million people or 1.8% in 1985 to 5.95 million workers or 3.1% in 2000 (Table 1).[24] However, more workers have been unemployed in cities (9.43%) compared with 1.15% in rural villages, according to estimates from the Chinese Academy of Social

Sciences.[25] The overall unemployment rate for the country as a whole has climbed up to 4.3% in 2003 reflecting a situation where more redundant workers face much difficulties in looking for re-employment. Table 2 shows the successful re-employment rate for redundant workers from 1995 to 2001. It has been dropped from a successful job-placement rate of 50% in 1998 to only 30.6% in 2001.

Table 1
Number and Percentage of Unemployed Workers in China, 1985–2000

	1985	1994	1995	1999	2000
Unemployment rate (%)	1.8%	2.8%	2.9%	3.1%	3.1%
No. of unemployed workers (in millions)	2.39	4.76	5.20	5.75	5.95
No. of people on unemployment insurance (in millions)	n.a.*	1.96	2.61	2.71	3.30

*Remark: n.a. = not applicable, as unemployment insurance was introduced only in 1986.

Source: State Statistical Bureau, *China Statistical Yearbook* (Beijing: State Statistical Publishers), various years.

Table 2
Successful Re-employment Rate, 1995–2001

Year	Yearly total no. of Redundant Workers	No. of Redundant Workers in SOEs	Cumulative total no. of Redundant Workers	No. of Re-employed Workers in SOEs	Successful Re-employment Rate (%)
1995	5,635,038	3,683,824	—	—	—
1996	8,147,998	5,419,636	—	—	—
1997	6,343,060	6,343,060	—	—	—
1998	7,389,228	5,622,148	8,769,314	6,099,000	50.0%
1999	7,814,733	6,185,709	9,371,765	4,920,000	42.0%
2000	5,122,882	4,452,293	9,113,104	3,610,000	35.4%
2001	8,314,496	7,343,136	7,416,781	2,270,000	30.6%

Source: *China Labour Statistical Report, 1996–2001*, China Statistical Publisher: Peking.

A new three-tier basic income support system had been set up during the years 1997 to 2000. Under this three-tier system, laid-off and redundant workers are encouraged to approach Labour Re-employment Service Centres set up by their enterprises and counties to attend retraining and reemployment services. They are also paid with a monthly basic living subsidy for up to a maximum of three years. The intention is that workers with such living allowances, will be able to receive retraining and take advantage of reemployment services without worrying about making a living. After the three years' lapse in re-training, if workers are still unable to find a job, they can receive unemployment insurance up to a maximum of two years. If this period also expires before they have found employment, they are to be referred to the last tier of basic income support, namely the Minimum Living Assistance package, which is the lowest level of cash assistance for the destitute living in metropolitan areas in China. The provision of this three-tier income support system, however, is not available in rural villages.

Although labour re-employment centres have been effective in enabling large number of unemployed and redundant workers find open employment after attending re-training courses, the problem of abuse in cases whereby some redundant workers are quite hesitant to lose their serving employment ties with near-bankrupting SOEs for fear of losing their hitherto entitlement in staff quarters, subsidised housing benefits, medical insurance and nursery services. Thus after the lapse of three years training experiences in these re-employment centres, quite a number of redundant workers are still with low motivation to look for open employment. Qiao Qing[26] observed that quite a number of such redundant workers are receiving double benefits with cash both from the training and cost of living assistance rates by the labour re-employment centres and those from their part-time jobs in a move to still maintain their housing and medical care benefit entitlements by their near-bankrupting SOEs.

A major change in policy took effect in 2000. Redundant workers and laid-off workers with their employment contracts formally terminated by bankrupting SOEs are to receive direct assistance by the unemployment insurance administered by the Provincial Ministry of Labour and Social Security for a maximum period of two years. They will not receive the cash living assistance from the labour re-employment centres. Redundant workers who are still not yet laid-off by near-bankrupting SOEs are still getting cash living benefits from labour re-employment centres but with a maximum period of three years. Cash benefit assistance will be withheld by these centres after the three-year period even if these redundant workers are still without open employment. Furthermore, they need to cut off their serving employment ties with their former near-bankrupting SOEs and cling on unemployment insurance as their living benefits to no more than 24 months. It reflects a strong determination by the Central government to push redundant workers looking for successful job placements and not cling on cash benefits by the labour re-employment centres. According to the writer's in-depth interviews with senior officials from the Guangdong Social Insurance Bureau and the Labour Department in 2002 in Guangzhou, the effect of this push policy for redundant workers to become formal unemployed workers is to push them to look for new jobs and "chopping off" their housing and medical entitlements with their former SOEs. It is anticipated that in the years to come, more cash benefits and re-employment training courses would be provided by the Ministry of Labour and Social Security in charge of the unemployment insurance whereas the scope of services by labour re-employment training centres by local enterprises would become smaller and belittle. This is the policy named as "putting redundant workers back to the proper care of unemployment insurance. Official statistics showed that the number of redundant workers receiving cash assistance support by labour re-employment training centres dropped to 1.9 million workers in 2003 when compared with a peak record of 6.57 million workers in 2000.[27] In the 11th Five-Year Programme 2006–10, the Ministry of Labour and Social Insurance will take an active role in providing unemployment insurance benefits to redundant and laid-off workers with an active move to push them for open-employment via re-employment training courses by their local labour district offices.

The intent is to bring unemployment benefits and re-employment work under the domain of one single Ministry and Department (Ministry of Labour), instead of branching out through fragmented and small labour re-employment training centres by enterprises. The ultimate goal, fundamentally, is to push redundant workers back to work.

How effective is this change in unemployment cash benefits for redundant workers? It has been noted by Wu[28] that in recent years, the total number of workers on unemployment insurance has been steadily declining. According to official statistics,[29] the number of people participating in the unemployment insurance plan decreased by 1.73 million compared with 2001. Thus at a first glance, it seems that this policy has some effect in reducing the number of people on unemployment insurance and get back to open employment. However, one should not have overlooked the fact that this is also due to a booming economy following China'a admission as a full member of the World Trade Organisation in November 2001 with more job opportunities available. Also, the success in opening up new jobs in community and amenity cleansing services, minor in-house repairs, baby-sitting and home care for frail elders and minor environmental anti-pollution works by community services centres set up by local street and district offices with the support from the Ministry of Labour and Social Security and the Ministry of Civil Affairs are also helping trainees in labour retraining courses to go back to open employment. Thus it is not a policy of pushing redundant workers to take away their weakening housing and medical benefit entitlement links with their near-bankrupting SOEs that is at work but more due to effective channels of opening up more jobs for regular employment that counts. The Ministry of Labour and Social Security should look for effective ways of opening new regular jobs for redundant workers apart from conducting labour retraining courses with living assistance benefits and unemployment insurance. It is a major challenge in the years to come in the 11th Five-Year Programme (2006–10).

How adequate is the level of benefits provided by unemployment insurance? Before answering this question, it is important to note that in May 1998, it was decided at the meeting on reemployment of laid-off workers of state-owned enterprises convened by the Ministry of Labour and Social Security that the rate of unemployment insurance contribution would be increased from 1% to 3% of total wages, of which 1% would be borne by individual workers. The uplifting in this contribution rate is considered necessary as unemployment insurance revenue was inadequate to meet expenditure, especially when a considerable portion of the living expenses of laid-off workers had to be covered by the unemployment insurance.[30] The other 2% are borne by workers' employing enterprises. However, cases of missing contribution by some irresponsible enterprises have been found. The Ministry of Labour and Social Security noted that there is a discrepancy in the actual unemployment insurance contribution revenue and the "should be" contribution from enterprises. The former is 20.3 billion yuan in 2003 and 24.9 billion yuan for the latter, a discrepancy of 4.6 billion yuan. The Chinese Academy of Social Sciences Blue Book study in 2004 found that the level of unemployment benefits are still at low to subsistence level approximating 30% to 40% of the average total wages which falls below the 50% former wage levels for unemployed workers set by the International Labour Office.[31] Moreover, for ordinary workers with less than ten years of contribution record for unemployment insurance, their maximum claim is 18 months. Only those workers with more than ten years' contribution record could get the maximum entitlement period of 24 months.

Despite the rise in contribution rates from 1% to 3% of total wages, expenses for meeting payments for unemployment insurance, medical subsidies, widow and survivors benefits, labour re-training living cost assistance and expenses for training centres and job-placement centres are on the meagre. Table 3 shows the pattern and proportion of expenses for unemployment insurance in 2001. As nearly all the revenue (81.83%) had been used as unemployment insurance payments, the remaining expenses for covering medical subsidies for redundant workers is as low as 4.84% of the total spending for unemployment insurance funds. This is considered as barely sufficient when most workers' medical insurance expenses are in the range of 8% to 10% of total wages. The level of medical subsidy for redundant and unemployed workers are significantly low when compared with workers in steady employment. It is thus understandable why so many redundant workers are reluctant to cut off their medical insurance benefits with their near-bankrupting enterprises. The improvement for a reasonable and comparable level of medical subsidy for unemployed and redundant workers should not be overlooked.

Table 3
Proportion of Unemployment Insurance Expenses, 2001

	$ (,000)	%
Unemployment insurance funds	832,563	81.83
Medical subsidies	49,260	4.84
Burial and survivors' dependent benefits	1,003	0.10
Training courses subsidies	81,812	8.04
Job placement service subsidies	52,752	5.18
Total	1,017,390	—

Source: *Yearbook of Ministry of Labour and Social Security*, 2000.

Policies and Improvement in the Level of Assistance Provided by the Minimum Living Assistance Scheme in Urban Cities

With massive economic reforms towards the development of a Socialist Market Economy, the benevolent intent by the Central Government to provide a basic subsistence allowance for the urban poor appeared imminent. In September 1997, the State Council called for the policy to establish a Minimum Living Assistance System for urban poor residents across the country, requiring that a minimum living guarantee system for urban residents in cities and towns be established during the period of the 9th Five-Year Plan. As of September 2002, the system had spread to almost all major cities in China, with 19.63 million poor people on the dole.[32] Among the recipients of this Minimum Living Assistance, 79% belong to the so-called new urban poor – redundant and laid-off workers whose unemployment insurance had expired and who are still awaiting for employment, with a per capita household income lower than the minimum living standard, pensioners falling under the old labour insurance system with meagre pension levels, and unemployed migrant workers.[33] The remaining 21% come from the destitute and the "three-nil" (older people with no family members, no income and no earning capacity). Thus, it seems that a cash safety-net has been established for urban poor residents.

Table 4 shows that the total spending on payments for the Minimum Living Standard Assistance scheme in urban cities in China is in the range of 18.5 to 20.5 billion yuan for the year 2004 to 2005.[34] This spending reflects the low assistance rate paid to recipients – the average minimum living standard nationwide was 154 yuan per capita per month, and the average minimum living allowance payment to beneficiaries nationwide was 65 to 70 yuan per capita per month, with fluctuation in the payment levels among affluent cities along the coast and the South, and poorer cities in the West and inner provinces.[35] Tong commented that this level of subsistence allowance is considered low (being only 22.2% of the average urban workers' income per month).[36] He further recommended that there is a need to raise the subsistence allowance to at least 30% of the average urban workers' monthly wage.

However, this safety-net subsistence allowance in urban cities is not without its inherent problems. First, in terms of source of financing, all payments are shouldered by local counties and metropolitan governments, which in turn tax enterprises to raise revenues, and from owners of all forms of enterprises (SOEs, collective enterprises and private enterprises). Enterprises thus face double taxes for social welfare, at both the national and local levels. Second, the protection level is low in metropolitan areas where government are in poor financial circumstances. Thus, only well-off cities in the Special Economic Zones were able to raise the benefit

Table 4
Expenditure in the Minimum Living Assistance Schemes, 2004 & 2005

		Cumulative Spending (in billion yuan)	Average Minimum Living Assistance (in yuan)	Average Monthly Living Supplement (in yuan)
2004	1st Quarter	413.7	—	—
	2nd Quarter	413.2	—	—
	3rd Quarter	415.9	—	—
	4th Quarter	486.2	—	—
2005	1st Quarter	462.8	154	70
	2nd Quarter	462.7	154	70
	3rd Quarter	462.6	154	70

Source: Ministry of Civil Affairs, *Annual Reports, 2004 & 2005*, Beijing, China.

levels by 30% in 1999. Many other cities were handicapped by a lack of sufficient funds. Tong found that there is a wide variation in benefit levels for the Minimum Living Assistance Scheme in December 2005 – it was 300 yuan in Shanghai but was 165 yuan in Sin Ling city in the west inner province.[37] He further commented that the assistance rate was as low as 10% to 14% of the average workers' wages in the cities. It was only barely sufficient for poverty-stricken families not to be starved for a basic living. Overall speaking, although a social assistance safety-net has been set up in urban cities for urban poor families, the prospect of effective social programmes to help these "new urban poor" people jump out of poverty remains dim as they are largely jobless people unable to find jobs in the open market with a long record of unemployment due to personal incapacities in view of their advancing age or disabilities.

Nevertheless, the rural poor families are even worse off in terms of an effective cash subsistence monthly scheme. To start with, the Minimum Living Assistance Scheme has only been set up in cities but not in rural counties. At the moment, most poor destitute families in rural areas have to cling on the decaying "Five

Guarantee" system which seeks to offer basic assistance to the destitute in the areas of food, clothing, shelter, medical care and funeral expenses, being mostly assistance in kind that cash benefits. This "Five Guarantee" system is in decay when the "family responsibility production system" was introduced since 1978 emphasizing the contribution of each peasant household in agricultural production. Lone elders without children appear much disadvantaged in terms of household agricultural producing. The problem of rural poverty, however, is a major concern. In 1985, rural poverty levels were defined as individual annual net incomes below 200 yuan. It was estimated that 125 million people, or 14.8% of the total population, were known to be living in poverty. The poverty line was raised to 530 yuan in 1995. According to this definition, about 65 million people, or 7.1% of the total population, were still known to be living in absolute poverty.[38] This level was revised to 550 yuan in 1997.[39] The Ministry of Agriculture estimated that at least 26 million farmers live in poverty in 2004, with average earnings of 579 yuan (US$71) a year whereas the expenses for living essentials was at least 602 yuan (US$74). It was further found that 72% of rural residents cannot afford to see doctors.[40] These are fundamental care problems which the Hu-Wen administration need to tackle.

At the annual session of the National People's Congress held on 5 March 2006, Premier Wen Jiabao declared a pledge to build a "new Socialist countryside" in the 11th Five-Year Prgoramme (2006–10) to address the problem of rural poverty and to speed up rural development to help raise farmers' living standards and productivity amid rising fears about the widening wealth gap between cities and rural areas and an upsurge in rural unrest. To implement this, Premier Wen pledged to increase rural spending by 14.2% to 339.7 billion yuan in 2006–07, a net increase of 42.2 billion yuan over the previous year.[41] The Central Government would make a major change to shift its priority in infrastructure investment from cities to the countryside to improve farmers' living conditions. Premier Wen also hailed the policy of scrapping the agricultural tax throughout the country starting in 2006 in a way to boost farmers' income. Besides, the Central Government will increase budget expenditure for nine-year compulsory education by 218.2 billion yuan (US$27 billion) in 2006–10 after waiving tuition and miscellaneous fees for all rural students by 2007. Premier Wen declared that the construction of rural infrastructure must be accelerated and the emphasis should be on projects most crucial to farmers' daily lives. It appears that the Hsu-Wen leadership is determined to build up a "new Socialist countryside" for a harmonious society with the aim to improve the livelihood of farmers. Premier Wen proclaimed that the Central government will allocate an additional 4.2 billion yuan to extend a pilot rural co-operative health system to 40% of the countryside, and to spend more than 20 billion yuan in the 11th Five-Year Programme on renovating hospital facilities in townships and counties.[42] These appear to be good news for people living in the countryside. But the crux of the problem is not on how much money to be further spent in additional infrastructure and hospital facilities but on how effective are these additional funds being able to create new job opportunities for countryside and township enterprises and on rising farmers' incomes and an affordable health and hospital care systems for farmers. The abolition of the agricultural tax is a good start but there should be detailed plans on ways to increase farmers' income.

Reforms in the Old Age Pension Plans

Massive reforms were launched in the early 1990s to revamp the hitherto enterprise-based Labour Insurance schemes into a national Old Age Insurance system, administered at the provincial level by Social Insurance bureaus. All pension-related receipts and payments on pensions are now the responsibility of these bureaus. This new arrangement immediately solved the pension debt problems of bankrupting SOEs and collective enterprises, as the burden of inadequate pension payments are to be met by the Provincial Social Insurance Bureaus, with payments coming from the unified Old Age Insurance Fund.[43] Major features of these reforms are summarised as follow:

- The introduction of an individual pension account with workers contributing 2% of their monthly wages in 1993, and incrementally increased to 8% in 2005;
- The creation of a Multi-tier Pension Accounts comprising a Basic and Supplementary pension account, and an individual pension account to allow a differing pension level among those workers who have a higher level of contribution;
- The introduction of multi-tier source of financing changing from sole contribution by enterprises to tripartite sources with "enterprise-workers-state" financing.
- Changing the Pay-as-you-go (PAYG) Labour Insurance system to a partially funded system with funds accumulated in workers' individual pension accounts in the national Old Age Insurance Fund.

The major intent of the above measures is to reduce the pension debt borne by bankrupting enterprises who faced difficulties in meeting the rising pension payments among its older retirees. It was envisaged that with the new policy requiring workers to make monthly contributions to their own individual pension accounts, the contribution rate would be increased by 1% in every two years since 1993, so that eventually it could be able to climb up to about 11% of their monthly wages. Correspondingly, the contribution load for enterprises could be able to be reduced from the 25% of total workers' wages to about 10% to 15%.[44] How effective are these changes? What is their prospect of success in the Hu-Wen administration?

To start with, the so-called unified national Old Age Insurance scheme is not yet fully implemented successfully throughout China. Administration of pension payments and receipts are still the work of Provincial Social Insurance Bureaus (now renamed as the Ministry of Labour and Social Security), and unified pension payments are still kept largely at local provincial levels. Transfer of payments among different provinces, especially from Provinces in the South to inner and poorer provinces in the West as in the case of migrant labours, are still not done effectively. According to the study by the Chinese Academy of Social Sciences,[45] in the year 2001, with the exception of the three provinces Fujian, Zhejiang and Shandong, nearly most provinces faced problems in making balanced payments among their annual receipts for pension claims. An accumulated annual deficit of 30 billion yuan was reported in 2001, especially among cities with older industries.[46] There is still room for improvement in extending the unified pension system from local cities and provinces to a national level.

Secondly, the problem of under-reporting and missing contribution in enterprise payments to the Old Age Insurance system has been identified from time to time by local Ministries of Labour and Social Security. This problem is particularly acute among those private enterprises employing large number of migrant workers without a registered household in the employing city. Some unfaithful private enterprises tend to under-report the total number of workers employed as gathered by the author's field studies done in Dongguan in the Pearl River Delta in 2005–06. The difference can be about 100 workers being under-reported among those employing over 500 workers. As a result, the Ministry of Labour has increased the number of regular spot checks on these enterprises. Yet the problem of under-reporting and missing contribution among enterprises are still reported from time to time.

Thirdly, the contribution load by enterprises does not reduce much whereas the contribution level by workers is on the constant increase. Enterprise contribution only falls slightly but not considerably from about 25% of total workers' wages to 20%. This is because the number of retirees are still large especially among older industries, and the pension rate can be as high as over 80% for long-serving cadets, and a rise in the annual pension deficit. However, the workers' field studies in Guangzhou city and Dongguan in 2005–06 found that some workers begin to complain on the steady rising pension monthly contribution, being now already 8% of their monthly wages in 2005. This, together with monthly deductions for medical insurance (3%) and housing allowances (5%), are adding almost to 16% of their total monthly wages. Some workers also complained that they need to spare at least 5% of their monthly salary to pay for their children's educational expenses. At least over 20% of their wages are eventually deduced to meet such social security, housing, medical and educational expenses, reducing their take-home pay and fewer money to be sent back to their host cities and rural counties, This explains why the workers' contribution rate for Old Age Pension is kept at a ceiling of 8% to 11% at the moment, despite the original plan to increase in by 1% in every two-year interval since 1993. In cases involving bankrupting enterprises which failed to keep regular employers' contribution to their workers' pension plans, the Central government has to pump in relevant funding as the last resort.

In the 11th Five-Year Programme (2006–10), Premier Wen pledged to proceed with Old Age Pension reforms in the following areas:

i) to improve the low pension rates for older cadets and retirees who retired before the 1993 pension reforms as their monthly salary was low,

ii) to promote the implementation of individual workers' saving accounts with effective computerisation throughout the country to allow mobility of workers among different provinces,

iii) to promote the maximum participation among all forms of enterprise and workers with a view to include individual entrepreneurs, and

iv) to promote the prospect for the development of effective multi-sources of financing in Old Age Pension Funds so as to spread the contribution load among employing enterprises, workers and the Central government.

Towards the Construction of a New "Socialist Countryside"

The Hu-Wen government pledged to build up a new countryside to improve rural living standards and spur demand being identified as its primary task in the 11th Five-Year Programme period (2006–10).

This was set in the context that in 2005, rural residents earned an average 3,255 yuan (US$402) per head, less than one-third of the urban average, with about 26 million farmers live in poverty. Their earnings averaged 579 yuan (US$71) a year, with expenses for essentials of at least 602 yuan (US$74).[47] Major development tasks in the road towards the construction of a New Countryside Development Plan in the captioned Five-Year Programme are as follow:

- Budget expenditure for agriculture, rural areas and farmers will total 339.7 billion yuan (US$42 billion), or 14% more than last year (2005); This additional spending will be spent on upgrading agriculture and rural social services;

- The Central Government will totally abolish agricultural tax starting in 2006;

- Charges on rural students receiving nine-year compulsory education will be eliminated in two years from 2006. The spending on compulsory education will increase by 218.2 billion yuan (US$26.9 billion) from 2006 to 2010;

- There is a need to push for the modernisation of agricultural production in the 11th Five-Year Programme. The construction of rural infrastructure must be accelerated and the emphasis should be on projects most crucial to farmers' daily lives so as to boost their income levels and spur demand for goods and services. The Central government will shift its priority in infrastructure investment from cities to the countryside to improve farmers' living conditions;

- The Central Government will spend at least 20 billion yuan on improving township health services during the period of the 11th Five-Year Programme. In 2004, the central government spent 3.7 billion yuan on subsidizing medical care in rural provinces. The aim is to develop an affordable health and hospital care system to rural citizens on renovating hospital facilities in townships and rural counties. An additional 4.2 billion yuan will be allocated to extend a pilot co-operative health system to cover 40% of rural population throughout the country.[48]

The Central government's bold determination to improve citizens' living in the countryside should be praised as recognizing the need for a balanced path for economic and social development not only in urban areas but also in rural farmlands and township industries. In the National People's Congress held in March 2006, President Hu Jintao called for a focus on the countryside through the captioned social development programmes to help raise farmers' living standards and productivity amid rising fears about the widening wealth gap and an upsurge in rural unrest. These developmental plans are enshrining the goal of creating a harmonious society initiated by President Hu. Premier Wen also pledged to apply the guiding policies of industry replenishing agriculture and the cities supporting the countryside.

Will farmers benefit from these higher spending to support rural infrastructure development in improving tap water, electricity supply and roads and in upgrading agricultural products, an affordable health care and hospital system, and the vision of higher income as a result of the abolition of the agricultural tax? Professor Lin Yufu, Director of the China Centre for Economic Research at Peking University, alerted that exclusively increasing farm output gives rise to the situation that low prices of grain hurt farmers. He pointed out that apart from increasing spending on infrastructure development in farmlands, the Central government should also aspires to promote employment structures and create new job opportunities by supporting township industries in rural counties. This will enable rural citizens have more choices in either new industrial employment or choosing to stay on the farmland with higher-yield agricultural products. All this will translate into sustained growth in income for farmers and ex-farmers. [49] Nonetheless, he agreed that the efforts to build a new countryside are bound to bring substantial benefits to the farmers.

The Hu-Wen government has set a new orientation in moving away from the hitherto heavy dependence on investment-driven economic growth in urban regions to a boost to promote economic and infrastructure development in the countryside by improving farmers' livelihood with additional funds from the Central government to improve their access to an affordable health and hospital care, compulsory education, increased job opportunities in rural township industries and abolishing the agricultural tax for farmers. This will seek to promote a harmonious society. In the years to come, the challenge lies in changing the mindset of local officials. Most of them still have a single-minded focus on building more factories and plants, as opposed to investing in existing operations to make them more efficient, and in education and health care to make the people more productive.[50]

An Affordable Health Care System for All?

Health care reforms in late 1980s and 1990s had made fundamental changes to the public health insurance system in China. As hospitals are made to be market-driven towards self-sufficiency, charges for operation and hospital expenses have been on the increase. Those people who are still being covered by the public health insurance system by their employing enterprises are still able to maintain affordable hospital care as such charges are mostly paid by their employing enterprises' medical insurance schemes, although they have to make few relevant charges. This remains the privileges of civil servants, employees of SOEs and those working in private enterprise with their own medical insurance schemes. However, dependants of SOEs employees were only entitled to 50% coverage and dependants of private company employees were not covered at all.[51] Besides, migrant workers often find themselves being caught in a "no-care" zone in medical and hospital charges especially for their young dependants as the latter are normally not included in private companies' medical insurance schemes The author's in-depth interviews with migrant workers in Dongguan in fall 2005 found that medical care applies basically to industrial accidents. Outpatient and hospital care for major illness are normally not included in their employing factories' medical schemes. This is especially the case for those migrant workers working in temporary jobs in the Pearl River Delta areas. One adolescent female migrant worker lamented: "We never go to hospital for normal illness. We have no medical insurance. If there is a family member suffering a major illness, we have to borrow money." She came from a village in Anhui province and is working on a temporary job in sewing industry in a factory in Dongguan.

On the other hand, abuses and unnecessary over-spending in medical expenses have been noted among hospitals who are driven to raise charges from patients covered by public medical insurance plans in their employing enterprises. It has been found that over-prescription of antibiotics is a serious problem, accounting for 36% of the total pharmaceutical market in 2202, compared with 17% in India and 5% worldwide, as commented by a MacKinsey Consultancy Report.[52] Another study by Zheng and Hillier found that hospitals without state subsidies were making up for their revenue shortfall by increased medicine sales and economic targeting by individual hospital departments by passing on the additional costs to service users.[53]

Caring of the sick is a problem in the countryside. Farmers seek medical treatment not according to the state of their health but according to its affordability.[54] The study by Han Jun, Director of the State Council Development Research Centre's Rural Development Institute in 2003, among 1,000 rural households in 118 villages in 25 provinces, found that 83% of respondents refused to go to hospital because of the fees, especially high for doing operations which can be as high as 7,000 yuan – much more than an ordinary farmer could be able to afford. In reality, most of the farmers did not have any kind of medical protection and it is very difficult for them to get access to state medical assistance because subsidised public hospitals are few and remote. In some poor rural areas, seriously ill farmers can only seek help from quacks or take local remedies.[55]

It is understandable that the move by Premier Wen to deliver an affordable health care system for farmers in the countryside is a timely and sensible move. In the period of the 11th Five-Year Programme (2006–10), the Central government will speed up the effective implementation of a network of rural medical insurance by establishing medical co-operatives, to which farmers would contribute 10 yuan a month and the government 20 yuan per person in the poorer western provinces. In return to farmers' monthly contribution, this scheme will cover farmers for about 3,000 yuan in medical costs. In June 2005, about 156 million farmers, or 20% of the rural population, were covered by this rural medical insurance.[56] It is envisaged that its effective coverage will be speed-up to 40% with the government's contribution rate increased from 20 yuan to 40 yuan per individual participant of the rural population. Besides, an additional 20 billion yuan will be spent to build up a network of subsidised public hospitals among rural counties and township areas in the countryside. The Central government aspires to build up an effective and affordable health care system for rural people by the year 2008 with full implementation of this medical co-operative insurance system amidst a more easily accessible network of subsidised public hospital services. If successful, this will certainly be a timely good public practice for the rural population.

Concluding Remark:
A Harmonious Society for All?

The Hu-Wen administration is not without its occasional turmoil in social unrest especially among land clearance disputes with local die-hearted residents fighting openly for their reasonable amount of compensation over lands cleared for development and compensated with small payouts. For example, in 1999, nearly 4 million square metres of farmland was requisitioned in the Guangzhou villages of Donghua and Xicheng to build the new Baiyun Airport.[57] Among these landless farmers, they have no social security schemes and are mostly unemployed and live in poverty. Official figures show that industrialisation and urbanisation in the past decade had forced 20 million farmers off their land nationwide. This could exceed 78 million farmers by 2030 if the existing situation continues.[58] A social security system for dispossessed farmers are urgently needed, apart from setting up effective machineries to review the level of reasonable compensation payments to farmlands cleared for re-development.

The next pragmatic measure is how to reduce the problem of aggravating income distribution among urban workers and rural farmers. The Gini coefficient, an indicator of income disparities, reached 0.53 in 2004, far higher than a dangerous level of 0.4.[59] In terms of net income, the urban-rural income gap has expanded from a ratio of 3.2:1 in 2003 to 3.3:1 in 2005.[60] Professor Lu Xueyi, Director of the Chinese Academy of Social Sciences (Sociology), alerted that the huge income gap between urban residents and 140 million rural migrants working in cities also gave rise to social conflicts and crimes, with about 70% of the suspects arrested for criminal offices in cities being migrant workers.[61] The wealth gap is not only between urban and rural areas, but also between the rich coastal cities and the poorer inland provinces. So the move by Premier Wen to proclaim the construction of a new Socialist countryside with a vision to bring in higher income levels and an affordable medical care system, compulsory and free education for rural children, better infrastructure for farmlands with improved facilities in roads, electricity, water, subsidised public hospitals in the counties, appear as essential ingredients in President Hu's path towards the building up of a harmonious society. The 11th Five-year Programme will be a major step for the Hu-Wen leadership to put in concrete terms how the following prime policy goals will be able to be achieved in the years 2006–10: an overall increase in income levels and living standards in urban and rural areas; maintain stable commodity prices; and significantly improve living conditions, transport, education, culture, health and hygiene, and the environment. The author would like to add one more concern: the plight of migrant workers in ineffective labour insurance coverage with mounting spending on hospital care and educational fees for their dependent children in their employing cities which they do not have a registered household status.

Acknowledgements

Data on migrant workers comes from a Strategic Research Grant funded by the City University of Hong Kong titled "Labour Mobility in the Pearl River Delta: Implications for Labour Supply Policy" (Project no.: 7001744) with Raymond Ngan, Stephen Ma and Law Pui Lam in the Research Team.

Notes and References

1. Sources based on *South China Morning Post* and *China Daily* reporting, October 12, 2005 on the Fifth Plenum of the 16th Central Communist Party.

2. "Party aims for leaner growth machine," *South China Morning Post*, 12 October 2005.

3. The 3-tier social security ssfety-net are created by (i) the Minimum Living Assistance scheme in cities, (ii) the unemployment insurance and (iii) a basic living subsidy provided by the Labour Re-employment Service Centres for redundant workers attending labour retraining courses. For details see P. Saunders and X. Shang, "Social security reform in China's transition to a market economy," *Social Policy & Administration*, 35 (3): (2001) pp. 274-289; R. Ngan and K.L. Tang, "Social security reforms and prospects in the twenty-first century", in Joseph Cheng (ed.), *China's Challenges in the Twenty-first Century* (Hong Kong: City University of Hong Kong Press, 2003), pp. 597–626.

4. Chinese Academy of Social Sciences, *Blue Book of China's Society 2006* (Beijing: China Social Sciences Academic Press, 2006).

5. "Challenges remain in steering growth, *South China Morning Post*, 27 January 2006. A12: Editorial.

6. *Ibid.*, see also Chinese Academy of Social Sciences, *Blue Book of China's Society 2005*.

7. J. Dixon, *The Chinese Welfare System 1949–1979* (New York: Praeger, 1981).

8. K.L. Tang and R. Ngan "China: developmentalism and social security," *International Journal of Social Welfare*, 10 (4) (2000), pp. 250–257.

9. R. Ngan, and K.L. Tang, "Social security reforms and prospects in the twenty-first century, " pp. 597–626.

10. N. Chow, *Socialist Welfare with Chinese Characteristics: The Reform of the Social Security System in China* (Hong Kong: Centre of Asian Studies, University of Hong Kong, 2000).

11. Chinese Academy of Social Sciences, *Green Book of China Social Security System, 2001–2004* (Beijing: China Social Sciences Academic Press, 2004).

12. H.L.Fung, *Decommodification Regime and Income Security in Urban China 1949 to 1995*. Unpublished Ph.D.. Thesis. City University of Hong Kong (2003).

13. N. Chow, The Administration and Financing of Social Security in China. (Hong Kong: Centre of Asian Studies, University of Hong Kong, 1987).

14. Redundant workers means workers who are without jobs with their current employers; yet the employers still maintain an employment contract with them giving them still entitlement rights to their housing medical and welfare schemes. See also Chinese Academy of Social Sciences, *Green Book of China Social Security System, 2001–2004*.

15. K.L. Tang and R. Ngan "China: developmentalism and social security."

16. P. Saunders and X. Shang, "Social security reform in China's transition to a market economy," pp. 274–289.

17. *Ibid.*

18. World Bank, *China 2020: Old Age Security* (Washington, D.C.: World Bank, 1997).

19. J. Leung, "The emergence of social assistance in China", paper presented at the Asia's Social Security Symposium: Social Policy and Poverty in East Asia organised by Chinese University of Hong Kong & University of California at Berkeley, 27–29 March 2006, Chinese University of Hong Kong; J. Tong, "Adjusting the basic support for the poor," in Chinese Academy of Social Sciences (ed.), *Blue Book of China's Society 2006*. (Beijing: China Social Sciences Academic Press, 2006), pp. 165–175.

20. H. Mok, *Study on Poverty Alleviation in Hong Kong* (in Chinese) (Hong Kong: Joint Publishing (H.K.) Co. Ltd., 1999).

21. Chinese Academy of Social Sciences, *Green Book of China Social Security System, 2001–2004*.

22. "Party aims for leaner growth machine," *South China Morning Post*, 12 October 2005.

23. J. Tong, "Approaches and policies to enhance social assistance system," in Chinese Academy of Social Sciences (ed.), *Green Book of China Social Security System* (Beijing: China Social Sciences Academic Press, 2004), pp. 21–46.

24. State Statistical Bureau, *China Statistical Yearbook 2004* (Beijing: State Statistical Publisher, 2004).

25. Chinese Academy of Social Sciences (2004), *Green Book of China Social Security System, 2001–2004*.

26. J. Qiao, "Report of the condition of the Chinese workers in 1998," in Chinese Academy of Social Sciences (ed.), *Blue Book of China's Society 1999* (Beijing: China Social Sciences Academic Press, 2004).

27. Chinese Academy of Social Sciences (2004), *Green Book of China Social Security System, 2001–2004*.

28. J.L. Wu, *Understanding and Interpreting Chinese Economic Reform*. (Singapore: Thomson South-western, 2005).

29. Ministry of Labour and Social Security, *Yearbook 2003* (Beijing: Ministry of Labour and Social Security, 2003).

30. J.L. Wu, *Understanding and Interpreting Chinese Economic Reform*.

31. The Chinese Academy of Social Sciences, *Blue Book* (2004).

32. J.L. Wu, *Understanding and Interpreting Chinese Economic Reform*.

33. *Shanghai Encyclopedia* (Shanghai: Shanghai Scientific Press, 1999).

34. Ministry of Civil Affairs, *Yearbook 2005* (Beijing: Ministry of Civil Affairs, 2005); J. Tong, "Adjusting the basic support for the poor."

35. J. Leung, "The emergence of social assistance in China"; J.L. Wu, *Understanding and Interpreting Chinese Economic Reform*.

36. J. Tong, "Adjusting the basic support for the poor."

37. *Ibid.*

38. Chinese Academy of Social Sciences, *Green Book of China Social Security System, 2001–2004*.

39. N. Chow, *Socialist Welfare with Chinese Characteristics: The Reform of the Social Security System in China*; K.S. Lau, "A study of rural social insurance in China," in Chinese Academy of Social Sciences (ed.), Blue Book of Chinese Society 2000 (Beijing: China Social Sciences Academic Press, 2000) pp. 159–166.

40. "Wen pledges prosperity for all," *China Daily*, 6 March 2006. A1–A12.

41. "Wen's vision will remain a dream for us, say poor," *South China Morning Post*, 6 March 2006. A5.

42. "Wen pledges prosperity for all," *China Daily*, 6 March 2006.

43. Wu Jinglian, *Understanding and Interpreting Chinese Economic Reform* (Mason, USA: Thomson Higher Education, 2005), pp. 337–345.

44. Guangdong Social Insurance Bureau, (1998).

45. Chinese Academy of Social Sciences, *Blue Book of China's Society 2005* (Beijing: China Social Sciences Academic Press, 2005).

46. Chinese Academy of Social Sciences, *Green Book of China Social Security System, 2001–2004*.

47. China Ministry of Agriculture, *Yearbook 2005* (Beijing: Ministry of Agriculture, 2005); see also Ministry of Civil Affairs, *Yearbook 2005* (Beijing: Ministry of Civil Affairs, 2005).

48. *China Daily*, 6 March 2006.

49. *Ibid*.

50. *South China Morning Post*, 27 January 2006. Editorial.

51. C.K. Wong, V.L. Lo and K.L. Tang, *China's Urban Health Care Reform: From State Protection to Individual Responsibility*. (London: Lexington Books, 2006).

52. "Few benefit from health-budget rise," *South China Morning Post*, 24 January 2006. A8.

53. Wong. C.K., Lo, V.L. & Tang, K.L. (2006). *China's Urban Health Care Reform: From State Protection to Individual Responsibility*; see also X. Zheng and S. Hillier (1995). "The Reforms of the Chinese health care system: county level changes: the Jiangxi study," *Social Science and Medicine* 41 (8) (1995), pp. 1057–1064.

54. Chinese Academy of Social Sciences, *Blue Book of China's Society 2006*.

55. "10 yuan can mean life or death for rural poor," *South China Morning Post*, 4 October 2005. A7.

56. *China Ministry of Health Year Book 2005*, (Beijing: Ministry of Health, 2005).

57. "Social Security System in sight for landless Guangdong farmers," *South China Morning Post*, 11 August 2005. A6.

58. *Ibid*.

59. Chinese Academy of Social Sciences, *Blue Book of China's Society 2005* (Beijing: China Social Sciences Academic Press, 2005); *South China Morning Post*, 12 December 2005)

60. Chinese Academy of Social Sciences, *Blue Book of China's Society 2005*

61. "Social Security System in sight for landless Guangdong farmers".

13

The Emergence of Non-state Welfare in China: Performance and Prospects for Civilian-run Care Homes for Elders

Linda WONG

Since the late 1990s, civilian-run care homes for seniors in Chinese cities have grown in leaps and bounds. This remarkable phenomenon arises as a result of a mismatch between the need for and the supply of publicly funded programmes. On the need side, the factors at work include rapid aging, rising incomes, changes in work and family life, and state reluctance to assume responsibility for welfare good provision. On the supply side, the weakness comes from diminished family ability, decline of work unit welfare, and government inability to cope with growing unmet needs. The lacuna in service shortfall has been met by the non-state sector using private resources to run care homes under the state policy of encouraging non-profit agencies.

The chapter draws on research findings on 137 non-state care homes in three Chinese cities and in-depth case studies of fourteen homes. The paper examines the agency characteristics, performance and future prospects. It is argued that agency survival and development prospects is affected by four factors: the extent to which care agencies are able to meet the needs of their users, successfully manage their human resources, ensure the agency's financial sustainability, and satisfy the expectation of their investors. The evidence from our data reveals a complicated picture. While agencies generally perform well in serving their customers and maintaining staff satisfaction, they encounter difficulties in financing and service operation that pose grave challenges to agency investors. The resultant problems and uncertainties cast a shadow over their future prospects and also raise questions on the state's nonprofit policy.

Residential Care for Chinese Elders – High Level of Unmet Demands

Since the late 1990s, civilian-run care homes for older people have grown in leaps and bounds in many Chinese cities. In 1999, 17,000 beds were run by civilians, amounting to 1.6% of the 1.09 million social welfare beds in the country. By 2001, the number had tripled to 51,000 beds, or 4.1% of total beds. [1] This remarkable phenomenon arises from the mismatch between the need for and the supply of publicly run programmes.

On the need side, the forces at work derives from a number of demographic and socio-economic dynamics. First, China has entered a stage of rapid aging as a result of improved health care, better living standards, and falling birth rate. In the fifth national census (2001), the proportion of people aged 60 and above rose to 10% and those aged 65 and over reached 7%, thrusting China into the rank of an aging society according to international norm. [2] In particular, longer life expectancy means there are more frail elders susceptible to chronic diseases and declining health who require residential care. According to official estimates, 40–50% of elders (60 and above) suffer from one or more chronic illness. [3] Another survey identifies some 25–27 million elders who suffer from bad health and severe illness, half of whom (12–13 million) require special care. [4] Second, rising incomes have raised the purchasing power of families for goods and services, including elder care. Third, changes in work and family life means that people now have to work longer and harder, increase their incomes through business, study and training, take more frequent work-related trips, or even migrate abroad. Fourth, the decision to launch market reforms has been driven by a desire to relax state control over civil society. This has created greater space for social organisations, including agencies that cater for the unmet social needs of a market society. All these changes fundamentally alter the context for old age care in the Chinese mainland.

On the supply side, the customary agents for old age care have seen their ability in this regard much weakened. First, Chinese families hard pressed with the burden of work, study and parenting are finding it more difficult to care for dependent parents at home, notwithstanding the cultural precept of filial piety. Often, failing health of a surviving parent after the onset of widowhood is what it takes to thrust a family into crisis. Second, the decline of the socialist work unit removes the support, in cash aid, care services, and emotional support, that used to buttress the resources of an urban family.[5] Nowadays, the work of overseeing retired enterprise workers is gradually taken over by street organisations. However, retiree management seldom goes beyond keeping their personal dossiers, dispensing social security, or holding irregular social activities for local elders.[6] Third, the government is not able and willing to take up the main role in providing old age care. State civil affairs agencies, which run welfare homes for destitute elders without families and work units, do not have the means and resolve to expand care homes for ordinary older people. They are painfully aware of their shortcomings – state welfare homes are expensive to run, management is poor, staff morale is low, and the attitude of managers is rigid, passive and fearful of change.[7]

Just how serious is the service shortfall? In 1998, social welfare homes run by the state and collective units came to less than a million. This means a shortfall of 3 to 4 million beds.[8] In respect of urban homes, the 2000 supply was a mere 327,902 beds,[9] enough for only 0.8% of the target population.[10] On the preference side, a national survey conducted by the Ministry of Civil Affairs identified some 12% of Chinese elders nationwide and 5 million urban elders who would like to enter a care facility. Admission rate is actually lower, at only 0.7%, much lower than the 5–7% in industrial societies.[11]

Recognising the grave constraints, the state's response has been to "socialise" welfare responsibility (*shehui fuli shehuihua*). Since 1990, the Ministry of Civil Affairs has adopted welfare socialisation as the cornerstone of its welfare delivery policy. What it means was that the contribution of societal actors other than the state in service provision, funding, and management will be fully exploited. Market demands will determine supply and consumption. Society actors such as social organisations, enterprises, local communities, social groups and private individuals are encouraged to provide services to meet hitherto unmet needs.[12] In 2003, the Ministry of Civil Affairs signalled a new move towards a public management approach. First, government function will change from direct provider to regulator and policy maker. In line with this, the responsibility for service provision will be borne mainly by civil society. Second, there should be higher participation of social forces to fill the vacuum created by state retreat. Third, public services will incorporate the approach of entrepreneurial management; the operation of welfare services will follow a market model. Finally, the government plans to assist community groups and the non-state sector to play a larger role in service provision.[13] The policy window for non-state services is now wide open.

To encourage expansion of non-state social services, including residential care, the state passed the Provisional Regulations on the Registration and Management of Civilian-run Non-Enterprise Units in 1998. This decree governs the formation of non-profit organisations (NPOs) whose mission is to deliver social services that use non-state funds. Institutional incentives take the form of exemption from tax and preferential utility charges. In return, service units must be non-profit making. This does not proscribe surplus earnings but requires that profits gained not be distributed as dividends and must be ploughed back into the business.[14]

Civilian-Run Care Homes for Chinese Elders: Research Findings

To explore the performance and prospects of private old age homes,

Wong and Tang conducted a questionnaire survey of 137 homes in Guangzhou, Tianjin and Shanghai in 2001–2002. Fourteen homes were also chosen for in-depth study. In each home, we interviewed about ten to twelve persons, comprising the founder/investor, superintendent, doctor, nurse, care workers, elderly residents and their family members. The personal interviews gauged the experiences and views of key stakeholders to assess how effectively these homes were meeting the expectations of various parties. The chapter begins with an examination of the service shortfall in light of a mismatch between supply and demand. It then identifies the characteristics of the sample homes. The core of the paper assesses the performance and prospects of these homes along four dimensions – whether they are meeting the needs of their users, how successful they are in resolving the staffing issues, the financial viability of the homes, and the extent to which performance matches the expectation of the founders. It is argued that these issues are critical to the survival and growth of a social service. The first criterion addresses the primary purpose of the organisation. Any agency that fails to meet the needs of its users will lose the raison d'etre for its existence.[15] The second and third variables supply the basic ingredients for an organisation to carry out its work and ensure continuity of service. Finally, if investors' expectations are not fulfilled, the agency loses the foundation for its support. Based on a holistic review of agency functioning, the author concludes that non-state homes in urban China are attaining satisfactory levels of performance in the main but their continuing prosperity cannot be assumed in light of multiple problems and constraints.

Characteristics of the Sample Homes

Our sample of 137 non-state care homes consists of 36 homes in Guangzhou, 51 homes in Shanghai and 50 homes in Tianjin. They were chosen from a list of non-state care homes kept by the municipal civil affairs department to arrive at a sample consisting of institutions of various sizes and auspices. The vast majority – 81.5% – was registered as civilian-run non-enterprise units, 11.1% registered as business enterprises and 7.4% registered as social organisations. Out of the 137 homes, fourteen were chosen as intensive case studies. The questionnaire survey and intensive interviews took place in 2001 and 2002.

In terms of auspices, the sample homes fell into five types. Individual-run units were started by individual entrepreneurs or investors using their own funds. Almost all investors used their own savings, family resources or loans from friends and relatives as start up capital. None borrowed from banks, claiming they had no collateral and were unable to pay the high interests. Community run homes were organised by neighbourhood agencies and received start up grants and land from the local state. Enterprise run homes were organised and funded by state owned enterprises with two purposes: to cater for the unit's retired employees and to place their redundant staff. Shareholders run units were formed by a number of persons jointly contributing capital divided into shares; the funding was mainly private. Joint ventures were formed by various partners. For example, private entrepreneurs teamed up with a street office, or individuals went into business with an enterprise, public institution or social organisation to run the programme. Even in joint ventures, the capital was raised privately. Except for community run units, all homes relied on fee charges as their primary income source. This meant that all homes had to operate on commercial lines in order to survive.

In the Western literature, an economic project that adopts a market mode of operation but embraced social objectives is referred to as a social enterprise. In a social enterprise, the business has primarily social objectives. The surpluses earned are reinvested in the business or in the community, rather than being driven by the need to deliver profits to shareholders and owners.[16] In starting and running a social enterprise, the driving force is the social entrepreneurs, who are commonly referred to as persons who are committed to a social mission, recognise and relentlessly pursue new opportunities, engage in the process of continuous innovation and adaptation, and act boldly without being limited by the resources available.[17] Our private care homes which operate on a market mode but embraces social objectives can be regarded as Chinese style social enterprises and their founders/investors the social entrepreneurs.[18]

Among the sample units, homes operated by individuals were the most numerous, at 36%. Neighbourhood run homes accounted for 28.7%. Units run by state enterprises amounted to 13.2%, a trifle higher than shareholders run facilities, at 12.5%. Only 9.6% of homes were joint ventures.

In terms of capacity, the sample homes supplied a total of 11,706 beds. The size of homes varied a great deal. The largest had capacity of over 1,000 beds while the smallest (a community-run home) had only four beds. The average capacity was 87 beds.

At the time of the survey, the homes (with data returned by 124 homes) cared for 8,646 residents. While the biggest project admitted 916 residents, the smallest unit had only four elders. The average utilisation rate was 72%. The range was rather extreme, from a high of 193% to a measly 8%.

According to the Ministry of Civil Affairs, in 2001, there were 1,620 civilian run care homes providing 60,000 beds that cared for 40,000 residents. The number of residents per home averaged 37 with a utilisation rate of 67%. This meant that our sample homes accounted for about one-fifth of all beds and residents. In comparison, the admission rate was higher than the national average. They were also larger in scale.

Meeting the Needs of the Users

Twenty-four elderly residents were interviewed to find out their characteristics, reasons for admission and satisfaction with the service. The gender split was 11 men against 13 women. Relating to marital status, twenty-one persons were widowed, two were single and one person had his spouse visiting a family member abroad.

Among the twenty-four interviewees, ten elders were in their eighties, nine were in their seventies, two were younger than 70, and three were below 60 but had very poor health. Fifteen elders were still capable of self care but the rest required varying levels of help. Apart from nine elders who did not report a chronic disease, the others suffered from different kinds of health problems. Three elders had heart disease, six were crippled, paralysed or wheelchair bound, and six had other ailments like diabetes, stroke, and epilepsy. Poor health was the most important factor necessitating admission.

Most of the interviewees, baring seven, had pension incomes. The size of the monthly pension was moderate: three persons had a pension below 500 yuan, five had 500 to 700 yuan, three had 700 to 1,000 yuan, and six had over 1,000 yuan. For most, their retirement benefit was not enough to meet the monthly charges, hence family members, mostly children, chipped in to pay the balance.

The idea of going into a home came largely from the elderly person and the immediate family. Fourteen elders initiated the request. For eight residents, the idea came from family members – by children in seven cases and by a sister in another case. In one case, the decision was taken by the person's work unit. Self initiation reflected the pragmatic attitudes of older persons who were unwilling to burden their family with the painful chore of looking after them. The reasons given by the elders included their sickness and frailty, need for constant care, death of the spouse who used to care for them, and sometimes the desire to avoid relationship conflicts.

Elders' children who proposed residential care often met with personal and family pressures. Under Chinese tradition, old people are supposed live out their twilight years in the family. Hence placing a parent in a home had to be justified by objective circumstances. Several reasons were often cited: their preoccupation with work, lack of skill and equipment in caring for sick parents, cramped living conditions, and the special needs of the parent. None of the residents were admitted against their will.

Almost all the residents we talked to felt they made the right decision to go into care. Living in a collective facility gave them the level of care they required, which could not be had in the original family context. As the homes were self-financing, the amount of space, quality of accommodation, food, and degree of care were determined by what charges the residents were willing and able to pay. All the residents seemed to accept the differential standards. A few had stayed in other homes before moving to the present one. In general, there were few complaints about the physical facilities. Residents tended to regard the space constraints as something they could do little about. Most were happy with the services they received, in particular the food and the care and attention of the staff. Homes that had a caring and capable boss who took personal charge of home operation were singled out for praise. Generally speaking, the level of satisfaction was high. The fact that we could only interview residents who were capable of talking to us may mean that the respondents tended to have better health than people whom we could not interview. Unhappy residents were also likely to have left the home.

Similar levels of satisfaction were found among family members who came to visit. Most family members thought fairly highly of the accommodation, facilities, cleanliness, diet, medical treatment, personal care, and human environment. Knowing that their parents were given round-the-clock care gave them peace of mind. In particular, the fact that homes would arrange for immediate treatment or even hospitalisation was a big relief. On the other hand, the question of fees was a concern for most. Apart from rent/bed charges which were fixed, payment for medical treatment, drugs, air conditioning, and consumables (like nappies, special diet) were variable and could be quite costly. A particularly vexing issue was medical treatment costs. In many homes, the treatment and drugs provided by the in-house doctor were not covered by social insurance. Some seniors did not have any health insurance at all and had to pay out of pocket for treatment and drugs. The financial burden often became a source of friction between family members and the home managers. Without authorisation from the family, the resident doctor could not prescribe the needed drugs and procedures.

In an extreme situation, family hardship, triggered by the unemployment of a paying member or financial crisis, could result in the senior being removed from the home.

In general, the in-depth interviews with the residents and their family members confirmed that both parties considered that the care homes were meeting the needs of the users. Satisfaction with the services provided was consistently high. However, many felt the financial pressure in meeting the hefty and variable costs of care, especially for medical services.

Staffing Issues

A care home is a human service. It delivers services to frail users through the mediation of human labour, skills, and attitudes of a highly personalised nature. The work is arduous, exhausting, emotionally draining and often unpleasant. Working hours are exceptionally long but pay is comparatively low. In the sample homes, the service team consists of administrators, doctors, nurses, care workers and support staff. Professional therapists like rehabilitation counsellors, physiotherapists, occupational therapists, dieticians, social workers, and activity coordinators found in the better endowed homes in industrial societies are entirely absent. The rather simple staffing structure of the Chinese facilities reflects the lower level of economic development and occupational professionalisation in China at the present time. Within the care team, doctors, nurses and care workers are core members whose performance and satisfaction is critical in determining the quality of care as well as the stability of the service.

The sample homes (137) employed a total of 220 doctors, 224 nurses and 1,674 care workers. This works out as fewer than two doctors and two nurses in each home. In half of the homes, there was only one doctor and one nurse. The number of care workers varied according to the size of the facility. In general, the care workers made up the bulk of the care staff.

Doctors

Among the doctors, females predominated (65.8%). Age distribution is skewed to the older age groups: 51.9% were aged 36 to 55, 23.3% were 56 and above, and only 24.8% were under 36. On education attainment, 75.5% had post-secondary and above qualification, 23% reached senior middle school level, and 1.5% had junior middle school and below schooling. 83.4% of the doctors were employed full time, with only 16.6% working part time. The typical profile of the sample doctors is a middle-aged female practitioner having a post-secondary qualification. The vast majority provided their services full time.

The interviews with the doctors reveal a number of salient points. First, most doctors were either very close to retirement age or have retired from active medical practice. Yet they were still keen to serve in a post that allowed them to make use of their skills and gave them an income. Second, none of the doctors had worked in a care home before. While it took them some time to readjust and learn new knowledge and skills to treat their elderly patients, they generally felt they were providing a vital service even though the work was demanding. Third, some doctors felt considerable frustration about the treatment they could provide at the home, given the lack of equipment and facilities. Doctors used to working in hospital settings wanted to do more for their patients but felt hamstrung. In particular, the impossibility of claiming home treatment costs from social insurance was a great disappointment because this meant that some patients would be denied treatment. Fourth, pay was regarded as low (at about 1,000 yuan a month) but the doctors did not feel too strongly about this because most were drawing a pension and health insurance benefits from their previous employment. Even those who had not reached retirement accepted the current salary given the difficulty in finding work at middle age. Fifth, most doctors expected to carry on working in the agency. These views suggested a significant level of contentment with the work nature and conditions of service among the home doctors.

Nurses

All the nurses (except one) were females. Home nurses were generally younger than the doctors: 67.6% were below 36, 27.9% were aged 36 to 55, and only 4.4% were older than 56. On education attainment, 52.9% had middle-school and equivalent level (including vocational middle school), 43% had post-secondary and above qualification, and only 4.1% completed lower secondary level and below. Practically all nurses, 93.8%, were employed full time. Thus the typical nurse in a non-state old age home is a female aged 36 and below who had completed senior middle school. Half of the homes employed only one nurse, 21.8% had two nurses, and 28.2% had three, reflecting a low level of nursing input in existing homes.

The interviews with the nurses identified these duties: nursing sick patients, dispensing medicine, giving minor treatment, overseeing rehabilitation exercises, liaising with family members, and even providing personal care. Some nurses saw their chores as overlapping those of care workers. In terms of background, most nurses obtained their training from nursing schools attached to medical schools. Many nurses came from the rural areas. According to them, getting a nursing job in a city hospital and clinic was not easy as there was an over-supply of nurses at the present time. These constraints explained why the nurses were willing to accept the unattractive pay in a care home. At 700–800 yuan per month, their salary was only marginally higher than what care workers got (600–800 yuan) and inferior to pay scales in medical settings. Working in a care home was physically and emotionally draining. Taking care of residents with dementia and difficult personalities was demanding. It was even harder to appease family members who were prone to complain and reluctant to pay for more costly but effective drugs and treatment. In short the work required a great deal of energy, patience and tact. While most nurses expressed reasonable satisfaction with their work, age seemed to affect their desire for job mobility. In general, the older nurses were more likely to envisage continued service with their employer. Some of the younger nurses were more ambivalent. A change of job or agency could not be ruled out when better opportunities arose.

Care Workers

The age and gender characteristics of care workers approximated those of doctors and nurses. Almost all, 91.8%, were women. In terms of age, mature workers outnumbered younger ones: 67.1% were between 36 and 55, 31.7% were younger than 36, and 1.2% were above 56. The education they received was inferior to doctors and nurses, as expected. The vast majority, 73.4%, had lower middle school and below schooling, 23.4% had senior middle school education, while 3.1% had post-secondary qualification. Thus carers in non-state homes were primarily middle-aged women with a rather elementary level of education. Most of the women came from the villages. A small number were redundant workers from state enterprises. All of them worked full time.

Working as a care worker in a home for older people is a round-the-clock affair. They worked non-stop the moment their charges woke up for the day. Depending on the self-care ability of the resident, care workers performed a range of tasks that included dressing, cleaning, feeding, bathing, toileting, exercising, washing and nursing. It was common for a worker to take care of four to eight residents with mixed abilities. Average pay ranged from 600 to 800 yuan a month, depending on work load and the amount of care required.

Our interviews revealed a number of salient features. First, most had no experience in residential care. Very few received any pre-service training. What they knew they learned on the job, picking up from what limited guidance they got from their bosses and supervisors. Second, the competitive edge of these women was their determination to perform any paid work that would allow them to support their family. Not equipped with any special skills, the hard life they had in the villages set them up with a tremendous ability to perform strenuous work and suffer hardship. Third, the women were generally happy with their pay, their reference point being the low income from farm work. Admittedly, furloughed urban workers wanted better pay but all were realistic enough to accept their age, schooling and skill limits. What they appreciated the most was the wage stability. The agencies always paid them punctually. None encountered the wage insecurity and defaults they suffered in their previous jobs. Fourth, even though the work was exhausting and difficult, once having adjusted, most carers actually saw the value of their work and derived satisfaction from serving their dependent charges. This applied to rural women more than women with an urban background.

Our interviews with the bosses and home administrator suggested there was considerable turn-over among the care staff. The principal reasons were the nature of the job and the harsh working conditions. For example, weekly rest days were unusual. Most homes could not release their staff during the Lunar New Year, when it is customary for peasant workers to pay home visits to their native village. Objectively speaking, living and working in the care home without a respite would be detrimental to the health and family life of the carers themselves. Their measly pay was poor compensation for the incredibly long hours they worked. Only the unlimited supply of cheap rural labour and their relatively low expectations ensured a steady pool of human resources needed to run a care home.

In general, the care homes were quite successful in resolving their staffing issues. The doctors and nurses tended to be older in age. Given keen job competition, recruitment and retention was not a problem. For many doctors, working in a care home was a second job after retirement from medical service. The comparative salary did not bother them too much as many had pensions and social insurance from their previous employment. Doctors were generally happy to work in a care home. For nurses, the over-supply of nurses meant that working in a care home was an acceptable option. The job nature was seen as demanding, and the pay inferior. While the older nurses were disposed to see a future in the home, the younger nurses would be attracted by better paying and more pleasant work if they had the choice. As far as personal carers were concerned, recruitment was eased by the vast pool of unskilled rural women. The rural background trained them for hard work, high tolerance and low expectation on working conditions. Many care workers had adjusted to their work and valued the wage stability. However given the low pay and incredibly long hours, it was not always easy to retain staff.

Financing Issues

The initial capital of the homes came from four sources: individual investment, enterprise funding, government subsidy, and social donations. Some homes had multiple funding. 66% of homes had individual investment, 39.6% of homes obtained start up capital from enterprises, 24.7% enjoyed a subsidy from the government, and 13.6% secured donations from society.

Initial capital was required for three types of expenditure. The first and most costly item was for building, repair and renovation of the premises. The second type of spending went to the purchase of furniture, beddings, equipment and consumables. The last item was staff salary. In Shanghai and Tianjin, it was uncommon for homes to ask for a one-off charge for the purchase of furniture and bedding. Only in Guangzhou was the homes authorised to charge an initial sum of several thousand yuan at the time of admission. Nevertheless, some homes preferred not to levy this charge because it would lead to dispute about refunds when the resident eventually left the home.

After the homes went into operation, continued injection of capital was needed to expand the scale of operation and to enhance amenities and services. Apart from neighbourhood run projects, all other care homes had to rely on fee income to keep their services afloat. Hence financial balance was extremely important. We discovered that it was rare for the government and enterprises to make further contribution after the initial capital outlay. Indeed, enterprises often set a time limit for the start up capital to be repaid. For most homes, the timing and frequency of further injection depended on the financial means of the investors and the income generation potential of the business.

Given that private care homes depended on unitary funding, effective control of costs became crucial to agency survival. Eight kinds of costs were reported. In descending order, these were: staff salaries (34%), food (24%), rent (20%), water, electricity and energy (9%), miscellaneous costs (6%), consumables and depreciation (4%), office and transport expenses (2%), and fee charges and taxes to government (1%). Rent and utility charges were most burdensome. Not only did they take up 29% of expenditure, they were almost impossible to trim. The majority of agencies (62%) used rented space. Insecure tenure exposed them to potential and actual ruinous rent hikes and eviction. In contrast, the free space enjoyed by state institutions was an important source of gripe. Private homes saw state welfare homes as having an unfair advantage because the premises were provided free and funding from the government was generous and stable. High utility charges were also a source of unhappiness. On paper, private care homes were eligible for the lower rate charged to civilian households. In reality, most utility companies simply refused to observe the policy and continued to levy the higher rate for commercial users. Such brazen flouting of state policy made operators frustrated and angry.

The financial health of the care homes turned out to be surprisingly fragile. When asked about their financial situation, only 16.9% of homes reported they were making a profit (revenue exceeding expenditure). The greatest proportion of homes, 46.9%, claimed they could balance income and outgoings. Slightly over one third, 36.9%, reported a loss (expenditure exceeding income). This state of affairs was undesirable.

An equally vital concern to a business investor, apart from achieving financial balance, was when the invested sums could be recovered. On this score, the answers we obtained were rather surprising. Only 20.2% of homes estimated they could recover their investment in the near future, 29.4% thought this would not happen any time soon, and 50.5% were not hopeful of recouping their investment in the long term.

Taking into account the homes' difficulty in controlling cost, their income and expenditure situation as well as the uncertain return of capital, they appeared to be financially vulnerable. Only a small proportion earned a profit. More than a third was in deficit and close to half only managed to break even. Long term viability was likewise uncertain. Even though some homes managed to expand incrementally, whether or not more investors would be attracted to the field was unclear if 80% of homes could not see clearly when they could repay their loans. Homes with weaker management might not survive. The more resourceful and savvy investors may not see much of a future in the business.

Meeting the Expectation of Agency Investors/Founders

The in-depth study of 14 homes revealed vital facts about the investors, or social entrepreneurs. It was these founder/investors who conceived of the idea to start a self-financing project, raised capital, took personal charge of planning and organizing, and frequently engaged in direct management. Almost all founders and their close kin took part in running the homes. They were known as the "bosses" or *laoban* to staff and residents alike. From our observation, most homes operated like a family enterprise.

Among the 14 social entrepreneurs, there were 10 women against four men. Relating to age, among the twelve who answered our question, five were between 40 and 50, four were aged 51 to 60, two were 39 years' old and one was 64. Thus the overwhelming majority were in their middle or late middle years. In terms of education, only two had junior middle or below qualifications (14%), five persons had senior middle or vocational middle schooling (36%), four persons (29%) had college and above schooling. The remaining three had unknown qualifications.

The employment status of the social entrepreneurs before they started the care homes revealed an interesting mix of career fortunes.

Among the 14 bosses, only five were serving employees (36%). The rest might be regarded as losers in the new market economy: they were near retirement, on the verge of redundancy, or have already left their job. Their job backgrounds were even more interesting. Among the thirteen who answered the question, four were ordinary workers; the rest were professionals and administrators. This suggested that the majority of the social entrepreneurs had high occupational status and managerial skills that were useful in the running of a care facility.

The founders were asked what prompted them to start their social project. Their response identified four important motivations. First, quite a number of founders have had the personal history of not being able to obtain residential care for an infirm parent. Starting a care home helped themselves and others in a similar situation. Second, most were confronted with job insecurity. At middle and late middle age, most were eager to find a form of employment that could earn an income, if not profit. Seen in this light, social entrepreneurship was a strategy for self-salvation. Third, most had acquired useful skills and experience in their work life. Many had worked as an administrative cadre or in a service-related post. Fourth, most had an entrepreneurial vision. The possession of business acumen and willingness to take risk were attributes shared by many investors.

Besides, the questionnaire survey found that 90% of agencies identified themselves as a non-profit organisation (NPO). The reasons why agencies were willing to accept NPO status further confirmed that they had a social mission in mind and that making a profit was of secondary importance. These include (multiple answers allowed): "the goal of founding the agency was not to make a profit" (69%), "providing a social service without compensation or with low compensation is a good thing" (63%), "the agency does not make a profit all along" (45%), "the agency can get tax exemption treatment" (40%), and "the agency can get state subsidy or societal donations" (38%).

When interviewed, all the investors acknowledged that they understood the NPO policy before they embarked on their enterprise. Yet, after starting the project, they realised that they had to wrestle with many problems to win the battle for survival. Many confessed they had underestimated the risks involved. To the investors, cost control was a big challenge, as discussed in the last section.   There were a few other difficulties as well. First, the vulnerability of caring for a high risk group – frail and accident-prone elderly people – exposed operators to lengthy and expensive litigation and compensation claims. Much as they wanted to obtain insurance cover, no insurance company was prepared to offer these products. Second, non-state programmes suffered from the public's lack of knowledge and trust in their work. In a service field dominated by the state, non-state services were often seen as being for-profit and not delivery a good service. Third, government was faulted for not giving nonprofits help in solving their resource problems. While agencies were realistic enough not to expect regular state subventions, any form of aid (start up capital, donations and help in finding space) and advice in sorting out their day to day problems was badly needed. The desire for state tutelage and protection was keenly felt by all social entrepreneurs in China's fledgling market economy as the state still controls vast resources and authority.

The hardships of running a social enterprise at the present time in China were vividly summarised by one founder:

> "In three sentences, civilian run care agencies face problems after problems (*kunnan chongchong*), suffering after suffering (*kunan chongchong*), and struggles after struggles (*monan chongchong*). To me, problems and suffering are no big deal. The struggles are really terrible.   As a civilian run agency, we need government and society support. If not, we just cannot survive. There is no fair competition between us. State homes do not pay rent. They pick the old people they want, often those with better health and self care. But for me, I can only accept the difficult cases in order to earn more money. I don't have any authority to turn to

> when I get into trouble. Had I known it to be so tough,
> I wouldn't have taken the plunge."

We do not know how many social entrepreneurs regretted their decision to run a self-financing social project. However the feeling of being overwhelmed by problems and not getting help from the government was widespread among the founders. Coupled with the fact that many homes were still not making any profit and the expectation of recouping the investment was remote, one had reason to believe that the expectation of investors was at best partially met. The fact that they had chosen to soldier on owed much to their perseverance and fear of the total loss of their investment. Their determination was also driven by their need for paid work after having suffered job insecurity in the labour market themselves. In the meantime, some were still hopeful that given more time and after having learned their lessons the hard way, they could successfully run their social project and make it viable.

Conclusion

The emergence of private care homes for older people plugged a huge gap in service provision for frail elders. In Chinese society, rapid aging and severe shortfall in state welfare services created room for private efforts. The state's policy to encourage nonprofits to run social services on a self-financing basis forces many to adopt an entrepreneurial approach as their modus operandi. The in-depth study of 14 care homes confirmed that these homes were meeting an important social need. Both the residents and their family members thought the services answered their need for care in a satisfactory way.

The homes were also successful in recruiting and retaining staff to man the care team. These included doctors, nurses and care workers, who, because of keen job competition, regarded employment in a care home as socially useful work. At the present time, the care homes appeared to be successful in resolving their staffing issues even though instability may occur in the nursing and care worker ranks.

In terms of financial stability, many private care homes still operate precariously. Many are still in deficit or barely breaking even. As far as return on capital goes, a lot of uncertainty still remains. These challenges present headaches for the investors whose continuing commitment determines the future of these projects.

Because of the high risks of operation and the unhelpful nonprofit policy, many investors experience a strong sense of anxiety and helplessness. Hence, the future of private care homes for older people is plagued by risks and uncertainty, as in any business venture in a market environment. In the case of China, the immaturity of welfare markets when average incomes remain low and government assistance is conspicuous by its absence make the operating environment for Chinese NPOs even more volatile.

The government's policy on nonprofits is problematic. While the state is keen to make use of nonprofits to provide the bulk of welfare services, it does not grant them financial aid beyond tax incentives. This irrational policy is the leading cause of agency insecurity. Given the vulnerability of the NPOs, the government may be overly optimistic in expecting the nonprofit sector to pick up the major responsibility to provide welfare services. There is a need to rethink the state nonprofit policy so that the state, civil society and market providers can work out a partnership framework that satisfies social needs of users and assures the viability of social enterprises.

Notes and References

1. *Zhongguo Minzheng Tongji Nianjian* (*China Civil Affairs Statistical Yearbook*), (Beijing, various years).

2. Tian, Z. H. and Ma, X. "Analysis of the influence of ageing problem on social security service system for the aged and its solutions", *Northwest Population*, Lanzhou, (2002), 2, pp.17–18.

3. *Journal of Nanhua University – Social Science Edition*, Vol. 2, No. 2, (2001), p. 92.

4. *China Social Work*, no. 4, (1998), p. 8

5. Lee, M. K., *Chinese Occcupational Welfare in Market Transition*, (London: Macmillan, 2000).

6. Linda Wong and Bernard Poon, "From Serving Neighbors to Recontrolling Urban Society", *China Information*, 2005, Vol. XIX (3), (2005), pp. 413–442.

7. *Zhongguo Minzheng* (*China Civil Affairs*), no. 8, (2002). See also Chang, Z. H., "The study and analysis of admission rates in old age care organisations. How to interpret these and what can be done", *Zhongguo Minzheng* (*China Civil Affairs*), (2000), 9, pp.30–31.

8. *China Social Work*, 1998, no. 4, p.8; *Northwest Population*, Lanzhou, (2001), no. 2, p. 21. and various issues.

9. *Zhongguo Minzheng Tongji Nianjian* (*China Civil Affairs Statistical Yearbook*) (Beijing, 2002), p. 104.

10. Chang, Z. H., "The study and analysis of admission rates in old age care organisations. How to interpret these and what can be done."

11. *Ibid.*

12. Linda Wong (1998), *Marginalization and Social Welfare in China"* (London and New York: Routledge and LSE, 1998). See also Linda Wong "Individualization of social rights in China", in S. Sargeson (ed.), *Collective Goods, Collective Future in Asia* (London and New York: Routledge, 2002).

13. Yan, Q. C., "Observations on Public Sector Reform and Social Welfare Socialization", *Zhongguo Minzheng* (*China Civil Affairs*), (2003), 7, pp. 25–26.

14. Linda Wong and Tang Jun, "Dilemmas Confronting Social Entrepreneurs: Care Homes for Elderly People in China", *Pacific Affairs*, Vol. 79, No. 4 (2007).

15. Alfred J. Kahn, *Social Policy and Social Services*, Second Edition, (New York: Random House, 1979).

16. Liao, M. N., Foreman, S. and Sargeant, A., "Market versus societal orientation in the nonprofit context", *International Journal of Nonprofit and Voluntary Sector Marketing*, (2001), 6: 3, pp. 254–258. See also *New Statesman*, 3 June 2002: pp. v–x.

17. Dees, G., Emerson, J. and Economy, P., *Enterprising Nonprofit: A Toolkit for Social Entrepreneurs* (New York: Wiley, 2001).

18. Linda Wong and Tang Jun, "Dilemmas Confronting Social Entrepreneurs: Care Homes for Elderly People in China".

14

Where is China's Rural Economy Heading for: A Brighter Future or Problems Unsolved?

Charles C. L. KWONG

The advent of rural economic reforms in the late 1970s has accomplished remarkable achievements in China's countryside, reflected by the rise in rural income, enhancement of living standard, and the rapid expansion of rural industry. However, the initial benefits that peasants gained from the early rural reforms have become less glamorous when rural-urban disparity and regional disparity in rural areas has been intensifying since the mid-1990s amid these encouraging results. The annual growth rate of per capita income of rural households, measured in real terms, rose from 11.5% in 1986 to its historic peak of 38.5% in 1995, but falls continuously since then to a meagre 0.72% in 2000. Though a mild rebound of 4.08 and 5.88% was recorded in 2001 and 2002 respectively, the growth rate tapered off again to 3.84% in 2003.[1] In relative term, rural residents have not gained a proportional share of the economic fruits generated by the two decades of reform. Per capita income and expenditure of rural households were only 30.9 and 29.8% respectively of their urban counterparts in 2003.[2]

This chapter argues that the sluggish growth of rural income is attributable to the slow growth of rural non-farm activities, which fail to absorb the surging surplus labour in the countryside. It is unveiled that the expansion of rural enterprises has been constrained by capital shortage, resulting from an underdeveloped rural financial market. The livelihood of rural residents is further aggravated by the extensive land expropriation and arbitrary tax and fees collection by local governments. The predatory behaviour of local cadres defeats the original purpose and the past achievements of China's rural reforms. The root of local governments' predatory behaviour stems from their stringent financial conditions due to the implementation of the tax-assignment system (TAS, *fengshuizhi*) in 1994, and a lack of institutions to enforce the property rights in China's countryside. The phasing out of agricultural tax since 2004 likely worsens the fiscal conditions of the debt-ridden local governments. This chapter concludes that if the legitimacy of the Chinese government rests on its ability to enhance people's livelihood, given the fact that a dominant share of population resides in the rural areas, the government must devise an institutional overhaul to protect the property rights of the rural residents by curbing local governments' predatory behaviour. The success of limiting local governments' predatory behaviour largely relies on a comprehensive fiscal reform, which enables the local governments to regain their financial health to meet their coffers. The livelihood of rural residents also hinges on the sustained growth of rural non-farm activities, which generate employment opportunities for the rural dwellers. To ensure ample capital channelling to fuel the future growth of rural enterprises, the Chinese government must acknowledge the dilatory financial reform in the countryside.

Two Decades Later:
Targets Achieved or Problems Unsolved?

On the eve of rural reform implemented in the late 1970s, the industrial sector had been performing quite well, at least in terms of output level, and the whole economy was far from reaching a crisis state. However, rural reform was fuelled by the stagnant living standards under the planned system since the early 1950s. The momentum behind the rural reform is best grasped by Hare:[3]

> Why [should] China embark on major reforms at its
> present stage of development [?] . . . The economy as a
> whole has grown very rapidly since 1950, with industry
> doing especially well . . . But China's traditional central
> planning system had failed to achieve significant
> advance in popular living standards since the early
> 1950s, and it is this glaring failure which the present
> reforms are seeking to rectify.

Per capita income of rural households exhibited a nearly
stagnant growth from 102.8 yuan in 1957 to 113 yuan in 1977,
measured at 1977 constant prices. The annual growth rate was only
about 0.5%.[4] The dominant share of population residing in the
countryside, with stagnant living standards, motivated both the
local and central leaders to re-institute the use of market and
material incentives in the late 1970s to boost production and
household income, through which solidifying the legitimacy of the
government. Judging from the aspects of income and welfare
enhancement, the initial results of rural reform are encouraging. The
average annual growth rates of per capita rural household income
and consumption, measured in real term, were 15.74% and 15.0%
respectively, during the period 1981–1997. However, such figures
plummeted to 4.1% and 3.4% in 1998–2003 (Table 1).[5] Rural
reforms have also been praised by its encouraging results in poverty
reduction. The number of rural residents living below official
poverty line shrank from 250 million in 1978 to 29 million in 2003,
representing a decline of poverty incidence from 30.7% to 3.1%.[6]
Few developing countries have been able to match China's
accomplishment in poverty reduction in the past two decades.
However, a less affirmative view will be taken when a higher and
widely-used standard of US$1 per day set by the World Bank is
applied. Based on the data of the rural household survey undertaken
by the National Bureau of Statistics, it is estimated that only 33% of
rural household could reached the US$1 per day standard in 2003
and the remaining 67% of rural residents are still living under

Table 1: Per Capita Income and Consumption of Rural Households 1980–2003

Year	Yr*	Growth of Yr (%)	Cr*	Growth of Cr (%)
1980	180.50		153.03	
1981	218.20	20.89	186.34	21.77
1982	265.07	21.49	216.12	15.98
1983	305.19	15.12	244.62	13.19
1984	345.65	13.26	266.34	8.88
1985	355.32	2.80	283.66	6.50
1986	396.04	11.46	333.60	17.60
1987	425.14	7.35	366.08	9.74
1988	451.48	6.20	394.91	7.88
1989	517.21	14.56	460.34	16.57
1990	677.50	30.99	577.13	25.37
1991	674.17	-0.49	589.71	2.18
1992	721.91	7.08	606.82	2.90
1993	793.82	9.96	662.92	9.24
1994	976.78	23.05	813.45	22.71
1995	1,350.80	38.29	1,121.88	37.92
1996	1,770.28	31.05	1,444.93	28.79
1997	2,027.28	14.52	1,568.38	8.54
1998	2,175.03	7.29	1,599.93	2.01
1999	2,239.45	2.96	1,598.20	-0.11
2000	2,255.68	0.72	1,671.80	4.61
2001	2,347.62	4.08	1,727.18	3.31
2002	2,485.57	5.88	1,841.37	6.61
2003	2,580.91	3.84	1,912.70	3.87

Source: Calculated based on the data from State Statistical Bureau, *Zhongguo tongji nianjian* (hereafter *ZGTJNJ*) (*Statistical Yearbook of China*), 1987 (Beijing: Zhongguo tongji chubanshe, 1987), p. 701; 1990. pp. 249, 314; 1995, p. 280; 1997, p. 314; 1998, p. 346; 2000, pp. 289, 332; 2002, p. 344; 2003, pp. 313, 368; 2004, pp. 323, 382; Rural Social and Economic Investigation Team of the State Statistical Bureau, *Zhongguo nongcun tongji nianjian* (hereafter *ZGNCTJNJ*) (Rural Statistical Yearbook of China),1985 (Beijing: Zhongguo tongji chubanshe, 1985), p. 197; 1989: 224.

Note:
*Yr = per capita income of rural household;
 Cr = per capital consumption of rural household;
Figures are measured at constant prices.

Table 2: Urban-Rural Income Ratio 1980–2004

Year	Urban-Rural Income Ratio
1980	2.50
1985	1.86
1989	2.28
1990	2.20
1991	2.40
1992	2.58
1993	2.80
1994	2.86
1995	2.71
1996	2.51
1997	2.47
1998	2.51
1999	2.65
2000	2.79
2001	2.90
2002	3.11
2003	3.23
2004	3.21

Source: Calculated based on the data from *ZGTJNJ* 2005, p. 335.

poverty.[7] The slow growth of rural income has magnified rural-urban disparity, as evident by the ongoing growth of the urban-rural income ratio. As revealed by Table 2, the ratio fell from 2.5 in 1980 to 1.86 in 1985 and continued to rise since then, reaching its historic peak in 2003. Rural residents could only earn one-third of the income of their urban counterparts in recent years. The gap in living standard is actually greater than the income ratios suggest since the urban population enjoy better services, both in terms of quality and quantity, in education, health and social welfare. A survey conducted by the central government indicates that per capita education in the eastern cities was 1.87 times higher than that in rural areas in 1995 and such figure escalated to 2.97 in 2002.[8] Another study by the Chinese Academy of Social Sciences reports that in terms of government expenditure on education and medical services, urban residents are six times better off than their rural counterparts.[9] Yawning income and welfare gaps imply that rural residents have not gained a proportional share of the economic fruits generated by the two decades of reform. Mounting discontent, fuelled by inequalities, among farmers heightens the risks of social and political instability, which has direct bearing on the legitimacy of the ruling party.

Then, what has hindered the rural income growth since the mid-1990s? The answer to this questions lies on the unintended repercussions of the fiscal and banking reforms implemented in 1994.

1994 Banking Reform: Impediment to Rural Industrial Growth

Enhanced rural income recorded from the early 1980s to the mid-1990s was attributable to the proliferation of non-farm activities, in particular rural industry. In 1985, 27% of rural household income comes from non-farm activities while such figure reached 45.2% in 2003.[10] From the early 1980s to the mid-1990s when China's rural financial system was in its infant stage, local governments played active roles in offering assistance to channel funds from local banks and Rural Credit Cooperatives (RCCs) to enterprises under their jurisdiction.[11] The assistance took several forms. First, local governments acted as intermediaries and facilitators to initiate the bargaining with and borrowing from the banks. Second, in some cases, local governments, on behalf of the local communities, used collective assets as collateral for loans. Third, local governments served as guarantors who shouldered the risk of default in such a way that local governments were held responsible for repaying the loans if the enterprises were unable to pay it. The backing of local governments in financial arrangement was particularly crucial for start-up business that faced an underdeveloped financial system in the countryside. Table 3 indicates that the growth of bank loans extended to rural enterprises was spectacular from 1985 to 1993, during which the proportion of loan financing in total capital had been in an uptrend. The relatively easy assess to capital rendered the rural enterprises an impressive annual growth of 37.9% for the period 1985–1994.

However, the momentous growth of rural enterprises has demonstrated signs of slow down since the mid-1990s. The average annual growth rate of the gross output value of rural enterprises tapered off to 18.6% for the period 1995–2002 down from 37.9% for the period 1985–1994.[12] The dearth of capital has been one of the major constraining factors for the growth of rural enterprises. The fundamental cause of capital shortage was resulted from China's banking reform in 1994, which aimed at commercialising the four state-owned specialised banks (SOCBs)[13] by separating commercial lending from policy lending, through which enhancing the efficiency of the ailing banking sector.[14] The reform insulated local governments from influencing local banks' decision on lending to local enterprises. Since the SOCBs were required to operate on commercial principles, 44,000 county branches of SOCBs ceased to operate during 1998–2001 to cut the operation costs. RCCs become the single most important financial institution in rural areas to meet the credit demand for rural enterprises. However, despite increase in deposit in RCCs, a rising amount of funds has been channelled out of rural areas through depositing funds into the People's Bank of China or purchasing bonds for which the returns are more stable and less risky. The estimated outflow of funds escalated from 328 billion yuan in 1997 to 447.7 billion yuan in 2002.[15] Capital shortage has become one of the primary constraining factors for the expansion of rural non-farm activities. It is evident that 20.7% of the capital of township-village enterprises (TVEs) were financed by bank loans in 1985 and reached a historic high of 30.7% in 1992, but the figure shrank to 12.1% in 2002 (Table 3). The efficiency-enhancing banking reform in 1994 lacks a parallel development of a

Table 3
Loan Financing in Rural Enterprises 1985–2002

Year	Gross Value of Fixed Assets (billion yuan) (a)	Circulating Funds (billion yuan) (b)	Total Capital (c) = (a) + (b)	Bank Loans (d)		(e) = (d)/(c)
1985	75.04	59.01	134.05	27.78		20.7
1986	94.67	76.98	171.65	40.83	(47.0)	23.8
1987	123.24	114.03	237.27	78.86	(93.1)	33.2
1988	158.43	154.06	312.49	102.74	(30.3)	32.9
1989	192.07	189.01	381.08	108.04	(5.2)	28.4
1990	220.20	224.47	444.67	124.81	(15.5)	28.1
1991	262.63	292.50	555.13	159.13	(27.5)	28.7
1992	349.07	409.53	758.60	233.15	(46.5)	30.7
1993	516.09	633.96	1,150.05	299.69	(28.5)	26.1
1994	661.35	845.89	1,507.24	305.83	(2.05)	20.3
1995	912.26	1,096.62	2,008.88	379.32	(24.0)	18.8
1996	1,114.94	1,261.02	2,375.96	432.69	(14.1)	18.2
1997	1,253.93	1,349.18	2,603.11	457.16	(5.7)	17.5
1998	1,344.31	1,385.79	2,730.10	456.82	(-0.07)	16.7
1999	1,391.58	1,402.40	2,793.98	453.74	(-0.7)	16.2
2000	1,368.53	1,367.30	2,735.83	410.87	(-9.4)	15.0
2001	1,351.44	1,329.59	2,681.03	376.81	(-8.3)	14.1
2002	1,355.72	1,334.95	2,690.67	327.84	(-13.0)	12.1

Source: *ZGTJNJ* (1986: 218–219; 1987: 208–209; 1995: 367); *ZGXZQYNJ* (1978–1987: 641–643; 1989: 108–109; 1990: 190–192; 1991: 198-200; 1992: 205–206; 1993: 237–238; 1994: 367–368; 1996: 254–256; 1997: 240, 242, 245; 1998: 202, 204, 206; 1999: 228, 230, 232; 2000: 232, 234, 236; 2001:210, 212, 214; 2002: 228, 230, 232; 2003: 229, 231, 233).

Note: Figures in parentheses are the respective growth rates of bank loans extended to rural enterprises.

Table 4
Average Size of a TVE (selected years)

	1986	1995	2002
Workers Employed	5.2	5.8	6.2
Gross Output Value (yuan)	22,367	312,872	658,487
Value Added (yuan)	n.a.	66,262	151,855
Fixed Assets (yuan)	7,996	58,296	167,387

Source: Calculated based on the data from *ZGXZQYNJ* (1978–1987: 569; 1996: 112, 115, 116, 118; 2003: 129).

full-fledged rural financial market to divert adequate financial resources to rural enterprises, particularly to the small- and medium-sized ones. Most of the TVEs are small-sized firms in terms of workers employed, output value, value added, and fixed assets (Table 4). Clear and accurate financial reports of the small-sized enterprises are rare in China's countryside either because it is unaffordable for the enterprises to have qualified accountants to compile their financial reports, or because they deliberately hide their "real" transactions to avoid possible taxes and fees collected by local governments. Local banks and RCCs thus incur very high transaction costs to evaluate the credit risks of each project. Because of adverse selection caused by asymmetric information, lenders in the countryside tend to extend loans to large enterprises which indicate low credit risks and high repayability. Additionally, though the value of fixed assets of a TVE increased by almost twenty times from 7,996 yuan in 1986 to 167,387 yuan in 2002, the absolute value remains relatively small. Further, most of the fixed assets, including machinery and equipment, of these small- and medium-sized rural enterprises (SMREs) are very specific for certain production purpose. This specific capital equipment unlikely generates high resale value. The meagre amount of fixed assets and the specific use of the machinery and equipment render the enterprises limited collateral available for loans. The problem of capital shortage runs into a vicious circle in which local banks and

Table 5: Workers Employed in TVEs 1985–2002

Year	Workers Employed (million)
1985	69.79
1986	79.37
1987	88.05
1988	95.45
1989	93.67
1990	92.65
1991	96.14
1992	106.25
1993	123.45
1994	120.17
1995	128.62
1996	135.08
1997	130.50
1998	125.37
1999	127.04
2000	128.20
2001	130.86
2002	132.87

Source: *ZGTJNJ* (2003: 448)

RCCs are unwilling to extend loans to the SMREs and the expansion of the enterprises is constrained owing to the lack of capital. The firm size and production scale thus remain small and local financial institutions are again reluctant to offer loans to the SMREs.

Shrinking growth of rural enterprises intensifies the already pressing problem of surplus labour in China's countryside. As estimated by the China's Ministry of Agriculture, surplus labour in rural China amounted to 150 million in 2004.[16] Revealed by Table

5, after reaching its peak in 1996, the number of workers employed in TVEs has demonstrated either a decline or a modest growth. The annual growth rate of workers employed by TVEs declined substantially from 9.2% to 1.3% for the periods 1985–1994 and 1995–2002 respectively.[17] The slow labour absorption rate defeats the original purpose of developing TVEs to lighten the problem of surplus labour in agriculture. Further, the impeded growth of rural enterprises constrains the plausibility of enhancing rural household income through the development non-farm activities. The growth rate of per capita income of rural households has been experiencing considerable decline after reaching its peak in 1995 (Table 1). Since increasing share of rural household income was derived from non-farm activities, which includes wage income earned from rural enterprises and income from household business, dwindling rural enterprises would unlikely bring impetus to enhance rural household income. It not only adversely affects the welfare of rural households, but also widens the rural-urban gap.

Tightening Fiscal Constraint: The Source of Local Government's Predatory Behaviour

Since 1978, the central share of national budgetary revenues had been rising and reached its peak at 40.5% in 1984. However, the share began to shrink since 1984, reaching a trough at 22% in 1993. To ensure an adequate and stable flow of budgetary revenues into the state finances, the central government implemented the TAS, which centralises the major revenue sources of turnover taxes (value-added and consumption taxes), but lacks a concomitant centralisation of expenditure responsibilities. Table 6 indicates that the central share of total budgetary revenue escalated from 22% in 1993 to 55.7% in 1994. Since then, the central government has collected about half of the total fiscal revenues. Nevertheless, local governments have been responsible for the major share, about 70%, of the total expenditure since the inception of the TAS.

Table 6
Central and Local Share
of Budgetary Revenue and Expenditure 1978–2004 (Percent)

Year	Central Government	Local Governments	Central Government	Local Governments
1978	15.5	84.5	47.4	52.6
1979	20.2	79.8	51.1	48.9
1980	24.5	75.5	54.3	45.7
1981	26.5	73.5	55.0	45.0
1982	28.6	71.4	53.0	47.0
1983	35.8	64.2	53.9	46.1
1984	40.5	59.5	52.5	47.5
1985	38.4	61.6	39.7	60.3
1986	36.7	63.3	37.9	62.1
1987	33.5	66.5	37.4	62.6
1988	32.9	67.1	33.9	66.1
1989	30.9	69.1	31.5	68.5
1990	33.8	66.2	32.6	67.4
1991	29.8	70.2	32.2	67.8
1992	28.1	71.9	31.3	68.7
1993	22.0	78.0	28.3	71.7
1994	55.7	44.3	30.3	69.7
1995	52.2	47.8	29.2	70.8
1996	49.4	50.6	27.1	72.9
1997	48.9	51.1	27.4	72.6
1998	49.5	50.5	28.9	71.1
1999	51.1	48.9	31.5	68.5
2000	52.2	47.8	34.7	65.3
2001	52.4	47.6	30.5	69.5
2002	55.0	45.0	30.7	69.3
2003	54.6	45.4	30.1	69.9
2004	54.9	45.1	27.7	72.3

Source: *ZGTJNJ* (2000: 267–68; 2001: 257–258; 2005: 276).

Table 7
Budget Balance of Local Governments 1978–2004 (billion yuan)

Year	LGR (1)	LGE (2)	LGR – LGE (3)	LGE/LGR (4)
1978	95.65	56.00	39.65	0.59
1979	91.50	62.67	28.83	0.68
1980	87.55	56.20	31.35	0.64
1981	86.47	51.28	35.19	0.59
1982	86.55	57.82	28.73	0.67
1983	87.69	64.99	22.70	0.74
1984	97.74	80.77	16.97	0.83
1985	123.52	120.90	2.62	0.98
1986	134.36	136.86	-2.50	1.02
1987	146.31	141.66	4.65	0.97
1988	158.25	164.62	-6.37	1.04
1989	184.24	193.50	-9.26	1.05
1990	194.47	207.91	-13.44	1.07
1991	221.12	229.58	-8.46	1.04
1992	250.39	257.18	-6.79	1.03
1993	339.14	333.02	6.12	0.98
1994	231.16	403.82	-172.66	1.75
1995	298.56	482.83	-184.27	1.62
1996	374.69	578.63	-203.94	1.54
1997	442.42	670.11	-227.69	1.51
1998	498.40	767.26	-268.86	1.54
1999	559.49	903.53	-344.04	1.61
2000	640.61	1,036.67	-396.06	1.62
2001	780.33	1,313.45	-533.12	1.68
2002	851.50	1,528.14	-676.64	1.79
2003	984.99	1,722.98	-737.99	1.75
2004	1,189.33	2,059.28	-869.95	1.73

Source: Calculated based on the data from *ZGTJNJ* (2001: 257–258; 2005: 276).

The TAS has imposed increased fiscal pressures on subnational, in particular subprovincial, finance.[18] Table 7 explores further the fiscal conditions of local governments. The extent of budget deficit (or surplus) is measured by the ratio of local government expenditure (LGE) to local government revenue (LGR) [column (4)], which represents a balanced budget if the ratio is equal to one. A ratio greater than one denotes a budget deficit and a larger figure indicates a budget deficit of greater extent. A ratio less than one reflects a budget surplus and a smaller figure registers a larger surplus. Local budget experienced deficits in six years in the fifteen years between 1978 and 1993 and the deficit was relatively mild, ranging from 1.02 to1.07 [column (4)]. Dramatically, local governments encountered deficits for all the years from 1994 to 2004 and the magnitude of the deficits was more immense than that before 1994. Though local government revenue (LGR) had increased in absolute terms since 1994, the escalation of local government expenditure (LGE) had more than outweighed the rise in LGR. An official estimate revealed that up to 2004, town and township governments accumulated about 200 billion yuan of debt. On average every town/township shouldered 4.5 million yuan of debt. The total debt amount of local governments is likely to double if the estimate covers the debts accrued to village level.[19] The deteriorating fiscal strength of local finance hampers the local governments' capability of enhancing the provision of social services such as education and medical care services, particularly in the impoverished rural areas.

To make ends meet, local government, particularly those at county level or below, collected fees, legally or illegally from farmers for various items and purposes. The fees charged are often higher than the formal tax. It is recorded that the fees collected in 1999 was 67 billion yuan while the tax revenue from agricultural tax was 42 billion yuan.[20] The 67 billion yuan of fees included only those collected legally. If illegal fees, estimated to be 20 billion yuan in 1999,[21] were included, the fees collected by local governments were more than double of the agricultural tax. The practice put unbearable burden on farmers and tenses up the relations between farmers and the local cadres. To curb the exorbitant fees, a tax-for-fees pilot reform was implemented in 2000, beginning in Anhui Province. The main plank of the reform was to abolish the illegal fees and adopt an uniform tax to replace most of the legal fees, through which restraining the local governments from charging fees and initiating fund-raising programmes at their own discretion.[22] The pilot reform accomplished initial success and was spread to all other provinces in 2003. In 2003, the tax-and-fees burden on farmers reduced by 14.5%.[23] The reform has achieved notable results in reducing about 30–40% of farmers' tax-and-fees burden by 2004.[24] The reform has lightened the burden of farmers by restraining excessive fees collection by local governments, but fails to harmonise the relations between farmers and local cadres. The financial conditions of the debt-ridden local governments were severely aggravated by the reduction in tax-and-fees collection in their jurisdiction. The abolition of agricultural special tax in 2004 and the gradual phasing out of agricultural tax puts extra burden on local finances.[25]

Stringent fiscal constraints trigger local governments to explore other sources to finance their coffers. Land requisition by local government becomes a commonly used means to raise local fiscal revenue. Though the revised Land Contract Law in 2003 stated clearly that land contracted out to farm households cannot be requisitioned by local governments and collectives during the contracted period,[26] the Land Management Law, however, entrusts the local governments to expropriate the contracted land for the reason of "public interest", which is ambiguously defined.[27] In practice, land is expropriated for commercial use and the proceeds of the land sales are then funnelled largely to the local governments. According to a survey conducted in Zhejiang Provinces, about 50 to 60% of the value-added from land requisition (i.e. the selling price of the land minus the cost of land requisition) is captured by the local governments and collectives while only about 5-10% was shared by farm households.[28] Being the major beneficiary, some local governments perceive land requisition as "second finance" (*dier caizhen*) on top of tax-and-fees collection. It has become an acute socio-economic problem in China's countryside that increasing number of cases has been reported that the local governments have expropriated land from the households without proper compensation. According to official statistics, the compensation needed for land requisition amounted to 14.8 billion yuan in 2004, but only 8.7 billion yuan are actually paid in recompense for the farmers' land losses, indicating that about 41% of the compensation is still unpaid.[29] It is estimated that about 40 million farmers are landless and jobless in rural China by 2004.[30] The landless peasants without apposite compensation have undermined the central government's effort in poverty alleviation and harmonizing the relations between farmers and local governments. Land requisition disputes replace tax-and-fees collection as the major trigger point for the confrontation between farmers and local cadres. The seriousness of the conflict is reflected by the recent crackdown of protests connected with land requisition in Shanwei in Guangdong Province in December 2005. Eight villagers were reportedly shot by local police officers. This event follows a similar protest in Dingzhou, Hebei Province in June 2005. The protest results in six dead and more than forty people injured.[31] The public security ministry recorded that the number of serious protests, mostly arising from land disputes and pollution issues, increased from 10,000 in 1994 to 58,000 in 2003 and further soared to 74,000 in 2004.[32] The near-daily occurrence of protests not only intensifies the social unrest in the countryside, but also poses a possible threat to the governance of the ruling party. Increasing surplus labour released from the farmland is another unintended repercussion of land expropriation. An estimate indicates that for each *mu* (0.0667 hectares) of requisitioned land, 1.4 farmers will lose their land for production.[33] Since labour absorption by rural enterprises has been impeded for the past few years, the newly generated landless farmers are likely to enlarge the pool of surplus labour in the countryside. Further, since land is nominally owned by the collectives who possess the right to reallocate the land to other farm households or to non-farm uses, the insecure property rights on farmland depress the farmers' incentives to commit long-term investment in their contracted land, which in turn impacts negatively on land productivity.

Recent Development: A Brighter Future?

The recently announced Eleventh Five-Year Blueprint (2006–2010) registers a policy shift from blindly searching for GDP growth to forging for a balanced growth which entails a development of a harmonised country.[34] This policy redirection represents the central leaders' recognition of the gravity of the widening rural-urban wealth gap, which has a direct bearing on the effective governance of the central government. The ever increasing Gini coefficient, which measures the degree of income inequality, reached its historic high of 0.53 in 2004 that is far higher than the critical level of 0.4.[35] Central leaders are willing to trade off economic growth for more even distribution of income to avoid escalating social unrest. Central funds transferred to support agriculture and infrastructure investment in the countryside was about 300 billion yuan in 2005. A budget deficit of 295 billion yuan is planned for 2006 and increasing fiscal resources will be funnelled for rural development and enhancing productivity.[36] Solely focusing on the growing central funds injected into rural areas, however, does not reveal exactly whether the funds are allocated for productive uses. Wen and Wang estimates that about 30% of the loans and central funds earmarked for rural development were finally converted into investment in the 1950s while the percentage has been declining for the past decades and reaches its trough of 5–10% in the 1980s with a mild rebound to 15% in the 1990s.[37] The huge discrepancy between the funds allocated for rural development and the amount effectively transformed in investment implies that the funds are either embezzled by local cadres or used for other projects favoured by local officials, or projects which enhance the reputation and profile of the cadres. Whether the increased fiscal inputs for rural areas can effectively be converted into productive investment, thus, depends on the close monitoring of the fund uses by higher level governments to avoid inappropriate diversion of the funding.

A practical step to alleviate local fiscal burden is the fundamental reform on education financing at local levels, which will be implemented in 2006. Before the 2000 tax-for-fees reform, education in rural areas were financed by town/township and village governments which relied mainly on the tax and fees collected from farm households. The burden of education financing at local levels was almost solely shouldered by farmers. After the reform, education fund-raising and surcharge were prohibited and the burden of education funds on farmers has shifted to local governments. To remedy the deteriorating fiscal condition of the local governments and to ensure ample financial inputs channelling to local education, the central government decides to assume a major role in financing rural education. School fees in rural areas in western provinces will be waived in 2006 and such policy will be extended to all provinces in 2007. Rural education funds will then be financed primarily by central and provincial vaults.[38] It provides a cure, at least partially, for the lasting fiscal imbalance at town/township and village levels and makes education more accessible to rural dwellers.

With the aim of easing the financial burden of the farmers at a faster pace, central leaders decided in the annual rural work conference, held in December 2005, to abolish the agricultural tax in 2006, instead of phasing out the tax by 2008 as originally scheduled.[39] The earlier elimination of agricultural tax will certainly benefit the farmers, but the blessing of the reform is achieved at the expense of the added financial burden on local governments, especially for those in agricultural based provinces. The central government plans to compensate the sub-provincial governments by fiscal transfer, but this practice will likely end up with costly negotiations between central and local governments in regard to the amount of fiscal transfer. Local governments will bargain for maximum fiscal inputs from the centre rather than minimizing local expenditure.[40] Mounting fiscal burden will eventually fall on the central vault.

To control the rampant protests arising from land disputes,

Guangdong party chief, Zhang Dejiang, announced that local cadres are required to ensure that all land requisitions must follow the formal procedures, and all compensation mutually agreed between farmers and local governments must be paid in full before the construction projects begin. Cadres fail to implement these newly announced procedures and trigger mass protest are subject to dismissal and further investigation.[41] It was followed by President Hu Jintao's speech at the Communist Party's Central Commission for Discipline Inspection held in January 2006 which highlighted the ongoing anti-graft investigation targeted to rural officials who involved in corruption and illicit land expropriation. Hu singled out the protests in Huanxi in Zhejiang Province and Shanwei in Guangdong Province in 2005,[42] which denotes that the central leaders are alarmed by the growing tension and grievances at the grassroots. The central government has conveyed a positive signal of protecting the benefits of the farmers, but the long-term solution to land expropriation disputes rests on a clearly delineated property rights on land and its efficacious enforcement, which in turn relies on an independent judicial system rendering impartial ruling. Nonetheless, political pressure on local judges is routine as their appointments are made by the local people's congresses and the budget of the court are provided by local governments.[43]

Conclusion

This chapter argues that growth and development in rural China has been spectacular after two decades of reform, but rural income started to stagnate in the late 1990s, which is attributable to a number of interconnected pressing problems facing China's rural economy. First, the 1994 banking reform has been heading to the right direction to improve the efficiency of China's banking sector by curtailing piles of non-performing loans and more prudent credit policy. While the banking reform has well squeezed the credits extended to rural enterprises by insulating local governments from influencing local banks' decision on lending to rural enterprises, it lacks a concomitant development of financial market in rural areas. Capital shortage becomes one of the major constraining factors for the development of rural non-farm activities. Reforms are needed to boost the development of financial institutions in the countryside and to train ample staff with finance expertise to monitor and manage the operation of RCCs, basing on the principles of creditworthiness and repayability. Without an efficient financial market, investment in rural industries and agricultural production will be inhibited, and the effects of any further effort to enhance rural income will be very marginal. Second, the TAS implemented in 1994 has led local governments into long-term fiscal imbalance, which induced local cadres to collect exorbitant and illicit fees to meet their expenditure. The tax-for-fees reform in 2000 has successfully alleviated the farmers' burden, but at the expense of aggravating the fiscal burden of local governments, which turns local governments to land requisition to generate additional fiscal income by reselling or redevelopment of the expropriated land. The earlier phasing out of agricultural tax in 2006 implies added burden on low-level governments and will likely intensify local governments' predatory behaviour. To curb the confrontation between farmers and local cadres, key reforms must be launched to ensure that farmland expropriated by local governments must be compensated at a level which is economically viable for the farmers. Achieving this requires a system of well-delineated and enforceable property rights on farmland, which will be conducive to farmers' long-term investment in their contracted land. Pertaining to the previous point, an institutional overhaul is needed to reform the existing central-local fiscal relationship to ensure that ample fiscal revenues are shared by local governments to accomplish their fiscal responsibilities, which to a certain extent, reduces their predatory behaviour in land expropriation. Without apposite reforms resolving these thorny problems, it is unlikely that China can achieve its target of establishing a harmonious society with balanced growth as blueprinted for the coming years.

Notes and References

1. See Table 1.

2. *ZGTJNJ* 2004, p. 355.

3. Paul Hare, "What Can China Learn from the Hungarian Economic reform?" in Stephan Feuchtwang , Athar Hussain, and Thierry Pairault (eds.), *Transforming China's Economy in the Eighties* (Boulder: Westview, 1988), p. 58.

4. S. Lee Travers, "Getting Rich through Diligence: Peasant Income after the Reforms" in Elizabeth J. Perry and Christine Wong (eds), *The Political Economy of Reform in Post-Mao China* (Cambridge: Harvard University Press, 1985), p. 111.

5. Calculated based on the data from Table 1.

6. Charles C L Kwong and Harry W C Lo. "China's Rural Economy at the Crossroads: Prospect and Bottlenecks," *The Chinese Economy* (forthcoming 2006). The poverty line is set in terms of net annual income per capita. The figures were 98 yuan, 206 yuan, and 250 yuan in 1978, 1985 and 1992 respectively. The present poverty line is set at 625 yuan. For further discussion on the calculation of poverty line, see Zhang, Mei, *China's Poor Regions: Rural-urban Migration, Poverty, Economic Reform and Urbanisation* (New York: RoutledgeCurzon, 2003), pp. 23–25.

7. Calculated based on the data from *ZGTJNJ* (2004, p. 381). See also the explanatory notes in *ZGTJNJ* (2004, pp. 353–4).

8. "China Moves Closer to Education for All," *South China Morning Post*, (29 November, 2005), A8.

9. "Wealth Gap Fuelling instability, Studies Warn," *South China Morning Post*, (22 December, 2005), A6.

10. Figures are calculated based on the data from *ZGTJNJ* (2000, p. 331; 2004, p.381).

11. See W. A. Byrd, and Lin, Qingsong, "China's Rural Industry: An Introduction," in W. A. Byrd and Lin, Qingsong (eds.), *China's Rural Industry: Structure, Development, and Reform,* (New York: Oxford University Press, 1990); Che, Jiahua and Qian, Yingyi, "Institutional Environment, Community Government, and Corporate Governance: Understanding China's Township-village Enterprises," *The Journal of Law, Economics, & Organisation*, Vol. 14, No. 1, (1998), p. 6; Barry Naughton, *Growing Out of the Plan: Chinese Economic Reform 1978–1993*, (Cambridge: Cambridge University Press, 1996, 152–154).

12. Charles C L Kwong. "Financial Constraints on China's Rural Enterprises: Causes and Cure," paper presented at the 15th Biennial Conference of the Asian Studies Association of Australia 29 June – 2 July 2004, Canberra, Australia.

13. The four SOCBs are Agricultural Bank of China (ABC), Industrial and Commercial Bank of China (ICBC), People's Construction Bank of China (PCBC), and Bank of China (BOC).

14. For a more detailed discussion of China's banking reform, see Lo, Wai Chung. "A Retrospect on China's Banking reform," *The Chinese Economy*, Vol. 34, No. 1 (January–February 2001), 15–28.

15. Kwong and Lo, "China's Rural Economy at the Crossroads: Prospect and Bottlenecks," p. 5.

16. Mathew Shane and Fred Gale. "China: A Study of Dynamic Growth," Electronic Outlook Report from the Economic Research Service, United States Department of Agriculture, October 2004.

17. Calculated based on the data from Table 5.

18. For a detailed discussion of the impacts of TAS on local finances, see Pak K Lee and Charles C L Kwong, "From Developmental to Predatory Government: An Institutional Perspective of Local Cadres' Strategic Economic Behaviour," in Joseph Y. S. Cheng (ed.), *China's Challenges in the Twenty-first Century*, (Hong Kong: City University of Hong Kong Press, 2003, 383–407).

19. Lian, Yumin and Wu, Jianzhong, *Zhongguo Guoqing Baogao* (Report on China's Condition), (Beijing: Zhongguo Shidai Chubanshe, 2005, 201).

20. M. Tanabe. "Technical Assistance to the People's Republic of China for the Agricultural Taxation Reform Project," Asian Development Bank, September 2004, p.1.

21. Institute for Rural Development of the Chinese Academy of Social Sciences (ed.) *Zhongguo Nongcun Fazhan Yanjiu Baogao No.4* (China's Rural Development Report No.4), (Beijing: Shehui Kexue Wenxian Chubanshe, 2004, 139).

22. Dian Tai. "Taxes, Fees No Longer to Target Farmers," *China Daily,* (7 July 2004) www.chinadaily.com.cn access on 23 December 2005); M. Tanabe. "Technical Assistance to the People's Republic of China for the Agricultural Taxation Reform Project," p. 2.

23. Institute for Rural Development of the Chinese Academy of Social Sciences and Rural Social and Economic Investigation Team of the State Statistical Bureau (eds.), *2003–2004: Zhongguo Nongcun Jingji Xingshi Fenxi Yu Yuce* (Analysis and Forecast of China's Rural Economic Conditions 2003–2004), (Beijing: Shehui Kexue Wenxian Chubanshe, 123).

24. M. Tanabe. "Technical Assistance to the People's Republic of China for the Agricultural Taxation Reform Project," p. 2.

25. See Note 24.

26. Chen, Xiwen. "*Zhongguo Nongcun Xuyao Jiejue Wu Da Wenti*," (The Five Problems in Rural China that Needed to be Solved), *Sannong Zhongguo* (Three Agriculture and China), No. 3 (December 2004), p. 20.

27. Jiang Ping, "*Nongcun Tudi Lifa San Nanti*" (Three Probems Regarding Enacting Laws on Rural Land), *Caijing* (Economics and Finance) No. 148 (December 2005), pp. 26–27; Shen Lang, "*Nongcun Tudi Lifa NanzaiNeili*," (What Are the Difficulties in Enacting Laws on Rural Land?), *Caijing* (Economics and Finance) No. 148 (December 2005), p. 27.

28. Lian, Yumin and Wu, Jianzhong, *Zhongguo Guoqing Baogao* (Report on China's Condition), p. 141.

29. http://www.wenweipo.com (accessed April 12, 2005)

30. See note 27.

31. "Villagers Reportedly Shot Dead During Land Dispute," *South China Morning Post*, (8 December, 2005), A5.

32. A. Bezlova, 'Development: Great Leap to Help Rural China.' www.ipsnews.net/print.asp?idnews=30559 (accessed October 13, 2005)

33. See note 27.

34. See note 32.

35. See note 9.

36. Wang, Chengyong and Li, qiyan, "*Zhongyang Caichi Zhouli Sannong*," (Central Budget Deficit Focusing on 'Three Agriculture'), *Caijing* (Economics and Finance) No. 149 (December 2005), p. 110.

37. Wen Tao and Wang Yuyu, "*Zhengfu Zhudao de Nongye Xindai Caizheng Zhinong Moshi de Jingji Xiaoying – Jiju Zhongguo 1952–2002 Nian de Jingyan Yuanzheng*," (Economic Effect of the Government-led Model on Agricultural Loans and Fiscal Transfer: An Empirical Study Based on 1952–2002 Data), *Zhongguo Nongcun Jingji* (Chinese Rural Economy) No. 10 (October 2005), p 28.

38. Cheng, Hongshe, "*Nongcun Yiwu Jiaoyu Mianfei Xinzheng*," (The New Policy on Free Rural Education), *Caijing* (Economics and Finance) No. 149 (December 2005), pp. 107–109.

39. "Farmers Win Pledge of More Investment," *South China Morning Post*, (30 December, 2005), A6.

40. See note 24.

41. "Party Chief Sets Rules on Land Acquisition," *South China Morning Post*, (6 January, 2006), A5.

42. "Leaders Need More Than Just Inspiring Words to Tackle Corruption," *South China Morning Post*, (9 January, 2006), A4.

43. "Minor Ruling Plants the Seeds of Reform for Judiciary," *South China Morning Post*, (29 November, 2005), A18; "Pledge to Speed up Judicial Reforms," *South China Morning Post*, (7 January, 2006), A5.

15

The Question of Land: An Alternative Model of Modernity?

Mobo GAO

Introduction

Let us first put our mind to a scenario in the West, the scenario of a fairly typical English countryside: a village pub around the corner, a church with a cemetery nearby, a newsagent combined with a post office, a clean street or two with or without a couple of local shops, lush lawns and beautifully maintained gardens dotted between houses. Surrounding the village there are hedged fields either of pastoral or crop land. It is a picture of forever green, orderly, quite, peaceful and relaxing rural landscape. Every aspiring English person in London would like to have a country house somewhere in Kent or Sussex or Essex for the weekends.

Now let us move our mind to the East and imagine the possibility of a similar scenario in China. Instantly our imagination folds up because even the possibility is not there. I cannot think of such a picture anywhere in China, north, south, west or east. This is not a question of whether there are moneyed people in China who would like a country life. In some villages in Kaiping County Guangdong province where there has been a long tradition of overseas Chinese remittance, imposing and even some breathtakingly beautiful blockhouses (*diao lou*) were built in the late eighteenth and early nineteenth centuries. Those buildings were built

413

to protect the wealthier families of the transnational migrants against bandits and robbers at that time. Comparatively large amount of money was remitted to these villages and much was spent on public works such roads, bridges, schools and even hospitals.[1] But no rural prosperity or rural style of life resulted from this kind of money. In villages of other counties of the *si yi* (the famous four counties that have many migrants overseas) in Guangdong where many villagers migrated internationally my recent field work research failed to find any rural prosperity or stability. The moneyed households or clans all turned their back to rural life.

This shifting of places immediately brings to our minds many sets of different issues that are relevant to this comparison between China and England. England is a little island that has more than enough moisture to make it green. China has deserts. China has huge mountains and powerful rivers that give life blood as well as destruction to the lives of millions. In China generally there is too much rain along the southeast coast and too little in the northwest. England is largely pastoral whereas in south China it is largely rice culture. English weather is mildly cold and mildly hot whereas almost everywhere in China the weather can go extremity either way. There is also the issue of agriculture subsidies (almost three $US dollars a day for every cow in England) and exploitation of the peasantry in China past or present. There is the issue of different level of industrialisation, the issue of different level of living standards and different perceptions of what are the priorities in life. And so on and so on.

However, the fundamental difference is the sharp lack of land resources for its huge population in China. The very factor places tremendous constraints on the style of life in rural China. According to one estimate, the per capita arable land in China is 0.106 hectare, being 43% of the world average figure.[2] But according to another estimate by NIE based on Washington, by 1990 per capital arable land in China was 0.08 hectares, and in comparison with 0.20 for India, 0.11 for Japan, 2.90 for Australia, 0.34 for France, 0.29 for Mexico, 0.34 for Nigeria, 0.13 for the Philippines, 0.15 for Saudi Arabia, 0.36 fro South Africa, 0.12 for the U.K. and 0.75 for the

U.S.[3]. The land to population ratio in China is so low that even the rapid industrialisation and urbanisation recent years do not seem to have an impact. According to Wen, currently 73% of the Chinese are registered as rural population, but only 64% of Chinese residents are actually living in rural China. The gap of this 103 million people is the number of rural migrant workers who live in urban areas temporarily. By 2030 China's population is expected to be 1.6 billion. Even if we assume that China's urbanisation will be so successful and so fast that 50% of the Chinese population will be urban by 2020 that still leaves 800 million Chinese rural.[4]

Land resources keep on shrinking as a result of rapid industrialisation. According to Liu Tian, in the past 20 years the state took away one hundred million *mu* of land for development.[5] The very factor of shortage of land under such tremendous population pressure in China has determined that rural life is under the strain of an economy of scarcity. In such an economy of scarcity rural existence is not a style of life that one may or may choose, but a way of survival, past and present.

Rural England and rural China are two different worlds. So why do we compare? I bring this comparison out because I want to show that it should not be taken for granted that the mode of modernity applies to every place the same way. It should not be taken for granted that Europe is more advanced and developed and places like China only need to catch up by developing. Rural England was enriched by colonisation in the past and by agricultural subsidies at the present whereas China was extracted by external colonisation in the past and what is sometimes called internal colonisation[6] at the present. China has to have its own approach to modernity, its own approach to what should be a good way of life. The Chinese elite may aspire European style of urban life and they apparently have been doing that dramatically successfully since the 1980s. However, it is rural China that it is a challenge to the nation's leadership and the fundamental issue of the challenge is the question of land. In this chapter I will discuss the issues surrounding this challenge and to explore the possibility of an alternative development model for China.

Much of the information in this chapter is from research on the internet as internet seems to be not only the fastest but also the freest in China and from two field research trips to China by the author in early 2005. One field research was conducted in January-February 2005 in the *si yi* areas of Guangdong. The other field research trip was made during February-March 2005 to Zhang Zhuang (Long Bow Village) in Shanxi province. The differences between the north and south China regarding the land situation are discussed later.

The Land Issue: A Brief Background

Let us assume that, leave the controversies of Tibet and Taiwan aside, the Chinese cannot and will not invade other countries to grab land resources (and this is what many fear and hence the China threat or the Yellow Peril) then there are only starkly two or three choices of action for the Chinese. One is to control their population and that is what they have been doing amongst many controversies. Successful or not, population control, as mentioned above, will not have a resource relieving impact for a couple decades to come. Instead, what can be seen already is negative impact such as imbalance of male and female gender, a growing population of the elderly who required to be looked after by fewer young people and personality problem of one child per family. Another option is to import grain and that is they have started doing. However there are two constraints on this option. One is that the Chinese have to have enough money to be able to depend on importing grain. The Chinese do not. The other constraint is that as a national strategy no Chinese leadership can afford to allow their country to slide on to the road of entirely or even largely dependent on importation to feed the Chinese population. Even Japan imports only about 50% of its grain and primary agricultural produces that it needs. Subsidiary and supplementary may be but not substantial importation for such a big country of so many people. The final option, the most feasible option is to find a way to make the best use of the existing land resources. To do that the issue of land ownership is crucial.

Currently land in rural China is theoretically collectively owned. That is, what was traditionally owned by all the people privately before the CPC took over power in any given village is collectively owned by all the people in that village. Within a village, land was distributed equally on a per capita basis during what is called the Land Reform period when the Communist Party of China (CPC) took over power from the mid 1940s to the early 1950s. Then the development of mutual aid, cooperatives and finally communes took place rapidly during what is called the Socialist Transformation from the early 1950s to the late 1950s. During the Commune period, which lasted from the late 1950s to the early 1980s, villages still owned their land collectively in reality though in theory a commune, usually consisting of several villages, owned the land. A village could then be a production team, or divided into two or more teams if a village was big, in a commune. Though production and distribution were carried out within a commune in name, in reality production and distribution were carried out in a village. Apart form some variations from region to region and from one political campaign to another, in general every villager was also entitled to a small amount of land as private plot to grow vegetables and economic crops for family consumption. The rest of the land was pooled together within a village for every one to work on and for every one to share the fruit of their labour.

Since the early 1980s the commune system was broken up and land was distributed to households on a per capita basis. Now individual households have become the owner of their plots of land though in theory the village still owns the land collectively. No households have the right to sell any land to any individual though they may rent it out for any given period of time. On the other hand if the state (the agents of this state can be anybody who has to the right to say that they are state: a developer who gets a permission from whoever has the authority or a head of a villager who wants to use or abuses his power) wants to use any land any individual has to give up that land and the village may or may not get some compensation and the individual involved will get some other piece of land from the village pool.

What are the consequences of such a land ownership arrangements? What is the implication for agricultural production and productivity? What is the implication for income and wealth distribution in rural China? What does this mean for internal migration from rural to the urban? What does it mean for the way of life of the millions of rural Chinese? What is the implication for China's modernisation? In a word, what are the advantages and problems for such a land ownership arrangements? This chapter aims to discuss, if not answer some of these important questions in the context of current leadership which shows tentatively that it has some idea of different direction of development from the previous one.

Land Ownership and Production

Senior rural economist Wen Tiejun states that the floor – or cost – prices of key farm products had already exceeded ceiling prices on the international market. Furthermore, according to Wen ". . . in 14 of China's 27 provinces and regions, land acreage per capita is already at subsistence level". Wen thinks that Chinese government agricultural polices have been exhausted and that China's agriculture is already unsustainable. It is under such circumstances that the issue of land ownership is heatedly debated. The bottom line of the issue is whether land should be unambiguously privatised. The president of the Chinese Land Economy Society and a long time party personnel on rural issues, Du Runsheng, called for urgent legislation on land ownership and rights. Du thinks that clarification of land rights is essential for handling land as a capital resource, so that some farmers could stay on the land and be able to borrow against its value while others would have to leave.[7]

One of the important criticisms against the current land use arrangements is that it defies the rationale of production scale.

Precisely because of the low ratio between land and people division of land on a per capita basis leads to division of many small plots dotted everywhere. Even the division of land to households instead of individuals does not increase much land ownership size. This is specially so in south and southwest of China. As land quality varies from one area to another surrounding even one village, from a hill side to a river bank for instance, a fair distribution means that every area has to be divided up. This leads to what is called *doufu kuai* of land size ownership, i.e., the land is divided into small pieces like toufu slices for individual households.

One immediate consequence is that mechanisation cannot be applied to these *toufu* slices. To start with, mechanisation will have to destroy plots boundaries. However, to destroy land plots boundaries ruins the very purpose of maintaining household distribution. Even in northern China where large size of plain land is available and where land quality variation is minimal and therefore land boundaries do not have to be physically maintained, division of land to individual households renders large scale mechanisation difficult if not impossible. This is the case because different households may have different plans for crops, different time and conditions of planting. Moreover, the coordination cost of applying mechanisation together is too high.

Secondly small household production also means that there cannot be large scale of specialisation. Every household produces what it considers good for its own needs. They would produce different crops at different times. Even they do produce the same crop at the same time there is no coordinated scale of production. As a result not only is productivity low; there is no specialisation and individual farmers cannot cope with the market. It is reported time and again in the media that many Chinese farmers go bankrupt as a result of responding to the market rationally but individually. For instance, when the farmers in one area see that watermelon fetch good price the previous year they all tend to produce watermelon the year after. Inevitably too much watermelon on the market leads to depression of price for every farmer.

Thirdly, as small plots of land require intensive labour usually by hand there is no incentive and no necessity for the introduction and development of new technology and new innovation. There is therefore no prospect of much an increase of productivity. Overall, the rural people in China seem to have condemned as beasts of burden involving in low-tech, labour intensive production that they have been engaging in thousand of years. The reversal of land ownership arrangements since the end of the era of Mao can hardly be called reform. The arrangements seem to have returned back to the agriculture to self-sufficiency and subsistence.

Argument For and Against Privatisation of Land

The current arrangements of land ownership in rural China have been attacked from all directions. However, what is to be done as a solution varies greatly from one's political stand. For example, the economist Li Yining 《我们有世界最大的金矿》 argues that rural China should be formed as different companies and individual households can join the company as share holders. These companies would be run by entrepreneurs who would then invest, develop new technology and open up new markets. Another representative of what is referred to as neo-liberals[8] Zhou Qiren 《农地制度以俄为师》 argues that, just as the Chinese learned from Russia the system of collectivisation they should also learn from the Russians privatisation of land. Therefore, all the Chinese have to do is make households the permanent owners of their land, not just temporary ownership of use right.

Wen Tiejun, however, argues that Zhou's solution reflects only wishful thinking. China cannot copy the Russian model of privatisation because China does not have that much land but has too many people. According to Wen, once the land is privatised, there will be land closure and land seizure and there will be landlords and at the same time large number of landless Chinese will fall into poverty and even starvation that no Chinese government will be able to cope with.

Land Ownership Problem:
Attack from Direction of the Right

Let us first examine what criticisms come from the neo-liberals since theirs has been the dominant discourse since the late 1990s. The main argument put forward by this dominant discourse is that ownership of the current arrangements is too ambiguous. Article 10 of the 1992 version o the Chinese Constitution[9] does not seem to be able to clarify the ambiguity:

> Land in the rural and suburban areas is owned by collectives except for those portions which belong to the state in accordance with the law; house sites and privately farmed plots of cropland and hilly land are also owned by collectives. The state may, in the public interest, requisition land for its use in accordance with the law. No organisation or individual may appropriate, buy, sell or unlawfully transfer land in other ways. The right to the use of the land may be transferred in accordance with the law.

Does the state own the land? Who is the state? Is it the collective village or anyone beyond the village? Individual households appear to own only the use right of land. Even that is not very clearly defined since every now and then the village as a collective can and does redistribute or reallocate land. Some villages for instance redistribute land in every five years to make adjustment to population change in households, change as a result of birth, death, marriage and migration. In some villages the insistence on non-change, say, for fifteen years causes concerns by some villagers because they argue adjustment has to be made more frequently to reflect population change.

What the rational economists such Steven Cheung (who admits that he was encouraged by Ronald Coase and Friedman to move from the U.S. to Hong Kong in the 1982 to influence China[10], Yang[11] and Dang[12] argue is that according to the Coase Theorem, private property rights is a necessary condition for the theorem of exchange to be operative. In Coase's own words: "The delimitation of rights is an essential prelude to market transactions."[13] The definition of property rights have to be clear in that 1) it is clear who has the right to use the land, 2) it is clear that who has the right to enjoy the benefit of the land and 3) it is clear that right to own the land can be transferred freely.[14]

According to Cheung, the very ambiguity of land ownership in rural China is the lack of freedom of transfer. Because of this ambiguity there is not only high transaction cost but also lack of incentive to invest in the land. The economists of this political persuasion also argue that without the right and freedom of selling and buying individual households will hold to their small plots. As a result, there will be no division of labour, no specialisation and no critical mass and there no scale of production.[15] Yang actually goes as far as to give figures for the benefit of privatisation of land by saying that if land can be allowed to change hand in the market net income of the Chinese peasantry could increase by at least 30%.[16] Therefore, the best solution is to hand the land to the farmers, define their rights and allow them to sell their land. The rest can be taken care of by the market, so Cheung declares.[17] Another well known essayist argues that property must belong to the private. Otherwise there would be no market economy, no economic development and therefore no freedom and prosperity.[18] Similar view is stated by Liu Junning that private right to property is the crux of market economy. Private ownership of property is thus the most crucial component of a civilised, just, free and prosperous society.[19]

Land Ownership Problem:
Attack from Direction of the Left

There are also criticisms from the left attacking the current land arrangements. This can be seen from the criticism by Hinton[20] who argues that the so-called rural reform in the early 1980s not only undid what had been achieved collectively but also made mechanisation impossible. Wen Tiejun argues that in the Chinese situation productivity has nothing to do with private ownership. He states that it is a myth that only through land privatisation can Chinese agriculture join international competition. As he sees it, even if Chinese land is privatised ten thousand times, China still won't be a player in international competition.[21] Wen tells the following story to illustrate his point:

> The second story is about my home province. The mountainous regions of Guizhou are known for their severe soil erosion, a problem that has worsened in recent years. Many deeply concerned international organisations, including NGOs, are engaged in poverty-alleviation efforts in Guizhou. I wonder if they understand why poverty-stricken Guizhou farmers have to do their farming on mountain slopes too steep even for farm oxen? Only humans can climb up on them, to dig some soil and plant some corn in the crevices of the rocks. Do you think they enjoy doing that? Guizhou people will tell you a story about a "straw-hat field." A man was given 28 pieces of land. So, he climbed up the slopes to till them. After doing 27 of them, he couldn't, for the life of him, find the last one. But when he picked up his straw hat, he saw that there it was, all covered up by his hat! This tells you how bad things are.[22]

For people like Wen, the main problem with Chinese agriculture is not the lack of production scale but that of poverty. What the mainstream neo-liberals take for granted is that privatisation will get rid of poverty eventually even if poverty may be a necessary condition at the initial stage of development. Wen thinks that privatisation would not solve the problem of poverty and even urbanisation alone would not solve the problem. For this argument Wen wants us to draw a comparison between China and Mexico:

In our eagerness to raise farmers' income by accelerating urbanisation, we need to look at other countries in the world. Mexico's urbanisation rate is 80%, whereas ours is only 40%. Mexico's per capita income had once hit $6,000, whereas ours is only $1,000. And yet, they still have farmers who go under. According to government statistics, their poverty rate is 34%, but researchers put it at over 50%, which is far higher than ours. They still have farmers' rebellions, battles waged by the mask-wearing combatants I mentioned earlier, and they still have slash-and-burn farming and native Indians have had to abandon their old tradition of living in harmony with nature. This is all due to problems in the system.[23]

Li Changping, another rural China specialist who made his name by writing to Zhu Rongji[24] and who subsequently wrote a very popular book[25], is against the ideology of privatisation. He argues, what is at stake is not just about ownership. In fact the current collective ownership acts to provide welfare for the most disadvantaged in rural China. For instance those who cannot work, the sick, the old and disabled can rent their land in return for grain to feed themselves. Some income from the collectively owned orchards, tea farms and fish farms are used to pay for the maintenance of roads, some medical facilities and irrigation infrastructure. Land is also the last resort for migrant workers who may not be able to find work, who may be disabled at work place or who may be simply not wanted after certain age. They can always return home and the small plots of land that cannot be taken away from them is the ultimate safety net for the vast majority of rural Chinese.[26]

What the right and left have to agree with is that Chinese farming is fundamentally small in scale: 900 million peasants, 230 million of whom are small farmers, and 0.5 hectare on average per family[27]. The debate between the increasingly influential left and still mainstream neo-liberals on the right on land ownership concerns not only the present but also the past and future. The right argues that since the responsibility system was implemented, even the rural Chinese have solved the problem of *wen bao* (meaning adequately fed and clothed, not exactly true for all the rural Chinese). Therefore, it is the success of *fen tian dao hu* (privatisation) that resulted in the growth of grain production in China. It has become an article of faith the Commune system encouraged laziness and free riders and that *fen tian dao hu*, though not very clear private ownership, was good enough an incentive for rapid rise of grain production. In order to support such propositions Du Rensheng had even organised a group of economists including Wen Tiejun and the well-known U.S. trained economist Justine Lin to examine the 1960s and 1970s year books of production teams to find evidence to support the belief that the Commune system was a high cost and low efficiency system of production of labour relationship. According to Wen though no evidence could be found by the team, but the assumptions have been taken as the truth ever since.[28]

However, the left argues that is not true. *Fen tian dao hu* was not the main reason or at least not the only reason for the fact that the Chinese have solved the *wenbao* issue. Chinese agriculture could perform better in the post-Mao era because the collective system laid the foundation for the latter days such as irrigation infrastructure and technology of chemical fertilisers.[29] It seems that the neo-liberals focus solely on ownership factor but ignore important factors such as technology and resources. According to Lao Tian, a very active internet participant who worked as a farmer before and after the reform, farmers work less after the reform to improve productivity and production but rely more on chemicals. In the area where he used to work farmer used only about 30 *jin* of chemical fertilisers for one *mu* of land. By the beginning of the 21st century they use more than 120 *jin* for one *mu* of land.[30]

Lao Tian argues that during the era of Mao the commune system worked very well and had solved the problem of production scale. In addressing Coase' argument that by participating market competition companies will reduce the transaction cost, Lao Tian argues that a production team in the Commune system was like a company that was able to reduce the transaction cost. It is the dismantling of the Commune system that has not only increased the transaction cost but also has made efficient large scale irrigation projects un-functional. Lao Tian lists several examples from He Xuefeng and Luo Xingzuo. One is a water pumping station built in 1976 which started to operate in 1978. A 1,800 metres long ditch was built for the water that was pumped from Han Jiang 24 meters below. The project could irrigate 14 thousand *mu* of land. Because of the division and distribution of land to individual households, it became too difficult to charge the cost of operating in accordance with the reward. The irrigation system virtually stopped function. Even in 1990 the pumping operated for 1251.9 hours. In 2003 it operated for only 21 hours.[31] The project is un-operable while a large amount of paddy fields go un-irrigated.

Hinton is also very critical of the so-called rural reform pushed by Deng. Hinton was very much involved in helping China addressing the issue of production scale and mechanisation and invested a lot of his time and efforts[32] on experimenting and demonstrative mechanisation. Therefore it really went to his heart when he saw the detrimental effects the so-called responsibility system (*fen tian dao hu*, distribution of land to individual households) had on the budding mechanisation in north China. In his book *Shenfan* documenting the change he had witnessed in Zhang Zhuang (Long Bow) village, a sequel to his influential *Fanshen* which documents the land reform that he had witnessed, Hinton was still not quite sure of the direction and consequences of the reform. But in his 1990 book *the Great Reversal* Hinton casts away his ambiguity and was very critical of the dismantling of the commune system.

Wang Jinhong, the Party Secretary of Long Bow from 1966 to 2003 (only briefly out of power in the early 1970s) agrees with Hinton[33]. Wang worked together with Hinton since the early 1970s to develop mechanisation in Long Bow. Wang, with Hinton's help, even developed his own mechanised corn dryer and mechanised irrigation system for Long Bow in the 1970s. In 1984, when the tide of the great reversal was rolling all of China Wang Jinhong resisted and managed to keep a portion of the land collective so that machines can be used. The arrangement worked well to provide enough grain to pay tax to the state so that individual households would not have to bother about paying agricultural taxes. However, mechanisation was reduced to smaller scale and eventually all the collective owned machines fell out of repair. Mechanisation is still partially applicable in Long Bow, only for plough and planting. This is possible because majority of the land is very level and of the same quality in Long Bow, unlike the situation in south and southwest China. Though land is divided up and boundaries are marked machines can still used in the two tasks. Households pay for the cost of these tasks according to their portion of the land that uses the machines which are owned by private operators. For the purpose of using machines in performing the two tasks households have to agree to grow the same kind of crop, which happens to be corn in Long Bow.

The debate of land ownership of course also concerns the future direction of China. The neo-liberal right argues that we should look to the model of Western development and speed up the process of urbanisation.[34] Western development model is that way to solve rural problems in China. However the left argues, to raise the living standards according to Western development is wishful thinking.[35] The very conditions in China and environmental and resource constraints mean that China cannot develop along the Western model. If all the Chinese become urban where does the energy and resources come from to maintain the living standard that the Chinese want?

The Challenge: A Model of Development

The challenge to the first Chinese leadership in the 21st century is to find a model that will solve the so-called *san nong wen ti* (three related agricultural and rural problems), which are the problem of raising the living standards of the majority of the Chinese who are currently rural, the problem of maintaining agricultural production adequate enough to feed China's huge population and the problem of bringing rural China into modernity. The three related problems have their root cause in the lower land to population ratio. But it is also closely related to a developmental model. The development models in both the era of Mao and the post-Mao have one thing in common: exploitation of rural China for the benefit of industrialisation and urban development. The hardship and poverty endured by rural people have been considered as the necessary sacrifice for the wealth and strength of the nation.

This kind of exploitation of the Chinese peasantry is sometimes called "internal colonisation (*nei zhimin*) i.e., colonial plunder of the rural by the urban.[36] For example, from 1997 to 2001 alone there was a transfer of more than 100 billion RMB from rural China to the urban through price regulations by the state.[37] Furthermore, the current land ownership situation enables urban China in the name of the state to generate enormous amount of income by turning agricultural land into commercial and urban land. For example, the total financial income of Shanghai from 1992 to 2002 was 360 billion and 120 billion of that was actually from land transaction.[38]

If there had been a consensus that exploitation of rural China was necessary for developing China that consensus has now been challenged for two main reasons. One main reason is that economically the exploitation of the peasantry is not viable anymore at this stage of China's economic development. The basic problem is that without a higher living standard for the rural people there is no internal market for industrial products. The rural Chinese are too poor to consume. The second main reason is that there is a danger that rural poverty will upset the political stability of China.

The challenge is therefore first whether to completely dismantle the Great Wall that has divided two Chinas, the rural and urban China.[39] Currently the rural people are allowed to work for limited range of jobs (the dirtiest, hardest and lowest paid) in urban areas but are not allowed to have access to any of the benefits that rural people might have, such as subsidised housing, minimum livelihood allowance when out of job, some entitlement of health care and virtually free primary and secondary education. In cities like

Shanghai where resident population growth has been negative there are not enough children going to existing schools. The authorities in Shanghai have chosen to merge or close down these schools rather than to let children of migrant workers in. Migrant parents are forced to leave their children behind in rural areas or give up their jobs to return for the sake their children's education. The second aspect of the challenge is, if the control of migration is relaxed, whether the urban sector able to cope with the sudden explosion of urban population with adequate energy and social infrastructure. There would be no point of having more urban residents if they are completely abandoned in ghettos. The final aspect of the challenge is that even if the urban sector is well prepared enough to allow all those who can find work and their families to become urban citizens the urbanisation could not be quick enough to absorb most of the rural people. If the Chinese population is to be expected to peak at 1.6 billion in 2020, a speed of urbanisation of 10 million a year means that by 2020 there will still be 800 million rural Chinese, as Wen estimates. In relation to all the three aspects of the challenge it is the issue of land ownership.

Conclusion

Both the new left and neo-liberals agree that one of the important reasons for the increasing polarisation between urban and rural China is that when agricultural land is taken away by the "state" for urban and commercial development the tremendous increase of value in this transaction benefits the urban alone. The rural residents are only given compensation at the rate of agricultural land. However, the new left and neo-liberals have different solutions to this "internal colonisation" problem. In fact some neo-liberals would not think this is a problem at all. They would argue instead that this is a necessary stage of development for which some have to make the sacrifice. Most neo-liberals, however, do think this is a problem that needs to be solved. Their suggested solution is clear and unambiguous private ownership of land. Once privatisation takes place the market will not be distorted and rural residents will benefit from the profit of land transaction when agricultural land is turned into urban commercial land. For the new left, this kind of fundamental marketism is at best ignorant of the Chinese situation and at worst brutal and lacking compassion. For the new left, urbanisation cannot be fast enough to absorb most of the rural Chinese. Unless the Chinese government has enough resources and the will to provide a socio-economic safety net for the rural Chinese household ownership of land is the last and only safety net available. If land is completely and clearly privatised many of the peasantry will first sell their land and then will be left with nothing for even a subsistence living. Why don't we see ghettos in Chinese cities, ghettos like the ones we see in some other developing countries where child feed on rubbish dumps? Because every family has a guaranteed piece of land at home to which migrant workers can return and at which children are left.

While the arguments of both the new left and neo-liberals are convincing from their value concern they seem to neglect to make a nuanced difference between agricultural land near urban centres/industrial centres and agricultural land in Chinese rural heartland. Agricultural land near urban and industrial centres can increase its value overnight tens and even hundred times, but the vast majority land in rural heartland will never be turned urban or commercial. The other missing link in this land ownership debate is the role and constitutional power of the state. Currently the Chinese state in theory has the power to take away from its citizen almost anything, private or public, land or property, at nominal or very little compensation.[40]

On 1 October 2005, there seems to be some breakthrough on the transaction of agricultural land into commercial and urban land in favour of rural residents. On that day Guangdong provincial government passed a document stipulating new measures concerns land transfer.[41] According to the old land regulation laws no agricultural land is allowed to be transferred to be commercial or urban land unless it is approved by the state. "The state" at various levels uses this right to confiscate land from rural residents and make profits by land transfer (as the case of Shanghai shows) while rural residents receive very little compensation. According to the new regulations in Guangdong, the collective, for instance a village, has the right to make land transfer decision and have the right to benefit from commercial transaction.[42] This will settle the land ownership debate between the neo-liberals and the new left as the villagers who "privately" own their land collectively will benefit from the profit of land transfer collectively. However, for the majority of the rural people whose collective land will not be transferred, privatisation or not is a challenge and the solution of which will determine the Chinese model of modernity.

Notes and References

1. Hsu, Madeline, Y., "Migration and native place: *Qiaokan* and the imagined community of Taishan Country, Guangdong, 1893–1993," *The Journal of Asian Studies*, Vol. 59, No. 2 (May 2000), pp. 307–331.

2. SOE, *Report on the State of the Environment in China*, 2002, http://www.zhb.gov.cn/english/SOE/soechina1999/land/landdown.htm. Accessed on 18 September 2005.

3. NIE, Committee for the National Institute for the Environment, http://www.cnie.org/pop/conserving/landuse4b.htm. Accessed on 18 September 2005.

4. Wen Tiejun, "Xue zhe xi lie fang tan zhi Wen Tiejun fang tan" ("Scholars interview series, interview with Wen Tiejun"), Shi ji xue tang, http://www.ccforum.org.cn/viewthread.php?tid–16618&extra=page%3D2, 20 July 2005. Accessed on 21 July 2005.

5. Cited in Lu Xueyi, Shi ji zhongguuo, zhong guo san nong wen ti de you lai he fa zhan ("The origin and development of the problems of rural China, agriculture and rural people") http://www.cc.org.cn/newcc/browwenzhang. php?articleid=4891 Lu Xueyi. Accessed on 22 September 2005.

6. Cao Jingqing, "zhongguo ongcun zhuanxing: zhuan xiang hefang?" ("Rural Chinese transition: to where?") a talk given in 2004 at Huazhong shifan daxue, *shiji zhongguo* (Century China net), http://www.cc.org.cn/newcc/browwenzhang.php?articleid=5116. Accessed on 1 November 2005.

7. BBC News, "Chinese farmers face bleak future" Thursday, 14 December, 2000, 18:05 GMT. Accessed on 17 September 2005.

8. Andrew Kipnis, "Neo-leftists versus Neo-Liberals: PRC Intellectual Debates in the 1990s", *Journal of Intercultural Studies*, 24, 3 (2003), pp. 239–51. See also Gao, Mobo C. F., "The rise of neo-nationalism and the new left: a post-colonial and postmodernism perspective" in Leong Liew and Shaoguang Wang (eds.), *Nationalism, Democracy and National Integration in China* (London: Routledge Curzon, 2004), pp. 44–62.

9. *Constitution of the People's Republic of China* online, article 10, http://www.usconstitution.net/china.html. Accessed on 17 September 2005.

10. Cheung is thriving among the young Chinese university students. This is what he says about himself: "Fifteen years ago the head of the Nobel Prize Committee came to see me and asked me to put my ideas into a collected volume. What he implied was that I would have a good chance of wining the prize if I did that. I was going to do that myself. But when I was asked to do that I dropped the very idea! (laughter and applause)". "There is one thing that I feel very proud of. I can be sure that six and seven of my articles will be read by people even a hundred years later. No Nobel Prize winners have the confidence to say that (laughter and applause.) See Cheung, N. S., 新周刊, 狂生傲语张五常只以文章论英雄 (the arrogant Steven Cheung only judges heroes by what has been written) http://www.stevenxue.com/ref_135.htm, 15th June 2001). Here I keep the Chinese version for appreciation. 15 年前, 诺贝尔奖评委会的头头来找我, 他叫我把我自己的论文思想写成一本书, 言下之意是如果我这样做的话, 获奖机会很大. 我本来是准备写的, 但你叫我写的话, 我就不写! (笑声, 掌声). 有件事情我是感到很骄傲的, 我可以肯定, 我起码有六七篇文章, 100 年后还会有人读. 没有一个诺贝尔奖的得主敢这么说的. (笑声, 掌声).

11. Yang, Xiao-kai and Wills' paper "A model formalizing the theory of property rights," *Journal of Comparative Economics*, Vol. 14, (1990), pp. 177–98.

12. Dang Guoying 土地制度对农民的剥夺 san nong zhongguo http://www.snzg.net/shownews.asp?newsid=7645, 8 September 2005. Accessed on 17 September 2005.

13. Quoted in Cheung, N. S., 新周刊, 狂生傲语张五常只以文章论英雄 (the arrogant Steven Cheung only judges heroes by what has been written) http://www.stevenxue.com/ref_135.htm, 15th June 2001. Also see "The Transaction Costs Paradigm: 1998 Presidential Address Western Economic Association" printed in 10 January 1998, *Economic Inquiry* Page 514.

14. *Ibid.*

15. Yang, Xiao-kai and Wills' paper "A model formalizing the theory of

property rights".

16. Dang Guoying 土地制度对农民的剥夺 san nong zhongguo.

17. Cheung, N. S., 新周刊, 狂生傲语张五常只以文章论英雄 ("the arrogant Steven Cheung only judges heroes by what has been written").

18. Wang Dingding 汪丁丁："哈耶克'扩展秩序'思想初论"(中),《经济民主与经济自由》,《公共论丛》第三辑, 1997 年).

19. Liu Junning, 财产权与个人幸福及人类文明 in《共和? 民主? 宪政 — 自由主义思想研究》, 上海三联书店, 1998 年).

20. William Hinton, *The Great Reversal: the Privatization of China, 1978–1989*, (New York: Monthly Review Press, 1990).

21. Wen Tiejun, Speech on Rural Development and Environmental Protection Presented at the 1st Green China Forum (25 October 2003) uploaded on 20 November 2003 China Study Group, http://www.chinastudygroup. org/article/66/. Accessed on 17 September, 2005.

22. *Ibid.*

23. *Ibid.*

24. Gao, Mobo, C. F., "Li Changping, Wo xiang zongli shuo shihua" ("I Told the Truth to the Premier") *The China Journal*, 48 (2002), pp. 175–77.

25. Li Changping, *Wo xiang zongli shuo shihua* (*I Told the Truth to the Premier*) (Beijing: Guangming ribao chubanshe, 2002).

26. Li Changping, 农业税和土地制度改革简单不得 san nong zhongguo, http://www.snzg.net/shownews.asp?newsid=7821, 16th September 2005, accessed on 17th September 2005.

27. Wen Tiejun, Speech on Rural Development and Environmental Protection Presented at the 1st Green China Forum (25 October 2003)

28. Wen Tiejun,《中国农村基本经济制度研究》(北京: 中国经济出版社, 2000).

29. Gao, Mobo C. F., "Shuxie lishi *Gao jia cun*" ("Writing history and *Gao village*"), in *Dushu* (*Readings*), No. 1 (January 2001), pp. 9–16.

30. Lao Tian, "三农研究中的视野屏蔽与问题意识局限" (世界中国, 2005).

31. Lao Tian, "cong jig e shui li dd xiao gu shi kan nong min de he zuo neng li wen ti (On the cooperative abilities of the farmer from several stories about irrigation), personal webpage http://laotianlaotian.yeah.net, 20 April 2004. Accessed on the 26th September 2005.

32. William Hinton, *Iron Oxen*: a *Documentary of Rrevolution in Chinese Farming* (New York: Vintage Books, 1971).

33. All the information concerning Wang Jinhong was obtained during my field research trip to the village in August 2005 where I stayed for 11 days. During the stay I lived in Wang's house and had nearly a hundred hours of conversation with Wang, his extended families, his friends, colleagues and villagers in Long Bow.

34. Dang Guoying 土地制度对农民的剥夺 san nong zhongguo.

35. Wen Tiejun, Speech on Rural Development and Environmental Protection Presented at the 1st Green China Forum (25 October 2003).

36. Cao Jingqing, "zhongguo ongcun zhuanxing: zhuan xiang hefang?" ("Rural Chinese transition: to where?")

37. *Ibid.*

38. *Ibid.*

39. Gao, Mobo C. F., "The great wall that divides two Chinas and the rural/urban disparity challenge," in Joseph Cheng (ed.), *China's Challenges in the Twenty-First Century* (Hong Kong: City University of Hong Kong Press, 2003), pp. 533–557.

40. 向救赎：中国城乡二元结构的转型——两个局外人的对谈录之十, 15 March 2005, http://www.snzg.net/shownews.asp?newsid=1229. Accessed on 2 November 2005.

41. The document is called 广东省集体建设用地使用权流转管理办法.

42. 中国青年报, 11 October 2005.

16

Fiscal Reforms, Rural Tension and Prospect for Stability

Ray YEP

Introduction

The conventional wisdom on the rising rural tension in China attributes the chaos in the countryside to the misbehaviour of local cadres. According to this logic, these predatory and corrupt officials are the major culprits provoking numerous violent responses of aggrieved Chinese peasants in recent years. And the logic follows that in addition to disciplinary actions against local bureaucracy, tightening of fiscal loopholes for excessive extraction should be introduced. This explains the experimentation of "tax-for-fee" reform and abolition of agricultural tax in recent years. This paper contends however, while corruption and abuses of power at local level are evident, one has to contextualise the rising tension in the backdrop of changing formula of rural finance: the replacement of hidden-taxation under collective framework with explicit extraction in reform era, the imperative of rural self-sufficiency and the consequent under-financing of rural administration. These changes play no lesser role than corruption in aggrieving the Chinese peasants. Put in this light, the recent well-intended measure of abolishing agricultural tax may fail to fulfil its mission of placating the peasantry. It may ironically, intensify rural tension if it is not supplemented by more fundamental changes in rural finance.

Fiscal Skepticism
in Post-commune Era

Mao's economy was renowned for its success in rural extraction. Its imperative of rapid industrialisation of socialist economies rendered the creation of effective organisation of agriculture a top priority and the collective framework of People's Commune provided the means for siphoning off agricultural surplus in Mao's China. During the collective era, economic life of Chinese peasants was highly regimentalised and agricultural production was fully dictated by the commune. Peasants were deprived of the ownership of lands, and even more significantly, their control over the appropriation of the harvest. Peasants were reimbursed according to the work points they earned from assigned labour. There was never a straight forward connection between amount of work points one had and his or her actual income. The worth of each work point remained unknown until the state and the collective had completed their extraction. A procurement quota of grain was imposed on each commune under the compulsory grain purchase system. The system guaranteed the state a direct access to agricultural surplus. The commune, brigade and team administrations then took their "fair shares" necessary for financing cadres' salaries, administrative expenses and other collective ventures. These were in effect, taxation on the peasants. Eventually, the residue would be shared among peasants and the size of the leftover determined the actual value of each earned point. The efficacy of this extractive mechanism was supported by a number of institutional features of Mao's economy. First, the deprivation of ownership of means of production of Chinese peasants made compliance with the dictate of the collective inevitable. De facto private ownership of land brought by Land Reform was soon brushed off by the collectivisation drive unleashed by Mao's radicalism. Second, the effective closure of private market rendered the room for income via illegitimate avenue a very difficult and dangerous pursuit. Both measures made labour under the collective framework the only viable way to maintain subsistence. Third, in return for their compliance, Chinese peasants were at least nominally, entitled to comprehensive welfare provisions financed by the collective. A typical package included communal dinning hall, nursery and clinic services, while a more generous collective may even provide hairdressing service, entertainment etc. This elaborate welfare regime helped legitimise the high level of extraction. An unintended consequence of the extraction mode was the relative acquiescence among Chinese peasants. The lack of transparency in local budgeting and thus the general ignorance of the actual intensity of hidden taxation helped diffuse the tension. Tolerance threshold of state exaction in the collective era rested by and large, on the physical limit of provoking starvation and famine. For example, the rape of the Chinese peasantry during the Great Leap Forward eventually came to a halt as a result of the millions of life lost during. According to Zhou, about 600 billion yuans were diverted from the agricultural sector to the industrial sectors in the form of price differential and tax in the pre-reform period.[1]

The advent of economic reforms however, made the collective mode of extraction untenable. The return to individual farming under the household responsibility system heralded a new ethos in rural finance, both in private and public realms. Individual household resumed its status as the basic accounting unit. Household income was now determined by its ability to thrive in market with the collective with no direct access to its harvest. The three pillars supporting the effective extraction also disappeared with decollectivisation. Means of production, land in particular, are now under *de facto* private ownership, and individual peasants regained their freedom in economic activities. Markets reopen in post-Mao years and the profits inherent in market transaction are reiterated as the incentive for production. Decollectivisation also comes with a price of termination of comprehensive welfare provision in the countryside and the main burden of financing contingency is now shifted back to one's family. The impact of these changes on peasant-cadre relationship is significant. Not only is the state deprived of the effective leverage of extraction, but there also emerges a different calculation towards financial obligations among Chinese peasants. Peasants are now fully aware of their direct financial contribution to the public coffers. The new fiscal regime is, in other words, much more explicit than the old practice. Transparency should breed confidence and trust, but it may also nurture shrewdness in payment. Peasants are now much better informed of the actual amount of their financial contribution than in the collective era.[2] Expectedly, such knowledge encourages "value-for-money" attitude towards financial obligations. And the mentality has been reflected in the rising complaints against redundancy of officials in local administration. There have been many reports of peasants challenging the necessity of maintaining a large corp of cadres after decollectivisation. While the paternalistic state of people commune may justify the present of a strong force, the retreat of the state in economic and social affairs inherent in decollectivisation process has provoked many queries on the need of supporting a huge establishment. The frustration is vividly reflected in a folklore ridiculing the cadres. Cadres are seen as unpleasant figures who only come with *san yao* (three "wants"): *yao qian* (they want payment of different charges and levies), *yao liang* (grain for fulfilling procurement quota) and *yao min* (ensuring birth control regulation).[3]

Such financial scepticism helps explain the discontent against the arbitrary imposition of levies and charges at rural grass root. Capricious extraction always breeds resentment. Unfortunately, unpredictable charges are the defining features of the extractive regime in the countryside in post-Mao era. Random charges on different justifications were rampant. Charges were imposed in principle, for peasants' consumption of specific service or violation of regulations. However, in most cases, most of the charges were ungrounded. By 1997, the total number of surcharges and fees with official approvals had reached 6,800 nationwide! The extra-budgetary nature of these incomes explains the pervasiveness of such practice at local level. For local governments, collection of fees and charges – mostly extra-budgetary in nature – implies more secured entitlement, freedom in application, flexibility in appropriation and most importantly, immunity from the watchful eyes of higher levels. In principle, their usage is confined to the related policy area, and they are not subject to sharing with higher levels of governments. Management of these funds has been erratic in most cases. Underreporting is common, as is illegitimate use of these funds for purposes other than those specified. Given the laxity of control, local governments see these funds as a convenient source of extra revenues. As a result, the total extra-budgetary revenues collected at sub-national levels jumped from 53.2 billion yuan to 315.5 billion yuan between 1982 and 1999.[4] And these charges were regarded by the central government as the major culprit for causing the rising financial burden of the peasants (*nongmin fudan*), and thus rural tension during the 1990s.

The Attempt of Tax-for-fee Reform

Tax-for-fee reform came as the first major attempt to placate the aggrieved peasants. The idea first emerged as a possible policy option in a joint document issued by the State Commission of Restructuring Economy, Ministry of Construction, Ministry of Finance and eight other ministries and commissions in 1995. In the document titled, *Xianchengzhen Zonghe Gaige Shidian Zhidao Yijian* (Document Relaying the Opinion on the Test Point of Comprehensive Reform of Small Towns, 1995), the idea of tax-for-fee was forwarded as an alternative for tackling the problem of chaotic fund-raising and excessive charges in the countryside. This early effort drew few sympathetic ears. Nevertheless, as in the history of rural reform, local initiative always preceded official endorsement. For example, Wugang Prefecture of Hunan Province had already piloted the idea since 1995. Under this experiment, township and village levies (*santi wutong*) were replaced by rural community development taxes.[5] These local experiments provided ammunition for advocates, and the idea gained further momentum when Premier Zhu Rongji singled out tax-for-fee as one of the major reforms for coming years at the National People's Congress meeting in 1998. This green light from the top encouraged further local experiments. By 1999, pilot projects were introduced in more than fifty counties and prefectures in seven provinces, including Anhui, Hunan, Inner Mongolia, Sichuan and Hebei.[6] In 2000, the State Council eventually decided to push the reform a step forward and designated Anhui Province as a test site. As Anhui has initiated the most comprehensive and systematic reforms in this direction so far, we will use its experience to evaluate the progress and achievement of this new policy option.

Anhui Province has a history as a pioneer of rural reform. Xiaogang Village of Fenyang County was first to introduce the household output-linked contract responsibility system in the late 1970s, which sparked off the nationwide rural reform in post-Mao years. Tax-for-fee reform experiments started in Anhui in 1993, and by the time it was designated as the provincial test point, the number of pilot counties and prefectures had already reached 15, comprising about 30% of pilot schemes across the country.[7] This may be a logical development for Anhui, as confrontations between local officials and peasants have been rampant in recent years, and the conflict over the collection of fees and levies was among the major causes of tension. For example, there were 624 petitions against excessive burdens in Huaiyuan County in 1997.[8] The rising threat of rural instability explains the urgency and enthusiasm for reform in the province.

The pilot scheme in Anhui consisted of several key components. First, most of the township levies and charges were abolished. Prior to the reform, peasants in Anhui were subject to five major township levies (*wutong*). These were fees collected on a per-capita basis for financing expenditure on local education, militia training, road construction and maintenance, welfare for veterans and birth control. The reform also forbade township governments to conduct other forms of fund-raising for public works and education. The slaughter-tax, which was applied to all local residents irrespective of their involvement in the poultry business, was also banned. Second, a plan was devised to phase out voluntary labour obligations in three year's time. A legacy of the collective era, each rural labourer was required to provide 10–20 days of labour a year, or its monetary equivalent, for afforestation and water conservation. These obligations are scheduled to be terminated by 2003. Third, as compensation for the loss of revenue due to these two changes, the agricultural tax was raised to 7% on average. Agricultural tax is determined by the size of the land leased by each household and its "expected output", rather than actual output. Expected output was calculated on the basis of average output level in the region in "normal years", which was in turn, based on obsolete data collected decades ago. Though the provincial nominal rate of agricultural tax was 15% on average before 2000,[9] the real rate was in the region of 2–3% due to the deliberate policy of under-estimating agricultural productivity.[10] Thus, the adjustment to the level of 7% in 2000 is a *de facto* rise in extraction. A province-wide reassessment of land distribution and productivity was launched, requiring monumental effort. 365 provincial and prefectural-level cadres were sent to rural areas, and 11,000 local cadres were involved in the exercise.[11] It was decided that the average productivity between 1993 and 1997 should be taken as the basis of calculation, with variation between counties allowed. Lastly, the village levies for financing collective investment, welfare and cadre compensation were also abolished. In return, a supplement to agricultural taxes equivalent to the maximum of 20% of the tax payment was imposed on peasants.[12]

Table 1 provides a summary of the changes introduced by the pilot scheme. It should be noted that, theoretically, the impact on township and village finance is minimal; the post-reform peasants' burden is in the region of 8.4% of their agricultural output value, which is very close to the pre-reform total of township and village levies and agricultural taxes. Local administrations will lose a substantial amount of revenue from extra-budgetary exaction under the new regime, but this is exactly the objective of the central government, which regards the arbitrariness of these charges as the major culprit behind peasant discontent. A more transparent and predictable fiscal regime is in place with greater budgetary control from above and certitude for below.

Table 1
Financial Obligations of Anhui Peasants
Before and After Tax-for-fee Reform

	Before the reform	After the reform
i. agricultural tax	nominal rate of 15% of average normal output value in the area; real rate: 2–3%	7%
ii. township levies	(ii) & (iii) should not exceed 5% of average annual per capita income	abolished
iii. village levies		maximum of 20% of agricultural tax
iv. 10–20 days	per capita basis	abolished in 2003 labour contribution
v. other charges	no fixed rate	mostly abolished

Abolishing Agricultural Tax

The ostensible success of the Anhui experiment in reducing peasant burden encourages more audacious programs. The experiment soon spread to all provinces in the country. However, in 2004, the central government came up with an even more daring decision to abolish agricultural tax. In the Second Meeting of the Tenth National People's Congress, Premier Wen Jiabo announced,

> "From this year onward, the tax rate of agricultural tax will be reduced gradually. On average, there should be an annual reduction by one per cent and the tax will be eventually abolished in five years time".[13]

Chinese peasants have endured numerous exploitative and discriminative measures such as under-pricing of agricultural products and *hukou* system. Not only were they deprived of access to the fruits of economic progress and modernisation by these measures, but they had also been coerced to shoulder the main burden of financing industrialisation in the past decades. The decision to abolish agricultural tax heralds a belated bestowal of justice. And it is consistent with the Party's reiterated concerns of improving the livelihood of the rural population and maintaining stability in the countryside. Economists supporting the move also highlight the incentive effect of the reduced cost of production on agricultural development.[14]

In immediate terms, these drastic fiscal innovations are certainly popular among peasants. The question however, remains. Like Tax-for-Fee reform, the utility of agricultural tax reform hinges upon its long term impact on the welfare of the rural population. Unfortunately, both measures suffer a major over-sight in analyzing the root cause of peasants' suffering. That is, the reality of under-funding of rural administration may play a more decisive role than abuse of power by individual cadres in arousing rural tension.

The cruel reality is that, despite the restriction on deficit budgeting for local governments, most administrations at county levels or below are in the red. A State Council Research Centre report estimates that 63% of all 2,074 county governments in the country are in deficit.[15] Findings of another survey conducted by the Ministry of Civil Affairs in 2001 are even more alarming. The report shows that the average amount of township government debt is four million yuan[16] – a ridiculous amount when one considers the average size of an annual township budget is in the region of one to two million yuan. Table 2 further reveals the growing paucity of financial resources available for lower-levels rural administrations since the mid-1980s. The gap between budgetary income and total expenditure of township governments has been growing since the early 1990s. The total expenditures grew at a speed of 22.5% during the ten-year period of 1986–1995, far exceeding the average annual growth of township budgetary income (15.6%). Budgetary incomes of township governments are no longer sufficient to fully finance local governance. As expected, township governments tried to make ends meet by raising extra-budgetary income. Its steady growth, averaging 25% a year, helps to maintain the aggregate

Table 2: Township Finance 1986–1995

Unit: billion yuan				
Year	(I) Total budgetary income	(II) Total extra-budgetary income	(III) Total Expenditure	(I)/(III)
1986	19.4	3.9	15.6	124.6%
1987	21.3 (9.8%)	4.4 (12.8%)	17.4 (11.5%)	122.3%
1988	27.0 (26.8%)	6.8 (15.5%)	33.8 (94.5%)	110.1%
1989	33.4 (23.7%)	10.6 (55.9%)	32.5 (-3.8%)	102.6%
1990	36.1 (8.1%)	12.3 (16.0%)	37.6 (15.7%)	96.0%
1991	39.9 (10.5%)	15.4 (25.2%)	43.9 (16.8%)	90.9%
1992	47.2 (18.3%)	18.9 (22.7%)	66.0 (50.3%)	89.0%
1993	64.8 (37.3%)	23.0 (21.7%)	68.1 (3.2%)	95.1%
1994	49.7 (-23.3%)	29.0 (26.1%)	84.0 (23.3%)	59.1%
1995	64.0 (28.8%)	38.1 (31.4%)	102.1 (21.5%)	62.7%
average growth rate	15.6%	25.3%	22.5%	-----

Note:
1. Extra-budgetary incomes also include self-raised fund.
2. ( ) – growth over previous year
Source: *Zhongguo Caizheng Nianjian*, various years

financial balance in the countryside. The ability to increase extra-budgetary income, in other words, holds the key to sustaining fiscal health for most rural administrations.

Why are most local administrations in red? There are a number of reasons. First, the overall size of government revenues has been in decline since the early days of market reform. Retreat of the state implies diminished control over national economy and the rapid shrinking of state sector further denotes less guaranteed income for the government. Second, the principle of self-sufficiency has always been enshrined in rural finance. It means fiscal transfers from industrial sector and central coffer have been limited and funding of rural administrations has been by and large, dependent on resources generated by rural economic development. The agricultural sector however, contributed not more 15% of the national total of GDP by 2002. Expectedly, slow growth in this sector can hardly sustain the administration of majority of the Chinese population living in the countryside. However, the self-sufficiency arrangement also generates perverse incentive for irresponsible adventurism in public investment among local officials. The principle of self-sufficiency inherent in the fiscal decentralisation process since the 1980s implies not only that "the less you collect the less you spend, rely on yourself to balance account (*xiaoshou xiaozhi, zili pingheng*)", the other side of the coin is "the more you collect the more you spend (*duoshou duozhi*)". Economic success may bring more fiscal resource and thus facilitates effective governance. There is also personal interest of leading officials at stake. Coupled with the fiscal incentive is the introduction of cadre responsibility system. Under this system, evaluation of leading cadres is directly linked up with his or her ability to fulfil specific economic indicators stipulated in the performance contract. Top of the list are growth of local industries and tax payment. In other words, there is a strong incentive for pushing rapid growth, and direct investment by government can always be an expedient option. And as seen in Table 2, the deficit of local finance is not really a result of slow growth in revenue, but more a consequence of rapid rise in the expenditure side.

Are Fiscal Reforms Really "Peasant-friendly"?

Assessment of desirability of fiscal reforms like Tax-for-Fee and abolition of agricultural tax thus should take the impact on local revenues into account. Unfortunately, both seemingly "peasant-friendly" efforts exert negative impact on local finance in general. The case of Anhui quoted above is illustrative of the effect. A total decrease of 1.84 billion yuan in revenue for village and township finances in the province was recorded after the first year of reform, i.e. a 30–40% drop on average for each village and township administration. Central finance allocated a special grant of 1.1

billion yuan, whereas the provincial government provided a 100 million yuan grant plus a 120 million yuan tax exemption for township and village administrations in 2001.[17] In addition to the extra increase in investment in education mentioned above, from 2001 onward, a three-year financial relief of 100 million yuan is provided for each prefecture. The exempted revenue is designated for financing local education.[18] As part of experiment, central finance allocated a special grant of 1.1 billion yuan, whereas the provincial government provided a 100 million yuan grant plus a 120 million yuan tax exemption for township and village administrations in 2001.[19] In addition to the extra increase in investment in education mentioned above, from 2001 onward, a three-year financial relief of 100 million yuan is provided for each prefecture. The exempted revenue is designated for financing local education.[20]

The damage inflicted by abolition of agricultural can be even more severe. Firstly, agricultural tax is a local tax (*difang shuo*). In other words, the full brunt of the impact will be, in principle, felt solely on sub-national administrations. Secondly, the importance of the contribution of this tax varies from province to province with the poorest regions showing a higher degree of dependence. Table 3 shows the variation in the degree of dependence on agricultural tax among selected provinces. On average, county coffers will suffer a loss of 16.3% in revenue if agricultural tax is to be abolished today. However, what is noteworthy here is that many provinces which suffer most from the reform turn out to be the less well off regions. For example, Yunnan, Guizhou, Jiangxi and Shaanxi are among the poorest in income per capita term in China. Common to these provinces is the heavy reliance on agriculture. In other words, local governments in these agricultural provinces will suffer the most severe blow of financial loss. The expected beneficiaries ironically, turn out to be the major victims of the reform.

The central government is hardly unaware of the impact of its reform on local finance. In fact, as seen in the case of Anhui experiment, special grant and transfer payment were allocated to compensate for the losses suffered by local government. The Chinese

Table 3: Importance of Agricultural Tax for County Finance

	Agricultural Tax as percentage of total fiscal income at county level
National Total	16.3%
Beijing	1.0%
Tinjian	5.9%
Hebei	22.7%
Shanxi	10.1%
Inner Mongolia	17.2%
Liaoning	8.9%
Heilongjiang	28.1%
Shanghai	6.5%
Zhejiang	9.2%
Anhui	31.7%
Fujian	10.5%
Jiangxi	21.5%
Shandong	17.6%
Henan	27.5%
Hubei	25.9%
Hunan	21.6%
Guangdong	7.2%
Guangxi	15.2%
Hainan	20.2%
Chongqing	22.0%
Sichuan	20.0%
Guizhou	10.3%
Yunnan	25.0%
Shaanxi	20.9%
Gansu	17.6%
Qinghai	14.5%
Ningxia	9.5%
Xinjiang	9.1%
Tibet	0.1%

Source: Calculated from data in *2002 County Financial Statistic*, p. 14

Financial Minister, Jin Renqing announced that a total of 40 billion RMB yuan would be released to local levels as part of the reform package in rural finance.[21] It is firstly, debatable whether the amount is sufficient to compensate the loss faced by local governments in the countryside. While it is true that the annual income from agricultural tax is in the region of 50–60 billion RMB yuan, the loss in income as a result of tax-for-fee reform which closes most of the loopholes in extra-budgetary extraction could possibly double the figure. Even if we assume the compensation is adequate, there is another consideration of whether the extra grant can really reach the targeted designations.

The main instruments for fiscal redistribution in China are earmarked grant and transfer payment. However, both are under-developed and fail to perform a significant redistributive function under the current system. Earmarked grants are usually allocated for the purpose of implementing specific policies. In 1994, they constituted about 15.4% of the total central subsidies. Their redistributive function, as pointed out by West and Wong, is rather limited.[22] The usual requirement of matching funds from the recipient is usually attached to these grants; local governments that are eligible for these grants may be deprived of these subsidies if they cannot meet the matching requirement. Table 4 shows vividly the non-progressive nature of the grant allocation. Four of the top five recipients of earmarked grants for county/prefecture levels in 1998 were in the coastal region – the most developed part of the country. Guangdong, the province with the fastest growth in the reform era, turned out to be the major winner, capturing the biggest share of more than 10% of the total grants. Ironically, the combined allocation for two of the poorest provinces, Guizhou and Qinghai, amounted less than 3% of the total. Financial need appears to assume little relevance in the allocation process.

The transfer payment system is equally underdeveloped. The amount involved remains extremely small, limiting its redistributive function. In 1998, the total amount of transfer payments constituted less than 2% of the total central financial subsidies (Table 5), and no more than 5% of the total local budgetary deficit.[23] As seen in

Table 4
Top Ten (County/prefecture-level)
Recipients of Earmarked Grants in 1998
(Unit: billion yuan)

	Amount received	As percentage of total earmarked grant for county/prefecture level
Guangdong	7.98	10.0%
Shanghai	5.74	7.2%
Zhejiang	4.27	5.4%
Yunnan	4.19	5.3%
Shandong	4.12	5.2%
Liaoning	4.06	5.1%
Sichuan	3.94	5.0%
Jiangsu	3.91	4.9%
Heilongjiang	3.00	3.8%
Inner Mongolia	2.94	3.7%

Source: *Quanguo Dishixian Caizheng Tongji Ziliao 1998* (National Statistics of Prefecture/County Finance 1998), p. 4.

Table 5
Transfer Payment 1995–1998

Unit: billion yuan			
Year	(I) Amount of Transfer Payment	(II) Total Central Financial Subsidies	(I)/(II)
1995	2.07	253.4	0.82%
1996	3.47	272.2	1.27%
1997	5.02	285.7	1.76%
1998	6.05	332.1	1.82%

Source: *Zhongguo Caizheng Nianjian 2000*, p. 465–6

Table 6
Distribution of Transfer Payment 1995–1998

	GDP Per Capita (yuan)	Total Transfer Payment Received 1995–98 (100 million yuan)	Percentage of Total Transfer Payment
1. Guizhou	2,816	16.12	9.7%
2. Gansu	3,838	6.38	3.8%
3. Tibet	4,483	4.87	2.9%
4. Yunnan	4,559	6.76	4.1%
5. Guangxi	4,567	8.43	5.1%
6. Shaanxi	4,607	7.34	4.4%
7. Ningxia	4,725	6.77	4.1%
8. Sichuan	4,815	12.21	7.4%
9. Jiangxi	4,838	6.62	4.0%
10. Shanxi	4,986	4.86	2.9%
11. Anhui	5,076	5.56	3.3%
12. Qinghai	5,089	9.86	5.9%
13. Chongqi	5,143	0.76	0.5%
14. Henan	5,551	11.33	6.8%
15. Hunan	5,733	6.84	4.1%
16. Inner Mongolia	5,897	16.91	10.2%
17. Hainan	6,588	1.51	0.9%
18. Jilin	6,676	2.72	1.6%
19. Xinjiang	7,086	17.24	10.4%
20. Hubei	7,094	8.78	5.3%
21. Hebei	7,594	4.86	2.9%
22. Heilongjiang	8,818	5.0	3.0%
23. Shandong	9,409	0	0
24. Liaoning	11,017	0	0
25. Guangdong	11,181	0	0
26. Fujian	11,294	0	0
27. Jiangsu	11,539	0	0
28. Zhejiang	12,906	0	0
29. Tianjin	16,377	0	0
30. Beijing	17,936	0	0
31. Shanghai	27,187	0	0

Note: Percentage does not add up to 100 due to rounding of figures
Source: *Zhongguo Tongji Nianjian 2001*, pp. 57 and 92, *Zhongguo Caizheng Nianjian 1999*, p. 465

Table 6, the scheme is more progressive than the earmarked grant allocation, as the more prosperous regions, like Shanghai and Guangdong, did not get any subsidy at all. Unfortunately, financial need is not the only consideration. Political concern is a major factor; regions with a large non-Han Chinese population emerged as major beneficiaries and enjoyed a disproportionately large share of the subsidies. Guizhou, Inner Mongolia and Xinjiang received the largest transfer payment allocation between 1995 and 1998, yet in terms of GDP per capita, the latter two are not among the poorest in the country. The eight major provinces with large ethnic groups together grasped 52.4% of the total allocation during this period.

Trickling Down of Burdens

Another possible unintended consequence of abolition of agricultural tax is a rise in financial burden faced by the administration at the very bottom. While it is uncertain whether the financial assistance of transfer payment and earmarked grant could reach the destinations at grass roots, it is highly likely that the administrations at the bottom have to face further financial squeeze attributed to the new round of fiscal reforms. An expected response of provincial governments which suffers a loss of tens of billion Yuan in local tax is to shift the loss downward to lower administrations. This is in fact, the reality even before the experiment of agricultural tax reform. Table 7 shows the financial details between levels of sub-national government in five of the poorest provinces in the country: Gansu, Yunnan, Shaanxi, Qinghai and Tibet. The health of the provincial finance appears to maintain at the expense of county administrations. The emphasis on fiscal discipline further facilitates the exaction of lower levels. Particularly for township and village administrations, there is a tendency to entrust the next higher level to maintain a hand-on approach in managing their coffers. In many cases, this implies their funds are physically deposited in the account of the supervising authority and any appropriation may require approval of the latter. This is common for village financial administration as the practice of township administration of village fund is getting more and more popular in recent years. And the tax-for-fee reform that deprives village administrations their independent source of income further exacerbates their vulnerability. With the abolition of administrative levies, villages now survive on the steady supply of financial support of the higher authorities. In principle, villages are entitled to receive the new surcharge on agricultural tax, which is introduced in order to compensate for their loss in levies incomes. However, as the surcharge is collected by the township administration, not by the villages directly, the former enjoys a decisive control on when and how the fund would eventually deliver to the latter. The allocation of financial subsidies follows a similar logic. A tight hierarchical control exists in the dissemination of grants and subsidies, even though village and township finance are the ultimate targets of the financial support. County level or above, are thus in a good position to retain or divert these fiscal resources, if they find it necessary. The sudden loss of tens of billion of agricultural tax and the influx of transfer payment as compensation appear to be a huge temptation for the provincial government to abuse the system.

Table 7: Finance of Selected Poor Provinces in 1995
(Unit: million yuan)

	Gansu	Yunnan	Shaanxi	Qinghai	Tibet
Aggregate Balance	−267	1,607	923	−45	230
Provincial Balance	612	1,942	1,073	126	245
County Balance	−879	−335	−150	−171	−15

Source: Wan Yu, "Difang Caizheng Guncun Chizi de Chengyin yu Duice Yanjiu" (Cause of deficit in local finance and policy recommendation) *Difang Caizheng* (*Local Finance*), No. 2 (1997), pp. 13–6.

Conclusion

The recent experiments of tax-for-fee reform and abolition of agricultural tax are certainly popular among peasants. In immediate term, these changes imply substantial reduction in financial burdens for peasants. The closing of loopholes for administrative charges and levies puts an end to random and arbitrary exaction by abusive officials, and abolition of agricultural tax heralds further relief for peasant households whose real income have been growing at a very slow pace over the last few years. Yet, conflicts with local officials go unabated. While tension over "peasant burden" and "unreasonable surcharges" may have diminished, the confrontation has taken a new form: land conflict. More and more reports on conflict over land transfer in the countryside are available, and in most cases, local officials are the focal points of tension. Most arguments concern the level of compensation for peasants and the legality of the transfer process. The new pattern of rural tension is illustrative. Firstly, it demonstrates the effectiveness of the recent efforts of fiscal reforms. The policy of abolishing irregular surcharges and levies has been faithfully implemented. However, it also reveals the lingering of the hunger for revenue among local governments. Land sales, appears to be the only viable way left for local administrators to secure sufficient revenue for effective governance. And given the collective ownership nature of rural land, local administration can still exert its influence over the process, and thus in a good position to grasp a big piece of the pie in any land deal. Peasants, on the other hand, who will only be compensated according to the level of farming income derived from the land concerned, are destined to be the major victims of the process. In short, the current fiscal reforms may have affected the form of extraction, but not the drive.

These populist efforts of reducing peasant burden are thus illusive. As seen from the above analysis, they do not touch upon the root of the issue – paucity of fiscal resources for effective governance. They may be effective in treating the symptoms, but not the cause of the disease. Local officials, driven by their survival instinct, are always quick to exploit loopholes and ready to trespass limits. Difficult decisions – creation of a more effective distributive leverage, re-ordering of fiscal formula between urban and rural finances, so far have been avoided. Postponement of these hard choices nonetheless comes with a heavy political cost. Ultimately, it is the Chinese peasants who suffer. However, the upsurge in rural violence in recent years demonstrates that they may not always swallow their frustration quietly.

Notes and References

1. Lin Yifu, Cai Fang and Li Zhou, *Zhongguo Jingji Gaige yu Fazhan* (*Chinese Economic Reform and Development*) (Taipei: Linking Press, 2000), pp. 148–9.

2. Certainly some forms of "hidden extraction" do linger. Under-pricing of the procurement portion and price-scissor between industrial and agricultural products can still serve as an indirect to extract surplus from the agriculture.

3. Author's interview, Shandong, 1999.

4. *Zhongguo Tongji Nianjian* 2001 (*China Statistical Yearbook 2001*), p. 261.

5. "Nongmin weishenme zhichi feigaishui" ("Why peasants support tax-for-fee reform"), *Xiangzhen Caizheng* (Township Finance), No. 5 (1997), pp. 44–6.

6. Liu Jianmin et al, "Feigaishui: Nongcun gonggong fehpei guanxi gaige di tupokou" (Tax-for-fee: a breakthrough in rural allocation), *Nongye Jingji Wenti* (*Problem of Agricultural Economy*) No. 2 (2000), pp. 34–41.

7. "Tax Reform in Anhui's Rural Areas," *Foreign Broadcasting Information Service* (FBIS) (China) (CHI-2000-0529) (27 July 2000).

8. *Ibid.*

9. Li Weiguang (ed.), *Ruhe Jisuan he Jiaona Nongmuye Shui (How to Calculate and Pay Agricultural (& Poultry) Tax)* (Beijing: Renmin Daxue Chubanshe, 2000), p. 30.

10. *Zhongguo Caizheng Nianjian* 2000 (*China's Financial Yearbook 2000*), p. 428.

11. *Anhui Ribao*, 5 June 2002.

12. Wu Hongchang, "Nongcun feishui faige libi fenxi jie chengce jianyi ("Analysis of the tax-for-fee reform and recommendation") *Nongye Jingji Wenti* (*Problem of Agricultural Economy*) No. 10 (2000), pp. 22–5; Song Hongyuan et al, "Nongcun jiceng shuifei gaige zhuyao zuofa" ("Major options of fiscal reform at rural grass roots"), *Nongcun gongzuo Tongxun* (*Newsletter of Rural Work*), No. 1 (1996), p. 41.

13. *Renmin Ribao*, 7 July 2004.

14. Song Ligan, "Jianmian nongyeshui hou jidai zhiding de peitao gaige zhengce" ("Supplementary measures for the abolition of agricultural tax"), *Nongcun Caizheng yu Caiwu (Rural Finance and Accounting)*, No. 8 (2004), pp. 17–18.

15. Xianji Caizheng Yanjiu Xiaozu (Task Force on the Study of County Finance), "Xianji caizheng weiji jiqi duice," ("County financial crisis and responses) *Caizheng Yanjiu (Fiscal Studies)*, No. 5 (1996), pp. 55–59.

16. *Ming Pao*, 20 June 2001.

17. *Anhui Ribao*, 23 February 2001.

18. *Anhui Ribao*, 5 June 2002.

19. *Anhui Ribao*, 23 February 2001.

20. *Anhui Ribao*, 5 June 2002.

21. *Xinwen Zhoukan (News Weekly)*, 29 March 2004, p. 46.

22. Loraine West and Christine Wong, "Equalization issues," in Christine Wong (ed.), *Financing Local Government*, op. cit., pp. 283–311.

23. Woguo Nongcun Caizheng Zhidu Chuangxin yu Zhengce Xuanze Ketizu (Research Team on Institutional Innovation and Policy Alternative of China's Rural Financial System), "Xiangzhen caizheng: zhidu kuangjia yu zhengce gaige" ("Finance at township level: the institutional framework and reform of policies) *Zhongguo Nongcun Jingji (Chinese Rural Economy)*, No. 4 (2002), pp. 4–10.

17

China's Ethnic Minorities: Policy and Challenges under the Fourth-generation Leadership

Colin MACKERRAS

This chapter takes up several aspects of policy and a few challenges regarding China's ethnic minorities under the new leadership of Hu Jintao since 2002. Discussion of policy focuses on national unity and the obsession about splittism and secession, a few foreign policy issues relevant to ethnic minorities, especially those of Xinjiang and Tibet, and economic development in the wake of the Great Western Development Strategy. The challenges the chapter considers include the continuing sensitivities about separatism and related matters, especially as regards the Uygurs of Xinjiang and the Tibetans, and the HIV/AIDS and drug crisis.

The chapter argues that the Hu Jintao leadership has mainly inherited policy from the previous period, but made a few changes in line with the new demands of the times and a new leadership emphasis on social values as opposed to an exclusive rise in the GDP.

Introduction

The census of 1 November 2000 put the population of China's 55 state-recognised ethnic minorities at 106.43 million, or 8.41% of China's total of 1.26583 billion, not counting Hong Kong, Macau or Taiwan.[1] The ethnic minority population may be large when compared with other countries but is small in Chinese terms. Yet, the areas where minorities live are about 60% of China's total, including some very sensitive borders. For these and other reasons the ethnic minorities are actually much more important for China's overall situation than their population might suggest. The PRC's overall policy towards the ethnic minorities is to grant them limited autonomy within the framework of a multinational unitary state. There are five autonomous regions for ethnic minorities, which are equivalent in level to provinces.

The present chapter takes up policy towards these ethnic minorities under the fourth-generation leadership of Hu Jintao, who became CPC general secretary at the 16th CPC Congress of November 2002 and has since expanded his power through taking over other crucial positions. It also looks at some of the main challenges the Chinese state faces in dealing with the ethnic minorities. It argues that continuity with the previous leadership of Jiang Zemin is greater than change. It also recognises some areas where the new leadership has made quite important changes in emphasis or faced dilemmas that have caused it to make adjustments in handling ethnic minority issues.

In discussions of China's ethnic minorities, especially the Islamic ones, a major background event was the September 11 Incidents of 2001, which saw hijacked aircraft fly into the twin World Trade Towers in New York, causing them to collapse. United States President George W. Bush immediately began a "war against terrorism," accusing Saudi Arabian-born Islamic extremist Osama bin-Laden and his al-Qaida network of responsibility for the outrage, soon afterwards launching an invasion of Afghanistan overthrowing the radical Islamist Taliban-led government there. China was enthusiastic to take part in this war against terrorism and was keen to have the suppression of separatism in Xinjiang, which will be discussed in some detail below, recognised as part of that struggle.

In discussing the Hu Jintao leadership, we can see three big-picture emphases that separate it from its predecessor.

- It has tried to rein in the provinces, especially in financial terms. In this endeavour Tibet, which is dominated by protégés of Hu Jintao, has been quite cooperative, but the autonomous regions are not as important as some of the richer southern provinces and municipalities, such as Guangdong and Shanghai.
- It has tended to be somewhat more suspicious of American-led globalisation and free trade. Its experience is that the United States and Europe are very keen on free trade when it suits their interests, but not so keen when it is China that is most likely to benefit.
- It has given a higher priority to social factors and those affecting social stability, because of the increasing demonstrations and protests from workers and peasants and even over ethnic issues.

Hu Jintao and Policy

The issue of social stability is relevant to the notion of the "harmonious society." This means affluence and a rise in living standards, people respecting each other, with society having "an ambiance of respecting labor, knowledge and creativity."[2] This idea, which State Council Premier (since 2003) Wen Jiabao emphasised at the National People's Congress meeting of early 2005, has definite Confucian overtones, and has its obverse in maintaining social stability. Sometimes, the two do not coincide and the Hu leadership is still convinced that social instability in the form of rioting or demonstrations against the government must be suppressed.

Thre has been considerable and apparently growing social instability in China in the 21st century, some of it discussed in other chapters. Although Xinjiang and Tibet have loomed largest in social instability in ethnic affairs, other places have also been affected. In particular, a serious incident took place in October 2004 in Henan Province between Hui (Sinic Muslims) and members of the Han majority. When a Hui Muslim driver ran over and killed a small Han girl, ethnic violence broke out, which lasted five days.

One factor highly relevant to minority affairs under Hu Jintao is Hu's own background. From the end of 1988 to 1992, Hu held the post of CPC Secretary in Tibet. This fact suggests a considerable interest in issues relevant to one of the most sensitive of all minority areas in China. However, the particular period of his tenure was a striking one. The man he succeeded was Wu Jinghua, an Yi national and the only non-Han who has ever held the position.[3] Under Wu serious rioting for independence had erupted in September and October 1987 and again in March 1988. Hu's top priority was to try and stabilise the situation.

Initially, the situation looked quite negative for Hu. March 1989 saw further serious disturbances, marking the 30th anniversary of a major rebellion against the Chinese that had seen the Dalai Lama leave Tibet and set up a government-in-exile in India. Hu Jintao's response to the rioting was to suppress it without mercy and, for the first time in the PRC's history, to declare martial law, which was not lifted until May 1990.

The policy Hu adopted for Tibet after he declared martial law was very much in accord with the direction things moved with the imposition of martial law in Beijing in May 1989 and the suppression of the student movement there and throughout China. These events followed the crisis in Tibet by less than three months. There were three strands to Hu's policy in Tibet. These were:

- Zero tolerance for separatism;
- Rapid economic development;[4] and
- The retention of a degree of autonomy, including a modicum of cultural and religious freedom as long as it did not threaten the Chinese state.

The first and second of these policies will be discussed separately below.

The autonomy policy gives members of the ethnic minorities the right to exert influence within their own regions. Under the Constitution, the government head of an autonomous area must belong to the relevant ethnic group. However, there are no such prescriptions concerning the CPC leadership in any ethnic area, which is actually much more important.[5]

In February 2001, the *Law on Regional National Autonomy*, initially adopted in 1984, was amended, with autonomy provisions slightly strengthened. For example, Article 22 of both the 1984 and 2001 versions deals with recruitment of ethnic minorities. The initial Article has the general stipulation to train large numbers of ethnic minority cadres, where as the new one adds the requirement to "give appropriate considerations" to members of ethnic minorities in recruiting new cadres.[6] The difference is not great but the requirement at least to consider members of ethnic minorities means that they cannot be ignored altogether.

A white paper issued by the State Council at the end of February 2005 emphasised the high policy priority in favour of ethnic autonomy in all its various aspects, including giving ethnic groups influence in their own areas. However, the figures it gives suggest that there is actually a deceleration and in some respects even a slowing down of ethnic minority influence. For instance, the white paper gives the number of minority cadres at the end of 2003 at 2.9 million, or an increase of 0.6% increase per year since 1999, and the number of non-Han members of the 2003 National People's Congress at 415, or 13.91% of the total.[7] Comparable official figures for the end of 1999 claim 2.824 million minority cadres, having risen at a rate of 3% per year since 1993,[8] and at the 1998 National People's Congress 428 or 14.37% of the total.[9]

What these figures suggest is that autonomy is still very much Hu Jintao's policy, but it does not necessarily receive the same priority as earlier. As China's economy has grown, the balance between modernisation and autonomy for ethnic minorities has tended to change towards favouring the former.

Chinese Unity and Separatism

The PRC has always put a good deal of emphasis on national unity, regarding itself as a multinational unitary state. In the late 1980s demonstrations for independence in Tibet sharpened its concern over national unity, especially because of the equivocal attitude towards whether Tibet was actually part of China taken up in capitals like Washington. Although the independence movement in Tibet was considerably weaker in the 1990s than in the late 1980s, popular support in the West for a Tibet separate from China remained very strong.

In the Western world and elsewhere, there is strong support for independence movements and hostility to states in general. Globalisation theory gathered momentum in the 1990s and appeared to suggest that the notion of the nation-state, which has been at the core of international relations since the mid-17th century, might be losing its grip. One globalisation specialist wrote that one implication of globalisation was "the breakdown of the basic assumptions whereby societies and states have been conceived, organised and experienced" as separate territorial units.[10] Though some theorists believe globalisation to be in retreat in the 21st century,[11] China's accession to that most globalised of bodies the World Trade Organisation in December 2001 has formalised and strengthened its integration into the international capitalist economy dominated by the United States.

The Hu Jintao leadership is less enthusiastic about American-led globalisation than its predecessor. When it comes to the nation-state, however, PRC leaderships are at one. Their concern is with *state sovereignty*, not with undermining, let alone breaking down, assumptions prevalent for centuries about nation-states. The implication is clear: the Chinese state wants nothing to do with independence for any part of its territory. It argues that to give independence to any territory implies that others will start asking to split off, the result being national fragmentation along the lines of the Soviet Union.

The clearest sign that the Hu Jintao leadership is just as enthusiastic about national unity as its predecessor, and possibly even more so, is the adoption of a formal law in March 2005, for the first time banning secession. The focus of the promotion of national unity is Taiwan. However, the law applies also to all places the Chinese state regards as its sovereign territory, or integral parts of China. Among the ethnic regions, the two most relevant are Xinjiang and Tibet. The key point is that China has no intention whatever of relaxing its emphasis on national unity.

The Concept of "Nationality" and Identity

The Chinese state uses the same concept of "nationality" it has done since 1949, namely that a "nationality" (*minzu*) is a historically constituted community of people having a common territory, a common language, a common economic life and a common culture. The definition is inherited from Stalin, who first put it forward in 1913. Like most definitions in so controversial a field as ethnicity, it is subject to criticism. For instance, the Hui, who are mainly distinguished by their adherence to Islam, do not really have a single "common territory" and their language is Chinese, so they do not have a "common language" either, at least not in the sense that their common language distinguishes them from other ethnic groups.[12] However, the Hu Jintao leadership is certainly showing no signs of altering the definition, because the policy of setting aside autonomous places for the ethnic minorities largely depends on it.

Ethnic identity has reasserted itself during the reform period. With the collapse of the Soviet Union in 1991, much worldwide strife based itself not on the liberal-communist divide as had been the case during the Cold War, but on ethnicity, and ethnic consciousness became even stronger in China. The government was generally tolerant of this growth of ethnic identity unless it threatened the state. In some cases like the Tibetans and Uygurs to be discussed in more detail below, ethnic challenges did indeed threaten the state through independence movements.

Very few of China's state-recognised ethnic minorities have any wish to secede from China, which does not mean they lack ethnic consciousness. Two examples at opposite ends of China are worth mentioning. One is the Zhuang, whose main concentrations are in the Guangxi Zhuang Autonomous Region. They are China's most populous ethnic minority with a population of 16,178,811 in the 2000 census. A major scholarly book on the Zhuang notes their neglect both in the West and within China itself, and continues that "today Zhuang peasants, intellectuals, workers, and cadres proudly assert their membership in an ancient and culturally rich minority group,"[13] in other words they have undergone a profound assertion of their ethnic identity.

Another very interesting example is the Manchus, most of whom live in the region now known as China's north-east and formerly known as Manchuria, their 2000 population being 10,682,262. The Manchus actually ruled China's last dynasty the Qing (1644–1911). During that time China as a country actually did very well out of Manchu rule in the sense that they more than doubled the physical size of China by adding such territories as Xinjiang and Tibet. Nevertheless, the nationalist revolution hated the Manchus and its initial aim was more to expel them and their regime than to destroy the monarchy as such and replace it with a republic.[14] While they were in control of the country, the Manchus became all but assimilated into China, largely losing their identity. During the Republican period, Manchu identity was frowned upon because of their role in China's last dynasty. This situation worsened when the last Manchu emperor headed a Japan-controlled state called Manzhouguo (Japanese Manchukoku) in northeast China.

From the late 1970s, Manchu consciousness revived to a major extent. This is reflected in the population figures for the Manchus in the 1982 and 1990 censuses, which show their population at 4,304,160 and 9,821,180 respectively. This enormous growth in population over just eight years is due not to fecundity but re-registration. In other words, many communities formerly registered as Han simply changed their ethnicity to Manchu. Groups of people who had earlier been reluctant to acknowledge their Manchu ancestry or roots now came forward claiming to be Manchu.[15] This trend is part of what Gladney describes as "a new feeling in China, a revalorisation of ancestral and ethnic ties."[16]

One scholar claims the Manchu middle classes as the drivers of this revival of Manchu identity. She argues that a "surge of ethnic-identity revival" has begun among the Manchus, with a "more assertive Manchu image."[17] What is particularly interesting is that its proponents argue that their contribution to China during the Qing dynasty should be more recognised and reflected in political influence within the PRC. She quotes one member of the middle class elite as complaining that the Manchus do not even have their own autonomous region, despite the fact that they "expanded and managed so large a territory" as Qing-dynasty China, whereas the Mongolians are comparatively very well represented.[18] It is an interesting point. Actually, among the 155 or so ethnic autonomous areas in China, there are no Manchu autonomous regions (province level) or autonomous prefectures. It is true there are 13 at county level,[19] but county is a low level and puts the Manchus in a very inferior position. The earliest nationalists may have hated them while they were actually in power, but it is far from generous of later generations not to recognise their contribution to China as a political and cultural entity.

In the cases of the Manchus and Zhuang, identity is most unlikely to lead to anything remotely resembling secession. It is hardly a challenge for Hu Jintao's leadership, who is most unlikely to look askance at identity revivals that do not threaten the Chinese state. On the other hand, the accelerating modernisation he is favouring is not likely to make him give ethnic political demands a high priority.

Foreign Policy and the Ethnic Minorities

Under the Hu Jintao leadership, Chinese influence has tended to increase internationally, both because of China's continued economic rise and a general improvement in its diplomacy. The rise of China does not originate from the Hu Jintao leadership, but it has accelerated under it.

The ethnic minorities are relevant to some important developments in China's foreign relations. Because of the flow-on from the September 11 Incidents, the struggle against separatism in the "Muslim borderland" area of Xinjiang illustrates some major features new to the 21st century.[20] The war against terrorism initially had a major positive effect on Sino-American relations. The foreign policy implications from the situation in the Tibetan areas are less damaging from China's point of view than in previous years.

Xinjiang's Ethnic Minorities and Foreign Policy

Partly as a response to the rise of Islamic extremism and threats of terrorism, the presidents of five countries began to meet annually in April 1996 to discuss mutual problems. These were Russia, China, Kazakhstan, Kyrgyzstan and Tajikistan. The first meeting was in Shanghai, with later ones in the capitals of each of the other countries. In June 2001, that is to say a few months before the September 11 Incidents, another meeting in Shanghai added Uzbekistan, the group of six forming the Shanghai Cooperation Organisation (SCO). In July 2005, at its meeting in the Kazakhstan capital Astana, the SCO gave observer status to three other countries: Iran, India and Pakistan.

When the war against terrorism began late in 2001, China and the other SCO members declared support for Washington. They were particularly anxious to win support from the United States for their own struggles against the "three evils," namely terrorism, extremism and separatism, in China the main region affected being Xinjiang. The United States reacted sympathetically towards China,[21] and cooperation in the war against terrorism has become a factor leading towards better bilateral relations. In August 2002, the United States froze all ETIM assets because of its activities as a terrorist organisation.[22] The United States acknowledged terrorists from Xinjiang among those it captured in Afghanistan and imprisoned in Guantanamo Bay in Cuba.

According to one noted observer, "Within Beijing's foreign policy establishment, it is well recognised that if former president Jiang Zemin could be called pro-U.S., then Hu is pro-Russian."[23]

Under the Hu Jintao leadership several factors have put strain on Sino-American relations, with the ethnic situation in Xinjiang being a major factor.

China was not enthusiastic about the way the Americans used the war against terrorism to set up bases in Kyrgyzstan, Tajikistan and Uzbekistan in Central Asia, an area traditionally in the Russian sphere of influence. The first two named countries border Xinjiang, which has Kirgiz, Tajik and Uzbek populations (according to the 2000 census, respectively 79,128, 41,028 and 12,370).[24] For China and Russia, American presence in Central Asia is a potential threat. At the July 2005 meeting of the SCO, both countries pushed for the Americans to set a timetable for withdrawal of its military bases in Central Asia, the United States responding that it would sort out the issue with the governments of the relevant countries.

In several other respects, the good relations following China's support for the war against terrorism began to wear thin under Hu Jintao. Most important of all is that China has consistently opposed the American-led military intervention in Iraq, which began early in 2003 and is a matter on which the United States feels very strongly. Late in 2003, the United States decided to release the Chinese Muslims in Guantanamo Bay, but refused to send them back to China, on the grounds that they would be persecuted or tortured there, even though China asked for them to be repatriated. The Americans did not themselves wish to give the detainees refuge and so tried to find asylum for them in numerous other countries, including Sweden, Finland, Switzerland and Turkey, but all refused. The result is that as of mid-2006, the men remain in custody in Guantanamo Bay in undesirable conditions,[25] apart from five allowed to go to Albania in May 2006. For China, it was also very important that in April 2004 the United States-government funded National Endowment for Democracy gave $75,000 to the Uyghur [Uygur]American Association. This was the first time the National Endowment has given a grant to a Uygur exile group, let alone one that advocates independence for Xinjiang. Not surprisingly, China was furious at this move, which seemed to counter its earlier support for China over ETIM's status as a terrorist group.

Hu Jintao's leadership has been keen to promote the already existing trend of increasing Chinese influence in the various countries of Central Asia. Late in 2002, China and Kyrgyzstan carried out joint military exercises along their mutual border. However, not all has been smooth for China. In 2003, when the Kyrgyzstan government ceded to China some border territory formerly in Kyrgyzstan, popular protest against the move erupted among many ordinary Kyrgyz people. China is worried about the popular movement of March 2005 that overthrew the government of President Askar Akaev, because of the possibility that a similar trend might spread to Xinjiang. One Chinese specialist wrote: "Observers warn that the East Turkistan terrorist forces may make the most of Kyrgyzstan's political disorder."[26]

Hu Jintao has moved to strengthen relations with Uzbekistan under President Islam Karimov. This is a country where terrorism based on militant Islam has been quite strong since the 1990s. One authority writes that by the beginning of the 21st century the radical Islamist Hizb ut-Tahrir al-Islami (Party for Islamic Freedom) has become "the most popular, widespread underground movement" in Uzbekistan, Kyrgyzstan and Tajikistan.[27] At the same time, although the United States has been quite supportive of Karimov's regime for its anti-terrorist stance, government crackdowns on real and supposed Islamic extremism have gained him notoriety for human rights abuses.

Just before the June 2004 SCO meeting, Hu and Karimov met and agreed to cooperate in combating terrorism, separatism and extremism, including against the Uygur separatists and terrorists in Xinjiang. Hu also agreed to give significant credits and humanitarian aid to Uzbekistan. Hu was supportive of Karimov when suicide bombers in the capital Tashkent struck the Israeli and United States embassies at the end of July. Perhaps more importantly, Hu strongly supported Karimov's suppression of the apparently popular movement in Andijan, Uzbekistan, in May 2005.

Another Islamic country in the region important for China is Pakistan, where President General Pervez Musharraf has taken a strong position in support of the American-led war on terrorism as well as of China's attempts to suppress any signs of Uygur or Islamic terrorism in Xinjiang. China-Pakistan relations have long been cordial, but appear to have moved even closer over the war against terrorism. In October 2003 Pakistan soldiers killed ETIM leader Hasan Mahsum during a raid against a suspected al-Qaida hideout in South Waziristan, Pakistan. In August 2004, Chinese and Pakistani troops held military exercises in a Tajik area in south-western Xinjiang near the border with Pakistan.

The Tibetans and Chinese Foreign Policy

Apart from Xinjiang, the ethnic area most relevant to China's foreign relations is Tibet. This has for long been a thorn in China's relations with a range of countries, including India and various Western countries, especially the United States. Dharamsala in India is the site of the Dalai Lama's government-in-exile. Although both India and all Western countries recognise Tibet as part of China, they are also home to Tibetan diaspora groups that have pushed Tibetan independence and castigated China for human rights abuses in the Tibetan areas.

Diplomatically, Tibet has been the source of many embarrassments for China since the Dalai Lama fled to India in 1959 following the suppression of the March uprising against Chinese rule. These difficulties reached a high point in the 1990s, after the Dalai Lama received the Nobel Peace Prize in December 1989. There was a crescendo in the reception of the Dalai Lama by various Western international leaders.[28] The Chinese choice of the Eleventh Panchen Lama in 1995 was greeted with hostility in the West. The late 1999 flight to India of the young Seventeenth Karmapa Lama (enthroned in 1992) was a severe setback for China's Tibet policy, since he was the third most influential lama in Tibetan Buddhism after the Dalai and Panchen and the Chinese had thought him loyal.

George W. Bush met with the Dalai Lama in May 2001, very early in his term as United States president and just at the time when the Chinese were celebrating the 50th anniversary of the agreement by which the Dalai Lama's administration had recognised Tibet as part of the PRC. However, the September 11 Incidents altered the texture and priority of Tibet's impact on China's relations with the outside world. The reason was very simply that they gave terrorism based on Islamic radicalism a much higher priority than ever before and pushed other factors to the sidelines. The United States wants China's support for its war against terrorism, and if that means downgrading the Tibet issue, then, so be it. Tibet specialist Tom Grunfeld is right to suggest that September 11 has led to a convergence of interests between the United States and China, with the likely result that "the Tibet issue will subside further and further into obscurity."[29]

This obscurity is by no means total. The Tibet issue actually remains an important one among many people in Western and other countries, with lively Tibet lobbies in many countries. Even Russia maintains some sympathy for the Dalai Lama, despite its cordial relations with China. Late in 2004, the Russian government gave the Dalai Lama a visa to visit the partly Buddhist region of Kalmykia in southern Russia.

However, there are signs that Western governments are taking more notice of Chinese pressure against meetings with the Dalai Lama by Western leaders. In July 2002, Australian Prime Minister John Howard was pointedly out of the country, attending independence celebrations in East Timor, when the Dalai Lama made a ten-day visit. Howard had met the Dalai Lama in 1996, shortly after winning power, and been publicly quite hostile to any Chinese pressure against the meeting. In May 2004, British Prime Minister Tony Blair also refused to meet the Dalai Lama during a visit to Britain. Although Blair declined on grounds of time constraints, many suggested that it was really Chinese pressure that had led to his decision.[30]

Tibet remains a thorn in the side of Sino-Indian relations, with India being the home of the Tibetan government-in-exile and of the bulk of the Tibetan diaspora. In February 2001 the Indian government granted the Karmapa Lama refugee status and allowed him freedom to travel, to China's irritation. However, generally India has tried to prevent the Karmapa Lama and the Tibet issue in general from damaging its relations with China. Recent years have seen a general warming of relations between China and India, which the Hu Jintao leadership is keen to promote.

Another country where the Tibet issue affects China's foreign relations is Nepal. The main reason is that Nepal shares a long border with Tibet and is culturally similar. Most refugees leaving Tibet go first to Nepal, though the majority then go on to India. In 2003 a high-profile case occurred showing the Nepali government handing back Tibetan refugees to the Chinese authorities, even though the Tibetan Refugee Centre in the capital Kathmandu had paid for them a fine imposed by the Nepali Immigration Department. The Centre requested that the refugees be given to the United Nations High Commissioner for Refugees, which would have enabled them to move on to India. In January 2005 the Nepali government closed down the Dalai Lama's office in Kathmandu and derecognised the Tibetan Refugee Centre. This measure was clearly calculated to please China and it is even possible that China had pressured Nepali King Gyanendra.

On 1 February 2005 the King dismissed his own prime minister's government for the second time in just over two years. He accused the government of being unable to control a Maoist-led insurgency and seized control of affairs into his own hands. This insurgency had already led to the deaths of over 10,000 people and is anathema to the Chinese leadership, which has no time at all for Maoists and regards it as insulting that these Nepali insurgents should use the name of the late CPC chairman. India was horrified by Gyanendra's move, but China adopted its standard line that the coup was Nepal's internal affair. Coming so soon after the incident over the Tibetan refugees, the coup seems to signal a rise in Chinese influence in Nepal and an improvement in Sino-Nepali relations. Certainly, it can hardly be welcome to refugees from Tibet.[31] An offer by the Maoist insurgents later in 2005 to lay down their arms led to major and sustained popular protests against the King's policies and demands for the reinstatement of democracy.

Economic Development and the Great Western Development Strategy

Rapid economic development has been the policy of the Chinese government for a long time, but the reality is that the last decades of the 20th century saw much greater progress in the areas along the eastern seaboard than in the interior or west of China. In the second half of 1999, the government announced its Great Western Development (*Xibu da kaifa*) strategy, which was put into operation in January 2000. Among the aims of the strategy was to reduce socio-economic inequalities and to bring the ethnic minority areas up to a level if not equal to the eastern seaboard at least high enough to avert potential social and political instability.

In his report to the government in March 2000, just after the strategy had begun, Premier Zhu Rongji emphasised the strategy as crucial to promoting sustained national economic growth and bringing about "coordinated development of regional economies for eventual common prosperity" as well as strengthening national unity and safeguarding social stability. Top of the list among objectives was infrastructure development, within which roads, railways, airport and gas trunk pipelines were first named. [32] Observers both inside and outside China have noted the importance of ethnic minorities in this strategy. [33] The places counted as "western" in this strategy include almost all the ethnic areas, which tend strongly to be poorer than the Han ones anyway.

According to David Goodman, this strategy is actually "more of an adjustment to the PRC's regional development policy than a radical change," [34] meaning that it does not mark nearly as drastic a departure from earlier policy as the Chinese government has claimed. The Hu Jintao leadership has retained the strategy as part of official policy. However, it has also declared that an emphasis on gross domestic product (GDP) should yield some ground to social factors and the impact of economic development on the environment. In 2004 the GDP target was lowered as part of a shift of focus to sustainable development, with a trend towards reducing success in raising GDP as a criterion of performance assessment for government officials. This may signal a slight change in the way the leadership wants the strategy implemented.[35]

It is important to note that the strategy operates with different emphases in the various western regions of China, making a local or at least provincial perspective necessary. Qinghai Province, which has a significant minorities population especially of Tibetans and Hui,[36] and Xinjiang, the politics of which is discussed elsewhere in this paper, are two good illustrative and contrasting examples. The Great Western Development strategy has probably been more beneficial economically in Qinghai than in Xinjiang.

Goodman suggests an important change in Qinghai's economic policy due to the Great Western Development strategy. He characterises it through "a commitment to a more gradual approach to development that encourages environmental sustainability, the improvement of the province's internal infrastructure, and the establishment of good communication links with the rest of the PRC." [37] Xinjiang has seen great economic progress, [38] but the government has been more concerned with the kind of development most likely to secure the region as part of China. Xinjiang has immense quantities of oil and gas, and the basis of its economy is extractive.[39] Moreover, the 3,000-kilometre oil pipeline, completed at the end of 2005, which takes oil from the Caspian Sea through Kazakhstan, ends in Xinjiang.[40] There the oil is refined or sent east through a 4,200-kilometre pipeline stretching from Xinjiang to Shanghai, itself possibly "the most significant project in China's quest for long-term energy security."[41]

For Tibet, probably the most important single project to derive from the Great Western Development strategy so far is the 1,100-kilometre railway from Golmud in Qinghai to the Tibetan capital Lhasa. The decision to embark on this project, which is enormously complex from an engineering point of view and the highest-lying extended railway ever built, was taken in 2001 and it came into operation in mid-2006. The railway will certainly benefit Tibet's economy, for example making the transfer of goods into and out of the region easier and expanding tourism greatly. It will also strengthen China's political hold over Tibet, because it will facilitate moving troops and people into (but also out of) the region.

Overview of the Challenges

The Hu Jintao leadership faces numerous challenges concerning the ethnic minorities. Most are neither exclusive to minorities nor very different from those faced under the Jiang Zemin leadership.[42] They include:

- Separatism and related issues in Xinjiang and Tibet;
- Economic and social inequalities;
- Poverty alleviation;
- Prevention of serious epidemics;
- Narcotics prevention;
- Human rights abuses; and
- Internal migration and population transfer.

I deal here directly only with separatism, religious extremism and terrorism in Xinjiang, separatism in Tibet and the HIV/AIDS and narcotics crisis. These have shown interesting developments under the Hu Jintao leadership that entitle them to treatment in a context where space is very limited. Several other topics, such as human rights, are considered in other chapters or treated briefly in this one.

Separatism and Allied Issues

One of the challenges China faces in the 21st century is separatism, which is directly correlated to the heavy emphasis the Chinese state has placed on national unity in recent times. It is perhaps worth noting that in the 21st century, only Xinjiang and Tibet are relevant to this challenge, other ethnic areas of China having hardly been troubled by separatism at all. Most of them are keener to do well out of being part of China than to secede from it. In the early 1990s, there was a small-scale separatist movement in Inner Mongolia, aimed at joining up with the State of Mongolia, with reported clashes between them and the government in May 1990.[43] However, this had all but disappeared by the end of the century, a study by a partly Western-educated Mongol arguing that any resistance to China assumes acceptance that Inner Mongolia is part of China. Such resistance "has not questioned the state's legitimacy in ruling the Mongols, only its methods of rule."[44]

Xinjiang

The area most affected by separatism in the 21st century is Xinjiang, since the early 1990s much more so than Tibet. And within Xinjiang virtually all serious separatist attempts have been by the Uygurs, not the Kazaks or other Islamic ethnic groups.[45] The Hui have traditionally been generally loyal to the Chinese state. I agree with the comment by one authority that "Few Hui support an independent Xinjiang" while the Kazaks there "would probably have little voice in an independent 'Uyguristan,'"[46] as a Uygur-dominated independent Xinjiang would possibly be called.

Since the suppression in April 1990 of a small-scale rebellion in Baren Township near Kashgar, almost certainly based on the Islamic doctrine of *jihad* or holy war against the infidel,[47] sporadic anti-government incidents have occurred, many of them wanting to separate Xinjiang from China. The Chinese government has used its state power against all disorder, especially attempts to secede.

A turning point came in 1996. In March the CPC Central Committee Politburo Standing Committee issued a confidential document (known generally as Document No. 7) charging international and domestic organisations with collaborating to carry out sabotage and terrorism against the government and claiming, in particular, that "illegal religious movements are rampant."[48] In May the Xinjiang CPC held a work conference in Xinjiang's capital Ürümqi at which it echoed Document No. 7 and proposed solutions to counter the problem, including improving the economy and treading on secessionist ideas savagely.[49] Despite these top-level decisions, there was a series of riots early in 1997 in Yining (or

Gulja) in north-western Xinjiang, which again the Chinese authorities suppressed. [50] However, though further incidents occurred, especially in the south, they appear to have been at a reduced level of violence, with the Chinese state attempting to improve the economy and at the same show zero tolerance and brutality for separatism, terrorism and the Islamic extremism it holds as largely responsible for the incidents.

In January 2002, not long after the September 11 Incidents, the Chinese government issued a long report claiming that, between 1990 and 2001, terrorist, separatist forces had carried out over 200 terrorist incidents in Xinjiang, which had killed over 160 people. [51] The report also named several organisations it believed were terrorist. Most importantly, it claimed that the East Turkistan Islamic Movement (ETIM), headed by Hasan Mahsum, was "supported and directed" by Osama bin Laden. [52]

Since Hu Jintao's accession to the leadership of the CPC late in 2002, policy on Xinjiang has remained essentially unchanged. However, there have been developments showing a slightly different emphasis. Domestically, China has continued to publicise attacks on terrorism. For instance, in a news conference on 13 September 2004 Xinjiang CPC Secretary Wang Lequan revealed that in the first eight months of the year, authorities had cracked 22 groups involved in terrorism separatism and sentenced over 50 people to death for the same crimes, an unusually high number. Wang defended the actions, claiming that worldwide terrorism was actually getting worse, and vowed that China would continue suppressing terrorists as long as it was necessary. He also rejected suggestions that the attacks on terrorism were to some extent actually attacks on the Uygurs, their culture and their religion. [53]

This last comment was partly aimed against the Uygur diaspora organisations based in the West and Turkey. Although generally fragmented, these groups have tried to act more coherently in the 21st century and in a large meeting held in Munich in April 2004 actually set up a World Uyghur Congress. Uygur diaspora groups tend to be secular, and generally disavow violence, let alone terrorism, but all are strongly anti-Chinese and most support independence for Xinjiang. In the 21st century they have been very active on the Internet in a phenomenon one scholar has called "cyber-separatism."[54]

Many scholars, human rights activists and journalists in the West believe that China's crackdown on terrorism has been unnecessarily severe and counterproductive. They believe that China has made use of the September 11 Incidents to strengthen attacks on Uygur culture and that Chinese authorities have not presented nearly enough evidence for their charge of separatism. Dru Gladney writes that among incidents of civil unrest, assassinations and bombings in China since 1990, "very few can be definitely traced to Uyghur separatist groups or events in Xinjiang." He believes they "apparently arise not from separatist sentiment but from more general forms of alienation."[55] Bodies like Amnesty International and Human Rights in China have issued reports very condemnatory of the Chinese government on human rights grounds. In particular, a special Human Rights in China report issued in April 2005 claimed that "China's efforts to control Uighur religion are so pervasive that they appear to go beyond suppression to a level of punitive control seemingly designed to entirely refashion Uighur religious identity to the state's purposes."[56]

Tibet

Whereas separatism in Xinjiang became a more serious challenge to China in the 1990s following the April 1990 Baren Township uprising, Tibet was beginning to move in the opposite direction with the lifting of martial law the month after. In Tibet, the 1990s saw much less separatist activity than in the 1980s or than in Xinjiang. The 30th anniversary of the 1959 uprising against Chinese rule had seen disturbances serious enough for the Chinese to impose martial law in Tibet in March 1989 for the first time in the PRC's history, the 40th anniversary in 1999 was conspicuous for its *lack* of anti-Chinese separatist demonstrations. Moreover, the 50th anniversary of the 17-Point Agreement of May 1951 witnessed many Chinese-organised demonstrations, but nothing significant on the other side.

I discussed earlier the policy Hu Jintao had followed while Tibet's CPC secretary. His successor Chen Kuiyuan held the post from 1992 to 2000 and energetically followed the dual policy of development and stability, succeeding in raising the standard of living and achieving double-digit economic growth rates over his eight years in office.[57] Guo Jinlong followed Chen, having one four-year term to December 2004, after which Yang Chuantang was appointed Tibet's CPC secretary, being transferred from the governorship of the very poor and partly Tibetan-inhabited province of Qinghai. The significance of Yang's appointment is that he is known as very close to Hu Jintao, with the implication of carrying out Hu's policies closely. Although these include economic development and no tolerance for separatist movements, they may also take more account of the needs of Tibetan society and culture than did Chen Kuiyuan, who was noted for his hard attitude towards Buddhism and his efforts to keep its clergy in line with Chinese rule through propaganda exercises like "patriotic education campaigns."

The signs concerning human rights abuses under Hu Jintao are still unclear. The U.S. Department of State's reports for 2003 and 2004 suggest a continuing grim situation but slight improvement when compared with earlier years. The report for 2003 acknowledges that restrictions on religious freedom in the Tibet Autonomous Region (TAR) were "somewhat less oppressive for lay followers" in 2003 than in earlier years,[58] while the corresponding report the next year noted a few minor improvements but made very few comparisons with the past. One particular point noted in this report is the claim made by government officials that possessing and displaying pictures of the Dalai was not illegal, and the statement by TAR Deputy Chairman Wu Jilie that not displaying pictures of the Dalai Lama was the voluntary choice of Tibetans.[59] Such claims may be pure sophistry, but nevertheless suggest a slight relaxation by comparison with 1996, when Chen Kuiyuan's regime imposed the ban on pictures of the Dalai Lama.

The same reports published by the United States Department of State claim "Tibetan Buddhists in many areas outside the TAR had fewer restrictions on their freedom to practice their faith"[60] and "Conditions were generally more relaxed in Tibetan autonomous areas outside the TAR."[61] As generalities, these may be true. However, it is worth noting that the number of monks and nuns per head of population is almost identical. At the beginning of the 21st century there were 60,000 clergy among the 3 million Tibetans outside the TAR (2%) as opposed to 46,000 among the 2.4 million in the TAR (1.9%).[62] It is striking that the human rights case to attract most international condemnation for the Tibetan areas since Hu Jintao became CPC general secretary was in Sichuan, not in the Tibet Autonomous Region itself. This concerns well respected Tibetan lama Tenzin Deleg Rinpoche and a younger monk, both from Litang Monastery in western Sichuan, who were tried secretly in December 2002 on charges of separatism and perpetrating bomb blasts. Both were sentenced to death, Tenzin Deleg Rinpoche with a two-year reprieve. After an appeal failed, the younger monk was executed in January 2003, but with the expiry of the two years in January 2005, Tenzin Deleg Rinpoche's sentence was changed to life imprisonment.

This case attracted protests both from within China and abroad on the grounds that the charges and evidence were fabricated and the trials secret.[63] It is clear that issues of separatism and human rights in Tibet remain a challenge for the Chinese authorities, even though less than formerly. A more positive but related challenge is to reach an accord with the Dalai Lama or his successor over the future of Tibet within China.

In a speech he made before the European Parliament in Strasbourg in 1988, the Dalai Lama proposed that Tibet should become a self-governing democratic unit in association with China, but withdrew the suggestion in 1991 due to opposition from among his own supporters, not to mention the Chinese. In July 1996, in a speech to the British Parliament he proposed "genuine autonomy" within China. The precise implications of this were not spelt out, but in contrast to his Strasbourg proposal he has never negated it. In fact, he has made several statements strengthening it. Early in 2005 he said in an interview to Hong Kong's *South China Morning Post*:

"This is the message I wish to deliver to China. . . . I am not in favour of separation. Tibet is a part of the People's Republic of China. It is an autonomous region of the People's Republic of China. Tibetan culture and Buddhism are part of Chinese culture."[64]

In the meantime, the Chinese leadership invited representatives of the Dalai Lama to visit China, including Tibetan areas, in September 2002 and May 2003. Both sides have expressed satisfaction with the visits. The United States Administration, along with many others, recognises Tibet as part of China but believes China and the Dalai Lama should negotiate with one another without preconditions "for a negotiated settlement on questions related to Tibet."[65] It believes the visits by the Dalai Lama's representatives are a step in the right direction.

The Chinese believe they are in a stronger position than formerly, because the September 11 Incidents have shifted attention away from Tibet and because the Dalai Lama is yielding ground. Like its predecessors, the Hu Jintao leadership believes that Tibet is an internal affair and that other countries should not interfere. Any negotiations with the Dalai Lama must be on the precondition that he recognises Tibet as part of China and Taiwan as a province of China.

Given that the Dalai Lama has recognised Tibet as part of China and retains a great deal of influence, there may still be benefits for China in negotiating with the Dalai Lama over his repatriation in return for a greater degree of autonomy for Tibet. Certainly there are influential people in China who believe that the Dalai Lama is the key to Tibet's future.[66] There are still challenges for the Chinese leadership in Tibet and its relationship with the Dalai Lama.

The HIV/AIDS and Drugs Crisis

The related areas of HIV/AIDS and drug use are among the most serious of all challenges for the Chinese government, including among the ethnic minorities. Initially the authorities were very slow to recognise and address the HIV/AIDS and drugs crisis, fearing that too much exposure would stir panic among the people and make China look bad internationally. However, as of 2005 there are signs that under the Hu Jintao leadership the Chinese government is aware of the problems and really concerned to confront them.

A report by China's State Council AIDS Working Committee Office and the United Nations Theme Group on HIV/AIDS in China, which consists of representatives from the ten international cosponsors of UNAIDS was published on 1 December 2004 (World AIDS Day), this report itself being a first in its scope and detail. According to that report the estimated number of HIV/AIDS cases at the end of 2003 ranged somewhere between 650,000 and 1.02 million, a reasonable estimate being 840,000.[67] Although it is true that many specialists and activists believe the real figure is much higher,[68] the report itself claims that the collection of data and "sentinel surveillance" improved greatly in 2004. It continues:

> The emerging picture is one of an epidemic that has reached high HIV prevalence levels among sub-groups in some areas of Yunnan, Xinjiang and Henan. In at least one instance, the prevalence among some high risk population groups is over 5% and in another the prevalence rate among pregnant women is over 1%. Based on UNAIDS standards, some localities have now entered the generalised epidemic stage. The main transmission route is still injecting drug use (IDU). Infection through commercial blood and plasma donors primarily occurred before 1996, so the number of AIDS patients and AIDS-related deaths may have reached its peak already in this group. There is now some evidence that the proportion of sexually transmitted HIV infections is increasing and that men who have sex with men are a particularly high-risk group.[69]

Although there is no reference here to ethnic groups, two of the province-level units mentioned have significant minority populations, namely Yunnan and Xinjiang. Moreover, the reason why Henan is so high is connected with a corruption scandal that involved the cover-up of illegal blood sales blood infected with the HIV virus through unsterile collection methods occurring, according to the above extract, before 1996.

Two specialists on Xinjiang have written that the Uygurs there are "in a fight for their very survival," not because of Chinese rule, Uygur militancy, terrorism or separatism, but because of the HIV/AIDS epidemic. [70] The main causes are use of drugs intravenously and through shared needles and casual sex. Economic development and the Great Western Development strategy has ironically helped the spread of HIV/AIDS, because it has contributed to large-scale migration, including truck drivers, soldiers, prostitutes, and it appears that both in developing and developed countries, migration is playing "a major role in the spread of the AIDS epidemic."[71] Up to now most victims in Xinjiang have been Uygurs. However, Han migration into and within Xinjiang is likely to increase the number of Han affected as well.

Yunnan is known as a major centre for the drug trade. It is, for instance, a major conduit for the transport of heroin from Myanmar to the eastern provinces. Truck drivers visiting prostitutes can also help spread HIV/AIDS unless they take precautions such as using condoms. Yunnan's borders with Myanmar, Laos and Vietnam also attract prostitutes from those countries, some of them infected with HIV/AIDS. Yunnan was a leading province in seeking international help to control HIV/AIDS through condom promotion and needle-exchange programmes.[72]

What is less clear is how much Yunnan's minorities are affected by HIV/AIDS. Prostitutes are numerous in Xishuang banna Dai Autonomous Prefecture and especially its capital Jinghong. In the late 1990s, one specialist claimed that there were 500 prostitutes in Jinghong, but went on that most of them were Han immigrants, some of them pretending to be Dai, with only a small number of Dai or other minority women.[73] Ruili in south-western Yunnan on the border with Myanmar is also known for drug addiction, the prevalence of HIV/AIDS, as well as gambling. Some of the prostitutes come over the border from Myanmar to ply their trade, of whom some are infected with HIV/AIDS. There are also Dai and Jingpo villages near or on the border where drug infection is common and HIV/AIDS very difficult to control.[74]

One of the important points to emerge from the 1 December 2004 report is that up to that time the prevalence of HIV/AIDS in China varies strongly from one province/ autonomous region to another. For instance, although incidence is highest in two of the places where there are most ethnic minorities, it is much less so in others. The province and autonomous regions to have reported less than 100 cases were Inner Mongolia, Ningxia, Qinghai and Tibet, all with significant minority populations.[75] The incidence among ethnic groups may vary wildly from one place to another and from one group to another. There is not enough evidence to suggest whether the incidence is higher among ethnic minorities or Han.

It is clear from the above that there is a close connection between HIV/AIDS and drug abuse. According to figures cited by Vice Minister of Public Security Luo Feng on 1 March 2004, there were in 2003 about 1.05 million drug abusers registered with authorities, with those not registered about four or five times greater. The number of registered users has grown rapidly from about 70,000 in 1990.[76] Most drug addicts are male, aged between ages 15 and 35, and in the border provinces of Yunnan, Guangxi and Xinjiang, and along drug trafficking routes in Sichuan, Guizhou, Hunan and Jiangxi.[77] Drugs in the border provinces come mainly from Myanmar, some being transported to Xinjiang. However, there are certainly drugs smuggled from Central Asian countries into Xinjiang as well, and mutual cooperation to prevent narcotics from circulating throughout Central Asia is one of the concerns of the Shanghai Cooperation Organisation.[78]

Other than Jiangxi, the provinces all have significant ethnic minority populations. It certainly does not follow that the ethnic minorities are more prone to drug-taking than the Han. However, in the case of Xinjiang government authorities put more blame on Uygurs than others for drug usage and for illegal smuggling of drugs across the borders from the Central Asian countries. Whether or not reality matches perception, this can only exacerbate tensions between the Uygurs and other ethnic groups and between the Uygurs and the Chinese state.

So is the government doing anything about these extremely serious challenges? While it may have been quite slow to act, the evidence suggests that the Hu Jintao leadership has been quite proactive in dealing with HIV/AIDS and drugs, much more so than its predecessor. Although authorities were starting to do something about HIV/AIDS before Hu Jintao became the CPC general secretary, it seems that the SARS scare in the first half of 2003 really motivated the new leadership to take action over the nation's health. This has increased the seriousness with which it views the HIV/AIDS epidemic and the related drugs problem.

Some of the signs of leadership concern are:

- In December 2003 Premier Wen Jiabao made a senior Chinese leader's first visit to an AIDS hospital;
- In February 2004, the government set up its State Council AIDS Working Committee to supervise the prevention and control of HIV/AIDS;
- In March 2004, the State Council issued a document setting out a comprehensive policy framework for HIV/AIDS prevention and control in China;
- In July 2004, several ministries began a campaign to promote condom usage, with a target of 100% usage among high-risk behaviour populations;
- Government funding of anti-HIV/AIDS work has greatly increased, for example being in 2004 more than double what it had been in 2002;
- A generalised education and communication programme has been undertaken to raise general awareness of HIV/AIDS among the general population;[79]
- In April 2005, Minister of Public Security Zhou Yongkang announced a "people's war" against drugs, thus making formal a crack-down on the trafficking and use of drugs that had been intensifying since mid-2004.

- Measures to reduce demand for drugs have been strengthened, including much bigger budgets for police training and equipment and the establishment of detoxification units.[80]

How successful such measures will be remains to be seen. There are many who remain deeply sceptical, even scornful, of government efforts. For example, journalist Jonathan Watts quotes AIDS activist Wan Yanhai, who had been arrested in 2002 for disclosing details of the epidemic at a time when authorities regarded them as a state secret, as saying that there were already 5 to 10 million HIV/AIDS cases in China in 2004 and would be 20 million by 2020.[81] However, what does appear clear is that measures to control both the HIV/AIDS epidemic and drug crisis have escalated under the Hu Jintao leadership, especially since early 2004. It is also apparent that leaders no longer regard the epidemic with nearly the same secrecy as used to be the case. It is likely that the major event bringing about the new attitude was the SARS scare, which broke out at almost exactly the same time as Hu Jintao became president and Wen Jiabao premier at the Tenth National People's Congress in March 2003.

Conclusion

Hu Jintao's leadership has not seen any really basic changes in approach to the minorities. The bulk of what is most striking about policy and reality among the ethnic minorities was already in place when Hu Jintao came to power. The determination to maintain Chinese unity was already characteristic of all Chinese regimes in modern times, although some have been more successful than others. The belief that economic development will help strengthen national integration dates from before Hu Jintao. The Great Western Development strategy also predates Hu Jintao's regime, but appears to be yielding some results in the ethnic minority areas, almost all of which are in the west as defined by the strategy.

Hu Jintao's leadership period has seen changes in emphasis in a few areas that are very significant for the ethnic minorities. He appears to have presided over a shift away from sympathy for the United States, characteristic of Jiang Zemin, and towards one for Russia. This has shown itself relevant to the developing situation in Central Asia, including how things are developing in Xinjiang. Perhaps the most important of all changes under Hu Jintao is an explosion of awareness of just how serious the HIV/AIDS and related narcotics abuse crisis is. While it is true that relevant international bodies have been urging openness for a long time, the SARS crisis of early 2003 no doubt also made it obvious that secrecy could not assist meeting challenges like those posed by serious epidemics.

The September 11 Incidents, the war against terrorism and in Iraq have affected the political climate of the 21st century to an enormous degree and some of the shifts in emphases in China's leadership policies and challenges follow from it. While there is absolutely nothing new about challenges of separatism in Xinjiang, the war against terrorism has impacted on the texture of developments with the ethnic minorities there, especially the Uygurs. Not only has the United States military moves into Central Asia affected relations with China and the Central Asian states, but also the way China has reacted towards Uygur separatism from China, either real or supposed. The Uygur diasporas have become much better organised and tried to put forward their views in a more systematic way; and they have apparently been more successful in getting their view heard in Washington.

Yet it is legitimate to ask just how big a threat separatism really poses to China's unity. My answer is that it is real, but not serious enough to warrant the rather extreme reaction against it, especially in Xinjiang. Economic development is of course both desirable and necessary, and it is succeeding in weakening separatism, especially in Tibet. To me it remains an open question whether the restrictions on Islam in Xinjiang or on Tibetan Buddhism in the Tibetan areas actually provoke resistance, as some commentators claim. But whatever the answer separatism seems unlikely to triumph while

China's rise persists to the extent we have seen in recent years. This is because the successful establishment of an independent Tibet or East Turkistan would require either the complete collapse of the Chinese state or outside intervention of some kind. And neither seems on the horizon unless and until China's rise is halted.

Notes and References

1. *Zhongguo tongji nianjian, China Statistical Yearbook 2004* (Beijing: Zhongguo tongji chubanshe, 2004), p. 97.

2. See Xiao Zhuoji, "Project of a harmonious society," *Beijing Review*, Vol. 48, No. 11 (17 March 2005), p. 18.

3. The main areas of Yi concentration are Yunnan, Sichuan and Guizhou. They speak a Tibeto-Burman language and numbered 7,762,272 in the 2000 census. For brief notes on all 55 ethnic minorities, including male, female and total populations in the 2000 census, see Colin Mackerras, *China's Ethnic Minorities and Globalisation* (London: RoutledgeCurzon, 2003), pp. 182–93.

4. See especially Tsering Shakya, *The Dragon in the Land of Snows*, A History of Modern Tibet Since 1947 (London: Pimlico, 1999), pp. 431–40.

5. See a more general explanation of the policy of autonomy and its limitations in Colin Mackerras, *China's Minorities, Integration and Modernisation in the Twentieth Century* (Hong Kong: Oxford University Press, 1994), pp. 153–9.

6. Compare Article 22 in the 1984 Law as given in Katherine Palmer Kaup, *Creating the Zhuang, Ethnic Politics in China* Boulder, London: Lynne Rienner, 2000), p. 189, with the 2001 version, as given in *Zhonghua renmin gongheguo minzu quyu zizhi fa Law of the People's Republic of China on Regional national Autonomy* (Beijing: Minzu chubanshe, 2001), pp. 9, 42. See also the discussion on comparison of the two versions of the law in Mackerras, *China's Ethnic Minorities and Globalisation*, p. 39.

7. Information Office of the State Council, "Regional Autonomy for Ethnic Minorities in China," *China Daily*, 1 March 2005.

8. See *Renmin ribao, Haiwai ban (People's Daily, Overseas Edition)*, 28 June 2000.

9. See the figures in Colin Mackerras, *The New Cambridge Handbook of Contemporary China* (Cambridge: Cambridge University Press, 2001), p. 96.

10. Ulrich Beck, trans. Patrick Camiller, *What is Globalisation?* (Cambridge, Oxford and Malden MA: Polity Press in association with Blackwell Publishers, 2000), p. 21.

11. For instance, see John Ralston Saul, *The Collapse of Globalism and the Reinvention of the World* (Viking, 2005).

12. On the question of Hui identity see Dru C. Gladney *Ethnic Identity in China, The Making of a Muslim Minority Nationality* (Fort Worth, TX: Harcourt Brace, 1998), pp. 44–54 and other works by the same author.

13. Kaup, *Creating the Zhuang*, p. 3.

14. The manifesto of the Chinese United League (*Tongmeng hui*), set up in August 1905 with Sun Yatsen as president, had four main points, the first being to expel the Manchus, and only the third to establish a republic. See Sun Zhongshan, *Guofu quanji* (*Complete Works of the Father of the Nation*) (Taibei: Guomindang Central Committee Party History Commission, 1973), Vol. 1, pp. 285–6.

15. See Mackerras, *China's Minorities*, pp. 238, 244.

16. Gladney *Ethnic Identity in China*, p. 20.

17. Lian Bai "Identity reproducers beyond the grassroots: The middle class in the Manchu revival since the 1980s," *Asian Ethnicity*, Vol. 6, No. 3 (October 2005), p. 186.

18. *Ibid.*, p. 187.

19. See the list of PRC autonomous areas in Mackerras, *The New Cambridge Handbook of Contemporary China*, pp. 254–6.

20. The term comes from the title of S Frederick Starr (ed.), *Xinjiang, China's Muslim Borderland* (Armonk, New York, London, England: M E Sharpe, 2004).

21. For instance, see U.S. Department of State, Counterterrorism Office, *Patterns of Global Terrorism 2001* (Washington: U.S. Department of State, 2002), pp. 16–17.

22. See Colin Mackerras, "Some issues of ethnic and religious identity among China's Islamic peoples," *Asian Ethnicity*, Vol. 6, No. 1 (February 2005), pp. 11–13.

23. Willy Lam, "Hu's Central Asian Gamble to Counter the U.S. 'Containment Strategy'", *China Brief*, Vol. 5, Issue 15 (5 July 2005), website jamestown.org, accessed 21 August 2005.

24. See Mackerras, *China's Ethnic Minorities*, pp. 186, 190–2.

25. See, for instance, Robin Wright, "Chinese detainees are men without a country," *Washington Post*, 24 August 2005.

26. Ding Zhitao, "Colorless revolution, Kyrgyzstan feels the domino effect of the revolutions that have toppled the governments of former Soviet republics," *Beijing Review*, Vol. 48, No. 14 (7 April 2005), p. 29.

27. Ahmed Rashid, *Jihad: The Rise of Militant Islam in Central Asia* (New Haven: Yale University Press, 2002), p. 115.

28. For a good account of the 1995 choice of Panchen Lama see Melvyn C Goldstein, *The Snow Lion and the Dragon, China, Tibet, and the Dalai Lama* (Berkeley: University of California Press, 1997), pp. 105–11. He also discusses the Tibet issue in Sino-American relations from 1989 through the first half of the 1990s pp. 117–31.

29. A T Grunfeld, "A brief survey of Tibetan relations with the United States," in Alex McKay (ed.), *Tibet and Her Neighbours: A History* (London: Edition Hansjörg Mayer, 2003), p. 204.

30. For instance, see Mark Townsend, "Dalai Lama visit riles China," *The Guardian*, 23 May 2004.

31. R Devraj, "Out comes the China card, *AsiaTimes Online*, 5 February 2005, http://www.atimes.com/atimes/South_Asia/GB05Df09.html, accessed March 2005.

32. Zhu Rongji, "Report on the work of the government," *Beijing Review*, Vol. 43, No. 14 (3 April 2000), p. 20.

33. See, for instance, economist Dong Funai quoted in "Focusing on western China," *Beijing Review*, Vol. 43, No. 15 (10 April 2000), p. 14. See also David Goodman, "The campaign to 'open up the west': national, provincial-level and local perspectives," *The China Quarterly*, No. 278 (June 2004), p. 321.

34. Goodman, "The campaign to 'open up the west,'" p. 317.

35. See Chai Mai, "More balanced development," *Beijing Review*, Vol. 47, No. 13 (1 April 2004), p. 24, where the author cites Qinghua University's China Studies Center Director Hu Angang as holding the view that blind pursuit of higher GDP in development has led to a raft of social problems, which can be solved only through much more balanced development that takes adequate account of the environment and society and reducing economic disparities. Actually, in the 1990s Hu wrote extensively on the problems of uneven development and, according to Goodman, "The campaign to 'open up the west,'" p. 326, his ideas formed part of the initial justification of the Great Western Development strategy.

36. According to the 2000 census, the population of Qinghai was 5,181,560 of whom 53% were Han, Tibetans 22% and Hui 16%. See *Qinghai ribao* (*Qinghai Daily*), 28 April 2001, as cited in David Goodman, "Qinghai

and the emergence of the west: nationalities, communal interaction and national integration," *The China Quarterly*, No. 178 (June 2004), p. 381.

37. Goodman, "Qinghai and the emergence of the west," p. 389.

38. See Colin Mackerras, "Ethnicity in China: the case of Xinjiang," *Harvard Asia Quarterly*, Vol. 8, No. 1 (Winter 2004), pp. 6–8.

39. See Calla Wiemer, "The economy of Xinjiang," in S Frederick Starr (ed.), *Xinjiang, China's Muslim Borderland* (Armonk, New York and London, England: M E Sharpe, 2004), p. 188.

40. See also Martin Andrew, "Beijing's growing security dilemma in Xinjiang," *China Brief*, Vol. 5, Issue 13 (7 June 2005), website jamestown.org, accessed 22 August 2005.

41. Nicolas Becquelin, "Staged development in Xinjiang," *The China Quarterly*, No. 178 (June 2004), p. 365.

42. For a consideration of these see Colin Mackerras, "Some problems on China's ethnic borders," in Joseph Y S Cheng (ed.) *China's Challenges in the Twenty-first Century* (Hong Kong: City University of Hong Kong Press, 2003), pp. 627–60.

43. See Katherine Palmer Kaup, *Creating the Zhuang*, p. 2.

44. Uradyn E Bulag, "Ethnic Resistance with Socialist Characteristics," in Elizabeth J Perry and Mark Selden (eds), *Chinese Society, Change Conflict and Resistance* (London: Routledge, 2000), p. 178.

45. See figures on Xinjiang's population by ethnic breakdown in Mackerras, "Ethnicity in China," p. 8.

46. Dru C. Gladney, "Responses to Chinese Rule, Patterns of Cooperation and Opposition," in S Frederick Starr (ed.), *Xinjiang, China's Muslim Borderland* (Armonk, New York and London, England: M E Sharpe, 2004), p. 393.

47. Journalist Michael Winchester interviewed a man he calls Turghun (not his real name), a follower of the rebellion's leader Zahideen Yusuf. Whereas Zahideen was killed in the rebellion, Turghun did not actually take part in it, though he supported it strongly. He told Winchester that Zahideen had been "Inspired by the idea of the 'holy war' practiced by the Afghan muhahideen against the infidel invader." See Michael Winchester, "Beijing vs. Islam," *Asiaweek*, Vol. 23, No, 42 (24 October 1997), p. 31. Human Rights in China, "Devastating blows, religious repression of Uighurs in Xinjiang," *Human Rights Watch*, Vol. 17, No. 2(C) (April 2005), p. 14 calls the Baren Township incident "a major, Islamic-inspired insurrection."

48. See the translation of an extract from Document No. 7 in Nicolas Becquelin, "Xinjiang in the nineties," *The China Journal*, No. 44 (July 2000), p. 87.

49. See also Michael Dillon, *Xinjiang: Ethnicity, Separatism and Control in Chinese Central* (Durham East Asian Papers, 1, Durham: Department of East Asian Studies, University of Durham, 1995), pp. 20–9.

50. See also Justin Rudelson and William Jankowiak, "Acculturation and Resistance, Xinjiang Identities in Flux," in S Frederick Starr (ed.), *Xinjiang, China's Muslim Borderland* (Armonk, New York and London, England: M E Sharpe, 2004), pp. 316–18.

51. Information Office of the State Council of the People's Republic of China, "'East Turkistan' Terrorist Forces Cannot Get Away with Impunity," *Beijing Review*, Vol. 45, No. 5 (31 January 2002), p. 15.

52. *Ibid.*, p. 19.

53. See, for instance, John Ruwitch, "China convicts 50 to death in 'terror crackdown'", Reuters from Urumqi, 13 September 2004.

54. Gladney, "Responses to Chinese rule," pp. 393–94.

55. *Ibid.*, p. 381.

56. Human Rights in China, "Devastating blows, religious repression of Uighurs in Xinjiang," p. 7.

57. Robert Barnett, "Chen Kuiyuan and the Marketisation of Policy," in Alex McKay (ed.), *Tibet and Her Neighbours: A History* (London: Edition Hansjörg Mayer, 2003), p. 231.

58. United States Department of State, *Country Reports on Human Rights Practices 2003: China (includes Tibet, Hong Kong, and Macau)* (Washington: Department of State, February 2004), http://www.state.gov/g/drl/rls/hrrpt/2003/27768.htm#Tibet, accessed January 2005.

59. United States Department of State Bureau of Democracy, Human Rights and Labor, *China (includes Tibet, Hong Kong, and Macau) Country Reports on Human Rights Practices 2004* (Washington: United States Department of State, February 2005), http://www.state.gov/g/drl/rls/hrrpt/2004/41640 htm#tibet, accessed 22 August 2005.

60. United States Department of State, *Country Reports*, 2004.

61. United States Department of State Bureau of Democracy, Human Rights and Labor, *China*, 2005.

62. For both figures see United States Department of State Bureau of Democracy, Human Rights and Labor, *China*, 2005.

63. See, for instance, Julian Gearing, "Tibetan lama dodges Chinese bullet," *Asia Times Online*, 28 January 2005, http://www.atimes.com/, accessed 31 January 2005.

64. Staff Reporter, "Dalai Lama yields ground on Tibet self-rule; We will

accept China's authority if it preserves our culture, he says," *South China Morning Post*, 14 March 2005.

65. United States Department of State, Bureau of East Asian and Pacific Affairs, *Report on Tibet Negotiations* (Washington: Department of State, 2004), http://www.state.gov/p/eap/rls/rpt/34266.htm, accessed on 22 August 2005.

66. See, for instance, Melvyn C Goldstein, Dawei Sherap and William R Siebenschuh, *A Tibetan Revolutionary, The Political Life and Times of Bapa Phüntso Wangye* (Berkeley, Los Angeles, London: University of California Press, 2004), pp. 315–17.

67. State Council AIDS Working Committee Office and UN Theme Group on HIV/AIDS in China, *HIV/AIDS Prevention, Treatment and Care in China (2004)*(Beijing: State Council AIDS Working Committee Office, National Center for AIDS/STD Prevention and Control, China CDC, UNAIDS China Office, 2004), p. 1.

68. For example, Edward Cody, "In China, an about-face on AIDS prevention," *Washington Post*, 8 December 2004. In "Chinese walls come down," *The Guardian*, 11 September 2004, Jonathan Watts notes the UN prediction that China could have 10 million HIV/AIDS cases by 2010 unless nothing is done to remedy the situation.

69. State Council AIDS Working Committee Office and UN Theme Group on HIV/AIDS in China, *HIV/AIDS Prevention, Treatment and Care in China (2004)*, p. 1.

70. Justin Rudelson and William Jankowiak, "Acculturation and resistance, Xinjiang identities in flux," in S Frederick Starr (ed.), *Xinjiang, China's Muslim Borderland* (Armonk, New York and London, England: M E Sharpe, 2004), p. 318.

71. Christopher J Smith and Xiushi Yang, "Examining the connection between temporary migration and the spread of STDs and HIV/AIDS in China," *The China Review*, Vol. 5, No. 1 (Spring 2005), p. 131.

72. See, for instance, Watts, "Chinese walls come down."

73. Grant Evans, "Transformation of Jinghong, Xishuangbanna, PRC," in Grant Evans, Christopher Hutton and Kuah Khun Eng (eds), *Where China Meets Southeast Asia, Social & Cultural Change in the Border Regions* (Bangkok: White Lotus, Singapore: Institute of Southeast Asian Studies, 2000), p. 170.

74. See, for instance, Rose Tang, "The cesspool diary," *The Standard* (Hong Kong), 7–8 May 2005.

75. State Council AIDS Working Committee Office and UN Theme Group on HIV/AIDS in China, *HIV/AIDS Prevention, Treatment and Care in China (2004)*, p. 1.

76. Drew Thompson, "The 'people's war' against drugs and HIV/AIDS," *China Brief*, Vol. 5, Issue 14 (21 June 2005), website jamestown.org, accessed 23 August 2005.

77. *People's Daily*, 13 February 2004, as cited in Thompson, "The 'people's war.'"

78. See, for instance, Pan Guang, "The Chinese perspective on the recent Astana summit," *China Brief*, Vol. 5, Issue 18 (16 August 2005), website jamestown.org, accessed 25 August 2005.

79. State Council AIDS Working Committee Office and UN Theme Group on HIV/AIDS in China, *HIV/AIDS Prevention, Treatment and Care in China (2004)*, pp. i–iii.

80. Thompson, "The 'people's war.'"

81. Watts, "Chinese walls come down."

18

The Triangular Relations among China, Taiwan and the Vatican: A Taiwan Perspective

Beatrice K. F. LEUNG
Marcus J. J. WANG

Introduction: History of the Triangle

The Vatican and the Republic of China established diplomatic relations in 1942, with Archbishop Celso Constantini as the first papal representative stationed in Nanjing, the national capital of the Republic of China.[1] Both the Vatican and the new Nanjing government had a positive attitude towards this diplomatic relationship. For the Vatican, the Catholic affairs in China could be free from the interference of foreign powers, e.g. "the French Protectorate."[2] For China, without the French Protectorate it meant to be free from some imperialist interference within its boundaries. Also, Chiang Kai-shek the head of the new National Government was a Christian and he would find it a privilege to have diplomatic relations with the Holy See, which is the symbol of moral authority in the international community. Within the Church's circle, Archbishop Paul Yupin of Nanjing was the leading figure between the Vatican and China to facilitate the establishment of the Sino-Vatican diplomatic relationship.[3]

After the Revolution of 1949, with the expulsion of the Papal Nuncio Archbishop Riberi from the Mainland in September 1951, Sino-Vatican diplomatic relations were disrupted. After pending in Hong Kong for a few months, the Papal Nuncio to China moved to Taipei in December 1952 and re-established the Papal Nunciature there until the present.[4] The Vatican is the only European state which has diplomatic relations with Taiwan. Nations which have diplomatic relations with Taiwan have shrunk to fewer than 30 small republics in Central America and Africa. From the point of view of the Taiwanese government, Sino-Vatican relations have been very important for Taiwan because they allow Taiwan's diplomatic presence and contacts in Europe. This chapter discusses the development of the Taiwanese-Vatican relations, which are under constant threat from Beijing.[5] The recent change of Taiwan's policy on the Vatican will be discussed to highlight Taiwan's perspective on the triangular relations among Beijing, Taipei and the Vatican.

Theoretical Review and Discussion

Most scholars regard relations between church and state historically as ranged from the relatively mild tension found in western democracies to the fundamental conflicts over authority found in authoritarian, especially communist states.[6] Ideological incompatibilities led to repeated clashes in Communist Party states between those who sought atheist communism and those who held religious beliefs.[7] Problems involving the Catholic Church, whose hierarchical structure posed extra challenges to the omniscience of the ruling communist party, were particularly common[8]. They were aggravated by the claim of the Vatican exercises authority over its clergy in organisational and theological terms coupled with the Vatican's sovereign status in International Law. The church-state differences in the Soviet Union and Eastern Europe were both ideological and political because the cultural heritage of these nation-states was fundamentally Christian. In China, however, church-state relations were additionally complicated by cultural factors.[9] The competition over authority was exacerbated by the Bolshevik's organisational behaviour which aimed at gaining power through the exercising of institutional weapons.[10]

In the midst of conflicting authority between the Vatican and Beijing, Taipei has been under a constant threat from Beijing. Bao Zhong He has a marriage scenario in the triangular relations of Taiwan's foreign relations with a third nation, vis-à-vis China.[11] According to Bao's theory, Taiwan would be left out if the Vatican establishes its diplomatic relations with Beijing. Thus it prompted Taipei to initiate a theory of accommodation, which requests Taiwan neither to react too strongly nor negatively on the possible Sino-Vatican rapprochement, but to support the Vatican's policy to promote religious freedom among Chinese (mainlanders and Taiwanese).[12]

The Forgotten Catholic History in Taiwan

Many studies have been devoted to the church history in the Mainland, but the church history of Taiwan has been forgotten by many Church historians. Spanish missionaries were the first to arrive at Taiwan, reaching the cities of Keelung and Tanshui in northern Taiwan in 1626. In 1642, after the Dutch occupation, they were arrested and deported to Batavia, Indonesia, after the controversy of the Chinese Rites. On 18 May 1859, Spanish Dominicans came from the Philippines, through Amoy, to Kaoshiung, where they established the Church. Indigenous Catholic faithful on the Island was limited into a few rural enclaves in the south, principally in villages close to Kaohsiung and Tainan. Those Catholic families were largely descendents of converts of the Spanish missionaries who first arrived in 1626 and named the island Formosa.[13]

In the Catholic hierarchy, Taiwan belonged originally to the Fukien Apostolic Vicariate, which was divided in 1883 into two vicariates of Fuchow and Amoy, Taiwan belonging to the latter. After the Japanese occupation of the island, on 19 July 1913 Taiwan became an independent apostolic prefecture, having successively two prefects Apostolic of Spanish nationality from 1913 to 1920. Under the pressure of the Japanese government, a Japanese prefect apostolic was appointed in the person of Msgr. Satowaki Asajiro (1941–46).[14]

After the Japanese surrender in 1946, a native Taiwanese priest was appointed to administrate the Taiwan Prefecture. In 1948, Jose Arregui, O.P. was appointed prefect. The arrival of National government to Taiwan with large number of Chinese civilian from the mainland in 1949 turned a new page of the Taiwan Catholic Church.[15]

With a warm church-state relationship in Taiwan under the Kuomintang (KMT) rule, the Catholic Church had a tremendous boost. The number of priests increased from 15 in 1948 to 296 in 1954, and Catholics increased from 1,300 to 32,310 within the same period. Those increased members in the Taiwanese Catholic Church came from various part of China.[16] The growth of the Catholic population between 1952 and1953 was 25%. In 1956, it reached the peak of growth at 65% with a Catholic population of 80,000 in the whole island. Until 1963 the growth rate had been kept to 10%. Then Taiwan was divided into seven prefectures which later turned into dioceses. Compared with the atheist Communist rule of Mao Zedong no religion was tolerated Taiwan's Catholic development was spectacular. Catholic leaders in Taiwan were largely from the Mainland. Since 1949, Taiwan has allowed its people to enjoy religious freedom. Archbishop Paul Yupin (later Cardinal) of Nanking and Cardinal Thomas Tien Kenghsin of Shangdong Province and a few outstanding priests-academicians, such as Father Fong Hou began to work in the island with fewer than 100,000 Catholics. In addition, American and European missionaries who moved to Taiwan with the KMT regime after 1949 found their new roots at the National Taiwan University and the newly established Catholic Fu Jen University[17] as members of the teaching faculty, as well as in mountain areas among aboriginals.

With the sudden increase of manpower, the Taiwanese Catholic Church was able to offer education, social and medical services to the local people as a means to evangelise them into Catholicism. The increase of Catholic faithful, in spite of the diligent work of Mainland priests and bishops who moved to Taiwan with the nationalist government, could not be considered as a significant missionary achievement.[18]

However, in spite of unsatisfactory success of conversion of the indigenous population,[19] the Holy See saw the importance of consecrating ethnic Chinese clergy and bishops to invigorate and to prepare the continuation of evangelisation of the Chinese people and to restore the Chinese Church. However, the backbone of the Taiwan church came from the Chinese priests coming from the Mainland until the 1990s.[20] The Vatican Apostolic Delegate in Taiwan perceived himself essentially as papal delegate to the Chinese Church in exile. Similarly, most of the native Taiwanese viewed the Catholic Church and its leaders as a church of the mainland, because pastoral care and evangelisation were mostly among the Mainlanders.[21] It is therefore safe to conclude that the relationship with the Vatican has always been the relationship between Rome and the Church in exile, Taiwan being non-Communist occupied territory where the Church could continue its evangelical missions.

After the evaluation of the Catholics in China and the amount of religious freedom Taiwanese Catholic enjoyed, the Vatican planned to change the nature of its relationship with Taiwan from that of diplomatic in nature to religious in nature on the date of the establishment of the Sino-Vatican relations.[22]

In view of the change of the nature to review the Taiwan-Vatican relations which are hinged on two issues: the Beijing-Vatican negotiations, and the bridging endeavour. The change of Taiwan's policy on the Vatican as suggested by the former ambassador of Taiwan to the Vatican, Mr. Raymond R.M. Tai suggested a new approach on the government-church relations in Taiwan.

The Taiwan-Vatican
Relationship under Threat

After the exile of Republic of China (ROC) to Taiwan in 1949, the Papal Nuncio to China was still in Nanjing waiting to establish diplomatic relations with the new regime of people's Republic of China (PRC) in Beijing. Unfortunately, the Papal Nuncio Archbishop Riberi was expelled in September 1951. After staying in Hong Kong for ten months, he went to Taipei to re-establish the Papal Nunciature in October 1952. From this period onwards, the Vatican relationship with China becomes a triangular relation among Beijing, Rome and Taipei. Even where there is a diplomatic relation between Taiwan and the Vatican, most of the attention of the Vatican has been given to the church in the Mainland China which was under persecution in the Maoist regime. In other words, the gravity triangular relation has been lopsided toward the Vatican and Beijing. In the Maoist regime, dialogue and rapprochement of the Sino-Vatican relationship was not possible, when Mao accepted no other ideology except dialectic Marxism-Leninism, and the Vatican for Mao was a symbol related to the Capitalist West, which was a target to be attacked.

The Vatican grasped every possible opportunity to approach Beijing and prepared to clear the ground for dialogue, even in Maoist era. In the 1950s, the Vatican ordered the exile of two anti-Communist Church leaders, Archbishop Yupin and Cardinal Thomas Tien for fear that the anti-Communist attitude and their lobby in the KMT government in Taiwan would jeopardise the Sino-Vatican contact. Pope Paul VI visited Hong Kong and delivered a speech towards China in December 1970.

On the contrary, during the period of 1950 to 1978 Taiwan had been very passive vis-à-vis the Vatican's China policy which tended to woo Beijing for negotiations.[23] After PRC replaced the ROC as a member of the Security Council of the United Nations in 1971, the Vatican withdrew the Pronuncio Cardinal Edward Cassidy and replaced him with Charge d'Affaires to downgrade the Taiwan-

Vatican diplomatic relations until the present. However, Taiwan did not retaliate, but rather kept the ambassador rank to its representative to the Vatican.

Since Deng's Modernisation Era, the Taiwan-Vatican relationship has been constantly threatened by Beijing, which demanded the severance of Taiwan-Vatican diplomatic relations as a condition for negotiations aimed at the normalisation of a Sino-Vatican relationship.[24] However, the Vatican has been cogently pursuing the normalisation of Sino-Vatican relations which aims at providing better church-state relations in China. It is because a warmer political environment for the normal development is needed for the development of the Chinese Catholic Church with a population of 12 ,000,000 Catholics. If a Sino-Vatican Concordat were formulated, the natural outcome might change the nature of the Taiwan-Vatican relation from a diplomatic nature to a religious and cultural nature as suggested recently by Taipei. Because there is a big concern for the Vatican to move the Papal Nunciature from Taipei to Beijing with minimal embarrassment to Taiwan.

However, the future relationship between the Vatican and Taiwan is closely associated with the development of Sino-Vatican relations. In spite of the fact that, since 1987 the Vatican has been trying very hard to normalise Sino-Vatican diplomatic relations. Due to domestic consideration, Beijing is not yet ready to establish the Sino-Vatican diplomatic relationship which has an implication on the loosening of state control on ideological matters including religious matters.[25] With ideological differences, up to now, after 18 years of negotiation (1987–2005) no rapprochement has been reaped. With changes in China's political landscape, both internally and externally, the normalisation of the Sino-Vatican relationship is only a matter of time.[26] Taipei has long realised that it is unrealistic to retain the diplomatic relations with the Vatican in the near future, and prepares to change its policy with the Vatican by supporting the Vatican's policy of promoting peace as well as Vatican's quest for religious freedom. Taipei prepares to replace the diplomatic relation with more intensive religious and cultural relations, if there is Sino-Vatican rapprochement.[27]

The Catholic Church
with Taiwan's Ruling Parties

Catholic Church and the Kuomintang (KMT)

Due to ideological incompatibility between atheist Marxism-Leninism and Catholicism, the Catholic Church led by the Vatican traditionally has not supported any Communist Party including the Communist Party of China (CPC). On the contrary, since the Nanjing Period (1911–1949), the same Catholic Church based on its traditional biblical teaching which demands obeying and cooperating with the legitimate National government headed by the KMT. (Romans 13:1–6) As early as in the Sino-Japanese War (1937–45), Catholics in Anguo County, Hebei Province, led by Fr. Lebb, a nationalised Belgian priest joined the Chinese ambulance service in the battle field to serve the wounded Chinese soldiers, while Catholics of the Fu Jen Catholic University in Beijing engaged in underground intelligence service for the Chinese. Archbishop of Nanjing, Paul Yupin, later Cardinal Yupin, went abroad to make international appeal for the support on the Chinese to combat Japanese militarism, which was an ally to Hitler.[28] The cooperation between the Chinese Catholic leaders and the National government in Nanjing during the Sino-Japanese War laid the foundation of their warm relationship in days to come, not only in the Mainland but even in the post-1949 period after both fled to Taiwan.

In Taiwan during the ruling period of the KMT, the Taiwanese Catholic Church had rendered various kinds of educational, social, and medical services to respond to the needs of those who had migrated to Taiwan from the Mainland. It was because the Church with the flooding in of large numbers of clerics and religious, both male and female, was able to enhance its service tremendously with the increase of manpower. Subsequently, the Catholic population experienced a sudden growth in the 1950s and1960s. On the other hand, the newly arrived Church personnel received assistance from the KMT government to establish themselves in different locations and various sectors of life in Taiwan.[29] For example with the help of the government the Catholic Fu Jen University re-established itself in Taipei in 1960 with Madam Chiang Kai Shek who became the chairperson of the Board of Directors after the death of Cardinal Thomas Tien, the ipso facto chairperson of Fu Jen's Board of Directors. Some bishops got the help of local officials in the matter of acquiring land and other matters in setting up of Church institutes.[30] Compared with the migrated Buddhist monks some of whom were under house arrested when they were suspected as subversive elements, the Catholic Church personnel received much better treatment. Cardinal Yupin was the Vice Chairman of the Anti-Communist Committee, and under his patronage, no Catholic personnel was detained for the suspicion of subversion.[31] Even the KMT were straight in scrutinizing subversive elements within civil organisations, the Taiwanese security police reported that the records of Catholic clergy and sisters were clean without suspicion.

The government later in the 1970s discovered that some foreign Catholic missionaries including Fr. Neil Magill, and Fr. Paul Duffy were sympathisers of the "illegal" opposition party, the predecessor of the DDP. They offered protection to political dissents who were involved in the issue of "Meilidao" [The Issue of the Beautiful Island] . With the pretext that Fr. Neil Magill supported the labour movement; the KMT refused to renew his passport and deported him by force. The deportation of Fr. Magill aroused the protest of the Chinese Bishops in Taiwan with the consent of the Archbishop of Taipei, Loukwong, a staunch supporter of KMT, the successor of Yupin.[32]

Within the church led by Loukwong and supported by a leading Chinese Catholic theologian Aloysius Chang, strong criticism was made to condemn the government for the deportation[33]. On the other hand, the Presbyterian Church, whose mainstream leaders supported the opposition and worked on the localisation of theology to justify the pro-independent DDP.[34] The Catholic Church, however, has its foreign missionaries who were aware of social justice services to the oppressed. Traditionally, the Catholic Church support the legitimate government but upholds the Christian principle of social justice and respect for human rights.

Catholic Church and the Democratic Progressive Party (DDP)

DDP officials have not formed warm relations with Catholic leaders, who have been traditionally supported the KMT. The economic growth in Taiwan in the 1970s to the 1990s experienced a stagnant growth and later the decline of the Catholic population.[35] In the presidential elections in 2000 and the problematic victory of Chen Shui Bien with the shooting incident on 19 March 2004, the whole nation was torn into the north and south. Most of the northern electors supported the KMT (the Blue Camp) and the related groups (pan-blue). The southern Taiwanese support the Democratic Progressive Party (DPP) (the Green Camp) Chen Shui Bien himself is a southerner. The cleavage is not for the interest of the people nor the nation.[36] Catholic Paul Cardinal Shan, S.J. the Chairman of the Taiwan Catholic Bishops Conference openly called for reconciliation.[37] However, his message became the lonely voice in the desert, very few Catholic priests have followed his footstep by preaching this message of reconciliation on the Sunday pulpit. On the contrary, the Presbyterian Christian church in Tainan advocated revenge to KMT after the victory of the DDP which they had supported with a heavy price.[38] On the other hand, the ruling party (DPP) does not understand the Catholic Church and the Vatican too well not to mention to have a warmer relation with the church. The presidential participation of Pope John Paul II's funeral can illustrate this statement.

Pope John Paul II's death on 2 April 2005 attracted 200 heads of states and a crowd of eight millions to flock to Rome. His funeral was the prime drawing room of international politics in which Chen Shui Bien, the President of Taiwan was able to present himself without being blocked by Beijing. It was through the careful maneuver of some Catholic priests and the Vatican's Charge d'Affaires in Taipei, Monsignor Ambrose Madtha.[39] However by comparing the U.S. presidential delegation, one can see that Taiwan could not distinguish the "sacred" and "profane" phases of the Vatican. President of Taiwan brought with him two aboriginal

Catholic priests, a Muslim religious leader and the Minister of Foreign Affairs on this occasion of gathering of world leaders. U.S. president Gorge W. Bush brought him with his wife, the Secretary of State Condoleezza Rice, together with Bill Clinton, and George Bush (former presidents). When the U.S. delegation armed with three presidents and a state secretary, it is a demonstration of its political relationship with the Vatican. The U.S. knew very well that the funeral of this distinguished religious leader is an occasion for political shoulder rubbing, and Taiwan political leader did not have this kind of political wisdom to know the nature of Vatican and failed to grasp the political nuisance of Pope John Paul II.

However, during the funeral, Vatican did not help Chen in his attempt to rub shoulders with other state leaders which was one of his main reasons to visit Rome. Vatican also denied Chen's request to meet senior officials and cardinals. Foreign reporters revealed that no body spoke to him, and he was put in a situation where he would be de facto isolated, and none of the big state leaders wanted to be seen talking to him.[40] On the other hand, shortly before the death of the Pope John Paul II, Cardinal Godfried Danneels of Belgium was sent to Beijing to meet the Chinese Vice Premier Hui Liangyu, and officials of Religious Affairs Bureau. The Hong Kong prelate Bishop Joseph Zen remarked that the possibility of the resuming of the Sino-Vatican relations was not impossible. All these signs indicated that it is time to review DDP's understanding of Vatican and provide suggestions to further development of the precarious Taiwanese-Vatican relation.

The Difficulties in the Sino-Vatican Negotiation

The course of the Sino-Vatican relationship has not been smooth due to the ideological nature. The fundamental difficulty rests in the ideological incompatibility between the dialectic materialism embedded in Marxism – Leninism and religious idealism. Catholicism aggravates the question by its hierarchical nature. The CPC and the Vatican are struggling for the teaching authority over the 12 millions Chinese Catholics.

When old problems in the Sino-Vatican negotiation have not been resolved, new questions were added. Changes in the international political landscape gave additional complications to the old questions after the toppling down of European Communism and the disintegration of the Soviet Union. In the "market competition" between the Chinese Communist Party and the Catholic Church in Deng-Jiang period, it reflected that the struggle on the exercising the teaching authority has been carrying on in China.[41]

In the process of struggle, at some stage, it seems that the Catholic Church was on the upper scale, when the party has been suffering from ideological hollowness resulting from internal discipline problems, corruption and abuse of power. During the years of informal and formal talks between Beijing and the Vatican, issues which were brought up for negotiation can be summarised into the following categories:

1) the arrangement to share power between Vatican and China in appointing Chinese bishops;

2) the method in unifying the official and no-official sectors of the Chinese Catholic Church;

3) the ways and means whereby the papal representative in Beijing relates to local bishop in the future;

4) the ways for moving the Papal Nunciature in Taiwan to Beijing with minimal disturbance and embarrassment to Taiwan.

Before some solution based on tolerance and accommodation could be thought of to resolve thorny issues stemming from these four categories, two new requests came from Beijing in August 1999 adding extra complexity to the unresolved problems. Beijing's two requests which stepped on Vatican's nerves were

a) the transference of the ecclesial administrative power of a local bishop to the civil authority.

b) Beijing's suggestion in the joint appointment of Chinese bishops of the usual practice of selecting bishop candidate by itself and the Vatican's continued validation of the government appointment.

In the first place, the Vatican could not go against the Cannon Law (The Catholic Constitutional Law) by accepting Beijing's suggestion simply because the papal authority would be undermined in the Chinese Catholic Church when Art. 333 Canon Law stipulates that: *By virtue of his office the Roman Pontiff not only has power over the universal Church, but also has pre-eminent ordinary power over all particular churches and their groupings.*"[42] Vatican refused to accept Beijing's two requests and it led to an abrupt brake on the Sino-Vatican negotiation. Then it precipitated the rows on the issues of self consecration of five Chinese bishops on 6th January 2000 and the canonisation of one hundred and two saints in China on 1 October 2000.

On the other hand, the Vatican also faces its own administrative difficulties. Inevitable personnel changes during the negotiation period (1987–2005) in the Propaganda Fides (The Department of the Evangelisation of Peoples) and the Council the States of the Vatican have reduced the Church's capacity to understand and deal with China. Also, the roman Curia has shifted its attention to its new relations with Eastern Europe and Russia.[43] The push towards rapprochement with China, with visible effort at the time of the meeting between Zhao Ziyang and Cardinal Sin in 1987, has faded. Changes in Hong Kong and Taiwan have added further new issues and dimensions to the Sino-Vatican negotiation.[44]

However, China is facing a tremendous socio-political problem which is aggravated by corruption. The real social picture in China was not as rosy as we expected when the gap between the rich and poor is the widest in the whole world. When a dissent writer spoke about creative writing in China, she revealed that the Party's Secretary General Hu Jintao has screwed up the ideological control in literary field.[45] Her criticism was proved to be valid when foreign reporters are continuously receiving news on the suppression of Uighurs in Xinjiang in the name of campaign against anti-terrorism.[46] Arrest of prominent underground Protestant leaders with raiding of the family churches have been taken place.[47] Leading intellectuals including Liu Xiaobo, were arrested. They were well known to the international community as political activists who request freedom of expression. The arrest aimed at silencing liberal voice on political reform. [48] In big cities like Shanghai, the surveillance on mobile phones, internet and E-mail communication to detect cyber dissents has been taken place.[49] State order was given to mass media to ban news reports on farmland seizures, and worker protests. Then news editors were instructed not to report on outspoken intellectuals who did not have the same voice with the party/government.[50] The internal control on the Catholic Church has been going on more intensively. In some places, church projects initiated by bridging endeavour were thwarted by local religious officials.[51] These issues of repression of dissents were taken place between July and December 2004 after Hu Jintao has firmly held the grip of power in China. Recently, internationally well known reporter of the Strait Times (Singapore) Ching Cheong, a Hong Kong SAR citizen was detained and sentenced as a spy[52]. It is also a warning to dissents in HKSAR. Hu also gave a footnote to his conservatism expressed in repression and suppression by saying that he was not prepared to allow democracy in China.

Traditionally religion has been a catalyst in a social movement, because it is capable to provide a frame to collect people from all directions to agitate for their demands The Yellow Turban Revolt in Han Dynasty, the Taiping Revolution in the Qing dynasty, the role of the Christian Churches in the collapse of European Communism 1989[53] and the rise of Falungong 1995.[54] proved that religion had its "framing" role to play for the success of a social change. All these religion - related movements inflicted a big challenge to the rule in China and in the Communist Europe. When seeds of social unrest are growing in the Chinese society, Jiang and Hu have valid reasons to keep the Chinese society abreast from religion for fear a frame might be provided for people to organise themselves to agitate for more freedom and democracy.[55]

The Party/state control in ideological issues in China forms a sharp contrast to the excessive economic openness in market economy. On the other hand the development of the Party's response to the Falungong is a yardstick to measure the Party's tolerance on religion. Aiming at drawing people away from the

Falungong, and mobilising some kind of "faith" to stabilise the society, more tolerance should be expanded to world religions, including Catholicism. A Sino-Vatican rapprochement with tolerance and concession would be a possible means to resolve religious questions internally.

Externally, Sino-Vatican reconciliation will boost China's image in the international community. Neither the Vatican nor China can any longer ignore the other's existence. Their representatives meet each face to face on many occasions in the international arena. Beijing being an ascending power, should acquire more confidence to deal with Catholicism with tolerance and accommodation.

The Bridging Endeavour and Its Shift of Gravity

Since 1984, with the suggestion of Pope John Paul II, a bridging endeavour with mainly on informal contacts between the overseas Chinese Catholics and the local church of China has been built aiming at assisting the revival of the Chinese Catholic Church.[56] The launch of the bridging enterprises coincided with the launching of the economic reform as the major part of Deng Xiaoping's modernisation programme in 1979. The Chinese Communist Party (CPC) is inevitably challenged by the ideological crisis, the by-product of China's openness, as a result of the spread of religion. CPC perceives that the revival of Catholic Church did not go along with the current religious policy of the Deng-Jiang Era which aims at eliminating the influence of religion in the socialist regime.[57]

The bridging endeavour mainly focused on supporting churches, training of church personnel and Catholic laity, sending religious literature and teachers, and giving financial aids for church operation and church related social service projects. The assistance, which is extended both to the official and unofficial sectors of the Church, has been playing a crucial role for the revival of Catholicism in China in the last two decades.

The actual extent of the revival and development of the Chinese Church are reflected in the following basic statistics. Religious activities were propagating very rapidly. In 1983 there were 300 Catholic Church buildings in China, by 1987 the number to have increased to 2,100, by 1992 to 3,900, by 1997, 5000, and 5,400 in 2004. The number of Catholic adherents was estimated to have risen from 3.3 million in 1986 to over 10 millions in 1992, and 12 millions in 2004 (including both the official and underground sectors). In 1997 there were 1,500 Catholic priests, the number increased to 2,200 in 2004, among them three quarters were ordained in the last twelve years.[58]

In the same year of 1998, it was recorded that in the official sector there was one national seminary, six regional seminaries and seven provincial seminaries and ten diocesan seminaries with 1,000 major seminarians and 600 minor seminarians under training. There were ten training centres for the underground sector with 800 seminarians (major and minor) under training. There were forty novitiates for religious sisters with 1,500 sisters under training in the official sector while twenty in the underground sector for the training of 1,000 sisters.[59] In 2004, there were 1,000 candidates in nineteen seminaries and five pre-seminaries while there were 800 in the ten underground seminaries. [60] In 2004, there were 3,300 sisters with forty convents in the open sector and 1,600 in twenty convents in the underground sector of the Chinese church (most of them are of the age under twenty five).[61]

The great expansion of the Catholic Church was the result of the effort of the bridging endeavours which has been donating huge amount of money in nation-wide building and restoring of churches both in rural and urban settings in responding to the needs of local Catholics who desperately need places of worship and pastoral care.

Due to geographic proximity, Hong Kong was the first one to start the bridging endeavour in 1978 before the Holy Father requested the cementing the local church in China with the universal church in 1984, then the church in Taiwan and Macau joined in. Hong Kong's efficient and effective communication attracts overseas bridge workers for meetings and for exchange of views. It gains a leading position in the bridging enterprise.

The launch out of the bridging enterprises coincided with the launching out of "openness" in socio-economic policies in the modernisation programme of Deng Xiaoping since 1979. When the Communist ideological crisis encountered the spread of religion, the Communist Party perceives that the revival of Catholic Church did not go along with the current religious policy of Deng-Jiang era which aims at eliminating the growth of religion in the socialist era.[62]

However, shortly before Hong Kong was transferred to the Chinese rule, Beijing gave it a signal that the bridging endeavour of Hong Kong should come to an end after July 1997.[63] Twelve months before Hong Kong's reversion to China, Ye Xiaowen, the head of Religious Affair Bureau, the State Council of China visited Hong Kong and indirectly warned Hong Kong Catholics that since mainland did not make Hong Kong conform to the Mainland's religious policy nor should Hong Kong Catholic attempt to transplant its religious practice to the Mainland. He frankly reminded the Hong Kong Catholics that after the transfer to Chinese rule in 1997 they should observe the principles of "mutual non-subordination, mutual non-interference and mutual respect" as stipulated in Art. 148, Basic Law of Hong Kong the Special Administrative Region of PRC.[64] This was the first indication from PRC to HKSAR to refrain from the bridging endeavour.

After the transfer of Hong Kong to Chinese rule, Bishop Joseph Zen, the Coadjutor Bishop of Hong Kong who had taught in the Mainland seminaries for the last ten years, were politely but firmly refused to visit Chinese seminaries in February 1998.[65] In October 1998, he was summoned to meet Ye Xiaowen, the head of Religious Affairs Bureau, in Shenzhen, the adjusting city of Hong Kong, for a private meeting. In the meeting, Ye warned Zen that Beijing was not holding a positive attitude towards Hong Kong's bridging endeavour.[66] This second indication was clearer than before by directly requesting Hong Kong to withdraw from the bridging endeavour. However, it seemed that the Hong Kong Catholics' bridging endeavour has been carrying on all the same when most Hong Kong Catholics did not take the warning of Beijing seriously. The recent development in Hong Kong Catholic Church and its relationship with the local government as well as its relations with Beijing under its new leadership, Bishop Joseph Zen Ze Kiun inflicts a negative implication on its role in the Bridging Enterprise. The result was restrictions imposed on Hong Kong Catholics became more severe compared with the bridging endeavour of Taiwan.

During the last two decades, the programmes of Bridging Endeavour of Hong Kong, Taiwan and Macau reflect the characteristics of individual churches. For example Hong Kong Church in the last two decades spent a large chunk of resource in training of its laity, so its laity engages in the formation programme in China, when the Bridging programmes in Macau and Taiwan have been mostly conducted by priests and sisters. When the size of Macau is so small that most of the projects have been small in size and its bishop yielded to the demand to Beijing and remarked that the bridging endeavour of Macau would be at the invitation from China only.[67] In Taiwan when most priests and sisters have links with their own hometowns in the Mainland, so it is easy for them to penetrate into the underground sector of the Chinese Church and offer assistance to them. Many religious orders in Taiwan even recruited candidates for their own congregation and were able to export them to abroad for training when the training environment in China is never satisfactory.[68] The contacts of the underground Catholics are not so common for the Hong Kong Bridging personnel compared with its counterparts in Taiwan. It is mainly because most of Hong Kong Catholics are Cantonese speaking and they could not penetrate to interior provinces so easily as Taiwan bridging personnel who are able to speak Putonghua, and their roots of cultural heritage go back to their own home provinces in the Mainland.

The Hong Kong Bridging programme increasingly received stricter control by the Mainland for various reasons. Firstly, the bridging endeavour does not all go along with the state/Party policy. China could not do anything when Hong Kong was under the British rule. Now Hong Kong has been in the process of amalgamating into China, subsequently the bridging endeavour is experiencing an increasingly hardship than before.

Discussion I:
The Unequal Triangle – The Vatican, Beijing and Taipei

As early as in the Maoist Era, the Vatican expressed its wish to overture Beijing when its concern has gone to the four million persecuted Chinese Catholics in a vast territory. The normalisation of the Sino-Vatican relations in the Post Maoist China is expected to result a warmer political environment for the normal growth of the Chinese Catholic Church who's twelve million Catholics. [69] According to the Lost Sheep Theory of the Bible, between Taiwan and China, Vatican regarded China with its persecuted church needed more attention and help.[70] The one lost sheep needs more care and attention in China than those ninety-nine who are safe in the pasture of the Taiwan Island enjoying reasonably high degree of religious freedom.

Then Hong Kong factor and Taiwan factor are in Vatican's considerations on its relations with China. Not only Hong Kong diocese is very important in the eye of the Vatican, but also its record in the bridging endeavor and its pastoral work are highly appreciated by the Vatican.[71] Some Chinese Catholic communities in major cities like Vancouver, Toronto, Sydney, Melbourne, New York, San Francisco and London are exemplary to local Catholic communities with their pillars coming from Hong Kong Catholic circles. Hong Kong Catholics migrated to these English speaking cities in the last few decades with their religious training from their Hong Kong Church, exercise their pastoral service among their fellow Chinese Catholics with minimal priestly assistance. A Vatican official also remarked that the volume of Catholic activities in one single Hong Kong diocese is equivalent to that of seven dioceses in Taiwan.[72] This Vatican official also noticed that the stagnation of the Catholic growth in Taiwan since in 1960s and the marginalisation of the Catholic Church since the 1970s during the island's economic boom. In short, according to the Vatican, Hong Kong Catholic Church has been more active than that of Taiwan, when the Catholic population in Hong Kong is eight percent and in Taiwan there is less than one percent. It would be natural for the

Vatican to take Hong Kong factor more seriously than that of Taiwan on the negotiation table with China.

Bishop Joseph Zen of Hong Kong not only did not dance with the government's tone as his counterpart bishops in the Mainland China, but also supported Hong Kong political dissents who request more freedom and human rights.[73] So Beijing suggested to the Vatican of Zen's removal from Hong Kong in exchange for the reopening of the Sino-Vatican negotiation as the removal of Joseph Zen would be a possible means to intimidate Hong Kong's pro-democrats. On the other hand, Zen is preparing to be taken to Rome and to be promoted as an archbishop without hooking into a diocese. However the removal has not happened; apparently the Vatican has its own considerations on Hong Kong rather than Taiwan in the context of the Sino-Vatican relations. In the Vatican's consideration on its relations with Beijing, Hong Kong factor has a stronger position than Taiwan factor. With Bao Zhong He's marriage scenario in the triangular relations among Vatican, Beijing and Taipei, Taiwan will be left out when the Vatican decided to "marry" with Beijing at its own time.[74]

Discussion II:
Taiwan's Changing Policy towards the Vatican

Above all, according to the Vatican, the breaking up of the Taiwan-Vatican diplomatic relationship would be called the change of the Taiwan-Vatican relationship from a diplomatic nature to religious nature. However, the Taiwanese church leaders did not quite follow the logic of the Vatican. When they have been closely allied with the KMT leaders since their arrival at Taiwan in the 1950s, they are torn in between in the breaking up of the Taiwan-Vatican relationship. It would be natural that they would serve as a channel for the Taipei's officials to lobby the Vatican to strengthen the precarious Taiwan-Vatican relations. The sensitive reactions of Taiwan on the Vatican's overturing Beijing aroused some degree of Vatican's resentment when ROC becomes the stumping block of the normalisation of the Sino-Vatican diplomatic relationship.[75]

The Chinese ambassador to the Vatican Raymond R.M. Tai (1996–2003) began to turn the tide. On private conversations and public occasions, he praised the objectives of Vatican's foreign relation for peace. He expressed his wish that it would be for the interest of the Chinese people, if Beijing and Taipei could start a dialogue on peace. Given the Vatican's overture to Beijing, he did not take it negatively as a zero-sum game, but he wishes to turn it into a win-win solution when he expressed that he would be delighted to see the dialogue between Beijing and Vatican would taken place to facilitate religious freedom in the Mainland. He reiterated that only if China embraces democracy, religious freedom could be ensured. He expressed that Taiwan is ready to cooperate with the Vatican to facilitate religious freedom in China.[76] Indeed, Raymond Tai's new approach is innovative. Although his statement would not alter the path of the development Sino-Vatican relations, however, his response to the inevitable situation is an act to preserve the dignity and self-esteem of Taiwan and enhance the international presence of Taiwan once the Sino-Vatican diplomatic relation is formulated.

Conclusions

The Sino-Vatican diplomatic relationship which was established in 1942 was ruptured with the expulsion of the Papal Nuncio Archbishop Riberi in 1951 from Nanjing. However, the bilateral relation resolved into triangular relations with the re-establishment of the Papal Nunciature in Taipei (1952) and Vatican has been harbouring the idea to overture Beijing leading to a concordat to save the persecuted Catholics in China. In spite of the fact that the downgrading of the diplomatic rank of the Vatican to Taiwan as the Charge d'Affaire, the Taipei treasures the relationship with the Vatican and keeps the ambassador rank to the Vatican all the same. However, Taiwan-Vatican diplomatic relation has been under a constant threat from Beijing which demands the break up of the

Taiwan-Vatican diplomatic relation as a condition for the Sino-Vatican rapprochement.

Both the Vatican and Beijing have different objectives in the Sino-Vatican negotiation. For Beijing, it is to sever the Taiwan-Vatican diplomatic relation as a means to further isolate Taiwan from the international arena. Vatican is the only European state which has diplomatic relations with Taiwan whose capacity in diplomatic interaction has been shrinking. The main motive for Vatican to negotiate with Beijing is to acquire a better political environment for the development of the budding of the Chinese Catholic Church after the formulation of a Sino-Vatican Concordat.

Old problems of negotiation have not been resolved, new difficulties were added to the negotiation when Vatican refused to accept Beijing's requests to transfer the church administration to civil authority and the method of appointing bishops.

Hong Kong factor and Taiwan factor are in Vatican's considerations about its relations with China. Taiwan cannot compare with Hong Kong in its religious development, when Hong Kong diocese not only has been most active among all Chinese dioceses round the world, but also its record in the bridging endeavour and its pastoral work are highly appreciated by the Vatican. However, Vatican has to consider that Taiwan has to take more shares in the bridging endeavour in days to come when Hong Kong SAR is more and more under the surveillance of Beijing which squeezes the Hong Kong Catholics to put a brake to its endeavour to assist the Chinese church.

In the triangle representing Vatican, China and Taiwan, all sides are unequal. Apparently Taiwan is on the weakest side. Once the "marriage" between Vatican and China will be take place, Taiwan would be left out mercilessly. Taiwan's new policy towards the Vatican by enhancing the religious relations with the Vatican is seen as a good strategy to preserve Taiwan's dignity and self-esteem vis-à-vis the inevitability. However, how to enhance Taiwan's religious relations with the Vatican to replace the diplomatic relations would be a good topic for further research.

Notes and References

1. The Secretariat of the Chinese Regional Bishops Conference (ed.), *Catholic Directory: Taiwan, Republic of China* (Taipei: The Secretariat of the Chinese Regional Bishops Conference,1997), p. 45–47.

2. Gianni Criveller, "China, the Holy See and France: The Giuanelli mission to the Chinese emperor and its aftermath (1885–1886)," in Angelo Lazzarotto et. al., *The Boxer Movement and Christianity in China* (Taipei: Fu Jen University Press, 2004) pp. 43–94.

3. Chen Fengzhong and Jiang Guoxiong, *Zhongfan Waijiao Guanxishi* (*History of the Sino-Vatican Diplomatic Relation*) (Taiwan: Commercial Press, 2003), pp. 25–30.

4. Chen Fengzhong and Jiang Guoxiong. *Zhongfan Waijiao Guanxishi* (*History of the Sino-Vatican Diplomatic Relation*)., pp. 25–30.

5. Beatrice Leung, "Sino-Vatican relations at the century's turn," *Journal of Contemporary China* (May 2005) vol. 14(43), pp. 353–370.

6. Michele Dillon, *Catholic Identity: Balancing Reason, Faith and Power* (Cambridge: Cambridge University Press, 1999); Eric Hanson, 1987. *Catholic Church and World Politics* (New Jersey: Princeton University Press, 1987); G. Moyer (ed.), 1990. *Politics and Religion in the Modern World* (London: Routlege, 1990); Robins & Robertson, *Church-State Relations: Tension and Transition* (Oxford and New Brunswick: Transaction Books, 1987).

7. Eric Hanson, *Catholic Politics in China and Korea* (New York: Orbis Books, 1980); H. Stchle, *Eastern politics of the Vatican 1917–1979.* Tran. S. Smith (Ohio: Ohio State University Press, 1987); Beatrice Leung, 1992 *Sino-Vatican Relations Problems of conflicting Authority (1976–1986)* (Cambridge: Cambridge University Press, 1992); Neils Nielsen, 1991. *Revolution in Eastern Europe: The Religious Roots* (New York: Orbis Books, 1991); George Weigel, *The Final Revolution: The Resistance Church and Collapse of Communism* (New York: Oxford University Press, 1992); Leo F. Goodstadt, "Politics and economic modernisation in 21st century Asia: potential conflict and their management" in Beatrice Leung (ed.,) *Church and State Relations in 21st Century Asia* (Hong Kong: Centre of Asian Studies, University of Hong Kong, 1996); Pedro Ramet and Sabrina Ramet (eds.), 1993 *Religious Policy in the Soviet Union* (Cambridge: Cambridge University Press, 1993); Pedro Ramet and Sabrina Ramet (eds.), *Religion and Nationalism in Soviet and East European Politics* (Durham: Duke University Press, 1989); Donald Treadgold, *The West in Russia and China: Religious and Secular Thought in Modern Times* (Cambridge: Cambridge University Press, 1973).

8. Pedro Ramet and Sabrina Ramet, 1990 *Catholicism and Politics in Communist Societies* (Durham, N.C.: Duke University Press, 1990);

Adam Michnik (ed.), *The Church and the Left*. Trans.b y David Ost (Chicago: Chicago University Press, 1993); Szajkowski Bogdan, *Next to God – Poland; Politics and Religion in Contemporary Poland* (New York: St. Martin's, 1983).

9. Chan Kim Kwong, *Towards a Contextual Ecclesiology: The Catholic Church in the People's Republic of China, 1979–1983: Its Life and Theological Implications* (Hong Kong: Phototech, 1987); Beatrice Leung, *Sino-Vatican Relations Problems of Conflicting Authority, 1976–1986* (Cambridge: Cambridge University Press, 1992); Wiest, Jean Paul and Edmond Tang (eds.), *The Catholic Church in Modern China: Perspectives*. (New York: Orbis Book, 1993).

10. Philip Selznick, *The Organizational Weapon: A Study of Bolshevik Strategy and Tactics* (Illinois: Free Press, 1960).

11. Bao Zhong He, "Janlou sanjiao jiaose zhuanbian yu leixing bianhua fengshi" ("Strategic triangle: the analysis of its role and form") in Bao Zhong He and Wu Yu Shan (eds.), *Centending Approaches to Cross Strait Relations* (Taipei: Wunan (2nd ed.), 2000), pp. 337–364.

12. Chen Fengzhong and Jiang Guoxiong, *Zhongfan Waijiao Guanxishi* (*History of the Sino-Vatican Diplomatic Relation*), pp. 27–30.

13. The Secretariat of the Chinese Regional Bishops Conference (ed.), *Catholic Directory: Taiwan, Republic of China*. p. 19.

14. *Ibid.*

15. *Ibid.*

16. Guo Wenban, *Taiwan de Tianjiujiao de Zhengjiao Guanxi* (*The Church and State Relations of Taiwan's Catholic Church*) *A Research Report of National Science Council*. Series No. NSC87-2412-H005A-004, p. 8.; Zhang Chuanzheng, *A Study of Everyday Life of Catholic Clergy in Taiwan 1950–1960*. M. Ph. Thesis, (Taiwan: Xisin University, 2003), p. 4.

17. Fu Jen Catholic University was a joint enterprise designed by Archbishop Yu Ping with the corporation of several religious societies that included the Society of Divine Word and the Society of Jesus. Then administration and teaching staff involved the Dominican Fathers and others which were almost all previously missionaries on the mainland before 1949.

18. Guo Wenban, *Taiwan de Tianjiujiao de Zhengjiao Guanxi* (*The Church and State Relations of Taiwan's Catholic Church*).

19. Kuo Wenban, *Taiwan Tianjujiao de Zhenjiao Guangxi* (*The Church-state Relations of Taiwan Catholic church*), Research Report of National Science Council, Taiwan, No. NSC87-2412-H005A-004.

20. Zhang Chuanzheng, *A Study of Everyday Life of Catholic Clergy in Taiwan 1950–1960*.

21. Chiu Hai Yuan, *Taiwan Zhongjiao Banqain de Xuewei Fenxi (The Socio-Political Analysis of the Change of Religious phenomena in Taiwan)* (Taipei: Kwaikwan 1997), pp. 209–46.

22. This was revealed by Raymond Tai Ruiming, the former Taiwan ambassador to the Holy See, when he was interviewed on 24 December 2004.

23. Chen Fengzhong and Jiang Guoxiong, *Zhongfan Waijiao Guanxishi (History of the Sino-Vatican Diplomatic Relation)*, pp. 27–30.

24. Beatrice Leung "The Sino-Vatican negotiations: old problems in a new context," *The China Quarterly*, no. 153 (March 1998), pp. 128–140.

25. Beatrice Leung, "Sino-Vatican relations at century's turn," *The Journal of Contemporary China*, (USA) *Journal of contemporary China.* (May 2005), 14(43), pp. 353–370.

26. *Ibid.*

27. It was revealed by Raymond Tai Ruiming, the former Taiwan ambassador to the Vatican, when he was interviewed in December 2004.

28. Kuo Wenban, *Taiwan Tianjujiao de Zhenjiao Guangxi (The Church-state Relations of Taiwan Catholic Church)*, Research Report of National Science Council, Taiwan, No. NSC87-2412-H005A-004, pp. 5-10.

29. Zhang Chuanzheng. *A Study of Everyday Life of Catholic Clergy in Taiwan 1950s–1960s*, pp. 27–34.

30. *Ibid.*

31. *Ibid.*

32. Human Right Group of Catholic Laity (ed.), *Behind the Veil of the News Story Related with Fr. Neil Magill SSC.* (Taiwan: Kwongchi Press, 1989).

33. *Ibid.*

34. On the brief history of the Presbyterian Church in Taiwan, http://www.ces.org.tw/main/mission/activity/article18.htm..

35. Chiu Hai Yuan, *Taiwan Zhongjiao Banqain de Xuewei Fenxi (The Socio-Political Analysis of the Change of Religious phenomena in Taiwan)* (Taipei: Kwaiguan, 1997, pp. 209–46).

36. Joseph Cheng and Camoes C.K. Tam, "The Taiwan presidential election and its implication for cross straits relations: a political cleavage perspective," *Asian Affairs, An American Review* (Spring 2005) vol. 32.1, pp. 3–24.

37. "Chongbai Yesu Shengti Guanhuai Shehui Dazhong" ("Adore the body of Christ and concern about the society," A pastoral letter of Chinese regional bishops' conference headed by Cardinal Paul Shan, 5 August 2005.

38. One of the authors, Beatrice Leung got this impression after she had an open dialogue with Rev. Huang Bohe, the Presbyterian theologian, a leader of the Pro-DDP, in a church-state relations conference held by Chang Jung Christian University in November 2004.

39. It was informed by a priest who was the architect of Chen's visit.

40. Francesco Sisci, "China, Catholic Church at a Crossroads," *Asia Times.* April 12, 2005.

41. Beatrice Leung, "China's religious freedom policy: an art of managing religious activity," *The China Quarterly,* No. 184, (December 2005), pp. 894–913.

42. Can. 333: Roamanus Pontifex, vi sui mueris, non modo in universam Ecclesiam potestate gaudet, sed et super omnes Ecclesias particulares earumque coetus ordinariae potestatis obtinet principatum . . . *Codex Iuris Canonici* (Typis Polyglottis Vaticanis, 1983).

43. Beatrice Leung, "Sino-Vatican relations at century's turn."

44. Beatrice Leung and Marcus J.J. Wang. "Hong Kong factor in the Sino-Vatican relations." (Manuscript for a book chapter. The book will be published in Hanover, Germany in 2007).

45. Zhang Yihe the dissent writer made this remark when she visited Taiwan in December 2004. See: *United Daily News* (Taiwan), 11 December 2004. TMP01.

46. *Financial Times,* 7 July 2004; *Agence France Presse-Asia.* 2 November 2004.

47. *Agence France Presse-Asia,* 12 December 2004.

48. *New York Times,* December 2004 Section A. p.10.

49. Associated Press News, 2 July, 2004.

50. *BBC Monitoring World Media,* 7 October 2004.

51. A Laity Formation programme from Hong Kong Catholic laity which was expected to be delivered in Chongqing was thwarted by the government.

52. *South China Morning Post,* 8, 9, 10 August 2005.

53. George Weigel, *The Final Revolution: The Resistance Church and Collapse of Communism* (New York: Oxford University Press, 1992).

54. Patricia M.Thornton, "Framing dissent in contemporary China: irony, ambiguity and metonymy," *The China Quarterly* no. 171, (September 2002), pp. 661.

55. It was revealed by Raymond Tai Ruiming when he was interviewed by one of the authors on 24 December 2004.

56. Pope John Paul II in February 1984 made this request when he received Taiwan bishops who made their "ad liminia" visit to the Holy See. For

details see Beatrice Leung, *Sino-Vatican Relations: Problems of Conflicting Authority 1976–1986* (Cambridge: Cambridge University Press, 1992), pp. 189–256

57. Ye Xiaowen, "Danqian de zongjiao wenti" ("The contemporary religious questions of the motherland") in *Zhonggong zhongyang dangxiao baogao xuan* (Selected Reports of the Party Central School) vol. 101, no. 5 (1996), pp.9–23 (internally circulated document). Ye Xiaowen is the current director of the Religious Affairs Bureau, the Council of the State, China.

58. "A chronology of the Catholic church in China in the context of selected dates in world and Chinese history," *Tripod*. Vol. XIII no. 76 (July–August 1993), pp. 19–76. China Catholic Communication, 1993 *Guide to the Catholic Church in China 1993* (Singapore, 1993), pp. 10–8. China Catholic Communication, *Guide to the Catholic Church in China 1997* (Singapore, 1997) pp. 10–8. China Catholic Communication, *Guide to the Catholic Church in China 2000* (Singapore, 2000) pp. 8–14, 18–20. China Catholic Communication. 2004 *Guide to the Catholic Church in China 2004* (Singapore, 2004), pp. 18–20.

59. *Ibid*.

60. *Ibid*. pp. 18–20.

61. *Ibid*.

62. Ye Xiaowen, "Danqian de zongjiao wenti" ("The contemporary religious questions of the motherland.")

63. The first author of this article jointed the Precious Blood Sisters of Hong Kong to make a visit to China in December 1996. She was informed on informal occasions by the deputy head of the Catholic Patriotic Association, Lui Bailien who conveyed her this message. Then on other occasions Catholics in Hong Kong also received the same message that the Hong Kong government wanted the Bridging Endeavour not be carried on after Hong Kong's handover.

64. *Sunday Examiner* (Hong Kong Catholic Weekly), 5 July 1996; *Yi: China Message*, Vol XV–XVII no. 6 (August 1996), pp.12–3.

65. The details of the issue was reported by Bishop Joseph Zen when he met the author in November 1998.

66. The meeting was informed by Bishop Joseph Zen to the author in November 1998.

67. 張士江 "澳門回歸之前訪林家駿主教" 《中國宗教》，總第 18 期，1999 年秋季號，頁 25-6.

68. In Manila a formation institute has been established for religious women training in which more than 50 novices of various congregations are under training. The recruits are mostly from the underground sector of the Chinese Church. This institute is closely related to Taiwan and has

nothing to do with Hong Kong and Macau. An expert in spirituality in Taiwan stationed there for the sister formation.

69. The government sponsored sector can be named as the open church while the non-government sponsored sector is the sector of Catholics who refuse to be manipulated by the government so that their activities are clandestine. It can be called the underground church.

70. Luke15:1–7.

71. It was revealed by an anonymous Vatican official in an interview in May 2004.

72. This message was expressed by Cardinal Cassidy, a retired Vatican official who had served the Vatican on Far East affairs for many years including some years in Taiwan serving as the Papal Pro-nuncio in Taiwan (1970–1971).

73. Beatrice Leung and Marcus J.J. Wang, "The Hong Kong factor in the Sino-Vatican relations. (Manuscript for a book chapter. The book will be published in Hanover, Germany).

74. Bao Zhong He. "Janlou sanjiao jiaose zhuanbian yu Leixing Bianhua Fengshi ("Strategic Triangle: The analysis of its role and form"), pp. 337–364.

75. It was revealed by a researcher who is close to the inner circle of the Vatican in an interview in November 2000.

76. It was revealed by Raymond Tai Ruiming to Beatrice Leung, when Tai was interviewed on 24 December 2004.

19

The Impact of Globalisation on the Educational Developments in China: Policy and Challenges

David CHAN

Introduction

For more than half a century, the People's Republic of China has been making great strides in developing an advanced educational system, in terms of both equity and quality, at all levels from pre-school to post-graduate education. During the early period of its nation-building, the Chinese educational authority, for various political reasons, cut off its link to the Western world and turned towards the former Soviet Union for its model of education. However, with China's adoption of its open door policy since 1978, its education has begun, once again, to be drawn closer to the Western world. With over two decades of its economic development, China has now become a major world force and is approaching to become the locus of the region. In the new century, China, as a new member of the World Trade Organisation (WTO), is keen to come into the arms of the world market and to further develop its education in order to deal with the new challenges of its political, social and economic developments. Since the new leaders, Hu Jintao and Wen Jiabao, have come into authority, China has undergone a series of educational reforms, which are given the tasks of facilitating and supporting economic growth and development of the country. As an extension and renewal of the economic reforms in the late 1990s, the educational reforms at the turn of the new century have also undergone major changes.

Over the last quarter century, the market-oriented economic reforms have contributed greatly to China's educational development. The sharp differentials and regional disparities that have existed among provinces and regions, between urban and rural areas, and within social classes, have become major social concerns for many decision-makers, policy-makers and researchers. Therefore, the new focus for its various social policies (including that on education) of the new government, as headed by Hu and Wen, is to ameliorate those gaps in order to assure that the benefits of the country's economic successes can be shared more equitably within the nation.

It was back in the year 2000 that Hu Jintao called on the cadres to have cool-headed assessments of China's harsh realities, and laid down two principles for them to follow, namely: the first one is that "we must ask leading cadres to arm their brains with scientific theory" by following the "scientific" path; while the second one is to ask cadres to break new grounds in reform by "grasping new opportunities, face new challenges, create new superior conditions, and realise new developments". Similarly, Wen Jiabao, in addressing an international investors' forum in 2001, mentioned that China must "enthusiastically" take part in globalisation by saying that "we must grasp the trends of global international development, take firm hold of the opportunities, and boldly accept challenges." This kind of new thinking has thus provided important underpinnings, upon which the main thrust has now been put on towards the development of a world-class education system for the 21st century in order to serve the country's long-term interests.

With the impact of globalisation, together with the rise of the knowledge-based economy, there will be a very keen competition among nation-states on the front of the global labour market. This will demand a whole new breed of human capital for manpower training: the rise of "knowledge creators" and "knowledge workers" in a network society in order to create new knowledge, which is now seen as a new kind of capital and wealth (the idea of "intellectual property") for further economic growth. Thus, the kind of institutions that need to cater for such kind of demands are the universities and research institutes, which will try to nurture this new breed of "knowledge workers" at the undergraduate level, while post-graduate education will try to breed this new kind of "knowledge creators" to advance knowledge for further economic growth.

In order to be able to compete globally in the labour market, various nation-states will need to establish their own "world-class universities", according to international benchmarks, in order to find a niche and get a stronghold and a firm footing for their competition in this global labour market. With the accession of China into the World Trade Organisation (WTO), China is now putting a great effort into developing its own "world-class universities" in order to build a firm foundation for its further growth and development, as well as to become more globally competitive in the 21st Century.

This chapter tries to examine the impact of globalisation on the recent educational developments and reforms in China by reflecting upon its global relevance in the globalisation agenda and discourse. There are five sections to this chapter. The first section provides an overview of the managerial and economic dimensions of globalisation. The second section provides the policy agenda of education by describing and examining the development of education since the implementation of economic reforms in 1978. The third section describes the recent reforms and development of policy on the various levels of primary, junior secondary and senior secondary education. The fourth section elaborates on the most recent developments of higher education, concerning its quantitative expansion and qualitative enhancement. Both Project 211 and Project 985, together with the strategy of massification of higher educational development are the main focus of this section. The final section sums up this chapter by concluding that there is a transformation of the state capacity in a new state-education relationship under the impact of globalisation.

Global Context of Education Reforms
under the Impact of Globalisation

Globalisation is an important concept to the development of education in this globalised world. Although the comprehensive concept of globalisation is far from clear and well defined, the changes brought by the global trend are obvious but complex and varied. As a tidal wide of development, globalisation provides a broad base for discussion and analysis on the different arenas of human activities. Various perspectives within the global context will bring about many facets and diverse images of globalisation within current literatures. Nevertheless, generally speaking, the concept of globalisation indicates that the various changes over the interconnected globe are creating new forms of interdependencies among actors, institutions and states.[1] This chapter will mainly emphasise on the two main dimensions of globalisation, namely: managerial globalisation and economic globalisation.

The managerial dimension of globalisation mainly focuses on the new extent of state capacity as well as governance framework within the global context. As a globalizing practice, managerial ideologies are widely adopted throughout the world.[2] Such concepts and ideas emphasise on the participation of non-state actors in the management and delivery of public services, as the nation-state is no longer the sole provider of public services. In association with the rise of the "New Public Management" (NPM) and managerialism within the tide of public sector reforms, nation-states have been undergoing a structural readjustment through the deregulation of legal and financial controls, the opening of markets and quasi-markets, the increasing notion of competition and the receding role of the nation-state in the globalisation discourse.[3] In the progress of this transformation and innovation of governance structure, practices and ideas in the private sector are introduced to modify and/or even replace the old rules and customs in the public sphere. The most significant instance of this change has been the emphasis on the "3Es" of "economy, efficiency and effectiveness" with a general goal of continual increase of productivity.[4]

In the educational sector, managerialism is upheld by adopting the policies of decentralisation, marketisation, privatisation and corporatisation. These policies can be reflected by the call for "the running of education is like the running of a business" which requires educational institutions to be more efficient and effective in decision-making and in response to the various changes of global challenge.[5] In this context, the "consumer ethos" is promoted as a commitment to the market-oriented provision of services in the ethics of educational governance. This is because both schools and universities have to face the reality of government cutback in funding for education. The original responsibility of educational provisions that used to be shouldered solely by the government is now being shared and delivered by other non-state sectors through various means, such as the adoption of the user-pay principle, the introduction of the private sector in educational provisions, and the mobilisation of social donations, among others.

As a result, educational institutions have to face up to the public request for showing maximum outputs from the resources and inputs given to them from both the government and the community at large. In this regard, various sorts of accountability practices (such as quality assurance mechanism) have become important indicators for the justification on the spending of public resources, particularly in the circumstance of financial stringency and during the process of the massification of higher education.[6] In response to the increased pressure of adopting managerial ideologies, there is a tendency to strengthen executive leadership or to centralise certain aspects of decision making within educational governance framework.[7] Without affecting the autonomous role of academics, senior administrators of educational institutions are more likely to transform their role into managers and chief executive officers who can behave more proactively in facing challenges, exercise more discretionary power in financial arrangements and decision-making process, and enjoy more freedom to innovate their organisations.[8] As a consequence, managerial accountability now begins to replace the traditional type of professional accountability that used to be exercised in the educational sector.[9] It is in this sense that the nation-state has gone through the process of "re-regulation" by strengthening the mechanisms of auditing and quality assurance (characterised by performance-based merit system), as well as the processes of marketisation, privatisation and corporatisation in order to uphold the notion of accountability, while adopting the policies of decentralisation and deregulation.

The impacts of economic globalisation on education can be generalised as a paradigm shift towards commercialisation, commodification, assimilation within the circumstance of worldwide competition and the emerging "borderless" education market.[10] It is noted that, with the rapid integration of the world economy with increasingly liberalised trade and commerce, the growth of dependency among nations, the emergence of newly-industrialised nations, the homogenisation of cultural developments, as well as the increasing importance of information driven by technological innovation, education is recognised as an important instrument for maintaining the national competitiveness in the global economy. Transnational skills or competences, such as the mastery of an international language (i.e. English), mastery of information and communications technology, as well as that of information, problem solving, creative and critical thinking, become important components to streamline society for national competition in the global economic race.[11]

Moreover, in terms of educational products, supplementary items (e.g. specialised programmes, vocational and competency-oriented training and modular course) have become more common and widely recognised, while traditional qualifications (degrees and diplomas) remain the most important products of higher education institutions (HEIs). This indicates that the demand for higher education not only grows quantitatively but also become more diverse with the increased need for "knowledge workers" in the global labour market. This explains why continuing and lifelong education, learning and training in different modes and at different levels have now become an area with a large growing capacity and there is the emergence of "diploma mills" in many developing countries. [12] In short, within the contextual background of worldwide competition, educational institutions are obliged to prioritise their economic aspects of activities above all else, including teaching and learning. Educational institutions thereby are undergoing a transformation to become a global "knowledge enterprise or industry", which primarily aims to nurture educated manpower for societal and economic needs.

Furthermore, the huge increase in the world-wide demand in higher education results in the prominence of market principles in the provisions of educational services. The emergence and making use of "borderless" higher education market is considered as a solution in solving the budgetary and capacity problems in many countries. With the opportunities created by new information and communication technologies, for-profit education providers in the developed world "take initiatives to reach out their educational provision to this international higher education market, by active recruitment of international, fee-paying students to the home institution, by establishing branch campuses or franchising and twining agreements with local institutions, or via distance education and e-learning and other transnational activities."[13] Meanwhile, due to the insufficient domestic supply but growing demand in the society, the developing world usually welcomes the foreign providers entering their educational market. This eventually leads to the processes of commercialisation, commodification and McDonaldisation of education, with higher education in particular,[14] which are characterised by the emphasis on market values, cost-effectiveness, transnational competition and trans-national assimilation.[15]

Our analysis shows that there is a paradigm shift in the education sphere. In the context of international competition in the global economy, public choice and competition are introduced in the education sector at both national and institutional levels. To combine the ideas of economic globalisation with managerialism, we thus summarise the globalizing practices in education as the dynamics in promoting cost-effectiveness and managerial accountability, decentralised authorities and responsibilities, together with an emphasis on competition, public accountability and the use of market forces.

Context and Policy Agenda of Educational Developments and Reforms in China

Prior to the economic reform of the late 1970s, the communist state developed a highly centralised education system through the adoption of the Soviet model in China's higher education. Given that education was regarded as an instrument to spread the official ideology of communism, the Soviet pattern was used to reinforce the tendencies toward the centralisation of knowledge and uniformity of thought and ideology. [16] In 1952, the Chinese government implemented a re-organisation of higher education in order to nationalise all higher educational institutions (HEIs), including all public, private and missionary universities and colleges, during the First Five-Year Plan (1953–1957). After the re-organisation, all universities and colleges became state-run institutions, which were made narrowly specialised according to the manpower planning derived from the "centrally-planned economy".[17] The administration of higher education was also based on a "centralised model", in which all the colleges and universities throughout the country were under the direct leadership of the central government in implementing the unitary instructional plans, course syllabi and textbooks. In regard to their governance, HEIs in this system were categorised into three main types:

- those under the direct administration of the Ministry of Education (MOE);
- those under the non-educational central ministries; and
- those under provincial and other local authorities.

This highly centralised education system has undergone both processes of decentralisation and marketisation since the economic reforms of the late 1970s. In its pursuit of economic development, the Chinese government realised that the centralised educational system was woefully inadequate to contribute to the new economic challenges and opportunities. Since the state alone was incapable to satisfy the increasing demands for education, structural changes in the education sector were needed. Under this kind of historical context, the Chinese authority issued the "Decision of the Central Committee of the Chinese Communist Party of China on the Reform of the Educational System" in 1985, which marked the beginning of a process of educational reform and gradually aligned the educational system with the newly-emerging "socialist market economy." The document called for the devolution of power to lower levels of government and a reduction in the rigid governmental controls over schools. To be illustrated as general policy guidelines, the 1985 reform focused on:

- linking education to economic reforms;
- implementing the nine-year compulsory education;
- decentralising educational finances and management;
- increasing vocational and technical education;
- increasing the number and quality of school teachers.[18]

Since then, the state has started to diversify educational services, allowing and encouraging the non-state sectors to establish and run educational institutions. Meanwhile, the state has deliberately devolved responsibility and power to local governments, local communities and other non-state parties by providing a necessary framework for educational development.[19]

To restate many of these policies in education reform, the Chinese authority issued the "Outline for Education Reform and Development in China" (*Outline*, hereafter) in 1993. This policy statement clearly stated that the national policy is to actively encourage and fully support social institutions and citizens to establish schools according to laws and to provide right guidelines and strengthen administration.[20] The state no longer insisted on its direct control over educational institutions, but instead upheld school management through legislation, funding, planning and advice on policies.[21] The retreat of the central state provided enough space for local levels, as well as non-state parties, to take more responsibilities for education governance activities, in terms of provision, financing and regulation. In this context, non-state parties started to provide education in the formal education sector, thereby leading to the emergence of *minban* (people-run) education.

On the basis of the *Outline*, the Ministry of Education (MOE) promulgated the "Regulations on Non-state Education in 1997 and the Non-state Education Promotion Law" in 2004 respectively, which further clarify the operational principles regarding the participation of the non-state sectors in education. For instance, both documents clearly stated that non-governmental institutions are important parts of the education system in China, and thus encouraged schools to engage in collaborations among different sectors, including public and private ones, as well as with overseas institutions. In fact, in this process of transformation, a variety of modes in the running of schools have slowly evolved. Generally speaking, there are several practices of non-state educational institutions with different degrees of state participation:

- "People-run schools with state support" (*minban gongzhu*), that is, at the initial stage, the local government provides financial or material-technical support to the school unit as it accumulates a pool of its own funds;
- A non-governmental educational institution is co-founded with either state enterprise or institution, and individuals or organisations, which invest a sum of capital (*gongban minzhu*).
- Individual or a group of individuals (*xieli ziban*) who found the schools;
- Chinese and overseas partner jointly establish non-governmental educational institutions on a shareholding basis;
- State schools or HEIs establish their non-governmental branches called "independent colleges".[22]

In 2003, there were over 70 thousand *minban* schools on different levels with over 14 million students throughout the country.[23] And the legislations in the past few years have provided a legal base for the participation of non-state parties in formal education, thus reflecting that the Chinese authority has employed a more legal and systemic strategy on the diversification of provisions in education. The involvement of non-state parties in educational provisions means the formation of a new financing system for education. With the emergence of self-financing students and non-state education providers, China's education has now undergone the process of marketisation.[24]

An Overview of Basic Education in China

The Chinese government nowadays gives a top priority to education in its policy agenda as it recognises that the provision of quality manpower is an essence for its economic development and global competitiveness in the 21st century. Currently, the government is still the major operators, providers and financiers of education at different levels, but non-governmental sectors are encouraged to participate in the running of schools. Yet, the administration of schools is based upon the governmental hierarchical structure as follows:

1) The central government exercises macro guidance over basic education. The MOE is responsible for formulating laws and regulations, policies and overall planning, and the basic elements of the education system; for establishing special funds for teacher training, and education in poor and minority areas, and for general supervision and guidance of the work of the local educational administrative departments;

2) The provincial governments are responsible for implementing basic education, including the design of development plans and teaching plans for local primary and secondary schools; the organisation of evaluation and acceptance of accomplishment of compulsory education; the establishment of educational special funds to help poor and minority areas and the provision of subsidies to counties with inadequate educational expenditure;

3) The county-level governments bear the main responsibilities for implementing compulsory education, including the overall management of educational finance, the deployment and management of school principals and teachers, and the provision of guidance to education and instruction in primary and secondary schools;

4) The township governments are mainly responsible for the implementation of compulsory education.

Overall speaking, education has been made part and parcel of the overall national plan for economic and social developments in order to assure that it fits in well with its economic development in the long run.

Since the promulgation of the "Compulsory Education Law" in 1986, the nine-years of compulsory education have been implemented. There is at least one school in each of the communities in most cities. Although universal enrolment of primary education has not yet been fully achieved, according to the statistics of 1998, the net enrolment rate of primary school age children has attained 98.9%. In fact, the Chinese government has put great efforts to primary education in the past few years. For example, regional disparity is a real problem in the development of education in China, with the Hope Project being most helpful to many poverty-stricken students in giving them opportunities to start or continue their studies in rural and mountainous areas.

Secondary education in China consists of three-years of junior secondary school (which is compulsory), plus three-years of senior secondary school. Accordingly, junior secondary education has been universalised by 73% of the national population. In many urban areas and economically developed coastal areas, the universal senior secondary education has been in progress. The compulsory education rate of China's basic education, which includes preschool education, the nine-years of compulsory education and special education, has now reached 85% of the Chinese population, thus reducing the country's rate of young and middle-aged illiterate adults to below 5% by the end of last century. By setting the year of 2010 as the future target for educational development, the Chinese government hopes to improve its basic education to that level of developed countries in the world. Apart from its quantitative growth, the Chinese government has also made improvements to the quality of its basic education.

In the past, the education system was very much examination-oriented, and had ignored the whole person development of individual students. Reforms now have been taken to pursue a more comprehensive education for all students. In the primary sector, a point-making system has now been replaced by a general grading system, in order to release the students from the pursuit of marks in examinations. Meanwhile, more teaching hours are devoted to non-academic subjects, such as sports, moral education, music, etc. In the secondary sector, the National College Entrance Examination has been reformed. Under the new examination system, students have more choices of subjects to take and, in response to the call for internationalisation, English has become an optional subjects of examination.[25]

Recent Educational Developments of Higher Education in China

As the economic reforms of the 1970s were initiated, the nation has slowly evolved into a major economic force, both regionally and world-wide. Currently, China is the world's seventh largest economy, and the second largest recipient of direct foreign investment. Given that the emergence of the "socialist market economy" represents a liberalisation of internal and external economic relationships, China has never been immune from the growing impact of globalisation, particularly when China's economy is becoming increasingly open to the global market. China's accession to the WTO can be seen as a landmark for its economic liberalisation, which helps to further boost an enormous need for human resources in order to achieve and retain rapid economic growth, which has been averaging at almost 9 to 10% per annum for the past years.

In line with the processes of marketisation and decentralisation,

China's education policy in general, and higher education in particular, has undergone several major changes during the Ninth Five-Year Plan (1996–2000).[26] Firstly, the financing of higher education has gone through a dramatic change. Presently, higher educational institutions (HEIs) are classified into different categories of status, and will accordingly receive differential funding from corresponding sources of central, provincial and local governments. Given that only about 100 HEIs are under the direct supervision of the MOE, most of the total 1,300 HEIs in the country are supervised and funded by either provincial or municipal governments. However, between 1995 and 2000, the governmental share of higher education revenue in public institutions has declined from 70% to 56%. With the continuous growth of the gross enrolment rate, it is predicted that the government is incapable to maintain this kind of proportion its educational financing. Meanwhile, the average tuition fee has increased rapidly during this period in order to help offset this shortage of funds. The decline of the government's share of education funding, as well as the dependence on institutional sources (e.g. tuition and other fees), not only have resulted in limited resources, but this also means that there needs to have some further readjustments of government funding. To achieve the aim of quality enhancement in its pursuit of the world standard, the Chinese authority upheld the targeted resource allocation by adopting special financing strategies for key universities. Secondly, structural changes have been taken place in the higher education sector, such that "comprehensive universities" were created through the merger of single disciplinary and professional HEIs. Thirdly, there was a dramatic shift from the previous kind of elite higher education towards mass higher education.

Strategy of Building World-Class Universities

The Chinese government has tactically prioritised education as one of key items in its policy agenda of national development since the 1990s. With over two decades of rich experiences in adopting reform measures, China has now accumulated a comparatively strong base in terms of finance and technology for the further development of higher education.[27] Moreover, alongside with the mega trend of integration with the global community, China is actively engaged in various sorts of international organisations and expands its participation in international collaboration and exchange for education. As part and parcel of international communication and cooperation, there is a promotion of the "internationalisation" of the Chinese higher education in order to integrate the domestic higher education sector with the world's academic and scholarly community.[28] This leads to frequent overseas studies or academic visits of academics, administrators and specialists/professionals from Chinese universities and research institutes. It is recognised that the ultimate goal of the "internationalisation" of higher education is to enhance the total quality of higher education and to boost its overall standard up to international standing. This provides a background and rationale for the strategy of building world-class universities in China.

In reviewing some of the Chinese literatures on the kind of characteristics that a world-class university is supposed to have, we can identify and generalise nine major criteria in order to define a world-class university. These are:

- Overall quality of teaching staff – the number of full-time staff, the ratio of doctoral degree holders, the number of publications, and so forth are important indicators;
- Quality of students – the entrance requirements are usually seen as a reflection of student quality. However, to be more comprehensive, students' achievements in other areas such as their contributions to community services, as well as their leadership quality are also part of this criterion;
- Number and diversity of programmes – it is realised that most top universities all over the world are "comprehensive universities" with a wide range of programmes and courses so that the students could have comprehensive knowledge and exposure in different fields of study;

- Performance in competition of research funding – top universities are usually actively engaged in many research projects and activities. In this sense, the amount of research funding gained could reflect on the level of their research activities;
- Ratio of teachers to students – universities with a long history (such as Oxford and Cambridge) keep a very low ratio of teachers to students;
- Quality and quantity of equipments and facilities – the book and serial collections of libraries, the equipments of scientific laboratories, as well as the instalment, usage of both hardware and software of computer facilities are all important indicators of this criterion;
- Financing channels – many top universities are private universities, and so their ability in soliciting private donations is crucial to their survival and development;
- Achievement and reputation of graduates and academic staff – for example, the number of Nobel Prize winners is used as one of those indicators;
- History and overall reputation of institutions – the management of university, its overall image, as well as its relationships with the government, the business and industrial sectors, as well as with the community as a whole could also be included.[29]

All these factors do not necessarily provide any solid policy initiatives for the Chinese higher education. Nevertheless, this pursuit of building world-class universities gives a higher level of platform for the development strategy of higher education in China in the 21st Century. However, there is a common understanding that China, at the present state, is not capable to enhance its overall quality of higher education up to the world standard. Instead, the government should concentrate its limited resources to develop and improve some selected HEIs to become world-class institutions. To this end, the Chinese government has issued additional funding schemes in the late 1990s.[30]

Project 211

Project 211 is the Chinese government's first endeavour in enhancing the quality of education and research in China's higher education since the 1990s. Project 211, which was first mentioned in the *Outline* of 1993, was later formally promulgated by the State Education Commission (SEC) in 1995.[31] It primarily aimed at strengthening about 100 HEIs and key disciplinary areas as a national priority for the 21st century. Generally speaking, Project 211 consists of three major components:

- Improving the overall institutional capacity by expanding the number of academics who have high academic attainments and prestige in both teaching and research; as well as in enhancing the infrastructure and other facilities which are indispensable for both teaching and research;
- Developing key disciplines which are considered to be necessary and crucial to social and economic developments, scientific and technological advancements, as well as national defence of the country;
- Strengthening the networking of, and collaboration among, HEIs and its public service delivery through the developments of the various systems, such as the Chinese Education and Research Network (CERNET), the Library and Documentation Support System (LDSS) and the Modern Equipment and Facilities Sharing System (MEFSS).

To be more specific, there are three main tasks in the Project 211. Firstly, top priority was given to intensively finance Peking University and Tsinghua University in order to enhance the two universities in reaching for the higher level of international standing and thus become world-class universities. Secondly, through provisions of additional funding, 25 other key universities were selected for upgrading their quality of teaching and research activities in key disciplines, which are closely related to economic development. Thirdly, further efforts would be made to enhance around 300 key disciplines in different institutions.[32] Accordingly, the Chinese government invested around 10.9 billion yuan during the period of 1996–2000.[33]

In terms of achievements, although only less than 10% of HEIs had benefited from this Project, these universities offered a high percentage of student enrolments; and captured most of the research funding and facilities in the country. The implementation of the Project 211 has also brought about a significant growth in the enrolment rate of students at various levels (e.g. undergraduate level: 61%; master's degree level: 108%; doctoral degree level: 101%). And the number of teachers with doctoral degrees and publications has increased significantly to 109% and 94% respectively during the period.[34] These figures have indicated that the Project 211, as the first key national project, has contributed significantly to the quality enhancement of higher education in China.

Project 985

The promulgation of Project 985 marked a second step of quality enhancement of higher education in China. In 1998, the former President Jiang Zemin made a speech on the 100th anniversary of Peking University, in which he addressed the need of establishing world-class universities in China. The MOE thereby worked out the *Action Plan of Education Promotion for the 21st Century* (*Action Plan*, hereafter), which stresses that, within the first two decades of the 21st Century, some Chinese universities and key areas of study shall reach a world-class level and be internationally recognised. Project 985, which literally means that the ideas of this Project were first initiated in May of 1998, was implemented afterwards. At its early stage, the two top universities of Peking University and Tsinghua University were, again, being selected to be intensively funded by the central authority. In accordance with the *Action Plan*, these two universities would be allocated a special budget of 1.8 billion yuan for enhancing their teaching and research activities. In 1999, seven more universities were also selected by the MOE to join in the Project through collaborative efforts with local authorities. Subsequently, more and more institutions have been encouraged and supported to enhance their quality in research and teaching, with the aim of becoming world-class universities in the future. By the year 2003, the number of universities listed in the Project 985 has increased to 34 institutions.[35] By now, Project 985 has started on its second stage (2004–2007), which will be mainly focused on the improvement of university management, the establishment of an innovative platform/basis for future development, and the refinement of the assessment and evaluation system. It also emphasises on building stronger teams of management and teaching through worldwide recruitments. In addition, the Project attempts to enhance the effectiveness of the existing laboratories, research centers and facilities through restructuring and establishing a well-structured coordinating mechanism. Finally, the Project further proposes to strengthen international cooperation among institutions through various exchange activities.[36]

Restructuring of Higher Education System

Prior to 1998, the higher education system in China was highly characterised by "matrix fragmentation" (*tiaokuai fenge*) in its educational governance. Administrative departments at the central level, together with local governments at either provincial or municipal levels, all provided education separately, and yet simultaneously involved in the administration of these HEIs. Previously, a large number of specialised economic management departments were established and maintained in China to implement government's direct intervention in business. In order to train professional manpower for the specific industries, these non-educational central departments established and administered their own universities. For example, the Ministry of Agriculture had a university specialising in management and technology of the agricultural sector, while the Ministry of Foreign Trade and Economic Cooperation could have its own university specialising in disciplines of international trade and economics. Similar structures permeated down to the provincial level. Too many of these single disciplinary and professional HEIs had led to functional overlapping, resources wastage, low economy and efficiency in the higher education sector.[37]

In response to these overlapping disciplines and lacking adequate economics of scale, the SEC issued a policy document entitled "Suggestions on Deepening Higher Education Structural Reform" (*Suggestions*, hereafter) in 1995. With the primary aim in rationalizing and strengthening the regulatory functions of China's higher education systems, the *Suggestions* recommended four major restructuring strategies, namely: "joint development" (*gongjian*), "restructuring" (*huazhuan*), "merging" (*hebing*) and "cooperation" (*hezuo*).

Joint Development (*gongjian*)

In order to resolve the problem of "matrix fragmentation", the strategy of "joint development" was proposed to strengthen the involvement of provincial, municipal and autonomous regional governments in higher education by introducing the dual-leadership scheme without change in the financing channels. Based on this idea, the provincial government would then place the universities under its local economic and social development plans, and thus provide the necessary capital investment funds for them. In return, the universities would need to cater for the demands of their local economic and social developments, in terms of their curriculum and programme design, admission, employment of graduates, and scientific research.[38] Apart from this kind of "joint development" by the central and local governments, some universities have been jointly run by the MOE and other central ministries. This arrangement allows the MOE to play a more important role in its educational service delivery in regards to their monitoring and facilitating.[39] By the year 2000, over 400 HEIs have been readjusted in accordance with this strategy of "joint development".[40]

Restructuring (*huazhuan*)

As mentioned earlier, different line ministries (including Ministry of Coal Industry, Ministry of Machine-Building Industry, Ministry of Metallurgical Industry, Ministry of Internal Trade, Light Industry Council and Textile Industry Council, Ministry of Posts and Telecommunications, and Ministry of Forestry, etc.) previously supervised and administered their own HEIs. With different purposes, the strategy of "restructuring" mainly took place at two levels. Firstly, in order to strengthen their role in the local economic development, the leadership of numerous universities was transferred from non-educational central ministries to the local governments. In 1998, the leadership of 151 universities, which was originally led by nine central ministries, was transferred to the local governments; while 81 of them were jointly developed and administered by both the central and local governments.[41] In 1999, 59 universities with military background were also transferred to be governed by local governments. In 2000, 97 universities originally run and led by different ministries at the central level became jointly developed and administered by both the central and local governments; while 55 institutions of adult higher learning previously run by ministries at the central level were transferred to local governments.[42] Secondly, to streamline the regulatory and management responsibilities to one central organisation, the leadership of HEIs was transferred from non-educational central ministries to the MOE. In 1998, the leadership of 10 key universities, originally run by different ministries, was transferred to the MOE.[43] In 2000, the leadership of an additional 66 HEIs previously run and led by central ministries was also transferred to the MOE.[44] The adoption of this restructuring strategy was a mark on the roll back of non-educational central ministries from the higher education sector. This consequently changed the relationship between the MOE, non-educational central ministries and provincial governments.

Mergers (*hebing*)

Merger, as a part of the structural reform of the Chinese higher education system, advocates a principle of "1 + 1 > 2", which stresses that, with the enhancement of efficiency and effectiveness, standard and competitiveness, an extra value could be added and "productivity gain" could be achieved through merger. Given that those single disciplinary and professional HEIs under the Soviet patterns were the major targets, merger was also seen as a way to readjust the strategic structure of higher educational institutions. Through merger, the number of HEIs has been decreased in order to respond to the problems of functional overlapping, narrowly specialised and small scale of institutions. The establishment of the new Zhejiang University in 1998 is a good case in point: the Zhejiang Project was established on the basis of the merger of the old Zhejiang University, Hangzhou University, Zhejiang Agricultural University and Zhejiang Medical University. As a "comprehensive university", the various programmes of the merged new Zhejiang University include arts, humanities, education, economics, management, law, agriculture, sciences, engineering and medicine. In addition, there are other areas that are well in place, such as national laboratories, research centres, post-doctoral stations in the areas of excellence at the university. The merger was considered to be successful in transforming the university to become a "comprehensive university" and to place it in a leading position in both size and diversity.[45]

Cooperation (*hezuo*)

The *Suggestions* of 1995 also promotes collaboration between universities by adopting the strategy of "cooperation". The adoption of this reform strategy can pull resources of those involved institutions together without a huge amount of investment that was required in university merger.[46] In addition, since "cooperation" does not involve reorganisation of institutional structure and personnel, the strategy is easier to be implemented.[47] For example, 13 HEIs at Xueyuan District of Beijing started a "teaching consortium" in 1999. Based on this kind of collaborative mechanism, students from the 13 involved institutions can enrol courses, and share various facilities, within the member institutions. In addition, the member institutions also jointly set up an academic accreditation mechanism so as to ensure and enhance their overall teaching quality.[48]

Massification of Higher Education

The two large projects and the nationwide restructuring of HEIs discussed above mainly focused on the qualitative enhancement[49] of China's higher education, but the massification of higher education was also an important characteristic of China's higher education policy by the 1990s.[50] The policy of massification of higher education was first mentioned in the *Action Plan* of 1998. It was later reconfirmed by the former Premier Zhu Rongji in 1999. According to the document, the enrolment rate of higher education in China will reach 15% by the year 2010. In fact, as indicated in Figure 1, there was a rapid growth of student enrolment in higher education during the 1990s, and so the target of 15% was achieved earlier than expected. In 2003, the gross enrolment rate of higher education (aged 18–22) has already reached 17%, which is still lower than that of many developed countries.[51] Yet, many scholars argue that China, as a developing country, has its own limitations in the expansion of higher education due to its limited education resources, with an extremely imbalanced environment between different regions (urban versus rural, or coastal areas versus hinterlands), and so many of them agree that 15% is already an indicator that China is entering into the stage of mass higher education.[52] Four reasons are identified to account for the dramatic expansion of China's higher education since the mid-1990s:

- Enrolment in China's higher education was too low prior to the mid-1990s;

- The rapid economic development brought on increasing demand for higher education;
- This was a way to postpone the students from entering into the labour market, and thus helped ease the high unemployment rate of young people;
- This can also be seen as a relaxation of the extremely competitive National College Entrance Examination.[53]

Figure 1
Gross Enrolment Rate of Higher Education (Aged 18–22)
in China (1990–2003)

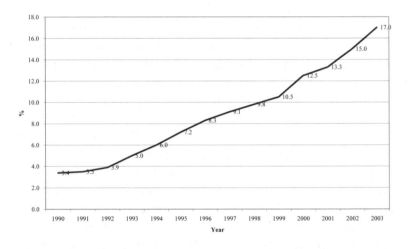

Source: Editorial Board of China Education Yearbook, *Chinese Education Yearbook 2004* (Beijing: Renmin Jiaoyu Chubanshe, 2004), p. 93.

It is noteworthy that there is no radical expansion of student numbers in the key universities that are directly run and administered by MOE and other ministries or agencies at the central level. For instance, the student enrolment rate of the key universities in Beijing (including Peking University, Tsinghua University, Beijing Normal University) has not changed since 2002.[54] In contrast, the expansion in the student enrolment rate occurred mostly in local universities and HEIs with lower prestige. Significant expansion of enrolment is achieved by the establishment of "independent colleges" attached to the existing regular universities. Accordingly, there were over 300 "independent colleges" with over 400 thousand students enrolled in 2003.[55] In addition to the expansion of regular programmes, many HEIs further expanded their size of student enrolment by providing non-degree programmes (e.g. higher vocational education or short courses) to meet the increasing needs of society. In 2003, there were 909 colleges of higher vocational education, with almost 60% of which being attached to existing regular HEIs.[56]

Challenges of China's Higher Education Reform

As can be seen from above, both qualitative improvement and quantitative growth are the main components of China's higher education reform since the late 1990s. However, equity, affordability, sustainability, accountability and efficiency are the main issues in the process of higher education reform.[57] This section will try to discuss the various issues under two major areas of concern: quality management in higher education and the marketisation of higher education.

Quality Management in Higher Education

Since the massification of higher education is adopted as a policy initiative in China, the issue on the quality of higher education has become a topic of public concern. In the case of China, higher education serves various socio-cultural, economic and political functions. This makes the issue of quality assurance more complicated and controversial. Firstly, the government's call for the expansion of higher education, together with the rapidly growing social needs for it, helped to generate strong political and social demands. Hence, the quantitative expansion of higher education as provided by HEIs grew at a very hasty speed, in order to fulfil the goal that was set up by the government, resulting in the lowering of standards for their programmes and graduates. Secondly, in the context of globalisation, China is going to be even more open to the rest of the world than ever before, and thus international competition is inevitable. Thus, the educational authorities have to catch up with the dynamic international environment in order to increase its competitiveness in the global marketplace. In order to ensure the quality assurance of China's higher education, three factors that are affecting this issue, namely: administrative structure, financial arrangements and the participation of non-state sectors, will need to be considered.

First of all, as discussed earlier, the structural reform of the higher education system since 1998 has fundamentally changed the higher education governance in China. The structural streamlining and the centralisation of the regulatory and management responsibilities to the MOE have improved the effectiveness of utilizing scarce resources, and thus allowed for the establishment of uniform qualification standards for both learning outcomes and accreditation for granting degrees. For example, under the current system, the Academic Degrees Committee of the State Council is responsible for setting the standards for academic degrees at different levels. While the MOE is responsible for the approval of doctoral and professional programmes, the provincial educational agencies are authorised to approve programmes at both master's and undergraduate levels. Starting in 2002, the MOE appointed the National Evaluation Institute of Degrees and Graduate Education, a non-governmental organisation established in 1994, to develop and execute a five-year cycle system of institutional assessment and evaluation as a mechanism for quality assurance. Furthermore, there are other three other types of institutional assessments, namely: *qualification assessment*, which is targeted at newly established HEIs; *excellence assessment*, which focuses on evaluating those institutions with longer history; and *random assessment*, which aims to assess those institutions not included in the first two categories.[58] The role and responsibilities of the MOE in these quality assurance activities reflect that the MOE has become more of a monitoring, coordinating and facilitating organisation, and less of a regulator and controller in the system of university governance. However, the distinction of "nationally accredited" versus "provincial/local accredited" HEIs remains to be a problem in the current system. On the one hand, this division of labour (that is, the authorisation of local governments to administer education via restructuring) helps improve the efficiency of education administration, particularly in terms of assessment and evaluation activities. Yet, on the other hand, with a strong mindset of accreditation by the MOC, such a decentralised nature of the reform makes people to be in doubt as to the creditability of quality control at the provincial and local levels.

This distinction between the central and the local levels of educational administration brings our discussion into the second factor of financial arrangement. In the former administrative system, the central government was responsible for all HEIs and their funding. With the new management system in place, it not only means that there is a decentralisation of managerial authority from the central government, but it also means that the central government shares its financial burden with the local governments. To achieve the utilisation of scarce resources, only a limited number of key universities or key disciplines can benefit from special funding, as in the cases with Project 211 and Project 985. In fact, these special funding have demonstrated an uneven pattern of resource allocation in China's higher education. Equity, in terms of locations (among provinces, and urban versus rural), types of institution (key versus non-key institutions) and areas of study (programmes that can make direct contributions to economic development versus those that may not), then becomes a critical issue.[59]

As a consequence, it is believed that HEIs in China are being distinguished into two levels: one is that of the key universities which will pursue world standard and excellence; while the other one is that of the non-key universities which are there to achieve mass higher education. In fact, there is a discussion of classification/stratification of HEIs within the academic community. From the eyes of both internal and external parties, being included in the Project 211/Project 985 has become an important symbol for the university's ranking, and is replacing the traditional identity of a key university. Figure 2, which shows China's higher education in the shape of a trapezium, briefly describes the classification of the higher education sector in accordance with the allocation of government funding and their level of awarding qualifications. In this regard, the special funding schemes, to certain extent, are exercising some functions of quality control in China's higher education.

Figure 2
Classification of Higher Education Sector in China

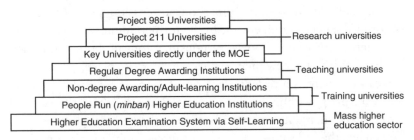

Source: Jingyao Yang, *The Study of China Higher Education* (Taibei: Gaodeng Jiaoyu Chuban, 2003).

Furthermore, the active participation of non-state actors in higher education (including enterprises, social organisations, individuals and foreign participants, etc.), as the third factor, makes its quality management more difficult. Since these *minban* HEIs are usually operated on a self-financing base, cost effectiveness and economy of budget will always be of the major concerns to these educational providers. For example, these HEIs tend to employ more part-time (often those who have full-time positions in regular HEIs) and/or retired faculty members. Although this arrangement can be understood as an usage of excessive personnel in the Chinese context, it is difficult to assure the quality of teaching since there has not been a well-developed quality assurance system of teaching during this transitional period. Similarly, in the case of foreign participation, many of them are run in partnership with domestic HEIs. Without a mature regulatory mechanism for their entrance[60], the quality of these HEIs with foreign participation is in doubt simply because some of these universities are corporate universities, which primarily aim to support the business goals of their own companies. It is in this sense that the status on the qualifications that are granted from this type of institutions remains unclear at the present stage.[61]

Bearing in mind these three factors, we can safely argue that the quality assurance mechanism of the higher education in China will most probably develop towards a more diversified system of assessment and evaluation through various channels and participants. The Chinese system previously adopted a government-driven pattern, in which institutional assessment and evaluation was primarily implemented by government officials, and so the evaluation exercises used to be bureaucratic, passive and homogenous. The recent developments, as mentioned above, will likely make the quality assurance mechanism of higher education in China tend to be more proactive and flexible.[62] The engagement of external/independent parties (such as the National Evaluation Institute of Degrees and Graduate Education) in the quality management practice represents an enhancement of the externality of the system. Meanwhile, reform of internal institutional administration further allows higher institutional autonomy on personnel matters. Institutions can, therefore, adopt a more performance-based approach towards personnel management. In sense, the administrative reform can be seen as a way of self-evaluation and self-improvement. More importantly, the emergence of the education market has led to an ideological transformation in which education is now seen more as a commodity, the schools and universities as service providers, with the parents and students as consumers and customers respectively.[63] As a result, students and parents, as well as the community at large, are hereby considered as stakeholders who should be included in the quality assurance mechanism of higher education as depicted in Figure 3.

Figure 3: Diversified Quality Assurance Mechanism of Higher Education

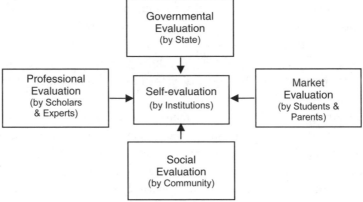

Source: Huiliang Jia, "Quality assurance in higher education and establishment of evaluation mechanism" ("Gaodeng jiaoyu zhiliang baozhang yu pingjia jizhi jianshe"), *Higher Education Review* (*Gaojiao Tansuo*), 2003, vol. 1, p. 20.

Marketisation of Higher Education

The development of recent education reforms in China could be interpreted as a process of marketisation. The Chinese government has attempted to diversify educational provision and financing by adopting the policy of decentralisation and making use of the market forces. In its policy of higher education finance, sustainability and efficiency are seemingly the major considerations by the Chinese government. In order to enable the sustainable growth of education, diversification of financing channels is used to achieve the goal. Hence, the central government has decentralised its authorities of education governance, and shifted parts of its financial burden to the local governments and the non-state sectors/actors. The retreat of the state from its educational financing has thus directly changed its traditional financing by introducing the "user-pay" principle, and so students have to pay their own tuition fees starting from the late 1980s.

Currently, public HEIs in China are financed through the following four main sources of funding:

- a per capital payment made to the institution by the central or provincial government, against an agreed quota of student;
- additional government funds provided (mainly) to the top universities, under the special funding schemes (e.g. Project 211 and Project 985);
- tuition fees that are fixed by provincial governments based on educational costs and students' affordability. The fees are currently set at about 25% of the total cost;
- additional incomes that universities and colleges raise through supplementary teaching, research and other activities.[64]

Under this kind of circumstance, tuition fees become an important part of revenue for many institutions. This is shown by the growth of non-state educational expenditures within a ten years' period (from 333 million yuan in 1993 to 17 billion yuan in 2002). In term of provision, *minban* institutions have now captured almost 8.3% of regular higher education and adult learning.[65] As there is a greater demand for higher education in the society, mobilizing the social investment through the diversification of educational provision and funding is being regarded as an efficient way to ensure the sustainable and rapid development of higher education in China.

Moreover, the changes of human resource management practices also have implications for the higher education sector. In past, the employment practices in China were characterised by centralised labour allocation, life tenure and low labour mobility.[66] Now, with the removal of this "iron rice bowl" employment system, this has created more flexibility in the labour market. Employers can now become an important stakeholder of higher education, and students would tend to choose those subjects with high market demands. It is in this way that student choices become a determining factor for the survival of an educational institution, thereby leading to the rise of "consumerism" as well as the "commodification/ commercialisation" of higher education. [67] In addition, the domination of market forces has sharpened inter-institutional competitions. Owing to the opening of the labour market, HEIs have to compete for quality staff and professors with good reputation. Similarly, with the emergence of an internal market in student admissions and government grants, universities are required to compete for quality students and government funding in order to maintain their ranking and competitiveness. In this regard, we can argue that these characteristics of marketisation provided effective allocation mechanism of educational resources through the making use of the market principles.

However, the present situation does not help to cope with any problems in regards to equity and affordability. At the national level, mobilisation of non-state investments in education releases the government from part of the pressures for educational demands in society. Actually, the government is trying to minimise its involvements in private education. As a facilitator and regulator, it is responsible for establishing the minimum standards for accreditation, and providing necessary information to the various stakeholders of students, parents and employers. While the former task is included in its quality assurance mechanism, the latter task is executed by the National Information and Career Centre for University Student under the guidance of the MOE. In terms of subsidy, the government would sponsor the private institutions in terms of land and facilities, rather than in cash.

At the regional level, the accessibility of higher education is an outstanding issue due to the distinction between urban and rural areas amongst provinces. In the present situation, students from urban areas, or economically advanced regions, have much higher opportunities to enter into universities. In the cases of intra-provincial differences, the provincial government, as an unit of interest, would be more willing to redistribute its resources to support the relatively poor and disadvantaged regions within the province. For example, the highly urbanised southern part of Jiangsu is capable to support the northern region, a backward part of the province, to promote mass higher education.[68] Nevertheless, the current financial arrangement cannot effectively solve the inter-provincial variations in terms of opportunities for higher education.

At the individual level, a loan scheme was started in 1999. Students in financial difficulties may apply and can get up to the full amount of their tuition fees and living costs during their period of study. But, since the loans are made by the national banks, the students are required to shoulder half of the interest, while the other half would be paid for by the government. Moreover, this loan scheme is considerably restrictive, as only a very low proportion of students (about 10–15%) can successfully apply for it.[69] Hence, equity in term of access remains to a problem in the policy of higher education finance. In short, the market mechanism does not provide effective solutions to solve the issues of equity and affordability. On the other hand, market failures may occur in China's delivery of its higher educational services

Apart from those attributes, the process of marketisation can also be analysed from the perspective of the state-education relationship. As discussed earlier, the participation of non-state sectors/actors in education represents a retreat or transformation of role of the nation-state in public/social policy. The adoption of market principles replaces the role of the nation-state to function as a mechanism of resources mobilisation and allocation. And yet, the nation-state in China remains to play a considerable strong role in education. For instance, the form of the "independent colleges" (usually called the "second-level colleges" [*erji xueyuan*]) in the higher education sector, which is the latest development of the practices of *minban* institutions, can be regarded as some sort of state-intervention in the emerging education market within the specific contexts of transitional communist societies. This type of institutions is usually jointly operated by the public universities and the non-state sectors, and occur in the form of an extended arm of the original institutions. Since many of them are run on a profit-making basis,[70] they are seen as a kind of "state invasion" to the profitable private education sector, which is considered as a way of strengthening the state with an accelerationist mode in the educational sphere.[71] This illustrates that the usual dichotomy between the market and the state is analytically problematic and practically unrealistic, particularly in such a socialist state like China.

Conclusion

The above observations and discussions have indicated that the development of higher education in China is spearheaded in two directions, i.e. qualitative enhancement and quantitative expansion. For the qualitative enhancement, much emphasis has been placed on a few selected HEIs and key disciplines. With the privileged support from the central government, these institutions enjoy many advantageous and favourable policies in all aspects of development, such as facilities and equipments, and staff recruitment. It is clear that the Chinese government tactically reserves elite education in these selected institutions in order to make the tip of the higher education sector capable of approaching the world standard in order to fulfil its goal of pursuing world-class universities. Meanwhile, the quantitative growth of higher education has taken place in various modes of policy initiatives. Owing to its financial constraints, the Chinese government obviously cannot retain its role as the sole provider in higher educational services while adopting the policy of massification. It, instead, adopted a very flexible policy to revitalise and mobilise different sectors/actors and resources to participate in its higher education expansion. This is shown by the wide variety of models in the running of *minban* schools during the process of reform.

In order to enable and empower a sound mass higher education system in China, the establishments of a quality assurance mechanism and an effective funding system have become a necessity. Our discussion has drawn us to the fact that the three factors of administrative structure, financial arrangements and the participation of non-state sectors have strong influences on the quality assurance of higher education in China. We also see the emergence of an alternative policy of a diversified assessment and evaluation system, which involves different actors/sectors in the quality assurance activities. In addition, we have shown how the Chinese government has attempted to use the process of marketisation to achieve sustainability and effectiveness. Through marketisation, it helps China to achieve sustainable development of education by mobilising non-state investments and allocate scarce resources with higher social and economic effectiveness. Yet, issues have emerged as the market is insufficient to guarantee equal opportunities in accessing high education with affordable fees.

By examining the recent development and reforms of higher education in China within the analytical framework of globalisation, we come to realise that the new Chinese leadership responds to the globalisation challenges by trying hard to embrace globalisation and meet the requirements of the world, through implementing the various education reform policies initiated in the late 1990s. To further streamline the education governance structure, the Chinese government reconstitutes its higher educational development on the theme of building world-class universities. Obviously, the diversification of actors and sectors in higher education could be seen as part of the global trend in terms of marketisation, corporatisation and privatisation. In fact, we have paid particular attention to the changing relationship between the state and the market. Rather than diminishing state capacity, we would suggest that the state in China still remains to have an active role as facilitator, enabler, regulator and even sponsor in education within the specific context of a "socialist market economy". Hence, through shifting and transformation of its role, the nation-state has even more flexibilities and options in its policy-making and implementation. This analysis reasserts the view of local diversity in policy agenda within the globalised context.

Appendix I: List of Institutions in "Project 985" (38)

▪ Peking University	▪ Tsinghua University
▪ Beijing Normal University	▪ Beijing Institute of Technology
▪ Beijing University of Aeronautics and Astronautics	▪ Renmin University of China
▪ National University of Defense Technology	▪ Central University for Nationalities
▪ Zhejiang University	▪ Fudan University
▪ Tongji University	▪ Shanghai Jiaotong University
▪ Harbin Institute of Technology	▪ Shandong University
▪ Nankai University	▪ Tianjin University
▪ Nanjing University	▪ Wuhan University
▪ Chongqing University	▪ Xi'an Jiaotong University
▪ Xiamen University	▪ University of Electronic Science and Technology of China
▪ Southeast University	▪ Huazhong University of Science and Technology
▪ Hunan University	▪ Ocean University of China
▪ Central South University	▪ Dalian University of Technology
▪ Jilin University	▪ Sichuan University
▪ Lanzhou University	▪ Northeastern University
▪ South China University of Technology	▪ Sun Yat-sen University
▪ Northwestern Polytechnical University	▪ China Agricultural University
▪ Northwest University of Science and Technology	▪ University of Agriculture and Forestry

Notes and References

1. Dirk Van Damme, "Higher Education in the Age of Globalisation: The Need for a New regulatory Framework for Recognition, Quality Assurance and Accreditation," in *Globalisation and Competition in Education*, Jan De Groof, Gracienne Lauwers and Germain Dondeilinger eds., (Nijmegen: Wolf Legal Publishers, 2003).

2. Jan Currie, Richard DeAngelis, Harry de Boer, Jeroen Huisman and Claude Lacotte, *Globalizing Practices and University Responses: European and Anglo-American Differences* (Westport: Praeger, 2002).

3. Ka-ho Mok and Anthony Welch (eds.), *Globalization and Educational Restructuring in the Asia Pacific Region* (Basingstoke, Hampshire: Palgrave Macmillan, 2003); Jurgen Enders and Oliver Fulton (eds.), *Higher Education in a Globalising World: International Trends and Mutual Observations: A Festschrift in Honour of Ulrich Teichler* (Dordrecht: Kluwer Academic Publishers, 2002).

4. See Andrea Beckmann and Charlie Cooper, "Globalisation, the New Managerialism and Education: Rethinking the Purpose of Education in Britain," *Journal for Critical Education Policy Studies*, 2004, vol. 2, no. 2, pp. 1–16; Mike Bottery, *Education, Policy and Ethics* (New York: Continuum, 2000).

5. Stephen J. Ball, *Politics and Policy Making in Education* (London: Routledge, 1990); Stephen J. Ball, "Big Politics/small World: An Introduction to International Perspectives in Education Policy," *Comparative Education*, vol. 34, no. 2, pp. 119–130; David Bridges and Terence H. McLaughlin (eds.), *Education and the Market Place* (London: The Falmer Press, 1994).

6. Jan Currie et al, *op. cit.*

7. *Ibid.*

8. Mike Bottery, op. cit; Jan Currie and Lesley Vidovich, "Micro-economic Reform through Managerialism in American and Australian Universities, in *Universities and Globalization: Critical Perspectives*, Jan Currie and Janice Newson (eds.), (Thousand Oaks, CA: Sage Publications, 1998).

9. David K. K. Chan, "Policy Implications of Adopting a Managerial Approach in Education," in *Globalization and Education: The Quest for Quality Education in Hong Kong*, Ka-ho Mok and David K. K. Chan (eds.) (Hong Kong: Hong Kong University Press, 2002); Jan Currie et al, *op. cit.*

10. Jan De Groof, Gracienne Lauwers and Germain Dondeilinger (eds.), *Globalisation and Competition in Education* (Nijmegen: Wolf Legal Publishers, 2003).

11. United Nations Educational, Scientific and Cultural Organisation, *Globalisation and Living Together: The Challenge for Educational Content in Asia* (Paris: United Nations Educational, Scientific and Cultural Organisation, 2000).

12. Dirk Van Damme, *op. cit.*

13. Cited in *ibid.*, p. 31.

14. Ka-ho Mok, "The Cost of Managerialism: The Implications for the 'McDonaldization' of Higher Education in Hong Kong," *Journal of Higher Education Policy and Management*, 1999, vol. 21, no. 1, pp. 117–127.

15. Madeleine Green, Peter Eckel and Andris Barblan, *The Brave New (and Smaller) World of Higher Education: A Transatlantic View* (Washington, DC: American Council on Education, 2002).

16. Ruth Hayhoe, *China's Universities and the Open Door* (New York: M.E. Sharpe, 1989).

17. Wei-fang Min, "People's Republic of China: Autonomy and Accountability: An Analysis of the Changing Relationships between the Government and Universities", in Guy Neave and Frans van Vught (eds.), *Government and Higher Education Relationships Across Three Continents: The Winds of Change* (Oxford: Pergamon, 1994).

18. Communist Party of China Central Committee, *The Decision of the Central Committee of the Communist Party of China on the Reform of Educational Structure* (Beijing: People's Press, 1985).

19. See David Chan and King-lun Ngok, "Towards Centralisation and Decentralisation in Educational Development in China: The Case of Shanghai," *Education and Society*, 2001, vol. 19, no. 3, pp. 59–78; John N. Hawkins, "Centralization, Decentralization, Recentralization: Educational Reform in China," *Journal of Educational Administration*, 2000, vol. 38, no. 5, pp. 442–454.

20. Communist Party of China Central Committee, *Outline for Reform and Development of Education in China* (Beijing: People's Press, 1993).

21. State Education Commission, Policies and Law Department, *Law and Regulation on Basic Education of the People's Republic of* China (Beijing, Beijing Normal University, 1993), p. 6.

22. Cited in Nina Borevskaya, "The Private Sector in the Chinese Educational System: Problem and Prospects", *Far Eastern Affairs*, 2003, vol. 31, no. 4, pp. 89–107.

23. Editorial Board of China Education Yearbook, *Chinese Education Yearbook 2004* (Beijing: Renmin Jiaoyu Chubanshe, 2004), pp. 277.

24. See Ka-ho Mok, "Marketization and Quasi-marketization: Educational Development in Post-Mao China," *International Review of Education*, 1997, vol. 43, no.5–6, pp. 547–567; Ka-ho Mok and David Chan, "Privatization or Quasi-marketisation," in Michael Agelasto and Bob Adamson (eds.), *Higher Education in Post-Mao China* (Hong Kong: University of Hong Kong Press, 1998); Ka-ho Mok and David Chan, "Educational Development and the Socialist Market in Guangdong," *Asia Pacific Journal of Education*, 2001, vol. 21, no. 1, pp. 1–18; David Chan and Ka-ho Mok, "Educational Reforms and Coping Strategies under the Tidal Wave of Marketisation: A Comparative Study of Hong Kong and the Mainland," *Comparative Education*, 2001, vol. 37, no. 1, pp. 21–41.

25. For the school management system in China, see Fengzhen Yang, "Education in China," *Educational Philosophy and Theory*, 2002, vol. 34, no. 2, pp. 135–144.

26. Organisation for Economic Cooperation and Development (OECD), *OECD Review of Financing and Quality Assurance Reforms in Higher Education in the People's Republic of China* (Paris: OECD, 2004), p. 8.

27. Financing of Chinese higher education is still facing constraints. Strong base here is in a comparison with the pre-reform period. See Zaohuan Zheng and Yingzhen Zhao, "Pursuing World Class Higher Education: China's Step Towards A Strong Education Nation" ("Lizhen Shijie Yiliu Gaodeng Jiaoyu: Zhongguo Dalu cong Jiaoyu Daguo Zhubu Zouxiang Jiaoyu Qiangguo"), paper presented to Hong Kong Educational Research Association's 20th Anniversary Regional Symposium on "Questing for World Class Education", Chinese University of Hong Kong, Hong Kong, 20 November 2004.

28. The idea of internationalisation is often interchangeably used or mixed up with the concept of globalisation. But Rui Yang points out that there are fundamental difference, as well as different rationales, impetus and effects between these two distinguished concepts. See Rui Yang, *Third delight: the internationalisation of higher education in China* (New York, London: Routledge, 2002). This chapter uses the internationalisation of higher education as an explicitly international frame of reference for describing and dealing with the international perspective of local development.

29. See Xueliang Zhu Ding, Shenme shi Shijie Yiliu Daxue (Beijing: Peking University Press, 2004); Zaohuan Zheng and Yingzhen Zhao, *op. cit.*; Jide Cha, "Zhongguo Daxue yu Shijie Yiliu Daxue de Chaiju ji qi Yinsu Fenxi", unpublished master's thesis, Southern China Normal University, 2002; Xueliang Zhu Ding, "On What's First?", *Higher Education Studies (Gaodeng Jiaoyu Yanjiu)*, 2001, vol. 3 pp. 5–9.

30. Two government projects, namely Project 211 and Project 985, are usually seen as the major projects of facilitating the pursuit of world-class universities. Some literatures also consider other non-governmental fund

schemes and donations such as the "Cheung Kong Scholar Award" as relevant programs. See Zaohuan Zheng and Yingzhen Zhao, op cit.

31. It is now renamed as the Ministry of Education (MOE).

32. Ministry of Education, *A Brief Introduction to Project 211*, 2004, available at www.moe.edu.cn, access on 1 August 2005. See also Lianmeng Zhang and Zuwu Shen (eds.), *Eryiyi Gongcheng Jianshe Guanli Tansuo yu Shijian*. (Wuhan: Wuhan University of Technology Press, 2003).

33. Including 2.8 billion of central government funding, 3.2 billion of departmental funding, 2.5 billion of local governments funding, 2.4 billion of self-financing by institutions and 0.1 billion from other channels, see National Planning Commission, Ministry of Education and Ministry of Finance, *The General Achievements of Project 211 and the Ninth Five-year Plan*, 2004, available at www.moe.edu.cn, access on 1 August 2005.

34. *Ibid.*

35. Futao Huang, "Qualitative Enhancement and Quantitative Growth: Changes and Trends of China's Higher Education", *High Education Policy*, 2005, vol. 18, pp. 117–130. For the latest information by mid-2005, this figure has already risen to 38. Please see Appendix I.

36. See Ministry of Education and Ministry of Finance, *Suggestions on Continuously Implementing the Items of Project 985*, 2004, available at www.moe.edu.cn, access on 1 August 2005.

37. Ka-ho Mok and Yat-wai Lo, "University Merging and Changing Higher Education Governance in China," *Education Policy Forum*, 2004, vol. 7, no. 1, pp. 83–100.

38. Yijuo Zhou, "Streamlining Administrative Structure and Quickening Higher Education Restructuring," *Chinese Administration and Management*, 2000, vol. 12, p. 15.

39. OECD, *op. cit.* p. 20.

40. Ka-ho Mok and Yat-wai Lo, *op. cit.*

41. General Office of the State Council, *State Education Commission's Suggestions on Higher Education Restructuring* (Beijing: General Office, State Council, 1998).

42. General Office of the State Council, *Suggestions on Restructuring of Higher Education Institutions run by Central Ministries of the State Council* (Beijing: General Office, State Council, 2000).

43. General Office of the State Council, *op. cit.* 1998.

44. By 2000, apart from the Ministry of Education, only eleven ministries, state commissions and bureaus (including Ministry of Foreign Affairs, State Commission of Science, Technology and Industry for National

Defence, Ministry of Public Security, Ministry of State Security, General Administration of Customs, Civil Aviation Administration of China, State Sports General Administration, Office of Overseas Chinese Affairs, Chinese Academy of Sciences and State Seismological Bureau) run their own higher educational institutions, see General Office of the State Council, *op. cit.*, 2000.

45. Yijuo Zhou, *op. cit.* p. 16.

46. Wei-fang Min, *Improving the Effectiveness of Higher Education Institutions through Inter-university Co-operation: The Case Study of Peking University* (Paris: UNESCO, 1999).

47. Changze Wang and Zuheng Mao, "The Study of Collaboration and Resources Sharing between Higher Education Institutions", *China Electronic Education*, 2001, vol. 4, pp. 11–13.

48. Songhua Shen, "A Case Study of the Teaching Consortium of the Beijing Xueyuan Road," *China University Education*, vol. 4, pp. 1–4.

49. See Futao Huang, *op. cit.*

50. OECD, *op. cit.* p. 8.

51. Many developed countries, such as Sweden, United Kingdom, France and Japan, has already reached 15% of enrolment rate in the 1970s. See Jianhua Hu, "An Analysis of the characteristics in the Progress from Elite to Mass Higher Education in China," *Journal of Higher Education*, 2002, vol. 23, no. 2, pp. 42–45.

52. Many Chinese academics, based on Trow's ideas, believe 15% of enrolment rate can be considered as an important indicator of massification of higher education. However, Trow himself does not recognize the significance of 15% in the development of higher education in China. For Trow's original ideas on massification of higher education, see Martin Trow, *Problems in the Transition from Elite to Mass Higher Education* (Berkley, C.A.: Carnegie Commission on Higher Education, 1973). For his view on China's current situation, see Daguang Wu, "Connotation and Value of Mass Higher Education Theory: the Conversation with Mr. Martin Trow," *Journal of Higher Education*, 2003, vol. 24, no. 6, pp. 6–9.

53. Langqing Li, *Interviews with Li Langqing on Education* (Beijing: People's Education Press, 2003).

54. *Beijing Youth Daily*, 3 April 2002.

55. Editorial Board of China Education Yearbook, *op. cit.*, pp. 277–279. See also Haibo Liu, *Gaodeng Jiaoyu Dazhonghua yu Gaodeng Jiaoyu Tizhi Gaige.* Unpublished PhD Thesis. (Beijing: Peking University, 2002).

56. Futao Huang, *op. cit.* p. 126.

57. OECD, *op. cit.* See also Daguang Wu (ed.) *Zhongguo Gaodeng Jiaoyu Dazhonghua Wenti Yanjiu.* (Beijing: Gaodeng Jiaoyu Chubanshe, 2004).

58. *Ibid.* pp.19–26. See also Zhixiang Xiong, *Gaodeng Jiaoyu Zhiliang Baozhang Tixi Yanjiu.* (Changsha: Hunan Renmin Chubanshe, 2005); Yukun Chen, Ruihua Dai, Xiaojiang Yang and Shengbing Tian, *Gaodeng Jiaoyu Zhiliang BaoZhang Tixi Gailun.* (Beijing: Peking Normal University Press, 2004); Zubin He (ed.), *Gaodeng Jiaoyu Dazhonghua yu Zhiliang Baozhang* (Guilin: Guangxi Normal University Press, 2004).

59. Fengqi Ma, "The Issue of Equity in the Progress of Massification of Higher Education in China (Woguo Gaodeng Jiaoyu Dazhonghua Guochengzhong de Gongping Wenti)", *Higher Education Review (Gaojiao Tansuo)*, 2001, vol. 2, pp. 16–18.

60. The MOE promulgated the "Regulations on Chinese-Foreign Cooperative Education" in 2004.

61. Sue Shaw, "The Corporate University: Global or Local Phenomenon?", *Journal of European Industrial Training,* 2005, vol. 29, no. 1, pp. 21–39.

62. Xin An, Tai Xiao and Guangqian Dong, "Issues of Quality Assurance in Higher Education (Shixi Gaodeng Jiaoyu Zhiliang Baozhang de Ruogan Wenti)", *Higher Education Studies (Gaodeng Jiaoyu Yanjiu),* 1998, vol. 6, pp. 64–68.

63. David Chan "Policy Implications of Adopting a Managerial Approach in Education", in Ka-ho Mok and David Chan (eds.), *Globalisation and Education: The Quest for Quality Education in Hong Kong* (Hong Kong: Hong Kong University Press, 2002).

64. Cited in OECD, *op. cit.* p. 38.

65. In 2003, there are 2,110 regular and adult HEIs in China, among which 175 are "people-run". But apart from them, 1,104 of non-state-run institutions are categorised as "other" people-run higher educational institutions (*qita minban gaodeng jiaoyu jiguo*). See Editoral Board of China Education Yearbook, *op. cit.* p. 90.

66. Sue Shaw, *op. cit.* p. 26.

67. King-lun Ngok, "The Relationship between Higher Education and Government in the Trend of Marketization of Education" in *The Marketization of Higher Education: A Comparative Study of Taiwan, Hong Kong and China*, Dai Xiaoxia, Mo Jiahao, Xie Anbang, (eds.), (Taibei: Higher Education Press, 2002). See also Aijuan Chen, *Zhongguo Gaodeng Jiaoyu Shichanghua Fazhan Mushi Xuanze yu Zhiduo Anpai.* Unpublished PhD Thesis (Xian: Xian Jiaotung University Press, 2003).

68. Hongzhi Yuan "The Targets and Choices of Mass Higher Education in Economically Disadvantaged Regions" ("Gaodeng Jiaoyu Dazhonghua de

Mubiao Dingwei huo Zhanlu Suanze"), *Higher Education Studies (Gaodeng Jiaoyu Yanjiu)*, 2004, pp. 38–40.

69. OECD, *op. cit.* p. 36–39.

70. The idea of profit-making here refers to the generation of additional financial resources. Education for profit-making is prohibited under the current legislations. School/university operators are requested to reinvest the profit to the institutions. See Nina Borevskaya, op cit, p. 103.

71. See Ka-ho Mok, "Globalisation and Educational Restructuring: University Merging and Changing Governance in China", *Higher Education*, vol. 50, no. 1, pp. 57–88.

20

Hu Jintao's Policy towards Intellectuals: Enlightenment, Deception, Disappointment

Jean-Philippe BÉJA

Government policy towards the intelligentsia has always been a harbinger of the political attitude of the leadership in countries ruled by Communist parties. For instance, the thaw that characterised Khruchtchev's rule after Stalin's death made itself feel first in the field of literature through the rehabilitation of writers such a Ilya Ehrenburg.

This can be explained by the fact that in this type of regime, ideology plays a determining role. In the years that immediately follow the conquest of power, one of the Party's main objectives consists in inculcating the new ideology to the citizens in order to control their hearts and minds. As ideology is the realm of the intelligentsia, control over this category is a pre-requisite to the consolidation of the regime. The Party needs to transform them in order to eradicate the ideology of the *ancien régime*, and to spread the new official credo in the populace and achieve its re-education, which is crucial to the consolidation of the new regime. This task was regarded as important in Stalin's USSR, but it became essential in Mao Zedong's China. One of the cardinal aspects of the Great Helmsman's thought was crystallised in his 1942 talks on the role of literature in Yan'an[1], a speech in which he outlined the framework of the Party's policy towards the intellectuals, and towards society. Ever since, every major turn of the Communist Party of China (CPC) policy has been first felt in its attitude towards the intelligentsia: it was the case with the Hundred Flowers campaign and the anti-rightist movement[2], the Cultural Revolution, the second bout of criticism of Deng Xiaoping in 1975–76 . . .

Under Mao, the radical twists of policy were first felt in the literary field. At the end of the Great Helmsman's rule, which had been characterised by the attempt to put all the aspects of social life under the control of the apparatus in order to create a "new man" and had resulted in the demoralisation of the population, his successors had to find a way to renew the regime legitimacy. And when Deng came back to power in 1977, one of his first gestures was to extend a hand towards the intellectuals. This was a symptom of his desire to change the emphasis of the government from an ideology-driven rule to the readiness to take reality into account: in order to re-start the modernisation process, Deng decided that the Party should grant a substantial degree of autonomy to the intelligentsia. To renew the legitimacy of communist rule, he set a new objective to the regime: the four modernisations[3], the old goal of *fuguo qiangbing* (a prosperous country and a strong military) that has been the essential agenda of most leaders since the British gunboats have defeated the Chinese fleet during the first opium war.

Deng's behaviour was conditioned by the laws of the evolution of communist regimes. In communist countries, after the demise of the charismatic leader, his successor usually promises to restore the rules ensuring Party cadres that their behaviour will be sanctioned by a predictable set of rewards and punishments, terminating the arbitrary rule that his predecessor had put in place. This policy was called "return to Leninism" by Khruchtchev, and denunciation of "leftism" by Deng Xiaoping.

However, as ideology played an even greater role in China than in the Soviet Union, Deng, in order to comfort his rule, openly appealed to intellectuals, theoreticians, writers who had been persecuted during Mao's days to support his policy of the Four modernisations. He launched the campaign for the "emancipation of thought"[4] to topple his neo-Maoist rivals in the Politburo and organised the Conference on Theoretical Work[5], where previously marginalised thinkers were rehabilitated and asked to help elaborate the ideological foundations of the new line. He also relaxed Party control over literary and artistic creation, and, as had happened in the years which followed Stalin's death, the ensuing thaw resulted in a flowering of literary creation and the development of reflection on the flaws of the regime which had led to the catastrophe (Stalin's repression, Mao's Cultural Revolution).

Following the return of a leader who promises to install a rational-bureaucratic rule, the intelligentsia tries to create an autonomous space which will prevent the return of the dictatorship of ideology. After the death of the charismatic leader, intellectuals support and help elaborate the reform programme whose goal is to improve the populace's standard of living and give more autonomy to society in order to mobilise its energies for the gigantic task of modernisation. In the 1980s China, a substantial part of the intelligentsia who had suffered at the hands of Mao Zedong after having supported him fanatically[6], collaborated with the new leadership in order to help it make the system more rational. And as Deng Xiaoping needed the support of society to break many taboos, he often turned a blind eye on the developing autonomy of the intelligentsia. During the 1980s, salons, unofficial associations advocating liberalisation, taboo-breaking writers were often subject to criricism[7], but did not become the targets of full fledged maoist type campaigns. The informal alliance between reformers inside the Party and intellectuals trying to develop an autonomous space resulted in the relaxation of CPC controls over many aspects of social life. The liberalised policy towards the intelligentsia was a symptom of the type of rule enforced by Deng Xiaoping and his reformer associates Hu Yaobang and Zhao Ziyang. At the end of the first decade of the reforms, despite a stop and go process which saw the recurrent denunciations of "bourgeois liberalisation"[8], the CPC rule was increasingly heading towards democratisation.

However, to Deng Xiaoping and most of his colleagues, the 1989 explosion of the pro-democracy movement showed that the relaxation of ideological controls and the granting of more freedom to the intelligentsia ended up in threatening the Party's rule.

Therefore, after the June 4th massacre, the patriarch and the leaders who supported him returned to a much stricter policy towards intellectuals, and tried to re-establish the overall rule of the party. The salons, associations, autonomous research centres which had flourished in the 1980s were dismantled, their promoters were prosecuted, control was re-established on the organs of public opinion and even on literary creation. Once again, the policy towards intellectuals was a harbinger of the degree of openness attained by the regime.

Intellectuals Enter the Middle Class

However the switch towards conservatism could not last long, and after two years of repression and of re-establishment of controls on the economy, Deng Xiaoping re-launched his policy of economic reform and opening to the world. This was symbolised by the Southern tour he made on the Chinese New Year of 1992. Having decided to put economic development back at the centre of his programme[9], he knew that he would need the support of the intelligentsia. In the years to come, the market was to provide new opportunities for intellectuals and therefore party policies would not exert such a direct influence on their material life as in the previous decade.

In order to enlist the support of the intellectuals who had been accused of all the evils and had been persecuted in the wake of the June 4th massacre, the Party had to give them some benefits. It was obviously impossible to give them back the margin of manoeuvre they had enjoyed in the realm of politics before 1989. However, if they accepted restrictions in this field, they would be granted the possibility to drastically improve their standards of living. At the end of the 1980s, there was an atmosphere of freedom and political discussion went rife, but the economic status of intellectuals had not been substantially improved if compared to the beginning of the decade. University professors' incomes were lower than many uneducated people who had taken advantage of the new economic policy and become self-employed (*geti hu*). Young professors and researchers, even those who had studied abroad, were finding it extremely difficult to find accommodation, and they often lived in crammed quarters where their books remained in crates. Young urban women were reluctant to marry scholars, and the intelligentsia complained that its rehabilitation by Deng in the late seventies had not been matched by an equivalent improvement in their social standing. Whereas under the last decade of Mao's rule, women wouldn't marry intellectuals because as "stinking ninth" they were the victims of ostracism from the rest of society, at the end of the first decade of the reforms, they were praised for their role in China's modernisation, but women wouldn't marry them all the same because they were too poor and seemed to have no future.

The situation radically changed after Deng's 1992 Southern tour. The opening to the market of the fields of high tech, import export and consultancy led many graduates, and a good number of scholars to "jump into the sea" (*xia hai*) of commerce, and take advantage of the opportunities to launch new firms.

Moreover, at the end of the nineties, the salaries of university professors and academic researchers were drastically improved. "Relevant figures from the Ministry of Education show that during the past two decades, the annual salary for college lecturers and professors soared 18.8 fold, and that of teachers in middle and primary schools went up 11.9 fold". According to the same source, in 2004 "in Beijing, even high school teachers, if willing to give some additional tutorial courses to their students on weekends or holidays, can earn up to some 10,000 yuan (or 1,200 US dollars) monthly, much more than ordinary government employees who average around 2,500 yuan (some 300 US dollars) [in the capital], and more even than some company white collar workers."[10] Besides, the new real estate policy gave huge material advantages to the intelligentsia. The privatisation of housing allowed them to take advantage of the immense difference of prices between "*danwei* accommodation" and "commercial housing". Most employees of universities and research centres were allowed to buy the apartments they lived in at very low prices, and to sell (or rent) them at market prices. During the same period (in the early 2000s), the government decided to create world standard universities and started building new campuses, including accommodation for teachers and research staff. These new institutions offered very good salaries (up to 8000 yuans monthly in Tsinghua University) and benefits such as lodging. The sale of their old apartments provided the staff of these "world-class" universities with capital. Besides, they were allowed to work as consultants for private firms and government organisations, improving their income and often multiplying them by two to three. In little more than a decade, most university professors moved from the poor to the upper middle class. This drastic improvement in their status had naturally important consequences on their attitude towards the regime.

Very few among them were ready to jeopardise their newly acquired wealth for the sake of the defence of principles. What was the point of abstractly denouncing the regime if one could help improve the situation by working within the system? After Deng's Southern tour, the Party enlisted the support of the intelligentsia to implement its policy which renewed with the old dream of the modernisation of China. It was all the more easy for the intelligentsia to accept this new contract as it had always dreamt of restoring the motherland to its due position on the international scene. Most intellectuals who had fought for democratisation in the 1980s had largely done so because they were convinced that it was the only way to achieve the country's modernisation. The experience of the Soviet Union in the early 1990s had cooled their enthusiasm for democracy. Coupled with the risks attached to the struggle against the regime, this led mainstream intellectuals to abandon their previous fight and support the new programme of the leadership. In 2000, Secretary General Jiang Zemin formalised the new social contract – a contract that Adam Michnik has called the "pact of the elites"[11]– with his formula of the "three represents": the Party represents the most advanced productive forces (the technical intelligentsia), the most advanced culture (the social science scholars, the writers) and the interests of the whole people. Of course, in order to be admitted in the new coalition, intellectuals had to refrain from criticising the Party rule and from questioning the regime legitimacy. In exchange, they were often consulted by the authorities. Therefore, only a very small proportion of the intelligentsia, the dissidents, a few liberal members of Zhao Ziyang and Hu Yaobang's networks, continued to claim for democratisation. But it can be said that the main body of the category was enlisted in the support of the Party programme.

The philosopher Xu Youyu summed up the situation quite well: "We do not have freedom of speech, and such a situation will last for a relatively long time, because the authorities are able to control most things . . . It is not the biggest problem for most ordinary people. And most professors are quite rich so they don't want to pay any cost by campaigning on an issue like that."[12]

It must be admitted that since 1992, Deng Xiaoping and Jiang Zemin have adopted a more sophisticated policy towards the intelligentsia. Since the mid-1990s, the scholars' academic freedom has increased – they now can take part in symposiums abroad, they are encouraged to join the international scientific community, foreign scholars are welcome in China – but they have been discouraged to re-establish the autonomous organisations such as the editorial boards, the specialists association and the salons which, during the 1980s had played an instrumental role in the development of political debate, of reflection on the flaws of the regime and on the ways to transform it. In a few words, academic research, studies by think tanks concerned with concrete problems have been encouraged, but political discussion has been hampered.

The new leadership under Hu Jintao has basically kept this policy unchanged. Despite the adoption of a new populist discourse, the social and economic status of university professors has continued to improve. In a show of respect for the professors, Hu has decided that they should be consulted on the challenges which confront the country. Members of the Politburo and of the cabinet attend monthly conferences made by famous professors from prestigious universities." Hu Jintao in person opens the meetings which involve lectures of sixty to ninety minutes and a question-

and-answer period." [13] They concern such subjects as global economics, crisis management, the consequences of new technologies etc. Many of the professors have studied or even taught in American Universities. Xue Lan, the executive associate dean of the School of Public Policy and Management at Tsinghua University who has given such a conference insists on the change that has taken place if compared with Mao's rule, when social sciences were considered bourgeois. "When you think that this sort of thing is being done now openly, regularly, pretty much monthly, I think it says the leadership is saying we need to learn, we want to draw on outside expertise. We need to make use of their suggestions." [14] Of course, these consultations depend totally on the will of the leadership, and the freedom granted to the professors in these forums cannot be exerted in the public sphere. But many intellectuals appreciate it, because they believe that convincing the decision makers is more efficient than trying to mobilise the forces of society in order to get things done. Most members of the intelligentsia particularly appreciate these forums because they comfort them in their conviction that they have to act as counsellors to the prince. When the prince gives weight to their advice, they have a tendency to support the prince, and be less interested in claiming for democracy.

Hu-Wen's Line:
Towards a Reform of the Political System?

Developing consultations was not the only way for Hu and Wen to make themselves popular among intellectuals. Their coming to power also raised large hopes of change: the fact that Hu Jintao had not been directly involved in the June 4th massacre, that Wen Jiabao had been the director of the Party General Office under Zhao Ziyang[15] helped create an atmosphere of expectation in a large part of the liberal intelligentsia who had been more or less silenced during the Jiang Zemin era. And as a matter of fact, developments in the period which immediately followed the 16th Party congress in November 2002 seemed to confirm these hopes.

In order to understand the rather liberal attitude adopted by the Hu-Wen leadership, one has to consider the general political situation. The 16th congress designed Hu as the number one of the Party as had been the wish of Deng Xiaoping, but Jiang Zemin was reluctant to abandon all his positions. Studying the example of the late patriarch, he refused to step down from the chairmanship of the Central military commission of the CPC, a position which allowed him to keep control over the People's Liberation Army (PLA). Besides, he stacked the Politburo Standing committee with his cronies, who had the majority in the ruling organ of the Party. Therefore, Hu's margin of manoeuvre appeared considerably limited, and he needed to find ways to extend the basis of his legitimacy. The history of the PRC has shown that transition periods as well as periods of acute power struggle provide spaces for society to voice its discontent. This is another reason why liberal members of the intelligentsia were expecting a more open attitude from the new leader. Besides, as Hu Jintao had been the general secretary of the Communist Youth League where the liberal Hu Yaobang had left a strong imprint, they hoped he would be as open-minded as his mentor. In the first months of his rule, they were proved right.

The way the new leadership reacted to the SARS crisis which burst in winter 2003 immediately after it came into power was the first positive sign. When the epidemic started, the initial reaction by the authorities conformed to the habit of secrecy of the Communist party, with the Guangdong provincial government refusing to admit the seriousness of the crisis and imposing a blackout on the press. This policy was said to have the support of Jiang Zemin as the Health Minister Zhang Wenkang who enforced it was one of his supporters. This might have been one of the reasons why Hu Jintao opposed it. When Jiang Yanyong[16], a military doctor, declared publicly that the SARS epidemic was actually much more serious than had been acknowledged till now, Hu did not conform to the traditional response by Party leaders which should have been to silence Jiang. Instead, showing a new commitment to transparency, he decided to face reality. On 17 April 2003, he summoned a meeting of the Politburo where "he acknowledged the government had lied about the disease and committed the Communist Party to an all-out war against an epidemic sweeping the country and the capital. Three days later, China's Communist leadership carried out its most significant political purge since the crackdown around Tiananmen Square in 1989. The capital's [vice] mayor [Meng Xuenong] and the country's health minister [Zhang Wenkang] were fired for covering up the epidemic of severe acute respiratory syndrome, or SARS."[17].

These resolute initiatives which demonstrated an interest in developing government accountability by the new General Secretary, confirmed the hopes of many intellectuals. The conservative theoretician Kang Xiaoguang, writing a few months later, gave a judgment which many of his colleagues shared in the wake of the SARS crisis:

"From the change of government in March to the victory on SARS in June, Hu Jintao demonstrated his charisma to the whole world and gained the respect and the support of the whole Chinese people."[18]. Such an opinion was not restricted to conservative thinkers. Wang Yi, a law professor at the University of Sichuan famous for the liberal opinions he often expresses on his website, had a very similar reaction: "In 2003, like other intellectuals, I had high expectations for Hu . . . But I didn't understand him – none of us did."[19]

The political developments that followed soon provided Hu Jintao with a new opportunity to display his attitude towards the intelligentsia. On 17 March 2003, a graphic designer from out of town, Sun Zhigang, was arrested in Canton, and taken to a Shelter and Repatriation camp for failing to show his residency permit (*hukou*). Three days later, he died in custody:

> "After the case was reported, Ai Xiaoming, a well-known Chinese scholar, wrote an article on the Internet strongly condemning those who caused his death. Subsequently, more Internet users joined the chorus in support for Ai's article, condemning police brutality.

On May 14th, three legal scholars in China wrote an open letter to the National People's Congress, calling on the legislature to investigate Sun's death, and to abolish, based on the Chinese constitution, the system of [shelter and repatriation]. On May 23rd, another five scholars wrote to the National People's Congress, calling for a constitutional review of [shelter and repatriation] regulations."[20]

This protest started on the Internet, and developed into the first collective large-scale mobilisation on a public issue by mainstream intellectuals since 1989. Under Jiang Zemin, it would have been met with an attempt at silencing the "culprits". But Hu and Wen's attitude was different. Instead of cracking down on this initiative which they could have regarded as a threat to the Party's monopoly on political affairs, they decided to take it into account. On June 20th, Wen Jiabao announced the suppression of the system of shelter and repatriation, a decision which largely surprised the public security apparatus which tried to oppose it. But it also surprised the scholars who had launched the petition.

This decision showed the intelligentsia that its hopes had not been misplaced, and that the new leadership was indeed ready to listen to its voice rather than resorting to repression. Enhanced by this success and encouraged by Hu-Wen's populist discourse, some long time liberal intellectuals tried to push their advantage by launching discussions on the amending of the constitution. Cao Siyuan, who had become famous in the 1980s for his draft law on bankruptcy[21] and for his attempts to obtain the convocation of the NPC during the 1989 pro-democracy movement[22], now the leader of a think tank on economics (the Beijing Siyuan Research Centre for Social Sciences) organised a symposium in Qingdao in June 2003 to discuss the ways to amend the constitution. During this meeting which was attended by Zhu Houze, former Director of the Central Propaganda Department of the CPC under Hu Yaobang, Cao argued for the election of the President of the Republic at universal suffrage[23]. In the following weeks, many meetings to discuss constitutional amendments took place, attended by legal scholars who asked for the establishment of a constitutional court which could put limitations to the power of the executive. But in August, the leadership put an end to the debate, advising the media not to report on it, and urging intellectuals to tackle other tasks. At the moment, this decision was interpreted as a move by Jiang and his supporters to oppose Hu. After all, it was Hu who, immediately after he had become Secretary General of the Party, had launched a campaign "to protect the constitution and the law". A party source quoted by Willy Lam, reinforced this interpretation: "The media must also avoid mentioning 'sensitive' names including . . . surgeon Jiang Yanyong, and even the detention centre victim Sun Zhigang." The same source insisted: "The former president has dismissed as 'bourgeois liberalisation' efforts by scholars to put into the constitution clauses guaranteeing internationally acknowledged civil rights"[24].

But, even though discussion about the ways to change the constitution had been suppressed in the summer, the NPC adopted amendments in its March 2004 session providing for the protection of human rights and the guarantee of private property. These were greeted by most liberal intellectuals as a victory for their cause.

The atmosphere was becoming increasingly euphoric. During the same month of March, an assistant professor of journalism at Peking University, Jiao Guobiao, posted a vehement denunciation of the Central Department of Propaganda[25] on the Internet. He wrote that "the Central Department of Propaganda is at present the only dead angle in China which does not function according to the law; it is the only kingdom of obscurity where the sun of the law doesn't shine"[26]. Jiao emphasised the fact that there were no Propaganda departments in the U.S., or in Europe. He reminded his readers that Nazi Germany had one, headed by Goebbels, and wrote: "Their censorship orders are totally groundless, absolutely arbitrary, at odds with the basic standards of civilisation, and as counter to scientific common sense as witches and wizardry"[27].

At the same time, the new leadership, which did not hesitate to use a populist discourse, was declaring its concern for the "vulnerable social groups" (*ruoshi qunti*), and enlisting the support of the "third sector" to fight the growing social polarisation that threatened the regime in its survival. The success of the struggle against the shelter and repatriation centres had encouraged a number of liberal intellectuals, lawyers, journalists, sociologists, to become wholeheartedly involved in the so-called non-governmental organisations (often Government operated) to help solve the concrete problems of migrant workers, and defend the rights of the farmers victimised by rural bureaucrats. Glad to be able to conciliate the traditional roles of counsellor to the prince and of spokesperson for the people dear to Chinese intellectuals, most members of the intelligentsia abandoned the terrain of political criticism to help solve the pressing social problems. In 2003–2004, a great number of non-governmental organisations (NGOs) were founded, often by lawyers or legal scholars who set up associations to advise migrant workers on their rights; charity organisations mushroomed in most big cities, enlisting the support of intellectuals. In September 2004, on the eve of the 4th plenum of the Central Committee which was to see the resignation of Jiang Zemin of his post of chairman of the Central Military Commission (CMC), most intellectuals had thrown their lot with Hu Jintao, whom they regarded as open-minded, against Jiang Zemin.

The claim for more freedom was becoming increasingly loud. In September, a Guangdong tabloid[28] published an article insisting on the need for China to have a consistent number of "public intellectuals", a term made popular in academic circles by the Shanghai political scientist Xu Jilin. The magazine declared that "the market economy had pushed the majority of intellectuals to the fringes of society, and that China desperately needed them to take an independent stand". It said that China had as many professors and experts "as there are hairs on a cow" but that those intellectuals who were brave enough to stand up for truth, "if they have not already vanished, have become the rarest of rarities". The magazine also heaped praise on American writer Susan Sontag, whom it called "the conscience of America" for her criticism of the U.S. government. The message could not have been clearer.[29]

The magazine also published a list of fifty "public intellectuals" among which many liberals such as Mao Yushi, the founder of the Unirule (Tianze) market studies centre, Cui Jian, the father of Chinese rock and roll, the "hooligan" writer Wang Shuo, doctor Gao Yaojie who had fought to make public the Henan AIDS crisis, the environmentalist Liang Congjie (Friends of Nature), and Wang Yi, the legal specialist from Sichuan who was very outspoken on the net. But it was careful not to include dissidents such as Liu Xiaobo, who, because he had been quite active during the 1989 pro-democracy movement, was considered a dangerous individual by the authorities Nor did it include Dr Jiang Yanyong, the SARS hero, who had dared post a letter denouncing the June 4th massacre that he had witnessed, and asking for the rehabilitation of the Tiananmen movement[30]. However, the publication of this list led to a heated debate on the Internet, without triggering any reaction from the Party. This silence reassured Chinese intellectuals who became convinced that a new era was coming.

The Fourth Plenum of the Central Committee: A Radical Change

Hu's political victory over his rival Jiang Zemin should have confirmed this liberal trend. But this didn't happen. The history of the People's Republic teaches us that when they are on their way towards supreme power, CPC leaders tend to lend a sympathetic ear to the voice of society, all the more so as they need its support (or at least, need to create a better image) to enhance their legitimacy against their predecessors. With the benefit of hindsight, Hu-Wen's relaxed policy towards intellectuals appears as another illustration of this mechanism.

The first disillusion came with the communiqué of the plenum which nominated Hu chairman of the CMC. It announced that the Communist Party should improve its capacity to govern by reinforcing its scientific management and introducing a measure of accountability. To those who had hoped that the new leadership would raise the issue of the reform or the political system, this decision was extremely disappointing:

"Existing rules and practices of democratic recommendation, multi-candidate selection, opinion solicitation on newly appointed officials, public selection of officials, public competition for official post, decision making through a vote by all members of a Party committee instead of arbitrary decision-making by the head of the committee, as well as democratic assessment of incumbent officials should continue to be enforced and further improved"[31]. No hint to the separation between the Party and the State which had been at the centre of Zhao Ziyang's report to the 13th congress in 1987.

Almost at the same time as Hu was crowned by the plenum, stripping his rival Jiang Zemin of his last position, the journalist Zhao Yan was arrested under the accusation of having revealed state secrets, a typical accusation used by hardliners[32] when they want to crackdown on dissent. The State secret that Zhao was accused of having revealed was that Jiang Zemin would step down from his position at the head of the CMC at the plenum. This piece of news was published in the *New York Times* before it was officially announced[33]. This harsh decision was not the first measure taken against the press since Hu's access to the general secretariat in November 2002. But Zhao Yan was not an ordinary journalist. He had distinguished himself as an aggressive reporter who had written well-documented exposés of the corruption of provincial and local cadres in the outspoken magazine *Gaige* (Reform). He had also been active in the civil rights movement (*weiquan yundong*) and had helped peasants bring their cases against corrupt officials, enduring the wrath of the leadership. Zhao's arrest appeared as the beginning of a campaign to curb the actions of the intellectuals involved in the civil rights movement[34]. As a matter of fact, two months later, Li Baiguang, a journalist and the leader of the Qimin Research Centre, a private organisation concerned with peasants' rights, was arrested in Fujian during a field trip to Lu'an[35]. These arrests came in the wake of arrests of other journalists, especially Cheng Yizhong, the editor of the *Nanfang Dushi bao*, which had published the report about Sun Zhigang in 2003. He was arrested on corruption charges on 19 March 2004[36] and was released in August of the same year. Yu Huafeng, the newspaper's general manager and deputy editor, was not so lucky and the day Cheng was arrested, he was sentenced to 12 years on charges of corruption, while Li Minying, the former director of the *Nanfang ribao* group, the paper's parent organisation, was sentenced to 11 years on charges connected to the other case[37].

On 29 September, a few days after Hu's victory at the Central Committee plenum, a document of the Committee announced that six intellectuals among whom the liberal author Yu Jie, the economist Mao Yushi, and Mao Zedong's former secretary, Li Rui, should not be allowed to publish their works in the official press or publishing houses[38].

In December, the editor of the *Zhongguo qingnian bao*, (*China Youth Daily*), Li Xueqian, was forced to step down and was replaced by Li Erliang, a former editor of *Market Daily*, a newspaper under the *People's Daily*, who later cracked down against aggressive reporting[39].   The editor of *Xin zhoubao*, (*Newsweek*) was also fired and replaced by a more docile personality[40].

During the same month, the chief editor of *Gaige* was taken into custody by the police and interrogated during a half day. Intimidation against these outspoken media came after the closure in August of the respected academic journal *Zhanlüe yu Guanli* (*Strategy and Management*), which had published many articles on farmers' resistance against local governments. The pretext was an article which severely criticised the North Korean leadership, but this decision was regarded as a serious blow to academic freedom. This restriction of freedom on campuses was reinforced by the fact that Jiao Guobiao was suspended from teaching at Peking University, whereas law professor Wang Yi, whose website regularly published articles to promote constitutionalism, was also suspended from his teaching position in Sichuan[41]. The latest instance of this wave of repression was the sentencing of Hunan journalist Shi Tao to ten years in jail for having made known abroad the contents of a Party document that limited the freedom of the press[42].

Contemporarily with the crackdown on the press, the

authorities turned to the Internet, where discussions on social conflicts has been rife in the last two years. In the spring of 2005, they decided to close Peking University BBS website *Yita hutu*, which was considered too outspoken. Besides, a new circular ordered that only students could post messages on universities BBS. But, to show that the government did not act only through the Central Department of Propaganda, and was serious about instauring the "rule of law", a new law has been passed at the end of September 2005 to restrict expression on the Internet. Its article 3 confirmed the previous rules (adopted in 1994) by stipulating: "Internet news information service work units that engage in Internet news information service shall abide by the constitution, laws, and regulations, persist in being oriented toward serving the people and serving socialism, persist in correctly guiding public opinion, and safeguard the nation's interests and the public interest."[43]. These new regulations, which put substantial limitations on citizens' basic freedoms show that the so-called rule of law is closer to rule by law, as the law is not based on the protection of basic human rights. As a matter of fact, besides using such old Maoist terms as "serving the people", the law gets more precise and adjoins the Internet to "disseminate healthy and civilised news information" whatever that means, and assigns various governments at all levels the task to enforce the new regulations. These new regulations give more details on what is prohibited in article 19: "(ix) inciting illegal assemblies, associations, marches, demonstrations, or gatherings that disturb social order; (x) conducting activities in the name of an illegal civil organisation;"[44]. These new provisions have clearly been enticed by the recent developments on the Internet, as many "right defenders" have been posting stories describing how peasants were victims of abuses by cadres, or how urban residents were expelled from their homes by real estate companies and municipal governments. These stories have stirred web surfers, propping many of them to criticise the authorities and to mobilise in order to defend the rights of the "vulnerable groups"[45]. Although the new leadership has attracted attention on the growing inequalities, it has shown that it is not ready yet to let citizens intervene in the public space to protect the rights of the weak. The new laws show that the Party won't allow pressure groups to emerge, even if they remain confined to the cyberspace. According to sources, last May, Hu Jintao delivered a speech at a Politburo meeting insisting on the necessity to get rid of the editors who don't heed to the injunctions of the propaganda department (without closing the news media concerned) and to control the civil rights activists, bourgeois liberals, and Falungong activists[46].

After having raised hopes among the liberal groups in China, the Hu-Wen leadership has tightened its grip on the various media, the press and the Internet.

Narrowing the Freedom of Expression of the Liberal Intelligentsia

These were already worrying signs about the new leadership's attitude towards freedom of expression. These signs were soon to be reinforced when, in mid-October, the unofficial Chinese pen-club organised a conference to grant a prize to Zhang Yihe, the famous rightist minister Zhang Bojun's daughter for her book entitled *The past is not like smoke* (*Wangshi bing bu ru yan*), a vigorous denunciation of the 1957 anti-rightist movement. The country's most famous dissident and liberal intellectuals attended the meeting which took place in the suburbs of Peking. The chairman of the pen-club, Liu Xiaobo, a dissident writer abhorred by the Jiang leadership, and its secretary general, Yu Jie, a prolific writer who had been ostracised in recent years, figured prominently at the meeting. The only fact that it was allowed to take place was, at the time, interpreted as a sign of the desire of the Hu-Wen leadership to send a positive sign to the liberal intelligentsia.

These hopes were soon going to be crushed, and as in the heyday of the Cultural Revolution, the reaction came in the guise of a Shanghai newspaper editorial[47]. After a period of relative liberalisation, the article re-stated the framework in which the intelligentsia was allowed to act under the leadership of the Communist Party. And, as in 1966, a few days after the editorial appeared in the city's *Jiefang ribao* (*Liberation Daily*), it was reprinted in the *People's Daily*[48], to make people clearly understand that the stand it had taken represented the line of the Central Government. What did the editorial say?

Its title already set the tone, developed in the article. "To raise the concept of 'public intellectual' means to sow discord in the relations between the intellectuals and the Party, and the vast masses of the people"[49].

The line was clear: intellectuals must submit to the Party authority and must not believe that they can act independently as defenders of the people. This editorial was soon to be transformed into an official Party document. This doesn't mean, of course, that Hu Jintao has taken China back to the days of Mao Zedong. If the Party sees such a necessity to crackdown on public intellectuals and on the media, it is because the latter can make their voices heard in China today. Journalists, to the difference of what happened under Mao, now dare criticise officials and denounce their abuses. Nobody can possibly imagine that another anti-rightist movement is possible in China.

However, or perhaps because Hu Jintao has shown that he has understood the seriousness of the challenge that the increasing social polarisation[50] represents for the regime, he has been especially careful, since 2004, to try and prevent the intelligentsia from working too closely with the "vulnerable groups". Zhao Yan is quite representative of the intellectuals who are ready to take chances to help peasants defend their basic rights. But he is not the only one. In January 2004, *Investigation on China's Farmers*, a book by two reportage writers[51] which denounced the abuses of peasants by local cadres in Anhui province was banned. Nevertheless, its huge success – even after having been banned, it sold hundreds of thousand copies – among urban dwellers shows that it is quite easy to mobilise the solidarity of society against persecution of peasants by Party cadres. This episode shows that the new leadership must walk a tight rope between its professed solidarity with the poor, and the risk that this discourse arouses criticism in society, and leads intellectuals to try to give a voice to the deprived.

In November 2004, dissident writer Liu Xiaobo, the chairman of the unofficial pen-club we mentioned above, launched a collective letter with Yu Jie and others to denounce the carelessness of local leaders and mine owners which caused hundreds of deaths in Shanxi. Are Hu Jintao and Wen Jiabao too conscious of the way the communist party developed in the twenties to let intellectuals get involved in the social question? Anyway, on December 13th, Liu Xiaobo and Yu Jie were taken into custody for 24 hours, and Liu was kept under surveillance for two weeks after that. This kind of repression is only a farce if compared to the way intellectuals were dealt with in Mao's days, or even during Deng's recurrent movements against "bourgeois liberalisation", but it shows that the Party leadership remains wary of the intelligentsia's behaviour.

Despite their attitude during the first year of their mandate, Hu and Wen have tightened the restrictions on the press, and many courageous journalists have been either arrested, threatened or sacked. One of the symbols of the leadership's change of mind is the fact that Ji Fangping's *Jiefang ribao* editorial on "public intellectuals" was awarded the title of "column of the year", an award given by the journalists' association of Shanghai[52]. This decision, obviously made by the communist party which controls the association, is a clear message to the intelligentsia. Coming after the reprint of the same editorial by the *People's Daily*, it is an obvious sign that the Central Government has no intention to let a group of critical public intellectuals emerge in the public sphere. But this is not the only sign that shows the restrictions imposed on intellectuals' freedoms by the new leadership.

A Crackdown on the "Third Sector"?

2004 has not only seen a limitation of the freedom of expression. The non-governmental associations which had been tolerated since the beginning of the twenty-first century have been subject to new restrictions. The official attitude towards them is ambiguous: the authorities have recognised that the "third sector" could be a valuable actor to solve social problems. As the Hu-Wen leadership has often asserted its dedication to improve the lot of the "vulnerable groups", it has encouraged the development of non-governmental organisations which try to help them. Many intellectuals, journalists, lawyers, have been active in Government Operated Non-Governmental Organisations (GONGOs) working with migrant workers[53], or helping to develop rural education[54]. Some are involved in more autonomous organisations, such as those which help migrant workers defend their rights[55], try to help AIDS victims[56], or are concerned with the protection of the environment[57]. During the last years of Jiang's rule, these associations mushroomed, but the majority were not registered as NGOs, as registration requires the sponsorship of an official work unit (the so-called dual management system) and the authorisation of the Ministry of Civil Affairs. Besides, since the 1998 law on associations, there can be only one association working in a certain field in one province. In March 2005, the National People's Congress (NPC) amended the 1998 law on NGOs[58], but despite lobbying by many scholars, it did not scrap the dual management system[59]. The new amendments which provide also for the registration of foreign NGOs do not make it easier for them to register. Until now, most of them had used the existing legal loopholes and had registered as companies. According to information from the Ministry of Civil Affairs, in 2005, there were three million NGOs in the whole country but only 280,000 had registered with it[60]. In 2003, the authorities had shown toleration for this procedure: Wan Yanhai, an activist whose aggressive defence of AIDS victims had landed him in jail, was allowed to register his NGO as a private company after international organisations had vehemently protested against his detention.

But recently, the government has changed attitude. On 21 March 2005, it issued a document ordering the research centres, associations and other NGOs registered as companies to report to the local bureaus of civil affairs. If they had not registered before March 30th, they would be closed down [61]. Despite this administrative order, many NGOs have kept their company status, but this decision shows the desire of the State to reinforce its control on the emerging civil society. Its action has been much tougher with the more radical associations, such as Hou Wenzhuo's Empowerment and Rights Institute (EARI) whose members do not hesitate to go to the villages where conflicts occur and advise the peasants on their rights. During the UN High Commissionner for torture Louise Arbour's visit to Peking, Hou Wenzhuo was put under house arrests. And more recently, during the Taishi (Panyu, Guangdong) villagers protest against the corruption of the village Party secretary, lawyer Guo Feixiong, who is linked to EARI, disappeared[62].

The last years definitely has not been auspicious for intellectuals involved in the civil rights movement. Incomplete statistics show that from the spring to the autumn of 2005 only, more than a dozen lawyers have been arrested because they tried to defend the rights of either urban dwellers threatened with expulsion, or peasants victims of local cadres' abuses[63].

After having raised large hopes among liberal intellectuals by daring to sack the leading cadres who had tried to conceal the truth during the SARS epidemic, the Hu-Wen leadership, once it succeeded in getting rid of Jiang Zemin, has adopted a much more rigid attitude towards the intelligentsia. Proceeding in the continuity of Jiang's attitude, it has not questioned the economic situation of university professors, which has continued to improve. However, whereas from 2002 to 2004, during his struggle against his predecessor, Hu had relaxed controls over NGOs and over the media (especially on the Internet), responding to the protests of intellectual opinion by suppressing the shelter and repatriation centres, he has suddenly changed attitude after his victory at the 4th plenum of the 16th Central Committee. Crackdown on the outspoken media, restriction of the freedom of the BBS, new laws to further curb expression on the Internet have been a shock to the liberal intelligentsia. Moreover, the frequent use of Marxist ideology to enforce conformity, the return of Maoists expressions such as "Serve the people", and the denunciation of "public intellectuals" have aroused the ire of writers and professors[64]. In the last two years, Hu has also increased control over the NGOs, trying to confine them to a role of subsidiary to State organisations, and has used the law to curb the freedom of the intelligentsia. Of course, no large-scale movement has been launched to scare the intellectual community; however, many outspoken journalists and lawyers have been arrested and given harsh sentences, professors have been prohibited from teaching[65], writers have been intimidated, even old cadres who dared ask for the rehabilitation of June 4th[66] or to demand the democratisation of the Party rule were criticised[67].

In 2005, there has been an obvious hardening in the policy towards intellectuals. This hardening was epitomised by the CPC's attitude after the demise of former Prime Minister and General Secretary Zhao Ziyang who died under house arrests on 17 January 2005. On this occasion, Hu showed that he had no intention to seize this opportunity to let Chinese society discuss its recent past. Zhao's death was not immediately reported, and, when it was, it was not in the front page of the *People's Daily*. Most of Zhao's collaborators and liberal intellectuals were not allowed to pay their respects to the former leader[68]. Only persons with invitations were allowed to go to the funeral[69]. It took a long time to the highest authorities in the Party to release the eulogy, and they insisted on the "mistakes" made by Zhao during the 1989 demonstrations[70]. To the risk of provoking the disappointment of the members of the former Premier's intellectual networks who had been active in the reforms of the 1980s, Hu Jintao has persisted in the attitude adopted by the CPC since June 4th, missing the opportunity to rally an important fraction of the Party behind his banner.

Under these circumstances, the decision by the new President to commemorate Hu Yaobang's ninetieth birthday is difficult to interpret. Why did Hu Jintao decide to celebrate the memory of one of the most radical reformers of the eighties? Even if there had been many contradictions between Hu and Zhao during that decade[71], they both had a comparable attitude towards students demonstrations. Hu was sacked from his position of General Secretary for having been too tolerant of "bourgeois liberalisation", whereas Zhao was put under house arrests for having refused to support the repression of the pro-democracy movement in 1989. Recently, the CPC highest authorities have refused to publish a biography of Hu Yaobang written by three professors of the central Party school, and only his selected works until 1976 have been published for the occasion[72]. Therefore, the celebration has not represented an opportunity to rehabilitate Hu's ideas on political reform, or study his attitude towards outspoken intellectuals.

As has often been the case in the PRC history, once a new leader has consolidated his position at the centre, he tries to eliminate any kind of opposition, and to install his hegemony on the ideological and political fields. Whereas the period of transition between Jiang and Hu provided society with opportunities to express itself and resulted in a relaxed policy towards intellectuals – conforming to the law of the Chinese communist regime that struggle at the top allows for opportunities at the bottom – the consolidation of the new leader's position has allowed him to take control of the propaganda apparatus and to prevent criticisms to be voiced. Worried about the increasing number of conflicts provoked by the continuing social polarisation, Hu Jintao has been eager to monopolise the discourse in favour of the poor, and to keep intellectuals from seizing the opportunity to act as their spokespeople to threaten the regime.

However, Hu's battle has not been won yet. Times have changed and those who are targeted by criticism do not submit as easily as a few decades ago to Party pressure. They sometimes can obtain the support of foreign or international organisations, whose weight grows because of China's increasing exposure to globalisation. For instance, in April 2005, UNESCO gave the World Press Freedom Price to *Nanfang dushi bao* editor Cheng Yizhong, who had been jailed by the authorities[73]. Whereas he was not allowed to attend the prize giving ceremony, he nevertheless sent a speech in which he compared his country to a "pigsty" where food is plentiful but freedom is absent. On 5 June 2005, 2,356 journalists sent an open letter to the Guangdong authorities complaining that the sentences which struck Yu Huafeng and Li Minying were "very unfair" and asking for their unconditional liberation[74]. This letter was the largest collective protest by intellectuals since 1989.

These reactions show that despite the hardening of Party policies towards the intelligentsia since Hu Jintao consolidated his position, many intellectuals, especially lawyers and journalists dare criticise official decisions. Whether these attitudes can become the seeds of an opposition movement in the years to come remains to be seen.

Notes and References

1. Mao Zedong "Talks at the Yenan Forum on Literature and Arts", *Selected Works of Mao Zedong*, http://www.marxists.org/reference/ archive/mao/selected-works/volume-3/mswv3_08.htm.

2. Cf Merle Goldman, *Literary Dissent in Communist China* (Cambridge: Harvard University Press, 1967).

3. First proposed by Zhou Enlai in 1964, this objective was announced after Deng's rehabilitation in 1973, and once again in 1977. The Four modernisations are the modernisations of agriculture, industry, national defence and science and technology.

4. An article entitled "Practice is the only criterion for truth" published in *Guangming Ribao* on May 11th, 1978 and reprinted the day after by *Renmin ribao* and *Jiefangjun bao* launched the campaign for the "emancipation of thought".

5. On this conference, see Yu Guangyuan, Wang Enmao, Li Desheng et al. 改变中国命运的四十一天 *Gaibian Zhongguo Mingyunde Sishiyi tian* (The 41 days that shook China) Shenzhen, Haitian chubanshe, 1998 and Merle Goldman, "Hu Yaobang's Intellectual Network and the Theory Conference of 1979", *China Quarterly*, No. 126, July 1991, pp. 219–242.

6. I am referring to the former Red Guards who denounced the regime after they were exiled to the countryside in the wake of the Cultural Revolution. Representative of this category are intellectuals like the founder of Peking Social and Economic Research Institute Chen Ziming, the 1980s leader of the Sitong research institute Cao Siyuan . . .

7. Cf Jean-Philippe Béja, *A la recherche d'une ombre chinoise. Le*

mouvement pour la démocratie en Chine (1919–2004) (Paris: Editions du Seuil, 2004), pp. 114–120.

8. The first large-scale movement against "bourgeois liberalisation" took place in 1981, with the denunciation of Bai Hua's *Unrequited Love*, followed by the movement against "spiritual pollution" in 1983–84, and the second movement against "bourgeois liberalisation" in 1987.

9. 发展是硬道理 *Fazhan shi ying daoli* (Development is the core logic) became the slogan of the day.

10. "Once low-income urban teachers better paid than white collar workers", *People's Daily*, 10 September 2004.

11. Adam Michnik, *Letters from Freedom*, (Berkeley, LA: University of California Press, 1998).

12. Richard McGregor, "A new push to enforce the unwritten rules", Financialexpress, Sept. 16, 2005, http://www.financialexpres.bd.com/index3.asp?cnd=9/16/2005&section_id=4&newsid=706&spcl=no consulted on 17 September 2005.

13. Howard French, "China Opens a Window on the Really Big Ideas", "Letter from Asia" *New York Times*, 2 June 2004.

14. *Ibid.*

15. Everybody in Peking recalled that Wen had gone to Tian'anmen with Zhao Ziyang on the last public appearance of the latter on 19 May 1989.

16. Joan Kaufman, "Can China Cure Its Severe Acute Reluctance to Speak?" *Washington Post*, 27 April 2003.

17. John Pomfret, "Outbreak Gave China's Hu an Opening", *Washington Post*, 13 May 2003.

18. 中国步入进步时代 (代序言) (*Zhongguo buru jinbu shidai (daixuyan)* China slowly heads towards a progressive period (preface) in 康晓光, 中国的道路, (*Zhongguo de daolu, China's Road*) p. 2.

19. Paul Mooney, "Hu Jintao good for peasants, bad for intellectuals", *Asia Times*, 10 March 2005.

20. Ding Dajun, "The Role of Chinese Intellectuals in the Hu-Wen Era", *China Strategy*, Vol. 1, January 2004. http://www.csis.org/isp/csn/040130.pdf.

21. He was then jokingly referred to as "Cao Pochan" Cao Bankruptcy.

22. Cf Béja, Bonnin, Peyraube, *Le Tremblement de terre de Pékin*, (*Peking Earthquake*) (Paris: Gallimard, 1991).

23. Cai Yongmei, 胡锦涛正在除下面纱 "Hu Jintao zhengzai chuxia miansha" ("Hu Jintao is taking off his veil"), 开放 *Kaifang*, 217, Janury 2005, p. 33.

24. Willy Wo-Lap Lam, "Setback for China's constitutional reform", *CNN*, 1 September 2003.

25. Sometime in 2000, the authorities issued a "circular" asking the foreign press to translate the term *xuanchuan bu*, department of propaganda, by "department of publicity". Of course, the Chinese name has remained, and the function too. However, many foreign journalist have accepted to use this benign term, which, I guess, helps them convince their readers that China has entered post-communism. This, and the adoption of the name "Beijing", show an amazing pusillanimity in the foreign press. (Do the Chinese say New York, or Paris in their language?).

26. From Jiao Guobiao's letter "Taohao Zhongxuanbu" which could be found on the website Observechina.com where it was posted on 9 April 2004.

27. The quotation comes from Joseph Kahn, "Let Freedom Ring? Not So Fast. China's Still China", *New York Times*, 4 May 2004.

28. 南方人物周刊 *Nanfang Renwu Zhoukan*, (*Southern People Weekly*) No. 7, 8 September 2004.

29. Paul Mooney, "Gagging China's intellectuals", *Asia Times*, 15 December 2004. http://atimes01.atimes.com/atimes/Front_Page/FF03Aa07.html.

30. Dr Jiang's letter was posted on the Internet on 24 February 2004, and translated into English on *CND*. The original version can be found on the URL http://my.cnd.org/modules/wfsection/article.php?articleid=5751.

31. "CPC pledges to focus on Party building for advancement of ruling capacity", *People's Daily on line*, 26 September 2004.

32. On 15 October 1979, Wei Jingsheng, the author of the *dazibao* "The Fifth Modernisation: Democracy" was sentenced to a jail term of 15 years for counter-revolutionary activities, and for revealing State secrets.

33. Cf. *The New York Times*, 7 September 2004. The decision was officially announced on the 19th.

34. Yu Wenxue, 胡锦涛推行毛式文化专政, ("Hu Jintao tuixing Maoshi wenhua zhuanzheng", "Hu Jintao enforces a Maoist type cultural dictatorship") 开放 (*Kaifang*) No. 222, June 2005, p. 15.

35. 4 January 2005, "People's Republic of China: Arrests of Writers" *International pen club*, http://www.internationalpen.org.uk/dev/viewArticles.asp?findID_=258. and Elaine Kurtenbach, "Chinese Journalist Detained by Police", *South China Morning Post* 20 December 2005.

36. Sophie Beach, "Southern Metropolis editors arrested" *China Digital Times*, March 22nd, 2004. http://chinadigitaltimes.net/2004/03/southern_metrop.php.

37. Edward Cody, "Arrest of Journalists Seen as Payback for A Bold Voice in China", *Washington Post*, 4 April 2005. However, because of the pressure, the sentences were reviewed and Yu's sentence was reduced from 12 to 8 years, whereas Li's was reduced from 11 to 6 years.

38. 乌苏里, 胡锦涛思恩仇报封杀李锐 ("Hu Jintao Sien choubao fengsha Li Rui, Repaying favors with vengeance", "Hu Jintao makes Li Rui silent"), 开放 (*Kaifang*) , No. 222, June 2005, pp.16–19.

39. See Li Datong, "A Letter To China Youth Daily's New Editor-in-Chief Li Erliang" (就中国青年报新的考评办法致李而亮总编辑的信, 李大同), *Observe China*, http://www.observechina.net/info/artshow.asp?ID=36159.

40. "Editors at outspoken newspapers reined in", *South China Morning Post*, 14 December 2004.

41. "The Role of China's Public Intellectuals at the Start of the Twenty-first Century", Testimony of Merle Goldman, congressional executive commission on China, 10 March 2005.

42. "Journalist gets 10 years in jail for leaking secrets", *China Daily*, 30 April 2005.

43. "Rules on the Administration of Internet News Information Services" promulgated on Sept. 25th, 2005, translated on *China Digital Space*, http://www.seedwiki.com/wiki/china_digital_space/.cfm?wpid=207566.

44. *Ibid.*

45. A serious instance was the conflict which took place in Taishi village, Panyu municipality, Guangdong province. As the news that villagers protested against the corruption of the village chief was posted on the Internet, Peking lawyers and Canton university professors tried to intervene on their behalf. The peasants were finally defeated. (September 2005).

46. 陈宇阳，胡锦涛力堵爆发颜色革命 ("Hu Jintao endeavours to prevent the colour revolution"), *Kaifang*, No. 223, July 2005, pp. 10–12. There was one more evidence of this policy when Li Datong (李大同) was sacked from his position of editor of *Bingdian* (冰点) in January 2006.

47. "Touguo biaoxiang kan shizhi: lun 'gonggong zhishifenzi lun" ("See reality through the appearances: about public intellectuals"), *Jiefang ribao*, 15 November 2004.

48. *Renmin Ribao*, 25 November 2004.

49. Touguo biaoxiang . . . , *art. cit.*

50. The official press has innumerable reports on this topic. For a recent example, cf." Party school journal warns against China's widening income gap", *People's Daily*, 20 September 2005.

51. Chen Kuaidi, Chuntao, *Zhongguo Nongmin Diaocha* (*Investigation on China's Farmers*) (Beijing, Renmin wenxue chubanshe, 1998).

52. See Richard McGregor, "A new push to enforce the unwritten rules", *financialexpress*, 16 September 2005, http://www.financialexpress-bd.com/index3.asp?cnd=9/16/2005&section_id=4&newsid=706&spcl=no.

53. For example, *Dagongmei zhi jia*, which is directly linked to the All China's Women Federation.

54. Such as the Hope (Xiwang) project, which is linked to the Communist Youth League.

55. For example, Beijing Facilitators, which was founded by former members of the *dagongmei zhi jia* or the Empowerment and Rights Institute in Peking headed by a Harvard and Oxford graduate in law, Hou Wenzhuo.

56. Such as Wan Yanhai's Aizhi, or the orphanages set up by Li Dan.

57. There are hundreds of such organisations in the whole of China.

58. Registration Administration of People-Run Non-Enterprise Units, promulgated in October 1998.

59. Josephine Ma, "NGOs to keep links to official agencies", *South China Morning Post*, 7 March 2005.

60. 南方周末 *Nanfang zhoumo* May 19th quoted in Yu Wenxue, 胡锦涛推行毛式文化专政, 开放 No. 222, June 2005, pp. 12–15.

61. Qiu Xin, "China curbs civil society groups", *Asia Times*, 19 April 2005.

62. 维权网信息交流平台 (Chinese Rights Defenders Information Bulletin), 21 September 2005. Gao has been arrested once more in September 2006.

63. Willy Lam, "Hu Boosts Power as he Scrambles to Maintain Social Stability", *China Brief*, Vol. V, Issue 19, 13 September 2005.

64. Many Peking writers and theoreticians told us that they were increasingly missing the "late Jiang era".

65. See supra.

66. Dr Jiang Yanyong wrote his letter in February, and was arrested for a few weeks in the spring of 2005.

67. Li Rui wrote a letter to the 16h congress in the fall of 2002. After the 4th plenum, publishers were advised not to publish his articles.

68. His secretary Bao Tong, who spent 7 years in jail after June 4th 1989, was not allowed to go and see his former boss.

69. Philip Pan, "Chinese Authorities Plan Invitation-Only Service for Zhao", *Washington Post*, 28 January 2005.

70. "In the political turbulence which took place in the late spring and early summer of 1989, Comrade Zhao committed serious mistakes." *Xinhua*, 29 January 2005.

71. See Jean-Philippe Béja, *A la recherche d'une ombre chinoise: le mouvement pour la démocratie en Chine* (In search of a Chinese shadow, the Chinse pro-democracy movement) (Paris: Seuil, 2004); and Ruan Ming, *Deng Xiaoping: chronique d'un empire* (Paris: Picquier, 1992).

72. Willy Lam, "Hu's Reformist Gimmick", *Asian Wall Street Journal*, 28 September 2005.

73. See p. 10.

74. 刘晓波 Liu Xiaobo, 新闻良知挑战新闻管制 ("Xinwen liangzhi tiaozhan xinwen guanzhi", "Journalistic conscience challenges the press management organs"), 争鸣 (*Zhengming*), No. 336, 10, 2005, pp. 21–22.

21

Interpreting Inequality and Crime in China: A Social and Cultural Capital Perspective[1]

Guoping JIANG
Tit Wing LO

Rising Inequality

China used to be one of most egalitarian societies in Mao's era. When Deng Xiaoping came into power in late 1970s, he started a process of reform to stimulate economic development that resulted in widening the income gap between the rich and the poor and thus threw off the shackles of Maoist egalitarianism.[2] Later on in 1984, Chinese government issued the "Decision of the Communist Party of China Central Committee on Reform of the Economic System" (Central Committee of the CPC, 1984) that further led to unequal distribution of income.[3] Needless to say, China's reform is success-ful in terms of economic development. As expected, the income gap has widened significantly since the reforms. The Gini coefficient is an indicator of income inequality that allows comparisons over time.[4] For example, from 1981 to 1984, according to the World Bank, the Gini coefficient for the whole country increased from 0.288 to 0.297,[5] which is within the normal range of expected fluctuation. However, while the annual increase rate of residents' income was below 1% from 1984 to 1989, the Gini coefficient increased from 0.297 to 0.349 over that period, indicating a rapid

Figure 1: Theil Inequality Index of China between 1987 and 2000

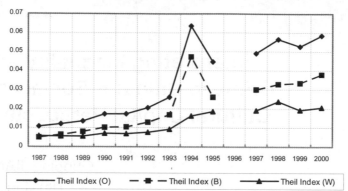

Source: UTIP-UNIDO University of Texas Inequality Project – United Nations Industrial Development Organisation. Retrieved October 20, 2005, from http://utip.gov.utexas.edu/data.html

Note:
1. Theil Index (O): Overal Theil Inequality Index for China
2. Theil Index (B): Between Province Component of Theil Inequality Index for China
3. Theil Index (W): Within Province Component of Theil Inequality Index for China
4. Data on 1996 is missing.

Figure 2: Total No. of Crimes in China between 1987 and 2003

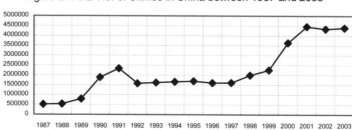

Source: *China Law Yearbook 1997, China Statistics Yearbook 1998, 1999, 2000, 2001, 2002, 2003* and *2004*

Total number of cases on crime is calculated by the Ministry of Public Security of China

growth in income inequality. The situation since 1989 has become worse even though residents' income increased speedily with the annual growth rate at 7%[6]. The Gini coefficient rose from 0.38[7] in 1995 to 0.403[8] in 1998.

Some other scholars[9] arrive at different Gini coefficients based on data from household sample surveys. However, the rising Gini coefficients and widening gaps in incomes are very similar across all these studies. Income inequality has not only come to the attention of academics, but also a daily reality for Chinese people. In Wong and Lee's study[10], 96.5% of a sample of respondents in Shanghai, the most developed metropolitan city in China, agreed that income disparities are large nowadays. Such a high level of income inequality is detrimental to the level of social connectedness across society.

Inequality is not only reflected in incomes, it also affects housing[11], education[12], gender differences[13], health care[14], regional variation[15], and so on. The inequality is so rampant that even officials admit that it has reached the alarm level. [16] It seems inevitable that the growing inequality at a time when over half of the population live in grinding poverty will exacerbate social problems and breed further uncertainty and instability in China. Overall, this trend of inequality is confirmed by the Theil Inequality Index constructed by the UN Industrial Development Organisation. According to this Index, inequality in China started to rise from 0.01 in 1987 to as high as 0.06 in 2000 (see Figure 1).

Rising Crime

Along with the booming economy and rising inequality is rising crime rate[17]. Figure 2 shows that the total number of crimes reported to the Ministry of Public Security rose from about 0.5 million in late 1980s to almost 4.5 million in early 2000s. Furthermore, the percentage of serious crime has also increased[18]. In Mao's era, Chinese could sleep without locking the door for they did not feel endangered but this is not true anymore. Robbery, homicide and rape occur everyday and everywhere. People are afraid to go out alone in late night. Children are not encouraged to go out for fun without an adult's surveillance. They do not feel safe anymore. There is no necessary linkage between economy boom and crime. Something more fundamental lies behind these changes. We suggest that social inequality is the fundamental construct that must be put into the framework. Further, we need to understand how social inequality is social structurally constructed, to explain why crime has increased in the economy boom period.

Along with economic developments, there has been a growth in corruption within China. As Gong states, "recent years have witnessed a spread of corruption into new economic areas as the scope of reform widened in China."[19] Corruption happens in the everyday life of the ordinary people and in important areas of economic activity, such as the stock market and real estate and international financial transactions. Corruption emerges in the form of graft, bribes, and also tax evasion and financial fraud. It is contended that "the 'second revolution,' initiated by Deng Xiaoping, precipitated a period of unprecedented social and economic change including increasing crime and corruption rate"[20]. Just because it is so rampant, "in the post-Mao era, political corruption has become one of the central concerns, even an obsession, for the citizens of the People's Republic of China"[21]. The studies by the People's University[22], He,[23] and Hsu[24] provide support for the above statement and demonstrate that corruption is one of the social problems which Chinese concerns most.

The relationship between economic deprivation and crime has been assessed by numerous empirical studies in the West. In particular, variables such as income inequality, income distribution, unemployment, GDP/GNP per capita and poverty have been examined[25]. However, studies on the relationship between economic deprivation, whether absolute or relative, and crime in China are few[26]. With the objective to enrich current research on this perspective, this chapter attempts to provide readers a background to the understanding of the reasons behind social change, rising inequality and increasing crime rate in China.

Definitions of Inequality

The idea of social inequality is so old that it can be traced back to Plato. More recently, it has been diversely defined within sociology. O'Rand categorised sociological definitions into three types. The first approach is to "define inequality in terms of the distribution of socially valued attributes such as power, wealth, and health"[27]; the second is to define inequality in terms of the relative position in social categories which "determine relations of dominance, such as class, race, and gender"[28]; the third is to define inequality as a "form of social relations rather than the attributes of individuals in those relations and to account for patterns of unequal relations without referring to oppositions"[29]. However, all the above definitions are based on well stratified societies, but may not be equally suitable for a society changing without any turmoil, especially one transforming from egalitarianism.

According to Marshall, social inequality occurs when there are "unequal rewards or opportunities for different individuals with a group or groups within a society",[30] while income inequality refers only to the extent of disparity between high and low incomes. Although the degree of income inequality is often regarded as an important aspect of the fairness of the society we live in, that does not mean income inequality alone is the critical dependent variable. In practice, there is a reciprocal relationship between income inequality and social inequality. Heller also puts emphasis on structural inequality: "the structure indicates an arrangement of elements: the inequality is not random but follows a pattern, displays relative constancy and stability, and is backed by ideas that legitimate and justify it"[31].

Moreover, as mentioned above, Deng Xiaoping's main view of reform is to get China on the road to becoming a market economy which takes modern economic liberalism as its doctrine. Under the doctrine of economic liberalism, all societies are expected to generate equal opportunities for all members to have access to social resources, including education, employment, housing, health care, upward mobility, human rights, justice, recreation and so forth[32].

The characteristics of liberalism emphasise meritocracy. This fits for the Chinese's desire of a fairer process of distribution in China after years of experience with vague and subjective criteria of virtuocracy during Mao's era[33]. Under the principle of meritocracy, there should be widespread procedural fairness in the evaluation of qualifications for positions[34]. The premise of liberalism is to enable fair competition among individuals for unequal positions or rewards in society. If this premise is not satisfied, inequality emerges. Inevitably people are differentiated in terms of biological characteristics such as sex, age, strength, and agility, and in every society they are also differentiated by social roles, work tasks, or occupations. Social inequality does not grow out of these differentiations, but out of life chances structured by social institutions or reward system non-justified by majority of society.

The Pre-reform Stratification

Human history is a continuous river. Any historical stage is based on its preceding stage. Current Chinese stratification is the continuity of pre-reform stratification. So, to analyze the social inequality or dynamics of stratification during the transformation of China, it is useful to describe the prior stratification. Mao Zedong, as a communist, treated eliminating class as his major duty after the foundation of People's Republic of China. Through a series of political movement, including "Three-Antis", "Five-Antis", "Four-Cleans", "Land Reforms", and "Socialist Transformation movement", Chinese government was seen as having reached the goal of the "classless society" in the late 1950s.[35]

Although classes in Marxian definition had been eliminated through "socialist transformation movement" by 1958, four major social groups have actually existed over the years. The first is "cadres" who are party members and who work at administrative work unit (*xingzheng danwei*), non-profit institutions (*shiye danwei*), profit enterprises (*qiye danwei*) or military units. The second group is industrial "workers" who live in cities with an urban household registration (*hukou*). Even though they do not have any power to allocate social resources, they are entitled to various welfare such as employment, public medical care and other subsidies distributed by state[36]. The third group is "peasants" and this was the largest one. They were not bound to the countryside out of choice, but as a result of a rigid household registration system (*hukou*) which had been limiting Chinese to the place where they were born since 1950s[37], and further separated peasants from the social resources available to other sectors. There were only a few opportunities for them to get an urban *hukou*[38], such as through admission to college or by marriage[39]. The fourth group is "intellectuals" who scatter in different work units and have higher status.

Social Stratification and the Four Capitals

The above descriptions of the different groups in pre-reform China were principally seen as horizontal. However, although these groups were not recognised as classes in a hierarchy system, they were hierarchically differentiated with regard to social resources. Or in Bourdieu's term, these groups had different amounts of assets including economic capital, social capital, cultural capital, and symbolic capital, as discussed below:

Economic Capital

Economic capital is the possession of productive property, money and material objects[40]. Before the reform, urban residents' (cadres, workers, and intellectuals) income was twice that of peasants[41]. In addition, urban residents, and especially the cadres, enjoyed many subsidies that were not available to peasants so that the true income gap would be larger, but still would not be that great compared to present income disparities. The income differences between provinces were not salient either.[42] According to Parish, "much of the inequality in income is among people in the same occupation rather than between occupations."[43] In other words, there was an elite section in all occupations that actually had an advantage in income even during this period.

Social Capital

Bourdieu refers social capital to "positions and relations in grouping and social network"[44]. Lin elaborated this concept as "resources accessible social connections" or "resources embedded in the ties of one's networks."[45] Previous studies on western society suggest that "social groups have different access to social capital because of their advantaged or disadvantaged structural positions and social networks"[46]. Similarly, cadres in China had far more social resources than peasants or workers do. They could help their sick relatives to be hospitalised easily; they could help their relatives to find a job somehow[47]; they could purchase scarce merchandise without the normally required goods stamps; and they could get their underperforming children into good schools[48]. In a rigid society without social mobility, all members develop their social network within their own sector. For example, Croll found that both urban and rural residents tried to select marriage partners from their own status group.[49] This further stabilised the difference in the social capital of different groups. Zhao found that the social networks of laid-off workers were mainly composed of relatives, while citizens in general had more members of their network from outside family[50]. Zhao also showed that "the laid-off workers have a rather low network resource score, which is also lower than that of the citizens in general."[51] Overall, laid-off workers have always belonged to the most disadvantaged group in society and always had the least amount of social capital.

Cultural Capital

Cultural capital, for Bourdieu, refers to "informal interpersonal skill, habits, manners, linguistic styles, educational credentials, tastes, and lifestyles"[52]. Cultural capital in its institutionalised state provides academic credentials and qualifications which create a "certificate of cultural competence which confers on its holder a conventional, constant, legally guaranteed value with respect to power"[53]. Although cultural capital is in part related to individual charisma, the amount of cultural capital each person holds is also socially determined. The cadres and their descendents have more opportunity to acquire interpersonal skills, manners and other socially valued elements just because of their positions in society. Moreover, they are also in the position to create the criteria that define accepted cultural capital which common people need to acquire in order to move up in the hierarchy. Further, these definitions favor their own interests and those of the members of their own network. Bourdieu also argues that "the scholastic yield from educational action depends on the cultural capital previously invested by the family"[54]. Cadres' offspring are getting a better education compared to workers' or peasants'. In this sense, the cadre group certainly have more cultural capital than the workers or peasants. In summary, workers and peasants, in general, have lower status with respect to cultural capital.

Symbolic Capital

Symbolic capital, as Turner defined it, is "the use of symbols to legitimate the possession of varying levels and configurations of the other three types of capital."[55] It can be seen as a special form of power which is not perceived as power but as a legitimate demand for recognition, deference, or the services of others. This invisible power is fundamentally available to the cadre group only. Workers and peasants, first, do not have as much social capital, cultural capital or economic capital as cadres do. For Bourdieu, just because of symbolic nature of capital, the interchangeability among other types of capital is possible. Moreover, the interchanges can be made in a legitimate way. Since workers and peasants do not have any symbolic capital advantage over cadres, their situations become worse because of their inability to use symbolic capital to acquire other benefits. On the other hand, the cadre group who are privileged in cultural capital are, thereby, likely to become more advantaged in economic capital or social capital too. The reciprocal reinforcements among capitals put workers and peasant into a more disadvantaged situation.

Based on the above analyses, we can see that the pre-reform Chinese society actually had a dual structure: the cadre group versus the worker and peasant group. Even though cadre group did not own the means of production or have a much greater advantage in income due to the "socialist transformation" and "de-stratification" movements[56], they were privileged in many other ways. Since their private property was not allowed in the pre-reform period, the advantages of capital was mainly reflected in access to welfare, health care, prestige, power, or the quality and quantity of personal networks, rather than in income. It is so dormant that people even did not notice its existence. However, these capital privileges do have a potential for enabling people to make money. They are like a sleeping volcano whose eruption may transform the world. It is this difference in capital privilege that laid the foundation for income disparity in later China. Further, although the urban workers benefit because of Hukou system and other institutional structures, these do not guarantee them advantages in capitals to a much greater degree than peasants. Basically, they are on the same level as peasants. That is why Li, Yang and Wang state that "in Chinese society the political system and the structure of social positions are identical."[57]

Inequality Institutionally Constructed

Reform is a process of adjustment. Inevitably, some groups will benefit from the reform, while others may suffer from it[58]. The Chinese economic reform has no exception. The main task of the reform was the establishment of the market system, a complex institution. Market, as an institution in general, requires certain organisational principles and sub-institutions governing human economic behaviours and possibly other kinds of activities. Wang summarised the changes as requiring the following conditions to be met:

(1) a legitimate purpose of maximizing profit for each producer;

(2) the opening of the economy to everyone's entry with an ideal of free flow or exchange of all economic resources;

(3) trading of economic resources and products based on mutually exclusive individual, or *legalis homo*, property rights;

(4) a changeable price system determined primarily by supply and demand;

(5) effective protection and enforcements of market transition such as contracts; and

(6) sufficient independence of economic activities from most of the non-economic concerns people may have.[59]

By comparing Chinese institutional changes in the past 26 years with the above market principles, we find that Chinese economic reform has sometimes been reluctant to adopt the above principles. It is understandable that Chinese government had to reform gradually and incompletely in order to avoid the political collapses that happened in European socialist countries. But, this incomplete reform was at the cost of the interests of the peasants or urban workers who had already been disadvantaged in society, and it has given rise to a pyramidal structure with 80% living at the bottom instead of the diamond shaped one where most were in the middle as before[60].

Income

The Chinese reform started from the rural area. The first stage of reform is characterised as "low growth and equality". Peasants' income increased due to commodity economy system, or more specifically, the household responsibility system and open market[61]. New agricultural policy allowed rural peasants to participate in sideline production and open market activities, which stimulated the peasants' enthusiasm to produce. As a result, the produce, like grain, cotton, and corn increased. Peasants were also allowed to sell the surplus production in private exchange markets[62]. Therefore, the income of peasants was raised.[63] Another positive consequence was that peasants were able to free themselves from land and move to the urban area for more earnings.

However, the "low growth and equality" period ended in 1984 when the income differences between peasants and the other sectors started to grow again. The reasons were that the commercialisation of produce did not increase the productivity in the rural sector[64] and that, contrary to Wang's fourth principle aforesaid, the produce price remained under the control of the state rather than being determined by supply and demand[65]. In addition, price increases of agricultural products have been much lower than that of industrial products[66]. Even though town-village enterprises (TVEs) began to emerge later, only TVEs on the coastal areas did well[67]. Surplus labour migrates to the metropolitan cities, but because the floating peasants are low in cultural capital, they can only fill low-income positions, such as babysitter, manual labour, restaurant worker, street cleaner, that urban residents are reluctant to take[68]. Due to the *hukou* system, they are not eligible for basic living rights as urban residents[69]. This, too, is contrary to the market principle of opening job opportunities to all in order to create a free flow of labour.

Moreover, peasants are taxed in unreasonable ways.[70] In these ways, the opportunities for peasants have been limited as follows:

- to stay at home and engage in agriculture;
- to migrate to the urban area to fill the lower positions;
- to find a job at a local TVE;
- to develop his/her own business.

No matter what choice he/she makes, he/she will encounter difficulties. Those who stay at home have to contend with the relatively lower price increase of agricultural products compared to that of industrial products and the limited amount of arable land limits the amount that can be produced. If they migrate to urban areas, they can only earn low wages and are not eligible for urban benefits. Joining a TVE is an option in well developed areas but since 1997 the profits earned by TVEs have been decreasing and a job at TVE does not provide access to social services or guarantee a high-income. The final option of starting one's own business requires social and cultural capitals that most peasants lack. Thus although the living conditions of peasants are better than that in Mao's era, relatively they have benefited less from the reforms than the other groups.

Then how about workers in urban areas? The economic reform in cities was carried out by first creating a number of distinct state owned enterprises (SOEs). There were four major policy goals implemented in relation to the SOEs:

- increased managerial autonomy so that the general manager was given power over production decisions, choice of materials, the sale of products, and also the employment of personnel;
- providing incentives to stimulate production by motivating employees (at first through profit retention, later replaced by a revised tax system);
- developing a share-holding system, which enabled the SOEs to move toward privatisation. As SOEs were privatised, it became apparent that the enterprising administrative and managerial cadres turned out to be shareholders of SOEs[71];
- reducing the numbers of employees in order to reduce costs. Zhang found that thirty million SOE employees were laid-off since the SOE reform and they had to search for new jobs.[72]

Although the performance of SOEs is now better than before the reform, not all SOEs revived. [73] And in many cases, workers' incomes were not significantly increased[74].

Then who is getting ahead in general? It is the administrative staff including cadres (*xingzheng danwei* and *shiye danwei*) and employees in work units monopolised by government departments related to telecommunications, cements, petroleum, finance, insurance, and stock, who are benefiting from the reforms. The administrative staff became rich because of decentralisation and the subsequent off-budget issue. Decentralisation aiming to revive local economy has two unintended consequences: fragmentation and off-budget transactions (often referred to as "little safe") [75] . Fragmentation is an administrative problem, but off-budget transactions are an income inequality issue. As long as each department has authority over its own administration, it will find reasons to charge or overcharge common people who need to get an authorisation (or "stamps").

Plenty of such cases can be identified. For instance, the Public Security Bureau may charge a prostitute 5,000 yuan when she is caught; an elementary school may charge migrant students an extra 3,000 yuan admission fee; the Family Planning Committee may charge newly married couple 2,000 yuan for sex education, and so on. Whether the corresponding department is actually authorised to impose these charge and the amount of any legitimate charge are very ambiguous matters. Usually, most departments just charge as much as they think people are prepared to pay. The fee collected will be put into department's "little safe", which will be used to provide staff bonuses that are often considerably larger than their salaries. That is why a common police can own a private luxury Mitsubishi SUV in Beijing[76]. However, workers or peasants, who do not have such power, have fallen way behind in terms of legitimate income.

Employees working at companies that are state monopolies are enjoying an income advantage too. The monopoly enterprises are making high-profits, but a large part of profit is being returned to employees. One justification is that their high wages are based on the excellent performance of the company. In part, the high payments may be related to social values (positions in those monopolised companies deserve high pay) that are accepted by society. However, these companies that have a monopoly have an unfair advantage compared to other SOEs that are not monopolies. This kind of mal-distribution is not likely to be seen as fair by the majority, especially when so many people are struggling for existence.

Another group who are getting exceedingly rich in a legitimate way deserved special attention. They are senior non-proprietor managerial staff or senior- and middle-level managerial personnel who work in large and medium-sized enterprises.[77] Privatisation and shareholding institutions help them achieve prosperity, or more exactly help them capitalise on their assets[78].

How about workers and peasants? Can they benefit from the privatisation? The answer is basically no. First, peasants do not work in the enterprises, and therefore are not qualified to take advantage of these opportunities. And the urban workers in the enterprises are qualified, but they have no symbolic capital and social capital to take advantage of the opportunity either. In practice, "state properties are becoming productive assets for officials' and managers' private gains". [79]

Many scholars have noticed the regional income disparities. It is so outrageous that middle and western parts of China are twenty years behind the coastal part in economic development[80]. However, the income disparities arise not just because of the market reforms, but also because of state policy. Deng Xiaoping had no idea how exactly to go about the reform when he initiated it. One of his famous sayings is that "passing the river by touching stone", which means moving steadily, or looking before you leap. So, China used Fujian and Guangdong as experiment sites and some Special Economic Zones were established at the same time. These districts were offered very preferential economic policies. As a result, investment flowed into these areas and the economy boomed there. People on the coast were soon making more money than those in inland areas[81]. Such income disparities are attributable to the policy favouritism. Now, it has been more than twenty years since the reform started in the coastal area but the western and middle provinces were not given equal opportunities for development.

Education

Education is of significance for individuals' career. Studies prove that there is a strong correlation between education and obtaining employment in China.[82] A lack of education is one of the reasons why peasants and workers and their descendents are unable to move upward. Their low educational level can be attributed to the effects of pre-reform stratification and also to the more recent educational reforms. The reform has made its impact through the following policies:

First, increases in the costs of tuition have prevented the children from disadvantaged groups continuing in school. This has happened at both pre-college level and at college level. Large numbers of pre-college students have had to drop out because their family cannot afford tuition costs or because their parents need them to work at minimum wage in order to ensure their family's continued existence. For college students, the Chinese government used to cover their tuition and also provide living expenses so that students at all economic levels were able to continue their schooling provided they were admitted. When the tuition was raised from 0 to 4000 yuan[83], many students who had been admitted to college but who came from a poor background were unable to enter. And some students with high scores but from a poor background had to choose the military colleges which charged no tuition and provided living expense.[84] Although the Chinese Government has developed a system of loans for poor students, this system has failed to enable poorer students to access higher education.

Second, privatisation, especially at elementary, middle, and high school level, separates students from the elite group from those who are in the disadvantaged group because of tuition costs. Private schools are able to attract the excellent teachers who have moved from the public to the private schools because of higher salaries in the private sector. Thus the creation of the private educational sector has resulted in children from the elite group receiving education that is different in kind and quality from that open to the disadvantaged group, and this has further differentially influenced the future career opportunities of both groups.

Third, different admission criteria for students at different places also affect educational opportunities. The criteria for admission are based on provincial boundaries[85]. The admission criteria for metropolitan city students like Beijing, Shanghai, and Tianjin are much lower than that in the undeveloped provinces, such as Jiangxi, Hunan, Shaanxi and Hubei. Let us elaborate it with a fictitious example. For example, in 2003, a student with a total of 560 admission scores in Hunan Province could only be admitted to a third tier school like Hunan Medical College, but this score would have been sufficient for a Beijing student to be admitted to Peking University, regarded as the best in China. This kind of institutional and geographical inequality renders the gap between elite and disadvantaged even wider.

Fourth, government funds are invested unevenly across country. Basically, better schools in better districts receive more funds from government. For example, a top high school in Beijing receives more funding than a regular school in Beijing which in turn receives more than a regular school in Nanchang which in turn receives more than an underperforming school at Qiyang County in Hunan Province. By the same logic, Peking University and Tsinghua University receive much more from the Ministry of Education than others, for example than Fudan University, or Nanjing University. The accumulated effect of all these factors entrenches privilege and widens and perpetuates the gap between the elite and disadvantaged groups.

Welfare

Welfare used to be universally provided in pre-reform China. In the urban areas, both administrative staff and workers at SOEs or collective enterprises received health care, housing, and pensions[86]. It was called "enterprises running society" which meant that work units functioned to provide for all aspects of needs. In rural areas, peasants were also covered with health insurance[87]. Since 1980s, rigorous reforms of the social security system have been launched[88]. Basically, government simplified the system by marketising social welfare. This led to increasing supply of modern health facilities and varieties of medicine. Unexpectedly, employers impose ceilings on the coverage of minor illnesses or require employees to pay part of minor medical expenses, such as out-patient registration fees or medicines[89]. Consequently, the improvements in health care now tend to benefit the people such as cadres who can afford to pay.

The above system of social security is also provided, for the most part, only to administrative staff, cadres and workers at the most productive SOEs or in foreign enterprises. Workers at collective or private enterprises often have no social security entitlements. It is found that the percentage of urban worker residents with health insurance decreased from 53% in 1993 to 42% in 1998[90]. It is worse for peasants; only 9% of peasants had health insurance in 1998. The percentage of welfare expense provided for peasants has become much less than before[91]. As health care becomes increasingly privatised, inequalities in health care and in health status have increased[92]. Moreover, health-care providers have become less interested in public health work compared to providing medical treatment for there is little or no remuneration for preventive services[93].

Housing used to be distributed by work units. Even though it was awarded on the basis of political ranking, seniority, professional expertise, and social capital[94], all the workers were still provided with housing. The housing reform terminated this part of the welfare system, and workers now acquire housing through estate market[95]. This works for the privileged group, but not for disadvantaged group who have been falling behind in income,[96] especially the unemployed.

Employment

As mentioned above, a major characteristic of market system is the rise of the meritocracy which becomes another social institution affecting people's behaviours. Chinese employers now pay more and more attention to the cultural capital possessed by applicants when recruiting employees, especially in foreign enterprises, joint ventures, SOEs and high-tech companies.[97] The administrative department is also stressing cultural capital in recruiting staff.[98] The emphasis on cultural capital means that opportunities are blocked for the disadvantaged people even though their disadvantage is itself a product of the institutional structure. However, although the recognition of the meritocracy has been reintroduced in China, this does not ensure that it is a dominating institution. Actually, in most undeveloped areas, political power has a much greater effect on the outcome of employment applications and this is yet another kind of social inequality. This will be further discussed below.

Social Inequality and Power Intervention

The preceding section describes the emergence of social inequality determined by institutions after the reform. It can be concluded that the people who were low in capitals (mainly in cultural capital and social capital) at the beginning of reform turned out to be lower in all capitals than before due to the institutional changes. Moreover, matters became worse when power intervened in all fields. The intervention of power implies unethical involvement of social capital in the social process. Lin argued that social capital works in the following ways: facilitating the flow of information, influencing the agents, reinforcing identity within the network, and providing social credentials, as in the following.[99]

In a market-oriented society, information is critical for competitors. In many cases, information means success. Individuals with social capital can always obtain important information from his/her network. For example, shareholders who can reach the policy maker will know the effect which the new policy is on any specific stock and thus pre-sell or pre-buy the affected stock.

A more common use of social capital is in the influence on agents. Person in power can write a letter to an agent (usually called note), can call the agent, or can dine with the agent and thus control the social process. Those with no such social capital will always build up personal social relationships (*guanxi*) to become part of the network and then maximise their own interests since *guanxi* with bureaucrats is very beneficial as a means of receiving preferential treatments as they may follow the practice of "opening one eye and closing the other," but not necessarily be involved in corruption[100]. Wank found that small entrepreneurs, in particular, sought political power in order to advance their business.[101] The person who helps an entrepreneur can receive a reward from the entrepreneur. Although bidding systems have been introduced, political power always makes the final decision.[102] Persons rich in social capital not only apply their power or influence on behalf of specific entrepreneurs, but also on behalf of their family members.

One outstanding instance is the inter-generational conversion of capital through influencing the agents. The cadres were able to use the power at hand to ensure their family members a smooth access to market opportunities and to become economic elite. One particular example is that leaders at all levels have helped their offspring to do business by using their power. It is called "one family, two systems" which means that the parents are in the government while their children are in business.[103] The influence on agents also reflects on employment. Even though the merit of the candidate has been accepted as determining employment, it does not mean that social capital cannot get around this. Lin and Bian found a strong father-son link in the work unit sector and a strong sector-to-occupation link across generations within families.[104] In fact, *guanxi*, a special incarnation of social capital, was "found to promote job and career opportunities for *guanxi* users, while constraining those who are poorly positioned in the networks of social relationships"[105].

The relations within the elite group help them to build their identity and recognise one another, which further separates them from disadvantaged group. One study shows that elite tend to interact with elite.[106] The group consciousness makes it hard for disadvantaged people to move up in the social hierarchy.

Crimes of the Disadvantaged: The Outcome of Income and Social Inequality

One significant outcome of income and social inequality is the rise of a large group of peasant migrants or transient people. Peasants are now moving to the urban and coastal areas for more earnings. Whilst China's total population had been rising gradually throughout the last decade, rural population had in fact decreased but urban population increased significantly. Zhang estimated that there were 60-million migrant peasant labours in China.[107] However, many of them fail to find regular jobs or are constrained in their job choices. Some become temporary workers, mainly in construction sites. Some turn to be casual labourers, including carpenters, painters and housemaids, among others. Other groups of workers become self-employed, selling fruits and vegetables (generally brought from their own village), goods (often smuggled from Taiwan and sold in subways or bridges), or repairing bicycles and shoes. Some just simply "search in the streets". They lack legal certification, a job, and a fixed living place, for which they are generally labelled as the 'three without' (*sanwu*). They work in the jobs that urban residents generally find inferior or distasteful. The nature of jobs determines that they cannot get rich, since their pay is always the lowest of all workers in the cities. Without an urban *hukou*, they are also deprived of the opportunities that were part of the basic levelling under the Maoist period, such as health care and education.

According to statistics from the Administers of Public Security, many of the migrant labours have been engaged in criminal behaviour. For example, 569,000 offenders arrested by the police in 1994 were transient people.[108] In Beijing, 44% of the crimes solved by the police were committed by transients. In Shanghai, this rate has been continually rising from 10% in the mid-1980s to 60%, even 80% in some districts by 1995. In Guangdong province, 90% of the prostitutes and drug traffickers were temporary residents. Burglary was the most serious crime in Guangzhou in 1994, with 80% of it being committed by transients.[109] Apparently, whereas the regular city residents are responsible for a portion of the crimes, the new migrants constitute a large majority of the problem in the major Chinese cities.

As with the surplus migrants from rural areas, the laid-off workers proved to be those with less cultural capital than those who were retained and this has made it very difficult for them to be re-employed, so they relied on their *guanxi* to seek jobs.[110] Some attempted to start their own business, with only a few successful cases. As a consequence, "a new urban poverty stratum is emerging from layoff labour and retired labour," and they feel "that they are truly proletarians".[111] Marginalised workers and peasants now make up 80% of the Chinese society and these groups live at the bottom of society[112], and they are vulnerable to committing crime if opportunities arise.

Conclusion

From the above analysis, we can see that in Mao's era, people were treated differently, especially those with "bad" origins. The differentiations were, essentially, embodied in the relation to social capital and cultural capital. Because of dominating Marxist egalitarianism which emphasises the importance of economic equality, the problem of income disparities did not exist. And people's attention was diverted from the latent differentiations of social capital and cultural capital among them, partly because these types of capital could not be converted into economic assets. However, after the reforms initiated in 1978 that stressed meritocracy and allowed private property, the two types of capitals began to have an impact in all aspects of life function.

In fact, the income disparity and social inequality in China are institutionally constructed. The new economic and social institutions have created opportunities and structures for members of the elite group to convert their social capital and cultural capital into economic capital. Yet the same institutions generated fewer opportunities in education, social security and welfare, and employment for the disadvantaged group who lacked the social and cultural capitals they needed to make advancement in the economic reforms. In addition, inflexible and incomplete bureaucratic system left space for the powerful to exert influence over social and political processes, and this further diminished opportunities for the less powerful to catch up. As such, institutional changes facilitated economic development, but on the other hand, they also created extreme social inequality. But the disadvantaged group still needed to survive in society. Most of them chose to migrate to urban and coastal areas and thus a "floating population" has emerged in the Mainland. Economic and industrial reforms also brought about a large group of laid-off workers. Migrant peasants and laid-off workers have increasingly become a problem group. Without social and cultural capital, they struggle to survive on the margins of society. To them, crime is an option if not the only solution.

Notes and References

1. This chapter is an extended and modified version of a paper published in the 2nd issue of Asian Journal of Criminology in 2006. The authors wish to thank Dr Gabrielle Maxwell for her substantive editing.

2. His famous instruction is that "let some people get rich first". See http://www.economist.com/World/asia/displayStory.cfm?Story_ID=63965 2. His another slogan is that "get rich is glorious". See "China's growing pains" *Economist*, 372(8389), (2004, August 21), pp. 11–12. See also Deng Xiaoping, *Deng Xiaoping Wenxuan, 1975–1982 (Selected Works of Deng Xiaoping, 1975–1982)* (Beijing, China: Renmin Chubanshe, 1983).

3. See Central Committee of the CPC, *Decision of the Chinese Communist Party Central Committee on reform of the economic system, (1984)*. Retrieved 22 October 2005. From http://www.people.com.cn/GB/shizheng/252/5301/5302/20010613/488130.html (in Chinese). "The justification for this policy was that poorer areas or those less developed would begin to benefit as richer areas began to profit; the growth and richness would then trickle down to these poorer regions and start the process of growth there." See M. Barnard and O. Shenkar, "The return of the red eye disease: wage in egalitarianism equality in the People's Republic of China." *Social Science Journal*, 34(1) (1997), p. 57.

4. According to Wang and Wang, China ranks third in terms of Gini Coefficient in the world. See F. Wang and T.F. Wang, *"Boundaries and categories: urban income inequality in China, 1986–1995"*. Paper presented at the American Sociological Association Annual Meeting, Anaheim (2001).

5. There are some explanations for this phenomenon. One major argument is that the initial stage of Chinese reform is featured as commodity economy, which allows common residents, especially peasants and disadvantaged people, to sell products in the limited market. See V. Nee

"The theory of market transition: from redistribution to markets in state socialism". *American Sociological Review*, 54, (1989), pp. 267–281.

6. According to the China Statistics Yearbook, the annual growth rate of the disposable income per capita in the urban areas is 15.3% from 1991 to 2001; the average wage of the urban employees grows at 15.9% per annum. See "The Challenge of China", *World Link*, 13(2), (Mar/Apr, 2000), pp. 42–43, *China Statistics Yearbook* (CSY) (1984–2002) (Beijing: China Statistical Publishing House).

7. *"Sharing rising incomes: disparities in China"*, (The World Bank, Washington D. C., 1997).

8. *"World Bank Development Indicators"*, (The World Bank, Washington D.C., 2001)

9. Z.S. Chen, *Income distribution in economic development*. (Shanghai, China: Shanghai Sanlian Bookstore, 1991), B. Gustafsson and Li S. "The anatomy of rising earnings inequality in urban China". *Journal of Comparative Economics*, 29 (2001), pp. 118–135, A.R. Khan and C. Riskin, "Income in China and its inequality", In Zhao R.W., Li S. and C. Riskin (Eds.), *Re-study on Income Distribution of Chinese Residents: Income Distribution in Economic Reform and Development*, (Beijing: China Finance and Economy Press, 1999), (pp. 72–108). Meng X., "Economic restructuring and income Inequality in urban China" (2001). Retrieved on December 12, 2005. From http://rspas.anu.edu.au/economics/staff/meng/inequal.pdf.

10. C.K. Wong and P.N.S. Lee, "Economic Reform and Social Welfare: the Chinese perspective portrayed through a social survey in Shanghai". *Journal of Contemporary China*, 10(28) (2001), pp. 517–532.

11. J. Logan, Y.J. Bian and F.Q. Bian, "Housing inequality in Urban China 1990s", *International Journal of Urban & Regional Research*, 23(1) (1999), pp. 7–25. Wu F.L. "Changes in the structure of public housing provision in urban China". *Urban Studies*, 33(9) (1996), pp. 1601–1627.

12. M. Wong, "Gender inequality in education in China: half a decade of 'half the sky' or have a chance?" *Education & Society*, 18(1) (2000), pp. 67–84.

13. R. Matthews and V. Nee, "Gender inequality and economic growth in rural China". *Social Science Research*, 29 (2000), pp. 606–632.

14. O. Anson and S.F. Sun, "Health inequalities in rural China: evidence from Hebei Province". *Health & Place*, 10 (2004), pp. 75–84.

15. Y.H. Wei, "Regional inequality in China". *Progress in Human Geography*, 23(1) (1999), pp. 49–59.

16. Former General Secretary of Chinese Communist Party, Jiang Zemin, expressed his concerns about the "unfairness" in the distribution process.

See Jiang Zemin, "Eliminate unfair income distribution". *Beijing Review*, 32 (August 28, 1989), pp. 19–24. J. Lewis and L.T. Xue, "Social change and political reform in China: Meeting the challenges of success". *The China Quarterly*, 176 (2003), pp. 930–942.

17. P.C. Friday, "Crime and crime prevention in China: A Challenge to the Development-Crime Nexus." *Journal of Contemporary Criminal Justice*, 14(3) (1998), pp. 296–315.

18. M. Dutton, "The basic character of crime in contemporary China". *China Quarterly*, 149 (1997), pp. 160–178.

19. T. Gong, "Forms and characteristics of China's corruption in the 1990s: change with continuity", *Communist and Post-communist Studies*, 30(3) (1997), p. 278.

20. P.C. Friday, "Crime and crime prevention in China: A Challenge to the Development-Crime Nexus". *Journal of Contemporary Criminal Justice*, 14(3) (1998), p. 296.

21. C.L. Hsu, "Political narratives and the production of legitimacy: the case of corruption in post-Mao China," *Qualitative Sociology*, 24(1) (2001), pp. 25–54.

22. The survey was conducted by the Institute of Opinion Research which is affiliated to the People's University of China. See "Survey finds corruption greatest concern to workers", *Foreign Broadcast Information Services Daily Report – China (June 14, 1996)*, (PrEx 7.10: FBS-CHI-96-115).

23. He states that up to now, "the corruption phenomenon is still much alive, and presently is seen as the second greatest public concern (behind unemployment)." See Z.K. He, "Corruption and anti-corruption in reform China", *Communist and post-communist Studies*, 33 (2000), pp. 243–270

24. Hsu did a fieldwork in 1997–98. His finding confirmed this fixation. See C.L. Hsu, "Political narratives and the production of legitimacy: the case of corruption in post-Mao China," *Qualitative Sociology*, 24(1) (2001), pp. 25–54.

25. D. Halpern, "Moral values, social trust and inequality: can values explain crime?" *British Journal of Criminology*, 41 (2) (2001), pp. 236–251. S.F. Messner, "Societal development, social equality, and homicide: a cross-national test of a Durkheimian model", *Social Forces*, 61 (1) (1982), pp. 225–241. S.F. Messner, "Economic discrimination and societal homicide rates: further evidences on the cost of inequality". *American Sociological Review*, 54 (1989), pp. 597–611. S.F. Messner, L.E. Raffalovich and P. Shrock, "Reassessing the cross-national relationship between income inequality and homicide rates: implications of data quality control in the measurement of income distribution." *Journal of Quantitative Criminology*, 18 (4) (2002), pp. 377–395. J.L. Neapolitan, "Cross-

national variation in homicides: the case of Latin America", *International Criminal Justice Review*, 4(1994), pp. 4–22.

26. See, for example, L.Q. Cao and Y.S. Dai, "Inequality and crime in China". In Liu J.H., Zhang L.N. and S.F. Messner (eds.), *Crime and social control in a changing China* (Westport, Conn.: Greenwood Press, 2001). pp. 73-88; Y.S.Chen and Y.Q. Luo, "Xiaoxin menhu zhongzai fangfan" ("Watch your doors and windows-burglary prevention is the focus") *Yangcheng Evening News* (1995, February 28), p. 5; D. Curran, "Economic reform, the floating population and crime," *Journal of Contemporary Criminal Justice*, 14 (1998), pp. 262–280.

27. A.M. O'Rand, "Social inequality", in *The Encyclopaedia of Sociology* (Volume 4), (New York: Macmillan Reference, 2000), p. 2691.

28. *Ibid*. p. 2692.

29. *Ibid*. p. 2693.

30. G. Marshall (ed.), *A dictionary of sociology*. (Oxford University Press, 1998), p. 313.

31. C.S. Heller, *Structured social inequality: a reader in comparative social stratification*, (New York: Macmillan, 1987), p. 4.

32. D.E. Mithaug, *Equal opportunity theory*. (Thousand Oaks, California: Sage Publications, 1996).

33. S. Shirk, "The decline of virtuocracy in China", in J. Watson (ed.), *Class and social stratification in post-revolution China*, (New York: Cambridge University Press, 1984), pp. 56–83.

34. J. Fishkin, *Justice, equal opportunity, and the family*. (New Haven: Yale University Press, 1983).

35. The Eighth National Congress of the Communist Party of China was held in Beijing from 15 to 27 September 1956. It analysed the situation following the basic completion of the socialist transformation of the ownership of the means of production. Please refer to Mao Zedong's original speech at http://listserv.cddc.vt.edu/marxists/www.marxists.org/reference/archive/mao/works/1956/0915.html. See also, R.C. Kraus, R.C., *Class conflict in Chinese socialism*, (New York, Columbia University press, 1981).

36. L.L. Li, X. Yang and F.Y. Wang, "The structure of socal strtification and the modernisation process in contemporary China", *International Sociology*, 6 (1) (1991), pp. 25–36.

37. T.J. Cheng and M. Selden, "The origins and social consequences of China's hukou system", *The China Quarterly*, 139 (1994), pp. 644–669; D.P. Han, ", *Journal of Developing Areas*, 33 (3) (1999), pp. 355–379.

38. It has long been regarded as an upward mobility for any peasant to

become an urban resident.

39. R.J.R. Kirkby, *Urbanisation in China*. (New York: Columbia University Press, 1985)

40. J.H. Turner, *The structure of sociological theory* (7th ed.). (Belmont, CA: Wadsworth Thomson Learning, 2003), p. 496.

41. Refer to the China Statistics Bureau website: http://www.stats.gov.cn/ndsj/information/zh1/i041a. Annual per capita income of the rural residents is 134 yuan in 1978, while that of the urban residents is 316 yuan.

42. See *China Statistics Yearbook*, (Beijing: China Statistical Publishing House, 1980)

43. W.L. Parish, W.L. "De-stratification in China", in J. Watson (ed.), *Class and social stratification in post-revolution China*, p. 90.

44. J.H. Turner, *The structure of sociological theory* (7th ed.) (Belmont, CA: Wadsworth Thomson Learning, 2003), p. 496.

45. Lin Nan *Social capital: a theory of social structure and action*. (Cambridge; NY: Cambridge University Press, 2001), p. 43.

46. *Ibid.*, p. 122.

47. X.G. Zhou, N.B. Tuma and P. Moen, "Stratification dynamics under state socialism: the case of urban China, 1949–1993", *Social Forces*, 74 (3) (1996), pp. 759–796.

48. Julia Kwong. "Is everyone equal before the system of grades: social background and opportunities in China", *British Journal of Sociology*, V34(1) (1983), p. 93; William L. Parish, "De-stratification in China", in James L. Watson, (ed), *Class & social stratification in post-revolution China*.

49. E.J. Croll, *The politics of marriages in contemporary China* (Cambridge: Cambridge University Press, 1981).

50. Zhao Y.D. "Measuring the social capital of laid-off Chinese workers", *Current Sociology*, 50(4) (2002), pp. 555–571.

51. *Ibid.* p. 563.

52. J.H. Turner, *The structure of sociological theory* (7th ed.) (Belmont, CA: Wadsworth Thomson Learning, 2003), p. 496.

53. P. Bourdieu, "The forms of capital", in J. Richardson (ed.) *Handbook of theory and research for the sociology of education* (New York: Greenwood Press, 1986), p. 248.

54. *Ibid.* p. 244.

55. J.H. Turner, *The structure of sociological theory* (7th ed.) (Belmont, CA:

Wadsworth Thomson Learning, 2003), p. 496.

56. William L. Parish, "De-stratification in China", pp. 84–120; M.K. Whyte, "De-stratification and re-stratification in China", in G.D. Berreman (ed.), *Social inequality: comparative and developmental approaches* (New York: Academic Press, 1981), pp. 309–336.

57. L.L. Li, X. Yang and F.Y. Wang "The structure of socal strtification and the modernisation process in contemporary China", *International Sociology*, 6 (1) (1991), p. 28.

58. S.C. Leng, *Reform and development in Deng's China*. (Lanham: Charlottesville, VA: University Press of America, Miller Center, University of Virginia, 1994).

59. F.L. Wang, *Institutions and institutional change in China*. (Houndmills & Hampshire: MacMillan Press, 1998), p. 20.

60. L.L. Li, X. Yang and F.Y. Wang "The structure of socal strtification and the modernisation process in contemporary China", pp. 25–36.

61. C. Aubert, *Rural China, 1985–1990: are the reforms really bogging down?* (Hong Kong: Hong Kong Institute of Asia-Pacific Studies, Chinese University of Hong Kong, 1991)

62. T.M. Kwong, "Markets and urban-rural inequality in China", *Social Science Quarterly*, 75 (4) (1994), pp. 820–837.

63. The average per capita net income of peasants increased from 134 yuan in 1978 to 424 yuan in 1986. See *China Statistics Yearbook* (1984).

64. P.C.C. Huang, *The peasant family and rural development in the Yangzi Delta, 1350–1988* (Stanford: Stanford University Press, 1990)

65. The produce price was released from state control in 1998 when China joined the WTO. But the produce price has been conditioned by international market.

66. J.C. Oi, *Rural China takes off: institutional foundations of economic reform* (Berkeley: University of California Press, 1999).

67. *Ibid.*

68. Z. Liang and Z.D. Ma, "China's floating population: new evidence from the 2000 census", *Population & Development Review*, 30(3) (2004), pp. 467–488.

69. W.L. Zhang, "Zhongguo shehui jieji jieceng yanjiu ershinian" ("Twenty years of research on Chinese class and strata"), *Sociological Research* (in Chinese), 1 (2000), pp. 24–39.

70. Local town governments always add more burdens on peasants by "Dabianche." Chinese Central government is planning to abolish tax on peasants completely in 2010 in order to increase their living conditions.

71. Q.J. Kong, "Quest for constitutional justification: privatisation with Chinese characteristics", *Journal of Contemporary China*, 12(36) (2003), pp. 537–551; S.Y. Ma,"The role of spontaneity and state initiative in China's shareholding system reform", *Communist & Post-Communist Studies*, 32(3) (1999), pp. 319–336.

72. W.L. Zhang, "Zhongguo shehui jieji jieceng yanjiu ershinian" ("Twenty years of research on Chinese class and strata"), pp. 24–39.

73. In the 16th Delegation Committee meeting of CPC in 2002, one topic about economic reform is to "grasp the big, and release the small", which allows small SOEs and collective enterprises to be privatised. See http://news.xinhuanet.com/newscenter/2002-11/21/content_636939.htm

74. C.A. Holz, "The impact of competition and labor remuneration on profitability in China's industrial state-owned enterprises", *Journal of Contemporary China*, 11(32) (2002), pp. 515–538.

75. X.B. Zhao and L. Zhang, "Decentralisation reforms and regionalism in China", *International Regional Science Review*, 22 (3) (1999), pp. 251–281.

76. See http://news.xinhuanet.com/legal/2005-05/14/content_2957194.htm

77. This group takes 1.5 percent of whole society population. See Lu P.P., "Ten strata of Chinese society". *Beijing Review,* (March 21, 2002). pp. 22–23.

78. See A.Y. So, *"The state, economic development and the changing patterns of classes and class conflict in China"*, Paper repented at the International Conference on Money, Growth, and Distribution, Academia Sinica, Taipei, (5–8 September 2001).

79. It mainly happened to the high-profit industries, like cement, mining, engineering, steel, oil and telecommunications. See Bian Yanjie, "Chinese social stratification and social mobility", *Annual Review of Sociology*, 28(2002), pp. 91–116.

80. Y.H. Wei, "Multiscale and multimechanisms of regional inequality in China: implications for regional policy", *Journal of Contemporary China*, 11(30) (2002), pp. 109–124.

81. S.M. Hauser and Y. Xie, "Temporal and regional variation in earnings inequality: urban China in transition between 1988 and 1995", *Social Science Research*, 34(1) (2005), pp. 44–79; S. Wang and A. Hu, *The political economy of uneven development: the case of China* (Armonk, NY: M.E. Sharpe, 1999).

82. Peter M. Blau and Ruan Danqing, "Inequality of opportunity in urban China and America", *Research on Social Stratification and Mobility*, 9(1990), pp. 3–32.

83. R.L. Holman "China ends tuition-free college", *Wall Street Journal-*

Eastern Edition, 229 (87) (5 May 1997), p. A14.

84. Usually military colleges have a lower admission score than other schools at the same level. For most students, military school is not their first choice.

85. Each province has its own admission criteria for different colleges (scores for the National Examination to College and University). But students across the nation basically take the same examination.

86. X. Li, "The transformation of ideology from Mao to Deng: impact on China's social welfare outcome", *International Journal of Social Welfare*, 8(2)(1999), pp. 86–97.

87. M. Beach, "China's rural health care gradually worsens", *Lancet*, 358(9281), (18 August 2001), p. 567.

88. R.C.M. Chau and S.W.K. Yu, "Social welfare and economic development in China and Hong Kong", *Critical Social Policy*, 19(1)(1999), pp. 87–107.

89. L. Liu, "New forms of social security in South China", *Social Security Bulletin*, 56(1)(1993), pp. 93–94.

90. Y.L. Liu, "China's public health-care system: facing the challenges", *Policy and Practice*, 82(7)(2004), pp. 532–538.

91. M. Beach, "China's rural health care gradually worsens", p. 567.

92. Gu E., "Market transition and the transformation of the health care system in urban China", *Policy Studies*, 22(3/4)(2001), pp. 197–215; Y.L. Liu, "China's public health-care system: facing the challenges", pp. 532–538; R. Tomlinson, "Health care in China is highly inequitable", *British Medical Journal*, 315 (7112)(1997), pp. 835–835.

93. Y.L. Liu, "China's public health-care system: facing the challenges", pp. 532–538.

94. J. Logan, Bian Yanjie and Bian Fuqin, "Housing inequality in Urban China 1990s", *International Journal of Urban & Regional Research*, 23(1)(1999), pp. 7–25; X.G. Zhou and O. Suhomlinova "Redistribution under state socialism: a USSR and PRC comparison", *Research on Social Stratification and Mobility*, 18(2001), pp. 163–204.

95. D.S. Davis, "Reconfiguring Shanghai households", in B. Entwisle and G.E. Henderson (eds.), *Re-drawing boundaries: work, household, and gender in China* (Berkeley, CA: University of California Press, 2000), pp. 245–60.

96. Mortgage is a tentative method to resolve the housing problem for middle class, but not for poor people. And there are still 30-million laid-off workers struggling for existence.

97. The enterprises open the jobs to the public; they choose employees based on their own criteria. Basically, their criteria are ability, education,

intelligence, and diligence, which belong to cultural capital. The enterprises open the jobs to the public; they choose employees based on their own criteria. Basically, their criteria are ability, education, intelligence, and diligence, which belong to cultural capital.

98. Public Functionary Test has been increasingly accepted by more and more government departments. However, it has not been spread to nationwide.

99. Lin Nan, *Social capital: a theory of social structure and action.* (Cambridge, NY: Cambridge University Press, 2001)

100. M.M. Yang, *The Art of social relationships and exchange in China.* (Berkeley, CA: University of California Press, 1986)

101. D.L. Wank "The institutional process of market clientelism: guanxi and private business in a South China city", *The China Quarterly*, 147(1996), pp. 820–839.

102. S.S. Han and Y. Wang, "The institutional structure of a property market in inland China: Chongqing", *Urban Studies*, 40(1)(2003), pp. 91–113.

103. He Qinglian, "China's listing social structure", *New Left Reviews*, 5(2000), pp. 69–100.

104. Lin Nan and Bian Yanjie, "Getting ahead in urban China", *American Journal of sociology*, 97(1991), pp. 657–688.

105. Bian Yanjie "Chinese social stratification and social mobility", *Annual Review of Sociology*, 28(2002), p. 107.

106. Yan Z.M., A *research on class and stratification in contemporary China* (Zhongguo xian jieduan jicji jieceng yanjiu) (Beijing: The CCP Central School Press, 2002) (Zhonggong Zhongyang Dangxiao Chubanshe).

107. W.L. Zhang, "Zhongguo shehui jieji jieceng yanjiu ershinian" ("Twenty years of research on Chinese class and strata"), pp. 24–39.

108. L. Xu "Ganhao liudong renkou wending shehui" ("Managing transient population, stabilising society"), *Legal Daily*. (10 July 1995). p. 1.

109. Y.S. Chen and Y.Q. Luo, "Xiaoxin menhu zhongzai fangfan" ("Watch your doors and windows-burglary prevention is the focus"), p. 5.

110. Y.D. Zhao, "Measuring the social capital of laid-off Chinese workers", *Current Sociology*, 50(4)(2002), pp. 555–571.

111. Bian Yanjie, "Chinese social stratification and social mobility", p. 96.

112. He Qinglian, "China's listing social structure", pp. 69–100.

Authors

Jean Philippe BÉJA is currently a senior researcher at CNRS, and works at the Centre for International Research (CERI) in Paris. He works on the relation between the citizen and the State in the People's Republic of China, and has also written extensively on the democratization of Hong Kong. He is the co-founder of *China Perspectives*, and regularly writes for *Esprit*. He supervises Ph.D. dissertations at Sciences-Po (Institute of Political Sciences) Paris, and at Ecole des Hautes Etudes en Sciences Sociales, Paris. His latest works include *A la recherche d'une ombre chinoise. Le mouvement pour la démocratie en Chine (1919-2004)* (In search of a Chinese shadow: the movement for democracy in China 1919-2004) (2004) and a special issue of *Social Research* 73(1) (Spring 2006) (New York), "China in Transition".

David CHAN is Associate Professor at the Department of Asian and International Studies at City University of Hong Kong. He is concurrently the Convenor of the Comparative Education Policy Research Unit at City University of Hong Kong, and is also the Chairperson of the Hong Kong Educational Research Association. He received his master degree from Stanford University and his Ph.D. from the University of Nottingham. His research interests include sociology of education, comparative education reforms and policies in various Asian countries, socio-cultural changes and social development of Asian societies. He has edited books and contributed in international and regional journals, including *Comparative Education, Journal of Contemporary China, Globalisation, Societies and Education, World Studies in Education, Asia Pacific Journal of Education, Education and Society*, among others.

Gerald CHAN is Professor of East Asian Politics and Director of the Centre for Contemporary Chinese Studies in the School of Government and International Affairs at Durham University, U.K. He is a Life Member of Clare Hall, Cambridge. He sits on the editorial board of five academic journals. He taught previously at Victoria University of Wellington, New Zealand, and has held visiting positions at Australian National University, Cambridge University, Chinese University of Hong Kong, National University of Singapore, and Peking University. He publishes widely in Chinese foreign policy, including *China's compliance in global affairs: trade, arms control, environmental protection, human rights* (Singapore: World Scientific, 2006). At present he works on a collaborative research on China and global governance. E-mail: gerald.chan@durham.ac.uk.

Lai-Ha CHAN is currently a Ph.D. candidate in the Department of International Business and Asian Studies at Griffith University in Brisbane, Australia. Her Ph.D. research is focused on China's engagement with global health governance.

She holds a Bachelor of Social Sciences from the University of Macau and a Master of Arts in International Relations from Victoria University of Wellington, New Zealand. She has recently published a monograph entitled "The Evolution of Health Governance in China: A Case Study of HIV/AIDS" in the Griffith Asia Institute Regional Outlook series.

Sylvia CHAN is a visiting research fellow of the Centre for Asian Studies at the University of Adelaide. Her research interest is in intellectual trends in contemporary China. In the last decade, she has been working on political reform in rural China. She has published many articles in English and Japanese academic journals and contributed book chapters to a number of books.

Joseph Y. S. CHENG is Chair Professor of Political Science and Coordinator of the Contemporary China Research Project, City University of Hong Kong. He is the founding editor of the *Hong Kong Journal of Social Sciences* and *The Journal of Comparative Asian Development*. He has published widely on political development in China and Hong Kong, Chinese foreign policy and local government in southern China. He has recently edited volumes on *China's Challenges in the Twenty-first Century* and *The July 1 Protest Rally – Interpreting a Historic Event*. In 2005-7, he served as the founding president of the Asian Studies Association of Hong Kong.

Mobo GAO studied at Xiamen University in China and completed his doctorate at Essex. He has taught part-time at a couple of universities in UK before he was employed full-time at Griffith University in 1991. He is currently Reader of Chinese Studies at the School of Asian Languages and Studies at University of Tasmania. He is the author of *Gao Village* and *Mandarin Chinese an Introduction* and numerous book chapters and journal articles. Gao is frequently invited by the international media to comment on China. His current research is on rural China, (Gao Village and Long Bow), the Chinese Cultural Revolution and early Chinese Migrants to Tasmania.

Yingjie GUO is a senior lecturer in Chinese Studies at the Institute for International Studies, University of Technology, Sydney. His research is related to nationalism in China and the domestic political impact of China's WTO membership. His recent publications include *Cultural Nationalism in Contemporary China: The Search for National Identity under Reform*, RoutledgeCurzon, 2004.

Guoping JIANG is a Ph.D. candidate at the City University of Hong Kong. He has been majoring in sociology since undergraduate education with great interests in how social issues are structurally constructed. He is writing his thesis on corruption in Mainland China from a critical perspective in the aim of finding out the essence of corruption and an effective way of corruption control with first hand data.

Charles C. L. KWONG is an assistant professor of economics in the School of Arts and Social Sciences at the Open University of Hong Kong. He received his Ph.D. from the Monash University, Australia. His research interest is mainly related to the growth and transformation of the Chinese economy, with emphasis on the rural and banking sectors. His recent publications include a co-edited (with Harry W.C. Lo) special issue titled "China's Rural Economy at the Crossroads" *The Chinese Economy*, 39(4) July-August 2006 and "Bad Loans Versus Sluggish Rural Industrial Growth: A Policy Dilemma of China's Banking Reform," *Journal of the Asia Pacific Economy*, 10(1), 2005 (with Pak K. Lee).

Willy Wo-Lap LAM is a specialist in areas including the Chinese Communist Party, foreign policy, the People's Liberation Army, as well as the country's economic and political reform. He has worked for international media including *Asiaweek, South China Morning Post*, and CNN. He is a Professor of China Studies at Akita International University, Japan; and an adjunct professor at the Chinese University of Hong Kong. He has just published the Western world's first book on the Hu Jintao administration, entitled *Chinese Politics in the Hu Jintao Era*. His views on China are often sought by global media including CNN, BBC, ABC, Bloomberg and Voice of America. He holds a Ph.D. in political economy from Wuhan University, and has published six books on China, including *The Era of Jiang Zemin*.

Pak K. LEE is Lecturer in Chinese Politics and International Relations/ International Political Economy in the Department of Politics and International Relations at the University of Kent, Canterbury, United Kingdom. Prior to this, he had taught for 14 years in the School of Arts and Social Sciences at the Open University of Hong Kong and in the Faculty of Social Sciences and Humanities, University of Macau. His recent publications on China have appeared in the *Journal of the Asia Pacific Economy* (2005) and *Pacific Review* (2005). He is currently working on a joint book project on China's participation in global governance.

Beatrice K. F. LEUNG was awarded a Ph.D. degree from the London School of Economics and Political Science in 1988. She had served as the chief editor of *Kung Kao Po* (the Chinese Catholic Weekly) as well as the founding executive secretary of the Holy Spirit Study Centre of the Hong Kong Catholic Diocese. Currently she is the professor of School of Management, Leadership and Government, Macau Inter-University Institute. She has published more than 40 academic papers on Church-State Relations of the Greater China in international academic journals, and has edited and written seven volumes. Her most recent publications include *The Chinese Catholic Church in Conflict: 1949-2001* (co-authored with William T. Liu) (2003) and "China's Religious Freedom Policy: An Art of Managing Religious Activity", *The China Quarterly* 184 (December 2005).

Guoli LIU is Professor of Political Science at the College of Charleston. He received his B.A. and M.A. degrees from Peking University and a Ph.D. in political science from the State University of New York at Buffalo. His main teaching and research interests are comparative politics and international relations. He is the author of *States and Markets: Comparing Japan and Russia* (Westview Press, 1994), and co-author of *United States Foreign Policy and Sino-American Relations* (China Social Sciences Press, 2000). His edited books include *Chinese Foreign Policy in Transition* (Aldine Transaction, 2004), (with Weixing Chen) *New Directions in Chinese Politics for the New Millennium* (Edwin Mellen, 2002), and (with Lowell Dittmer) *China's Deep Reform: Domestic Politics in Transition* (Rowman and Littlefield, 2006).

Tit Wing LO is a professor at City University of Hong Kong, teaching Criminology and Social Work. He graduated with an M.Phil. in Criminology from Hull in 1984 and a Ph.D. in Criminology from Cambridge in 1991. Before joining City University in 1990, he had been a social worker and a street gang worker for 17 years. Over the last ten years, he had led over twenty research projects. Many of them were large-scale projects or blueprint studies commissioned by the government. Over the years, he has published over 100 journal papers, research monographs, books and book chapters. He also serves as a member of a number of advisory committees in the Government and NGOs.

Colin MACKERRAS (Fellow of the Australian Academy of Humanities) gained his Ph.D. from the Australian National University, Canberra, in 1972. He worked as Foundation Professor in Asian Studies at Griffith University, Queensland, Australia, from 1974 to 2004, becoming professor emeritus in the Department of International Business and Asian Studies at Griffith University upon his retirement in 2004. He has written very widely on Asian studies in general, and especially on Chinese history, local theatre, culture and ethnic studies, and Western images of China. His several authored books on ethnicity include *China's Ethnic Minorities and Globalisation*, RoutledgeCurzon, London and New York, 2003, and his edited works include *Ethnicity in Asia*, RoutledgeCurzon, London and New York, 2003.

Raymond NGAN is Associate Professor at the Department of Applied Social Studies, City University of Hong Kong. He is the Vice-President of the Hong Kong Association of Gerontology since 1992, and was the former Chairman of the Committee on Social Security, Hong Kong Council of Social Service. He had also been the Chief Editor, *Hong Kong Journal of Social Work* (1996-99). His work has appeared in international journals, including *International Journal of Social Welfare*, *Journal of Aging and Social Policy*, *International Social Work*, and *Journal of Gerontological Social Work*. His research interests are in social security, reforms in old age pension, long term care and comparative welfare. He was awarded the Outstanding Research Award in Gerontology (1997) and the Outstanding Paper Presentation Award in the Annual Congress (2004) by the Hong Kong Association of Gerontology.

Alvin Y. SO received his PhD in sociology from UCLA. He has taught at the University of Hawaii before joining the Hong Kong University of Science and Technology. His research interests include economic development, democratization, and globalization of the Greater China. His recent publications include *China's Developmental Miracle: Origins, Transformations, and Challenges* (editor, M.E. Sharpe 2003), *Crisis and Transformation in China's Hong Kong* (co-editor, M.E. Sharpe 2002) and *The Chinese Triangle of Mainland-Taiwan-Hong Kong: Comparative and Institutional Analyses* (co-editor, Greenwood 2001).

Guiguo WANG is Professor (Chair) of Chinese and Comparative Law, City University of the Hong Kong, Chairman of the Hong Kong WTO Research Institute and Distinguished Professor of Law of Hunan Normal University. Holding a J.S.D. degree from Yale Law School and an LL.M. degree from Columbia Law School, Wang is a Member of the International Academy of Comparative Law. He is also an Honorary Advisor to the Ombudsman of Hong Kong, Adjudicator of the Immigration Tribunal of Hong Kong and the Country Advisor to Butterworths. His major publications include *Wang's Business Law of China* (4th ed.), *International Investment Law*, *International Monetary and Financial Law* (2nd ed.), *International Trade Law*, and *The Law of the WTO: China and the Future of Free Trade*.

Marcus J. J. WANG obtained his Ph.D. from the Department of Philosophy, Fu Jen Catholic University, Taiwan in 2005. He is the Director of the Division of the Junior College, and Associate Professor of the Center of General Education, Wenzao Ursuline College of Languages, Taiwan. His research interest spreads to the relations between philosophy and various disciplines of social sciences and humanities such as religion, morality, church-state relations and law. His research papers were published in international academic journals. The most recent on is "The Influence of Catholicism on the Natural Moral Law" *Universitas* (March 2006). Currently, he is engaging in an international research project jointly sponsored by the National Science Council, Taiwan and The British Academy to study the priests and sisters in Catholic Church in China.

Linda WONG is a Professor in the Department of Public and Social Administration in City University of Hong Kong. She received her Ph.D. in Social Policy in the London School of Economics and Political Science. Her teaching and research interests span the fields of social welfare, comparative social policy, and China studies. A long-standing researcher in social welfare and social development in China, she has completed empirical studies on social welfare reform, migrant workers, unemployment, non-state welfare development, and comparative social policy between Shanghai and Hong Kong. Her books include *Social Change and Social Policy in Contemporary China*, *Marginalization and Social Welfare in China*, *The Market in Chinese Social Policy*, and *Social Policy Reform in Hong Kong and Shanghai: A Tale of Two Cities*.

Ray YEP is Associate Professor in the Department of Public and Social Administration, City University of Hong Kong. His latest articles on rural development and local finance in China could be found in *China Quarterly, Public Administration Review* and *Public Administration & Development.* He is also the author of *Manager Empowerment in China: Political Implications of Rural Industrialization in the Reform Era* (London & New York: RoutledgeCurzon, 2003).

YOU Ji is senior lecturer in School of Political Science at the University of New South Wales. He has published widely on China's political, economic, military, and foreign affairs. He is author of three books including *China's Enterprise Reform: Changing State/Society Relations after Mao* (1998) and *The Armed Forces of China* (1999); and numerous articles. The most recent ones include: "The Anti-Secession Law and the Risk of War in the Taiwan Strait", *Contemporary Security Policy* (August 2006); "East Asian Community: A New Platform for Sino-Japanese Cooperation and Contention", *Japanese Studies* (May 2006); "Hu Jintao's Succession and Power Consolidation Strategy", in *China's Political and Social Change in Hu Jintao Era* (2006); and "The PLA as an Interests Group in China's Domestic Politics", in *The Chinese Communist Party in a New Era: Renewal and Reform* (2006).

Graham YOUNG received his Ph.D. from the Flinders University of South Australia. He has held academic positions at Flinders University and in the Contemporary China Centre, Australian National University. He is currently Senior Lecturer in Political and International Studies, University of New England, Australia, where his main teaching is on international relations and Chinese politics. He has published articles and chapters on the Chinese Communist Party, contemporary Chinese political thought, and international human rights, and is editor of *China: Dilemmas of Modernisation* (1985) and *Legitimation and the State* (2005) and co-author of *China since 1978: Reform, Modernisation and "Socialism with Chinese Characteristics"* (2nd ed., 1998).

Chinese Names
of People Mentioned in the Text

Ai Xiaoming	艾晓明,	576
Baihua	白桦,	157
Bao Zhong He	包宗和,	497, 514
Bo Xilai	薄熙来,	7
Cao Siyuan	曹思源,	577
Chang, Aloysius	张春申,	503
Chen Liangyu	陈良宇,	6, 51
Chen Shui Bien	陈水扁,	504
Cheng Yizhong	程益中,	581, 590
Chiang Kai-shek	蒋介石,	495
Ching Cheong	程翔,	508
Cui Jian	崔健,	580
Dang Guoying	党国英,	
Deng Xiaogang	邓小刚,	40
Deng Xiaoping	邓小平,	5, 23, 29, 31, 38, 84, 180, 184, 208, 210, 212, 216, 217, 231, 246, 247, 248, 249, 253, 509, 511, 568, 569, 570, 573, 575, 597, 600, 601, 611, 614
Du Runsheng	杜润生,	418
Fong Hou	方豪,	498
Gao Qiang	高强,	318
Gao Xiqing	高西庆,	42
Gao Yaojie	高耀洁,	321, 322, 580
Gong Li	宫力,	265
Guo Shuqing	郭树青,	42
Han Zheng	韩正,	42, 51
Hao Peng	郝鹏,	40

Li Baiguang	李柏光,	581
Li Changchun	李长春,	6, 37
Li Changping	李昌平,	424
Li Deshui	李德水,	256
Li Erliang	李而亮,	582
Li Minying	李民英,	582, 591
Li Peng	李鹏,	41, 213, 228, 250
Li Rui	李锐,	52, 582
Li Weiwen	李伟文,	80
Li Xiannian	李先念,	41
Li Yining	李亦宁,	420
Li Yizhong	李毅中,	53
Li Yuanchao	李源潮,	44, 46–48, 55
Liang Congjie	梁从诫,	580
Ling Jihua	令计划,	44, 50
Liu Guchang	刘古昌,	307
Liu Huaqing	刘华清,	41, 284
Liu Junning	刘军宁,	422
Liu Mingkang	刘明康,	55
Liu Peng	刘鹏,	44
Liu Shaoqi	刘少奇,	41
Liu Xiaobo	刘晓波,	507, 580, 584, 586
Liu Yandong	刘延东,	50
Liu Yazhou	刘亚洲,	41, 56
Liu Yuan	刘源,	41
Liu Yunshan	刘云山,	6, 37
Lou Jiwei	楼继伟,	42, 55
Loukwong	罗光,	503
Lu Hao	陆昊,	40, 45
Lu Nanquan	陆南泉,	309
Lu Xueyi	陆学艺,	361
Luo Gan	罗干,	7, 37
Luo Xingzuo	罗星左,	426

Wen Jiabao	温家宝,	3–4, 6, 10, 12, 35, 42, 50, 63, 66, 72, 87, 97, 125, 170, 179–180, 188, 190, 194, 232, 237, 258, 263, 308, 319, 323, 337, 351, 459, 484–485, 523–524, 574, 577, 586
Wen Tiejun	温铁军,	418, 420, 423, 425
Wu Aiying	吴爱英,	46, 50
Wu Bangguo	吴邦国,	7, 42
Wu Heping	武和平,	3
Wu Xiaoling	吴晓灵,	43
Wu Yi	吴仪,	50, 319–320, 321
Xi Jinping	习近平,	41
Xi Zhongxun	习仲勋,	41
Xie Zhenhua	解振华,	7
Xu Jilin	许纪霖,	579
Xu Youyu	徐友渔,	573
Yan Haiwang	阎海旺,	46
Ye Kedong	叶克冬,	40
Ye Xiaowen	叶小文,	511
Yu Huafeng	喻华锋,	582, 591
Yu Jie	余杰,	582, 584, 586, 588
Yu Zhengsheng	俞正声,	7
Yupin	于斌,	495, 498, 500, 502, 503
Zen, Joseph	陈日君,	505, 511, 514
Zeng Qinghong	曾庆红,	7, 41, 42, 50, 180
Zhan Chengfu	詹成付,	66
Zhang Dejiang	张德江,	6, 406
Zhang Qingli	张庆黎,	44, 51
Zhang Qingwei	张庆伟,	53
Zhang Taolin	张桃林,	43
Zhang Wenkang	张文康,	575
Zhang Yihe	章诒和,	584
Zhang Zhuang	张庄,	416, 426

Subject Index

A

Administrative Litigation Law, 113–115, 118
adverse selection, 397
afforestation, 441
Afghanistan, 156, 196, 209, 458, 466
agricultural tax 农业税, 72, 351–352, 356–358, 390, 402, 406, 408, 427, 435, 441–443, 445–446, 448, 451–452
AIDS, 48, 297, 314–324, 457, 474, 480–486, 580, 587
Amnesty International, 477
Amoy (now Xiamen) 厦门, 497–498
Anhui 安徽, 20, 25, 47–48, 52, 54, 318, 359, 403, 440, 442, 445–447, 450, 585
arms control, 199, 208, 230, 233, 289
Asian financial crisis, 164, 223, 226, 251–252, 301
Association of Southeast Asian Nations (ASEAN), 169–171, 193–196, 219–227, 301, 316
Autonomous Region, 51, 463, 478, 479
autonomy, 8, 66, 70, 110, 137–138, 166, 324, 458, 460, 461, 479, 480, 551, 568, 569, 609

B

Baihua 白桦 (油田), 157
Bank of China, 43, 46, 55, 395
barefoot doctor, 315

Basic Law, 511
basic living subsidy, 344
Beijing, 17, 30, 39–40, 43, 44, 48–49, 52, 54, 71, 75, 87, 100, 109, 141, 171–172, 181–182, 188, 190, 193, 195, 222, 225–227, 229–230, 249, 254, 257, 259, 263–264, 277–278, 288, 290, 301, 303, 307–309, 311–313, 316, 321–322, 343, 350, 392, 447, 450, 460, 466, 496–497, 499–502, 504–507, 509, 511–516, 545–546, 558, 571, 577, 610, 612–613, 617
bianzhi 编制, 73
bourgeois liberalisation, 43, 569, 578, 586, 590
Buddhism, 469, 478, 480, 486
budget deficit, 402, 405
business enterprise, 372

C

cadre, 5, 6, 7–8, 29, 31, 35–40, 42, 43, 45, 47, 49–50, 52, 53, 54, 55, 56, 57, 64, 73–76, 80, 82, 182, 217, 384, 390, 403–406, 408, 435, 436–438, 441, 443, 445, 461, 464, 524, 568, 581, 583, 585, 588, 602–606, 609, 614, 616
capitalist class, 182
capitalist world-economy, 137
care homes, 367–371, 373, 376–378, 380–384, 386–387
care workers, 379–380

State Organisation Chart of China

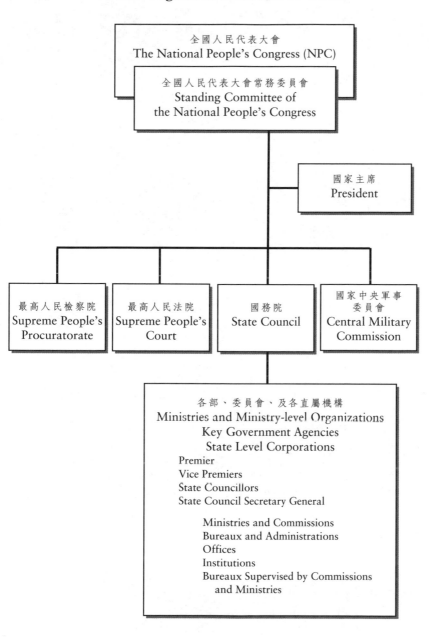

全國人民代表大會
The National People's Congress (NPC)

全國人民代表大會常務委員會
Standing Committee of
the National People's Congress

國家主席
President

最高人民檢察院
Supreme People's
Procuratorate

最高人民法院
Supreme People's
Court

國務院
State Council

國家中央軍事
委員會
Central Military
Commission

各部、委員會、及各直屬機構
Ministries and Ministry-level Organizations
Key Government Agencies
State Level Corporations
Premier
Vice Premiers
State Councillors
State Council Secretary General

Ministries and Commissions
Bureaux and Administrations
Offices
Institutions
Bureaux Supervised by Commissions
and Ministries

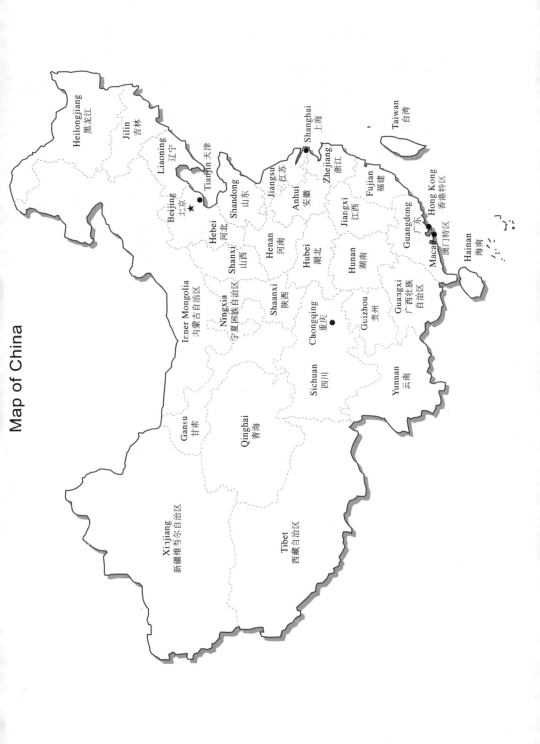

Map of China

Heilongjiang 黑龙江

Jilin 吉林

Liaoning 辽宁

Tianjin 天津

Beijing 北京

Hebei 河北

Shandong 山东

Shanxi 山西

Jiangsu 江苏

Anhui 安徽

Shanghai 上海

Zhejiang 浙江

Fujian 福建

Jiangxi 江西

Henan 河南

Hubei 湖北

Hunan 湖南

Guangdong 广东

Hong Kong 香港特区

Macau 澳门特区

Hainan 海南

Taiwan 台湾

Inner Mongolia 内蒙古自治区

Ningxia 宁夏回族自治区

Shaanxi 陕西

Chongqing 重庆

Guizhou 贵州

Guangxi 广西壮族自治区

Sichuan 四川

Yunnan 云南

Gansu 甘肃

Qinghai 青海

Xinjiang 新疆维吾尔自治区

Tibet 西藏自治区